The Earth and Its Peoples

A Global History

The Earth and Its Peoples

A Global History

THIRD EDITION

Volume I: To 1550

Richard W. Bulliet
Columbia University

Pamela Kyle Crossley
Dartmouth College

Daniel R. Headrick
Roosevelt University

Steven W. Hirsch
Tufts University

Lyman L. Johnson
University of North Carolina–Charlotte

David Northrup
Boston College

Houghton Mifflin Company   Boston   New York

Publisher: Charles Hartford
Editor-in-Chief: Jean L. Woy
Senior Sponsoring Editor: Nancy Blaine
Senior Development Editor: Jennifer Sutherland
Editorial Associate: Annette Fantasia
Senior Project Editor: Carol Newman
Editorial Assistant: Trinity Peacock-Broyles
Senior Design Coordinator: Jill Haber
Senior Designer: Henry Rachlin
Manufacturing Manager: Florence Cadran
Senior Marketing Manager: Sandra McGuire

Cover illustration: *Encampment of a Prince,* Turkish School, 15th century. Painted silk. Topkapi Palace Museum, Istanbul, Turkey/Giraudon/Bridgeman Art Library.

Part opener credits
Pt. 1, p. 1: Gian Berto Vanni/Corbis; Pt. 2, p. 115: © Corbis; Pt. 3, p. 205: Tokyo National Museum/DNP Archives; Pt. 4, p. 333: Bibliothèque nationale de France.

Chapter opener credits
Ch. 1, p. 4: David Coulson/Robert Estall Photo Agency; Ch. 2, p. 27: Giraudon/Art Resource, NY; Ch. 3, p. 55: Courtesy of the Trustees of the British Museum; Ch. 4, p. 81: Woodfin Camp & Associates; Ch. 5, p. 118: Bibliotèque nationale de France; Ch. 6, p. 150: © Dennis Cox/ChinaStock; Ch. 7, p. 178: Dinodia Photo Library; Ch. 8, p. 208: Allan Eaton/Ancient Art & Architecture; Ch. 9, p. 229: Suleymaniye Library, Istanbul. Courtesy, Karen Pinto, History Department, Columbia University; Ch. 10, p. 249: Musée de Bayeaux/Michael Holford; Ch. 11, p. 280 Fujita Art Museum; Ch. 12, p. 305: Justin Kerr; Ch. 13, p. 336: Imperial Household Agency/International Society for Educational Information, Japan; Ch. 14, p. 366: Imperial Household Collection, Kyoto; Ch. 15, p. 391: Copyright Brussels, Royal Library of Belgium; Ch. 16, p. 417: G. Dagli Orti/The Art Archive.

Printed in U.S.A.

Library of Congress Catalog Card Number: 2003115591

ISBN: 0-618-42765-1

5 6 7 8 9—VH—2008 2007 2006

Brief Contents

Contents

PART ONE
The Emergence of Human Communities, to 500 B.C.E.
1

PART TWO
The Formation of New Cultural Communities, 1000 B.C.E.–400 C.E.
115

Maps

Environment and Technology

Diversity and Dominance

Issues in World History

Preface

Reaching the point of preparing the third edition of a textbook is particularly gratifying for its authors. The sustained appeal of their writing tells them that they have done something good and useful. But that in turn prompts them to ponder what they can do to make their book still better. Fortunately, feedback from teachers and students provides a regular stream of helpful suggestions. We have tried to respond to the most frequent and constructive of these suggestions in preparing the third edition.

Our overall goal remains unchanged: to produce a textbook that not only speaks for the past but speaks to today's student and today's teacher. Students and instructors alike should take away from this text a broad vision of human societies beginning as sparse and disconnected communities reacting creatively to local circumstances; experiencing ever more intensive stages of contact, interpenetration, and cultural expansion and amalgamation; and arriving at a twenty-first century world in which people increasingly visualize a single global community.

Process, not progress, is the keynote of this book: a steady process of change over time, at first differently experienced in various regions, but eventually connecting peoples and traditions from all parts of the globe. Students should come away from this book with a sense that the problems and promises of their world are rooted in a past in which people of every sort, in every part of the world, confronted problems of a similar character and coped with them as best they could. We believe that our efforts will help students see where their world has come from and learn thereby something useful for their own lives.

Central Themes

We subtitled *The Earth and Its Peoples* "A Global History" because the book explores the common challenges and experiences that unite the human past. Although the dispersal of early humans to every livable environment resulted in a myriad of different economic, social, political, and cultural systems, all societies displayed analogous patterns in meeting their needs and exploiting their environments. Our challenge was to select the particular data and episodes that would best illuminate these global patterns of human experience.

To meet this challenge, we adopted two themes to serve as the spinal cord of our history: "technology and the environment" and "diversity and dominance." The first theme represents the commonplace material bases of all human societies at all times. It grants no special favor to any cultural group even as it embraces subjects of the broadest topical, chronological, and geographical range. The second theme expresses the reality that every human society has constructed or inherited structures of domination. We examine practices and institutions of many sorts: military, economic, social, political, religious, and cultural, as well as those based on kinship, gender, and literacy. Simultaneously we recognize that alternative ways of life and visions of societal organization continually manifest themselves both within and in dialogue with every structure of domination.

With respect to the first theme, it is vital for students to understand that technology, in the broad sense of experience-based knowledge of the physical world, underlies all human activity. Writing is a technology, but so is oral transmission from generation to generation of lore about medicinal or poisonous plants. The magnetic compass is a navigational technology, but so is Polynesian mariners' hard-won knowledge of winds, currents, and tides that made possible the settlement of the Pacific islands.

All technological development has come about in interaction with environments, both physical and human, and has, in turn, affected those environments. The story of how humanity has changed the face of the globe is an integral part of our first theme. Yet technology and the environment do not explain or underlie all important episodes of human experience. The theme of "diversity and dominance" informs all our discussions of politics, culture, and society. Thus when narrating the histories of empires, we describe a range of human experiences within and beyond the imperial frontiers without assuming that imperial institutions are a more fit topic for discussion than the economic and social organization of pastoral nomads or the lives of peasant women. When religion and culture occupy our narrative, we focus not only on the dominant tradition but also on the diversity of alternative beliefs and practices.

Changes in the Third Edition

A reader comparing the second and third editions will notice changes in both structure and coverage. Most apparent among the structural changes are two new features. In each chapter a two-page primary source feature, "Diversity and Dominance," has replaced the brief "Society and Culture" excerpts of the previous edition. The new feature fills two needs. First, it gives students extended documentary selections on which to hone their analytical skills. This, we believe, will serve well the desire of many teachers to expose their students to the raw material with which historians work. Second, it provides a focus for students to consider the many forms of dominance that have developed over time and the many ways in which human diversity has continued to express itself regardless of these forms of dominance. The topics covered under "Diversity and Dominance" range from "Hierarchy and Conduct in the Analects of Confucius" (Chapter 3) and "Archbishop Adalbert of Hamburg and the Christianization of the Scandinavians and Slavs" (Chapter 10) to "The Afro-Brazilian Experience, 1828" (Chapter 24) and "Women, Family Values, and the Russian Revolution" (Chapter 30).

"Issues in World History," the second new feature, comprises original essays that appear at the end of Parts One through Seven. As we surveyed the burgeoning field of global history, we became aware of issues of such broad significance, often involving new kinds of historical evidence, that they could not easily be discussed in a chapter concentrating on a specific time and place. We therefore highlight seven of these issues in part-ending essays: "Animal Domestication," "Oral Societies and the Consequences of Literacy," "Religious Conversion," "Climate and Population, to 1500," "The Little Ice Age," "State Power, the Census, and the Question of Identity," and "Famines and Politics." We believe that teachers and students will be stimulated to see the great reach and exciting potential of the field of global history and be encouraged to pose broader questions of their own.

We sifted through a mass of helpful suggestions on how to revise and reorganize the content itself. Along with hundreds of minor revisions and clarifications, we effected a number of major changes:

- Chapters 3 and 4 have been rethought and reorganized: Chapter 3 now deals with several civilizations that emerged independently in different parts of the world in the second and first millennia B.C.E., while Chapter 4 focuses on the same time period in Western Asia and the Mediterranean, giving greater stress to continuity and interaction in that region.
- Chapter 10, on early medieval Europe, has been reorganized so that it opens with Byzantium and proceeds from there to western Europe. Two new maps have been added—one on German kingdoms, c. 530, and the other on Kievan Russia and the Byzantine Empire in the eleventh century.
- We greatly increased the coverage of Russian history, including expanded discussions in Chapters 10 and 21 and an entirely new section in Chapter 26.
- The history and impact of the Mongols are now covered in a single chapter, Chapter 13, "Mongol Eurasia and Its Aftermath, 1200–1500." Combining previously separated materials allowed us to make more evident the parallels and contrasts between the impact of the Mongols in the west and in the east.
- Chapter 17, on early modern Europe, has been reorganized and streamlined.
- Coverage of the United States in the late nineteenth century, previously in two separate chapters, has been reorganized and consolidated in Chapter 24.
- Chapter 26 now includes an extended discussion of the beginnings of European impact on Egypt.
- Discussions of the modernization of Japan in the late nineteenth century have been combined in Chapter 27. The discussion of nationalism now includes coverage of the unification of Italy as well as two new maps on the unifications of Italy and Germany.
- Chapter 33 brings the account of threats and strains to the global environment up to the present, including a new map showing stresses on the world's fresh water supplies.
- The final chapter, Chapter 34, "Globalization at the Turn of the Millennium," has been entirely rewritten to reflect current developments in global politics, the global economy, and global culture. New maps have been added showing regional trade associations and the unequal distribution of wealth around the world. The terrorist attacks of September 11 and the responses to them receive special attention.
- Suggested Reading lists were updated with important recent scholarship.

Organization

The Earth and Its Peoples uses eight broad chronological divisions to define its conceptual scheme of global historical development. In **Part One: The Emergence of Human Communities, to 500 B.C.E.,** we examine important patterns of human communal organization in both the Eastern and Western Hemispheres. Small, dispersed human communities living by foraging spread to most parts of the world over tens of thousands of years. They responded to enormously diverse environmental conditions, at different times in different ways, discovering how to cultivate plants and utilize the products of domestic animals. On the basis of these new modes of sustenance, population grew, permanent towns appeared, and political and religious authority, based on collection and control of agricultural surpluses, spread over extensive areas.

Part Two: The Formation of New Cultural Communities, 1000 B.C.E.–400 C.E., introduces the concept of a "cultural community," in the sense of a coherent pattern of activities and symbols pertaining to a specific human community. While all human communities develop distinctive cultures, including those discussed in Part One, historical development in this stage of global history prolonged and magnified the impact of some cultures more than others. In the geographically contiguous African-Eurasian land mass, the cultures that proved to have the most enduring influence traced their roots to the second and first millennia B.C.E.

Part Three: Growth and Interaction of Cultural Communities, 300 B.C.E.–1200 C.E., deals with early episodes of technological, social, and cultural exchange and interaction on a continental scale both within and beyond the framework of imperial expansion. These are so different from earlier interactions arising from more limited conquests or extensions of political boundaries that they constitute a distinct era in world history, an era that set the world on the path of increasing global interaction and interdependence that it has been following ever since.

In Part Four: Interregional Patterns of Culture and Contact, 1200–1550, we look at the world during the three and a half centuries that saw both intensified cultural and commercial contact and increasingly confident self-definition of cultural communities in Europe, Asia, and Africa. The Mongol conquest of a vast empire extending from the Pacific Ocean to eastern Europe greatly stimulated trade and interaction. In the West, strengthened European kingdoms began maritime expansion in the Atlantic, forging direct ties with sub-Saharan Africa and beginning the conquest of the civilizations of the Western Hemisphere.

Part Five: The Globe Encompassed, 1500–1750, treats a period dominated by the global effects of European expansion and continued economic growth. European ships took over, expanded, and extended the maritime trade of the Indian Ocean, coastal Africa, and the Asian rim of the Pacific Ocean. This maritime commercial enterprise had its counterpart in European colonial empires in the Americas and a new Atlantic trading system. The contrasting capacities and fortunes of traditional land empires and new maritime empires, along with the exchange of domestic plants and animals between the hemispheres, underline the technological and environmental dimensions of this first era of complete global interaction.

In Part Six: Revolutions Reshape the World, 1750–1870, the word *revolution* is used in several senses: in the political sense of governmental overthrow, as in France and the Americas; in the metaphorical sense of radical transformative change, as in the Industrial Revolution; and in the broadest sense of a perception of a profound change in circumstances and worldview. Technology and environment lie at the core of these developments. With the rapid ascendancy of the Western belief that science and technology could overcome all challenges—environmental or otherwise—technology became an instrument not only of transformation but also of domination, to the point of threatening the integrity and autonomy of cultural traditions in nonindustrial lands.

Part Seven: Global Diversity and Dominance, 1850–1945, examines the development of a world arena in which people conceived of events on a global scale. Imperialism, world war, international economic connections, and world-encompassing ideological tendencies, such as nationalism and socialism, present the picture of a globe becoming increasingly interconnected. European dominance took on a worldwide dimension, seeming at times to threaten the diversity of human cultural experience with permanent subordination to European values and philosophies, while at other times triggering strong political or cultural resistance.

For Part Eight: Perils and Promises of a Global Community, 1945 to the Present, we divided the last half of the twentieth century into three time periods: 1945–1975, 1975–1991, and 1991 to the present. The challenges of the Cold War and post-colonial nation building dominated most of the period and unleashed global economic, technological, and political forces that became increasingly important in all aspects of human life. Technology plays a central role in Part Eight, because of its integral role in the growth of a global community and because its many benefits in improving the quality of life seem clouded by real and potential negative impacts on the environment.

Formats

To accommodate different academic calendars and approaches to the course, *The Earth and Its Peoples* is available in three formats. There is a one-volume hard-cover version containing all 34 chapters, along with a two-volume paperback edition: Volume I: *To 1550* (Chapters 1–16) and Volume II: *Since 1500* (Chapters 16–34). For readers at institutions with the quarter system, we offer a three-volume paperback version: Volume A: *To 1200* (Chapters 1–12); Volume B: *From 1200 to 1870* (Chapters 12–26); and Volume C: *Since 1750* (Chapters 22–34). Volume II includes an Introduction that surveys the main developments set out in Volume I and provides a groundwork for students studying only the period since 1500.

Supplements

We have assembled an array of supplements to aid students in learning and instructors in teaching. These supplements, including our new *History Companion*, a *Study Guide*, an *Instructor's Resource Manual*, *Test Items*, *Blackboard* and *Web CT* course cartridges, and *Map Transparencies* provide a tightly integrated program of teaching and learning.

In keeping with Houghton Mifflin's goal of being your primary source for history, we are proud to announce the *History Companion*, your new primary source for history technology solutions. History instructors have enough to do without having to master new software or download the latest plug-in to gain access to primary sources, maps, and other tools of the trade. The *History Companion* provides hundreds of resources with only a few clicks of your mouse. The *History Companion* has three components:

The *Instructor Companion* is an easily searchable CD-ROM that makes hundreds of historical images and maps instantly accessible in PowerPoint format. Each image is accompanied by notes that place it in its proper historical context and tips for ways it can be presented in the classroom. This CD is free to instructors with the adoption of this or any Houghton Mifflin history textbook. In addition to visual presentation materials, the CD includes our *HM Testing* program; a computerized version of the *Test Items* to enable instructors to alter, replace, or add questions; as well as resources from the *Instructor's Resource Manual*.

The *Student Research Companion* is a free Internet-based tool with 100 interactive maps and 500 primary sources. The primary sources include headnotes that provide pertinent background information and questions that students can answer and email to their instructors.

The *Student Study Companion* is a free online study guide that contains ACE self-tests, which feature 25 to 30 multiple-choice questions per chapter with feedback, an audio pronunciation guide, web-based flashcards, chapter chronologies, and web links. In addition, *History WIRED: Web Intensive Research Exercises and Documents*, updated by John Reisbord (Ph.D. Northwestern University), offers text-specific links to visual and written sources on the World Wide Web, along with exercises to enhance learning. These study tools will help make your students succeed in the classroom.

The *Study Guide*, authored by Michele G. Scott James of MiraCosta College, contains learning objectives, chapter outlines (with space for students' notes on particular sections), key-term identifications, multiple-choice questions, short-answer and essay questions, and map exercises. Included too are distinctive "comparison charts" to help students organize the range of information about different cultures and events discussed in each chapter. The *Study Guide* is published in two volumes, to correspond to Volumes I and II of the textbook: Volume I contains Chapters 1–16; Volume II, Chapters 16–34.

The *Instructor's Resource Manual*, thoroughly revised by John Reisbord (Ph.D. Northwestern University), provides useful teaching strategies for the global history course and tips for getting the most out of the text. Each chapter contains instructional objectives, a detailed chapter outline, discussion questions, in-depth learning projects, and audio-visual resources.

Our *Test Items*, prepared by Jane Scimeca of Brookdale Community College, offers 20 to 25 key-term identifications, 5 to 10 essay questions with answer guidelines, 35 to 40 multiple-choice questions, and 2 to 3 history and geography exercises.

We have designed *Blackboard* and *WebCT* course cartridges for institutions using these platforms, so that students and instructors can access a wealth of resources including learning objectives, chapter outlines, and Internet assignments, in addition to our testing and quizzing programs.

Finally, a set of transparencies of all the maps in the textbook is available on adoption.

Acknowledgments

In preparing the third edition, we benefited from the critical readings of many colleagues. Our sincere thanks go in particular to the following instructors: Joseph Adams, Walton High School, Cobb County, Georgia; William H. Alexander, Norfolk State University; Corinne Blake, Rowan University; Olwyn M. Blouet, Virginia State University; Eric Bobo, Hinds Community College; James Boyden, Tulane University; Craige B.

Champion, Syracuse University; Eleanor A. Congdon, Youngstown State University; Philip Daileader, The College of William and Mary; Donald M. Fisher, Niagara County Community College; Nancy Fitch, California State University, Fullerton; Jay Harmon, Catholic High School, Baton Rouge, Louisiana; Carol A. Keller, San Antonio College; Susan Maneck, Jackson State University; Laurie S. Mannino, Magruder High School, North Potomac, Maryland; Margaret Malamud, New Mexico State University; Randall McGowen, University of Oregon; Diethelm Prowe, Carleton College; Michael D. Richards, Sweet Briar College; William Schell, Jr., Murray State University; Jeffrey M. Shumway, Brigham Young University; Jonathan Skaff, Shippensburg University of Pennsylvania; Tracy L. Steele, Sam Houston State University; and Peter von Sivers, University of Utah.

When textbook authors set out on a project, they are inclined to believe that 90 percent of the effort will be theirs and 10 percent that of various editors and production specialists employed by their publisher. How very naïve. This book would never have seen the light of day had it not been for the unstinting labors of the great team of professionals who turned the authors' words into beautifully presented print. Our debt to the staff of Houghton Mifflin remains undiminished in the third edition. Nancy Blaine, Senior Sponsoring Editor, has offered us firm but sympathetic guidance throughout the revision process. Jennifer Sutherland, Senior Development Editor, offered astute and sympathetic assistance as the authors worked to incorporate many new ideas and subjects into the text. Carol Newman, Senior Project Editor, moved the work through the production stages to meet what had initially seemed like an unachievable schedule. Carole Frolich did an outstanding job of art and photo research. Jill Haber, Senior Production Design Coordinator, dealt with many of the technological issues that arise in producing a text of this size. We also recognize the invaluable contributions of Senior Designer Henry Rachlin, who created the book's elegant new design, Editorial Associate Annette Fantasia, who oversaw the review process and the preparation of supplemental material, and Florence Cadran, Manufacturing Manager, who saw to it that the text was printed on schedule.

We thank also the many students whose questions and concerns, expressed directly or through their instructors, shaped much of this revision. We continue to welcome all readers' suggestions, queries, and criticisms. Please contact us at our respective institutions or at this e-mail address: college_history@hmco.com

About the Authors

Richard W. Bulliet Professor of Middle Eastern History at Columbia University, Richard W. Bulliet received his Ph.D. from Harvard University. He has written scholarly works on a number of topics: the social history of medieval Iran *(The Patricians of Nishapur)*, the historical competition between pack camels and wheeled transport *(The Camel and the Wheel)*, the process of conversion to Islam *(Conversion to Islam in the Medieval Period)*, and the overall course of Islamic social history *(Islam: The View from the Edge)*. He is the editor of the *Columbia History of the Twentieth Century*. He has published four novels, co-edited *The Encyclopedia of the Modern Middle East*, and hosted an educational television series on the Middle East. He was awarded a fellowship by the John Simon Guggenheim Memorial Foundation.

Pamela Kyle Crossley Pamela Kyle Crossley received her Ph.D. in Modern Chinese History from Yale University. She is Professor of History and Rosenwald Research Professor in the Arts and Sciences at Dartmouth College. Her books include *A Translucent Mirror: History and Identity in Qing Imperial Ideology; The Manchus; Orphan Warriors: Three Manchu Generations and the End of the Qing World;* and (with Lynn Hollen Lees and John W. Servos) *Global Society: The World Since 1900*. Her research, which concentrates on the cultural history of China, Inner Asia, and Central Asia, has been supported by the John Simon Guggenheim Memorial Foundation and the National Endowment for the Humanities.

Daniel R. Headrick Daniel R. Headrick received his Ph.D. in History from Princeton University. Professor of History and Social Science at Roosevelt University in Chicago, he is the author of several books on the history of technology, imperialism, and international relations, including *The Tools of Empire: Technology and European Imperialism in the Nineteenth Century; The Tentacles of Progress: Technology Transfer in the Age of Imperialism; The Invisible Weapon: Telecommunications and International Politics;* and *When Information Came of Age: Technologies of Knowledge in the Age of Reason and Revolution, 1700–1850*. His articles have appeared in the *Journal of World History* and the *Journal of Modern History,* and he has been awarded fellowships by the National Endowment for the Humanities, the John Simon Guggenheim Memorial Foundation, and the Alfred P. Sloan Foundation.

Steven W. Hirsch Steven W. Hirsch holds a Ph.D. in Classics from Stanford University and is currently Associate Professor Classics and History at Tufts University. He has received grants from the National Endowment for the Humanities and the Massachusetts Foundation for Humanities and Public Policy. His research and publications include *The Friendship of the Barbarians: Xenophon and the Persian Empire,* as well as articles and reviews in the *Classical Journal,* the *American Journal of Philology,* and the *Journal of Interdisciplinary History.* He is currently working on a comparative study of ancient Mediterranean and Chinese civilizations.

Lyman L. Johnson Professor of History at the University of North Carolina at Charlotte, Lyman L. Johnson earned his Ph.D. in Latin American History from the University of Connecticut. A two-time Senior Fulbright-Hays Lecturer, he also has received fellowships from the Tinker Foundation, the Social Science Research Council, the National Endowment for the Humanities, and the American Philosophical Society. His recent books include *Death, Dismemberment, and Memory; The Faces of Honor* (with Sonya Lipsett-Rivera); *The Problem of Order in Changing Societies; Essays on the Price History of Eighteenth-Century Latin America* (with Enrique Tandeter); and *Colonial Latin America* (with Mark A. Burkholder). He also has published in journals, including the *Hispanic American Historical Review,* the *Journal of Latin American Studies,* the *International Review of Social History, Social History,* and *Desarrollo Económico.* He recently served as president of the Conference on Latin American History.

David Northrup Professor of History at Boston College, David Northrup earned his Ph.D. in African and European History from the University of California at Los Angeles. He earlier taught in Nigeria with the Peace Corps and at Tuskegee Institute. Research supported by the Fulbright-Hays Commission, the National Endowment for the Humanities, and the Social Science Research Council led to publications concerning pre-colonial Nigeria, the Congo (1870–1940), the Atlantic slave trade, and Asian, African, and Pacific Islander indentured labor in the nineteenth century. A contributor to the *Oxford History of the British Empire* and *Blacks in the British Empire,* his latest book is *Africa's Discovery of Europe, 1450–1850.* For 2004 and 2005 he serves as president of the World History Association.

Note on Spelling and Usage

Where necessary for clarity, dates are followed by the letters C.E. or B.C.E. The abbreviation C.E. stands for "Common Era" and is equivalent to A.D. (*anno Domini,* Latin for "in the year of the Lord"). The abbreviation B.C.E stands for "before the Common Era" and means the same as B.C. ("before Christ"). In keeping with our goal of approaching world history without special concentration on one culture or another, we chose these neutral abbreviations as appropriate to our enterprise. Because many readers will be more familiar with English than with metric measurements, however, units of measure are generally given in the English system, with metric equivalents following in parentheses.

In general, Chinese has been romanized according to the *pinyin* method. Exceptions include proper names well established in English (e.g., Canton, Chiang Kai-shek) and a few English words borrowed from Chinese (e.g., kowtow). Spellings of Arabic, Ottoman Turkish, Persian, Mongolian, Manchu, Japanese, and Korean names and terms avoid special diacritical marks for letters that are pronounced only slightly differently in English. An apostrophe is used to indicate when two Chinese syllables are pronounced separately (e.g., Chang'an).

For words transliterated from languages that use the Arabic script—Arabic, Ottoman Turkish, Perisan, Urdu—the apostrophe indicating separately pronounced syllables may represent either of two special consonants, the *hamza* or the *ain.* Because most English-speakers do not hear the distinction between these two, they have not been distinguished in transliteration and are not indicated when they occur at the beginning or end of a word. As with Chinese, some words and commonly used place-names from these languages are given familiar English spellings (e.g., Quran instead of Qur'an, Cairo instead of al-Qahira). Arabic romanization has normally been used for terms relating to Islam, even where the context justifies slightly different Turkish or Persian forms, again for ease of comprehension.

Before 1492 the inhabitants of the Western Hemisphere had no single name for themselves. They had neither a racial consciousness nor a racial identity. Identity was derived from kin groups, language, cultural practices, and political structures. There was no sense that physical similarities created a shared identity. America's original inhabitants had racial consciousness and racial identity imposed on them by conquest and the occupation of their lands by Europeans after 1492. All of the collective terms for these first American peoples are tainted by this history. *Indians, Native Americans, Amerindians, First Peoples, and Indigenous Peoples* are among the terms in common usage. In this book the names of individual cultures and states are used wherever possible. *Amerindian* and other terms that suggest transcultural identity and experience are used most commonly for the period after 1492.

There is an ongoing debate about how best to render Amerindian words in English. It has been common for authors writing in English to follow Mexican usage for Nahuatl and Yucatec Maya words and place-names. In this style, for example, the capital of the Aztec state is spelled Tenochtitlán, and the important late Maya city-state is spelled Chichén Itzá. Although these forms are still common even in the specialist literature, we have chosen to follow the scholarship that sees these accents as unnecessary. The exceptions are modern place-names, such as Mérida and Yucatán, which are accented. A similar problem exists for the spelling of Quechua and Aymara words from the Andean region of South America. Although there is significant disagreement among scholars, we follow the emerging consensus and use the spellings khipu (not quipu), Tiwanaku (not Tiahuanaco), and Wari (not Huari). However, we keep Inca (not Inka) and Cuzco (not Cusco), since these spellings are expected by most of our potential readers and we hope to avoid confusion.

The Earth and Its Peoples

A Global History

The Emergence of Human Communities, to 500 B.C.E.

Human beings evolved over several million years from primates in Africa. Differing from other primates in their ability to walk upright on two legs and their possession of large brains, hands with opposable thumbs, and the capacity for speech, early humans used teamwork and created tools that enabled them to survive in diverse environments. They spread relatively quickly to almost every habitable area of the world, sustaining themselves by hunting and by gathering wild plant products. Then, around 10,000 years ago, some human groups began to cultivate plants, domesticate animals, and make pottery vessels for storage. One consequence of this shift to agriculture was the emergence of permanent settlements—at first small villages but eventually larger towns as well.

The earliest complex societies arose in the great river valleys of Asia and Africa, around 3100 B.C.E. in the valley between the Tigris and Euphrates Rivers in Mesopotamia and along the Nile River in Egypt, somewhat later in the valley of the Indus River in Pakistan, and on the floodplain of the Yellow River in China. In these arid regions, agriculture depended on irrigation with river water, and centers of political power arose to organize the massive human labor required to dig and maintain channels to carry water to the fields.

Kings and priests dominated these early societies. Kings controlled the military forces; priests managed the temples and the wealth of the gods. Within the urban centers—in the midst of palaces, temples, fortification walls, and other monumental buildings—lived administrators, soldiers, priests, merchants, craftsmen, and others with specialized skills. The production of surplus food grown on rural estates by a dependent peasantry sustained the activities of these groups. Professional scribes kept administrative and financial records and preserved their civilization's religious and scientific knowledge.

Over time, certain centers extended their influence and came to dominate broad expanses of territory. The rulers of these early empires were motivated primarily by the need to secure access to raw materials, especially tin and copper, from which to make bronze. A similar motive accounts for the development of long-distance trade and diplomatic relations between major powers. Fueling long-distance trade was the desire for bronze, which had both practical and symbolic importance. From bronze, artisans made weapons, tools and utensils, and ritual objects. Ownership of bronze items was a sign of wealth and power. Trade and diplomacy helped spread culture and technology from the core river-valley areas to neighboring regions, such as southern China, Nubia, Syria-Palestine, Anatolia, and the Aegean.

In the Western Hemisphere, different geographical circumstances called forth distinctive patterns of technological and cultural response in the early civilizations of the Olmec in southern Mexico and Chavín in the Andean region of South America. Nevertheless, the challenges of organizing agriculture and trade led to many of the same features of complex societies—social stratification, specialization of labor, urbanization, monumental building, technological development, and artistic achievement.

	8000 B.C.E.	7000 B.C.E.	6000 B.C.E.	5000 B.C.E.
Americas		• 7000 Incipient plant domestication in Peru		• 5000 Maize, beans, and squash domestication in Mesoamerica
Europe	Spread of Indo-European languages		• 6000 Farming in southern Europe	
Africa	• 8000 Farming in eastern Sahara		• 5500 Farming in Egypt	
Middle East	• 8000 Domestication of plants and animals in Fertile Crescent			• 5000 Irrigation in Mesopotamia
Asia and Oceania		• 6500 Rice cultivation in China		• 5000 Farming in India

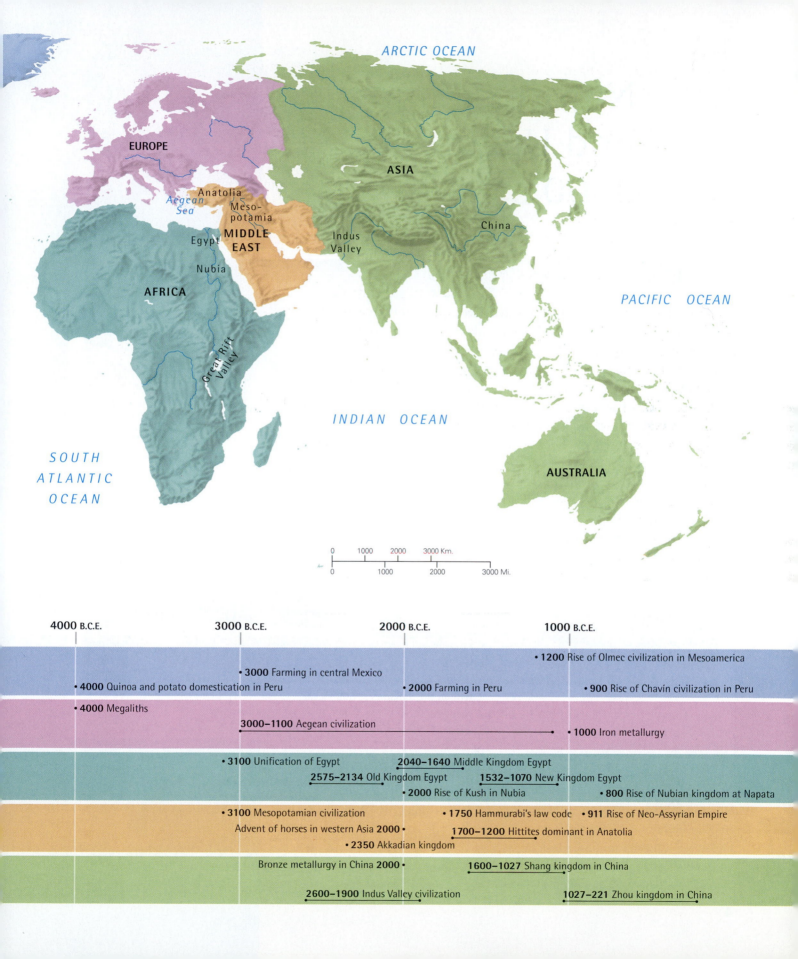

ARCTIC OCEAN

EUROPE

Aegean Sea

ASIA

Anatolia

Meso-
potamia

MIDDLE
EAST

Egypt

China

Indus
Valley

Nubia

AFRICA

PACIFIC OCEAN

Great Rift Valley

INDIAN OCEAN

SOUTH
ATLANTIC
OCEAN

AUSTRALIA

0   1000   2000   3000 Km.

0   1000   2000   3000 Mi.

4000 B.C.E.	3000 B.C.E.	2000 B.C.E.	1000 B.C.E.

• **1200** Rise of Olmec civilization in Mesoamerica

• **3000** Farming in central Mexico

• **4000** Quinoa and potato domestication in Peru

• **2000** Farming in Peru

• **900** Rise of Chavín civilization in Peru

• **4000** Megaliths

3000–1100 Aegean civilization

• **1000** Iron metallurgy

• **3100** Unification of Egypt

2040–1640 Middle Kingdom Egypt

2575–2134 Old Kingdom Egypt

1532–1070 New Kingdom Egypt

• **2000** Rise of Kush in Nubia

• **800** Rise of Nubian kingdom at Napata

• **3100** Mesopotamian civilization

• **1750** Hammurabi's law code   • **911** Rise of Neo-Assyrian Empire

Advent of horses in western Asia **2000** •

1700–1200 Hittites dominant in Anatolia

• **2350** Akkadian kingdom

Bronze metallurgy in China **2000** •

1600–1027 Shang kingdom in China

2600–1900 Indus Valley civilization

1027–221 Zhou kingdom in China

1

Nature, Humanity, and History to 3500 B.C.E.

Cattle in the Sahara, ca. 5000 B.C.E.
During a rainy era when grass grew in what is now desert unknown artists enscribed rock outcroppings with images of the herds that roamed there.

4

According to a story handed down by the Yoruba° people of West Africa, at one time there was only water below the sky. Then the divine Owner of the Sky let down a chain by which his son Oduduwa° descended along with sixteen male companions. Oduduwa scattered a handful of soil across the water and set down a chicken that scratched the soil into the shape of the land. A palm nut that he planted in the soil grew to become the bountiful forest that is the home of the Yoruba people. Oduduwa was their first king.

At some point in their history most human societies began telling similar stories about their origins. Some related that the first humans came down from the sky, others that they emerged out of a hole in the ground. Historical accuracy was not the point of such creation myths. Like the story of Adam and Eve in the Hebrew Bible, their primary purpose was to define the moral principles that people thought should govern their dealings with the supernatural world, with each other, and with the rest of nature. In addition, they provided an explanation of how a people's way of life, social divisions, and cultural system arose.

In the nineteenth century evidence started to accumulate that human beings had quite different origins. Natural scientists were finding remains of early humans who resembled apes rather than gods. Other evidence suggested that the familiar ways of life based on farming and herding did not arise within a generation or two of creation, as the myths suggested, but tens of thousands of years after humans first appeared. Although such evidence has long stirred controversy, a careful questioning of it reveals insights into human identity that may be as meaningful as those propounded by the creation myths.

As you read this chapter, ask yourself the following questions:

- What is the significance of the fact that humans evolved as part of the natural world, subject to its laws?

- How did the physical and mental abilities that humans gradually evolved give them a unique capacity to adapt to new environments by altering their

way of life rather than by evolving physically as other species did?

- After nearly 2 million years of physical and cultural development, how did human communities in different parts of the world learn how to manipulate the natural world, domesticating plants and animals for their food and use? In short, how did people's relationship with their environments change?

AFRICAN GENESIS

The discovery in the mid-nineteenth century of the remains of ancient creatures that were at once humanlike and apelike generated both excitement and controversy. The evidence upset many people because it challenged accepted beliefs about human origins. Others welcomed the new evidence as proof of what some researchers had long suspected: the physical characteristics of modern humans, like those of all other creatures, had evolved over incredibly long periods of time. Until recently, the evidence was too fragmentary to be convincing.

Interpreting the Evidence

In 1856 in the Neander Valley of what is now Germany, laborers discovered fossilized bones of a creature with a body much like that of modern humans but with a face that, like the faces of apes, had heavy brow ridges and a low forehead. Although we now know these "Neanderthals" were a type of human common in Europe some 40,000 years ago, in the mid-nineteenth century the idea that humans so different in appearance from modern people could have existed was so novel that some of the scholars who first examined them thought they must be deformed individuals from recent times.

Three years after the Neanderthal finds, Charles Darwin, a young English naturalist (student of natural history), published *On the Origin of Species*. In this work he argued that the time frame for all biological life was far longer than most persons had supposed. Darwin based his conclusion on pioneering naturalists' research and on his own investigations of fossils and living plant and animal species in Latin America. He proposed that the great diversity of living species and the profound changes in them over time could be explained by **evolution,** the process by which biological variations that enhance a population's ability to survive became dominant in that species. He theorized that, over very long periods

---

Yoruba (yoh-roo-bah) **Oduduwa** (oh-DOO-doo-wah)

Fossilized Footprints   Archaeologist Mary Leakey (shown at top) found these remarkable footprints of a hominid adult and child at Laetoli, Tanzania. The pair had walked through fresh volcanic ash that solidified after being buried by a new volcanic eruption. Dated to 3.5 million years ago, the footprints are the oldest evidence of bipedalism yet found.   (John Reader/Photo Researchers, Inc.)

of time, the changes brought about by evolution could lead to distinct new species.

Turning to the sensitive subject of human evolution in *The Descent of Man* (1871), Darwin summarized the growing consensus among naturalists that human beings had also come into existence through the same process of natural selection. Because humans shared so many physical similarities with African apes, he proposed that Africa must have been the home of the first humans, even though there was no fossil evidence at the time to support his hypothesis.

Instead, the next major discoveries pointed to Asia, rather than Africa, as the original human home. On the Southeast Asian island of Java in 1891 Eugene Dubois uncovered an ancient skullcap of what was soon called "Java man," a find that has since been dated to 1.8 mil-

lion years ago. In 1929 near Peking (Beijing°), China, W. C. Pei discovered a similar skullcap of what became known as "Peking man."

By then, even older fossils had been found in southern Africa. In 1924, while examining fossils from a lime quarry, Raymond Dart found the skull of an ancient creature that he named *Australopithecus africanus*° (African southern ape), which he argued was transitional between apes and early humans. For many years most specialists disputed Dart's idea, because, although *Australopithecus africanus* walked upright like a human, its brain was ape-size. Such an idea went against their expectations that large brains would have evolved first and that Asia, not Africa, was the first home of humans.

Since 1950, Louis and Mary Leakey and their son Richard, along with many others, have discovered a wealth of early human fossils in the exposed sediments of the Great Rift Valley of eastern Africa. These finds are strong evidence for Dart's hypothesis and for Darwin's guess that the tropical habitat of the African apes was the cradle of humanity.

The development of precise archaeological techniques has enhanced the quantity of evidence currently available. Rather than collect isolated bones, modern researchers literally sift the neighboring soils to extract the remains of other creatures existing at the time, locating fossilized seeds and even pollen by which to document the environment in which the humans lived. They can also measure the age of most finds by the rate of molecular change in potassium, in minerals in lava flows, or in carbon from wood and bone.

By combining that evidence with the growing understanding of how other species adapt to their natural environments, scientists can describe with some precision when, where, and how human beings evolved and how they lived. As the result of this new work, it is now possible to trace the evolutionary changes that produced modern humans during a period of 4 million years. As Darwin suspected, the earliest transitional creatures have been found only in Africa; the later human species (including Java man and Peking man) had wider global distribution.

Human Evolution

Evidence that humans evolved gradually over millions of years caused much debate about how species should be defined. Biologists now classify **australopithecines**° and humans as members of a fam-

---

Beijing (bay-jeeng)   *Australopithecus africanus* (aw-strah-loh-PITH-uh-kuhs ah-frih-KAH-nuhs)   **Australopithecine** (aw-strah-loh-PITH-uh-seen)

CHRONOLOGY

	Geological Epochs	Species and Migrations	Technological Advances
3,000,000 B.C.E.			
		2,500,000 B.C.E. early *Homo habilis*	**2,500,000** B.C.E. earliest stone tools; hunting and gathering (foraging) societies
2,000,000 B.C.E.	**2,000,000–9000** B.C.E. Pleistocene (Great Ice Age)	**1,900,000 to 350,000** B.C.E. *Homo erectus*	
1,000,000 B.C.E.		**400,000–130,000** B.C.E. archaic *Homo sapiens*	**500,000** B.C.E. use of fire for cooking
		150,000 B.C.E.–**present** modern *Homo sapiens* in Africa	
100,000 B.C.E.		**after 100,000** B.C.E. modern humans in Eurasia	**70,000** B.C.E. first known cave art
		by 50,000 B.C.E. modern humans in Australia	**35,000** B.C.E. first cave paintings
10,000 B.C.E.	**9000** B.C.E.–**present** Holocene	**by 13,000** B.C.E. modern humans in Americas	**8000–2000** B.C.E. Neolithic (New Stone) Age; earliest agriculture

ily of primates known as **hominids°**. Primates are members of a family of warm-blooded, four-limbed, social animals known as mammals that first appeared about 65 million years ago. The first hominids date to about 7 million years ago.

Within the primate kingdom modern humans are most closely related to the African apes—chimpanzees and gorillas. Since Darwin's time it has been popular (and controversial) to say that we are descended from apes. Modern research has found that over 98 percent of human DNA, the basic genetic blueprint, is identical to that of the great apes.

But three traits distinguish humans from apes and other primates. As Dart's australopithecines demonstrated, the earliest of these traits to appear was **bipedalism** (walking upright on two legs). This frees the forelimbs from any necessary role in locomotion and enhances an older primate trait: a hand that has a long thumb that can work with the fingers to manipulate objects skillfully. Modern humans' second distinctive trait was a very large brain. Besides enabling humans to think abstractly, experience profound emotions, and construct complex social relationships, this larger brain controls the fine motor movements of the hand and of the tongue, increasing humans' tool-using capacity and facilitating the development of speech. The physical possibility of language, however, depends on a third distinctive human trait: the location of the human larynx (voice box). It lies much lower in the neck than does the larynx of any other primate. This trait is associated with many other changes in the face and neck.

---

hominid (HOM-uh-nid)

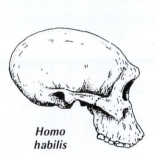
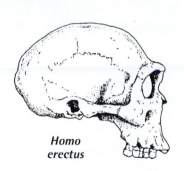
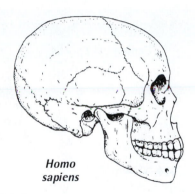

Homo habilis   *Homo erectus*   *Homo sapiens*

Evolution of the Human Brain   These drawings of skulls show the extensive cranial changes associated with the increase in brain size during the 3 million years from *Homo habilis* to *Homo sapiens sapiens.*

How and why did these immensely important biological changes take place? Scientists still employ Darwin's concept of natural selection, attributing the development of distinctive human traits to the preservation of genetic changes that enhanced survivability. Although the details have not been fully worked out, it is widely accepted that major shifts in the world's climate led to evolutionary changes in human ancestors and other species. About 10 million years ago, falling temperatures in temperate regions culminated in the **Great Ice Age,** or Pleistocene° epoch, extending from about 2 million to about 11,000 years ago (see Chronology). The Pleistocene included more than a dozen very cold periods, each spanning several thousand years, separated by warmer periods. These temperature changes and the altered rainfall and vegetation that accompanied them imposed great strains on existing plant and animal species. As a result, large numbers of new species evolved.

During the Pleistocene, massive glaciers of frozen water spread out from the poles and mountains. At their peak such glaciers covered a third of the earth's surface and contained so much frozen water that ocean levels were lowered by over 450 feet (140 meters), exposing land bridges between many places now isolated by water (see Map 1.1).

Although the glaciers did not extend beyond the arctic and temperate zones, the equatorial regions of the world probably also experienced altered climates during the Pleistocene epoch. Between 3 million and 4 million years ago, several new species of bipedal australopithecines evolved in southern and eastern Africa. In a re-

markable find in northern Ethiopia in 1974, Donald Johanson unearthed a well-preserved skeleton of a twenty-five-year-old female, whom he nicknamed "Lucy." Mary Leakey's related discovery of fossilized footprints in Tanzania in 1977 provided spectacular visual evidence that australopithecines walked on two legs.

Bipedalism evolved because it provided australopithecines with some advantage for survival. Some studies suggest that walking and running on two legs is very energy efficient. Another theory is that bipeds survived better because they could carry armfuls of food back to their mates and children. Whatever its decisive advantage, bipedalism led to other changes.

Climate changes between 2 million and 3 million years ago led to the evolution of a new species, the first to be classified in the same genus (*Homo*) with modern humans. At Olduvai° Gorge in northern Tanzania in the early 1960s, Louis Leakey discovered the first fossilized remains of this creature, which he named **Homo habilis°** (handy human). What most distinguished *Homo habilis* from the australopithecines was a brain that was nearly 50 percent larger. A larger brain would have added to the new species' intelligence. What was happening in this period that favored greater mental capacity? Some scientists believe that the answer had to do with food. Greater intelligence enabled *Homo habilis* to locate a vast number of different kinds of things to eat throughout the seasons of the year. They point to seeds and other fossilized remains in ancient *Homo habilis* camps that indicate that the new species ate a greater variety of more nutritious seasonal foods than did the australopithecines.

Pleistocene (PLY-stuh-seen)

Olduvai (ol-DOO-vy)   ***Homo habilis*** (HOH-moh HAB-uh-luhs)

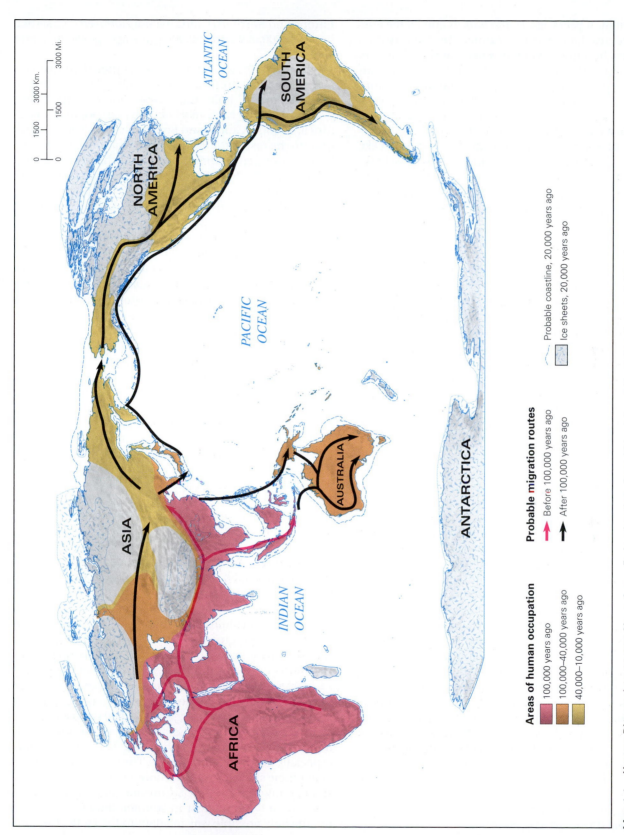

Map 1.1   Human Dispersal to 10,000 Years Ago   Early migrations from Africa into southern Eurasia were followed by treks across land bridges during cold spells, when giant ice sheets had lowered ocean levels. Boats may also have been employed.

By 1 million years ago *Homo habilis* and all the australopithecines had become extinct. In their habitat lived a new hominid, **Homo erectus**° (upright human), which had first appeared in eastern Africa about 1.9 million years ago. These creatures possessed brains a third larger than those of *Homo habilis,* which presumably accounted for their better survivability. A nearly complete skeleton of a twelve-year-old male of the species discovered by Richard Leakey in 1984 on the shores of Lake Turkana in Kenya shows that *Homo erectus* closely resembled modern people from the neck down. *Homo erectus* was very successful in dealing with different environments and underwent hardly any biological changes over a million years.

However, by a long, imperfectly understood evolutionary process between 400,000 and 130,000 years ago, a new human species emerged: **Homo sapiens**° (wise human). The brains of *Homo sapiens* were a third larger than those of *Homo erectus,* whom they gradually superseded. Indeed, these brains were more than three times the size one would expect in another primate of comparable body size and gave *Homo sapiens* tremendous capacity for speech.

This slow but remarkable process of physical evolution, which distinguished humans by a small but significant degree from other primates, was one part of what was happening. Equally remarkable was the way in which humans were extending their habitat.

Migrations from Africa

Early humans first expanded their range in eastern and southern Africa. Then they ventured out of Africa, perhaps following migrating herds of animals or searching for more abundant food supplies in a time of drought. The reasons are uncertain, but the end results are vividly clear: Humans successfully colonized environments, including deserts and arctic lands (see Map 1.1). This dispersal demonstrates early humans' talent for adaptation.

Homo erectus was the first human species to inhabit all parts of Africa and the first to be found outside Africa. Java Man and Peking Man were members of this species. By migrating overland from Africa across southern Asia, *Homo erectus* reached Java as early as 1.8 million years ago. At that time, because of the great volume of water trapped in ice-age glaciers, sea levels were so low that Java was not an island but was part of the Southeast Asian mainland. Java's climate would have been no colder than East Africa's. The harsh winters of northern

Europe and northern China, where *Homo erectus* settled between 700,000 and 300,000 years ago, posed a greater challenge.

DNA and fossil evidence suggest that *Homo sapiens* spread outward from an African homeland, although some scientists hold that *Homo sapiens* may have evolved separately from *Homo erectus* populations in Africa, Europe, China, and Southeast Asia. Their migrations to the rest of the world would have been made easier by a wet period that transformed the normally arid Sahara and Middle East into fertile grasslands until about 40,000 years ago. The abundance of plant and animal food during this wet period would have promoted an increase in human populations.

By the end of the wet period, further evolutionary changes had produced fully modern humans (*Homo sapiens sapiens*). This new species displaced older human populations, such as the Neanderthals in Europe, and penetrated for the first time into the Americas, Australia, and the Arctic.

During glacial periods when sea levels were low, hunters would have been able to cross a land bridge from northeastern Asia into North America. Recently a hypothesis has been advanced that some early colonizers of the Americas may also have come by boat along the Pacific coast. As these pioneers from East Asia and later migrants moved southward (penetrating southern South America by at least 12,500 years ago), they passed through lands teeming with life, including easily hunted large animal species. Meanwhile, traveling by boat from Java, other modern humans colonized New Guinea and Australia when both were part of a single landmass, and they crossed the land bridge then existing between the Asian mainland and Japan. Australia was reached by about 50,000 years ago. For a time, new waves of migrants entered the Americas and Australia. Then, when the glaciers melted, the seas rose and the lands underwent a long period of isolation from the rest of humanity.

As populations migrated, they may have undergone some minor evolutionary changes that helped them adapt to extreme environments. One such change was in skin color. The deeply pigmented skin of today's indigenous inhabitants of the tropics (and presumably of all early humans who evolved there) is an adaptation that reduces the harmful effects of the harsh tropical sun. At some point, possibly as recently as 5,000 years ago, especially pale skin became characteristic of Europeans living in northern latitudes that had far less sunshine, especially during winter months. The loss of pigment enabled their skin to produce more vitamin D from sunshine, though it exposed Europeans to a greater risk of sunburn and skin cancer in sunnier climates. This was not the only possible way to adapt to the arctic. Eskimos

---

Homo erectus (HOH-moh ee-REK-tuhs)
Homo sapiens (HOH-moh SAY-pee-enz)

who began moving into northern latitudes of North America no more than 5,000 years ago retain the deeper pigmentation of their Asian ancestors but are able to gain sufficient vitamin D from eating fish and sea mammals.

As distinctive as skin color seems, it represents a very minor biological change. What is far more remarkable is that these widely dispersed populations vary so little. Instead of needing to evolve physically like other species in order to adapt to new environments, modern humans have been able to change their eating habits and devise new forms of clothing and shelter. As a result, human communities have become culturally diverse while remaining physically homogeneous.

HISTORY AND CULTURE IN THE ICE AGE

Evidence of early humans' splendid creative abilities first came to light in 1940 near Lascaux in southern France. Examining a newly uprooted tree, youths discovered the entrance to a vast underground cavern. Once inside, they found that its walls were covered with paintings of animals, including many that had been extinct for thousands of years. Other cave paintings have been found in Spain and elsewhere in southern France.

Modern observers have been struck by the artistic quality of these ancient cave paintings. To even the most skeptical person, such rich finds are awesome demonstrations of richly developed imagination and skill. The ancient cave art is vivid evidence that the biologically modern people who made such art were intellectually modern as well (see Diversity and Dominance: Cave Art, page 16).

These ancient people's specialized tools and complex social relations may be less striking visually, but they also display uniquely human talents. The production of similar art and tools over wide areas and long periods of time demonstrates that skills and ideas were not simply bursts of individual genius but were deliberately passed along within societies. These learned patterns of action and expression constitute **culture.** Culture includes both material objects, such as dwellings, clothing, tools, and crafts, and nonmaterial values, beliefs, and languages.

Although it is true that some animals also learn new ways, their activities are determined primarily by inherited instincts. Among humans the proportions are reversed: instincts are less important than the cultural traditions that each generation learns from its elders. All living creatures are part of natural history, which traces biological development, but only human communities display profound cultural developments over time. The development, transmission, and transformation of cultural practices and events are the subject of **history.**

Food Gathering and Stone Tools

When archaeologists examine the remains of ancient human sites, the first thing that jumps out at them is the abundant evidence of human toolmaking—the first recognizable cultural activity. Because the tools that survive are made of stone, the extensive period of history from the appearance of the first fabricated stone tools around 2 million years ago until the appearance of metal tools around 4 thousand years ago has been called the **Stone Age.**

Making Stone Tools   About 35,000 years ago the manufacture of stone tools became highly specialized. Small blades chipped from a rock core were mounted in a bone or wooden handle. Not only were such composite tools more varied than earlier all-purpose hand axes, but the small blades required fewer rock cores—an important consideration in areas where suitable rocks were scarce. (From Jacques Bordaz, *Tools of the Old and New Stone Age.* Copyright 1970 by Jacques Bordaz. Redrawn by the permission of Addison-Wesley Educational Publishers, Inc.)

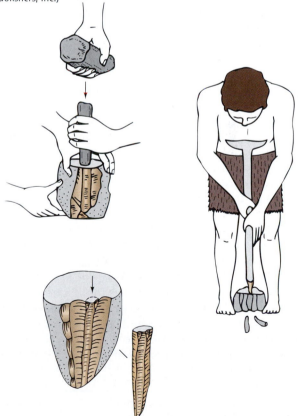

The name can be misleading. In the first place, not all tools were made of stone. Early humans would also have made useful objects and tools out of bone, skin, wood, and other natural materials less likely than stone to survive the ravages of time. In the second place, this period of nearly 2 million years contains many distinct periods and cultures. Early students recognized two distinct periods in the Stone Age: the **Paleolithic**° (Old Stone Age) down to 10,000 years ago and the **Neolithic**° (New Stone Age) associated with agriculture. Modern scientists have found evidence for many more subdivisions.

Most early human activity centered on gathering food. Like the australopithecines, early humans depended heavily on vegetable foods such as leaves, seeds, and grasses, but one of the changes evident in the Ice Age is the growing consumption of highly nutritious animal flesh. Moreover, unlike australopithecines, humans regularly made tools. These two changes—increased meat eating and toolmaking—appear to be closely linked.

The first crude tools made their appearance with *Homo habilis*. Most stone tools made by *Homo habilis* have been found in the Great Rift Valley of eastern Africa, whose sides expose sediments laid down over millions of years. One branch of this valley, the Olduvai Gorge in Tanzania, explored by Louis and Mary Leakey, has yielded evidence that *Homo habilis* made tools by chipping flakes off the edges of volcanic stones. Modern experiments show that the razor-sharp edges of such flakes are highly effective for skinning and butchering wild animals. Later human species made much more sophisticated tools.

Lacking the skill to hunt and kill large animals, small-brained *Homo habilis* probably obtained animal protein by scavenging meat from kills made by animal predators or resulting from accidents. There is evidence that they used large stone "choppers" for cracking open bones to get at the nutritious marrow. The fact that many such tools are found together far from the outcrops of volcanic rock suggests that people carried them long distances for use at kill sites and camps.

Homo erectus were also scavengers, but their larger brains would have made them cleverer at it—capable, for example, of finding and stealing the kills that leopards and other large predators dragged up into trees. They also made more effective tools for butchering large animals, although the stone flakes and choppers of earlier eras continued to be made. The stone tool most associated with *Homo erectus* was a hand ax formed by removing chips from both sides of a stone to produce a sharp outer edge.

Modern experiments show the hand ax to be an efficient multipurpose tool, suitable for skinning and butchering animals, for scraping skins clean for use as clothing and mats, for sharpening wooden tools, and for digging up edible roots. Since a hand ax can also be hurled accurately for nearly 100 feet (30 meters), it might also have been used as a projectile to fell animals. From sites in Spain there is evidence that *Homo erectus* even butchered elephants, which then ranged across southern Europe, by driving them into swamps where they became trapped and died.

Homo sapiens were far more skillful hunters. They tracked and killed large animals (such as mastodons, mammoths, and bison) throughout the world. Their success reflected their superior intelligence and use of an array of finely made tools. Sharp stone flakes chipped from carefully prepared rock cores were often used in combination with other materials. Attaching a stone point to a wooden shaft made a spear. Embedding several sharp stone flakes in a bone handle produced a sawing tool.

Indeed, *Homo sapiens* were so skillful and successful as hunters that they may have caused or contributed to a series of ecological crises. Between 40,000 and 13,000 years ago the giant mastodons and mammoths gradually disappeared, first from Africa and Southeast Asia and then from northern Europe. In North America the sudden disappearance around 11,000 years ago of highly successful large-animal hunters known as the Clovis people was almost simultaneous with the extinction of three-fourths of the large mammals in the Americas, including giant bison, camels, ground sloths, stag-moose, giant cats, mastodons, and mammoths. In Australia there was a similar event. Since these extinctions occurred during the last series of severe cold spells at the end of the Ice Age, it is difficult to measure which effects were the work of global and regional climate changes and which resulted from the excesses of human predators.

Finds of fossilized animal bones bearing the marks of butchering tools clearly attest to the scavenging and hunting activities of Stone Age peoples, but anthropologists do not believe that early humans depended primarily on meat for their food. Modern **foragers** (hunting and food-gathering peoples) in the Kalahari Desert of southern Africa and the Ituri Forest of central Africa derive the bulk of their day-to-day nourishment from wild vegetable foods; meat is the food of feasts. It is likely that the same was true for Stone Age peoples, even though the tools and equipment for gathering and processing vegetable foods have left few traces because they were made of materials unable to survive for thousands of years.

Paleolithic (pay-lee-oh-LITH-ik)   **Neolithic** (nee-oh-LITH-ik)

Like modern foragers, ancient humans would have used skins and mats woven from leaves for collecting fruits, berries, and wild seeds. They would have dug edible roots out of the ground with wooden sticks. Archaeologists believe that donut-shaped stones often found at Stone Age sites may have been weights placed on wooden digging sticks to increase their effectiveness.

Both meat and vegetables become tastier and easier to digest when they are cooked. The first cooked foods were probably found by accident after wildfires, but there is new evidence from East and South Africa that humans may have been setting fires deliberately between 1 million and 1.5 million years ago. The wooden spits and hot rocks that they would have used for roasting, frying, or baking are not distinctive enough to stand out in an archaeological site. Only with the appearance of clay cooking pots some 12,500 years ago in East Asia is there hard evidence of cooking.

Gender Roles and Social Life

Some researchers have studied the organization of nonhuman primates for clues about very early human society. Gorillas and chimpanzees live in groups consisting of several adult males and females and their offspring. Status varies with age and sex, and a dominant male usually heads the group. Sexual unions between males and females generally do not result in long-term pairing. Instead, the strongest ties are those between a female and her children and among siblings. Adult males are often recruited from neighboring bands.

Very early human groups likely shared some of these primate traits, but by the time of modern *Homo sapiens* the two-parent family would have been characteristic. How this change from a mother-centered family to a two-parent family developed over the intervening millennia can only be guessed at, but it is likely that physical and social evolution were linked. Larger brain size was a contributing factor. Big-headed humans have to be born in a less mature state than other mammals so they can pass through the narrow birth canal. Other large mammals are mature at two or three years of age; humans are not able to care for themselves until the age of twelve to fifteen. Human infants' and children's need for much longer nurturing makes care by mothers, fathers, and other family members a biological imperative.

The human reproductive cycle also became unique at some point. In other species sexual contact is biologically restricted to a special mating season of the year or to the fertile part of the female's menstrual cycle. As well, among other primates the choice of mate is usually not a matter for long deliberation. To a female baboon in heat (estrus) any male will do, and to a male baboon any receptive female is a suitable sexual partner. In contrast, adult humans can mate at any time and are much choosier about their partners. Once they mate, frequent sexual contact promotes deep emotional ties and long-term bonding.

An enduring bond between human parents made it much easier for vulnerable offspring to receive the care they needed during the long period of their childhood. Working together, mothers and fathers could nurture dependent children of different ages at the same time, unlike other large mammals whose females must raise their offspring nearly to maturity before beginning another reproductive cycle. Spacing births close together also ensured offspring a high rate of survival and would have enabled humans to multiply more rapidly than other large mammals.

Other researchers have studied the few surviving present-day foragers for models of what such early societies could have been like. They infer that Ice Age women would have done most of the gathering and cooking (which they could do while caring for small children). Older women past childbearing age would have been the most knowledgeable and productive food gatherers. Men, with stronger arms and shoulders, would have been more suited than women to hunting, particularly for large animals. Some early cave art shows males in hunting activities.

Other aspects of social life in the Ice Age are suggested by studies of modern peoples. All recent hunter-gatherers have lived in small groups or bands. The community had to have enough members to defend itself from predators and to divide responsibility for the collection and preparation of animal and vegetable foods. However, if it had too many members, it risked exhausting the food available in its immediate vicinity. Even a band of optimal size had to move at regular intervals to follow migrating animals and take advantage of seasonally ripening plants in different places. Archaeological evidence from Ice Age campsites suggests early humans, too, lived in highly mobile bands.

Hearths and Cultural Expressions

Because frequent moves were necessary to keep close to migrating herds and ripening plants, early hunting and gathering peoples usually did not lavish much time on housing. Natural shelters under overhanging rocks or in caves in southern Africa and southern France are known to have been favorite camping places to which bands returned at regular intervals.

Where the climate was severe or where natural shelters did not exist, people erected huts of branches, stones, bones, skins, and leaves as seasonal camps. More elaborate dwellings were common in areas where protection against harsh weather was necessary.

An interesting camp dating to 15,000 years ago has been excavated in the Ukraine southeast of Kiev. Its communal dwellings were framed with the bones of elephant-like mammoths, then covered with hides. Each oblong structure, measuring 15 to 20 feet (4.5 to 6 meters) by 40 to 50 feet (12 to 15 meters), was capable of holding fifty people and would have taken several days to construct. The camp had five such dwellings, making it a large settlement for a foraging community. Large, solid structures were common in fishing villages that grew up along riverbanks and lakeshores, where the abundance of fish permitted people to occupy the same site year-round.

Making clothing was another necessary technology in the Stone Age. Animal skins were an early form of clothing, and the oldest evidence of fibers woven into cloth dates from about 26,000 years ago. An "Iceman" from 5,300 years ago, whose frozen remains were found in the European Alps in 1991, was wearing many different garments made of animal skins sewn together with cord fashioned from vegetable fibers and rawhide (see Environment and Technology: The Iceman).

Although accidents, erratic weather, and disease took a heavy toll on a foraging band, there is no reason to believe that day-to-day existence was particularly hard or unpleasant. Some studies suggest that, under the conditions operating on the African savannas and in other game-rich areas, securing necessary food, clothing, and shelter would have occupied only from three to five hours a day. This would have left a great deal of time for artistic endeavors as well as for toolmaking and social life.

The foundations of what later ages called science, art, and religion were also built during the Stone Age. Basic to human survival was extensive and precise knowledge about the natural environment. Gatherers needed to know which local plants were best for food and the seasons when they were available. Successful hunting required intimate knowledge of the habits of game animals. People learned how to use plant and animal parts for clothing, twine, and building materials, as well as

Interior of a Neolithic House   This stone structure from the Orkney Islands off Scotland shows a double hearth for cooking and a small window in the center, along with stone partitions. Elsewhere, few Neolithic houses were made of stone, but wood was scarce in the Orkneys.   (Ronald Sheridan/Ancient Art & Architecture)

The Iceman

The discovery of the well-preserved remains of a man at the edge of a melting glacier in the European Alps in 1991 provides unusually detailed information about everyday technologies of the fourth millennium B.C.E. Not just the body of this "Iceman" was well preserved. His clothing, his tools, and even the food in his stomach survived in remarkably good condition.

Dressed from head to toe for the cold weather of the mountains, the fifty-year-old man was wearing a fur hat fastened under the chin with a strap, a tailored vest of different colored deerskins, leather leggings and loincloth, and a padded cloak made of grasses. On his feet were calfskin shoes also padded with grass for warmth and comfort. The articles of clothing had been sewn together with fiber and leather cords. He carried a birch-bark drinking cup.

Most of his tools were those of the late Stone Age. In a sort of leather fanny pack he carried small flint tools for cutting, scraping, and punching holes, as well as some tinder for making a fire. He also carried a leather quiver with flint-tipped arrows, but his 6-foot (1.8-meter) bow was unfinished, lacking a bowstring. In addition he had a flint knife and a tool for sharpening flints. His most sophisticated tool was of the age of metals that was just dawning: a copper-bladed ax with a wooden handle.

Further investigations of the body have revealed that a small arrowhead lodged in his shoulder caused the Iceman's death. In his stomach, researchers found the remains of the meat-rich meal he had eaten not long before he died.

The Iceman This is an artist's rendition of what the Iceman might have looked like. Notice his tools, remarkable evidence of the technology of his day. (Weislav Smetek/STERN)

which natural substances were effective for medicine, consciousness altering, dyeing, and other purposes. Knowledge of the natural world included identifying minerals suitable for paints, stones for making the best tools, and so forth. Given humans' physical capacity for speech, it is likely that the transmission of such prescientific knowledge involved verbal communication, even though direct evidence for language appears only in later periods.

Early music and dance have left no traces, but there is abundant evidence of painting and drawing (see Diversity and Dominance: Cave Art). The oldest known cave paintings in Europe and North Africa date to 32,000 years ago, and there are many others from later times in other parts of the world. Because many cave paintings feature wild animals such as oxen, reindeer, and horses that were hunted for food, some believe that the art was meant to record hunting scenes or that it formed part of

DIVERSITY AND DOMINANCE

CAVE ART

Were the people who lived tens of thousands of years ago different from people today? Biologically, *Homo sapiens sapiens* seem not to have become more diverse over time. But what were prehistoric people like inside—in their thoughts, imaginations, and emotions? Did their eyes see beauty, their ears hear music, and their imaginations wonder at the meaning of the world and the celestial bodies above them?

Very little evidence exists to answer these important questions except in one form: cave paintings. First discovered in France in the late nineteenth century, such art immediately suggested that those who drew it were sophisticated modern people like ourselves. Just as the skeletal remains of *Homo sapiens* of a hundred thousand years ago show they had modern bodies, the art they made suggests they had modern minds.

The oldest cave paintings discovered in southeastern France date from 30,000 years ago—a very long time measured in human lifetimes, but a small part of human existence. The oldest recognizable human art, a carefully crosshatched bone from Blombos Cave east of Cape Town, South Africa, dates from over 70,000 years ago. Even as the temporal distance from us increases, the evidence supports the conclusion that these early people had minds and imaginations no different from those of people today.

We may sense these cave artists' common humanity with ourselves, but it is not easy to understand the cultural context of their work. Why did they draw what they did? And why in caves? In his book *From Black Land to Fifth Sun* (1998), archaeologist Brian Fagan suggests three approaches to bridging the gap, based on his own examination of cave paintings.

His first suggestion is that the context in which the art was made tells us a great deal. Throughout the world, early artists drew, carved, and painted on many surfaces, many fairly inaccessible. The decision to work inside dark caves that the artists could illuminate only with crude torches was not an accident. The fact that the hidden caves protected and preserved their art for tens of thousands of years could not have been part of their plan. Rather, Fagan suggests, the artists went deep underground "to feel the power of the earth." Unlike contemporary urban people who have lost a sense of nature's spiritual power, the cave painters would have believed that the wild animals and the earth itself were full of spiritual energy. The dark and enclosed caves would have heightened the sense of nature's mystery and power with which they informed their paintings. It is thus likely that the artists were already the spiritual guides of their communities.

As for the art itself, one should begin with the cautionary remark that even today's art conveys many messages. Still, Fagan believes, since the artists and original viewers were part of a community, it is likely that the common culture they shared enabled them to understand art in the same ways. He cites the example of the rock art traditions of the San artists of southern Africa that continued into the twentieth century to suggest that other cave art concerned the mystical relationship of humans with the animals they hunted. The form of the paintings and the ingredients that went into them meant that humans could absorb something of the power of the bears, antelope, bison, or other animals depicted in the caves by viewing or touching them.

Finally, Fagan says, we need to consider what these caves were used for and why cave artists returned over many generations, filling the walls and ceilings with their works. In magical and religious rites to ensure successful hunting. However, a newly discovered cave at Vallon Pont-d'Arc° in southern France features rhinoceros, panthers, bears, owls, and a hyena, which probably were not the objects of hunting. Still other drawings include people dressed in animal skins and smeared with paint. In many caves there are stencils of human hands. Are these the signatures of the artists or the world's oldest graffiti? Some scholars suspect that other marks in cave paintings and

---

Vallon Pont-d'Arc (vah-LON pon-DAHRK)

The Lion Panel in Chauvet Cave, France (Jean Cottes/Ministere de la Culture/Corbis)

some places, later artists even painted over earlier works. Fagan compares the decorated caverns of remote antiquity with the Sistine Chapel in the Vatican, beautifully decorated by the artist Michelangelo, where many religious ceremonies are staged, including the election of the pope. The decorated caverns were not galleries where people went to view art, but holy places where religious ceremonies were performed and where those present would have had powerful religious experiences.

The scenes reproduced here from the large tableau of animal drawings known as the "Lion Panel" show the skill techniques and the variety of art in the Chauvet Cave. From the right come a band of female lions on the hunt, approaching a herd of bison, who turn to regard them. Across a cleft in the rock the panel resumes with a herd of rhinoceroses and another group of lions at the far left of the panel.

QUESTIONS FOR ANALYSIS

1. Is there anything in the depiction of the animals that suggests whether the artists were in awe of them, felt superior to them, or felt at one with them?
2. Are all the animals ones that people hunted to eat? How persuasive are Fagan's explanations?

on bones from this period may represent efforts at counting or writing.

Newer theories suggest that cave and rock art represent concerns with fertility, efforts to educate the young, or elaborate mechanisms for time reckoning. Another approach to understanding such art draws on the traditions of peoples like the San—hunters, gatherers, and artists in southern Africa since time immemorial.

Some cave art suggests that Stone Age people had well-developed religions, but without written religious texts it is difficult to know exactly what they believed. Sites of deliberate human burials from about 100,000 years ago give some hints. The fact that an adult was often buried with stone implements, food, clothing, and red-ochre powder suggests that early people revered their leaders enough to honor them after death and may imply a belief in an afterlife.

Today we recognize that the Stone Age, whose existence was scarcely dreamed of two centuries ago, was a formative period. Important in its own right, it also laid the basis for major changes ahead as human communities passed from being food gatherers to being food producers. Future discoveries are likely to add substantially to our understanding of these events.

THE AGRICULTURAL REVOLUTIONS

For most of history people ate only wild plants and animals. But around 10,000 years ago global climate changes seem to have induced some societies to enhance their food supplies with domesticated plants and animals. More and more people became food producers over the next millennium. Although hunting and gathering did not disappear, this transition from foraging to food production was one of the great turning points in history because it fostered a rapid increase in population and greatly altered humans' relationship to nature (see Map 1.2).

What should this historic transformation be called? Because agriculture arose in combination with new kinds of stone tools, archaeologists called the period the "Neolithic" and the rise of agriculture the "Neolithic Revolution." But that name can be misleading: first, stone tools were not its essential component, and second, it was not a single event but a series of separate transformations in different parts of the world. A better term is **Agricultural Revolutions,** which emphasizes that the central change was in food production and indicates that agriculture arose independently in many different places. In most cases agriculture included the domestication of animals for food as well as the cultivation of new food crops.

The Transition to Plant Cultivation

Food gathering gave way to food production in stages spread over hundreds of generations. The process may have begun when forager bands returning year after year to the same seasonal camps took measures to encourage the nearby growth of the foods they liked. They deliberately scattered the seeds of desirable plants in locations where they would thrive, and they discouraged the growth of competing plants by clearing them away. Such techniques of semicultivation could have supplemented food gathering for many generations. Families choosing to concentrate their energies on food production, however, would have had to settle permanently near their fields.

Settled agriculture required new, specialized tools. Indeed, it was the presence of new tools that first alerted archaeologists to the beginning of a food production revolution. Many specialized stone tools were developed or improved for agricultural use, including polished or ground stone heads to work the soil, sharp stone chips embedded in bone or wooden handles to cut grain, and stone mortars to pulverize grain. However, stone axes were not very efficient for clearing away shrubs and trees. To do that, farmers used a much older technology: fire. Fires got rid of unwanted undergrowth, and the ashes were a natural fertilizer. After the burn-off farmers could use blades and axes to cut away new growth.

Also fundamental to the success of agriculture was selecting the highest-yielding strains of wild plants, which led to the development of valuable new domesticated varieties over time. As the principal gatherers of wild plant foods, women probably played a major role in this transition to plant cultivation, but the heavy work of clearing the fields would have fallen to the men.

The transition to agriculture occurred first in the Middle East. By 8000 B.C.E. human intervention transformed certain wild grasses into higher-yielding domesticated grains, now known as emmer wheat and barley. Farmers there also discovered that alternating the cultivation of grains and pulses (plants yielding edible seeds such as lentils and peas) helped maintain soil fertility.

Plants domesticated in the Middle East spread to adjacent lands. Farmers in Greece were cultivating wheat and barley as early as 6000 B.C.E. Shortly after 4000 B.C.E. farming developed in the light-soiled plains of Central Europe and along the Danube River. As forests receded because of climate changes and human clearing efforts, agriculture spread to other parts of Europe over the next millennium.

Early farmers in Europe and elsewhere practiced shifting cultivation, also known as swidden agriculture. After a few growing seasons, the fields were left fallow (abandoned to natural vegetation), and new fields were cleared nearby. In the Danube Valley of Central Europe between 4000 and 3000 B.C.E., for example, communities of from forty to sixty people supported themselves on about 500 acres (200 hectares) of farmland, cultivating a third or less each year while leaving the rest fallow to restore its fertility. From around 2600 B.C.E. people in Central Europe began using ox-drawn wooden plows to till heavier and richer soils.

Although the lands around the Mediterranean seem

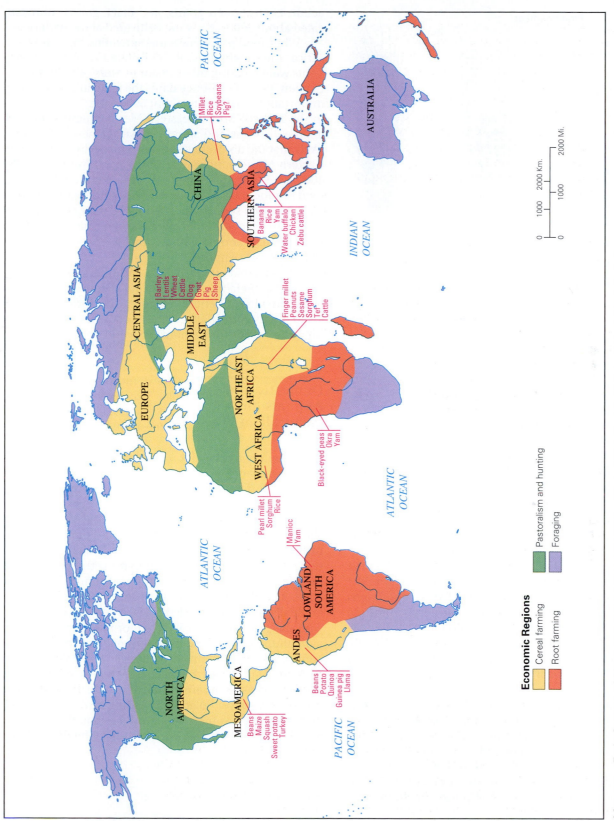

Map 1.2   Early Centers of Plant and Animal Domestication   Many different parts of the world made original contributions to domestication during the Agricultural Revolutions that began about 10,000 years ago. Later interactions helped spread these domesticated animals and plants to new locations. In lands less suitable for crop cultivation, pastoralism and hunting remained more important for supplying food.

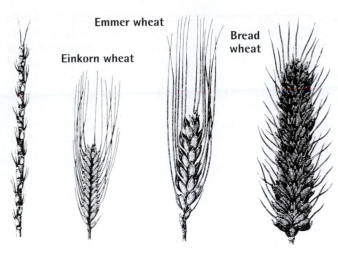

Emmer wheat

Einkorn wheat

Bread wheat

Wild wheat — Later domesticated varieties

Domestication of Wheat Through selection of the largest seeds of this wild grass, early farmers in the Middle East were able to develop varieties with larger edible kernels. Bread wheat was grown in the Nile Valley by 5000 B.C.E. (From Iris Barn, *Discovering Archaeology,* © 1981)

to have shared a complex of crops and farming techniques, wheat and barley could not spread farther south because the rainfall patterns in most of the rest of Africa were unsuited to the growth of these grains. Instead, separate agricultural revolutions took place in Saharan and sub-Saharan Africa, beginning almost as early as in the Middle East. During a particularly wet period after 8000 B.C.E. people in what is now the eastern Sahara began to cultivate sorghum, a grain they derived from wild grasses they had previously gathered. Over the next 3,000 years the Saharan farmers domesticated pearl millet, black-eyed peas, a kind of peanut, sesame, and gourds. In the Ethiopian highlands farmers domesticated finger millet and a grain called tef. The return of drier conditions about 5000 B.C.E. led many Saharan farmers to move to the Nile Valley, where the annual flooding of the Nile River provided moisture for cereal farming. In the rain forests of equatorial West Africa there is early evidence of indigenous domestication of yams and rice.

Eastern and southern Asia were also major centers of plant domestication, although the details are not as clearly documented as in the Middle East. Rice was first domesticated in southern China, the northern half of Southeast Asia, or northern India, possibly as early as 10,000 B.C.E. but more likely closer to 5000 B.C.E. Rice cultivation thrived in the warm and wet conditions of southern China. In India several pulses (including hy-acinth beans, green grams, and black grams) domesticated about 2000 B.C.E. were cultivated along with rice.

While food production was spreading in Eurasia and Africa, the inhabitants of the isolated American continents were creating other major centers of crop domestication. Recent evidence dates the cultivation of several important food crops to about 5000 B.C.E.: maize° (corn) in the Tabasco area of eastern Mexico, manioc in Panama, and beans and squash in Mesoamerica. It seems likely that the domestication of maize occurred earlier in western Mexico and manioc originated from Brazil. By 4000 B.C.E., the inhabitants of Peru were developing a food production system based on potatoes and quinoa°, a protein-rich seed grain. In so far as their climates and soils permitted, other farming communities throughout the Americas adopted such crops as these, along with tomatoes and peppers.

The fact that people in Asia, the Americas, and Africa developed their own domesticated plants in isolation from outside influences added to the variety of cultivated plants. After 1500 C.E. many of these crops became important foods throughout the world.

Domesticated Animals and Pastoralism

The domestication of animals also expanded rapidly during these same millennia. The first domesticated animal was probably the dog, tamed to help early hunters track game. Later animals were domesticated to provide meat, milk, and energy. Like the domestication of plants, this process is best known in the Middle East.

Refuse heaps outside some Middle East villages show fewer and fewer wild gazelle bones during the centuries after 7000 B.C.E. This probably reflects the depletion of such wild animals through overhunting by the local farming communities, but meat eating did not decline. The deposits show that sheep and goat bones gradually replaced gazelle bones. It seems likely that as wild sheep and goats scavenged for food scraps around agricultural villages, the tamer animals accepted human control and protection in exchange for a ready supply of food. Differences between the bones of wild and newly tamed species are too slight to date domestication precisely. However, selective breeding for desirable characteristics such as high milk production and long wooly coat eventually led to clearly distinct breeds of sheep and goats.

---

maize (mayz) **quinoa** (kee-NOH-uh)

Elsewhere, other animal species were domesticated during the centuries before 3000 B.C.E. Wild cattle were domesticated in northern Africa or the Middle East; donkeys in northern Africa; water buffalo in China; and humped-back Zebu° cattle in India. As in the case of food plants, varieties of domesticated animals spread from one region to another. Zebu cattle, for example, grew important in sub-Saharan Africa after about 2,000 years ago.

Once cattle became tame enough to be yoked to plows, they became essential to successful grain production. In addition, animal droppings provided valuable fertilizer. These developments and the widespread use of wool and milk from domesticated animals occurred much later than initial domestication. However, there were two notable deviations from the pattern of mixed agriculture and animal husbandry. One variation was in the Americas. There, comparatively few species of wild animals were suitable for domestication, and domesticated animals could not be borrowed from elsewhere because the land bridge to Asia had submerged as melting glaciers raised sea levels. Domesticated llamas provided transport and wool, while guinea pigs and turkeys furnished meat. Hunting remained the most important source of meat for Amerindians.

The other notable variation from mixed farming occurred in the more arid parts of Africa and Central Asia. There, pastoralism, a way of life dependent on large herds of small and large stock, predominated. As the Sahara approached its maximum dryness around 2500 B.C.E., pastoralists replaced farmers who migrated southward (see Chapter 8). Moving their herds to new pastures and watering places throughout the year made pastoralists almost as mobile as foragers and discouraged accumulation of bulky possessions and construction of substantial dwellings. Like modern pastoralists, early cattle-keeping people probably relied more heavily on milk than on meat, since killing animals diminished the size of their herds. During wet seasons, they may also have done some hasty crop cultivation or bartered meat and skins for plant foods with nearby farming communities.

Agriculture and Ecological Crisis

Why did the Agricultural Revolutions occur? Some theories assume that people were drawn to food production by its obvious advantages. For example,

it has recently been suggested that people in the Middle East might have settled down so they could grow enough grains to ensure themselves a ready supply of beer. Beer drinking is frequently depicted in ancient Middle Eastern art and can be dated to as early as 3500 B.C.E.

However, most researchers today believe that climate change drove people to abandon hunting and gathering in favor of agriculture or pastoralism. Temperatures warmed so much at the end of the Great Ice Age that geologists give the era since about 9000 B.C.E. a new name: the **Holocene°.** There is evidence that temperate lands were exceptionally warm between 6000 and 2000 B.C.E., the era when people in many parts of the world adopted agriculture. The precise nature of the crisis probably varied. Shortages of wild food in the Middle East caused by a dry spell or population growth may have prodded people to take up food production. Elsewhere, a warmer, wetter climate could turn grasslands into forest, thereby reducing supplies of game and wild grains.

Additional support for an ecological explanation comes from the fact that in many drier parts of the world, where wild food remained abundant, people did not take up agriculture. The inhabitants of Australia continued to rely exclusively on foraging until recent centuries, as did some peoples on all the other continents. Many Amerindians in the arid grasslands from Alaska to the Gulf of Mexico hunted bison, while in the Pacific Northwest others took up salmon-fishing. Abundant supplies of fish, shellfish, and aquatic animals permitted food gatherers east of the Mississippi River to become increasingly sedentary. In Africa conditions favored retention of the older ways in the equatorial rain forest and in the southern part of the continent. The reindeer-based societies of northern Eurasia were also unaffected by the spread of farming.

Whatever the causes, the gradual adoption of food production transformed most parts of the world. A hundred thousand years ago there were fewer than 2 million people, and their range was largely confined to the temperate and tropical regions of Africa and Eurasia. The population may have fallen even lower during the last glacial epoch, between 32,000 and 13,000 years ago. Then, as the glaciers retreated and people took up agriculture, their numbers rose. World population may have reached 10 million by 5000 B.C.E. and then mushroomed to between 50 million and 100 million by 1000 B.C.E.[1] This increase led to important changes to social and cultural life.

Zebu (ZEE-boo)

Holocene (HAWL-oh-seen)

LIFE IN NEOLITHIC COMMUNITIES

Evidence that an ecological crisis may have driven people to food production has prompted a reexamination of the assumption that farmers enjoyed better lives than foragers. Modern studies demonstrate that food producers have to work much harder and for much longer periods than do food gatherers. Long days spent clearing and cultivating the land yielded meager harvests. Guarding herds from wild predators, guiding them to fresh pastures, and tending to their many needs imposed similar burdens.

Early farmers were less likely to starve because they could store food between harvests to tide people over seasonal changes and short-term droughts, but their diet was less varied and nutritious than that of foragers. Skeletal remains show that Neolithic farmers were shorter on average than earlier food-gathering peoples. Farmers were also more likely to die at an earlier age because people in permanent settlements were more exposed to diseases. Their water was contaminated by human waste; disease-bearing vermin and insects infested their bodies and homes; and they could catch new diseases from their domesticated animals (especially pigs and cattle).

So how did farmers displace foragers? Some researchers have envisioned a violent struggle between practitioners of the two ways of life; others have argued for a more peaceful transition. Some violence was likely, especially as the amount of cleared land reduced the wild foods available to foragers. Conflicts among farmers for control of the best land must also have occurred. In most cases, however, farmers seem to have displaced foragers by gradual infiltration rather than by conquest.

The key to the food producers' expansion may have been the simple fact that their small surpluses gave them a long-term advantage in population growth by ensuring slightly higher survival rates during times of drought or other crisis. The respected archaeologist Colin Renfrew argues, for example, that over a few centuries farming-population densities in Europe could have increased by a factor of fifty to one hundred. In his view, as population densities rose, individuals who had to farm at a great distance from their native village would have formed a new farming settlement on the outskirts. A steady, nonviolent expansion of only 12 to 19 miles (20 to 30 kilometers) a generation could have repopulated the whole of Europe from Greece to Britain between 6500 and 3500 B.C.E.[2] The process would have been so gradual that it need not have provoked any sharp conflicts with existing foragers, who simply could have stayed clear of the agricultural frontier or gradually adopted agriculture themselves. New studies that map genetic changes also support the hypothesis of a gradual spread of agricultural people across Europe from southeast to northwest.[3]

Like forager bands, the expanding farming communities were organized around kinship and marriage. Nuclear families (parents and their children) probably lived in separate households, but felt great solidarity with all those who were related to them by descent from common ancestors several generations back. These kinship units, known as lineages° or clans, acted together to defend their common interests and land.

Even if one assumes stable marriage patterns, tracing descent is a complex matter. Because each person has two parents, four grandparents, eight great-grandparents, and so on, each individual has a bewildering number of ancestors. Some societies trace descent equally through both parents, but most give greater importance to descent through either the mother (matrilineal° societies) or the father (patrilineal° societies).

Some scholars have argued that very ancient peoples traced descent through women and may have been ruled by women. For example, the traditions of Kikuyu° farmers on Mount Kenya in East Africa relate that women ruled until the Kikuyu men conspired to get all the women pregnant at once and then overthrew them while the women were unable to fight back. No evidence exists to prove or disprove legends such as this, but it is important not to confuse tracing descent through women (matrilineality) with the rule of women (matriarchy°).

Cultural Expressions

Kinship systems influenced early agricultural people's outlook on the world. When old persons died, their burials might be occasions for elaborate ceremonies that expressed their descendants' group solidarity. Plastered skulls found in the ancient city of Jericho° (see Map 2.1) may be evidence of such early ancestor reverence or worship.

A society's religious beliefs tend to reflect relations to nature. The religions of food gatherers tended to center on sacred groves, springs, and wild animals. Pastoralists tended to worship the Sky God who controlled the rains and guided their migrations. In contrast, the religious activities of many farming communities centered

---

lineage (LIN-ee-ij)   matrilineal (mat-ruh-LIN-ee-uhl)
patrilineal (pat-ruh-LIN-ee-uhl)   Kikuyu (ki-KOO-yoo)
matriarchy (MAY-tree-ahr-key)   Jericho (JER-ih-koh)

Stonehenge, in Southern England This view from the center of the megalithic circle looks through an arch to the Heel Stone, which marks the precise place where the sun rises on the horizon on the summer solstice, the beginning of summer. The changing of the seasons was an important part of religion in Neolithic Europe. (© Mick Sharp)

on the Earth Mother, a female deity believed to be the source of all new life, and on other gods and goddesses representing fire, wind, and rain.

The story in an ancient Hindu text about the burning of a large forest near modern India's capital, New Delhi°, may preserve a memory of the conflict between old and new beliefs. In the story the gods Krishna° and Arjuna° are picnicking in the forest when Agni, the fire-god, appears in disguise and asks them to satisfy his hunger by burning the forest and every creature in it. As interpreted by some scholars, this story portrays both the clearing of the land for cultivation and the destruction of the wildlife on which food gatherers depended.[4]

The worship of ancestors, gods of the heavens, and earthly nature and fertility deities varied from place to place, and many societies combined the different elements in their religious practices. A recently discovered complex of stone structures in the Egyptian desert that was in use by 5000 B.C.E. includes burial chambers presumably for ancestors, a calendar circle, and pairs of upright stones that frame the rising sun on the summer solstice. The calendar and the structure aligned with the solstice reflect a strong devotion to the cycle of the seasons and knowledge of how they were linked to the

Delhi (DEL-ee)   **Krishna** (KRISH-nuh)   **Arjuna** (AHR-joo-nuh)

movement of heavenly bodies. Other **megaliths** (meaning "big stones") were erected elsewhere. Observation and worship of the sun is evident at the famous Stonehenge monolithic site in England constructed about 2000 B.C.E. Megalithic burial chambers dating from 4000 B.C.E. are evidence of ancestor rituals in western and southern Europe. The early ones appear to have been communal burial chambers, which descent groups may have erected to mark their claims to farmland. In the Middle East, the Americas, and other parts of the world, giant earth burial mounds may have served similar functions.

Another fundamental cultural contribution of the Neolithic period was the dissemination of the large language families that form the basis of most languages spoken today. The root language of the giant Indo-European language family (from which the Germanic, Romance, and Celtic languages are derived) arose around 5000 B.C.E. Its westward spread across Europe may have been the work of pioneering agriculturalists. In the course of this very gradual expansion, Celtic, Germanic, Slavic, and Romance languages developed. Similarly, the Afro-Asiatic language family of the Middle East and northern Africa may have been the result of the food producers' expansion, as might the spread of the Sino-Tibetan family in East and Southeast Asia.

Early Towns and Specialists

Most early farmers lived in small villages, but in some geographically favored parts of the world a few villages grew into towns, which were centers of trade and specialized crafts. These towns had elaborate dwellings and ceremonial buildings, as well as many large structures for storing surplus food until the next harvest. Baskets and other woven containers held dry foods; pottery jugs, jars, and pots stored liquids. Residents could make most of these structures and objects in their spare time, but in large communities some craft specialists devoted their full time to making products of unusual complexity or beauty.

Two towns in the Middle East that have been extensively excavated are Jericho on the west bank of the Jordan River and Çatal Hüyük° in central Anatolia (modern Turkey). (Map 2.1 shows their locations.) The excavations at Jericho revealed an unusually large and elaborate early agricultural settlement. The round, mud-brick dwellings characteristic of Jericho around 8000 B.C.E. may have been modeled on the tents of hunters who once had camped near Jericho's natural spring. A millennium later, rectangular rooms with finely plastered walls and floors and wide doorways opened onto central courtyards. A massive stone wall surrounding the 10-acre (4-hectare) settlement helped defend it against attacks.

The ruins of Çatal Hüyük, an even larger Neolithic town, date to between 7000 and 5000 B.C.E. and cover 32 acres (13 hectares). Its residents also occupied plastered mud-brick rooms with elaborate decorations, but Çatal Hüyük had no defensive wall. Instead, the outer walls of the town's houses formed a continuous barrier without doors or large windows, so invaders would have found it difficult to break in. Residents entered their house by means of ladders through holes in the roof.

Çatal Hüyük prospered from long-distance trade in obsidian, a hard volcanic rock that craftspeople skillfully chipped, ground, and polished into tools, weapons, mirrors, and ornaments. Other residents made fine pottery, wove baskets and woolen cloth, made stone and shell beads, and worked leather and wood. House sizes varied, but there is no evidence that Çatal Hüyük had a dominant class or a centralized political structure.

Agriculture was the basis of Çatal Hüyük's existence. Fields around the town produced crops of barley and emmer wheat, as well as legumes° and other vegetables. Pigs were kept along with goats and sheep. Yet wild foods still featured prominently in the diet of the town's resi-

Neolithic Goddess Many versions of a well-nourished and pregnant female figure were found at Çatal Hüyük. Here she is supported by twin leopards whose tails curve over her shoulders. To those who inhabited the city some 8,000 years ago the figure likely represented fertility and power over nature. (C. M. Dixon)

dents. Archaeologists have dug up remains of acorns, wild grains, and wild game animals.

Representational art at Çatal Hüyük makes it clear that hunting retained a powerful hold on people's minds. Elaborate wall paintings of hunting scenes are remarkably similar to earlier cave paintings. Scenes depict men or women adorned with the skins of wild leopards. Also, men were buried with weapons of war and hunting, not with the tools of farming.

Perhaps the most striking finds at Çatal Hüyük are those that reveal religious practices. There is a religious shrine for every two houses. At least forty rooms contained shrines with depictions of horned wild bulls, female breasts, goddesses, leopards, and handprints. Rituals involved burning grains, legumes, and meat as offerings, but there is no evidence of live animal sacrifice. Statues of plump female deities far outnumber statues of male deities, suggesting that the inhabitants

---

Çatal Hüyük (cha-TAHL hoo-YOOK)   **legume** (LEG-yoom)

venerated a goddess as their principal deity. The site's principal excavator believed that, although male priests existed, "It seems extremely likely that the cult of the goddess was administered mainly by women."[5]

Metalworking became an important specialized occupation in the late Neolithic period. At Çatal Hüyük objects of copper and lead—metals that occur naturally in a fairly pure form—can be dated to about 6400 B.C.E. In many parts of the world silver and gold were also worked at an early date. Because of their rarity and their softness, those metals did not replace stone tools and weapons but instead were used primarily to make decorative or ceremonial objects. The discovery of many such objects in graves suggests they were symbols of status and power.

Towns, specialized crafts, and elaborate religious shrines added to the workload of agriculturalists. Extra food had to be produced for nonfarmers, such as priests and artisans. Added labor was needed to build permanent houses, town walls, and towers, not to mention megalithic monuments. Stonehenge, for example, may have taken 30,000 person-hours to build. It is not known whether these tasks were performed freely or coerced.

CONCLUSION

This chapter covers a far longer period than do all the chapters in the rest of the book combined. The reason for including so much time is that the rate of change was much slower during this era and the number of people on earth was much smaller than would be true in later times. Compressing so long a period into a single chapter also highlights the evolution of the fundamental relationships between humans and their natural environment that still underlie all human history.

In the first stage of human existence, hominids had to evolve physically to survive changing environments. Next, early humans began to use their distinctive physical and mental abilities to adapt culturally to many different natural environments. Societies passed down and slowly improved their tools, techniques, and specialized technical knowledge. By the late Paleolithic period all hominid species had become extinct except one: *Homo sapiens sapiens*. They were the least varied biologically of any living organism, yet they were earth's most widely dispersed mammals. Cultural diversity permitted humans to thrive in all the habitable continents.

Environmental forces still played a powerful role. To survive the climate changes that began the Holocene, humans in several different parts of the world successfully made the complex technological change from food collection to food production. In turn, the spread of agriculture greatly modified the natural environment and led to great new cultural changes.

Agriculture brought many toils and hardships, but it enabled people to manipulate plants, animals, and the surface of the planet and to greatly increase their own numbers. Besides bringing still greater changes in technology, farming and settled life led to increased social and cultural diversity. The patterns of language and belief, of diet, dress, and dwelling that emerged in the Neolithic period shaped the next several millennia. As Chapters 2 and 3 detail, specialization made possible by settled life also gave rise to significant advances in architecture and metallurgy, to artistic achievements, and to the growth of complex religious and political systems.

◼ Key Terms

evolution	history
australopithecine	Stone Age
hominid	Paleolithic
bipedalism	Neolithic
Great Ice Age	forager
Homo habilis	Agricultural Revolutions
Homo erectus	Holocene
Homo sapiens	megalith
culture	

◼ Suggested Reading

Useful reference works for this period are the *Encyclopedia of Human Evolution and Prehistory* (1988) and the *Cambridge Encyclopedia of Human Evolution* (1992). Reliable textbooks are Brian Fagan's *People of the Earth: An Introduction to World Prehistory,* 9th ed. (1997), and Robert J. Wenke, *Patterns in Prehistory: Humankind's First Three Million Years,* 4th ed. (1999).

Accounts of the discoveries of early human remains written for nonspecialists by eminent researchers include Brian Fagan, *The Journey from Eden* (1990), Donald Johanson, Leorna Johanson, and Blake Edgar, *In Search of Human Origins* (1994), based on the *Nova* television series of the same name; and Richard Leakey and Roger Lewin, *Origins Reconsidered: In Search of What Makes Us Human* (1992). Other useful books that deal with this subject include George D. Brown, Jr., *Human Evolution* (1995), for a precise biological and geological perspective; Adam Kuper, *The Chosen Primate: Human Nature and Cultural Diversity* (1994), for an anthropological analysis; Glyn Daniel and Colin Renfrew, *The Idea of Prehistory,* 2d ed. (1988), detailing the development of the discipline and relying primarily on European examples; and Robert Foley, *Another Unique Species: Patterns in Human Evolutionary Ecology* (1987), a thoughtful and readable attempt to bring together archaeological evidence and biological processes.

More analytical overviews of the evolutionary evidence are James L. Newman, *The Peopling of Africa: A Geographical Interpretation* (1995); L. Luca Cavalli-Sforza and Francesco Cavalli-Sforza, *The Great Human Diasporas: The History of Diversity and Evolution* (1995), for genetic evidence; Richard G. Klein, *The Human Career: Human Biological and Cultural Origins* (1989); and Paul Mellars, ed., *The Emergence of Modern Humans* (1991). Thoughtful explorations of key issues are Colin Renfrew, *Archaeology and Language: The Puzzle of Indo-European Origins* (1988); and Marija Gimbutas, *The Civilization of the Goddess: The World of Old Europe* (1991). Margaret Ehrenberg, *Women in Prehistory* (1989), and M. Kay Martin and Barbara Voorhies, *Female of the Species* (1975), provide interesting, though necessarily speculative, discussions of women's history.

Cave and rock art and their implications are the subjects of many works. A broad, global introduction is Hans-Georg Bandi, *The Art of the Stone Age: Forty Thousand Years of Rock Art* (1961). Ann Sieveking, *The Cave Artists* (1979), provides a brief overview of the major European finds. Other specialized studies are Robert R. R. Brooks and Vishnu S. Wakankar, *Stone Age Painting in India* (1976); R. Townley Johnson, *Major Rock Paintings of Southern Africa* (1979); J. D. Lewis-Williams, *Believing and Seeing* (1981) and *Discovering Southern African Rock Art* (1990); Mario Ruspoli, *The Cave Art of Lascaux* (1986); and Jean-Marie Chauvet, Eliette Brunel Deschamps, and Christian Hillaire, *Dawn of Art: The Chauvet Cave, the Oldest Known Paintings in the World* (1996).

For the transition to food production see Jared Diamond, *Guns, Germs, and Steel: The Fates of Human Societies* (1997), and Allen W. Johnson and Timothy Earle, *The Evolution of Human Societies: From Foraging Group to Agrarian State* (1987). Jean-Pierre Mohen, *The World of Megaliths* (1990), analyzes early monumental architecture. James Mellaart, the principal excavator of Çatal Hüyük, has written an account of the town for the general reader: *Çatal Hüyük: A Neolithic Town in Anatolia* (1967). A pioneering work on human ecology, the early sections of which are about this period, is Madhav Gadgil and Ramachandra Guha, *This Fissured Land: An Ecological History of India* (1992).

■ Notes

1. Colin McEvedy and Richard Jones, *Atlas of World Population History* (New York: Penguin Books, 1978), 13–15.
2. Colin Renfrew, *Archaeology and Language: The Puzzle of Indo-European Origins* (New York: Cambridge University Press, 1988), 125, 150.
3. Luigi Cavalli-Sforza, L. Luca, Paolo Menozzi, and Alberto Piazza, *The History and Geography of Human Genes* (Princeton, NJ: Princeton University Press, 1994).
4. Madhav Gadgil and Ramachandra Guha, *This Fissured Land: An Ecological History of India* (Berkeley: University of California Press, 1992), 79.
5. James Mellaart, *Çatal Hüyük: A Neolithic Town in Anatolia* (New York: McGraw-Hill, 1967), 202.

The First River-Valley Civilizations, 3500–1500 B.C.E.

Painted Wooden Models from the Tomb of an Egyptian Nobleman, ca. 2000 B.C.E.
Meketre, seated at right, oversees inspection of his cattle with the help of herdsmen and other servants.

CHAPTER OUTLINE

Mesopotamia

Egypt

The Indus Valley Civilization

DIVERSITY AND DOMINANCE: **Violence and Order in the Babylonian New Year's Festival**

ENVIRONMENT AND TECHNOLOGY: **Environmental Stress in the Indus Valley**

One of the oldest surviving works of literature, the *Epic of Gilgamesh*, whose roots date to before 2000 B.C.E., provides a definition of *civilization* as the people of ancient Mesopotamia (present-day Iraq) understood it. Gilgamesh, an early king, sends a temple-prostitute to tame Enkidu°, a wild man who lives like an animal in the grasslands. After using her sexual charms to win Enkidu's trust, the temple-prostitute tells him:

> Come with me to the city, to Uruk°,
> to the temple of Anu and the goddess Ishtar . . .
> to Uruk, where the processions are and music,
> let us go together through the dancing
> to the palace hall where Gilgamesh presides.[1]

She then clothes Enkidu and teaches him to eat cooked food, drink brewed beer, and bathe and oil his body. By her words and actions she indicates some of the behavior that ancient Mesopotamians associated with civilized life.

The tendency of the Mesopotamians, like other peoples throughout history, to equate civilization with their own way of life should serve as a caution for us. What assumptions are hiding behind the frequently made claim that the "first" civilizations, or the first "advanced" or "high" civilizations, arose in western Asia and northeastern Africa sometime before 3000 B.C.E.? *Civilization* is a loaded and ambiguous concept, and the idea that the first civilizations emerged in ancient Mesopotamia and Egypt needs to be carefully explained.

Scholars agree that the following political, social, economic, and technological phenomena are indicators of **civilization:** (1) cities that served as administrative centers, (2) a political system based on control of a defined territory rather than on kinship connections, (3) a significant number of people engaged in specialized, non-food-producing activities, (4) status distinctions, usually linked to the accumulation of substantial wealth by some groups, (5) monumental building, (6) a system for keeping permanent records, (7) long-distance trade, and (8) major advances in science and the arts. The earliest societies in which those features are apparent developed in the floodplains of great rivers in Asia and Africa: the Tigris° and Euphrates° in Iraq, the Indus in Pakistan, the Yellow (Huang He°) in China, and the Nile in Egypt (see Map 2.1). The periodic flooding of the rivers brought benefits—deposits of fertile silt and water for agriculture—but also threatened lives and property. To protect themselves and channel these powerful forces of nature, people living near the rivers created new technologies and forms of political and social organization.

In this chapter we trace the rise of complex societies in Mesopotamia, Egypt, and the Indus River Valley from approximately 3500 to 1500 B.C.E. Our starting point roughly coincides with the origins of writing, so we can observe aspects of human experience that scholars cannot deduce from archaeological evidence alone. Because the independent emergence of civilization based on river floods and irrigation occurred somewhat later in China than in Mesopotamia, Egypt, and the Indus Valley, early China is taken up in the next chapter.

As you read this chapter, ask yourself the following questions:

- Why did the earliest civilizations arise in such challenging environments?

- How did the need to organize labor resources shape the political and social structures of these societies?

- To what degree did new technologies, such as metallurgy, writing, and monumental construction, contribute to the power and wealth of elite groups?

- How is the interaction of these societies with the environment reflected in their religious beliefs and worldviews?

Enkidu (EN-kee-doo)   Uruk (OO-rook)

Tigris (TIE-gris)   Euphrates (you-FRAY-teez)
Huang He (hwang huh)

C H R O N O L O G Y

	Mesopotamia	Egypt	Indus Valley
3500 B.C.E.			
3000 B.C.E.	3000–2350 B.C.E. Early Dynastic (Sumerian)	3100–2575 B.C.E. Early Dynastic	
2500 B.C.E.		2575–2134 B.C.E. Old Kingdom	2600 B.C.E. Beginning of Indus Valley civilization
	2350–2230 B.C.E. Akkadian (Semitic)	2134–2040 B.C.E. First Intermediate Period	
2000 B.C.E.	2112–2004 B.C.E. Third Dynasty of Ur (Sumerian)	2040–1640 B.C.E. Middle Kingdom	
	1900–1600 B.C.E. Old Babylonian (Semitic)	1640–1532 B.C.E. Second Intermediate Period	1900 B.C.E. End of Indus Valley civilization
1500 B.C.E.	1500–1150 B.C.E. Kassite	1532–1070 B.C.E. New Kingdom	

MESOPOTAMIA

Because of the unpredictable nature of the Tigris and Euphrates Rivers and the weather, the peoples of ancient Mesopotamia saw the world as a hazardous place where human beings were at the mercy of gods who embodied the forces of nature. One of their explanations for the origins and characteristics of their world is what we know as the Babylonian Creation Epic (see Diversity and Dominance: Violence and Order in the Babylonian New Year's Festival—**Babylon** was the most important city in southern Mesopotamia in the second and first millennia B.C.E.). The high point of the myth is a cosmic battle between Marduk, the chief god of Babylon, and Tiamat°, a female figure who personifies the salt sea. Marduk cuts up Tiamat and from her body fashions the earth and sky. He then creates the divisions of time, the celestial bodies, rivers, and weather phenomena, and from the blood of a defeated rebel god he creates human beings. Creation myths of this sort provided the ancient inhabitants of Mesopotamia with a satisfactory explanation for the environment in which they were living.

Settled Agriculture in an Unstable Landscape

Mesopotamia is a Greek word meaning "land between the rivers." It reflects the centrality of the Euphrates and Tigris Rivers to the way of life in this region (see Map 2.2). Mesopotamian civilization developed in the plain along and between the rivers, which originate in the mountains of eastern Anatolia (modern Turkey) and empty into the Persian Gulf. This is an alluvial plain—a flat, fertile expanse built up over many millennia by silt that the rivers deposited.

Mesopotamia lies mostly within modern Iraq. To the north and east, an arc of mountains extends from northern Syria and southeastern Anatolia to the Zagros° Mountains, which separate the plain from the Iranian Plateau. The Syrian and Arabian deserts lie to the west and southwest, and the Persian Gulf is in the southeast.

Tiamat (TEE-ah-mat)

Zagros (ZAG-ruhs)

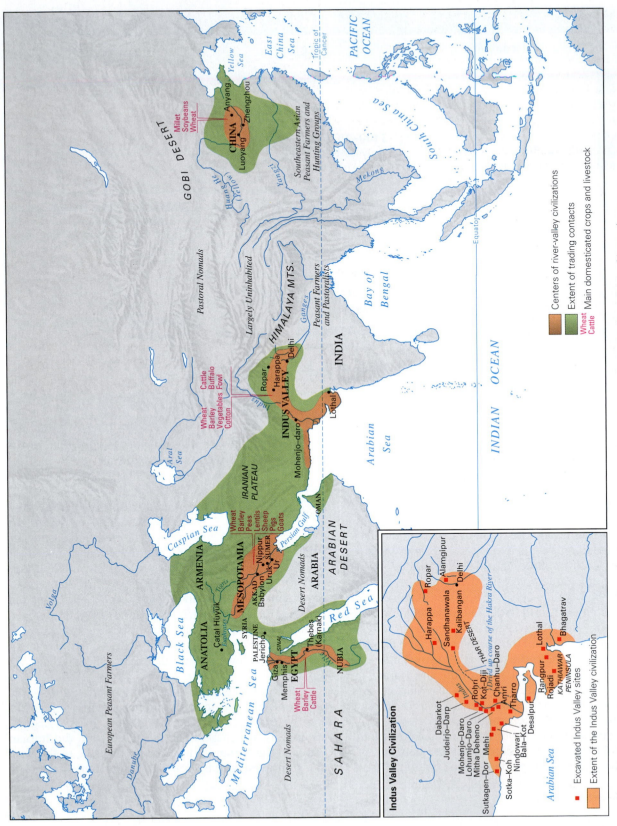

Map 2.1 River-Valley Civilizations, 3500–1500 B.C.E. The earliest complex societies arose in the floodplains of large rivers: in the fourth millennium B.C.E. in the valley of the Tigris and Euphrates Rivers in Mesopotamia and the Nile River in Egypt, in the third millennium B.C.E. in the valley of the Indus River in Pakistan, and in the second millennium B.C.E. in the valley of the Yellow River in China.

Floods can be sudden and violent and tend to come at the wrong time for grain agriculture—in the spring when the crop is ripening in the field. The floods sometimes cause the rivers to suddenly change course, cutting off fields and population centers from supplies of water and avenues of communication.

The first domestication of plants and animals took place in the "Fertile Crescent" region of northern Syria and southeastern Anatolia around 8000 B.C.E. Agriculture did not come to Mesopotamia until approximately 5000 B.C.E. Since agriculture requires annual rainfall of at least 8 inches (20 centimeters), it depended on irrigation—the artificial provision of water to crops—in hot, dry southern Mesopotamia. At first, people probably took advantage of the occasional flooding of the rivers into nearby fields, but shortly after 3000 B.C.E. they learned to construct canals to carry water to more distant parcels of land.

By 4000 B.C.E. farmers were using plows pulled by cattle to turn over the earth. A funnel attached to the plow dropped a carefully measured amount of seed. Barley was the main cereal crop in southern Mesopotamia because of its ability to tolerate hot, dry conditions and withstand the salt drawn to the surface when the fields were flooded. Fields were left fallow (unplanted) every other year to replenish the nutrients in the soil. Date palms provided food, fibers, and some wood. Small garden plots produced vegetables. Reed plants, which grew on the river banks and in the marshy southern delta, could be woven into mats, baskets, huts, and boats. Fish from the rivers and marshes were an important part of people's diet. Herds of sheep and goats, which grazed on the fallow land and beyond the zone of cultivation, provided wool and milk. Cattle and donkeys carried or

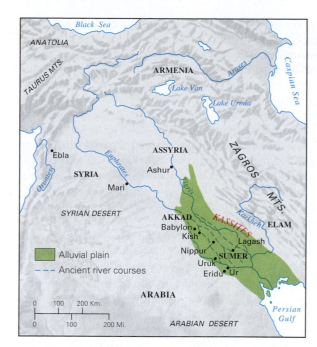

Map 2.2 Mesopotamia The Sumerians of southern Mesopotamia developed new technologies, complex political and social institutions, and distinctive cultural practices, responding to the need to organize labor resources to create and maintain an irrigation network in the Tigris-Euphrates Valley, a land of little rain.

pulled burdens; in the second millennium B.C.E. they were joined by newly introduced camels and horses.

The earliest people living in Mesopotamia in the "historical period"—the period for which we have written evidence—are the **Sumerians.** Archaeological evidence

Reed Huts in the Marshes of Southern Iraq Reeds growing along the riverbanks or in the swampy lands at the head of the Persian Gulf were used in antiquity—and continue to be used today—for a variety of purposes, including baskets and small watercraft as well as dwellings. (Courtesy, Dominique Collon)

places them in southern Mesopotamia by 5000 B.C.E. and perhaps even earlier. The Sumerians created the main framework of civilization in Mesopotamia during a long period of dominance in the fourth and third millennia B.C.E. However, they were not the only ethnic and linguistic group inhabiting the Tigris-Euphrates Valley. The names of individuals recorded in inscriptions from northerly cities from as early as 2900 B.C.E. suggest the presence of Semites, people who spoke a **Semitic**° language. (The term *Semitic* refers to a family of related languages that have long been spoken in parts of western Asia and northern Africa. These languages include ancient Hebrew, Aramaic°, and Phoenician°; the most widespread modern Semitic language is Arabic.) Historians believe that these Semites descended from nomadic peoples who had migrated into the Mesopotamian plain from the western desert. There is little indication of ethnic conflict between Sumerians and Semites. The Semites assimilated to Sumerian culture and sometimes achieved positions of wealth and power.

By 2000 B.C.E. the Semitic peoples had become politically dominant, and from this time forward the Semitic language Akkadian° took precedence over Sumerian, although the Sumerian cultural legacy was preserved. Sumerian-Akkadian dictionaries were compiled and Sumerian literature was translated. The characteristics and adventures of the Semitic gods borrow heavily from Sumerian precedents. This cultural synthesis parallels a biological merging of Sumerians and Semites through intermarriage. Other ethnic groups, including mountain peoples such as the Kassites° as well as Elamites° and Persians from Iran, played a part in Mesopotamian history. But not until the arrival of Greeks in the late fourth century B.C.E. was the Sumerian/Semitic cultural heritage of Mesopotamia fundamentally altered.

Cities, Kings, and Trade

Mesopotamia was a land of villages and cities. Groups of farming families banded together in villages to protect each other, share tools and facilities such as barns and threshing floors, and help each other at key times in the agricultural cycle. Villages also provided companionship as well as a pool of potential marriage partners.

Most cities evolved from villages. When a successful village grew, small satellite villages developed nearby,

and eventually the main village and its satellites coalesced into an urban center. Cities and villages were dependent upon one another. Cities depended on agriculture. The earliest known urban centers in the Middle East, such as Jericho° and Çatal Hüyük°, sprang up shortly after the first appearance of agriculture (see Chapter 1), and many early Mesopotamian city dwellers went out each day to labor in nearby fields. In villages almost everyone engaged in the basic tasks of subsistence, gathering or growing enough food to feed themselves and their families. In cities, on the other hand, some urban residents did not engage in food production but instead specialized in such activities as metallurgy (creating useful objects from metal), crafts, administration, and serving the gods, and they depended on the surplus food production of the villagers. Mesopotamian cities controlled the agricultural land and collected crop surpluses from the villages in their vicinity. In return, the city provided rural districts with military protection against bandits and raiders and a market where villagers could trade surplus products for manufactured goods produced by urban specialists.

The term **city-state** refers to an independent urban center and the agricultural territories it controlled. Stretches of open and uncultivated land, either desert or swamp, served as buffers between the many small city-states of early Mesopotamia. However, disputes over land, water rights, and movable property often sparked hostilities between neighboring cities and prompted most to build protective walls of sun-dried mud bricks. Cities also cooperated in various ways, sharing water and allowing safe passage of trade goods through their territories.

Mesopotamians opened new land to agriculture by building and maintaining an extensive irrigation network. Canals brought water to fields far away from the rivers. Dams raised the water level of the river so that gravity would cause the water to flow into the irrigation canals. Drainage ditches carried water away from flooded fields before evaporation could draw salt and minerals harmful to crops to the surface of the soil. Dikes protected young plants in fields near the riverbanks from floods. A machine with counterweights was invented to lift heavy buckets of water—for example, up from the river and over the dike to the land beyond. Because the rivers carried so much silt, channels got clogged and needed constant dredging.

Successful operation of this sophisticated irrigation system depended on leaders capable of compelling and

---

Semitic (suh-MIT-ik) Aramaic (ar-uh-MAY-ik)
Phoenician (fi-NEE-shuhn) Akkadian (uh-KAY-dee-uhn)
Kassite (KAS-ite) Elamite (EE-luh-mite)

Jericho (JER-ih-koe) Çatal Hüyük (cha-TAHL hoo-YOOK)

organizing large numbers of people to work together. Other projects also required cooperation: the harvest, sheep shearing, the erection of fortification walls, the construction of large public buildings, and warfare. Little is known about the political institutions of early Mesopotamian city-states, although there are traces of some sort of citizens' assembly that may have evolved from the traditional village council. The two centers of power for which there are written records are the temple and the palace of the king.

Each Mesopotamian city had one or more centrally located temples that housed the cult (a set of religious practices) of the deity or deities who watched over the community. The temples owned extensive tracts of agricultural land and stored the gifts that worshipers donated. The importance of cults is confirmed by the central location of the temple buildings. The leading priests, who controlled the shrine and managed the deity's considerable wealth, appear to have been the most prominent political and economic forces in early Mesopotamian communities.

In the third millennium B.C.E. the *lugal*°, or "big man"—we would call him a king—emerged in Sumerian cities. How this position evolved is not clear, but it may have been related to an increase in the frequency and scale of warfare as ever-larger communities quarreled over land, water, and raw materials. According to one plausible theory, certain men chosen by the community to lead the armies in time of war extended their authority in peacetime and assumed key judicial and ritual functions. The position of lugal was not automatically hereditary, but capable sons could succeed their fathers. The location of the temple in the city's heart and the less prominent location of the king's palace symbolize the later emergence of royalty. The king's power grew at the expense of the priesthood because the army backed him. The priests and temples retained influence because of their wealth and religious mystique, but they gradually became dependent on the palace. Some Mesopotamian kings claimed divinity, but this concept did not take root. Normally, the king portrayed himself as the deity's earthly representative and assumed responsibility for the upkeep and building of temples and the proper performance of ritual. Other key royal responsibilities included maintenance of the city walls and defenses, upkeep and extension of the irrigation channels, preservation of property rights, and protection of the people from outside attackers and from perversions of justice at home.

The *Epic of Gilgamesh* provides glimpses of both the restless ambition and the value to the community of this new breed of ruler. Gilgamesh, who was probably based on a historical king of Uruk, is depicted as the strongest man in his community. He stirs resentment by exercising the royal prerogative to have sex with new brides, but his subjects depend on his wisdom and courage to protect them. In his quest for everlasting glory, Gilgamesh builds magnificent walls around the city and stamps his name on all the bricks. His journey to the distant Cedar Mountains reflects the king's role in bringing valuable resources to the community.

Over time some political centers became powerful enough to extend their control over other city-states. Sargon°, ruler of the city of Akkad° around 2350 B.C.E., was the first to unite many cities under the control of one king and capital. His title, "King of Sumer and Akkad," symbolized his claim to universal dominion. Sargon and the four members of his family who succeeded him over a period of 120 years secured their power in a number of ways. They razed the walls of conquered cities and installed governors backed by garrisons of Akkadian troops. They gave land to soldiers to ensure their loyalty. Because Sargon and his people were of Semitic stock, the cuneiform° system of writing used for Sumerian (discussed later in the chapter) was adapted to express their language. A uniform system of weights and measures and standardized formats for official documents facilitated tasks of administration such as the assessment and collection of taxes, recruitment of soldiers, and organization of large labor projects.

For reasons that are not completely clear, the Akkadian state fell around 2230 B.C.E. The Sumerian language and culture were dominant again in the cities of the southern plain under the Third Dynasty of Ur (2112–2004 B.C.E.). Based on a combination of campaigns of conquest and alliances cemented by marriage, the dynasty encompassed five kings who ruled for a century. This state did not control territories as extensive as those of its Akkadian predecessor, but a rapidly expanding bureaucracy of administrators led to tight government control of a wide range of activities and obsessive record-keeping. A corps of messengers and well-maintained road stations facilitated rapid communication, and an official calendar, standardized weights and measures, and uniform writing practices enhanced the effectiveness of the central administration. As the southern plain came under increasing pressure from Semitic Amorites°

lugal (LOO-gahl)

Sargon (SAHR-gone) **Akkad** (AH-kahd)
cuneiform (kyoo-NEE-uh-form) **Amorite** (AM-uh-rite)

in the northwest, the kings erected a great wall 125 miles (201 kilometers) in length to keep out the nomadic invaders. In the end, though, the Third Dynasty of Ur succumbed to the combined pressure of nomadic incursions and an Elamite attack from the southeast.

The Amorites founded a new city at Babylon, not far from Akkad. Toward the end of a long reign, **Hammurabi°** (r. 1792–1750 B.C.E.) initiated a series of aggressive military campaigns, and Babylon became the capital of what historians have named the "Old Babylonian" state, which stretched beyond Sumer and Akkad into the north and northwest from 1900 to 1600 B.C.E. Hammurabi is best known for his Law Code, inscribed on a polished black stone pillar. The Code provides a fascinating window on the activities of everyday life, anticipating a wide range of problems that might need to be resolved: false accusations, bad judicial decisions, crimes, physical injury, property damage, debt, inheritance, ransom of prisoners-of-war, real estate, business deals, wages and prices, marriage, adoption, sexual misconduct, medical malpractice, shoddy construction, and shipwreck. Though probably not a comprehensive list of all the laws of the time, Hammurabi's Code provided judges with a lengthy set of examples illustrating principles to use in deciding cases. Some call for severe physical punishments and, not infrequently, the death penalty. These Amorite principles of justice differed from the monetary penalties prescribed in earlier codes from Ur.

The far-reaching conquests of some Mesopotamian states were motivated, at least in part, by the need to obtain vital resources. The alternative was to trade for raw materials, and long-distance commerce did flourish in most periods. Evidence of boats used in sea trade goes back as far as the fifth millennium B.C.E. Wool, cloth, barley, and oil were exported in exchange for wood from cedar forests in Lebanon and Syria, silver from Anatolia, gold from Egypt, copper from the eastern Mediterranean and Oman (on the Arabian peninsula), and tin from Afghanistan (in south-central Asia). Chlorite, a greenish stone from which bowls were carved, came from the Iranian Plateau, and for jewelry and carved figurines, black diorite was imported from the Persian Gulf, blue lapis lazuli° from eastern Iran and Afghanistan, and reddish carnelian from Pakistan.

In the third millennium B.C.E. merchants were primarily in the employ of the palace or temple, which were the only two institutions with the financial resources and long-distance connections to organize the collection, transport, and protection of goods. Merchants exchanged the surplus from the agricultural estates of kings or priests for vital raw materials and luxury goods. In the second millennium B.C.E. more commerce came into the hands of independent merchants, and merchant guilds became powerful forces.

Modern scholars do not know whether the most important commercial activities took place in the area just inside the city gates or in the vicinity of the docks. Wherever they occurred, commercial activity was accomplished without the benefit of money. Coins—pieces of metal whose value the state guarantees—were not invented until the sixth century B.C.E. and did not reach Mesopotamia until several centuries later. For most of Mesopotamian history, items could be bartered—traded for one another—or valued in relation to fixed weights of precious metal, primarily silver, or measures of grain.

Mesopotamian Society

A persistent feature of urbanized civilizations is the development of social divisions—that is, obvious variations in the status and privileges of different groups of people due to differences in wealth, social functions, and legal and political rights. The rise of cities, specialization of function, centralization of power, and use of written records enabled some groups to amass wealth on an unprecedented scale. Mesopotamian temple leaders and kings controlled large agricultural estates, and the palace administration collected various taxes from subjects. Mesopotamians who made up what we might call an elite class acquired large holdings of land. Debtors who could not pay what they owed forfeited their land, and soldiers and religious officials received plots of land in return for their services.

The Law Code of Hammurabi in eighteenth century B.C.E. Babylonia reflects social divisions that may have been valid for other places and times. Society was divided into three classes: (1) the free, landowning class, which included royalty, high-ranking officials, warriors, priests, merchants, and some artisans and shopkeepers; (2) the class of dependent farmers and artisans, who were legally attached to land that belonged to king, temple, or elite families and made up the primary rural work force; and (3) the class of slaves, primarily employed in domestic service. Penalties for crimes prescribed in the Law Code depended on the class of the offender. The most severe punishments were reserved for the lower orders.

Slavery was not as prevalent and fundamental to the economy as it would be in the later societies of Greece and Rome (see Chapters 5 and 6). Many slaves came from mountain tribes and had either been captured in

---

Hammurabi (HAM-uh-rah-bee)   **lapis lazuli** (LAP-is LAZ-uh-lee)

war or sold by slave traders. There was a separate category of slavery for people who were unable to pay their debts. Under normal circumstances, slaves were not chained or otherwise constrained, but they had to wear a distinctive hair style. If they were given their freedom, a barber shaved off the telltale mark. In the surviving documents it is often hard to distinguish slaves or dependent workers from free laborers because all were compensated with commodities such as food and oil in quantities proportional to their age, gender, and tasks. In the Old Babylonian period, as the class of people who were not dependent on the great institutions of temple or palace grew in numbers and importance, the amount of land and other property in private hands increased, and there was a greater tendency to hire free laborers.

It is difficult to reconstruct the life experiences of ordinary Mesopotamians, especially those who lived in villages or on large estates in the countryside, because they left few archaeological or literary traces. Rural peasants built their houses out of materials such as mud brick and reed, which quickly disintegrate, and they possessed little in the way of metals. Being illiterate, they were not able to write about their lives. It is particularly difficult to discover much about the experiences of women. The written sources are the product of male **scribes**—trained professionals who applied their reading and writing skills to tasks of administration—and for the most part reflect elite male activities. Archaeological remains provide only limited insight into women's status and activities and attitudes toward them.

Anthropologists theorize that women lost social standing and freedom in societies where agriculture superseded hunting and gathering (see Chapter 1). In hunting-and-gathering societies women provided most of the community's food from their gathering activities, and this work was highly valued. But in Mesopotamia the provision of food required dragging around a plow and digging irrigation channels, and that sort of hard physical labor usually was done by men. Food surpluses permitted families to have more children, and bearing and rearing children became the primary occupation of many women, preventing most from acquiring the specialized skills of the scribe or artisan.

Women had no political role, but they were able to own property, maintain control of their dowries (sums of money given by the woman's father to support her in her husband's household), and even engage in trade. Some worked outside the household in textile factories and breweries or as prostitutes, tavern keepers, bakers, or fortunetellers. Nonelite women who stayed at home

Mesopotamian Cylinder Seal   Seals indicated the identity of an individual and were impressed into wet clay or wax to "sign" legal documents or to mark ownership of an object. This seal, produced in the period of the Akkadian Empire, depicts Ea (second from right), the god of underground waters, symbolized by the stream with fish emanating from his shoulders; Ishtar, whose attributes of fertility and war are indicated by the date cluster in her hand and the pointed weapons showing above her wings; and the sun-god Shamash, cutting his way out of the mountains with a jagged knife, an evocation of sunrise.   (Courtesy of the Trustees of the British Museum)

must have engaged in tasks other than child care, such as helping with the harvest, planting vegetable gardens, cooking and baking, cleaning the house, fetching water, tending the household fire, and weaving baskets and textiles.

The standing of women seems to have declined further in the second millennium B.C.E. This development may have been linked to the rise of an urbanized middle class and an increase in private wealth. The husband became more dominant in the household and marriage and divorce laws favored his rights. Although Mesopotamian society was generally monogamous, a man could take a second wife if the first gave him no children, and in later Mesopotamian history kings and others who could afford to do so had several wives. Marriages that were arranged for the purpose of creating alliances between families made women instruments for preserving and increasing family wealth. Or a family could decide to avoid a daughter's marriage—and the resulting loss of a dowry—by dedicating the girl to the service of a deity as "god's bride." Some scholars believe that the constraints on women that eventually became part of the Islamic tradition, such as the expectation that they confine themselves to the household and wear veils in public (see Chapter 9), may have originated in the second millennium B.C.E.

Gods, Priests, and Temples

The Sumerian gods embodied the forces of nature: Anu was the sky, Enlil the air, Enki the water, Utu the sun, and Nanna the moon. The emotional impulses of sexual attraction and violence were the domain of the goddess Inanna. When the Semitic peoples became dominant, they equated their deities with those of the Sumerians. For example, Nanna and Utu became the Semitic Sin and Shamash, and Inanna became Ishtar. The myths of the Sumerian deities were transferred to their Semitic counterparts, and many of the same rituals continued to be practiced.

People believed the gods were anthropomorphic°—like humans in form and conduct. They thought the gods had bodies and senses, sought nourishment from sacrifice, enjoyed the worship and obedience of humanity, and were driven by lust, love, hate, anger, and all the other emotions that motivated human beings. The Mesopotamians feared their gods. They believed the gods were responsible for the natural disasters that occurred without warning in the landscape in which they lived, and they sought to appease the deities by any means.

The public, state-organized religion is most visible in the archaeological record. Each city built temples and showed devotion to one or more patron divinities who protected the community. All the peoples of Sumer venerated Nippur (see Map 2.2) as a religious center because of its temple of the air-god Enlil. The temple was considered the residence of the god, and the cult statue in a special interior shrine was believed to embody the deity's life-force. Priests tried to anticipate and meet every need of this physical image of the divinity in a daily cycle of waking, bathing, dressing, feeding, moving around, entertaining, soothing, and revering. These efforts reflected the emphatic claim of the Babylonian Creation Myth that humankind had been created to serve the gods. Several thousand priests may have staffed a large temple like that of the chief god Marduk at Babylon.

The office of priest was hereditary; fathers passed along sacred lore to their sons. Priests were paid in food raised on the deity's estates. The amount depended on an individual's rank within a complicated hierarchy of status and specialized function. The high priest performed the central acts in the great rituals. Certain priests made music to please the gods. Others exorcised evil spirits. Still others interpreted dreams and divined the future by examining the organs of sacrificed animals, reading patterns in the rising incense smoke, or casting dice.

A high wall surrounded the temple precinct, which included the shrine of the chief deity; open-air plazas; chapels for lesser gods; housing, dining facilities, and offices for the priests and other members of the temple staff; and craft shops, storerooms, and service buildings. The most visible part of the temple compound was the **ziggurat**°, a multistory, mud-brick, pyramid-shaped tower approached by ramps and stairs. Modern scholars are not certain of the ziggurat's function and symbolic meaning.

Even harder to determine are the everyday beliefs and religious practices of the common people. Modern scholars do not know how accessible the temple buildings were to the general public. Individuals placed votive statues in the sanctuaries. They believed that these miniature replicas of themselves could continually beseech and seek the favor of the deity. The survival of many **amulets** (small charms meant to protect the bearer from evil) and representations of a host of demons suggest widespread belief in magic—the use of special words and rituals to manipulate and control the

---

anthropomorphic (an-thruh-puh-MORE-fik)

ziggurat (ZIG-uh-rat)

forces of nature. A headache, for example, was believed to be caused by a demon that could be driven out of the ailing body. Lamashtu, who was held responsible for miscarriages, could be frightened off if a pregnant woman wore an amulet with the likeness of the hideous but beneficent demon Pazuzu. In return for an appropriate gift or sacrifice, a god or goddess might be persuaded to reveal information about the future. The elite and the ordinary people came together in great festivals such as the twelve-day New Year's Festival held each spring in Babylon to mark the beginning of a new agricultural cycle (see Diversity and Dominance: Violence and Order in the Babylonian New Year's Festival).

Technology and Science

The term *technology* comes from the Greek word *techne*, meaning "skill" or "specialized knowledge." It normally refers to the tools and machinery that humans use to manipulate the physical world. Many scholars now use the term more broadly to encompass any specialized knowledge that is used to transform the natural environment and human society. Ancient Mesopotamian use of irrigation techniques that expanded agricultural production fit the first definition; priests' belief that they could enhance prosperity through prayers and rituals the second.

A particularly important example of the broader type of technology is writing, which first appeared in Mesopotamia before 3300 B.C.E. The earliest inscribed tablets, found in the chief temple at Uruk, date from a time when the temple was the most important economic institution in the community. According to a plausible recent theory, writing originated from a system of tokens used to keep track of property—such as sheep, cattle, or wagon wheels—when increases in the amount of accumulated wealth and the volume and complexity of commercial transactions strained people's memories. The tokens, made in the shape of the commodity, were inserted and sealed in clay envelopes, and pictures of the tokens were incised on the outside of the envelopes as a reminder of what was inside. Eventually, people realized that the incised pictures were an adequate record of the transaction and that the tokens inside the clay envelope were redundant. These pictures were the first written symbols. The earliest symbols represented various objects, and they also could stand for the sound of the word for an object if the sound was part of a longer word. For example, the symbols *shu* for "hand" and *mu* for "water" could be combined to form *shumu*, the word for "name."

The most common method of writing involved pressing the point of a sharpened reed into a moist clay tablet. Because the reed made wedge-shaped impressions, the early pictures were increasingly stylized into a combination of strokes and wedges that evolved into **cuneiform** (Latin for "wedge-shaped") writing. Mastering this system required years of training and practice. Several hundred signs were in use at any one time, as compared to the twenty-five or so signs required for an alphabetic system. In the "tablet-house," which may have been attached to a temple or palace, students were taught writing and mathematics by a stern headmaster and were tutored and bullied by older students called "big brothers." The prestige and regular employment that went with their position may have made scribes reluctant to simplify the cuneiform system. In the Old Babylonian period, the growth of the private commercial sector was accompanied by an increase in the number of people who could read and write, but only a small percentage of the population was literate.

Cuneiform is not a language but rather a system of writing. Developed originally for the Sumerian language, it was later adapted to the Akkadian language of the Mesopotamian Semites as well as other languages of western Asia such as Hittite, Elamite, and Persian. The remains of the ancient city of Ebla° in northern Syria (see Map 2.2) illustrate the Mesopotamian influence on other parts of western Asia. Ebla's buildings and artifacts follow Mesopotamian models, and thousands of tablets are inscribed with cuneiform symbols in Sumerian and the local Semitic dialect. The high point of Ebla's wealth and power occurred from 2400 to 2250 B.C.E., roughly contemporary with the Akkadian Empire. Ebla controlled extensive territory and derived wealth from agriculture, manufacture of woolen cloth, and trade with Mesopotamia and the Mediterranean.

The earliest Mesopotamian documents are economic, but cuneiform came to have wide-ranging uses beyond its initial purpose. In the early period, legal acts had been validated by the recitation of oral formulas and the performance of symbolic actions. After the development of cuneiform, written documents marked with the seal of the participants became the primary proof of legitimacy. Cuneiform also served political, literary, religious, and scientific purposes.

Other technologies enabled the Mesopotamians to meet the challenges of their physical environment. Irrigation, indispensable to agriculture, called for the construction and maintenance of canals, dams, and dikes. Carts and sledges drawn by cattle were a common means of transportation in some locations. In the south,

Ebla (EH-bluh)

VIOLENCE AND ORDER IN THE BABYLONIAN NEW YEAR'S FESTIVAL

The twelve-day Babylonian New Year's Festival was one of the grandest and most important religious celebrations in ancient Mesopotamia. Complex rituals, both private and public, were performed in accordance with detailed formulas. Fragmentary Babylonian documents of the third century B.C.E. (fifteen hundred years after Hammurabi) provide most of our information about the festival, but because of the continuity of culture over several millennia, the later Babylonian New Year's Festival is likely to preserve many of the beliefs and practices of earlier epochs.

In the first days of the festival, most of the activity took place in inner chambers of the temple of Marduk, patron deity of Babylon, attended only by ranking members of the priesthood. A particularly interesting ceremony was a ritualized humiliation of the king, followed by a renewal of the institution of divinely sanctioned kingship:

On the fifth day of the month Nisannu . . . they shall bring water for washing the king's hands and then shall accompany him to the temple Esagil. The *urigallu*-priest shall leave the sanctuary and take away the scepter, the circle, and the sword from the king. He shall bring them before the god Bel [Marduk] and place them on a chair. He shall leave the sanctuary and strike the king's cheek. He shall accompany the king into the presence of the god Bel. He shall drag him by the ears and make him bow to the ground. The king shall speak the following only once: "I did not sin, lord of the countries. I was not neglectful of the requirements of your godship. I did not destroy Babylon. The temple Esagil, I did not forget its rites. I did not rain blows on the cheek of a subordinate." . . . [The *urigallu*-priest responds:] "The god Bel will listen to your prayer. He will exalt your kingship. The god Bel will bless you forever. He will destroy your enemy, fell your adversary." After the *urigallu*-priest says this, the king shall regain his composure. The scepter, circle, and sword shall be restored to the king.

Also in the early days of the festival, in conjunction with rituals of purification and invocations to Marduk, a priest recited the entire text of the Babylonian Creation Epic to the image of the god. After relating the origins of the gods from the mating of two primordial creatures, Tiamat, the female embodiment of the salt sea, and Apsu, the male embodiment of fresh water, the myth tells how Tiamat gathered an army of old gods and monsters to destroy the younger generation of gods.

When her labor of creation was ended, against her children Tiamat began preparations of war . . . all the Anunnaki [the younger gods], the host of gods gathered into that place tongue-tied; they sat with mouths shut for they thought, "What other god can make war on Tiamat? No one else can face her and come back" . . . Lord Marduk exulted, . . . with racing spirits he said to the father of gods, "Creator of the gods who decides their destiny, if I must be your avenger, defeating Tiamat, saving your lives, call the Assembly, give me precedence over all the rest; . . . now and for ever let my word be law; I, not you, will decide the world's nature, the things to come. My decrees shall never be altered, never be annulled, but my creation endures to the ends of the world" . . . He took his route towards the rising sound of Tiamat's rage, and all the gods besides, the fathers of the gods pressed in around him, and the lord approached Tiamat. . . . When Tiamat heard him her wits scattered, she was possessed and shrieked aloud, her legs shook from the crotch down, she gabbled spells, muttered maledictions, while the gods of war sharpened their weapons. . . . The lord shot his net to entangle Tiamat, and the pursuing tumid wind, Imhullu, came from behind and beat in her face. When the mouth gaped open to suck him down he drove Imhullu in, so that the mouth would not shut but wind raged through her belly; her carcass blown up, tumescent. She gaped. And now he shot the arrow that split the belly, that pierced the gut and cut the womb.

Now that the Lord had conquered Tiamat he ended her life, he flung her down and straddled the carcass; the leader was killed, Tiamat was dead her rout was shattered, her band dispersed. . . . The lord rested; he gazed at the huge body, pondering how to use it, what to create from the dead carcass. He split it apart like a cockle-shell; with the upper half he constructed the arc of sky, he pulled down the bar and set a watch on the waters, so they should never escape. . . . He projected positions for the Great Gods conspicuous in the sky, he gave them a starry aspect as constellations; he measured the year, gave it a beginning and an end, and to each month of the twelve three rising stars. . . . Through her ribs he opened gates in the east and west, and gave them strong bolts on the right and left; and high in the belly of Tiamat he set the zenith. He gave the moon the luster of a jewel, he gave him all the night, to mark off days, to watch by night each month the circle of a waxing waning light. . . . When Marduk had sent out the moon, he took the sun and set him to complete the cycle from this one to the next New Year. . . .

Then Marduk considered Tiamat. He skimmed spume from the bitter sea, heaped up the clouds, spindrift of wet and wind and cooling rain, the spittle of Tiamat. With his own hands from the steaming mist he spread the clouds. He pressed hard down the head of water, heaping mountains over it, opening springs to flow: Euphrates and Tigris rose from her eyes, but he closed the nostrils and held back their springhead. He piled huge mountains on her paps and through them drove water-holes to channel the deep sources; and high overhead he arched her tail, locked-in to the wheel of heaven; the pit was under his feet, between was the crotch, the sky's fulcrum. Now the earth had foundations and the sky its mantle. . . . When it was done, when they had made Marduk their king, they pronounced peace and happiness for him, "Over our houses you keep unceasing watch, and all you wish from us, that will be done."

Marduk considered and began to speak to the gods assembled in his presence. This is what he said, "In the former time you inhabited the void above the abyss, but I have made Earth as the mirror of Heaven, I have consolidated the soil for the foundations, and there I will build my city, my beloved home. A holy precinct shall be established with sacred halls for the presence of the king. When you come up from the deep to join the Synod you will find lodging and sleep by night. When others from heaven descend to the Assembly, you too will find lodging and sleep by night. It shall be BABYLON the home of the gods. The masters of all crafts shall build it according to my plan". . . . Now that Marduk has heard what it is the gods are saying, he is moved with desire to create a work of consummate art. He told Ea the deep thought in his heart.

"Blood to blood
I join,
blood to bone
I form
an original thing,
its name is MAN,
aboriginal man
is mine in making.

"All his occupations
are faithful service . . ."

Ea answered with carefully chosen words, completing the plan for the gods' comfort. He said to Marduk, "Let one of the kindred be taken; only one need die for the new creation. Bring the gods together in the Great Assembly; there let the guilty die, so the rest may live."

Marduk called the Great Gods to the Synod; he presided courteously, he gave instructions and all of them listened with grave attention. The king speaks to the rebel gods, "Declare on your oath if ever before you spoke the truth, who instigated rebellion? Who stirred up Tiamat? Who led the battle? Let the instigator of war be handed over; guilt and retribution are on him, and peace will be yours for ever."

The great Gods answered the Lord of the Universe, the king and counselor of gods, "It was Kingu who instigated rebellion, he stirred up that sea of bitterness and led the battle for her." They declared him guilty, they bound and held him down in front of Ea, they cut his arteries and from his blood they created man; and Ea imposed his servitude. . . .

*M*uch of the subsequent activity of the festival, which took place in the temple courtyard and streets, was a reenactment of the events of the Creation Myth. The festival occurred at the beginning of spring, when the grain shoots were beginning to emerge, and the essential symbolism of the event concerns the return of natural life to the world. The Babylonians believed that time moved in a circular path and that the natural world had a life cycle consisting of birth, growth, maturity, and death. In winter the cycle drew to a close, and there was no guarantee that it would repeat and that life would return to the world. Babylonians hoped that the New Year's Festival would encourage the gods to grant a renewal of time and life, in essence to recreate the world.

QUESTIONS FOR ANALYSIS

1. According to the Creation Epic, how did the present order of the universe come into being? What does the violent nature of this creation tell us about the Mesopotamian view of the physical world and the gods?

2. How did the symbolism of the events of the New Year's Festival, with its ritual reading and recreation of the story of the Creation Myth, validate such concepts as kingship, the primacy of Babylon, and mankind's relationship to the gods?

3. What is the significance of the distinction between the "private" ceremonies celebrated in the temple precincts and the "public" ceremonies that took place in the streets of the city? What does the festival tell us about the relationship of different social groups to the gods?

Source: Adapted from James B. Pritchard, ed., *Ancient Near Eastern Texts Relating to the Old Testament*, 3d ed. (Princeton, NJ: Princeton University Press, 1969), 332–334. Copyright © 1969 by Princeton University Press. Reprinted by permission of Princeton University Press.

Plaque Showing Harpist, ca. 2000–1600 B.C.E. This image can be attributed to the Old Babylonian period by the style of fringed robe and cap worn by the performer, but harps existed in Mesopotamia and Egypt thousands of years earlier. Clay plaques such as this were mass-produced from a mold. (Courtesy of the Oriental Institute, University of Chicago)

where numerous water channels cut up the landscape, boats and barges were used. In northern Mesopotamia, donkeys were the chief pack animals for overland caravans in the centuries before the advent of the camel (see Chapter 8).

The Mesopotamians had to import raw metal ore, but they became skilled in metallurgy, refining ores composed of copper and arsenic or copper and tin to make **bronze,** which is more malleable than stone. Liquid bronze can be poured into molds, and hardened bronze takes a sharper edge than stone, is less likely to break, and is more easily repaired. Stone implements continued to be produced for the poorest members of the population, who usually could not afford bronze.

Resource-poor Mesopotamians possessed one commodity in abundance: clay. Mud bricks, dried in the sun or baked in an oven for greater durability, were the primary building material. Construction of city walls, temples, and palaces required practical knowledge of architecture and engineering. For example, the reed mats that Mesopotamian builders laid between the mud-brick layers of ziggurats served the same stabilizing purpose as girders in modern high-rise construction. Because of the abundance of good clay, pottery was the most common material for dishware and storage vessels. The potter's wheel, a revolving platform that made possible the rapid production of vessels with precise and complex shapes, was in use by 4000 B.C.E.

In the military sphere, there were innovative developments in organization, tactics, and weapons and other machinery of warfare. Early military forces were militias made up of able-bodied members of the community called up for short periods when needed. The powerful states of the later third and second millennia B.C.E. built up armies of well-trained and well-paid full-time soldiers. In the early second millennium B.C.E. horses appeared in western Asia, and the horse-drawn chariot came into vogue. Infantry found themselves at the mercy of swift chariots carrying a driver and an archer who could get close and unleash a volley of arrows. Using increasingly effective siege machinery, Mesopotamian soldiers could climb over, undermine, or knock down the walls protecting the cities of their enemies.

In other ways, too, the Mesopotamians sought to control their physical environment. They used a base-60 number system (the origin of the seconds and minutes we use today), in which numbers were expressed as fractions or multiples of 60 (in contrast to our base-10 system). Advances in mathematics and careful observation of the skies made the Mesopotamians sophisticated practitioners of astronomy. Mesopotamian priests compiled lists of omens or unusual sightings on earth and in the heavens, together with a record of the events that coincided with them. They consulted these texts at critical times, for they believed that the recurrence of such phenomena could provide clues to future developments. The underlying premise was that the elements of the material universe, from the microscopic to the macrocosmic, were interconnected in mysterious but undeniable ways.

EGYPT

No place exhibits the impact of the natural environment on the history and culture of a society better than ancient Egypt. Located at the intersection of Asia and Africa, Egypt was protected by surrounding barriers of desert and a harborless, marshy seacoast. Where Mesopotamia was open to migration or invasion and was dependent on imported resources, Egypt's natural isolation and essential self-sufficiency fostered a unique culture that for long periods had relatively little to do with other civilizations.

The Land of Egypt: "Gift of the Nile"

The fundamental geographical feature of Egypt is the Nile River. The world's longest river, the Nile originates from Lake Victoria and from several large tributaries in the highlands of tropical Africa and flows northward, carving a narrow valley between the chain of hills on either side, until it reaches the Mediterranean Sea (see Map 2.3). The land through which it flows is mostly desert, but the river makes green a narrow strip on its banks. About 100 miles (160 kilometers) from the Mediterranean the Nile divides into channels to form a triangular delta. Nearly the entire population of the region lives in that twisting, green ribbon alongside the river or in the Nile Delta. The rest of the country, 90 percent or more, is a bleak and inhospitable desert of mountains, rocks, and dunes. The ancient Egyptians recognized the stark dichotomy between the low-lying, life-sustaining soil of the "Black Land" along the river and the elevated, deadly "Red Land" of the desert. With justification and insight the fifth-century B.C.E. Greek traveler Herodotus° called Egypt the "gift of the Nile."

The river was the main means of travel and communication, and the most important cities were located considerably upstream. Because the river flows from south to north, the Egyptians called the southern part of the country "Upper Egypt" and the northern delta "Lower Egypt." In most periods the southern boundary of Egypt was the First Cataract of the Nile, the northernmost of a series of impassable rocks and rapids below Aswan° (about 500 miles [800 kilometers] south of the Mediterranean). At times Egyptian control extended farther south into what was called "Kush" (later Nubia, the southern part of the modern state of Egypt and northern Sudan). The Egyptians also settled a number of large oases, green and habitable "islands" in the midst of the desert, some distance west of the river.

While the hot, sunny climate favored agriculture, rain rarely falls south of the delta, and agriculture was entirely dependent on river water. Throughout Egyptian history irrigation channels were dug to carry water out

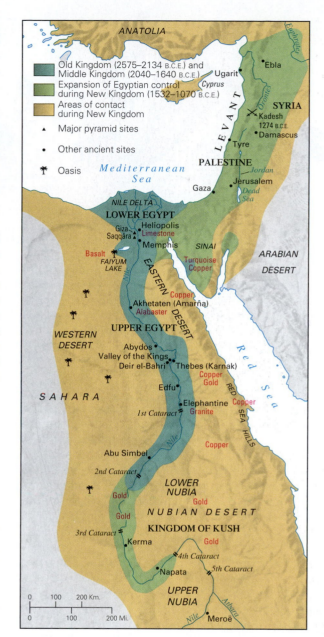

Map 2.3 Ancient Egypt The Nile River, flowing south to north, carved out of the surrounding desert a narrow green valley that became heavily settled in antiquity.

into the desert to increase the amount of land suitable for planting. Drainage techniques reduced the size of Lake Faiyum°, a large depression west of the Nile, allowing more land to be reclaimed for agriculture.

Herodotus (he-ROD-uh-tuhs)   **Aswan** (AS-wahn)   **Faiyum** (fie-YOOM)

Model of Egyptian River Boat, ca. 1985 B.C.E.   This model was buried in the tomb of a Middle Kingdom official, Meketre, who is shown in the cabin being entertained by musicians. The captain stands in front of the cabin, the helmsman on the left steers the boat with the rudder, while the lookout on the right lets out a weighted line to determine the river's depth. The vessel is being rowed downstream (northward); the white post in the middle would support a mast and sail when traveling upstream.   (The Metropolitan Museum of Art, Rogers Fund and Edward S. Harkness Gift, 1920 (20.3.1). Photograph © 1992 The Metropolitan Museum of Art.

Each September the river overflowed its banks, spreading water into the bordering depressed basins. Unlike the Mesopotamians, the Egyptians did not need to construct dams to lift river water to channels and fields. And unlike the Tigris and Euphrates, whose flood came at a disadvantageous time, the Nile flooded at exactly the right time for grain agriculture. When the waters receded, they left behind a moist, fertile layer of mineral-rich silt, where farmers could easily plant their crops. The Egyptians' many creation myths commonly featured the emergence of a life-supporting mound of earth from a primeval swamp.

The level of the flood's crest determined the abundance of the next harvest. "Nilometers," stone staircases with incised units of measure, were placed along the river's edge to gauge the flood surge. When the flood was too high, dikes protecting inhabited areas were washed out, and much damage resulted. When the floods were too low for several years, less land could be cultivated, and the country experienced famine and decline. The ebb and flow of successful and failed regimes seems to have been linked to the cycle of floods. Nevertheless, remarkable stability characterized most eras, and Egyptians viewed the universe as an orderly and beneficent place.

Egypt was well endowed with natural resources. Egyptians used reeds that grew in marshy areas and along the banks of the river to make sails, ropes, and a kind of paper. Hunters pursued the wild animals and birds that abounded in the marshes and on the edge of the desert, and fishermen netted fish from the river. Building stone could be quarried and floated downstream from a number of locations in southern Egypt. Clay for mud bricks and pottery could be found almost everywhere. Copper and turquoise deposits in the Sinai desert to the east and gold from Nubia to the south were within reach, and the state organized armed expeditions and mustered forced labor to exploit these resources. Thus Egypt was considerably more self-sufficient than Mesopotamia.

The farming villages that appeared in Egypt as early as 5500 B.C.E. relied on domesticated plant and animal species that had emerged several millennia earlier in western Asia. However, Egypt's emergence as a focal point of civilization was due, at least in part, to a climate change that took place gradually from the fifth to the third millennium B.C.E. Until then, the Sahara, the vast region that is now the world's largest desert, had a relatively mild and wet climate, and its lakes and grasslands supported a variety of plant and animal species as well as populations of hunter-gatherers (see Chapter 8). As the climate changed and the Sahara began to dry up and become a desert, displaced groups migrated into the Nile Valley, where they developed a sedentary way of life.

Divine Kingship

The increase in population produced new, more complex levels of political organization, including a form of local kingship. Later generations of Egyptians saw the conquest of these smaller units and the unification of all Egypt by Menes°, a ruler from the south, as a pivotal event. Although some scholars question whether Menes was a historical or a mythical figure, many authorities equate Menes with Narmer, a historical ruler around 3100 B.C.E., who is shown on a decorated slate palette exulting over defeated enemies. Later kings of Egypt were referred to as "Rulers of the Two Lands"—Upper and Lower Egypt—and were depicted with two crowns and implements symbolizing the unification of the country. In contrast to Mesopotamia, Egypt was unified early in its history.

The system that historians use to organize Egyptian history is based on thirty dynasties (sequences of kings from the same family) identified by Manetho, an Egyptian from the third century B.C.E. The rise and fall of dynasties often reflects the dominance of different parts of the country. At a broader level of generalization, scholars refer to the "Old," "Middle," and "New Kingdoms," each a period of centralized political power and brilliant cultural achievement, punctuated by "Intermediate Periods" of political fragmentation and cultural decline. Although experts disagree about specific dates for these periods, the chronology (on page 29) reflects current opinion.

The central figure in the Egyptian state was the king (often known as the **pharaoh,** from an Egyptian phrase meaning "palace," which began to be used in the New Kingdom). From the time of the Old Kingdom, if not earlier, Egyptians considered the king to be a god come to earth, the incarnation of Horus and the son of the sun-god Re°. They believed that their king had been placed on earth by the gods to maintain **ma'at°**, the divinely authorized order of the universe. He was the indispensable link between his people and the gods, and his benevolent rule ensured the welfare and prosperity of the country. The Egyptians' conception of a divine king who was the source of law and justice may explain the apparent absence in Egypt of an impersonal code of law comparable to Hammurabi's Code in Mesopotamia.

So much depended on the king that his death evoked elaborate efforts to ensure the well-being of his spirit on its perilous journey to rejoin the gods. Massive resources were poured into the construction of royal tombs, the celebration of elaborate funerary rites, and the sustenance of kings' spirits in the afterlife by perpetual offerings in funerary chapels attached to the royal tombs. Early rulers were buried in flat-topped, rectangular tombs made of mud brick. Around 2630 B.C.E. Djoser°, a Third Dynasty king, ordered the construction of a spectacular stepped **pyramid** consisting of a series of stone platforms laid one on top of the other for himself at Saqqara°, near Memphis. Rulers in the Fourth Dynasty filled in the steps to create the smooth-sided, limestone pyramids that have become the most memorable symbol of ancient Egypt. Between 2550 and 2490 B.C.E. the pharaohs Khufu° and Khefren° erected huge pyramids at Giza, several miles north of Saqqara, the largest stone structures ever built by human hands. Khufu's pyramid originally reached a height of 480 feet (146 meters).

Egyptians accomplished this construction with stone tools (bronze was still expensive and rare) and no machinery other than simple levers, pulleys, and rollers. What made it possible was almost unlimited human muscle power. Calculations of the human resources needed to build a pyramid within the lifetime of the ruler suggest that large numbers of people must have been pressed into service for part of each year, probably during the flood season when no agricultural work could be done. Although this labor was compulsory, the Egyptian masses probably regarded it as a kind of religious service that helped ensure prosperity. Most of the country's surplus resources went into the construction of these artificial mountains of stone. The age of the great pyramids lasted only about a century, although pyramids continued to be built on a smaller scale for two millennia.

Administration and Communication

Ruling dynasties usually placed their capitals in the area of their original power base. **Memphis,** on the Lower Nile near the apex of the delta (close to Cairo, the modern capital), held this central position during the Old Kingdom. **Thebes,** far to the south, came to prominence during much of the Middle and New Kingdom periods (see Map 2.3).

A complex bureaucracy kept detailed records of the resources of the country. The extensive administrative apparatus began at the village level and progressed to the districts into which the country was divided and, finally, to the central government based in the capital city. Bureaucrats in the central administration kept track of

---

Menes (MEH-neez)   Re (ray)   ma'at (muh-AHT)

Djoser (JO-sur)   Saqqara (suh-KAHR-uh)   Khufu (KOO-foo)
Khefren (KEF-ren)

Pyramids of Menkaure, Khafre, and Khufu at Giza, ca. 2500 B.C.E. With a width of 755 feet (230 meters) and a height of 480 feet (146 meters), the Great Pyramid of Khufu is the largest stone structure ever built. The construction of these massive edifices depended on relatively simple techniques of stonecutting, transport (the stones were floated downriver on boats and rolled to the site on sledges), and lifting (the stones were dragged up the face of the pyramid on mud-brick ramps). However, the surveying and engineering skills required to level the platform, lay out the measurements, and securely position the blocks were very sophisticated and have withstood the test of time. (Carolyn Clarke/Spectrum Colour Library)

land, labor, products, and people, extracting a substantial portion of the country's annual revenues—at times as much as 50 percent—in taxes. The income subsidized the palace, bureaucracy, and army, built and maintained temples, and raised great monuments celebrating the ruler's reign. The government maintained a monopoly over key sectors of the economy and controlled long-distance trade. This was quite different from Mesopotamia, where commerce increasingly fell into the hands of an acquisitive urban middle class.

The hallmark of the administrative class was literacy. A system of writing had been developed by the beginning of the Early Dynastic period. **Hieroglyphics°**, the earliest form of this writing system, were picture symbols standing for words, syllables, or individual sounds. Our ability to read ancient Egyptian writing is due to the decipherment, in the early nineteenth century C.E.,

of the Rosetta Stone, a document from the second century B.C.E. with hieroglyphic and Greek versions of the same text.

Hieroglyphic writing long continued to be used on monuments and ornamental inscriptions. By 2500 B.C.E., however, a cursive script, in which the original pictorial nature of the symbol was less readily apparent, had been developed for the everyday needs of administrators and copyists. They worked with ink on a writing material called **papyrus°**, after the reed from which it was made. The stems of the papyrus reed were laid out in a vertical and horizontal grid pattern and then pounded with a soft mallet until the moist fibers formed a sheet of writing material. The plant grew only in Egypt but was in demand throughout the ancient world and was exported in large quantities. Indeed, the word *paper* is derived from Greek and Roman words for papyrus.

---

hieroglyphics (high-ruh-GLIF-iks)

papyrus (puh-PIE-ruhs)

The Egyptians used writing for many purposes other than administrative recordkeeping. Their written literature included tales of adventure and magic, love poetry, religious hymns, and manuals of instruction on technical subjects. Scribes in workshops attached to the temples made copies of traditional texts.

When the monarchy was strong, officials were appointed and promoted on the basis of merit and accomplishment. They received grants of land from the king and were supported by dependent peasants who worked the land. Low-level officials were assigned to villages and district capitals; high-ranking officials served in the royal capital. When Old Kingdom officials died, they were buried in tombs around the monumental tomb of the king so that they could serve him in death as they had done in life.

Throughout Egyptian history there was an underlying tension between the centralizing power of the monarchy and the decentralizing tendencies of the Egyptian bureaucracy. One sign of the breakdown of centralized power in the late Old Kingdom and First Intermediate Period was the placement of officials' tombs in their home districts, where they spent much of their time and exercised power more or less independently, rather than near the royal tomb. Another sign was the tendency of administrative posts to become hereditary. The early monarchs of the Middle Kingdom responded to the fragmentation of the preceding period by reducing the power and prerogatives of the old elite and creating a new middle class of administrators.

Egypt has often been called a land of villages without real cities because the political capitals were primarily extensions of the palace and central administration. In comparison with Mesopotamia, a far larger percentage of Egyptians lived in rural villages and engaged in agriculture, and the essential wealth of Egypt resided to a higher degree in the land and its products. But there were towns and cities in ancient Egypt, although they were less crucial to the economic and cultural dynamism of the country than were Mesopotamian urban centers. Unfortunately, archaeologists have been unable to excavate many ancient urban sites in Egypt because they have been continuously inhabited and lie beneath modern communities.

During the Old and Middle Kingdoms, Egypt's foreign policy was essentially isolationist. Technically, all foreigners were considered to be enemies. When necessary, local militia units backed up a small standing army of professional soldiers. Nomadic tribes living in the eastern and western deserts and Libyans living in the northwest were a nuisance rather than a real danger and were readily handled by the Egyptian military. The king maintained limited contact with the other advanced civilizations of the region. Egypt's interests abroad focused primarily on maintaining access to valuable resources rather than on acquiring territory. Trade with the coastal towns of the Levant° (modern Israel, the Palestinian territories, Lebanon, and Syria) brought in cedar wood. In return, Egypt exported grain, papyrus, and gold.

In all periods the Egyptians had a particularly strong interest in goods that came from the south. Nubia had rich sources of gold (Chapter 3 examines the rise of a civilization in Nubia that, though considerably influenced by Egypt, created a vital and original culture that lasted for more than two thousand years), and the southern course of the Nile offered the only easily passable corridor to sub-Saharan Africa.

In the Old Kingdom, Egyptian noblemen living at Aswan on the southern border led donkey caravans south to trade for gold, incense, and products of tropical Africa such as ivory, dark ebony wood, and exotic jungle animals. A line of forts along the southern border protected Egypt from attack. In the early second millennium B.C.E. Egyptian forces struck south into Nubia, extending the Egyptian border as far as the Third Cataract of the Nile and taking possession of the gold fields. Still farther to the south, perhaps in the coastal region of present-day Sudan or Eritrea, lay the fabled land of Punt°, source of the fragrant myrrh resin that priests burned on the altars of the Egyptian gods.

The People of Egypt

The million to million and a half inhabitants of Egypt included various physical types, ranging from dark-skinned people related to the populations of sub-Saharan Africa to lighter-skinned people akin to the populations of North Africa and western Asia. Although Egypt did not experience the large-scale migrations and invasions common in Mesopotamia, settlers periodically trickled into the Nile Valley and assimilated with the people already living there.

Although some Egyptians had higher status and more wealth and power than others, in contrast to Mesopotamia no formal class structure emerged. At the top of the social hierarchy were the king and high-ranking officials. In the middle were lower-level officials, local leaders, priests and other professionals, artisans, and well-to-do farmers. At the bottom were peasants, who made up the vast majority of the population.

Levant (luh-VANT)   **Punt** (poont)

Peasants lived in rural villages, where they engaged in the seasonally changing tasks of agriculture: plowing, sowing, tending emerging shoots, reaping, threshing, and storing grain or other products of the soil. The irrigation network of channels, basins, and dikes had to be maintained, improved, and extended. Domesticated animals—cattle, sheep, goats, and fowl—and fish supplemented a diet based on wheat or barley, beer, and garden vegetables. Villagers probably shared implements, work animals, and storage facilities and helped one another at peak times in the agricultural cycle and in the construction of houses and other buildings. They prayed and feasted together at festivals to the local gods and other public celebrations. Periodically they were required to contribute labor to state projects, such as construction of the pyramids. If taxation or compulsory service was too great a burden, flight into the desert was the only escape.

This account of the lives of ordinary Egyptians is largely conjectural; the villages of ancient Egypt, like those of Mesopotamia, left few traces in the archaeological or literary record. Tomb paintings of the elite sometimes depict common people. The artists employed pictorial conventions to indicate status, such as obesity for the possessors of wealth and comfort, and baldness and deformity for members of the working classes. Egyptian poets frequently used metaphors of farming and hunting, and legal documents on papyrus preserved in the hot, dry sands tell of property transactions and legal disputes among ordinary people.

Slavery existed on a limited scale but was of little economic significance. Prisoners of war, condemned criminals, and debtors could be found on the country estates or in the households of the king and wealthy families. Treatment of slaves was relatively humane, and they could be freed.

Some information is available about the lives of women of the upper classes, but it is filtered through the brushes and pens of male artists and scribes. Tomb paintings show women of the royal family and elite classes accompanying their husbands and engaging in typical domestic activities. They are depicted with dignity and affection, though they are clearly subordinate to the men. The artistic convention of depicting men with a dark red and women with a yellow flesh tone implies that the elite woman's proper sphere was indoors, away from the searing sun. In the beautiful love poetry of the New Kingdom, lovers address each other in terms of apparent equality and express emotions akin to our own ideal of romantic love. We cannot be sure how accurately this poetry represents the prevalent attitude of other periods of Egyptian history or among groups other than the educated elite.

Legal documents show that Egyptian women could own property, inherit from their parents, and will their property to whomever they wished. Marriage, usually monogamous, was not confirmed by any legal or religious ceremony and essentially constituted a decision by a man and woman to establish a household together. Either party could dissolve the relationship, and the divorced woman retained rights over her dowry. At certain times queens and queen-mothers played significant behind-the-scenes roles in the politics of the royal court, and priestesses sometimes supervised the cults of female deities. In general, the limited evidence suggests that women in ancient Egypt were treated more respectfully and had more legal rights and social freedom than women in Mesopotamia and other ancient societies.

Belief and Knowledge

The religion of the Egyptians was rooted in the landscape of the Nile Valley and in the vision of cosmic order that this environment evoked. The consistency of their environment—the sun rose every day in a clear and cloudless sky, and the river flooded on schedule every year, ensuring a bounteous harvest—persuaded the Egyptians that the natural world was a place of recurrent cycles and periodic renewal. The sky was imagined to be a great ocean surrounding the inhabited world. The sun-god Re traversed this blue waterway in a boat by day, then returned through the Underworld at night, fighting off the attacks of demonic serpents so that he could be born anew in the morning. In one especially popular story Osiris°, a god who once ruled Egypt, was slain by his jealous brother Seth, who then scattered the dismembered pieces. Isis, Osiris's devoted sister and wife, found and reconstructed the remnants, and Horus, his son, took revenge on Seth. Osiris was restored to life and installed as king of the Underworld, and his example gave people hope of a new life in a world beyond this one.

The king, who was seen as Horus (son of Osiris) and as the son of Re, was thus associated with both the return of the dead to life and the life-giving and self-renewing symbolism of the sun-god. He was the chief priest of Egypt, intervening with the gods on behalf of his land and people. When a town attained special significance as the capital of a ruling dynasty, the chief god of that town became prominent across the land. Thus did Ptah° of Memphis, Re of Heliopolis°, and Amon° of Thebes be-

---

Osiris (oh-SIGH-ris)   **Ptah** (puh-TAH)
Heliopolis (he-lee-OP-uh-lis)   **Amon** (AH-muhn)

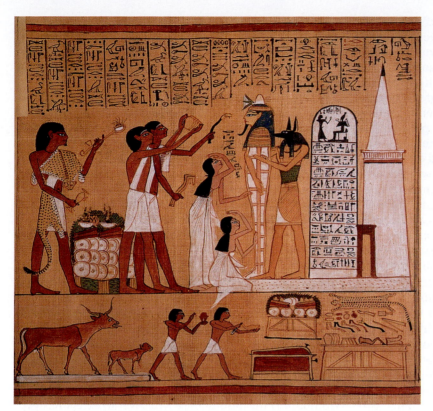

Scene from the Egyptian Book of the Dead, ca. 1300 B.C.E. The mummy of a royal scribe named Hunefar is approached by members of his household before being placed in the tomb. Behind Hunefar is jackel-headed Anubis, the god who will conduct the spirit of the deceased to the afterlife. The Book of the Dead provided Egyptians with the instructions they needed to complete this arduous journey and gain a blessed existence in the afterlife. (Courtesy of the Trustees of the British Museum)

come gods of all Egypt, serving to unify the country and strengthen the monarchy.

Egyptian rulers were especially interested in building new temples, refurbishing old ones, and making lavish gifts to the gods, as well as overseeing the construction of their own monumental tombs. A considerable portion of the wealth of Egypt was used in a ceaseless effort to win the gods' favor, maintain the continuity of divine kingship, and ensure the renewal of the life-giving forces that sustained the world.

The many gods of ancient Egypt were diverse in origin and nature. Some were normally depicted with animal heads; others were always given human form. Few myths about the origins and adventures of the gods have survived, but there must have been a rich oral tradition. Many towns had temples in which locally prominent deities were thought to reside. The fluidity of the metaphysical realm allowed local deities to be viewed as manifestations of the great gods, and gods could be merged to form hybrids, such as Amon-Re. Cult activities were carried out in the private inner reaches of the temples, off limits to all but the priests who served the needs of the deity by attending to his or her statue. Food offered to the image was later distributed to temple staff. As in

Mesopotamia, some temples possessed extensive landholdings worked by dependent peasants, and the priests who administered the deity's wealth were influential locally and sometimes even throughout the land.

During great festivals, the priests paraded a boat-shaped litter carrying the shrouded statue and cult items of the deity. Such occasions brought large numbers of people into contact with the deity in an outpouring of devotion and celebration. Little is known about the day-to-day beliefs and practices of the common people. In the household family members revered and made small offerings to Bes, the grotesque god of marriage and domestic happiness, to local deities, and to the family's ancestors. Amulets and depictions of demonic figures were supposed to protect the bearer and ward off evil forces. In later times Greeks and Romans commented that the devotion to magic was especially strong in Egypt.

Egyptians believed in the afterlife, and they made extensive preparations for safe passage to the next world and a comfortable existence once they arrived there. One common belief was that death was a journey beset with hazards. The Egyptian Book of the Dead, present in many excavated tombs, contained rituals and spells to protect the journeying spirit. The final and most important challenge was the weighing of the deceased's heart (believed to be the source of personality, intellect, and emotion) in the presence of the judges of the Underworld to determine whether the person had led a good life and deserved to reach the ultimate blessed destination.

Obsession with the afterlife produced great concern about the physical condition of the cadaver. Egyptians perfected techniques of mummification to preserve the dead body. The idea probably grew out of the early practice of burying the dead in the hot, dry sand on the edge of the desert, where bodies decomposed slowly. The elite classes utilized the most expensive kind of mummification. Vital organs were removed, preserved, and stored in stone jars laid out around the corpse. Body cavities were filled with various packing materials. The cadaver was immersed for long periods in dehydrating and preserving chemicals and eventually was wrapped in linen. The **mummy** was then placed in one or more decorated wooden caskets and was deposited in a tomb.

The tombs, which usually were built at the edge of the desert so as not to tie up valuable farmland, were filled with pictures, food, and the objects of everyday life so that the deceased would have whatever he or she might need in the next life. Archaeologists and historians have gleaned much of what is now known about ancient Egyptian life from this practice of stocking tombs with utilitarian and luxury household objects. Small figurines called shawabtis° were included to play the part of servants and to take the place of the deceased in case the regimen of the afterlife included periodic calls for compulsory labor. The elite classes ordered chapels attached to their tombs and left endowments to subsidize the daily attendance of a priest and offerings of foodstuffs to sustain their spirits for all eternity.

The form of a tomb also reflected the wealth and status of the deceased. Common people had to make do with simple pit graves or small mud-brick chambers. Members of the privileged classes built larger tombs and covered the walls with pictures and inscriptions. Kings erected pyramids and other grand edifices, employing subterfuge to hide the sealed chamber containing the body and treasures, as well as curses and other magical precautions to foil tomb robbers. Rarely did they succeed, however. Archaeologists have seldom discovered an undisturbed royal tomb.

The ancient Egyptians made remarkable advances in many areas of knowledge and developed an array of advantageous technologies. They learned about chemistry through experiments on preserving dead bodies.

The process of mummification also provided opportunities to learn about human anatomy, and Egyptian doctors were in demand in the courts of western Asia because of their relatively advanced medical knowledge and techniques.

The Egyptians sought ways to control and profit from the Nile flood and worked hard at constructing, maintaining, and expanding the network of irrigation channels and holding basins. They needed mathematics to survey and measure the dimensions of fields and calculate the quantity of agricultural produce owed to the state. By careful observation of the stars they constructed the most accurate calendar in the world, and they knew that the appearance of the star Sirius on the horizon shortly before sunrise meant that the Nile flood surge was imminent.

Pyramids, temple complexes, and other monumental building projects called for great skill in engineering and architecture. Vast quantities of earth had to be moved to make the construction sites level. Large stones had to be quarried, dragged on rollers, floated downstream on barges, lifted into place along ramps of packed earth, and then carved to the exact size needed and made smooth. Long underground passageways were excavated to connect mortuary temples by the river with tombs near the desert's edge. On several occasions Egyptian kings dredged out a canal more than 50 miles (80 kilometers) long in order to join the Nile Valley to the Red Sea and expedite the transport of goods.

Relatively simple technologies facilitated the transportation of goods and people. River barges were used to carry stones from quarries to construction sites. Lightweight ships equipped with sails and oars were well suited for travel on the peaceful Nile and sometimes were used for voyages on the Mediterranean and Red Seas. Carts and sledges pulled by draft animals were of limited use in a landscape interrupted by canals and flooded basins. Archaeologists recently discovered an 8-mile (13-kilometer) road made of slabs of sandstone and limestone connecting a rock quarry with Faiyum Lake. Dating to the second half of the third millennium B.C.E., it is the oldest known paved road in the world.

THE INDUS VALLEY CIVILIZATION

Civilization arose almost as early in South Asia as in Mesopotamia and Egypt. Just as each of the Middle Eastern civilizations was centered on a great river valley, so civilization in the Indian subcontinent originated on a fertile floodplain. In the valley of the Indus River, settled

---

shawabtis (shuh-WAB-tees)

farming created the agricultural surplus essential to urbanized society.

Natural Environment

A plain of more than 1 million acres (400,000 hectares) stretches from the mountains of western Pakistan east to the Thar° Desert in the central portion of the Indus Valley, the Sind° region of modern Pakistan (see Map 2.1). Over many centuries silt carried downstream and deposited on the land by the Indus River has elevated the riverbed and its containing banks above the plain. Twice a year the river overflows its banks and spreads as far as 10 miles (16 kilometers). In March and April melting snow feeds the river's sources in the Pamir° and Himalaya° mountain ranges. Then in August, the great monsoon (seasonal wind) blowing off the ocean to the southwest brings rains that swell the streams flowing into the Indus. As a result, farmers in this region of little rainfall are able to plant and harvest two crops a year. In ancient times the Hakra° River (sometimes referred to as the Saraswati), which has since dried up, ran parallel to the Indus about 25 miles (40 kilometers) to the east and provided a second area suitable for intensive cultivation.

Adjacent regions shared many cultural traits with this core area. To the northeast is the Punjab, where five rivers converge to form the main course of the Indus. Lying beneath the shelter of the towering Himalaya range, the Punjab receives considerably more rainfall than the central plain but is less prone to flooding. From there settlements spread as far as Delhi° in northwest India. Settlement also extended south into the great delta where the Indus empties into the Arabian Sea, and southeast into India's hook-shaped Kathiawar° Peninsula, an area of alluvial plains and coastal marshes. The territory covered by the Indus Valley civilization is roughly equivalent in size to modern France—much larger than the zone of Mesopotamian civilization.

Material Culture

The Indus Valley civilization flourished from approximately 2600 to 1900 B.C.E. Although archaeologists have located several hundred sites, the culture is best known from the archaeological remains of two great cities first discovered eighty years ago. The ancient names of these cities are unknown, so they are

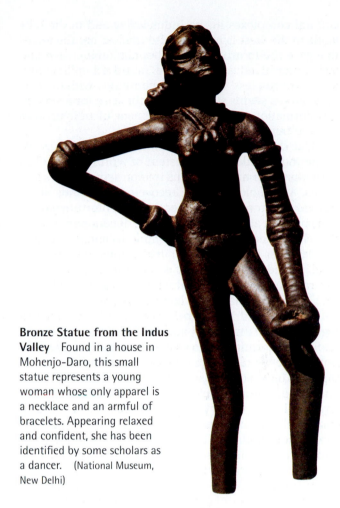

Bronze Statue from the Indus Valley   Found in a house in Mohenjo-Daro, this small statue represents a young woman whose only apparel is a necklace and an armful of bracelets. Appearing relaxed and confident, she has been identified by some scholars as a dancer.   (National Museum, New Delhi)

referred to by modern names: **Harappa** and **Mohenjo-Daro°**. Unfortunately, the high water table at these sites makes excavation of the earliest levels of settlement nearly impossible.

Scholars once assumed that the people who created this civilization were related to speakers of the Dravidian° languages whose descendants were driven into central and southern India by invading Indo-European herders around 1500 B.C.E. Skeletal evidence, however, indicates that the population of the Indus Valley remained stable from ancient times to the present, and it is now believed that settled agriculture in this part of the world dates back to at least 5000 B.C.E. The precise relationship between the Indus Valley civilization and earlier

---

Thar (tahr)   **Sind** (sinned)   **Pamir** (pah-MEER)
Himalaya (him-uh-LAY-uh)   **Hakra** (HAK-ruh)   **Delhi** (DEL-ee)
Kathiawar (kah-tee-uh-WAHR)

Mohenjo-Daro (moe-hen-joe–DAHR-oh)
Dravidian (druh-VID-ee-uhn)

cultural complexes in the Indus Valley and in the hilly lands to the west is unclear. Also unclear are the forces that gave rise to urbanization, population increase, and technological advances in the mid-third millennium B.C.E. Nevertheless, the case for continuity with the earlier cultures seems stronger than the case for a sudden transformation due to the movement of new peoples into the valley.

Like the Mesopotamians and Egyptians, the people of the Indus Valley had a system of writing. They used more than four hundred signs to represent syllables and words. Archaeologists have recovered thousands of inscribed seal stones and copper tablets. Unfortunately, no one has been able to decipher these documents.

This society produced major urban centers. Harappa was 3.5 miles (5.6 kilometers) in circumference and may have housed a population of 35,000. Mohenjo-Daro was several times larger. High, thick brick walls surrounded each city. The streets were laid out in a rectangular grid pattern. Covered drainpipes carried away waste. The regular size of the streets and length of the city blocks and the uniformity of the mud bricks used in construction have been taken as evidence of a strong central authority. The seat of this authority may have been the citadel—an elevated, enclosed compound containing large buildings. Nearby were well-ventilated structures that scholars think were storehouses of grain for feeding the urban population and for export. The presence of barracks may point to some regimentation of the skilled artisans.

It is often assumed that these urban centers controlled the rural farmlands around them, though there is no proof that they did. Various factors may account for the location of the chief centers, and different centers may have had different functions. Mohenjo-Daro seems to dominate the great floodplain of the Indus. Harappa, which is nearly 500 miles (805 kilometers) from Mohenjo-Daro, is on a frontier between farmland and herding land, and no other settlements have been found west of it. Harappa may have served as a "gateway" to the copper, tin, and precious stones of the northwest. Coastal towns to the south also would have had commercial functions, gathering fish and highly prized seashells and expediting seaborne trade with the Persian Gulf.

Mohenjo-Daro and Harappa have been extensively excavated, and published accounts on the Indus Valley civilization tend to treat them as the norm. Most people, however, lived in smaller settlements, which exhibit the same artifacts and the same standardization of styles and shapes as the large cities. Some scholars attribute this standardization to extensive exchange and trading of goods within the zone of Indus Valley civilization, rather than to a strong and authoritarian central government.

There is a greater abundance of metal in the Indus Valley than in Mesopotamia and Egypt, and most of the metal objects that archaeologists have found are utilitarian tools and other everyday objects. In contrast, more jewelry and other decorative metal objects have been unearthed in Mesopotamia and Egypt. Moreover, metal objects were available to a large cross-section of the population in the Indus Valley, while they were primarily reserved for the elite in the Middle East.

The civilization of the Indus Valley possessed impressive technological capabilities. The people were adept in the technology of irrigation, used the potter's wheel, and laid the foundations of large public buildings with mud bricks baked in kilns (sun-dried bricks would have dissolved quickly in floodwaters). Smiths worked with gold, silver, copper, and tin. The varying ratios of tin to copper in their bronze objects suggest that they were acutely aware of the hardness of different mixtures and used the smallest amount possible of the relatively rare tin, making, for example, axes harder than knives.

The people of the Indus Valley had widespread trading contacts. Utilizing passes through the mountains in the northwest, they had ready access to the valuable resources of eastern Iran and Afghanistan as well as to ore deposits in western India. These resources included metals (such as copper and tin), precious stones (lapis lazuli, jade, and turquoise), building stone, and timber. Goods were moved on rivers within the zone of Indus Valley culture. It has been suggested that the undeciphered writing on seal stones may represent the names of merchants who stamped their wares.

The inhabitants of the Indus Valley and of Mesopotamia obtained raw materials from some of the same sources. Indus Valley seal stones have been found in the Tigris-Euphrates Valley, and some scholars believe that Indus Valley merchants served as middlemen in the long-distance trade, obtaining raw materials from the lands of west-central Asia and shipping them to the Persian Gulf.

Little is known about the political, social, economic, and religious structures of Indus Valley society. Attempts to link artifacts and images to cultural features characteristic of later periods of Indian history (see Chapter 7)—including sociopolitical institutions (a system of hereditary occupational groups, the predominant role of priests), architectural forms (bathing tanks like those later found in Hindu temples, private interior courtyards in houses), and religious beliefs and practices (depictions of gods and sacred animals on the seal stones, a cult of the mother-goddess)—are highly speculative.

ENVIRONMENT + TECHNOLOGY

Environmental Stress in the Indus Valley

The three river-valley civilizations discussed in this chapter were located in arid or semiarid regions. Such regions are particularly vulnerable to changes in the environment. Scholars' debates about the existence and impact of changes in the climate and landscape of the Indus Valley illuminate some of the possible factors at work, as well as the difficulties of verifying and interpreting such long-ago changes.

One of the points at issue is climatic change. An earlier generation of scholars believed that the climate of the Indus Valley was considerably wetter during the height of that civilization than it is now. As evidence, they cited the enormous quantities of timber, cut from extensive forests, that would have been needed to bake the millions of mud bricks used to construct the cities (see photo), the distribution of human settlements on land that is now unfavorable for agriculture, and the representation of jungle and marsh animals on decorated seals. This approach assumes that the growth of population, prosperity, and complexity in the Indus Valley in the third millennium B.C.E. required wet conditions, and it concludes that the change to a drier climate in the early second millennium B.C.E. pushed this civilization into decline.

Other experts, skeptical about radical climate change, countered with alternative calculations of the amount of timber needed and evidence of plant remains—particularly barley, a grain that is tolerant of dry conditions. However, recent studies of the stabilization of sand dunes, which occurs in periods of heavy rainfall, and analysis of the sediment deposited by rivers and winds have been used to strengthen the claim that the Indus Valley used to be wetter and that in the early- to mid-second millennium B.C.E. it entered a period of relatively dry conditions that have persisted to the present.

A much clearer case can be made for changes in the landscape caused by shifts in the courses of rivers. These shifts are due, in many cases, to tectonic forces such as earthquakes. Dry channels, whether detected in satellite photographs or by on-the-ground inspection, reveal the location of old riverbeds, and it appears that a second major river system, the Hakra, once ran parallel to the Indus some distance to the east. The Hakra, with teeming towns and fertile fields along its banks, appears to have been a second axis of this civilization. Either the Sutlej, which now feeds into the Indus, or the Yamuna, which now pours into the Ganges, may have been the main source of water for this long-gone system before undergoing a change of course. The consequences of the drying-up of this major waterway must have been immense— the loss of huge amounts of arable land and the food that it

Mud-Brick Fortification Wall of the Citadel at Harappa
Built upon a high platform, this massive and towering construction required large numbers of bricks and enormous man-hours of labor. *The Cambridge History of India: The Indus Civilization*, 3d ed. (1968), by Sir Mortimer Wheeler. With permission of the Syndics of the Cambridge University Press.

produced, the abandonment of cities and villages and consequent migration of their populations, shifts in the trade routes, and desperate competition for shrinking resources.

As for the Indus itself, the present-day course of the lower reaches of the river has shifted 100 miles (161 kilometers) to the west since the arrival of the Greek conqueror Alexander the Great in the late fourth century B.C.E., and the deposit of massive volumes of silt has pushed the mouth of the river 50 miles (80 kilometers) farther south. Such a shift of the river bed and buildup of alluvial deposits also may have occurred in the third and second millennia B.C.E.

A recent study concludes: "It is obvious that ecological stresses, caused both climatically and technically, played an important role in the life and decay" of the Indus civilization.

Source: Quotation from D. P. Agarwal and R. K. Sood in Gregory L. Possehl, ed., *Harappan Civilization: A Contemporary Perspective* (Warminster, England: Aris and Phillips, 1982), 229.

Further knowledge about this society awaits additional archaeological finds and the deciphering of the Indus Valley script.

Transformation of the Indus Valley Civilization

The Indus Valley cities were abandoned sometime after 1900 B.C.E. Archaeologists once thought that invaders destroyed them, but now they believe that the civilization suffered "systems failure"—the breakdown of the fragile interrelationship of the political, social, and economic systems that sustained order and prosperity. The cause may have been one or more natural disasters, such as an earthquake or massive flooding. Gradual ecological changes may also have played a role as the Hakra river system dried up and salinization (an increase in the amount of salt in the soil, inhibiting plant growth) and erosion increased (see Environment and Technology: Environmental Stress in the Indus Valley).

When towns were no longer on the river, ports were separated from the sea by silt deposits in the deltas, and regions lost fertile soil and water, large numbers of people would have had to relocate, and those who remained would need new ways of making a living. The causes, patterns, and pace of change probably varied in different areas. Urbanization is likely to have persisted longer in some regions than in others. But in the end, the urban centers could not be sustained, and village-based farming and herding took their place. As the interaction between regions lessened, distinct regional variations replaced the standardization of technology and style of the previous era.

Historians can do little more than speculate about the causes behind the changes and the experiences of the people who lived in the Indus Valley around 1900 B.C.E. It is important to keep two tendencies in mind. In most cases like this, the majority of the population adjusts to the new circumstances. But members of the political and social elite, who depended on the urban centers and complex political and economic structures, lose the source of their authority and are merged with the population as a whole.

CONCLUSION

It is surely no accident that the first civilizations to develop high levels of political centralization, urbanization, and technology were situated in river valleys where rainfall was insufficient for dependable agriculture. Dependent as they were on river water to irrigate the cultivated land that fed their populations, Mesopotamia, Egypt, and the Indus Valley civilization channeled significant human resources into the construction and maintenance of canals, dams, and dikes. This work required expertise in engineering, mathematics, and metallurgy, as well as the formation of political centers that could organize the necessary labor force.

The unpredictable and violent floods in the Tigris-Euphrates Basin were a constant source of alarm for the people of Mesopotamia. In contrast, the predictable, opportune, and gradual Nile floods were eagerly anticipated events in Egypt. The relationship with nature stamped the worldview of both peoples. Mesopotamians nervously tried to appease their harsh deities so as to survive in a perverse world. Egyptians largely trusted in and nurtured the supernatural powers that, they believed, guaranteed orderliness and prosperity.

In both Egypt and Mesopotamia, kingship emerged as the dominant political form. The Egyptian king's divine origins and symbolic association with the forces of renewal made him central to the welfare of the entire country and gave him a religious monopoly superseding the authority of the temples and priests. Egyptian monarchs lavished much of the country's wealth on their tombs, believing that a proper burial would ensure the continuity of kingship and the attendant blessings that it brought to the land and people. Mesopotamian rulers, who were not normally regarded as divine, built new cities, towering walls, splendid palaces, and religious edifices as lasting testaments to their power.

The religious outlook of both cultures included a hierarchy of gods, ranging from protective demons and local deities to the gods of the state, whose importance rose or fell with the power of the political centers with which they were associated. Cheered by the essential stability of their environment, the Egyptians tended to have a more positive conception of the gods' designs for humankind. The Egyptians believed that although the journey to the next world was beset with hazards, the righteous spirit that overcame them could look forward to a blessed existence. In contrast, Gilgamesh, the hero of the Mesopotamian epic, is tormented by terrifying visions of the afterlife: disembodied spirits of the dead stumbling around in the darkness of the Underworld for all eternity, eating dust and clay, and slaving for the heartless gods of that realm.

Although the populations of Egypt and Mesopotamia were ethnically heterogeneous, both regions experienced a remarkable degree of cultural continuity. New immigrants readily assimilated to the dominant language, belief system, and lifestyles of the civilization. People were identified by culture, not physical appearance. Mesopotamian women's apparent loss of freedom and legal privilege in the second millennium B.C.E. may have been related to the higher degree of urbanization and class stratification in this society. In contrast, Egyptian pictorial documents, love poems, and legal records indicate respect and greater equality for women in the valley of the Nile.

In the second millennium B.C.E., as the societies of Mesopotamia and Egypt consolidated their cultural achievements and entered new phases of political expansion, and as the Indus Valley centers went into irreversible decline, a new and distinctive civilization, based likewise on the exploitation of the agricultural potential of a floodplain, was emerging in the valley of the Yellow River in eastern China. We turn our attention to that area in Chapter 3.

■ Key Terms

civilization	pharaoh
Babylon	ma'at
Sumerians	pyramid
Semitic	Memphis
city-state	Thebes
Hammurabi	hieroglyphics
scribe	papyrus
ziggurat	mummy
amulet	Harappa
cuneiform	Mohenjo-Daro
bronze	

■ Suggested Reading

Jack M. Sasson, ed., *Civilizations of the Ancient Near East*, 4 vols. (1993), contains up-to-date articles and bibliography on a wide range of topics. An excellent starting point for geography, chronology, and basic institutions and cultural concepts in ancient western Asia is Michael Roaf, *Cultural Atlas of Mesopotamia and the Ancient Near East* (1990). Amelie Kuhrt, *The Ancient Near East, c. 3000–330 B.C.*, 2 vols. (1995), is the best and most up-to-date introduction to the historical development of western Asia and Egypt, offering a clear and concise historical outline and a balanced presentation of continuing controversies. Other general historical introductions can be found in A. Bernard Knapp, *The History and Culture of Ancient Western Asia and Egypt* (1988); Hans J. Nissen, *The Early History of the Ancient Near East, 9000–2000 B.C.* (1988); and H. W. F. Saggs, *Civilization Before Greece and Rome* (1989).

Georges Roux, *Ancient Iraq*, 3d ed. (1992), traces the long history of ancient Mesopotamia, while Joan Oates, *Babylon* (1979),

focuses on the most important of all the Mesopotamian cities. J. N. Postgate, *Early Mesopotamia: Society and Economy at the Dawn of History* (1992), offers deep insights into the political, social, and economic dynamics of Mesopotamian society. Susan Pollock, *Ancient Mesopotamia: The Eden That Never Was* (1999), applies anthropological theory and models to early Mesopotamia. Marc van de Mierop, *The Ancient Mesopotamian City* (1997), explores the political, social, and economic dimensions of Mesopotamian urbanism. Daniel C. Snell, *Life in the Ancient Near East 3100–322 B.C.E.* (1997), emphasizes social and economic matters for those already familiar with the main outlines of ancient Near Eastern history. Stephanie Dalley, ed., *The Legacy of Mesopotamia* (1998), explores the interactions of the Mesopotamians with other peoples of the ancient world.

The most direct and exciting introduction to the world of early Mesopotamians is through the *Epic of Gilgamesh*, in the attractive translation of David Ferry, *Gilgamesh: A New Rendering in English Verse* (1992). Thorkild Jacobsen, *The Treasures of Darkness: A History of Mesopotamian Religion* (1976), is a classic study of the evolving mentality of Mesopotamian religion. Stephanie Dalley, *Myths from Mesopotamia* (1989), and Henrietta McCall, *Mesopotamian Myths* (1990), deal with the mythical literature. Jeremy Black and Anthony Green, *Gods, Demons and Symbols of Ancient Mesopotamia* (1992), is a handy illustrated encyclopedia of myth, religion, and religious symbolism. Pierre Amiet, *Art of the Ancient Near East* (1980), offers a richly illustrated introduction to a wide spectrum of artistic media. Dominique Collon, *First Impressions: Cylinder Seals in the Ancient Near East* (1988), explores a class of common objects that reveal much about art and daily life.

C. B. F. Walker, *Cuneiform* (1987), is a concise guide to the Mesopotamian system of writing. James B. Pritchard, *Ancient Near Eastern Texts Relating to the Old Testament*, 3d ed. (1969), contains an extensive collection of translated documents and texts from western Asia and Egypt. Karen Rhea Nemet-Nejat, *Daily Life in Ancient Mesopotamia* (1998), is an introduction to social history. Attitudes, roles, and the treatment of women are taken up by Karen Rhea Nemet-Nejat, "Women in Ancient Mesopotamia," in Bella Vivante, ed., *Women's Roles in Ancient Civilizations: A Reference Guide* (1999), and Barbara Lesko, "Women of Egypt and the Ancient Near East," in *Becoming Visible: Women in European History*, 2d ed., ed. Renata Bridenthal, Claudia Koonz, and Susan Stuard (1994). The significance of ancient Syria as a region with its own cultural vitality as well as indebtedness to Mesopotamia is taken up in Harvey Weiss, ed., *Ebla to Damascus: Art and Archaeology of Ancient Syria* (1985), and Giovanni Pettinato, *Ebla: A New Look at History* (1991).

A fine and lavishly illustrated introduction to the many facets of ancient Egyptian civilization is David P. Silverman, ed., *Ancient Egypt* (1997). John Baines and Jaromir Malek, *Atlas of Ancient Egypt* (1980), and T. G. H. James, *Ancient Egypt: The Land and Its Legacy* (1988), are primarily organized around the sites of ancient Egypt and provide general introductions to Egyptian civilization. Donald B. Redford, ed., *The Oxford Encyclopedia of Ancient Egypt*, 3 vols. (2001), and Kathryn A. Bard, ed.,

Encyclopedia of the Archaeology of Ancient Egypt (1999), are comprehensive reference tools. Historical treatments include B. G. Trigger, B. J. Kemp, D. O'Connor, and A. B. Lloyd, *Ancient Egypt: A Social History* (1983); Barry J. Kemp, *Ancient Egypt: Anatomy of a Civilization* (1989); Nicholas-Cristophe Grimal, *A History of Ancient Egypt* (1992); Erik Hornung, *History of Ancient Egypt: An Introduction* (1999); and Ian Shaw, ed., *The Oxford History of Ancient Egypt* (2000). John Romer, *People of the Nile: Everyday Life in Ancient Egypt* (1982); Miriam Stead, *Egyptian Life* (1986); Eugen Strouhal, *Life of the Ancient Egyptians* (1992); and Lionel Casson, *Everyday Life in Ancient Egypt* (2001), emphasize social history. For women see the article by Lesko cited above; Barbara Watterson, *Women in Ancient Egypt* (1991); Gay Robins, *Women in Ancient Egypt* (1993); and the articles and museum exhibition catalogue in Anne K. Capel and Glenn E. Markoe, eds., *Mistress of the House, Mistress of Heaven: Women in Ancient Egypt* (1996).

Stephen Quirke, *Ancient Egyptian Religion* (1990), is a highly regarded treatment of a complex subject. Erik Hornung and Betsy M. Bryan, eds., *The Quest for Immortality: Treasures of Ancient Egypt* (2002), is the lavishly illustrated and annotated catalogue of an exhibition that focused on Egyptian funerary practices and beliefs about the afterlife. George Hart, *Egyptian Myths* (1990), gathers the limited written evidence for what must have been a thriving oral tradition. Maria C. Betro, *Hieroglyphics: The Writings of Ancient Egypt* (1996), introduces the complex and alluring writing system. Pritchard's collection, cited above, and Miriam Lichtheim, *Ancient Egyptian Literature: A Book of Readings, vol. 1, The Old and Middle Kingdoms* (1973), provide translated original texts and documents. William Stevenson Smith, *The Art and Architecture of Ancient Egypt* (1998); Gay Robins, *The Art of Ancient Egypt* (1997); Jaromir Malek, *Egyptian Art* (1999); and Dieter Arnold, *The Encyclopedia of Ancient Egyptian Architecture* (2003), are introductions to the visual record.

For the Indus Valley civilization there is a brief treatment in Stanley Wolpert, *A New History of India*, 3d ed. (1989). Mortimer Wheeler's *Civilizations of the Indus Valley and Beyond* (1966) and *The Indus Civilization*, 3d ed. (1968), though still useful, are now largely superseded by Jonathan Mark Kenoyer, *Ancient Cities of the Indus Valley Civilization* (1998); Jane McIntosh, *A Peaceful Realm: The Rise and Fall of the Indus Civilization* (2002); and Gregory L. Possehl, *The Indus Civilization: A Contemporary Perspective* (2002). Possehl also has edited two collections of articles by Indus Valley scholars: *Ancient Cities of the Indus* (1979) and *Harappan Civilization: A Contemporary Perspective* (1982).

■ Notes

1. David Ferry, *Gilgamesh: A New Rendering in English Verse* (New York: Noonday Press, 1992).

3

New Civilizations in the Eastern and Western Hemispheres, 2200–250 B.C.E.

Wall Painting of Nubians Arriving in Egypt with Rings and Bags of Gold, Fourteenth Century B.C.E.
This image decorated the tomb of an Egyptian administrator in Nubia.

Around 2200 B.C.E. an Egyptian official named Harkhuf°, who lived at Aswan° on the southern boundary of Egypt, set out for a place called Yam, far to the south in the land that later came to be called Nubia. He had made this trek three times before, so he was familiar with the route and skillful in dealing with various Nubian chieftains along the way. He brought gifts from the Egyptian pharaoh for the ruler of Yam, and he returned home with three hundred donkeys loaded with incense, dark ebony wood, ivory, panthers, and other exotic products from tropical Africa. While this exchange was couched in the diplomatic fiction of gifts, we should probably regard it as a form of trade and Harkhuf as a brave and enterprising caravan leader. On this particular trip he returned with something so special that the eight-year-old boy pharaoh, Pepi II, could not contain his excitement. He wrote:

> Come north to the residence at once! Hurry and bring with you this pygmy whom you brought from the land of the horizon-dwellers live, hale, and healthy, for the dances of the god, to gladden the heart, to delight the heart of king Neferkare [Pepi] who lives forever! When he goes down with you into the ship, get worthy men to be around him on deck, lest he fall into the water! When he lies down at night, get worthy men to lie around him in his tent. Inspect ten times at night! My majesty desires to see this pygmy more than the gifts of the mine-land and of Punt![1]

Although the precise location of Yam is uncertain, scholars are beginning to identify it with Kerma, later the capital of the kingdom of Nubia, on the upper Nile in modern Sudan. From the Egyptian point of view, Nubia was a wild and dangerous place. Yet we can see that it was developing features of more complex political organization, and that the burgeoning trade between Nubia and Egypt was important to both societies.

In contrast to the river-valley civilizations of Mesopotamia, Egypt, and the Indus Valley surveyed in the previous chapter, the complex societies examined in this chapter subsequently emerged in ecological conditions quite a bit more diverse, sometimes independently, sometimes under the influence of the older centers. Whereas the river-valley civilizations were originally largely self-sufficient, each of the new civilizations discussed in this chapter and the next was shaped by the development of networks of long-distance trade.

In the second millennium B.C.E. a civilization based on irrigation agriculture arose along the valley of the Yellow River and its tributaries in northern China. In the same epoch, in Nubia (southern Egypt and northern Sudan), the first complex society in tropical Africa continued to develop from the roots observed earlier by Harkhuf. The first millennium B.C.E. witnessed the spread of Celtic peoples across much of continental Europe, as well as the flourishing of the earliest complex societies of the Western Hemisphere, the Olmec of Mesoamerica and the Chavín culture on the flanks of the Andes Mountains in South America. These societies had no contact with one another, and they represent a variety of responses to different environmental and historical circumstances. Thus, their stories will necessarily be separate. However, as we shall see, they have certain features in common and collectively point to a distinct stage in the development of human societies.

As you read this chapter, ask yourself the following questions:

- How did the peoples of early China, Nubia, Celtic Europe, and the Olmec and Chavín civilizations each develop distinctive political and social institutions, cultural patterns, and technologies in response to the challenges of the environment?

- What was the basis of the status, power, and wealth of elite groups in each society, and how did they dominate the rest of the population?

- In the case of Nubia and the Celts, how did the technological and cultural influences of older centers affect the formation of the new civilizations?

- Why did societies in the Eastern and Western Hemispheres acquire complex organizations and potent technologies at different times and in different sequences?

Harkhuf (HAHR-koof)   **Aswan** (AS- wahn)

CHRONOLOGY

	China	Nubia	Celtic Europe	Americas
	8000–2000 B.C.E. Neolithic cultures	**4500 B.C.E.** Early agriculture in Nubia		**3500 B.C.E.** Early agriculture in Mesoamerica and Andes
2500 B.C.E.		**2200 B.C.E.** Harkhuf's expeditions to Yam		**2600 B.C.E.** Rise of Caral
2000 B.C.E.	**2000 B.C.E.** Bronze metallurgy			
	1750–1027 B.C.E. Shang dynasty	**1750 B.C.E.** Rise of kingdom of Kush based on Kerma		
1500 B.C.E.		**1500 B.C.E.** Egyptian conquest of Nubia		
				1200–900 B.C.E. Rise of Olmec civilization, centered on San Lorenzo
1000 B.C.E.	**1027–221 B.C.E.** Zhou dynasty	**1000 B.C.E.** Decline of Egyptian control in Nubia	**1000 B.C.E.** Origin of Celtic culture in Central Europe	**900–600 B.C.E.** La Venta, the dominant Olmec center
		750 B.C.E. Rise of kingdom based on Napata		**900–250 B.C.E.** Chavín civilization in the Andes
	600 B.C.E. Iron Metallurgy	**712–660 B.C.E.** Nubian kings rule Egypt	**500 B.C.E.** Celtic elites trade for Mediterranean goods	**600–400 B.C.E.** Ascendancy of Tres Zapotes and Olmec decline
500 B.C.E			**500–300 B.C.E.** Migrations across Europe	**500 B.C.E.** Early metallurgy in Andes
		300 B.C.E.–350 C.E. Kingdom of Meroë	**390 B.C.E.** Celts sack Rome	

EARLY CHINA, 2000–221 B.C.E.

On the eastern edge of the great Eurasian landmass, Neolithic cultures developed as early as 8000 B.C.E. A more complex civilization evolved in the second millennium B.C.E. Under the Shang and Zhou monarchs many of the institutions and values of classical Chinese civilization emerged and spread south and west. As in Mesopotamia, Egypt, and the Indus Valley, the rise of cities, specialization of labor, bureaucratic government, writing, and other advanced technologies depended on the exploitation of a great river system—the Yellow River (Huang He°) and its tributaries—to support intensive agriculture. Although there is archaeological evidence of some movement of goods and ideas between western and eastern Asia, developments in China were largely independent of the complex societies in the Middle East and the Indus Valley.

Geography and Resources

China is isolated from the rest of the Eastern Hemisphere by formidable natural barriers: the Himalaya° mountain range on the southwest; the Pamir° and Tian° mountains and the Takla Makan° Desert on the west; the Gobi° Desert and the treeless and grassy hills and plains of the Mongolian steppe on the northwest (see Map 3.1). To the east lies the Pacific Ocean. Although China's separation was not total—trade goods, people, and ideas moved back and forth between China, India, and Central Asia— in many respects its development was distinctive.

Most of East Asia is covered with mountains, making overland travel, transport, and communications difficult and slow. The great river systems of eastern China, however—the Yellow and the Yangzi° Rivers and their tributaries—facilitate east-west movement. In the eastern river valleys dense populations could practice intensive agriculture; on the steppe lands of Mongolia, the deserts and oases of Xinjiang°, and the high plateau of Tibet sparser populations engaged in different forms of livelihood. The climate zones of East Asia range from the dry, subarctic reaches of Manchuria in the north to the lush, subtropical forests of the south, and support a rich variety of plant and animal life adapted to these zones.

Within the eastern agricultural zone, the north and the south have strikingly different environments. Each zone produced distinctive patterns for the use of the land, the kinds of crops that could flourish, and the organization of agricultural labor. The monsoons that affect India and Southeast Asia (see Chapter 2) drench southern China with heavy rainfall in the summer, the most beneficial time for agriculture. Northern China, in contrast, where rainfall is much more erratic, receives less moisture. As in Mesopotamia and the Indus Valley, where technological and social developments unfolded in relatively adverse conditions, China's early history unfolded on the northern plains, a demanding environment that stimulated important technologies and political traditions as well as the philosophical and religious views that became hallmarks of Chinese civilization. By the third century C.E., however, the gradual flow of population toward the warmer southern lands caused the political and intellectual center to move south.

The eastern river valleys and North China Plain contained timber, stone, scattered deposits of metals, and, above all, potentially productive land. Since prehistoric times, winds blowing from Central Asia have deposited a yellowish-brown dust called **loess**° (these particles suspended in the water give the Yellow River its distinctive hue and name). Over the ages a thick mantle of soil has accumulated that is extremely fertile and soft enough to be worked with wooden digging sticks. The lack of compactness of this soil accounts for the severity of earthquake damage in this region.

In this landscape, agriculture demanded the coordinated efforts of large groups of people. In parts of northern China forests had to be cleared. Recurrent floods on the Yellow River necessitated the construction of earthen dikes and channels to carry off the overflow. To cope with the periodic droughts, catch basins (reservoirs) were dug to store river water and rainfall. As the population grew, people built retaining walls to partition the hillsides into tiers of flat arable terraces.

The staple crops in the northern region were millet, a grain indigenous to China, and wheat, which had spread to East Asia from the Middle East. Rice requires a warmer climate and prospered in the south. The cultivation of rice in the Yangzi River Valley and the south required a great outlay of labor. Rice paddies—the fields where rice is grown—must be absolutely flat and surrounded by water channels to bring and lead away water according to a precise schedule. Seedlings sprout in a nursery, and are transplanted one by one to the paddy, which is then flooded. Flooding eliminates weeds and rival plants and supports microscopic organisms that keep the soil fertile. When the crop is ripe, the paddy is drained; the rice stalks are harvested with a sickle; and

---

Huang He (hwahng-HUH) **Himalaya** (him-uh-LAY-uh)
Pamir (pah-MEER) **Tian** (tee-en)
Takla Makan (TAH-kluh muh-KAHN) **Gobi** (GO-bee)
Yangzi (yang-zuh) **Xinjiang** (shin-jyahng)

loess (less)

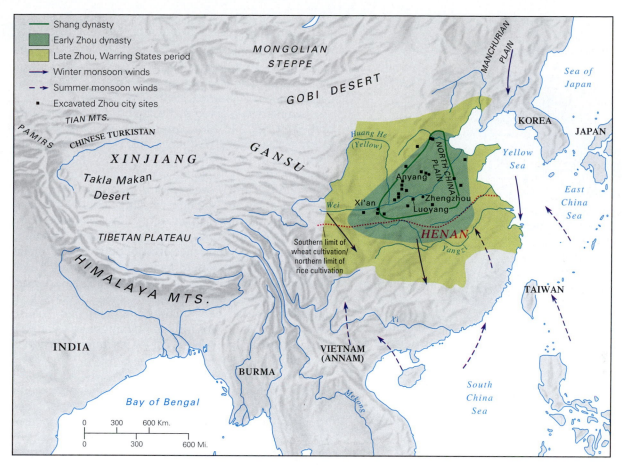

Map 3.1   China in the Shang and Zhou Periods, 1750–221 B.C.E.   The Shang dynasty arose in the second millennium B.C.E. in the floodplain of the Yellow River. While southern China benefits from the monsoon rains, northern China depends on irrigation. As population increased, the Han Chinese migrated from their eastern homeland to other parts of China, carrying their technologies and cultural practices. Other ethnic groups predominated in more outlying regions, and the nomadic peoples of the northwest constantly challenged Chinese authority.

the edible kernels are separated out. The reward for this effort is a spectacular yield. Rice can feed more people per cultivated acre than any other grain, which explains why the south eventually became more populous and important than the north.

The Shang Period, 1750–1027 B.C.E.

Archaeologists have identified several Neolithic cultural complexes in China, primarily on the basis of styles of pottery and forms of burial. These early populations grew millet, raised pigs and chickens, and used stone tools. They made pottery on a wheel and fired it in high-temperature kilns. They pioneered the production of silk cloth, first raising silkworms on mul-

berry trees, then carefully unraveling their cocoons to produce silk thread. The early Chinese built walls of pounded earth by hammering the soil inside temporary wooden frames until it became hard as cement. By 2000 B.C.E. they had begun to make bronze (roughly a thousand years after the beginnings of bronze-working in the Middle East).

Later generations of Chinese told stories about the ancient dynasty of the Xia, said to have ruled the core region of the Yellow River Valley. The validity of those stories is difficult to gauge, though some archaeologists identify the Xia with the Neolithic Longshan cultural complex in the centuries before and after 2000 B.C.E. Chinese history proper begins with the rise to power of the Shang clans, which coincides with the earliest written records anywhere in China.

Bronze Vessel from the Shang Period, 13th–11th Century B.C.E. Vessels such as this large wine jar were used in rituals that allowed members of the Shang ruling class to make contact with their ancestors. Signifying both the source and the proof of the elite's authority, these vessels were often buried in Shang tombs. The complex shapes and elaborate decorations testify to the artisans' skill. (Tokyo National Museum Image: TNM Image)

The **Shang**° originated in the part of the Yellow River Valley that lies in the present-day province of Henan°. After 1750 B.C.E. they extended their control north into Mongolia, west as far as Gansu°, and south to the Yangzi River Valley. Shang society was dominated by a warrior aristocracy whose greatest pleasures were warfare, hunting (for recreation and to fine-tune skills required for war), exchanging gifts, feasting, and wine-filled revelry.

The king and his court ruled the core area of the Shang state directly. Aristocrats served as generals, ambassadors, and supervisors of public projects. Other members of the royal family and high-ranking nobility governed outlying provinces. The most distant regions were governed by native rulers who swore allegiance to the Shang king. The king was often on the road, traveling to the courts of his subordinates to reinforce their loyalty.

Frequent military campaigns provided the warrior aristocracy with a theater for brave achievements and yielded considerable plunder. The nomadic peoples who occupied the steppe and desert regions to the north and west were periodically rolled back and given a demon-

stration of Shang power. (Chinese sources refer to these peoples as "barbarians." Modern readers should be wary of the Chinese claim that these nomads were culturally backward and morally inferior to the Chinese.) Large numbers of prisoners of war were taken in these campaigns and used as slaves in the Shang capital.

Various cities served as the capital of the Shang kingdom. The last and most important was near modern Anyang° (see Map 3.1). Shang cities were centers of political control and religion. Surrounded by massive walls of pounded earth, they contained palaces, administrative buildings and storehouses, royal tombs, shrines of gods and ancestors, and houses of the nobility. The common people lived in agricultural villages outside these centers. Because stone was in short supply, buildings were set on foundation platforms of pounded earth and constructed with wooden posts and dried mud. These cities, which were laid out on a grid plan aligned with the north polar star and had gates opening to the cardinal directions, are an early manifestation of the Chinese concern with the orientation of buildings known as *feng shui*,° and they symbolized the order imposed by gods and monarchs.

A key to effective administration was the form of writing developed in this era. Pictograms (pictures representing objects and concepts) and phonetic symbols representing the sounds of syllables were combined to form a complex system of hundreds of signs. Only a small, educated elite had the time to master this system. Despite substantial changes through the ages, the fundamental principles of the Chinese system still endure today. As a result, people speaking essentially different languages, such as Mandarin and Cantonese, can read and understand the same text. In contrast, the cuneiform of Mesopotamia and the hieroglyphics of Egypt were eventually replaced by simpler alphabetic scripts.

The Shang ideology of kingship glorified the king as the indispensable intermediary between the people and the gods. The Shang royal family and aristocracy worshiped the spirits of their male ancestors. They believed that these ancestors were intensely interested in the fortunes of their descendants and had special influence with the gods. Before taking any action, the Shang rulers used **divination** to determine the will of the gods (see Environment and Technology: Divination in Ancient Societies). They made ritual sacrifices to their gods and ancestors in order to win divine favor. Burials of kings also entailed sacrifices, not only of animals but also of humans, including noble officials of the court, women, servants, soldiers, and prisoners of war.

Possession of bronze objects was a sign of authority

Shang (shahng) **Henan** (heh-nahn) **Gansu** (gahn-soo)   **Anyang** (ahn-yahng)   **feng shui** (fung shway)

Women Beating Chimes　This scene, from a bronze vessel of the Zhou era, illustrates the important role of music in festivals, religious rituals, and court ceremonials. During the politically fragmented later (Eastern) Zhou era, many small states marked their independence by having their own musical scales and distinctive arrangements of orchestral instruments.　(Courtesy, Sichuan Museum)

and nobility. Bronze weapons allowed the state to assert its authority, and bronze vessels were used in rituals seeking the support of ancestors and gods. The quantity of bronze objects found in Shang tombs is impressive. The relatively modest tomb of one queen contained 450 bronze articles (ritual vessels, bells, weapons, and mirrors)—remarkable because copper and tin, the principal ingredients of bronze, were not plentiful in northern China. (Also found in the same tomb were numerous objects in jade, bone, ivory, and stone; seven thousand cowrie shells; sixteen sacrificed men, women, and children; and six dogs!) The Shang elite expended huge effort to find and mine deposits of copper and tin, refine them into pure metal, transport the ingots to the capital, and commission the creation of weapons and beautifully decorated objects.

Artisans worked in foundries outside the main cities. They poured the molten bronze into clay molds, and joined together the hardened pieces as necessary. Shang artisans made weapons, chariot fittings, musical instruments, and the ritual vessels used in religious ceremonies. Many of these elegant vessels were vividly decorated with stylized depictions of real and imaginary animals.

Far-reaching networks of trade sprang up across China, bringing the Shang valued commodities such as jade, ivory, and mother of pearl (a hard, shiny substance from the interior of mollusk shells) used for jewelry, carved figurines, and decorative inlays. Some evidence suggests that Shang China may have exchanged goods and ideas with distant Mesopotamia. The horse-drawn chariot, which the Shang may have adopted from Western Asia, was a formidable instrument of war.

The Zhou Period, 1027–221 B.C.E.

Shang domination of central and northern China lasted more than six centuries. In the eleventh century B.C.E. the last Shang king was defeated by Wu, the ruler of **Zhou**°, a dependent state in the Wei° River Valley. The Zhou line of kings (ca. 1027–221 B.C.E.) was the longest lasting and most revered of all dynasties in Chinese history. Just as the Semitic peoples in Mesopotamia had adopted and adapted the Sumerian legacy (see Chapter 2), the Zhou preserved the essentials of Shang culture and added new elements of ideology and technology.

The positive image of Zhou rule was skillfully constructed by propagandists for the new regime. The early Zhou monarchs had to justify their seizure of power to the restive remnants of the Shang clans. The chief deity was now referred to as "Heaven"; the monarch was called the "Son of Heaven"; and his rule was called the "**Mandate of Heaven.**" According to the new theory, the ruler had been chosen by the supreme deity and would retain his backing as long as he served as a wise, principled, and energetic guardian of his people. The proof of divine favor was the prosperity and the stability of the kingdom. If the ruler misbehaved, as the last Shang ruler had done, his right to rule could be withdrawn. Corruption, violence, arrogance, and insurrection, such as had occurred under the last Shang king, were signs of divine displeasure and validated the ruler's replacement by a new dynasty that was committed to just rule.

The Zhou kings continued some of the Shang ritu-

Zhou (joe)　**Wei** (way)

Divination in Ancient Societies

The ancient inhabitants of China, the Middle East, Europe, and the Americas, as well as many other peoples throughout history, believed that the gods controlled the forces of nature and shaped destinies. Starting from this premise, they practiced various techniques of divination—the effort to interpret phenomena in the natural world as signs of the gods' will and intentions. Through divination the ancients sought to communicate with the gods and thereby anticipate—even influence—the future.

The Shang ruling class in China frequently sought information from shamans, individuals who claimed the ability to make direct contact with ancestors and other higher powers. The Shang monarch himself often functioned as a shaman. Chief among the tools of divination used by a shaman were oracle bones. The shaman touched a tortoiseshell or the shoulder bone of an animal (sometimes holes had been drilled in it ahead of time) with the heated point of a stick. The shell or bone would crack, and the cracks were "read" as a message from the spirit world.

Tens of thousands of oracle bones survive. They are a major source of information about Shang life; usually the question, the resulting answer, and often confirmation of the accuracy of the prediction were inscribed on the back of the shell or bone. The rulers asked about the proper performance of ritual, the likely outcome of wars or hunting expeditions, the prospects for rainfall and the harvest, and the meaning of strange occurrences.

In Mesopotamia in the third and second millennia B.C.E. the most important divination involved the close inspection of the form, size, and markings of the organs of sacrificed animals. Archaeologists have found models of sheep's livers accompanied by written explanations of the meaning of various features. Two other techniques of divination were following the trail of smoke from burning incense and examining the patterns that resulted when oil was thrown on water.

From about 2000 B.C.E. Mesopotamian diviners foretold the future from their observation of the movements of the sun, moon, planets, stars, and constellations. In the centuries after 1000 B.C.E. celestial omens were the most important source of predictions about the future, and specialists maintained precise records of astronomical events. Mesopotamian mathematics, essential for calculations of the movements of celestial bodies, was the most sophisticated in the ancient Middle East. Astrology, with its division of the sky into the twelve segments of the zodiac and its use of the position of the stars and planets to predict an individual's destiny, developed out of long-standing Mesopotamian attention to the movements of celestial objects. Horoscopes—charts with calculations and predictions based on an individual's date of birth—have been found from shortly before 400 B.C.E. In the Hellenistic period (323–30 B.C.E.), Greek settlers flooding into western Asia built on this Mesopotamian foundation and greatly advanced the study of astrology.

Greek and Roman sources make occasional references to practices of divination among the Celts. Prediction of the future is one of the many religious functions attributed to the Druids, but certain sources distinguish a specialized group of "seers." Among their methods were careful observation of the patterns of flight of birds through the sky and the ap-

als, but there was a marked decline in the practice of divination and in extravagant and bloody sacrifices and burials. The priestly power of the ruling class, the only ones who had been able to make contact with the spirits of ancestors during the Shang period, faded away. The resulting separation of religion and government promoted the development of important philosophical and mystical systems in the Zhou period. The bronze vessels that had been sacred implements in the Shang period now became family treasures.

The early period of Zhou rule, the eleventh through ninth centuries B.C.E., is sometimes called the Western Zhou era because of the location of the capitals in the western part of the kingdom. These centuries saw the development of a sophisticated administrative apparatus. The Zhou built a series of capital cities with pounded-earth foundations and walls. The major buildings all faced south, in keeping with an already ancient concern to orient structures so that they would be in a harmonious relationship with the terrain, the forces of wind, water, and sunlight, and the invisible energy perceived to be flowing through the natural world. All gov-

pearance of sacrificial offerings. In Ireland a ritual specialist ate the meat of a freshly-killed bull, lay down to sleep on the bull's hide, then had prophetic dreams. The most startling form of Celtic divination is described by the geographer Strabo:

> The Romans put a stop to [the] customs . . . connected with sacrifice and divination, as they were in conflict with our own ways: for example, they would strike a man who had been consecrated for sacrifice in the back with a sword, and make prophecies based on his death-spasms.

Reports about this and other Celtic practices, such as human sacrifice and the display of heads of conquered enemies, were used by the Romans to justify the conquest of Celtic peoples in order to "civilize" them.

Little is known for certain about the divinatory practices of early American peoples. The Olmec produced polished stone mirrors whose concave surfaces gave off reflected images that were thought to emanate from a supernatural realm. Painted basins found in Olmec households have been

compared to those attested for later Mesoamerican groups. In the latter, women threw maize kernels onto the surface of water-filled basins and noted the patterns by which they floated or sank, in order to ascertain information useful to the family, such as the cause and cure of illness, the right time for agricultural tasks or marriage, and propitious names for newborn children.

It may seem surprising that divination is being treated here as a form of technology. Most modern people would regard such interpretations of patterns in everyday phenomena as mere superstition. However, within the context of the laws of nature as understood by ancient societies (the gods control and direct events in the natural world), divination involved the application of principles of causation to the socially beneficial task of acquiring information about what would happen in the future. These techniques were usually known only to a class of experts whose special training and knowledge gave them high status in their society.

Chinese Divination Shell After inscribing questions on a bone or shell, the diviner applied a red-hot point and interpreted the resulting cracks as a divine response. (Institute of History and Philology, Academia Sinica)

ernment officials, including the king, were supposed to be models of morality, fairness, and concern for the welfare of the people.

Like the Shang, the Zhou regime was highly decentralized. Members and allies of the royal family ruled more than a hundred largely autonomous territories. The court was the scene of elaborate ceremonials, embellished by music and dance, that impressed on observers the glory of Zhou rule and reinforced the bonds of obligation between rulers and ruled.

Around 800 B.C.E. Zhou power began to wane. Ambi-

tious local rulers operated ever more independently and waged war on one another, while nomadic peoples attacked the northwest frontiers (see Map 3.1). The following five hundred years are sometimes referred to as the Eastern Zhou era. In 771 B.C.E. members of the Zhou lineage relocated to a new, more secure, eastern capital near Luoyang°, where they continued to hold the royal title and received at least nominal homage from the real power

---

Luoyang (LWOE-yahng)

brokers of the age. This was a time of political fragmentation, rapidly shifting centers of power, and fierce competition and warfare among numerous small and independent states. Historians conventionally divide Eastern Zhou into the "Spring and Autumn Period," from 771 to 481 B.C.E., after a collection of chronicles that give annual entries for those two seasons, and the "Warring States Period," from 480 to the unification of China in 221 B.C.E.

The many states of the Eastern Zhou era contended with one another for leadership. Cities, some of them quite large, spread across the Chinese landscape. Long walls of pounded earth, the ancestors of the Great Wall of China, protected the kingdoms from each other and from northern nomads. The Chinese also learned from the steppe nomads to put fighters on horseback. By 600 B.C.E. iron began to replace bronze as the primary metal for tools and weapons. There is mounting evidence that ironworking came to China from the nomadic peoples of the northwest. Subsequently, metalworkers in southern China, which had limited access to copper and tin for making bronze, were the first in the world to forge steel by removing carbon during the iron-smelting process.

In many of the states, bureaucrats expanded in number and function. Codes of law were written down. Governments collected taxes from the peasants directly, imposed standardized money, and managed large-scale public works projects. The wealth and power of the state and its demands for obedience were justified by an authoritarian political philosophy that came to be called **Legalism.** Legalist thinkers maintained that human nature is essentially wicked and that people behave in an orderly fashion only if compelled by strict laws and harsh punishments. Legalists believed that every aspect of human society ought to be controlled and personal freedom sacrificed for the good of the state.

Confucianism, Daoism, and Chinese Society

The governments of the major Zhou states took over many of the traditional functions of the aristocracy. To maintain their influence, aristocrats sought a new role as advisers to the rulers. One who lived through the political flux and social change of this anxious time was Kongzi (551–479 B.C.E.)— known in the West by the Latin form of his name, **Confucius.** Coming from one of the smaller states, he had not been particularly successful in obtaining administrative posts. His doctrine of duty and public service, initially aimed at fellow aristocrats, was to become a central influence in Chinese thought (see Diversity and Dominance: Hierarchy and Conduct in the Analects of Confucius).

Many elements in Confucius's teaching had roots in earlier Chinese belief, including folk religion and the rites of the Zhou royal family, such as the veneration of ancestors and elders and worship of the deity Heaven. Confucius drew a parallel between the family and the state. Just as the family is a hierarchy, with the father at its top, sons next, then wives and daughters in order of age, so too the state is a hierarchy, with the ruler at the top, the public officials as the sons, and the common people as the women.

Confucius took a traditional term for the feelings between family members (*ren*) and expanded it into a universal ideal of benevolence toward all humanity, which he believed was the foundation of moral government. Government exists, he said, to serve the people, and the administrator or ruler gains respect and authority by displaying fairness and integrity. Confucian teachings emphasized benevolence, avoidance of violence, justice, rationalism, loyalty, and dignity. Confucius, who held a far more optimistic view of the basic goodness of human nature than the adherents of Legalism, sought to affirm and maintain the political and social order by improving it.

It is ironic that Confucius, whose ideas were to become so important in Chinese thought, actually had little influence in his own time. His later follower Mencius (Mengzi, 371–289 B.C.E.), who opposed despotism and argued against the authoritarian political ideology of the Legalists, made Confucius's teachings much better known. In the era of the early emperors, Confucianism became the dominant political philosophy and the core of the educational system for government officials (see Chapter 6).

The Warring States Period also saw the rise of the school of thought known as **Daoism°**. According to tradition, Laozi°, the originator of Daoism (believed to have lived in the sixth century B.C.E., though some scholars doubt his existence), sought to stop the warfare of the age by urging humanity to follow the *Dao*, or "path." Daoists accept the world as they find it, avoiding useless struggles and adhering to the "path" of nature. They avoid violence if at all possible and take the minimal action necessary for a task. Rather than fight the current of a stream, a wise man allows the onrushing waters to pass around him. This passivity arises from the Daoist's sense that the world is always changing and lacks any absolute morality or meaning. In the end, Daoists believe, all that matters is the individual's fundamental understanding of the "path."

The original Daoist philosophy was greatly expanded in subsequent centuries to incorporate popular

Daoism (DOW-izm)   **Laozi** (low-zuh)

beliefs, magic, and mysticism. Daoism represented an important stream of thought throughout Chinese history. By idealizing individuals who find their own "path" to right conduct, it offered an alternative to the Confucian emphasis on hierarchy and duty and to the Legalist approval of force.

Social organization also changed in this period. The kinship structures of the Shang and early Zhou periods, based on the clan (a relatively large group of related families), gave way to the three-generation family of grandparents, parents, and children as the fundamental social unit. A related development was the emergence of the concept of private property. Land was considered to belong to the men of the family and was divided equally among the sons when the father died.

Little is known about the conditions of life for women in early China. Some scholars believe that women may have acted as shamans, entering into trances to communicate with supernatural forces, making requests on behalf of their communities, and receiving predictions of the future. By the time written records begin to illuminate our knowledge of women's experiences, they show women in a subordinate position in the strongly patriarchal family.

Confucian thought codified this male-female hierarchy. Only men could conduct rituals and make offerings to the ancestors, though women could help maintain the household's ancestral shrines. Fathers held authority over the women and children, arranged marriages for their offspring, and could sell the labor of family members. A man was limited to one wife but was permitted additional sexual partners, who had the lower status of concubines. The elite classes used marriage to create political alliances, and it was common for the groom's family to offer a substantial "bride-gift," a proof of the wealth and standing of his family, to the family of the prospective bride. A man whose wife died had a duty to remarry in order to produce male heirs to keep alive the cult of the ancestors.

These differences in male and female activities were explained by the concept of **yin** and **yang,** the complementary nature of male and female roles in the natural order. The male principle (yin) was equated with the sun, active, bright, and shining; the female principle (yang) corresponded to the moon, passive, shaded, and reflective. Male toughness was balanced by female gentleness, male action and initiative by female endurance and need for completion, and male leadership by female supportiveness. In its earliest form, the theory considered yin and yang as equal and alternately dominant, like day and night, creating balance in the world. However, as a result of the changing role of women in the

Zhou period and the pervasive influence of Confucian ideology, the male principle came to be seen as superior to the female.

The classical Chinese patterns of family, property, and bureaucracy took shape during the long centuries of Zhou rule and the competition among small states. At the end of this period the state of Qin°, whose aggressive and disciplined policies made it the premier power among the warring states, defeated all rivals and unified China (see Chapter 6).

NUBIA, 3100 B.C.E.–350 C.E.

Since the first century B.C.E. the name *Nubia* has been applied to a thousand-mile (1,600-kilometer) stretch of the Nile Valley lying between Aswan and Khartoum° and straddling the southern part of the modern nation of Egypt and the northern part of Sudan (see Map 3.2). The ancient Egyptians called it Ta-sety, meaning "Land of the Bow," after the favorite weapon of its warriors. Nubia is the only continuously inhabited stretch of territory connecting sub-Saharan Africa (the lands south of the vast Sahara Desert) with North Africa. For thousands of years it has served as a corridor for trade between tropical Africa and the Mediterranean. Nubia was richly endowed with natural resources such as gold, copper, and semiprecious stones.

Nubia's location and natural wealth, along with Egypt's quest for Nubian gold, explain the early rise of a civilization with a complex political organization, social stratification, metallurgy, monumental building, and writing. Nubia traditionally was considered a periphery, or outlying region, of Egypt, and its culture was regarded as derivative. Now, however, most scholars emphasize the interactions between Egypt and Nubia and the mutually beneficial borrowings and syntheses that took place, and there is growing evidence that Nubian culture drew on influences from sub-Saharan Africa.

Early Cultures and Egyptian Domination, 2300–1100 B.C.E.

The central geographical feature of Nubia, as of Egypt, is the Nile River. This part of the Nile flows through a landscape of rocky desert, grassland, and fertile plain. River irrigation

Qin (chin)   **Khartoum** (kahr-TOOM)

령이 대중 앞에 나타나거나 애국심
을 고취하는 노래만을 내보내던 방
송마저 중단됐다.

파운드폭탄 4발 투하… 두 아들과 함께 사망 기

진지 구축… 이틀째 시가戰

라크 전후 대책
의에서는 전후
영국 주도로

DIVERSITY AND DOMINANCE

HIERARCHY AND CONDUCT IN THE ANALECTS OF CONFUCIUS

The Analects are a collection of sayings of Confucius, probably compiled and written down several generations after he lived, though some elements may have been added even later. They cover a wide range of matters, including ethics, government, education, music, and rituals. Taken as a whole, they are a guide to living a proper, honorable, virtuous, useful, and satisfying life. While subject to reinterpretation according to the circumstances of the times, Confucian principles have had a great influence on Chinese values and behavior ever since.

Chinese society in Confucius's time was very attuned to distinctions of status. Confucius assumed that hierarchy is innate in the order of the universe and that human society should echo and harmonize with the natural world. Each person has a role to play, with prescribed rules of conduct and proper ceremonial behavior, in order to maintain the social order. The following selections illuminate the particular attention paid by Confucius to the important status categories in his society, the proper way for individuals to treat others, and the necessity of hierarchy and inequality.

1:6 Confucius said: "A young man should serve his parents at home and be respectful to elders outside his home. He should be earnest and truthful, loving all, but become intimate with *ren* [an inner capacity, possessed by all human beings, to do good]. After doing this, if he has energy to spare, he can study literature and the arts."

4:18 Confucius said: "When you serve your mother and father it is okay to try to correct them once in a while. But if you see that they are not going to listen to you, keep your respect for them and don't distance yourself from them. Work without complaining."

2:5 Meng Yi Zi asked about the meaning of filial piety. Confucius said, "It means 'not diverging (from your parents).'" Later, when Fan Chi was driving him, Confucius told Fan Chi, "Meng asked me about the meaning of filial piety, and I told

him 'not diverging.'" Fan Chi said, "What did you mean by that?" Confucius said, "When your parents are alive, serve them with propriety; when they die, bury them with propriety, and then worship them with propriety."

1:2 Master You said: "There are few who have developed themselves filially and fraternally who enjoy offending their superiors. Those who do not enjoy offending superiors are never troublemakers. The Superior Man concerns himself with the fundamentals. Once the fundamentals are established, the proper way (*dao*) appears. Are not filial piety and obedience to elders fundamental to the enactment of *ren*?"

1:8 Confucius said: "If the Superior Man is not 'heavy,' then he will not inspire awe in others. If he is not learned, then he will not be on firm ground. He takes loyalty and good faith to be of primary importance, and has no friends who are not of equal (moral) caliber. When he makes a mistake, he doesn't hesitate to correct it."

4:5 Confucius said, "Riches and honors are what all men desire. But if they cannot be attained in accordance with the *dao* they should not be kept. Poverty and low status are what all men hate. But if they cannot be avoided while staying in accordance with the *dao*, you should not avoid them. If a Superior Man departs from *ren*, how can he be worthy of that name? A Superior Man never leaves *ren* for even the time of a single meal. In moments of haste he acts according to it. In times of difficulty or confusion he acts according to it."

15:20 Confucius said: "The Superior Man seeks within himself. The inferior man seeks within others."

16:8 Confucius said: "The Superior Man stands in awe of three things:

(1) He is in awe of the decree of Heaven.
(2) He is in awe of great men.
(3) He is in awe of the words of the sages.

66

The inferior man does not know the decree of Heaven; takes great men lightly and laughs at the words of the sages."

4:14 Confucius said: "I don't worry about not having a good position; I worry about the means I use to gain position. I don't worry about being unknown; I seek to be known in the right way."

7:15 Confucius said: "I can live with coarse rice to eat, water for drink and my arm as a pillow and still be happy. Wealth and honors that one possesses in the midst of injustice are like floating clouds."

4:17 Confucius said: "When you see a good person, think of becoming like her/him. When you see someone not so good, reflect on your own weak points."

13:6 Confucius said: "When you have gotten your own life straightened out, things will go well without your giving orders. But if your own life isn't straightened out, even if you give orders, no one will follow them."

12:2 Zhonggong asked about the meaning of *ren*. The Master said: "Go out of your home as if you were receiving an important guest. Employ the people as if you were assisting at a great ceremony. What you don't want done to yourself, don't do to others. Live in your town without stirring up resentments, and live in your household without stirring up resentments."

1:5 Confucius said: "If you would govern a state of a thousand chariots (a small-to-middle-size state), you must pay strict attention to business, be true to your word, be economical in expenditure and love the people. You should use them according to the seasons."

2:3 Confucius said: "If you govern the people legalistically and control them by punishment, they will avoid crime, but have no personal sense of shame. If you govern them by means of virtue and control them with propriety, they will gain their own sense of shame, and thus correct themselves."

12:7 Zigong asked about government.

The Master said, "Enough food, enough weapons and the confidence of the people."

Zigong said, "Suppose you had no alternative but to give up one of these three, which one would be let go of first?"

The Master said, "Weapons."

Zigong said "What if you had to give up one of the remaining two which one would it be?"

The Master said, "Food. From ancient times, death has come to all men, but a people without confidence in its rulers will not stand."

12:19 Ji Kang Zi asked Confucius about government saying: "Suppose I were to kill the unjust, in order to advance the just. Would that be all right?"

Confucius replied: "In doing government, what is the need of killing? If you desire good, the people will be good. The nature of the Superior Man is like the wind, the nature of the inferior man is like the grass. When the wind blows over the grass, it always bends."

2:19 The Duke of Ai asked: "How can I make the people follow me?" Confucius replied: "Advance the upright and set aside the crooked, and the people will follow you. Advance the crooked and set aside the upright, and the people will not follow you."

2:20 Ji Kang Zi asked: "How can I make the people reverent and loyal, so they will work positively for me?" Confucius said, "Approach them with dignity, and they will be reverent. Be filial and compassionate and they will be loyal. Promote the able and teach the incompetent, and they will work positively for you."

QUESTIONS FOR ANALYSIS

1. What are the important social categories and status distinctions in early China? What kinds of behaviors are expected of individuals in particular social categories toward individuals in other categories?

2. How does Confucius explain and justify the inequalities among people? Why is it important for people to behave in appropriate ways toward others?

3. How does the experience of family life prepare an individual to conduct himself or herself properly in the wider spheres of community and state?

4. Which personal qualities and kinds of actions will allow a ruler to govern successfully? Why might Confucius's passionate concern for ethical behavior on the part of officials and rulers arise at a time when the size and power of governments was growing?

Source: From "Hierarchy and Conduct in the Analects of Confucius," translated by Charles Muller, as seen at http://www.human.toyogakuen-u.ac.jp/~acmuller/contao/analects.htm.

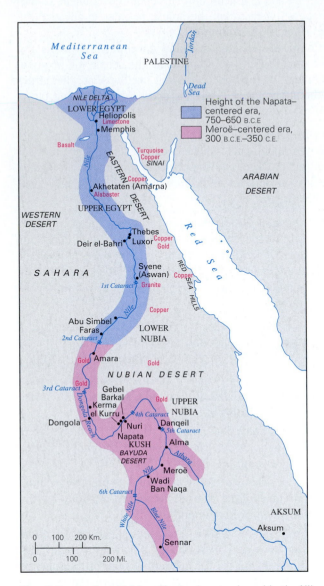

Map 3.2   Ancient Nubia   The land route alongside the Nile River as it flows through Nubia has long served as a corridor connecting sub-Saharan Africa with North Africa. The centuries of Egyptian occupation, as well as time spent in Egypt by Nubian hostages, mercenaries, and merchants, led to a marked Egyptian cultural influence in Nubia.   (Based on Map 15 from *The Historical Atlas of Africa*, ed. by J. F. Ajyi and Michael Crowder. Reprinted by permission of Addison Wesley Longman Ltd.)

In the fourth millennium B.C.E. bands of people in northern Nubia made the transition from seminomadic hunting and gathering to a settled life based on grain agriculture and cattle herding. From this time on, the majority of the population lived in agricultural villages alongside the river. Even before 3000 B.C.E. Nubia served as a corridor for long-distance commerce. Egyptian craftsmen of the period were working in ivory and in ebony wood—products of tropical Africa that had to have come through Nubia.

Nubia enters the historical record around 2300 B.C.E. in Old Kingdom Egyptian accounts of trade missions to southern lands. At that time Aswan, just north of the First Cataract, was the southern limit of Egyptian control. As we saw with the journey of Harkhuf at the beginning of this chapter, Egyptian noblemen stationed there led donkey caravans south in search of gold, incense, ebony, ivory, slaves, and exotic animals from tropical Africa. This was dangerous work, requiring delicate negotiations with local Nubian chiefs in order to secure protection, but it brought substantial rewards to those who succeeded.

During the Middle Kingdom (ca. 2040–1640 B.C.E.), Egypt adopted a more aggressive stance toward Nubia. Egyptian rulers sought to control the gold mines in the desert east of the Nile and to cut out the Nubian middlemen who drove up the cost of luxury goods from the tropics. The Egyptians erected a string of mud-brick forts on islands and riverbanks south of the Second Cataract. The forts protected the southern frontier of Egypt against Nubians and nomadic raiders from the desert, and regulated the flow of commerce. There seem to have been peaceable relations but little interaction between the Egyptian garrisons and the indigenous population of northern Nubia, which continued to practice its age-old farming and herding ways.

Farther south, where the Nile makes a great U-shaped turn in the fertile plain of the Dongola Reach (see Map 3.2), a more complex political entity was evolving from the chiefdoms of the third millennium B.C.E. The Egyptians gave the name **Kush** to the kingdom whose capital was located at Kerma, one of the earliest urbanized centers in tropical Africa. Beginning around 1750 B.C.E. the kings of Kush marshaled a labor force to build monumental walls and structures of mud brick. The dozens or even hundreds of servants and wives sacrificed for burial with the kings, as well as the rich objects found in their tombs, testify to the wealth and power of the rulers of Kush and suggest a belief in some sort of afterlife in which attendants and possessions would be useful. Kushite craftsmen were skilled in metalworking, whether for weapons or jewelry, and their pottery surpassed anything produced in Egypt.

was essential for agriculture in a climate that was severely hot and, in the north, nearly without rainfall. Six cataracts, barriers formed by large boulders and rapids, obstructed boat traffic. Commerce and travel were achieved by boats operating between the cataracts and by caravan tracks alongside the river or across the desert.

Temple of the Lion-Headed God Apedemak at Naqa in Nubia, First Century C.E. Queen Amanitore (right) and her husband, Natakamani, are shown slaying their enemies. The architectural forms are Egyptian, but the deity is Nubian. The costumes of the monarchs and the important role of the queen also reflect the trend in the Meroitic era to draw upon sub-Saharan cultural practices. (P. L. Shinnie)

During the expansionist New Kingdom (ca. 1532–1070 B.C.E.) the Egyptians penetrated more deeply into Nubia (see Chapter 4). They destroyed Kush and its capital and extended their frontier to the Fourth Cataract. A high-ranking Egyptian official called "Overseer of Southern Lands" or "King's Son of Kush" ruled Nubia from a new administrative center at Napata°, near Gebel Barkal°, the "Holy Mountain," believed to be the home of a local god. In an era of intense commerce among the states of the Middle East, when everyone was looking to Egypt as the prime source of gold, Egypt exploited the mines of Nubia at considerable human cost. Fatalities were high among native workers in the brutal desert climate, and the army had to ward off attacks from desert nomads.

Five hundred years of Egyptian domination in Nubia left many marks. The Egyptian government imposed Egyptian culture on the native population. Children from elite families were brought to the Egyptian royal court to guarantee the good behavior of their relatives in Nubia; they absorbed Egyptian language, culture, and religion, which they later carried home with them. Other Nubians served as archers in the Egyptian armed forces. The manufactured goods that they brought back to Nubia have been found in their graves. The Nubians built towns on the Egyptian model and erected stone temples to Egyptian gods, particularly Amon. The frequent depiction of Amon with the head of a ram may reflect a blending of the chief Egyptian god with a Nubian ram deity.

The Kingdom of Meroë, 800 B.C.E.–350 C.E.

Egypt's weakness after 1200 B.C.E. led to the collapse of its authority in Nubia. In the eighth century B.C.E. a powerful new native kingdom emerged in southern Nubia. The story of this civilization, which lasted for over a thousand years, can be divided into two parts. During the early period, between the eighth and fourth centuries B.C.E., Napata, the former Egyptian headquarters, was the primary center. During the later period, from the fourth century B.C.E. to the fourth century C.E., the center was farther south, at **Meroë°**, near the Sixth Cataract.

For half a century, from around 712 to 660 B.C.E., the kings of Nubia ruled all of Egypt as the Twenty-fifth Dynasty. They conducted themselves in the age-old manner of Egyptian rulers. They were addressed by royal titles, depicted in traditional costume, and buried ac-

---

Napata (nah-PAH-tuh)   **Gebel Barkal** (JEB-uhl BAHR-kahl)   **Meroë** (MER-oh-ee)

cording to Egyptian custom. However, they kept their Nubian names and were depicted with physical features suggesting peoples of sub-Saharan Africa. They inaugurated an artistic and cultural renaissance, building on a monumental scale for the first time in centuries and reinvigorating Egyptian art, architecture, and religion. The Nubian kings resided at Memphis, the Old Kingdom capital, while Thebes, the New Kingdom capital, was the residence of a celibate female member of the king's family who was titled "God's Wife of Amon."

The Nubian dynasty made a disastrous mistake in 701 B.C.E. when it offered help to local rulers in Palestine who were struggling against the Assyrian Empire. The Assyrians retaliated by invading Egypt and driving the Nubian monarchs back to their southern domain by 660 B.C.E. Napata again became the chief royal residence and religious center of the kingdom. Egyptian cultural influences remained strong. Court documents continued to be written in Egyptian hieroglyphs, and the mummified remains of the rulers were buried in modestly sized sandstone pyramids along with hundreds of shawabti° figurines.

By the fourth century B.C.E. the center of gravity had shifted south to Meroë, perhaps because Meroë was better situated for agriculture and trade, the economic mainstays of the Nubian kingdom. As a result, sub-Saharan cultural patterns gradually replaced Egyptian ones. Egyptian hieroglyphs gave way to a new set of symbols, still essentially undeciphered, for writing the Meroitic language. People continued to worship Amon as well as Isis, an Egyptian goddess connected to fertility and sexuality. But those deities had to share the stage with Nubian deities like the lion-god Apedemak, and elephants had some religious significance. Meroitic art combined Egyptian, Greco-Roman, and indigenous traditions.

Women of the royal family played an important role in Meroitic politics, another reflection of the influence of sub-Saharan Africa. The Nubians employed a matrilineal system in which the king was succeeded by the son of his sister. Nubian queens sometimes ruled by themselves and sometimes in partnership with their husbands. Greek, Roman, and biblical sources refer to a queen of Nubia named Candace. Since these sources relate to different times, *Candace* was probably a title rather than a proper name. At least seven queens ruled between 284 B.C.E. and 115 C.E. They played a part in warfare, diplomacy, and the building of temples and pyramid tombs. They are depicted in scenes reserved for male rulers in Egyptian imagery, smiting enemies in battle and being suckled by the mother-goddess Isis. Roman sources marvel at the fierce resistance put up by a one-eyed warrior-queen.

Meroë was a huge city for its time, more than a square mile in area, overlooking fertile grasslands and dominating converging trade routes. Much of the city is still buried under the sand. In 2002 archaeologists using a magnetometer to detect buried structures discovered a large palace and will soon begin excavation. Great reservoirs were dug to catch precious rainfall. The city was a major center for iron smelting (after 1000 B.C.E. iron had replaced bronze as the primary metal for tools and weapons). The Temple of Amon was approached by an avenue of stone rams, and the enclosed "Royal City" was filled with palaces, temples, and administrative buildings. The ruler, who may have been regarded as divine, was assisted by a professional class of officials, priests, and army officers.

Meroë collapsed in the early fourth century C.E. It may have been overrun by nomads from the western desert who had become more mobile because of the arrival of the camel in North Africa. Meroë had already been weakened when profitable commerce with the Roman Empire was diverted to the Red Sea and to the rising kingdom of Aksum° (in present-day Ethiopia). In any case, the end of the Meroitic kingdom, and of this phase of civilization in Nubia, was as closely linked to Nubia's role in long-distance commerce as had been its beginning.

CELTIC EUROPE, 1000–50 B.C.E.

The southern peninsulas of Europe—present-day Spain, Italy, and Greece—are surrounded on three sides by the Mediterranean Sea, share in the relatively mild climate of all the Mediterranean lands, and are separated from "continental" Europe to the north by high mountains (the Pyrenees and Alps). For all these reasons, the history of southern Europe in antiquity is primarily connected to that of the Middle East, at least until the Roman conquests north of the Alps (see Chapters 4, 5, and 6).

Continental Europe (including the modern nations of France, Germany, Switzerland, Austria, the Czech Republic, Slovakia, Hungary, Poland, and Romania—see Map 3.3) is well-suited to agriculture and herding. It contains broad plains with good soil and has a temperate climate with cold winters, warm summers, and ample rainfall. It is well-endowed with natural resources, such as timber and metals, and large, navigable rivers

---

shawabti (shuh-WAB-tee)

Aksum (AHK-soom)

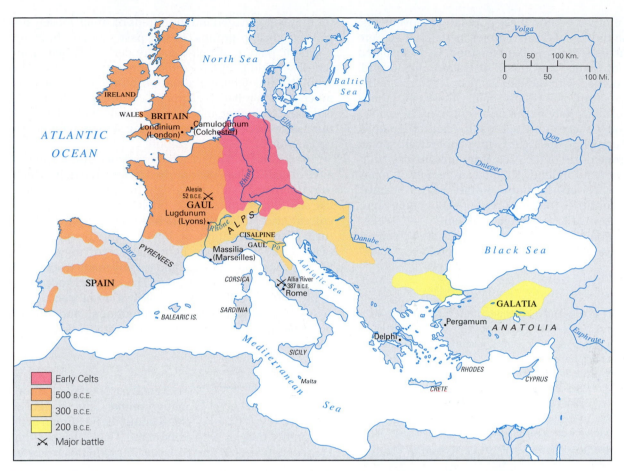

Map 3.3   The Celtic Peoples   Celtic civilization originated in Central Europe in the early part of the first millennium B.C.E. Around 500 B.C.E. Celtic peoples began to migrate, making Celtic civilization the dominant cultural style in Europe north of the Alps. The Celts' interactions with the peoples of the Mediterranean, including Greeks and Romans, encompassed both warfare and trade.   (From *Atlas of Classical History*, Fifth Edition, by Michael Grant. Copyright © 1994 by Michael Grant. Used by permission of Oxford University Press, Inc.)

(the Rhone, Rhine, and Danube) facilitate travel and trade.

Humans were living in this part of Europe for many thousands of years (see Chapter 1), but their lack of any system of writing severely limits our knowledge of the earliest inhabitants. Around 500 B.C.E. Celtic peoples spread across a substantial portion of Europe and, by coming into contact with the literate societies of the Mediterranean, entered the historical record. Information about the early **Celts**° comes from the archaeological record, the accounts of Greek and Roman travelers and conquerors, and the Celtic literature of Wales and Ireland that originated in oral traditions and was written down during the European Middle Ages.

Celts (kelts)

The Spread of the Celts

The term *Celtic* is a linguistic designation, referring to a branch of the Indo-European family of languages found throughout Europe and in west and south Asia. Scholars link the Celtic language group to archaeological remains first appearing in parts of present-day Germany, Austria, and the Czech Republic after 1000 B.C.E. (see Map 3.3). Many early Celts lived in or near hill-forts—lofty natural locations made more defensible by earthwork fortifications. By 500 B.C.E. Celtic elites were trading with Mediterranean societies for crafted goods and wine. This contact may have stimulated the new styles of Celtic manufacture and art that appeared at this time.

These new cultural features coincided with a period in which Celtic groups migrated to many parts of Europe. The motives behind these population movements, the precise timing, and the manner in which they were carried out are still not well understood. Celts occupied nearly all of France and much of Britain and Ireland, and they merged with indigenous peoples to create the Celtiberian culture of northern Spain. Other Celtic groups overran northern Italy in the fifth century B.C.E., raided into central Greece, and settled in central Anatolia (modern Turkey). By 300 B.C.E. Celtic peoples were spread across Europe north of the Alps, from present-day Hungary to Spain and Ireland. Their traces remain in many place names: rivers (Danube, Rhine, Seine, Thames, Shannon); countries (Belgium); regions (Bohemia, Aquitaine); and towns (Paris, Bologna, Leiden).

These widely diffused Celtic groups shared elements of language and culture, but there was no Celtic "state,"

Celtic Hill-Fort in England   Hundreds of these fortresses have been found across Europe. They served as centers of administration, gathering points for Celtic armies, manufacturing centers, storage depots for food and trade goods, and places of refuge. The natural defense offered by a hill could be improved, as here, by the construction of ditches and earthwork walls. Particularly effective was the so-called Gallic Wall, made of a combination of earth, stone, and timber to create both strength and enough flexibility to absorb the pounding from siege engines.   (English Heritage)

for they were divided into hundreds of small, loosely organized kinship groups. In the past scholars built up a generic picture of Celtic society derived largely from the observations of Greek and Roman writers. Current scholarship is focusing attention on the differences as much as the similarities among Celtic peoples. Indeed, it is doubtful whether ancient Celts would have identified themselves as belonging to anything akin to our modern conception of "Celtic civilization."

Greek and Roman writers were struck by the appearance of male Celts—their burly size, long red hair (which they often made stiff and upright by applying a cement-like solution of lime), shaggy mustaches, and loud, deep voices. Also striking was their strange apparel: pants (usually an indication of horse-riding peoples) and twisted gold neck collars. Particularly terrifying were the warriors who fought naked and eagerly made trophies of the heads of defeated enemies. The surviving accounts of the Celts describe them as wildly fond of war, courageous, childishly impulsive and emotional, and fond of boasting and exaggeration, yet quick-witted and eager to learn.

Celtic Society

The greatest source of information about Celtic society is the account of the Roman general Julius Caesar, who conquered Gaul (present-day France) between 58 and 51 B.C.E. Many Celtic groups in Gaul had once been ruled by kings, but by about 60 B.C.E. they periodically chose public officials, perhaps under Greek and Roman influence.

Celtic society, according to Greek and Roman commentators, was divided into an elite class of warriors, professional groups of priests and bards (singers of poems about glorious deeds of the past), and commoners (the largest group of all). The warriors owned land and flocks of cattle and sheep and monopolized both wealth and power. The common people labored on their land. The Celts built houses (usually round in Britain, rectangular in France) out of wattle and daub—a wooden framework filled in with clay and straw—with thatched straw roofs. An enclosure containing several such houses belonging to related families might be surrounded by a wooden fence to protect people and domestic animals from wild animals.

The warriors of Welsh and Irish legend reflect a stage of political and social development less complex than that of the Celts in Gaul. They raided one another's flocks, reveled in drunken feasts, and engaged in contests of strength and wit. At banquets warriors would fight to the death just to claim the choicest cut of the meat, the "hero's portion."

This silver vessel was found in a peat bog in Denmark, but must have come from elsewhere. It is usually dated to the second or first century B.C.E. On the inside left are Celtic warriors on horse and on foot, with lozenge-shaped shields and long battle-horns. On the inside right is a horned deity, possibly Cernunnos. (The National Museum of Denmark)

Druids, the Celtic priests in Gaul and Britain, formed a well-organized fraternity that performed religious, judicial, and educational functions. Trainees spent years memorizing prayers, secret rituals, legal precedents, and other traditions. The priesthood was the one Celtic institution that crossed tribal lines. The Druids sometimes headed off warfare between feuding groups and served as judges in cases involving Celts from different groups. In the first century C.E. the Roman government attempted to stamp out the Druids, probably because of concern that they might serve as a rallying point for Celtic opposition to Roman rule, as well as because of their involvement in human sacrifices.

The Celts were successful farmers, able to support large populations by tilling the heavy but fertile soils of continental Europe. Their metallurgical skills probably surpassed those of the Mediterranean peoples. Celts living on the Atlantic shore of France built sturdy ships that braved ocean conditions, and they developed extensive trade networks along Europe's large, navigable rivers. One lucrative commodity was tin, which Celtic traders from southwest England brought to Greek buyers in southern France. By the first century B.C.E some hill-forts were evolving into urban centers.

Women's lives were focused on child rearing, food production, and some crafts. Celtic women did not have true equality with men, but their situation was superior to that of women in the Middle East and in the Greek and Roman Mediterranean. Greek and Roman sources depict Celtic women as strong and proud. Welsh and Irish tales portray self-assured women who sat at banquets with their husbands, engaged in witty conversation, and provided ingenious solutions to vexing problems. Marriage was a partnership to which both parties contributed property. Each party had the right to inherit the estate if the other died. Celtic women also had greater freedom in their sexual relations than did their southern counterparts.

Tombs of elite women have yielded rich collections of clothing, jewelry, and furniture for use in the next world. Daughters of the elite were married to leading members of other tribes to create alliances. When the Romans invaded Celtic Britain in the first century C.E., they sometimes were opposed by Celtic tribes headed by queens, although some experts see this as an abnormal circumstance created by the Roman invasion itself.

Belief and Knowledge

Historians know the names of more than four hundred Celtic gods and goddesses, mostly associated with particular localities or kinship groups. More widely revered deities included Lug°, the god of light, crafts, and inventions; the horse-goddess Epona°; and the horned god Cernunnos°. "The Mothers," three goddesses depicted together holding symbols of abundance, probably played a part in a fertility cult. Halloween and May Day preserve the

Lug (loog) **Epona** (eh-POH-nuh) **Cernunnos** (KURN-you-nuhs)

ancient Celtic holidays of Samhain° and Beltaine° respectively, which took place at key moments in the agricultural cycle.

The early Celts did not build temples, but instead worshipped wherever they felt the presence of divinity—at springs, groves, and hilltops. At the sources of the Seine and Marne Rivers in France, archaeologists have found huge caches of Celtic wooden statues thrown into the water by worshippers.

The burial of elite members of early Celtic society in wagons filled with extensive grave goods suggests belief in some sort of afterlife. In Irish and Welsh legends, heroes and gods pass back and forth between the natural and supernatural worlds much more readily than in the mythology of other cultures, and magical occurrences are commonplace. Celtic priests set forth a doctrine of reincarnation—the rebirth of the soul in a new body. In contrast, other ancient peoples in Europe and western Asia believed that the barrier separating life from death could not be crossed.

The Roman conquest from the second century B.C.E. to the first century C.E. of Spain, southern Britain, France, and parts of Central Europe curtailed the evolution of Celtic society. The peoples in these lands were largely assimilated to Roman ways (see Chapter 6). That is why the inhabitants of modern Spain and France speak languages that are descended from Latin. From the third century C.E. on, Germanic invaders diminished the Celts still further, and the English language has a Germanic base. Only on the western fringes of the European continent—in Brittany (northwest France), Wales, Scotland, and Ireland—did Celtic peoples maintain their language, art, and culture into modern times.

FIRST CIVILIZATIONS OF THE AMERICAS: THE OLMEC AND CHAVÍN, 1200–250 B.C.E.

Humans reached the Western Hemisphere through a series of migrations from Asia (see Chapter 1). Some scholars believe that the first migrations occurred as early as 35,000 to 25,000 B.C.E., but most accept a later date of 20,000 to 13,000 B.C.E. Although some limited contacts with other cultures—for example, with Polynesians—may have occurred later, the peoples in the Western Hemisphere were virtually isolated from the rest of the world for at least fifteen thousand years. The duration and comprehensiveness of their isolation distin-

guishes the Americas from the world's other major cultural regions. While technological innovations passed back and forth among the civilizations of Asia, Africa, and Europe, the peoples of the Americas faced the challenges of the natural environment on their own.

Over thousands of years the population of the Americas grew and spread throughout the hemisphere, responding to environments that included frozen regions of the polar extremes, tropical rain forests, and high mountain ranges as well as deserts, woodlands, and prairies. Two of the hemisphere's most impressive cultural traditions developed in Mesoamerica (Mexico and northern Central America) and in the mountainous Andean region of South America. Well before 1000 B.C.E. the domestication of new plant varieties, the introduction of new technologies, and a limited development of trade led to greater social stratification and the beginnings of urbanization in both regions. Cultural elites associated with these changes used their increased political and religious authority to organize great numbers of laborers to construct large-scale irrigation and drainage works, to clear forests, and to unleash the productive potential of floodplains and steeply pitched hillsides. These transformed environments provided the economic platform for the construction of urban centers dominated by monumental structures devoted to religious purposes and to housing for members of the elite. By 1000 B.C.E. the major urban centers of Mesoamerica and the Andes had begun to project their political and cultural power over broad territories: they had become civilizations. The cultural legacies of the two most important of these early civilizations, the Olmec of Mesoamerica and Chavín of the Andes, would persist for more than a thousand years.

The Mesoamerican Olmec, 1200–400 B.C.E.

Mesoamerica is a region of great geographic and climatic diversity. It is extremely active geologically, experiencing both earthquakes and volcanic eruptions. Mountain ranges break the region into micro environments, including the temperate climates of the Valley of Mexico and the Guatemalan highlands, the tropical forests of the Peten and Gulf of Mexico coast, the rain forest of the southern Yucatán and Belize, and the drier scrub forest of the northern Yucatán (see Map 3.4).

Within these ecological niches, Amerindian peoples developed specialized technologies that exploited indigenous plants and animals, as well as minerals like obsidian, quartz, and jade. Eventually, contacts across these environmental boundaries led to trade and cultural ex-

Samhain (SAH-win)   **Beltaine** (BEHL-tayn)

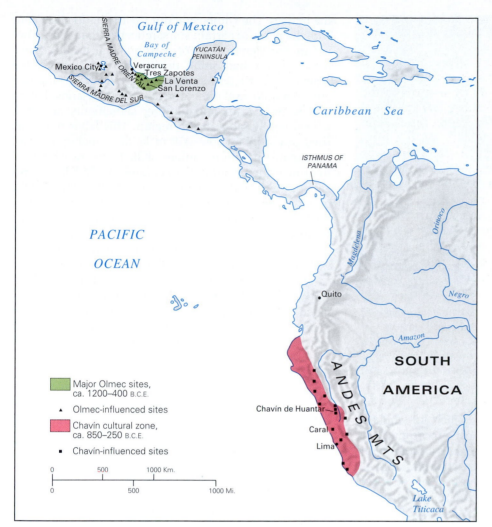

Map 3.4   Olmec and Chavín Civilizations   The regions of Mesoamerica (most of modern Mexico and Central America) and the Andean highlands of South America have hosted impressive civilizations since early times. The civilizations of the Olmec and Chavín were the originating civilizations of these two regions, providing the foundations of architecture, city planning, and religion.

change. Enhanced trade, increasing agricultural productivity, and rising population led, in turn, to urbanization and the gradual appearance of powerful political and religious elites. Although a number of militarily powerful civilizations developed in Mesoamerica, the region was never unified politically. All Mesoamerican civilizations, however, shared fundamental elements of material culture, technology, religious belief and ritual, political organization, art, architecture, and sports.

The most influential early Mesoamerican civilization was the **Olmec,** flourishing between 1200 and 400 B.C.E. (see Map 3.4). The center of Olmec civilization was located near the tropical Atlantic coast of what are now the Mexican states of Veracruz and Tabasco. Olmec cultural influence reached as far as the Pacific coast of Central America and the Central Plateau of Mexico.

Olmec urban development was made possible by earlier advances in agriculture. Original settlements depended on the region's rich plant diversity and on fishing. Later, by 3500 B.C.E or earlier, the staples of the Mesoamerican diet—corn, beans, and squash—were domesticated. Recent research indicates that manioc, a calorie-rich root crop, was also grown in the floodplains of the region, multiplying food resources. The ability of farmers to produce dependable surpluses of these products permitted the first stages of craft specialization and social stratification. As religious and political elites emerged, they used their prestige and authority to organize the population to dig irrigation and drainage canals, develop raised fields in wetlands that could be farmed more intensively, and construct the large-scale religious and civic buildings that became the cultural signature of Olmec civilization.

The cultural core of the early Olmec civilization was located at San Lorenzo but included smaller centers

Olmec Head Giant heads sculpted from basalt are a widely recognized legacy of Olmec culture. Sixteen heads have been found, the largest approximately 11 feet (3.4 meters) tall. Experts in Olmec archaeology believe the heads are portraits of individual rulers, warriors, or ballplayers. (Georg Gerster/Photo Researchers, Inc.)

the masses. The Olmec laid out their cities in alignment with the paths of certain stars, reflecting their strong belief in the significance of astronomical events. Since these centers had small permanent populations, the scale of construction suggests that the Olmec elite was able to require and direct the labor of thousands of men and women from surrounding settlements and dispersed family plots in the region. This labor pool was used primarily for low-skill tasks like moving dirt and stone construction materials. Skilled artisans who lived in or near the urban core decorated the buildings with carvings and sculptures. They also produced the high-quality crafts, such as exquisite carved jade figurines, necklaces, and ceremonial knives and axes, that distinguished Olmec culture. Archaeological evidence suggests the existence of a class of merchants who traded with distant peoples for obsidian, jade, and pottery.

Little is known about Olmec political structure, but it seems likely that the rise of major urban centers coincided with the appearance of a form of kingship that combined religious and secular roles. Finely crafted objects decorated the households of the elite and distinguished their dress from that of the commoners who lived in dispersed small structures constructed of sticks and mud. The authority of the rulers and their kin groups is suggested by a series of colossal carved stone heads, some as large as 11 feet (3.4 meters) high. Since each head is unique and suggestive of individual personality, most archaeologists believe they were carved to memorialize individual rulers. This theory is reinforced by the location of the heads close to the major urban centers, especially San Lorenzo. These remarkable stone sculptures are the best-known monuments of Olmec culture.

The organization of collective labor by the Olmec elites benefited the commoners by increasing food production and making it more reliable. People also enjoyed a more diverse diet. Ceramic products such as utilitarian pots and small figurines as well as small stone carvings associated with religious belief have been found in commoner households. This suggests that at least some advantages gained from urbanization and growing elite power were shared broadly in the society.

The Olmec elite used elaborate religious rituals to control this complex society. Thousands of commoners were drawn from the countryside to attend awe-inspiring ceremonies at the centers. The elevated platforms and mounds with carved stone veneers served as potent backdrops for these rituals. Rulers and their close kin came to be associated with the gods through bloodletting and human sacrifice, evidence of which is found in all the urban centers. The Olmec were polytheistic, and most of their deities had dual (male and female) natures. Human and animal characteristics were also blended.

nearby (1200–900 B.C.E.). La Venta°, which developed at about the same time, became the most important Olmec center after 900 B.C.E. when San Lorenzo was abandoned or destroyed. Tres Zapotes° was the last dominant center, rising to prominence after La Venta collapsed or was destroyed around 600 B.C.E. The relationship among these centers is unclear. Scholars have found little evidence to suggest that they were either rival city states or dependent centers of a centralized political authority. It appears that each center developed independently to exploit and exchange specialized products like salt, cacao (chocolate beans), clay for ceramics, and limestone. Each major Olmec center was eventually abandoned, its monuments defaced and buried and its buildings destroyed. Archaeologists interpret these events differently; some see them as evidence of internal upheavals or military defeat by neighboring peoples, and others suggest that they were rituals associated with the death of a ruler.

Large artificial platforms and mounds of packed earth dominated Olmec urban centers and served to frame the collective ritual and political activities that brought the rural population to the cities at special times in the year. Some of the platforms also served as foundations for elite residences, in effect lifting the elite above

La Venta (LA BEN-tah) **Tres Zapotes** (TRACE zah-POE-tace)

Surviving representations of jaguars, crocodiles, snakes, and sharks suggest that these powerful animals provided the most enduring images used in Olmec religious representation. The ability of humans to transform themselves into these animals is a common decorative motif. Rulers were especially associated with the jaguar.

An important class of shamans and healers attached to the elite organized religious life and provided practical advice about the periodic rains essential to agricultural life. They directed the planning of urban centers to reflect astronomical observations and were responsible for developing a form of writing that may have influenced later innovations among the Maya (see Chapter 12). From their close observation of the stars, they produced a calendar that was used to organize ritual life and agriculture. The Olmec were also the likely originators of a ritual ball game that became an enduring part of Mesoamerican ceremonial life.

There is little evidence for the existence of an Olmec empire. Given the limited technological and agricultural base of the society, it is unlikely that the power of the Olmecs could have been projected over significant distances militarily. However, the discovery of Olmec products and images, such as jade carvings decorated with the jaguar-god, as far away as central Mexico provides evidence that the Olmec did exercise cultural influence over a wide area. This influence would endure for centuries.

Early South American Civilization: Chavín, 900–250 B.C.E.

Geography played an important role in the development of human society in the Andes. The region's diverse environment—a mountainous core, arid coastal plain, and dense interior jungles—challenged human populations, encouraging the development of specialized regional production as well as complex social institutions and cultural values that facilitated interregional exchanges and shared labor responsibilities. These adaptations to environmental challenge became enduring features of Andean civilization.

The earliest urban centers in the Andean region were villages of a few hundred people built along the coastal plain or in the foothills near the coast. The abundance of fish and mollusks along the coast of Peru provided a dependable supply of food that helped make the development of early cities possible. The coastal populations traded these products as well as decorative shells for corn, other foods, and eventually textiles produced in the foothills. The two regions also exchanged ceremonial practices, religious motifs, and aesthetic ideas. Recent discoveries demonstrate that as early as 2600 B.C.E. the vast site called Caral in the Supe Valley had developed many of the characteristics now viewed as the hallmarks of later Andean civilization, including ceremonial plazas, pyramids, elevated platforms and mounds, and extensive irrigation works. The scale of the public works in Caral suggests a population of thousands and a political structure capable of organizing the production and distribution of maritime and agricultural products over a broad area.

Chavín, one of the most impressive of South America's early urban civilizations (see Map 3.4), inherited many of the cultural and economic characteristics of Caral. Its capital, Chavín de Huantar°, was located at 10,300 feet (3,139 meters) in the eastern range of the Andes north of the modern city of Lima. Between 900 and 250 B.C.E., a period roughly coinciding with Olmec civilization in Mesoamerica, Chavín dominated a densely populated region that included large areas of the Peruvian coastal plain and Andean foothills. Chavín de Huantar's location at the intersection of trade routes connecting the coast with populous mountain valleys and the tropical lowlands on the eastern flank of the Andes allowed the city's rulers to control trade among these distinct ecological zones and gain an important economic advantage over regional rivals.

Chavín's dominance as a ceremonial and commercial center depended on earlier developments in agriculture and trade, including the introduction of maize cultivation from Mesoamerica. Maize increased the food supplies of the coast and interior foothills, allowing greater levels of urbanization. As Chavín grew, its trade linked the coastal economy with the producers of quinoa (a local grain), potatoes, and llamas in the high mountain valleys and, to a lesser extent, with Amazonian producers of coca (the leaves were chewed, producing a mild narcotic effect) and fruits.

These developments were accompanied by the evolution of reciprocal labor obligations that permitted the construction and maintenance of roads, bridges, temples, palaces, and large irrigation and drainage projects as well as textile production. The exact nature of these reciprocal labor obligations at Chavín is unknown. In later times groups of related families who held land communally and claimed descent from a common ancestor organized these labor obligations. Group members thought of each other as brothers and sisters and were obligated to aid each other, providing a model for the organization of labor and the distribution of goods at every level of Andean society.

The increased use of **llamas** to move goods from one ecological zone to another promoted specialization of

---

Chavín de Huantar (cha-BEAN day WAHN-tar)

production and increased trade. Llamas were the only domesticated beasts of burden in the Americas, and they played an important role in the integration of the Andean region. They were first domesticated in the mountainous interior of Peru and were crucial to Chavín's development, not unlike the camel in the evolution of trans-Saharan trade (see Chapter 8). Llamas provided meat and wool and decreased the labor needed to transport goods. A single driver could control ten to thirty animals, each carrying up to 70 pounds (32 kilograms); a human porter could carry only about 50 pounds (22.5 kilograms).

The enormous scale of the capital and the dispersal of Chavín's pottery styles, religious motifs, and architectural forms over a wide area suggest that Chavín imposed some form of political integration and trade dependency on its neighbors that may have relied in part on military force. Most modern scholars believe that, as in the case of the Olmec civilization, Chavín's influence depended more on the development of an attractive and convincing religious belief system and related rituals. Chavín's most potent religious symbol, a jaguar deity, was dispersed over a broad area, and archaeological evidence suggests that Chavín de Huantar served as a pilgrimage site.

The architectural signature of Chavín was a large complex of multilevel platforms made of packed earth or rubble and faced with cut stone or adobe (sun-dried brick made of clay and straw). Small buildings used for ritual purposes or as elite residences were built on these platforms. Nearly all the buildings were decorated with relief carvings of serpents, condors, jaguars, or human forms. The largest building at Chavín de Huantar measured 250 feet (76 meters) on each side and rose to a height of 50 feet (15 meters). About one-third of its interior is hollow, containing narrow galleries and small rooms that may have housed the remains of royal ancestors.

American metallurgy was first developed in the Andean region. The later introduction of metallurgy in Mesoamerica, like the appearance of maize agriculture in the Andes, suggests sustained trade and cultural contacts between the two regions. Archaeological investigations of Chavín de Huantar and smaller centers have revealed remarkable three-dimensional silver, gold, and gold alloy ornaments that represent a clear advance over earlier technologies. Improvements in both the manufacture and the decoration of textiles are also associated with the rise of Chavín. The quality of these products, probably used only by the elite or in religious rituals, added to the reputation and prestige of the culture and aided in the projection of its power and influence. The most common decorative motif in sculpture, pottery, and textiles was a jaguar-man similar in conception to the Olmec symbol. In both civilizations and in many other cultures in the Americas, this powerful predator

provided an enduring image of religious authority and a vehicle through which the gods could act in the world of men and women.

Class distinctions appear to have increased during this period of expansion. A class of priests directed religious life. Modern scholars also see evidence that both local chiefs and a more powerful chief or king dominated Chavín's politics. Excavations of graves reveal that superior-quality textiles as well as gold crowns, breastplates, and jewelry distinguished rulers from commoners. These rich objects, the quality and abundance of pottery, and the monumental architecture of the major centers all suggest the presence of highly skilled artisans as well.

There is no convincing evidence, like defaced buildings or broken images, that the eclipse of Chavín (unlike the Olmec centers) was associated with conquest or rebellion. However, recent investigations have suggested that increased warfare throughout the region around 200 B.C.E. disrupted Chavín's trade and undermined the authority of the governing elite. Regardless of what caused the collapse of this powerful culture, the technologies, material culture, statecraft, architecture, and urban planning associated with Chavín influenced the Andean region for centuries.

CONCLUSION

The civilizations of early China, Nubia, the Celts, the Olmec, and Chavín emerged in very different ecological contexts in widely separated parts of the globe, and the patterns of organization, technology, behavior, and belief that they developed were, in large part, responses to the challenges and opportunities of those environments.

In the north China plain, as in the river-valley civilizations of Mesopotamia and Egypt, the presence of great, flood-prone rivers and the lack of dependable rainfall led to the formation of powerful institutions capable of organizing large numbers of people to dig and maintain irrigation channels and build dikes. An authoritarian central government has been a recurring feature of Chinese history, beginning with the Shang monarchy and warrior elite.

In Nubia, the initial impetus for the formation of a strong state was the need for protection from desert nomads and from the Egyptian rulers who coveted Nubian gold and other resources. Control of these resources and of the trade route between sub-Saharan Africa and the north, as well as the agricultural surplus to feed administrators and specialists in the urban centers, made the rulers of Kush, Napata, and Meroë wealthy and formidable.

The Celtic peoples of continental Europe never developed a strong state. They occupied fertile lands with adequate rainfall for agriculture, grazing territory for flocks, and timber for fuel and construction. Kinship groups dominated by warrior elites and controlling compact territories were the usual form of organization.

While the ecological zones in Mesoamerica and South America in which the Olmec and Chavín cultures emerged were quite different, both societies created networks that brought together the resources and products of disparate regions. Little is known about the political and social organization of these societies, but archaeological evidence makes clear the existence of ruling elites that gathered wealth and organized labor for the construction of monumental centers.

In most complex societies small groups achieve a level of wealth and prestige that allows them to dominate the majority. It is important to understand how these elite groups maintain and justify their position.

Among both the early Chinese and the Celts a warrior aristocracy, with wealth based on land and flocks, controlled significant numbers of human laborers. When the Zhou overthrew the Shang, they curtailed the power of the warrior elite, and over time a new elite of educated government officials evolved. Much less is known about the emergence of elite groups in Nubia and the states of the Olmec and Chavín. However, it is likely that they played key roles in the organization of trade and the construction of the irrigation networks that greatly increased the food supply available to their communities.

In the Eastern Hemisphere, the production of metal tools, weapons, and luxury and ceremonial implements were vital to the success of elite groups. Bronze metallurgy began at different times—in western Asia around 2500 B.C.E., in East Asia around 2000 B.C.E., in northeastern Africa around 1500 B.C.E. Possession of bronze weapons with hard, sharp edges enabled the warriors of Shang and Zhou China, like the royal armies of Egypt and Mesopotamia, to dominate the peasant masses. In Shang China bronze was also used to craft the vessels that played a vital role in the rituals of contact with the spirits of ancestors.

Throughout history, elites have used religion to bolster their position. The Shang rulers of China were indispensable intermediaries between their kingdom and powerful and protective gods and ancestors. Their Zhou successors developed the concept of the ruler as divine Son of Heaven who ruled in accord with the Mandate of Heaven. The rulers of Nubia, drawing on Egyptian concepts, claimed to be gods on earth. In the Olmec and Chavín zones there is some evidence of religious rituals performed to affirm the position of the ruling class. Human sacrifice was practiced among the Celts and in Shang China, Nubia, and Olmec Mesoamerica. This, too, was a mechanism by which ruling elites inspired fear and obedience in their subjects.

The construction and use of "urban" centers and monumental spaces and structures for dramatic religious rituals and colorful political events also propagated the ideologies of power. Ceremonies involving impressive pageantry communicated a message of the "superiority" of the elite and the desirability of being associated with them. In early China and the Olmec and Chavín civilizations, the centers appear to have been the sites of palaces, shrines, and the dwellings of the elite.

Scholars have debated why powerful civilizations appeared many centuries later in the Western Hemisphere than in the Eastern Hemisphere. Recent theories have focused on environmental differences. The Eastern Hemisphere was home to a far larger number of wild plant and animal species that were particularly well suited to domestication. In addition, the natural east-west axis of the huge landmass of Europe and Asia allowed for the relatively rapid spread of domesticated plants and animals to climatically similar zones along the same latitudes. Settled agriculture led to population growth, more complex political and social organization, and increased technological sophistication. In the Americas, by contrast, there were fewer wild plant and animal species that could be domesticated, and the north-south axis of the continents made it more difficult for domesticated species to spread because of variations in climate at different latitudes. As a result, the processes that foster the development of complex societies evolved somewhat more slowly.

The comparison of the two hemispheres leads to another important realization. The complex societies of the Western Hemisphere did not necessarily develop technologies in the same sequence as their Eastern Hemisphere counterparts. The Olmec and Chavín peoples did not possess large draft animals, wheeled vehicles, or metal weapons and tools. Nevertheless, they created sophisticated political, social, and economic institutions that rivaled those developed in the Eastern Hemisphere in the third and second millennia B.C.E.

■ Key Terms

loess	Confucius	Celts
Shang	Daoism	Druids
divination	yin/yang	Olmec
Zhou	Kush	Chavín
Mandate of Heaven	Meroë	llama
Legalism		

■ Suggested Reading

Caroline Blunden and Mark Elvin, *Cultural Atlas of China* (1983), contains general geographic, ethnographic, and historical information about China through the ages, as well as many maps and illustrations. Conrad Schirokauer, *A Brief History of Chinese Civilization* (1991), and John King Fairbank, *China: A New History* (1992), offer useful chapters on early China. Edward L. Shaughnessy and Michael Loewe, eds., *The Cambridge History of Ancient China* (1998), approaches the subject in far greater depth. Nicola Di Cosmo, *Ancient China and Its Enemies: The Rise of Nomadic Power in East Asian History* (2002), sets the development of Chinese civilization in the broader context of interactions with nomadic neighbors. Jessica Rawson, *Ancient China: Art and Archaeology* (1980), Kwang-chih Chang, *The Archaeology of Ancient China*, 4th ed. (1986), and Ronald G. Knapp, *China's Walled Cities* (2000), emphasize archaeological evidence. W. Thomas Chase, *Ancient Chinese Bronze Art: Casting the Precious Sacral Vessel* (1991), contains a brief but useful discussion of the importance of bronzes in ancient China, as well as a detailed discussion of bronze-casting techniques. Robert Temple, *The Genius of China: 3,000 Years of Science, Discovery, and Invention* (1986), explores many aspects of Chinese technology, using a division into general topics such as agriculture, engineering, and medicine. Anne Behnke Kinney, "Women in Ancient China," in *Women's Roles in Ancient Civilizations: A Reference Guide*, ed. Bella Vivante (1999), and Patricia Ebrey, "Women, Marriage, and the Family in Chinese History," in *Heritage of China: Contemporary Perspectives on Chinese Civilization*, ed. Paul S. Ropp (1990), address the very limited evidence for women in early China. Michael Loewe and Carmen Blacker, *Oracles and Divination* (1981), addresses practices in China and other ancient civilizations. Simon Leys, *The Analects of Confucius* (1997), provides a translation of and a commentary on this fundamental text. Benjamin I. Schwartz, *The World of Thought in Ancient China* (1985), is a broad introduction to early Chinese ethical and spiritual concepts.

After a long period of scholarly neglect, with an occasional exception such as Bruce G. Trigger, *Nubia Under the Pharaohs* (1976), the study of ancient Nubia is now receiving considerable attention. David O'Connor, *Ancient Nubia: Egypt's Rival in Africa* (1993); Joyce L. Haynes, *Nubia: Ancient Kingdoms of Africa* (1992); Karl-Heinz Priese, *The Gold of Meroë* (1993); P. L. Shinnie, *Ancient Nubia* (1996); Derek A. Welsby, *The Kingdom of Kush: The Napatan and Meroitic Empires* (1996); and Timothy Kendall, *Kerma and the Kingdom of Kush, 2500-1500 B.C.: The Archaeological Discovery of an Ancient Nubian Empire* (1997), all reflect the new interest of major museums in the art and artifacts of this society. Robert Morkot, "Egypt and Nubia," in *Empires: Perspectives from Archaeology and History*, ed. Susan E. Alcock (2001), examines the political dimension of Egyptian domination, while John H. Taylor, *Egypt and Nubia* (1991), also emphasizes the fruitful interaction of the Egyptian and Nubian cultures.

Simon James, *The World of the Celts* (1993), is a concise, well-illustrated introduction to Celtic civilization. Fuller treatments can be found in Barry W. Cunliffe, *The Ancient Celts* (1997), and Peter Ellis, *The Celtic Empire: The First Millennium of Celtic History, c. 1000 B.C.–51 A.D.* (1990). Miranda J. Green, *The Celtic World* (1995), is a large and comprehensive collection of articles on many aspects of Celtic civilization. Philip Freeman, *War, Women, and Druids: Eyewitness Accounts and Early Reports on the Ancient Celts* (2002), collects the ancient textual evidence. John Haywood, *Atlas of the Celtic World* (2001), is a useful reference. Simon James, *The Atlantic Celts: Ancient People or Modern Invention* (1999), reflects the current scholarly emphasis on articulating the important differences between Celtic groups and deconstructing the modern "myth" of a monolithic Celtic identity. On Celtic religion and mythology see Bernhard Maier, *Dictionary of Celtic Religion and Culture* (1997); James MacKillop, *Dictionary of Celtic Mythology* (1998); Proinsias Mac Cana, *Celtic Mythology* (1983); Paul R. Lonigan, *The Druids: Priests of the Ancient Celts* (1996); and two books by Miranda Green: *The Gods of the Celts* (1986) and *Celtic Myths* (1993). Peter Ellis, *Celtic Women: Women in Celtic Society and Literature* (1996), collects and evaluates the evidence for women's roles. Celtic art is covered by Ruth and Vincent Megaw, *Celtic Art: From Its Beginnings to the Book of Kells* (1989), and I. M. Stead, *Celtic Art* (1985). For translations and brief discussion of Celtic legends see Patrick K. Ford, *The Mabinogi and Other Medieval Welsh Tales* (1977), and Jeffrey Gantz, *Early Irish Myths and Sagas* (1981).

A number of useful books provide an introduction to the early Americas. In *Prehistory of the Americas* (1987) Stuart Fiedel provides an excellent summary of the early history of the Western Hemisphere. *Early Man in the New World*, ed. Richard Shutler, Jr. (1983), is also a useful general work. *Atlas of Ancient America* (1986), by Michael Coe, Elizabeth P. Benson, and Dean R. Snow, offers a compendium of maps and information. George Kubler, *The Art and Architecture of Ancient America: The Mexican, Maya, and Andean Peoples* (1984), is an essential tool, though dated.

For the Olmecs see Jacques Soustelle, *The Olmecs: The Oldest Civilization in Mexico* (1984). More reliable is Michael Coe, *The Olmec World* (1996). Richard W. Keatinge, ed., *Peruvian Prehistory* (1988), provides a helpful introduction to the scholarship on Andean societies. The most useful summary of recent research on Chavín is Richard L. Burger, *Chavín and the Origins of Andean Civilization* (1992).

Jared Diamond, *Guns, Germs, and Steel: The Fates of Human Societies* (1997), tackles the difficult question of why technological development occurred at different times and took different paths of development in the Eastern and Western Hemispheres.

■ Notes

1. Quoted in Miriam Lichtheim, ed., *Ancient Egyptian Literature: A Book of Readings* (Berkeley: University of California Press 1978).

The Mediterranean and Middle East, 2000–500 B.C.E.

The Mortuary Temple of Queen Hatshepsut at Deir el–Bahri, Egypt, ca. 1460 B.C.E.
This beautiful complex of terraces, ramps, and colonnades featured relief sculptures
and texts commemorating the famous expedition to Punt.

Ancient peoples' stories—even those that are not historically accurate—provide valuable insights into how people thought about their origins and identity. One famous story concerned the city of Carthage° in present-day Tunisia, which for centuries dominated the commerce of the western Mediterranean. Tradition held that Dido, a member of the royal family of the Phoenician city-state of Tyre° in southern Lebanon, fled with her supporters to the western Mediterranean after her husband was murdered by her brother, the king of Tyre. Landing on the North African coast, the refugees made friendly contact with local people, who agreed to give them as much land as a cow's hide could cover. By cleverly cutting the hide into narrow strips, they were able to mark out a substantial piece of territory for Kart Khadasht, the "New City" (called *Carthago* by their Roman enemies). Later, faithful to the memory of her dead husband, Dido committed suicide rather than marry a local chieftain.

This story highlights the spread of cultural patterns from older centers to new regions, and the migration and resettlement of Late Bronze Age and Early Iron Age peoples in the Mediterranean lands and western Asia. Just as Egyptian cultural influences helped transform Nubian society, influences from the older centers in Mesopotamia and Egypt penetrated throughout western Asia and the Mediterranean. Far-flung trade, diplomatic contacts, military conquests, and the relocation of large numbers of people spread knowledge, beliefs, practices, and technologies.

By the end of the second millennium B.C.E. many of the societies of the Eastern Hemisphere had entered the **Iron Age:** they had begun to use iron instead of bronze for tools and weapons. Iron offered several advantages. It was a single metal rather than an alloy and thus was simpler to obtain; and there were many potential sources of iron ore. Once the technology of iron making had been mastered—iron has to be heated to a higher temperature than bronze, and its hardness depends on the amount of carbon added during the forging process—iron tools were found to have harder, sharper edges than bronze tools.

These advantages were not discovered all at once. The Hittites of iron-rich Anatolia had learned to make iron implements by 1500 B.C.E. but did not share their knowledge. Some scholars believe that, in the disrupted period after 1200 B.C.E., blacksmiths from the Hittite core area migrated and spread the technology. Others speculate that metalworkers who could not obtain copper and tin turned to dumps of slag (the byproduct of bronze production) containing iron residue and found that they could create useful objects from it. As its usefulness became recognized and techniques were perfected, iron came to be used on an ever wider scale, though bronze also continued to be used.

The first part of this chapter resumes the story of Mesopotamia and Egypt in the Late Bronze Age, the second millennium B.C.E.: their complex relations with neighboring peoples, the development of a prosperous, "cosmopolitan" network of states in the Middle East, and the period of destruction and decline that set in around 1200 B.C.E. We also look at how the Minoan and Mycenaean civilizations of the Aegean Sea were inspired by the technologies and cultural patterns of the older Middle Eastern centers and prospered from participation in long-distance networks of trade. The remainder of the chapter examines the resurgence of this region in the early Iron Age, from 1000 to 500 B.C.E. The focus is on three societies: the Assyrians of northern Mesopotamia; the Israelites of Israel; and the Phoenicians of Lebanon and Syria and their colonies in the western Mediterranean, mainly Carthage. After the decline or demise of the ancient centers dominant throughout the third and second millennia B.C.E., these societies evolved into new political, cultural, and commercial centers.

As you read this chapter, ask yourself the following questions:

- What environmental, technological, political, and cultural factors led these societies to develop their distinctive institutions and values?

Carthage (KAHR-thuhj)   Tyre (tire)

CHRONOLOGY

	Western Asia	Egypt	Syria–Palestine	Mediterranean
2000 B.C.E.	**2000 B.C.E.** Horses in use	**2040–1640 B.C.E.** Middle Kingdom		**2000 B.C.E.** Rise of Minoan civilization on Crete; early Greeks arrive in Greece
	1700–1200 B.C.E. Hittites dominant in Anatolia	**1640–1532 B.C.E.** Hyksos dominate northern Egypt **1532 B.C.E.** Beginning of New Kingdom		**1600 B.C.E.** Rise of Mycenaean civilization in Greece
1500 B.C.E.	**1500 B.C.E.** Hittites develop iron metallurgy **1460 B.C.E.** Kassites assume control of southern Mesopotamia	**1470 B.C.E.** Queen Hatshepsut dispatches expedition to Punt **1353 B.C.E.** Akhenaten launches reforms	**1500 B.C.E.** Early "alphabetic" script developed at Ugarit **1250–1200 B.C.E.** Israelite occupation of Canaan	**1450 B.C.E.** Destruction of Minoan palaces in Crete
	1200 B.C.E. Destruction of Hittite kingdom	**1200–1150 B.C.E.** Sea Peoples attack Egypt **1070 B.C.E.** End of New Kingdom	**1150 B.C.E.** Philistines settle southern coast of Israel	**1200–1150 B.C.E.** Destruction of Mycenaean centers in Greece
1000 B.C.E.	**1000 B.C.E.** Iron metalurgy begins		**1000 B.C.E.** David establishes Jerusalem as Israelite capital	**1000 B.C.E.** Iron metallurgy
	911 B.C.E. Rise of Neo-Assyrian Empire **744–727 B.C.E.** Reforms of Tiglath-pileser **668–627 B.C.E.** Reign of Ashurbanipal **626–539 B.C.E.** Neo-Babylonian kingdom **612 B.C.E.** Fall of Assyria	**750 B.C.E.** Kings of Kush control Egypt **671 B.C.E.** Assyrian conquest of Egypt	**969 B.C.E.** Hiram of Tyre comes to power **960 B.C.E.** Solomon builds First Temple **920 B.C.E.** Division into two kingdoms of Israel and Judah **721 B.C.E.** Assyrian conquest of northern kingdom **701 B.C.E.** Assyrian humiliation of Tyre	**814 B.C.E.** Foundation of Carthage
600 B.C.E.			**587 B.C.E.** Neo-Babylonian capture of Jerusalem **515 B.C.E.** Deportees from Babylon return to Jerusalem **450 B.C.E.** Completion of Hebrew Bible; Hanno the Phoenician explores West Africa	**550–300 B.C.E.** Rivalry of Carthaginians and Greeks in western Mediterranean

- In what ways were the societies of this era more interconnected and interdependent than before, and what were the consequences—positive and negative—of these connections?

- What were the causes and consequences of large-scale movements of peoples to new homes during this era?

- Why were certain cultures destroyed or assimilated while others survived?

THE COSMOPOLITAN MIDDLE EAST, 1700–1100 B.C.E.

Both Mesopotamia and Egypt succumbed to outside invaders in the seventeenth century B.C.E. (see Chapter 2). Eventually the outsiders were either ejected or assimilated, and conditions of stability and prosperity were restored. Between 1500 and 1200 B.C.E. a number of large territorial states dominated the Middle East (see Map 4.1). These centers of power controlled the smaller city-states, kingdoms, and kinship groups as they competed with, and sometimes fought against, one another for control of valuable commodities and trade routes.

Historians have called the Late Bronze Age in the Middle East a "cosmopolitan" era, meaning a time of widely shared cultures and lifestyles. Extensive diplomatic relations and commercial contacts between states fostered the flow of goods and ideas, and elite groups shared similar values and enjoyed a relatively high standard of living. The peasants in the countryside who comprised the majority of the population may have seen some improvement in their standard of living, but they reaped far fewer benefits from the increasing contacts and trade.

Western Asia

By 1500 B.C.E. Mesopotamia was divided into two distinct political zones: Babylonia in the south and Assyria in the north (see Map 4.1). The city of Babylon had gained political and cultural ascendancy over the southern plain under the dynasty of Hammurabi in the eighteenth and seventeenth centuries B.C.E. Subsequently there was a persistent inflow of Kassites°, peoples from the Zagros° Mountains to the east

who spoke a non-Semitic language, and by 1460 B.C.E a Kassite dynasty had come to power in Babylon. The Kassites retained names in their native language but otherwise embraced Babylonian language and culture and intermarried with the native population. During their 250 years in power, the Kassite lords of Babylonia defended their core area and traded for raw materials, but they did not pursue territorial conquest.

The Assyrians of the north had more ambitious designs. As early as the twentieth century B.C.E. the city of Ashur,° the leading urban center on the northern Tigris, anchored a busy trade route across the northern Mesopotamian plain and onto the Anatolian Plateau. Representatives of Assyrian merchant families maintained settlements outside the walls of important Anatolian cities. The Assyrians exported textiles and tin, used since about 2500 B.C.E. to make bronze, which they exchanged for silver from Anatolia. In the eighteenth century B.C.E. an Assyrian dynasty briefly gained control of the upper Euphrates River near the present-day border of Syria and Iraq. This "Old Assyrian" kingdom, as it is now called, illustrates the importance of the trade routes connecting Mesopotamia to Anatolia and the Syria-Palestine coast. After 1400 B.C.E. a resurgent "Middle Assyrian" kingdom again engaged in campaigns of conquest and expansion of its economic interests.

Other ambitious states emerged on the periphery of the Mesopotamian heartland, including Elam in southwest Iran and Mitanni° in the broad plain between the upper Euphrates and Tigris Rivers. Most formidable of all were the **Hittites°,** speakers of an Indo-European language, who became the foremost power in Anatolia from around 1700 to 1200 B.C.E. From their capital at Hattusha°, near present-day Ankara° in central Turkey, they deployed the fearsome new technology of horse-drawn war chariots. The Hittites exploited Anatolia's rich deposits of copper, silver, and iron to play an indispensable role in international commerce. Many historians believe that the Hittites were the first to develop a technique for making tools and weapons of iron. They heated the ore until it was soft enough to shape, pounded it to remove impurities, and then plunged it into cold water to harden. The Hittites were anxious to keep knowledge of this process secret since it provided both military and economic advantages.

During the second millennium B.C.E. Mesopotamian political and cultural concepts spread across much of western Asia. Akkadian° became the language of diplo-

---

Kassite (KAS-ite)   **Zagros** (ZAH-groes)

Ashur (AH-shoor)   **Mitanni** (mih-TAH-nee)   **Hittite** (HIT-ite)
Hattusha (haht-tush-SHAH)   **Ankara** (ANG-kuh-ruh)
Akkadian (uh-KAY-dee-uhn)

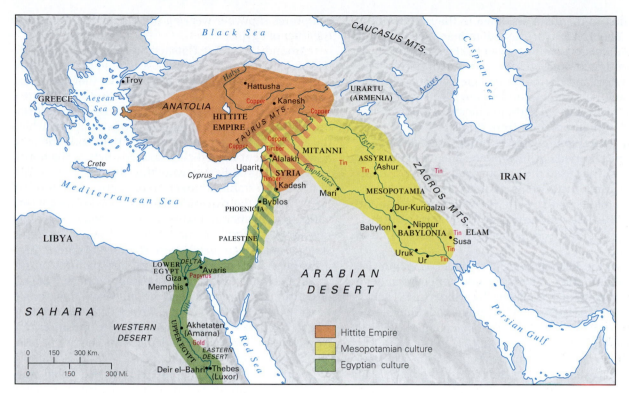

Map 4.1   The Middle East in the Second Millennium B.C.E.   Although warfare was not uncommon, treaties, diplomatic missions, and correspondence in Akkadian cuneiform fostered cooperative relationships between states. All were tied together by extensive networks of exchange centering on the trade in metals, and peripheral regions, such as Nubia and the Aegean Sea, were drawn into the web of commerce.

macy and correspondence between governments. The Elamites° and Hittites, among others, adapted the cuneiform system to write their own languages. In the Syrian coastal city of Ugarit° thirty cuneiform symbols were used to write consonant sounds, an early use of the alphabetic principle and a considerable advance over the hundreds of signs required in conventional cuneiform and hieroglyphic writing. Mesopotamian myths and legends and styles of art and architecture were widely imitated. Newcomers who had learned and improved on the lessons of Mesopotamian civilization often put pressure on the old core area. The small, fractious city-states of the third millennium B.C.E. had been concerned only with their immediate neighbors in southern Mesopotamia. In contrast, the larger states of the second millennium B.C.E. interacted politically, militarily, and economically in a geopolitical sphere encompassing all of western Asia.

Elamite (EE-luh-mite)   **Ugarit** (OO-guh-reet)

New Kingdom Egypt

After flourishing for nearly four hundred years (see Chapter 2), the Egyptian Middle Kingdom declined in the seventeenth century B.C.E. As high-level officials in the countryside became increasingly independent and new groups migrated into the Nile Delta, central authority broke down, and Egypt entered a period of political fragmentation and economic decline. Around 1640 B.C.E. Egypt came under foreign rule for the first time, at the hands of the Hyksos°, or "Princes of Foreign Lands."

Historians are uncertain about who the Hyksos were and how they came to power. Semitic peoples had been migrating from the Syria-Palestine region (sometimes called the Levant, present-day Syria, Lebanon, Israel, and the Palestinian territories) into the eastern Nile Delta for centuries. In the chaotic conditions of this time, other peoples may have joined them and established

Hyksos (HICK-soes)

control, first in the delta and then in the middle of the country. The Hyksos possessed military technologies that gave them an advantage over the Egyptians, such as the horse-drawn war chariot and a composite bow, made of wood and horn, that had greater range and velocity than the simple wooden bow. The process by which the Hyksos came to dominate much of Egypt may not have been far different from that by which the Kassites first settled and gained control in Babylonia. The Hyksos intermarried with Egyptians and assimilated to native ways. They used the Egyptian language and maintained Egyptian institutions and culture. Nevertheless, in contrast to the relative ease with which outsiders were assimilated in Mesopotamia, the Egyptians, with their strong ethnic identity, continued to regard the Hyksos as "foreigners."

As with the formation of the Middle Kingdom five hundred years earlier, the reunification of Egypt under a native dynasty was accomplished by princes from Thebes. After three decades of warfare, Kamose° and Ahmose° expelled the Hyksos from Egypt and inaugurated the New Kingdom, which lasted from about 1532 to 1070 B.C.E.

A century of foreign domination had shaken Egyptian pride and shattered the isolationist mindset of earlier eras. New Kingdom Egypt was an aggressive and expansionist state, extending its territorial control north into Syria-Palestine and south into Nubia and winning access to timber, gold, and copper (bronze metallurgy took hold in Egypt around 1500 B.C.E.) as well as taxes and tribute (payments from the territories it had conquered). The occupied territories provided a buffer zone, protecting Egypt from attack. In Nubia, Egypt imposed direct control and pressed the native population to adopt Egyptian language and culture. In the Syria-Palestine region, in contrast, the Egyptians stationed garrisons at strategically placed forts and supported local rulers willing to collaborate.

The New Kingdom was a period of innovation. Egypt fully participated in the diplomatic and commercial networks that linked the states of western Asia. Egyptian soldiers, administrators, diplomats, and merchants traveled widely, exposing Egypt to exotic fruits and vegetables, new musical instruments, and new technologies, such as an improved potter's wheel and weaver's loom.

At least one woman held the throne of New Kingdom Egypt. When Pharaoh Tuthmosis° II died, his queen, **Hatshepsut°,** served as regent for her young stepson and soon claimed the royal title for herself (r. 1473–1458 B.C.E.). In inscriptions she often used the male pronoun to refer to herself, and drawings and sculptures show her wearing the long, conical beard of the ruler of Egypt.

Around 1460 B.C.E. Hatshepsut sent a naval expedition down the Red Sea to the fabled land that the Egyptians called "Punt°." Historians believe that Punt may have been near the coast of eastern Sudan or Eritrea. Hatshepsut was seeking the source of myrrh°, a reddish-brown resin from the hardened sap of a local tree, which the Egyptians burned on the altars of their gods and used as an ingredient in medicines and cosmetics. She hoped to bypass the middlemen who drove up the price exorbitantly, and establish direct trade between Punt and Egypt. When the expedition returned with myrrh and various sub-Saharan luxury goods—ebony and other rare woods, ivory, cosmetics, live monkeys, panther skins—Hatshepsut celebrated the achievement in a great public display and in words and pictures on the walls of the mortuary temple she built for herself at Deir el-Bahri°. She may have used the success of this expedition to bolster her claim to the throne. After her death, in a reaction that reflected some official opposition to a woman ruler, her image was defaced and her name blotted out wherever it appeared.

Another ruler who departed from traditional ways ascended the throne as Amenhotep° IV. He soon began to refer to himself as **Akhenaten°** (r. 1353–1335 B.C.E.), meaning "beneficial to the Aten°" (the disk of the sun). Changing his name was one of the ways in which he sought to spread his belief in Aten as the supreme deity. He closed the temples of other gods, challenging the age-old supremacy of the chief god Amon° and the power and influence of the priests of Amon.

Some scholars have credited Akhenaten with the invention of monotheism—the belief in one exclusive god. It is likely, however, that Akhenaten was attempting to reassert the superiority of the king over the priests and to renew belief in the king's divinity. Worship of Aten was confined to the royal family: the people of Egypt were pressed to revere the divine ruler.

Akhenaten built a new capital at modern-day Amarna°, halfway between Memphis and Thebes (see Map 4.1). He transplanted thousands of Egyptians to construct the site and serve the ruling elite. Akhenaten and his artists created a new style that broke with the conventions of earlier art: the king, his wife Nefertiti°, and their daughters were depicted in fluid, natural poses with strangely elongated heads and limbs and swelling abdomens.

Kamose (KAH-mose)   Ahmose (AH-mose)
Tuthmosis (tuth_MOE-sis)   Hatshepsut (hat-SHEP-soot)

Punt (poont)   myrrh (murr)   Deir el-Bahri (DARE uhl–BAH-ree)
Amenhotep (ah-muhn-HOE-tep)   Akhenaten (ah-ken-AHT-n)
Aten (AHT-n)   Amon (AH-muhn)   Amarna (uh-MAHR-nuh)
Nefertiti (nef-uhr-TEE-tee)

Colossal Statues of Ramesses II at Abu Simbel   Strategically placed at a bend in the Nile River so as to face the southern frontier, this monument was an advertisement of Egyptian power. A temple was carved into the cliff behind the gigantic statues of the pharaoh. Within the temple, a corridor decorated with reliefs of military victories leads to an inner shrine containing images of the divine ruler seated alongside three of the major gods. In a modern marvel of engineering, the monument was moved to higher ground in the 1960s C.E. to protect it from rising waters when a dam was constructed upriver.   (Susan Lapides/Woodfin Camp & Associates)

Akhenaten's reforms were strongly resented by government officials, priests, and others whose privileges and wealth were linked to the traditional system. After his death the temples were reopened; Amon was reinstated as chief god; the capital returned to Thebes; and the institution of kingship was weakened to the advantage of the priests. The boy-king Tutankhamun° (r. 1333–1323 B.C.E.), one of the immediate successors of Akhenaten and famous solely because his was the only royal tomb found by archaeologists that had not been pillaged by tomb robbers, reveals both in his name (meaning "beautiful in life is Amon") and in his insignificant reign the ultimate failure of Akhenaten's revolution.

In 1323 B.C.E. the general Haremhab seized the throne and established a new dynasty, the Ramessides°. The rulers of this line renewed the policy of conquest and expansion that Akhenaten had neglected. The greatest of these monarchs, **Ramesses° II**—sometimes called Ramesses the Great—ruled for sixty-six years (r. 1290–1224 B.C.E.) and dominated his age. Ramesses looms large in the archaeological record because he undertook monumental building projects all over Egypt. Living into his nineties, he had many wives and concubines and may have fathered more than a hundred children. Since 1990 archaeologists have been excavating a network of more than a hundred corridors and chambers carved deep into a hillside in the Valley of the Kings where many sons of Ramesses were buried.

Commerce and Communication

Early in his reign Ramesses II fought a major battle against the Hittites at Kadesh in northern Syria (1285 B.C.E.). Although Egyptian scribes presented this encounter as a great victory, the lack of territorial gains suggests that it

---

Tutankhamun (tuht-uhnk-AH-muhn)   **Ramesside** (RAM-ih-side)   **Ramesses** (RAM-ih-seez)

was essentially a draw. In subsequent years Egyptian and Hittite diplomats negotiated a treaty, which was strengthened by Ramesses' marriage to a Hittite princess. At issue was control of Syria-Palestine, strategically located at a crossroads between the great powers of the Middle East and at the end of the east-west trade route across Asia. The inland cities of Syria-Palestine—such as Mari° on the upper Euphrates and Alalakh° in western Syria—were active centers of international trade. The coastal towns—particularly Ugarit and the Phoenician towns of the Lebanese seaboard—served as transshipment points for trade to and from the lands ringing the Mediterranean Sea.

In the eastern Mediterranean, northeastern Africa, and western Asia in the Late Bronze Age, any state that wanted to project its power needed metal to make tools and weapons. Commerce in metals energized the long-distance trade of the time. We have seen the Assyrian traffic in silver from Anatolia and the Egyptian passion for Nubian gold (see Chapter 3). Copper came from Anatolia and Cyprus, tin from Afghanistan and possibly the British Isles. Both ores had to be carried long distances and pass through a number of hands before reaching their final destinations.

New modes of transportation expedited communications and commerce across great distances and inhospitable landscapes. Horses arrived in western Asia around 2000 B.C.E. Domesticated by nomadic peoples in Central Asia, they were brought into Mesopotamia through the Zagros mountains and reached Egypt by 1600 B.C.E. The speed of travel and communication made possible by horses contributed to the creation of large states and empires. Soldiers and government agents could cover great distances quickly, and swift, maneuverable horse-drawn chariots became the premier instrument of war. The team of driver and archer could ride forward and unleash a volley of arrows or trample terrified foot soldiers.

Sometime after 1500 B.C.E in western Asia, but not for another thousand years in Egypt, people began to make common use of camels, though the animal may have been domesticated a millennium earlier in southern Arabia. Thanks to their strength and ability to go long distances without water, camels were able to travel across barren terrain. Their physical qualities eventually led to the emergence of a new kind of desert nomad and the creation of cross-desert trade routes (see Chapter 8).

THE AEGEAN WORLD, 2000–1100 B.C.E.

In this era of far-flung trade and communication, the influence of Mesopotamia and Egypt was felt as far away as the Aegean Sea, a gulf of the eastern Mediterranean. The emergence of the Minoan° civilization on the island of Crete and the Mycenaean° civilization of Greece is another manifestation of the fertilizing influence of older centers on outlying lands and peoples, who then struck out on their own unique paths of cultural evolution

The landscape of southern Greece and the Aegean islands is mostly rocky and arid, with small plains lying between ranges of hills. The limited arable land is suitable for grains, grapevines, and olive trees. Flocks of sheep and goats graze the slopes. Sharply indented coastlines, natural harbors, and small islands within sight of one another made the sea the fastest and least costly mode of travel and transport. With few deposits of metals and little timber, Aegean peoples had to import these commodities, as well as food, from abroad. As a result, the rise, success, and eventual fall of the Minoan and Mycenaean societies were closely tied to their commercial and political relations with other peoples in the region.

Minoan Crete

By 2000 B.C.E. the island of Crete (see Map 4.2) housed the first European civilization to have complex political and social structures and advanced technologies like those found in western Asia and northeastern Africa. The **Minoan** civilization had centralized government, monumental building, bronze metallurgy, writing, and recordkeeping. Archaeologists named this civilization after Greek legends about King Minos, who was said to have ruled a vast naval empire, including the southern Greek mainland, and to have kept the monstrous Minotaur° (half-man, half-bull) beneath his palace in a mazelike labyrinth built by the ingenious inventor Daedalus°. Thus later Greeks recollected a time when Crete was home to many ships and skilled craftsmen.

The ethnicity of the Minoans is uncertain, and their writing has not been deciphered. But their sprawling

---

Mari (MAH-ree)   **Alalakh** (UH-luh-luhk)

Minoan (mih-NO-uhn)   **Mycenaean** (my-suh-NEE-uhn)
Minotaur (MIN-uh-tor)   **Daedalus** (DED-ih-luhs)

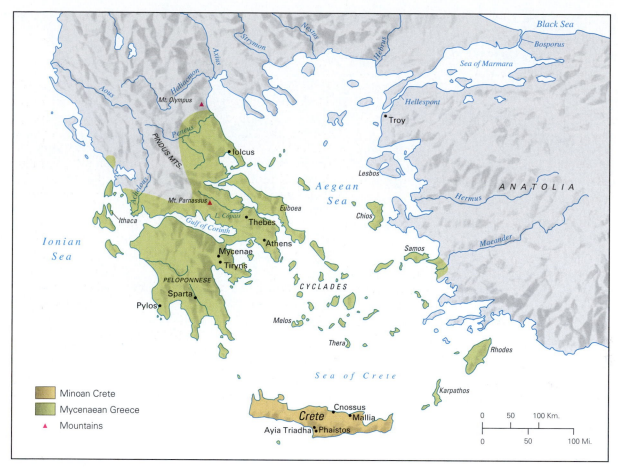

Map 4.2   Minoan and Mycenaean Civilizations of the Aegean   The earliest complex civilizations in Europe arose in the Aegean Sea. The Minoan civilization on the island of Crete evolved in the later third millennium B.C.E. and had a major cultural influence on the Mycenaean Greeks. Palaces decorated with fresco paintings, a centrally controlled economy, and the use of a system of writing for recordkeeping are some of the most conspicuous features of these societies.

palace complexes at Cnossus°, Phaistos°, and Mallia° and the distribution of Cretan pottery and other artifacts around the Mediterranean and Middle East testify to widespread trading connections. Egyptian, Syrian, and Mesopotamian influences can be seen in the design of the Minoan palaces, centralized government, and system of writing. The absence of identifiable representations of Cretan rulers, however, contrasts sharply with the grandiose depictions of kings in the Middle East and suggests a different conception of authority. Also noteworthy is the absence of fortifications at the palace sites and the presence of high-quality indoor plumbing.

Statuettes of women with elaborate headdresses and serpents coiling around their limbs may represent fertility goddesses. Colorful frescoes (paintings done on a moist plaster surface) on the walls of Cretan palaces portray groups of women in frilly, layered skirts engaged in conversation or watching rituals or entertainment. We do not know whether pictures of young acrobats vaulting over the horns and back of an onrushing bull show a religious activity or mere sport. Scenes of servants carrying jars and fishermen throwing nets and hooks from their boats suggest a joyful attitude toward work, but this portrayal may say more about the tastes of the elite than about the reality of daily toil. The stylized depictions of plants and animals on Minoan vases—plants with swaying leaves and playful octopuses whose tentacles wind around the surface of the vase—seem to reflect a delight in the beauty and order of the natural world.

Cnossus (NOSS-suhs)   **Phaistos** (FIE-stuhs)   **Mallia** (mahl-YAH)

Fresco from the Aegean Island of Thera, ca. 1650 B.C.E. This picture, originally painted on wet plaster, depicts the arrival of a fleet in a harbor as people watch from the walls of the town. The Minoan civilization of Crete was famous in later legend for its naval power. The fresco reveals the appearance and design of ships in the Bronze Age Aegean. In the seventeenth century B.C.E., the island of Thera was devastated by a massive volcanic explosion, thought by many to be the origin of the myth of Atlantis sinking beneath the sea. (Archaeological Receipts Fund, Athens)

All the Cretan palaces except Cnossus, along with the houses of the elite and peasants in the countryside, were deliberately destroyed around 1450 B.C.E. Because Mycenaean Greeks took over at Cnossus, most historians regard them as the likely culprits.

Mycenaean Greece

Most historians believe that speakers of an Indo-European language ancestral to Greek migrated into the Greek peninsula around 2000 B.C.E., although some argue for earlier and later dates. Through intermarriage, blending of languages, and melding of cultural practices, the indigenous population and the newcomers created the first Greek culture. For centuries this society remained simple and static. Farmers and shepherds lived in Stone Age conditions, wringing a bare living from the land. Then,

sometime around 1600 B.C.E., life changed relatively suddenly.

More than a century ago a German businessman, Heinrich Schliemann°, set out to prove that the *Iliad* and the *Odyssey* were true. These epics attributed to the poet Homer, who probably lived shortly before 700 B.C.E., spoke of Agamemnon°, the king of **Mycenae**° in southern Greece. In 1876 Schliemann stunned the scholarly world by discovering at Mycenae a circle of graves at the base of deep, rectangular shafts. These **shaft graves** contained the bodies of men, women, and children and were filled with gold jewelry and ornaments, weapons, and utensils. Clearly, some people in this society had acquired wealth, authority, and the capacity to mobilize human labor. Subsequent excavation uncovered a large

Schliemann (SHLEE-muhn) **Agamemnon** (ag-uh-MEM-non)
Mycenae (my-SEE-nee)

palace complex, massive walls, more shaft graves, and other evidence of a rich and technologically advanced civilization that lasted from around 1600 to 1150 B.C.E.

How can the sudden rise of Mycenae and other centers in mainland Greece be explained? Despite legends about the power of King Minos of Crete, there is no archaeological evidence of Cretan political control of the Greek mainland. But Crete exerted a powerful cultural influence. The Mycenaeans borrowed the Minoan idea of the palace, centralized economy, and administrative bureaucracy, as well as the Minoan writing system. They adopted Minoan styles and techniques of architecture, pottery making, and fresco and vase painting. This explains where the Mycenaean Greeks got their technology. But how did they suddenly accumulate power and wealth? Most historians look to the profits from trade and piracy and perhaps also to the pay and booty brought back by mercenaries (soldiers who served for pay in foreign lands).

The first advanced civilization in Greece is called "Mycenaean" largely because Mycenae was the first site excavated. Excavations at other centers have revealed that Mycenae exemplifies the common pattern of these citadels: built at a commanding location on a hilltop and surrounded by high, thick fortification walls made of stones so large that later Greeks believed that the giant, one-eyed Cyclopes° of legend had lifted them into place. The fortified enclosure provided a place of refuge for the entire community in time of danger and contained the palace and administrative complex. The large central hall with an open hearth and columned porch was surrounded by courtyards, living quarters for the royal family and their retainers, and offices, storerooms, and workshops. The palace walls were covered with brightly painted frescoes depicting scenes of war, the hunt, and daily life, as well as decorative motifs from nature.

Nearby lay the tombs of the rulers and leading families: shaft graves at first; later, grand beehive-shaped structures made of stone and covered with a mound of earth. Large houses, probably belonging to the aristocracy, lay just outside the walls. The peasants lived on the lower slopes and in the plain below, close to the land they worked.

Additional information about Mycenaean life is provided by over four thousand baked clay tablets written in a script now called **Linear B.** Like its predecessor, the undeciphered Minoan script called Linear A, Linear B uses pictorial signs to represent syllables, but it is recognizably an early form of Greek. The extensive palace bureaucracy kept track of people, animals, and objects in

---

Cyclopes (SIGH-kloe-pees)

Lion Gate at Mycenae View over the massive fortification wall encircling the citadel. Above the entrance a large stone depicts a Minoan-style column with lions on either side, thought to signify royal power. Just inside the gate on the right is one of the shaft grave circles containing the treasure-filled tombs of the elite. (Dimitrios Harissiadis/Benaki Museum)

exhaustive detail and exercised a high degree of control over the economy of the kingdom. The tablets list everything from the number of chariot wheels in palace storerooms, the rations paid to textile workers, and the gifts dedicated to various gods, to the ships stationed along the coasts.

The government organized and coordinated grain production and controlled the wool industry from raw material to finished product. Scribes kept track of the flocks in the field, the sheared wool, the allocation of raw wool to spinners and weavers, and the production, storage, and distribution of cloth articles.

The tablets say almost nothing about individual people—not even the name of a single Mycenaean king—and very little about the political and legal systems, social structures, gender relations, and religious beliefs. They tell nothing about particular historical events and relations with other Mycenaean centers or peoples overseas.

The evidence for a broad political organization of Greece in this period is contradictory. In Homer's *Iliad*, Agamemnon, the king of Mycenae, leads a great expedition of Greeks from different regions against the city of Troy in northwest Anatolia. To this can be added the cultural uniformity of all the Mycenaean centers: a remarkable similarity in the shapes, decorative styles, and production techniques of buildings, tombs, utensils, tools, clothing, and works of art. Some scholars argue that such cultural uniformity could have occurred only in a context of political unity. The plot of the *Iliad*, however, revolves around the difficulties Agamemnon has in asserting control over other Greek leaders. Moreover, the archaeological remains and the Linear B tablets give strong indications of independent centers of power at Mycenae, Pylos°, and elsewhere. Cultural uniformity might simply have resulted from extensive contacts and commerce between the various Greek kingdoms.

Long-distance contact and trade were made possible by the seafaring skill of Minoans and Mycenaeans. Commercial vessels depended primarily on wind and sail. In general, ancient sailors preferred to sail in daylight hours and keep the land in sight. Their light, wooden vessels had little storage area and decking, so the crew had to go ashore to eat and sleep every night. With their low keels the ships could run up onto the beach.

Cretan and Greek pottery and crafted goods are found not only in the Aegean but also in other parts of the Mediterranean and Middle East. At certain sites the quantity and range of artifacts suggest settlements of Aegean peoples. The oldest artifacts are Minoan; then Minoan and Mycenaean objects are found side by side; and eventually Greek wares replace Cretan goods altogether. Such evidence indicates that Cretan merchants pioneered trade routes and established trading posts and then admitted Mycenaean traders, who eventually supplanted them in the fifteenth century B.C.E.

What commodities formed the basis of this widespread commercial activity? The numerous Aegean pots found throughout the Mediterranean and Middle East must once have contained such products as wine and olive oil. Other possible exports include weapons and other crafted goods, as well as slaves and mercenary soldiers. Minoan and Mycenaean sailors also may have made tidy profits by transporting the trade goods of other peoples.

As for imports, amber (a hard, translucent, yellowish-brown fossil resin used for jewelry) from northern Europe and ivory carved in Syria have been discovered at Aegean sites, and the large population of southwest Greece and other regions probably relied on imports of grain. Above all, the Aegean lands needed metals, both the gold prized by rulers and the copper and tin needed to make bronze. A number of sunken ships carrying copper ingots have been found on the floor of the Mediterranean. Scholars believe that these ships were transporting metals from Cyprus to the Aegean (see Map 4.2). As in early China, the elite classes were practically the only people who owned metal goods, which may have been symbols of their superior status. The bronze tripods piled up in the storerooms of the Greek heroes in Homer's epic poems bring to mind the bronze vessels buried in Shang tombs.

In this era, trade and piracy were closely linked. Mycenaeans were tough, warlike, and acquisitive. They traded with those who were strong and took from those who were weak. This may have led to conflict with the Hittite kings of Anatolia in the fourteenth and thirteenth centuries B.C.E. Documents found in the archives at Hattusha, the Hittite capital, refer to the king and land of Ahhijawa°, most likely a Hittite rendering of *Achaeans*°, the term used most frequently by Homer for the Greeks. The documents indicate that relations were sometimes friendly, sometimes strained, and that the people of Ahhijawa were aggressive and tried to take advantage of Hittite preoccupation or weakness. The *Iliad*, Homer's tale of the Achaeans' ten-year siege and eventual destruction of Troy, a city on the fringes of Hittite territory that controlled the sea route between the Mediterranean and Black Seas, should be seen against this backdrop of Mycenaean belligerence and opportunism. Archaeology has confirmed a destruction at Troy around 1200 B.C.E.

The Fall of Late Bronze Age Civilizations

Hittite difficulties with Ahhijawa and the Greek attack on Troy foreshadowed the troubles that culminated in the destruction of many of the old centers of the Middle East and Mediterranean around 1200 B.C.E. In this period, for reasons that historians do not completely understand, large numbers of people were on the move. As migrants swarmed into one region, they displaced other peoples, who then joined the tide of refugees.

Around 1200 B.C.E. unidentified invaders destroyed Hattusha, and the Hittite kingdom in Anatolia came crashing down. The tide of destruction moved south into Syria, and the great coastal city of Ugarit was swept away.

Pylos (PIE-lohs)

Ahhijawa (uh-key-YAW-wuh)   **Achaeans** (uh-KEY-uhns)

Egypt managed to beat back two attacks. Around 1220 B.C.E., Merneptah°, the son and successor of Ramesses II, repulsed an assault on the Nile Delta. His official account identified the attackers as "Libyans and Northerners coming from all lands." About thirty years later Ramesses III checked a major invasion of Palestine by the "Sea Peoples." Although he claimed to have won a great victory, the Philistines° were able to occupy the coast of Palestine. Egypt soon surrendered all its territory in Syria-Palestine and lost contact with the rest of western Asia. The Egyptians also lost their foothold in Nubia, opening the way for the emergence of the native kingdom centered on Napata (see Chapter 3).

Among the invaders listed in the Egyptian inscriptions are the Ekwesh°, who could be Achaeans—that is, Greeks. In this time of troubles it is easy to imagine opportunistic Mycenaeans taking a prominent role. Whether or not the Mycenaeans participated in the destructions elsewhere, their own centers collapsed in the first half of the twelfth century B.C.E. The rulers had seen trouble coming; at some sites they began to build more extensive fortifications and took steps to guarantee the water supply of the citadels. But their efforts were in vain, and nearly all the palaces were destroyed. The Linear B tablets survive only because they were baked hard in the fires that consumed the palaces.

Scholars are not in agreement about how these events came about. The archaeological record contains no trace of foreign invaders. An attractive explanation combines external and internal factors, since it is likely to be more than coincidence that the collapse of Mycenaean civilization occurred at roughly the same time as the fall of other great civilizations in the region. Since the Mycenaean ruling class depended on the import of vital commodities and the profits from trade, the destruction of major trading partners and disruption of trade routes would have weakened their position. Competition for limited resources may have led to internal unrest and, ultimately, political collapse.

The end of Mycenaean civilization illustrates the interdependence of the major centers of the Late Bronze Age. It also serves as a case study of the consequences of political and economic collapse. The destruction of the palaces ended the domination of the ruling class. The massive administrative apparatus revealed in the Linear B tablets disappeared, and the technique of writing was forgotten, since it had been known only to a few palace officials and was no longer useful. Archaeological studies indicate the depopulation of some regions of Greece and an inflow of people to other regions that had escaped destruction. The Greek language persisted, and a thousand years later people were still worshiping gods mentioned in the Linear B tablets. People also continued to make the vessels and implements that they were familiar with, although there was a marked decline in artistic and technical skill in the new, much poorer society. The cultural uniformity of the Mycenaean Age gave way to regional variations in shapes, styles, and techniques, reflecting increased isolation of different parts of Greece.

Thus perished the cosmopolitan world of the Late Bronze Age in the Mediterranean and Middle East. Societies that had long prospered through complex links of trade, diplomacy, and shared technologies now collapsed in the face of external violence and internal weakness, and the peoples of the region entered a centuries-long "Dark Age" of poverty, isolation, and loss of knowledge.

THE ASSYRIAN EMPIRE, 911–612 B.C.E.

A number of new centers emerged in western Asia and the eastern Mediterranean in the centuries after 1000 B.C.E. The chief force for change was the powerful and aggressive **Neo-Assyrian Empire** (911–612 B.C.E.). Although historians sometimes apply the term *empire* to earlier regional powers, the Assyrians of this era were the first to rule over far-flung lands and diverse peoples (see Map 4.3).

The Assyrian homeland in northern Mesopotamia differs in essential respects from the flat expanse of Sumer and Akkad to the south. It is hillier, has a more temperate climate and greater rainfall, and is more exposed to raiders from the mountains to the east and north and from the arid plain to the west. Peasant farmers, accustomed to defending themselves against marauders, provided the foot-soldiers for the revival of Assyrian power in the ninth century B.C.E. The rulers of the Neo-Assyrian Empire struck out in a ceaseless series of campaigns: westward across the steppe and desert as far as the Mediterranean, north into mountainous Urartu° (modern Armenia), east across the Zagros range onto the Iranian Plateau, and south along the Tigris River to Babylonia.

These campaigns largely followed the most important long-distance trade routes in western Asia and

---

Merneptah (mehr-NEH-ptuh)   Philistine (FIH-luh-steen)
Ekwesh (ECK-wesh)

Urartu (ur-RAHR-too)

Map 4.3 The Assyrian Empire From the tenth to the seventh century B.C.E. the Assyrians of northern Mesopotamia created the largest empire the world had yet seen, extending from the Iranian Plateau to the eastern shore of the Mediterranean and containing a diverse array of peoples.

provided immediate booty and the prospect of tribute and taxes. They also secured access to vital resources such as iron and silver and brought the Assyrians control of international commerce. As noted earlier in this chapter, Assyria already had a long tradition of commercial and political interests in Syria and Anatolia. What started out as an aggressive program of self-defense and reestablishment of old claims soon became far more ambitious. Driven by pride, greed, and religious conviction, the Assyrians defeated all the great kingdoms of the day—Elam (southwest Iran), Urartu, Babylon, and Egypt. At its peak their empire stretched from Anatolia, Syria-Palestine, and Egypt in the west, across Armenia and Mesopotamia, as far as western Iran. The Assyrians created a new kind of empire, larger in extent than anything seen before and dedicated to the enrichment of the imperial center at the expense of the subjugated periphery.

God and King

The king was literally and symbolically the center of the Assyrian universe. All the land belonged to him, and all the people, even the highest-ranking officials, were his servants. Assyrians believed that the gods chose the king to rule as their earthly representative. Normally the king chose one of his sons to be his successor, and his choice was confirmed by divine oracles and the Assyrian elite. In the revered ancient city of Ashur the high priest anointed the new king by sprinkling his head with oil and gave him the insignia of kingship: a crown and scepter. The kings were buried in Ashur.

Every day messengers and spies brought the king information from every corner of the empire. He made decisions, appointed officials, and heard complaints. He dictated his correspondence to an army of scribes and received and entertained foreign envoys and high-ranking government figures. He was the military leader, responsible for planning campaigns, and he often was away from the capital commanding operations in the field.

Among the king's chief responsibilities was supervision of the state religion. He devoted much of his time to elaborate public and private rituals and to overseeing the upkeep of the temples. He made no decisions of state without consulting the gods through elaborate rituals. All state actions were carried out in the name of Ashur, the chief god. Military victories were cited as proof of Ashur's superiority over the gods of the conquered peoples.

Relentless government propaganda secured popular support for military campaigns that mostly benefited the king and the nobility. Royal inscriptions posted throughout the empire catalogued recent military victories, extolled the charisma and relentless will of the king, and promised ruthless punishments to anyone who resisted him. Art, too, served the Assyrian state. Relief sculptures depicting hunts, battles, sieges, executions, and deportations covered the walls of the royal palaces at Kalhu° and Nineveh°. Looming over most scenes was the king, larger than anyone else, muscular and fierce, with the appearance of a god. Few visitors to the Assyrian court could fail to be awed—and intimidated.

Conquest and Control

The Assyrians' unprecedented conquests were made possible by their superior military organization and technology. Early Assyrian armies consisted of men who served in return for grants of land, and peasants and slaves whose service was contributed by large landowners. Later, King Tig-

---

Kalhu (KAL-oo)   **Nineveh** (NIN-uh-vuh)

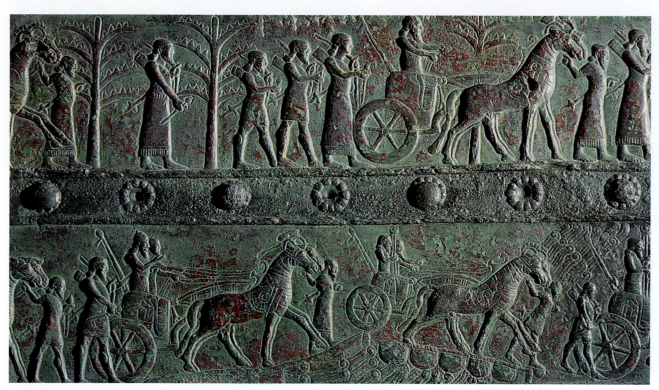

Section of Balawat Gates Bronze bands with images of military campaigns and court life were affixed to the cedar-wood gates of a palace built by the Assyrian king Shalmaneser III (r. 858–824 B.C.E.). (British Museum/Michael Holford)

lathpileser° (r. 744–727 B.C.E.) created a core army of professional soldiers made up of Assyrians and the most formidable subject peoples. At its peak the Assyrian state could mobilize a half-million troops, including light-armed bowmen and slingers who launched stone projectiles, armored spearmen, cavalry equipped with bows or spears, and four-man chariots.

Iron weapons gave Assyrian soldiers an advantage over many opponents, and cavalry provided unprecedented speed and mobility. Assyrian engineers developed machinery and tactics for besieging fortified towns. They dug tunnels under the walls, built mobile towers for their archers, and applied battering rams to weak points. The Assyrians destroyed some of the best-fortified cities of the Middle East—Babylon, Thebes in Egypt, Tyre in Phoenicia, and Susa in Elam (see Map 4.3). Couriers and signal fires provided long-distance communication, while a network of spies gathered intelligence.

The Assyrians used terror tactics to discourage resistance and rebellion, inflicting swift and harsh retribution and publicizing their brutality: civilians were thrown into fires, prisoners were skinned alive, and the severed heads of defeated rulers hung on city walls. **Mass deportation**—forcibly uprooting entire communities and resettling them elsewhere—broke the spirit of rebellious peoples. This tactic had a long history in the ancient Middle East—in Sumer, Babylon, Urartu, Egypt, and the Hittite Empire—but the Neo-Assyrian monarchs used it on an unprecedented scale. Surviving documents record the relocation of over 1 million people, and historians estimate that the true figure exceeds 4 million. Deportation also shifted human resources from the periphery to the center, where the deportees worked on royal and noble estates, opened new lands for agriculture, and built new palaces and cities. Deportees who were craftsmen and soldiers could be assigned to the Assyrian army.

To control their empire the Assyrians had to contend with vast distances, diverse landscapes, and an array of peoples with different languages, customs, religions, and political organization. The Assyrians never found a single, enduring method of governing an empire that included nomadic and sedentary kinship groups, temple-states, city-states, and kingdoms. Control tended to be tight and effective at the center and in lands closest to the core area, and less so farther away. The Assyrian kings waged many campaigns to reimpose control on territories subdued in previous wars.

Tiglathpileser (TIG-lath-pih-LEE-zuhr)

Wall Relief from the Palace of Sennacherib at Nineveh   Against a backdrop of wooded hills representing the landscape of Assyria, workers are hauling a huge stone sculpture from the riverbank to the palace under the watchful eyes of officials and soldiers. They accomplish this task with simple equipment—a lever, a sledge, and thick ropes—and a lot of human muscle power.   (Courtesy of the Trustees of the British Museum)

Assyrian provincial officials oversaw the payment of tribute and taxes, maintained law and order, raised troops, undertook public works, and provisioned armies and administrators that were passing through their territory. Provincial governors were subject to frequent inspections by royal overseers.

The elite class was bound to the monarch by oaths of obedience, fear of punishment, and the expectation of rewards, such as land grants or shares of booty and taxes. Skilled professionals—priests, diviners, scribes, doctors, and artisans—were similarly bound.

The Assyrians ruthlessly exploited the wealth and resources of their subjects. Military campaigns and administration had to be funded by plunder and tribute. Wealth from the periphery was funneled to the center, where the king and nobility grew rich. Proud kings used their riches to expand the ancestral capital and religious center at Ashur and to build magnificent new royal cities encircled by high walls and containing ornate palaces and temples. Dur Sharrukin°, the "Fortress of Sargon,"

Dur Sharrukin (DOOR SHAH-roo-keen)

was completed in a mere ten years, thanks to a massive labor force composed of prisoners of war and Assyrian citizens who owed periodic service to the state.

Nevertheless, the Assyrian Empire was not simply parasitic. There is some evidence of royal investment in provincial infrastructure. The cities and merchant classes thrived on expanded long-distance commerce, and some subject populations were surprisingly loyal to their Assyrian rulers.

Assyrian Society and Culture

Surviving sources shed light on the deeds of kings, victories of armies, and workings of government. A few things are known about the lives and activities of the millions of Assyrian subjects. In the core area people belonged to the same three classes that had existed in Hammurabi's Babylon a millennium before (see Chapter 2): (1) free, landowning citizens, (2) farmers and artisans attached to the estates of the king or other rich landholders, and (3) slaves. Slaves—debtors and prisoners of war—had legal rights and, if sufficiently talented, could rise to positions of influence.

The government normally did not distinguish between native Assyrians and the increasingly large number of immigrants and deportees residing in the Assyrian homeland. All were referred to as "human beings," entitled to the same legal protections and liable for the same labor and military service. Over time the inflow of outsiders changed the ethnic makeup of the core area.

The vast majority of subjects worked on the land. The agricultural surpluses they produced allowed substantial numbers of people—the standing army, government officials, religious experts, merchants, artisans, and all manner of professionals in the towns and cities—to engage in specialized activities.

Individual artisans and small workshops in the towns manufactured pottery, tools, and clothing, and most trade took place at the local level. The state fostered long-distance trade, since imported luxury goods—metals, fine textiles, dyes, gems, and ivory—brought in substantial customs revenues and found their way to the royal family and elite classes. Silver was the basic medium of exchange, weighed out for each transaction in a time before the invention of coins.

Building on the achievements of their Mesopotamian ancestors, Assyrian scholars created and preserved lists of plant and animal names, geographic terms, and astronomical occurrences, and made original contributions in mathematics and astronomy. Their assumption that gods or demons caused disease obstructed the investigation of natural causes, but in addition to exorcists trained to expel demons, another type of physician experimented with medicines and surgical treatments to relieve symptoms.

Some Assyrian temples may have had libraries. When archaeologists excavated the palace of Ashurbanipal° (r. 668–627 B.C.E.), one of the last Assyrian kings, at Nineveh, they discovered more than twenty-five thousand tablets or fragments of tablets. The **Library of Ashurbanipal** contained official documents as well as literary and scientific texts. Some were originals that had been brought to the capital; others were copies made at the king's request. Ashurbanipal was an avid collector of the literary and scientific heritage of Mesopotamia, and the "House of Knowledge" referred to in some of the documents may have been an academy that attracted learned men to the imperial center. Much of what we know about Mesopotamian art, literature, and science and earlier Mesopotamian history comes from discoveries at Assyrian sites.

Ashurbanipal (ah-shur-BAH-nee-pahl)

ISRAEL, 2000–500 B.C.E.

On the western edge of the Assyrian Empire lived a people who probably seemed of no great significance to the masters of western Asia but were destined to play an important role in world history. The history of ancient Israel is marked by two grand and interconnected dramas that played out from around 2000 to 500 B.C.E. First, a loose collection of nomadic kinship groups engaged in herding and caravan traffic became a sedentary, agricultural people, developed complex political and social institutions, and became integrated into the commercial and diplomatic networks of the Middle East. Second, these people transformed the austere cult of a desert god into the concept of a single, all-powerful, and all-knowing deity, in the process creating the ethical and intellectual traditions that underlie the beliefs and values of Judaism and Christianity.

The land and the people at the heart of this story have gone by various names: Canaan, Israel, Palestine; Hebrews, Israelites, Jews. For the sake of consistency, the people are referred to here as *Israelites*, the land they occupied in antiquity as **Israel.**

Israel is a crossroads, linking Anatolia, Egypt, Arabia, and Mesopotamia (see Map 4.4). Its location has given Israel an importance in history out of all proportion to its size. Its natural resources are few. The Negev Desert and the vast wasteland of the Sinai° lie to the south. The Mediterranean coastal plain was usually in the hands of others, particularly the Philistines, throughout much of this period. At the center are the rock-strewn hills of the Shephelah°. Galilee to the north, with its sea of the same name, was a relatively fertile land of grassy hills and small plains. The narrow ribbon of the Jordan River runs down the eastern side of the region into the Dead Sea, so named because its high salt content is toxic to life.

Origins, Exodus, and Settlement

Information about ancient Israel comes partly from archaeological excavations and references in contemporary documents such as the royal annals of Egypt and Assyria. However, the fundamental source is the collection of writings preserved in the **Hebrew Bible** (called the Old Testament by Christians). The Hebrew Bible is a compilation of several collections of materials that originated with different groups, employed distinctive vocabularies, and advocated particular interpretations of past events.

Sinai (SIE-nie) **Shephelah** (sheh-FEH-luh)

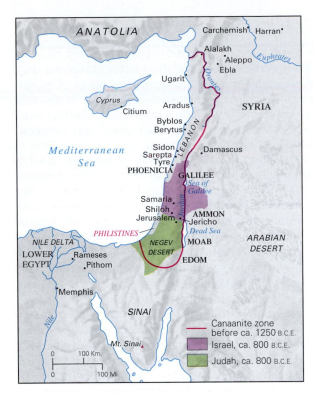

Map 4.4   Phoenicia and Israel   The lands along the eastern shore of the Mediterranean Sea—sometimes called the Levant or Syria-Palestine—have always been a crossroads, traversed by migrants, nomads, merchants, and armies moving between Egypt, Arabia, Mesopotamia, and Anatolia.

Traditions about the Israelites' early days were long transmitted orally. Not until the tenth century B.C.E. were they written down in a script borrowed from the Phoenicians. The text that we have today dates from the fifth century B.C.E., with a few later additions, and reflects the point of view of the priests who controlled the Temple in Jerusalem. Historians disagree about how accurately this document represents Israelite history. In the absence of other written sources, however, it provides a foundation to be used critically and modified in light of archaeological discoveries.

The Hebrew language of the Bible reflects the speech of the Israelites until about 500 B.C.E. It is a Semitic language, most closely related to Phoenician and Aramaic (which later supplanted Hebrew in Israel), more distantly related to Arabic and the Akkadian language of the Assyrians. This linguistic affinity probably parallels the Israelites' ethnic relationship to the neighboring peoples.

In some respects the history of ancient Israel is unique, but it also reflects a familiar pattern in the an-

cient Middle East, a story of nomadic pastoralists who occupied marginal land between the inhospitable desert and settled agricultural areas. Early on, these nomads raided the farms and villages of settled peoples, but eventually they settled down to an agricultural way of life and later developed a unified state.

The Hebrew Bible tells the story of the family of Abraham. Born in the city of Ur in southern Mesopotamia, Abraham rejected the traditional idol worship of his homeland and migrated with his family and livestock across the Syrian desert. Eventually he arrived in the land of Israel, which, according to the biblical account, had been promised to him and his descendants as part of a "covenant," or pact, with the Israelite god, Yahweh.

These "recollections" of the journey of Abraham (who, if he was a real person, probably lived in the twentieth century B.C.E.) may compress the experiences of generations of pastoralists who migrated from the grazing lands between the upper reaches of the Tigris and Euphrates Rivers to the Mediterranean coastal plain. Abraham, his family, and his companions were following the usual pattern in this part of the world. They camped by a permanent water source in the dry season, then drove herds of domesticated animals (sheep, cattle, donkeys) to a well-established sequence of grazing areas during the rest of the year. The animals provided them with milk, cheese, meat, and cloth.

The early Israelites and the settled peoples of the region were suspicious of one another. This friction between nomadic herders and settled farmers, as well as the Israelites' view of their ancestors as having been nomads, comes through in the story of the innocent shepherd Abel, who was killed by his farmer brother Cain, and in the story of Sodom° and Gomorrah°, two cities that Yahweh destroyed because of their wickedness.

Abraham's son Isaac and then his grandson Jacob became the leaders of this wandering group of herders. In the next generation the squabbling sons of Jacob's several wives sold their brother Joseph as a slave to passing merchants heading for Egypt. According to the biblical account, through luck and ability Joseph became a high official at Pharaoh's court. Thus he was in a position to help his people when drought struck Israel and forced the Israelites to migrate to Egypt. The sophisticated Egyptians feared and looked down on these rough herders and eventually reduced the Israelites to slaves, putting them to work on the grand building projects of the pharaoh.

Sodom (SOE-duhm)   **Gomorrah** (guh-MORE-uh)

That is the version of events given in the Hebrew Bible. Several points need to be made about it. First, the biblical account glosses over the period from 1700 to 1500 B.C.E., when Egypt was dominated by the Hyksos. Since the Hyksos are thought to have been Semitic groups that infiltrated the Nile Delta from the northeast, the Israelite migration to Egypt and later enslavement could have been connected to the Hyksos' rise and fall. Second, although the surviving Egyptian sources do not refer to Israelite slaves, they do complain about Apiru°, a derogatory term applied to caravan drivers, outcasts, bandits, and other marginal groups. The word seems to designate a class of people rather than a particular ethnic group, but some scholars believe there may be a connection between the similar-sounding terms *Apiru* and *Hebrew*. Third, the period of alleged Israelite slavery coincided with the era of ambitious building programs launched by several New Kingdom pharaohs. However, there is little archaeological evidence of an Israelite presence in Egypt.

According to the Hebrew Bible, the Israelites were led out of captivity by Moses, an Israelite with connections to the Egyptian royal family. The narrative of their departure, the Exodus, is overlaid with folktale motifs, including the ten plagues that Yahweh inflicted on Egypt to persuade the pharaoh to release the Israelites and the miraculous parting of the waters of the Red Sea that enabled the refugees to escape. It is possible that oral tradition may have preserved memories of a real emigration from Egypt followed by years of wandering in the wilderness of Sinai.

During their reported forty years in the desert, the Israelites became devoted to a stern and warlike god. According to the Hebrew Bible, Yahweh made a covenant with the Israelites: they would be his "Chosen People" if they promised to worship him exclusively. This pact was confirmed by tablets that Moses brought down from the top of Mount Sinai. Written on the tablets were the Ten Commandments, which set out the basic tenets of Jewish belief and practice. The Commandments prohibited murder, adultery, theft, lying, and envy, and demanded respect for parents and rest from work on the Sabbath, the seventh day of the week.

The biblical account tells how Joshua, Moses's successor, led the Israelites from the east side of the Jordan River into the land of Canaan° (modern Israel and the Palestinian territories). They attacked and destroyed Jericho° and other Canaanite° cities. Archaeological evidence confirms the destruction of some Canaanite towns between 1250 and 1200 B.C.E., though not precisely the towns mentioned in the biblical account. Shortly thereafter, lowland sites were resettled and new sites were established in the hills, thanks to the development of cisterns carved into nonporous rock to hold rainwater and the construction of leveled terraces on the slopes to expand the cultivable area. The material culture of the new settlers was cruder but continued Canaanite patterns.

Most scholars doubt that Canaan was conquered by a unified Israelite army. In a time of widespread disruption, movements of peoples, and decline and destruction of cities throughout this region, it is more likely that Israelite migrants took advantage of the disorder and were joined by other loosely organized groups and even refugees from the Canaanite cities.

In a pattern common throughout history, the new coalition of peoples invented a common ancestry. The "Children of Israel," as they called themselves, were divided into twelve tribes supposedly descended from the sons of Jacob and Joseph. Each tribe installed itself in a different part of the country and was led by one or more chiefs. Such leaders usually had limited power and were primarily responsible for mediating disputes and seeing to the welfare and protection of the group. Certain charismatic figures, famed for their daring in war or genius in arbitration, were called "Judges" and enjoyed a special standing that transcended tribal boundaries. The tribes also shared access to a shrine in the hill country at Shiloh°, which housed the Ark of the Covenant, a sacred chest containing the tablets that Yahweh had given Moses.

Rise of the Monarchy

The time of troubles that struck the eastern Mediterranean around 1200 B.C.E. also brought the Philistines to Israel. Possibly related to the pre-Greek population of the Aegean Sea region and likely participants in the Sea People's attack on Egypt, the Philistines occupied the coastal plain of Israel and came into frequent conflict with the Israelites. Their wars were memorialized in Bible stories about the long-haired strongman Samson, who toppled a Philistine temple, and the shepherd boy David, whose slingshot felled the towering warrior Goliath.

A religious leader named Samuel recognized the need for a stronger central authority to lead the Israelites against the Philistine city-states and anointed Saul as the first king of Israel around 1020 B.C.E. When Saul perished in battle, the throne passed to David (r. ca. 1000–960 B.C.E.).

Apiru (uh-PEE-roo) **Canaan** (KAY-nuhn) **Jericho** (JEH-rih-koe)
Canaanite (KAY-nuh-nite)

Shiloh (SHIE-loe)

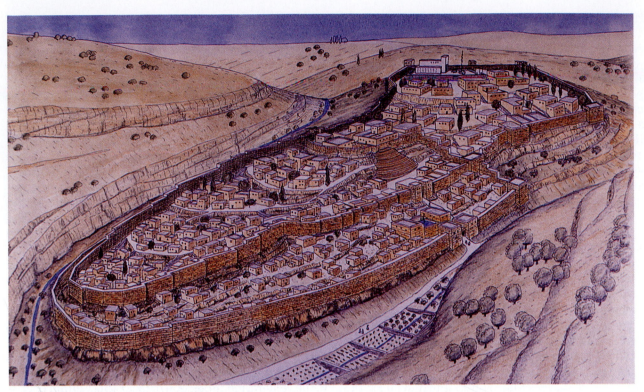

Artist's Rendering of Solomon's Jerusalem   Strategically located in the middle of lands occupied by the Israelite tribes and on a high plateau overlooking the central hills and the Judaean desert, Jerusalem was captured around 1000 B.C.E. by King David, who made it his capital (the City of David is at left, the citadel and palace complex at center). The next king, Solomon, built the First Temple to serve as the center of worship of the Israelite god, Yahweh. Solomon's Temple (at upper right) was destroyed during the Neo-Babylonian sack of the city in 587 B.C.E. The modest structure soon built to take its place was replaced by the magnificent Second Temple, erected by King Herod in the last decades of the first century B.C.E. and destroyed by the Romans in 70 C.E.   (Ritmeyer Archaeological Design, London)

A gifted musician, warrior, and politician, David oversaw Israel's transition from a tribal confederacy to a unified monarchy. He strengthened royal authority by making the captured hill city of Jerusalem, which lay outside tribal boundaries, his capital. Soon after, David brought the Ark to Jerusalem, making the city the religious as well as the political center of the kingdom. A census was taken to facilitate the collection of taxes, and a standing army, with soldiers paid by and loyal to the king, was instituted. These innovations enabled David to win a string of military victories and expand Israel's borders.

The reign of David's son Solomon (r. ca. 960–920 B.C.E.) marked the high point of the Israelite monarchy. Alliances and trade linked Israel with near and distant lands. Solomon and Hiram, the king of Phoenician Tyre, together commissioned a fleet that sailed into the Red Sea and brought back gold, ivory, jewels, sandalwood, and exotic animals. The story of the visit to Solomon by the queen of Sheba, who brought gold, precious stones,

and spices, may be mythical, but it reflects the reality of trade with Saba° in south Arabia (present-day Yemen) or the Horn of Africa (present-day Somalia). Such wealth supported a lavish court life, a sizeable bureaucracy, and an intimidating chariot army that made Israel a regional power. Solomon undertook an ambitious building program employing slaves and the compulsory labor of citizens. To strengthen the link between religious and secular authority, he built the **First Temple** in Jerusalem. The Israelites now had a central shrine and an impressive set of rituals that could compete with other religions in the area.

The Temple priests became a powerful and wealthy class, receiving a share of the annual harvest in return for making animal sacrifices to Yahweh on behalf of the community. The expansion of Jerusalem, new commercial op-

Saba (SUH-buh)

portunities, and the increasing prestige of the Temple hierarchy changed the social composition of Israelite society. A gap between urban and rural, rich and poor, polarized a people that previously had been relatively homogeneous. Fiery prophets, claiming revelation from Yahweh, accused the monarchs and aristocracy of corruption, impiety, and neglect of the poor (see Diversity and Dominance: An Israelite Prophet Chastizes the Ruling Class).

The Israelites lived in extended families, several generations residing together under the authority of the eldest male. Marriage, usually arranged between families, was an important economic as well as social institution. When the groom, in order to prove his financial worthiness, gave a substantial gift to the father of the bride, her entire family participated in the ceremonial weighing out of silver or gold. The wife's dowry often included a slave girl who attended her for life.

Male heirs were of paramount importance, and firstborn sons received a double share of the inheritance. If a couple had no son, they could adopt one, or the husband could have a child by the wife's slave attendant. If a man died childless, his brother was expected to marry his widow and sire an heir.

In early Israel women provided a vital portion of the goods and services that sustained the family. As a result, women were respected and enjoyed relative equality with their husbands. Unlike men, however, they could not inherit property or initiate divorce, and a woman caught in extramarital relations could be put to death. Working-class women labored with other family members in agriculture or herding in addition to caring for the house and children. As the society became urbanized, some women worked outside the home as cooks, bakers, perfumers, wet nurses (usually a recent mother, still producing milk, hired to provide nourishment to another person's child), prostitutes, and singers of laments at funerals. A few women reached positions of influence, such as Deborah the Judge, who led troops in battle against the Canaanites. Women known collectively as "wise women" appear to have composed sacred texts in poetry and prose. This reality has been obscured, in part by the male bias of the Hebrew Bible, in part because the status of women declined as Israelite society became more urbanized.

Fragmentation and Dispersal

After Solomon's death around 920 B.C.E., resentment over royal demands and the neglect of tribal prerogatives split the monarchy into two kingdoms: Israel in the north, with its capital at Samaria°; and Judah° in the southern territory

---

Samaria (suh-MAH-ree-yuh) Judah (JOO-duh)

around Jerusalem (see Map 4.4). The two were sometimes at war, sometimes allied.

This period saw the final formulation of **monotheism,** the absolute belief in Yahweh as the one and only god. Nevertheless, religious leaders still had to contend with cults professing polytheism (the belief in multiple gods). The ecstatic rituals of the Canaanite storm-god Baal° and the fertility goddess Astarte° attracted many Israelites. Prophets condemned the adoption of foreign ritual and threatened that Yahweh would punish Israel severely.

The small states of Syria and the two Israelite kingdoms laid aside their rivalries to mount a joint resistance to the Neo-Assyrian Empire, but to no avail. In 721 B.C.E. the Assyrians destroyed the northern kingdom of Israel and deported much of its population to the east. New settlers were brought in from Syria, Babylon, and Iran, changing the area's ethnic, cultural, and religious character and removing it from the mainstream of Jewish history. The kingdom of Judah survived for more than a century longer, sometimes rebelling, sometimes paying tribute to the Assyrians or the Neo-Babylonian kingdom (626–539 B.C.E.) that succeeded them. When the Neo-Babylonian monarch Nebuchadnezzar° captured Jerusalem in 587 B.C.E., he destroyed the Temple and deported to Babylon the royal family, the aristocracy, and many skilled workers such as blacksmiths and scribes.

The deportees prospered so well in their new home "by the waters of Babylon" that half a century later most of their descendants refused the offer of the Persian monarch Cyrus (see Chapter 5) to return to their homeland. This was the origin of the **Diaspora°**—a Greek word meaning "dispersion" or "scattering." This dispersion outside the homeland of many Jews—as we may now call these people, since an independent Israel no longer existed—continues to this day. To maintain their religion and culture outside the homeland, the Diaspora communities developed institutions like the synagogue (Greek for "bringing together"), a communal meeting place that served religious, educational, and social functions.

Several groups of Babylonian Jews did make the long trek back to Judah, where they met with a cold reception from the local population. Persevering, they rebuilt the Temple in modest form and drafted the Deuteronomic° Code (*deuteronomic* is Greek for "second set of laws") of law and conduct. The fifth century B.C.E. also saw the

---

Baal (BAHL) Astarte (uh-STAHR-tee)
Nebuchadnezzar (NAB-oo-kuhd-nez-uhr)
Diaspora (die-ASS-peh-rah)
Deuteronomic (doo-tuhr-uh-NAHM-ik)

DIVERSITY AND DOMINANCE

AN ISRAELITE PROPHET CHASTIZES THE RULING CLASS

Israelite society underwent profound changes in the period of the monarchy. A loosely organized society of village-based farmers and herders was transformed relatively rapidly into a centrally controlled state with urban centers, a standing army, an administrative bureaucracy supported by taxation, and involvement in long-distance trade networks. A central religious shrine emerged with a hierarchy of priests and other religious specialists maintained at public expense. The new opportunities for some to acquire considerable wealth led to greater disparities between rich and poor.

Throughout this period a series of prophets publicly challenged the behavior of the Israelite ruling elite. They denounced the changes in Israelite society as corrupting people and separating them from the religious devotion and moral rectitude of an earlier, better time. The prophets often spoke out on behalf of the uneducated, inarticulate, illiterate, and powerless lower classes, and thus provide valuable information about the experiences of different social groups. Theirs was not objective reporting, but rather the angry, anguished, visions of unconventional individuals.

The following excerpts from the Hebrew Bible are taken from the book of Amos. A herdsman from the southern kingdom of Judah (in the era of the divided monarchy), Amos was active in the northern kingdom of Israel in the mid-eighth century B.C.E., when Assyria threatened the Syria-Palestine region.

1:1 The following is a record of what Amos prophesied. He was one of the herdsmen from Tekoa. These prophecies about Israel were revealed to him during the time of King Uzziah of Judah and King Jeroboam son of Joash of Israel, two years before the earthquake. . . .

3:1 Listen, you Israelites, to this message which the Lord is proclaiming against you. This message is for the entire clan I brought up from the land of Egypt: 3:2 "I have chosen you alone from all the clans of the earth. Therefore I will punish you for all your sins" . . .

3:9 Make this announcement in the fortresses of Ashdod and in the fortresses in the land of Egypt. Say this: "Gather on the hills around Samaria! [capital of the northern kingdom]

Observe the many acts of violence taking place within the city, the oppressive deeds occurring in it."

3:10 "They do not know how to do what is right. They store up the spoils of destructive violence in their fortresses."

3:11 Therefore," says the sovereign Lord, "an enemy will encircle the land. Your power, Samaria, will be taken away; your fortresses will be looted."

3:12 This is what the Lord says: "Just as a shepherd salvages from the lion's mouth a couple of leg bones or a piece of an ear, so the Israelites who live in Samaria will be salvaged. They will be left with just a corner of a bed, and a part of a couch" . . .

3:14 "Certainly when I punish Israel for their treaty violations, I will destroy Bethel's altars. The horns of the altars will be cut off and fall to the ground.

3:15 I will destroy both the winter and summer houses. The houses filled with ivory will be ruined, the great houses will be swept away." The Lord is speaking!

4:1 Listen to this message, you "cows of Bashan" who live on Mount Samaria! You oppress the poor; you crush the needy. You say to your husbands, "Bring us more to drink so we can party!"

4:2 The sovereign Lord confirms this oath by his own holy character: "Certainly the time is approaching! You will be carried away in baskets, every last one of you in fishermen's pots.

4:3 Each of you will go straight through the gaps in the walls; you will be thrown out toward Harmon" . . .

5:10 The Israelites hate anyone who arbitrates at the city gate; they despise anyone who speaks honestly.

5:11 Therefore, because you make the poor pay taxes on their crops and exact a grain tax from them, you will not live in the houses you built with chiseled stone, nor will you drink the wine from the fine vineyards you planted.

5:12 Certainly I am aware of your many rebellious acts and your numerous sins. You torment the innocent, you take bribes, and you deny justice to the needy at the city gate.

5:13 For this reason whoever is smart keeps quiet in such a time, for it is an evil time.

5:15 Hate what is wrong, love what is right! Promote justice at the city gate! Maybe the Lord, the God who leads armies, will have mercy on those who are left from Joseph [the Israelites] . . .

5:21 "I absolutely despise your festivals. I get no pleasure from your religious assemblies.

5:22 Even if you offer me burnt and grain offerings, I will not be satisfied; I will not look with favor on the fattened calves you offer in peace.

5:23 Take away from me your noisy songs; I don't want to hear the music of your stringed instruments.

5:24 Justice must flow like water, right actions like a stream that never dries up . . ."

6:3 You refuse to believe a day of disaster will come, but you establish a reign of violence.

6:4 They lie around on beds decorated with ivory, and sprawl out on their couches. They eat lambs from the flock, and calves from the middle of the pen.

6:5 They sing to the tune of stringed instruments; like David they invent musical instruments.

6:6 They drink wine from sacrificial bowls, and pour the very best oils on themselves.

6:7 Therefore they will now be the first to go into exile, and the religious banquets where they sprawl out on couches will end.

7:10 Amaziah the priest of Bethel sent this message to King Jeroboam of Israel: "Amos is conspiring against you in the very heart of the kingdom of Israel! The land cannot endure all his prophecies.

7:11 As a matter of fact, Amos is saying this: 'Jeroboam will die by the sword and Israel will certainly be carried into exile away from its land.'"

7:12 Amaziah then said to Amos, "Leave, you visionary! Run away to the land of Judah! Earn money and prophesy there!

7:13 Don't prophesy at Bethel any longer, for a royal temple and palace are here!"

7:14 Amos replied to Amaziah, "I was not a prophet by profession. No, I was a herdsman who also took care of sycamore fig trees.

7:15 Then the Lord took me from tending flocks and gave me this commission, 'Go! Prophesy to my people Israel!'

7:16 So now listen to the Lord's message! You say, 'Don't prophesy against Israel! Don't preach against the family of Isaac!'

7:17 "Therefore this is what the Lord says: 'Your wife will become a prostitute in the streets and your sons and daughters will die violently. Your land will be given to others and you will die in a foreign land. Israel will certainly be carried into exile away from its land.'"

8:4 Listen to this, you who trample the needy, and get rid of the destitute in the land.

8:5 You say, "When will the new moon festival be over, so we can sell grain? When will the Sabbath end, so we can open up the grain bins? We're eager to sell less for a higher price, and to cheat the buyer with rigged scales.

8:6 We're eager to trade silver for the poor, a pair of sandals for the needy. We want to mix in some chaff with the grain."

8:7 The Lord confirms this oath by the arrogance of Jacob: "I swear I will never forget all you have done!

8:8 Because of this the earth will quake, and all who live in it will mourn. The whole earth will rise like the River Nile, it will surge upward and then grow calm, like the Nile in Egypt.

8:9 In that day," says the sovereign Lord, "I will make the sun set at noon, and make the earth dark in the middle of the day.

8:10 I will turn your festivals into funerals, and all your songs into funeral dirges. I will make everyone wear funeral clothes and cause every head to be shaved bald. I will make you mourn as if you had lost your only son; when it ends it will indeed have been a bitter day.

8:11 Be certain of this, the time is coming," says the sovereign Lord, "when I will send a famine through the land. I'm not talking about a shortage of food or water, but an end to divine revelation.

8:12 People will stagger from sea to sea, and from the north around to the east. They will wander around looking for a revelation from the Lord, but they will not find any . . ."

9:8 "Look, the sovereign Lord is watching the sinful nation, and I will destroy it from the face of the earth. But I will not completely destroy the family of Jacob," says the Lord.

9:9 "For look, I am giving a command and I will shake the family of Israel together with all the nations. It will resemble a sieve being shaken, when not even a pebble falls to the ground.

9:10 All the sinners among my people will die by the sword, the ones who say, 'Disaster will not come near, it will not confront us.'

9:11 In that day I will rebuild the collapsing hut of David. I will seal its gaps, repair its ruins, and restore it to what it was like in days gone by."

QUESTIONS FOR ANALYSIS

1. For whom is Amos's message primarily intended? How does the ruling class react to Amos's prophetic activity, and how does he respond to their tactics?

2. What does Amos see as wrong in Israelite society, and who is at fault? Why are even the religious practices of the elite criticized?

3. What will be the means by which God punishes Israel, and why does God punish them this way? What grounds for hope remain?

Source: http://www.netbible.com. Reprinted courtesy of Biblical Studies Press, L.L.C.

compilation of much of the Hebrew Bible in roughly its present form.

The loss of political autonomy and the experience of exile had sharpened Jewish identity, with an unyielding monotheism as the core belief. Jews lived by a rigid set of rules. Dietary restrictions forbade the eating of pork and shellfish and mandated that meat and dairy products not be consumed together. Ritual baths were used to achieve spiritual purity, and women were required to take ritual baths after menstruation. The Jews venerated the Sabbath (Saturday, the seventh day of the week) by refraining from work and from fighting, following the example of Yahweh, who, according to the Bible, rested on the seventh day after creating the world (this is the origin of the concept of the weekend). These strictures and others, including a ban on marrying non-Jews, tended to isolate the Jews from other peoples, but they also fostered a powerful sense of community and the belief that they were protected by a watchful and beneficent deity.

PHOENICIA AND THE MEDITERRANEAN, 1200–500 B.C.E.

While the Israelite tribes were being forged into a united kingdom, the people who occupied the coast of the Mediterranean to the north were developing their own distinctive civilization. Historians refer to a major element of the ancient population of Syria-Palestine as **Phoenicians°,** though they referred to themselves as "Can'ani"—Canaanites. Despite the sparse written record and the disturbance of the archaeological record by frequent migrations and invasions, enough of their history survives to reveal major transformations.

The Phoenician City-States

When the eastern Mediterranean entered a period of violent upheaval and mass migrations around 1200 B.C.E. (discussed earlier), many Canaanite settlements were destroyed. Aramaeans°—nomadic pastoralists similar to the early Israelites—migrated into the interior portions of Syria. Farther south, Israelites settled in the interior of present-day Israel as herders and farmers. At the same time, the Philistines occupied the coast and introduced iron-based metallurgy to this part of the world.

By 1100 B.C.E. Canaanite territory had shrunk to a narrow strip of present-day Lebanon between the mountains and the sea (see Map 4.4). The inhabitants of this densely populated area adopted new political forms and turned to seaborne commerce and new kinds of manufacture for their survival. Sometime after 1000 B.C.E. the Canaanites encountered the Greeks, who referred to them as *Phoinikes,* or Phoenicians. The term may mean "red men" and refer to the color of their skin, or it may refer to the highly valued purple dye they extracted from the murex snail (see Environment and Technology: Ancient Textiles and Dyes).

Rivers and rocky spurs of Mount Lebanon sliced the coastal plain into a series of small city-states, chief among them Byblos°, Berytus°, Sidon°, and Tyre. A thriving trade in raw materials (cedar and pine, metals, incense, papyrus), foodstuffs (wine, spices, salted fish), and crafted luxury goods (textiles, carved ivory, glass) brought considerable wealth to the Phoenician city-states and gave them an important role in international politics.

The Phoenicians developed earlier Canaanite models into an "alphabetic" system of writing with about two dozen symbols, in which each symbol represented a sound. (The Phoenicians represented only consonants, leaving the vowel sounds to be inferred by the reader. The Greeks added symbols for vowel sounds, thereby creating the first truly alphabetic system of writing—see Chapter 5.) Little Phoenician writing survives, however, probably because scribes used perishable papyrus. Some information in Greek and Roman documents may be based on Phoenician sources

Before 1000 B.C.E. Byblos had been the most important Phoenician city-state. It was a distribution center for cedar timber from the slopes of Mount Lebanon and for papyrus from Egypt. The English word *bible* comes from the Greek *biblion,* meaning "book written on papyrus from Byblos." After 1000 B.C.E. Tyre, in southern Lebanon, surpassed Byblos. King Hiram, who came to power in 969 B.C.E., was responsible for Tyre's rise to prominence. According to the Bible, he formed a close alliance with the Israelite king Solomon and provided skilled Phoenician craftsmen and cedar wood for building the Temple in Jerusalem. In return, Tyre gained access to silver, food, and trade routes to the east and south. In the 800s B.C.E. Tyre took control of nearby Sidon and monopolized the Mediterranean coastal trade.

Located on an offshore island, Tyre was practically impregnable. It had two harbors, one facing north, the other south, connected by a canal. The city boasted a large

---

Phoenician (fi-NEE-shun) **Aramaean** (ah-ruh-MAY-uhn)

Byblos (BIB-loss) **Berytus** (buh-RIE-tuhs) **Sidon** (SIE-duhn)

ENVIRONMENT + TECHNOLOGY

Ancient Textiles and Dyes

Throughout human history the production of textiles—cloth for clothing, blankets, carpets, and coverings of various sorts—may have required an expenditure of human labor second only to the amount of work necessary to provide food. Nevertheless, textile production in antiquity has left few traces in the archaeological record. The plant fibers and animal hair used for cloth are organic and quickly decompose except in rare and special circumstances. Some textile remains have been found in the hot, dry conditions of Egypt, the cool, arid Andes of South America, and the peat bogs of northern Europe. But most of our knowledge of ancient textiles depends on the discovery of equipment used in textile production—such as spindles, loom weights, and dyeing vats—and on pictorial representations and descriptions in texts.

The production of cloth usually has been the work of women for a simple but important reason. Responsibility for child rearing limits women's ability to participate in other activities but does not consume all their time and energy. In many societies textile production has been complementary to child-rearing activities, for it can be done in the home, is relatively safe, does not require great concentration, and can be interrupted without consequence. For many thousands of years cloth production has been one of the great common experiences of women around the globe. The growing and harvesting of plants such as cotton or flax (from which linen is made) and the shearing of wool from sheep and, in the Andes, llamas are outdoor activities, but the subsequent stages of production can be carried out inside the home. The basic methods of textile production did not change much from early antiquity until the late eighteenth century C.E., when the fabrication of textiles was transferred to mills and mass production began.

When textile production has been considered "women's work," most of the output has been for household consumption. One exception was in the early civilizations of Peru,

Ancient Peruvian Textiles The weaving of Chavín was famous for its color and symbolic imagery. Artisans both wove designs into the fabric and used paint or dyes to decorate plain fabric. This early Chavín painted fabric was used in a burial. Notice how the face suggests a jaguar and the headdress includes the image of a serpent. (Private collection)

where women weavers developed new raw materials, new techniques, and new decorative motifs around three thousand years ago. They began to use the wool of llamas and alpacas in addition to cotton. Three women worked side by side and passed the weft from hand to hand in order to overcome limitations to the width of woven fabric imposed by the back-strap loom. Women weavers also introduced embroidery, and they decorated garments with new religious motifs, such as the jaguar-god of Chavín. Their high-quality textiles were given as tribute to the elite and were used in trade to acquire luxury goods as well as dyes and metals.

More typically, men dominated commercial production. In ancient Phoenicia, fine textiles with bright, permanent colors became a major export product. These striking colors were produced by dyes derived from several species of snail. Most prized was the red-purple known as Tyrian purple because Tyre was the major source. Persian and Hellenistic kings wore robes dyed this color, and a white toga with a purple border was the sign of a Roman senator.

The production of Tyrian purple was an exceedingly laborious process. The spiny dye-murex snail lives on the sandy Mediterranean bottom at depths ranging from 30 to 500 feet (10 to 150 meters). Nine thousand snails were needed to produce 1 gram (0.035 ounce) of dye. The dye was made from a colorless liquid in the snail's hypobranchial gland. The gland sacs were removed, crushed, soaked with salt, and exposed to sunlight and air for some days; then they were subject to controlled boiling and heating.

Huge mounds of broken shells on the Phoenician coast are testimony to the ancient industry. It is likely that the snail was rendered nearly extinct at many locations, and some scholars have speculated that Phoenician colonization in the Mediterranean may have been motivated in part by the search for new sources of snails.

Phoenician Scarab Representing a Sea Deity This carved gemstone, made of green jasper and mounted on a gold hoop, would have been pressed into clay or wax to impress the owner's seal, the ancient equivalent of a signature. Made in Phoenicia but showing influences from Greek art, it depicts a bearded sea deity holding a conical cup and wreath accompanied by a dolphin or fish. (Bibliotheque Nationale de France)

marketplace, a magnificent palace complex with treasury and archives, and temples to the gods Melqart° and Astarte. Some of its thirty thousand or more inhabitants lived in suburbs on the mainland. Its one weakness was its dependence on the mainland for food and fresh water.

Little is known about the internal affairs of Tyre and other Phoenician cities. The names of a series of kings are preserved, and the scant evidence suggests that the political arena was dominated by leading merchant families. Between the ninth and seventh centuries B.C.E. the Phoenician city-states contended with Assyrian aggression, followed in the sixth century B.C.E. by the expansion of the Neo-Babylonian kingdom and later the Persian Empire (see Chapter 5). The Phoenician city-states preserved their autonomy by playing the great powers off against one another when possible and accepting a subordinate relationship to a distant master when necessary.

Expansion into the Mediterranean

After 900 B.C.E. Tyre began to turn its attention westward, establishing colonies on Cyprus, a copper-rich island 100 miles (161 kilometers) from the Syrian coast (see Map 4.4) that was strategically located on a major trade route. Phoenician merchants sailing into the

Aegean Sea are mentioned in Homer's *Iliad* and *Odyssey* around 700 B.C.E. By that time a string of settlements in the western Mediterranean formed a "Phoenician triangle" composed of the North African coast from western Libya to Morocco; the south and southeast coast of Spain, including Gades° (modern Cadiz°) on the Strait of Gibraltar, controlling passage between the Mediterranean and the Atlantic Ocean; and the islands of Sardinia, Sicily, and Malta off the coast of Italy (see Map 4.5). Many of these new settlements were situated on promontories or offshore islands in imitation of Tyre. The Phoenician trading network spanned the entire Mediterranean.

State enterprise and private initiative made Tyrian expansion possible. Frequent and destructive Assyrian invasions of Syria-Palestine and the lack of arable land to feed a swelling population probably made it necessary. Overseas settlement provided an outlet for excess population, new sources of trade goods, and new trading partners. Tyre maintained its autonomy until 701 B.C.E. by paying tribute to the Assyrian kings. In that year it finally fell to an Assyrian army that stripped it of much of its territory and population, allowing Sidon to become the leading city in Phoenicia.

The Phoenicians' activities in the western Mediterranean often brought them into conflict with the Greeks, who were also expanding trade and establishing colonies.

Melqart (MEL-kahrt)

Gades (GAH-days)   Cadiz (kuh-DEEZ)

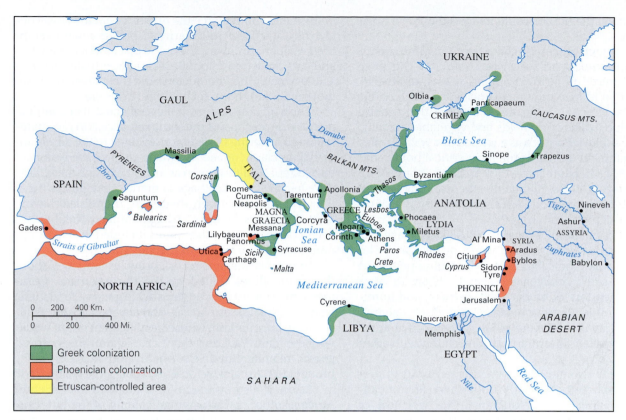

Map 4.5   Colonization of the Mediterranean   In the ninth century B.C.E., the Phoenicians of Lebanon began to explore and colonize parts of the western Mediterranean, including the coast of North Africa, southern and eastern Spain, and the islands of Sicily and Sardinia. The Phoenicians were primarily interested in access to valuable raw materials and trading opportunities.

The focal point of this rivalry was Sicily. Phoenicians occupied the western end of the island, Greeks its eastern and central parts. For centuries Greeks and Phoenicians fought for control of Sicily in some of the most savage wars in the history of the ancient Mediterranean. Surviving accounts tell of atrocities, massacres, wholesale enslavements, and mass deportations. The high level of brutality suggests that each side believed its survival to be at stake. Both communities survived, but the Phoenician colony of Carthage in Tunisia, which led the coalition of Phoenician communities in the western Mediterranean, controlled all of Sicily by the mid-third century B.C.E.

Carthage's Commercial Empire

Historians know far more about **Carthage** and the other Phoenician colonies than they do about the Phoenician homeland. Much of this knowledge comes from Greek and Roman reports of their wars with the western Phoenician communities. For example, the account of the origins of Carthage that begins this chapter comes from Roman sources (most famously Virgil's epic poem *The Aeneid*) but probably is based on a Carthaginian original. Archaeological excavation has roughly confirmed the city's traditional foundation date of 814 B.C.E. Just outside the present-day city of Tunis in Tunisia, Carthage controlled the middle portion of the Mediterranean where Europe comes closest to Africa. The new settlement grew rapidly and soon dominated other Phoenician colonies in the west.

Located on a narrow promontory jutting into the Mediterranean, Carthage stretched between Byrsa°, the original hilltop citadel of the community, and a double harbor. The inner harbor could accommodate up to 220 warships. A watchtower allowed surveillance of the surrounding area, and high walls made it impossible to see in from the outside. The outer commercial harbor was filled with docks for merchant ships and shipyards. In

Byrsa (BURR-suh)

case of attack, the harbor could be closed off by a huge iron chain.

Government offices ringed a large central square where magistrates heard legal cases outdoors. The inner city was a maze of narrow, winding streets, multistory apartment buildings, and sacred enclosures. Farther out was a sprawling suburban district where the wealthy built spacious villas amid fields and vegetable gardens. This entire urban complex was enclosed by a wall 22 miles (35 kilometers) in length. At the most critical point—the 2½-mile-wide (4-kilometer-wide) isthmus connecting the promontory to the mainland—the wall was over 40 feet (13 meters) high and 30 feet (10 meters) thick and had high watchtowers.

With a population of roughly 400,000, Carthage was one of the largest cities in the world by 500 B.C.E. The population was ethnically diverse, including people of Phoenician stock, indigenous peoples likely to have been the ancestors of modern-day Berbers, and immigrants from other Mediterranean lands and sub-Saharan Africa. Contrary to the story of Dido's reluctance to remarry, Phoenicians intermarried quite readily with other peoples.

Each year two "judges" were elected from upper-class families to serve as heads of state and carry out administrative and judicial functions. The real seat of power was the Senate, where members of the leading merchant families, who sat for life, formulated policy and directed the affairs of the state. An inner circle of thirty or so senators made the crucial decisions. From time to time the leadership convened an Assembly of the citizens to elect public officials or vote on important issues, particularly when the leaders were divided or wanted to stir up popular enthusiasm for some venture.

There is little evidence at Carthage of the kind of social and political unrest that later plagued Greece and Rome (see Chapters 5 and 6). This perception may be due in part to the limited information in existing sources about internal affairs at Carthage. However, a merchant aristocracy (unlike an aristocracy of birth) was not a closed circle, and a climate of economic and social mobility allowed newly successful families and individuals to push their way into the circle of politically influential citizens. The ruling class also made sure that everyone benefited from the riches of empire, and the masses were usually ready to defer to those who made prosperity possible.

Carthaginian power rested on its navy, which dominated the western Mediterranean for centuries. Phoenician towns provided a chain of friendly ports. The Carthaginian fleet consisted of fast, maneuverable galleys—oared warships. A galley had a sturdy, pointed ram in front that could pierce the hull of an enemy vessel below the water line, while marines (soldiers aboard a ship) fired weapons. Innovations in the placement of benches and oars made room for 30, 50, and eventually as many as 170 rowers. The Phoenicians and their Greek rivals set the standard for naval technology in this era.

Carthaginian foreign policy reflected its economic interests. Protection of the sea lanes, access to raw materials, and fostering trade mattered most to the dominant merchant class. Indeed, Carthage claimed the waters of the western Mediterranean as its own. Foreign merchants were free to sail to Carthage to market their goods, but if they tried to operate on their own, they risked having their ships sunk by the Carthaginian navy. Treaties between Carthage and other states included formal recognition of this maritime commercial monopoly.

The archaeological record provides few clues about the commodities traded by the Carthaginians. Commerce may have included perishable goods—foodstuffs, textiles, animal skins, slaves—and raw metals such as silver, lead, iron, and tin, whose Carthaginian origin would not be evident. We know that Carthaginian ships carried goods manufactured elsewhere and that products brought to Carthage by foreign traders were reexported.

There is also evidence for trade with sub-Saharan Africa. Hanno°, a Carthaginian captain of the fifth century B.C.E., claimed to have sailed through the Strait of Gibraltar into the Atlantic Ocean and to have explored the West African coast (see Map 4.5). His report includes vivid descriptions of ferocious savages, drums in the night, and rivers of fire. Scholars have had difficulty matching up Hanno's topographic descriptions and distances with the geography of West Africa, and some regard his account as outright fiction. Others believe that he misstated distances and exaggerated the dangers to deter other explorers from following his route and competing for the trade in West African gold. Other Carthaginians explored the Atlantic coast of Spain and France and secured control of an important source of tin in the "Tin Islands," probably Cornwall in southwestern England.

War and Religion

Unlike Assyria, Carthage did not directly rule a large amount of territory. A belt of fertile land in northeastern Tunisia, owned by Carthaginians but worked by native peasants and imported slaves, provided a secure food supply. Beyond this core area the Carthaginians ruled most of their "empire" indirectly,

---

Hanno (HA-noe)

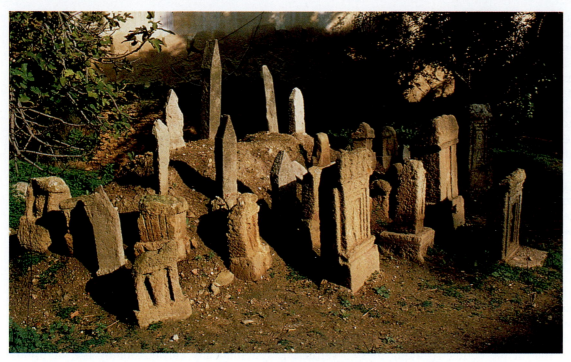

The Tophet of Carthage   Here, from the seventh to second centuries B.C.E., the cremated bodies of sacrificed children were buried. Archaeological excavation has confirmed the claim in ancient sources that the Carthaginians sacrificed children to their gods at times of crisis. Stone markers, decorated with magical signs and symbols of divinities as well as family names, were placed over ceramic urns containing the ashes and charred bones of one or more infants or, occasionally, older children.   (Martha Cooper/Peter Arnold, Inc.)

and allowed other Phoenician communities in the western Mediterranean to remain independent. These Phoenician communities looked to Carthage for military protection and followed its lead in foreign policy. Only Sardinia and southern Spain were put under the direct control of a Carthaginian governor and garrison, presumably to safeguard their agricultural, metal, and manpower resources.

Carthage's focus on trade may explain the unusual fact that citizens were not required to serve in the army: they were of more value in other capacities, such as trading activities and the navy. Since the indigenous North African population was not politically or militarily well organized, Carthage had little to fear from potential enemies close to home. When Carthage was drawn into a series of wars with the Greeks and Romans from the fifth through third centuries B.C.E., it relied on mercenaries from the most warlike peoples in its dominions or from neighboring areas—Numidians from North Africa, Iberians from Spain, Gauls from France, and various Italian peoples. These well-paid mercenaries were under the command of Carthaginian officers.

Another sign that war was not the primary business of the state was the separation of military command from civilian government. Generals were chosen by the Senate and kept in office for as long as they were needed. In contrast, the kings of Assyria and the other major states of the ancient Middle East normally led military campaigns.

Carthaginian religion fascinated Greek and Roman writers. Like the deities of Mesopotamia (see Chapter 2), the gods of the Carthaginians—chief among them Baal Hammon°, a male storm-god, and Tanit°, a female fertility figure—were powerful and capricious entities who had to be appeased by anxious worshipers. Roman sources report that members of the Carthaginian elite would sacrifice their own male children in times of crisis. Excavations at Carthage and other western Phoenician towns have turned up *tophets*°—walled enclosures where thousands of small, sealed urns containing the burned bones of children lay buried. Although some

Baal Hammon (BAHL ha-MOHN)   **Tanit** (TAH-nit)
tophet (TOE-fet)

scholars argue that these were infants born prematurely or taken by childhood illnesses, most maintain that the western Phoenicians practiced child sacrifice on a more or less regular basis. Originally practiced by the upper classes, child sacrifice seems to have become more common and to have involved broader elements of the population after 400 B.C.E.

Plutarch°, a Greek who lived around 100 C.E., long after the demise of Carthage, wrote the following on the basis of earlier sources:

> The Carthaginians are a hard and gloomy people, submissive to their rulers and harsh to their subjects, running to extremes of cowardice in times of fear and of cruelty in times of anger; they keep obstinately to their decisions, are austere, and care little for amusement or the graces of life.[1]

We should not take the hostile opinions of Greek and Roman sources at face value. Still, it is clear that the Carthaginians were perceived as different and that cultural barriers, leading to misunderstanding and prejudice, played a significant role in the conflicts among these peoples of the ancient Mediterranean. In Chapter 6 we follow the protracted and bloody struggle between Rome and Carthage for control of the western Mediterranean.

FAILURE AND TRANSFORMATION, 750–550 B.C.E.

The extension of Assyrian power over the entire Middle East had enormous consequences for all the peoples of this region and caused the stories of Mesopotamia, Israel, and Phoenicia to converge. In 721 B.C.E. the Assyrians destroyed the northern kingdom of Israel and deported a substantial portion of the population, and for over a century the southern kingdom of Judah was exposed to relentless pressure. Assyrian threats and demands for tribute spurred the Phoenicians to colonize and exploit the western Mediterranean. Tyre's fall to the Assyrians in 701 B.C.E. accelerated the decline of the Phoenician homeland, but the western colonies, especially Carthage, lying far beyond Assyrian reach, flourished.

Even Egypt, for so long impregnable behind its desert barriers, fell to Assyrian invaders in the mid-seventh century B.C.E. Thebes, its ancient capital, never recovered. The southern plains of Sumer and Akkad, the birthplace of Mesopotamian civilization, were reduced

to a protectorate, while Babylon was alternately razed and rebuilt by Assyrian kings of differing dispositions. Urartu and Elam, Assyria's great-power rivals close to home, were destroyed.

By 650 B.C.E. Assyria stood unchallenged in western Asia. But the arms race with Urartu, the frequent expensive campaigns, and the protection of lengthy borders had sapped Assyrian resources. Assyrian brutality and exploitation aroused the hatred of conquered peoples. At the same time, changes in the ethnic composition of the army and the population of the homeland had reduced popular support for the Assyrian state.

Two new political entities spearheaded resistance to Assyria. First, Babylonia had been revived by the Neo-Babylonian, or Chaldaean°, dynasty (the Chaldaeans had infiltrated southern Mesopotamia around 1000 B.C.E.). Second, the Medes°, an Iranian people, were extending their kingdom eastward across the Iranian Plateau in the seventh century B.C.E. The two powers launched a series of attacks on the Assyrian homeland that destroyed the chief cities by 612 B.C.E.

The rapidity of the Assyrian fall is stunning. The destruction systematically carried out by the victorious attackers led to the depopulation of northern Mesopotamia. Two centuries later, when a corps of Greek mercenaries passed by mounds that concealed the ruins of the Assyrian capitals, the Athenian chronicler Xenophon° had no inkling that their empire had ever existed.

The Medes took over the Assyrian homeland and the northern steppe as far as eastern Anatolia, but most of the territory of the old empire fell to the **Neo-Babylonian kingdom** (626–539 B.C.E.), thanks to the energetic campaigns of kings Nabopolassar° (r. 625–605 B.C.E.) and Nebuchadnezzar (r. 604–562 B.C.E.). Babylonia underwent a cultural renaissance. The city of Babylon was enlarged and adorned, becoming the greatest metropolis of the world in the sixth century B.C.E. Old cults were revived, temples rebuilt, festivals resurrected. The related pursuits of mathematics, astronomy, and astrology reached new heights.

CONCLUSION

This chapter traces developments in the Middle East and the Mediterranean from 2000 to 500 B.C.E. The patterns of culture that originated in the river-valley civilizations of Egypt and Mesopotamia persisted into this era. Peoples such as the Amorites, Kassites, and Chal-

---

Plutarch (PLOO-tawrk)

Chaldaean (chal-DEE-uhn)   **Mede** (MEED)
Xenophon (ZEN-uh-fahn)   **Nabopolassar** (NAB-oh-poe-lass-uhr)

daeans, who migrated into the Tigris-Euphrates plain, were largely assimilated into the Sumerian-Semitic cultural tradition, adopting the language, religious beliefs, political and social institutions, and forms of artistic expression. Similarly, the Hyksos, who migrated into the Nile Delta and controlled much of Egypt for a time, adopted the ancient ways of Egypt. When the founders of the New Kingdom finally ended Hyksos domination, they reinstituted the united monarchy and the religious and cultural traditions of earlier eras.

Yet the Middle East was in many important respects a different place after 2000 B.C.E. New centers of political and economic power had emerged—the Elamites in southwest Iran, the Assyrians in northern Mesopotamia, Urartu in present-day Armenia, the Hittites of Anatolia, and the Minoan and Mycenaean peoples of the Aegean Sea. These new centers often borrowed heavily from the technologies and cultural practices of Mesopotamia and Egypt, creating dynamic syntheses of imported and indigenous elements. The entire Middle East was drawn together by networks of trade and diplomacy, a situation that provided general stability and raised the standard of living for many. Ultimately, though, the very interdependence of these societies made them vulnerable to the destructions and disorder of the decades around 1200 B.C.E. The entire region slipped into a "Dark Age" of isolation, stagnation, and decline that lasted several centuries.

The early centuries after 1000 B.C.E. saw a resurgence of political organization and international commerce, and the spread of technologies and ideas. The Neo-Assyrian Empire, the great power of the time, represented a continuation of the Mesopotamian tradition, though the center of empire moved to the north. Israel and Phoenicia, on the other hand, reflected the influence of Mesopotamia and Egypt but also evolved distinctive cultural traditions.

Throughout this era people were on the move, sometimes voluntarily and sometimes under compulsion. The Assyrians deported large numbers of prisoners of war from outlying subject territories to the core area in northern Mesopotamia. The Phoenicians left their overpopulated homeland to establish new settlements in North Africa, Spain, and islands off the coast of Italy. In their new homes the Phoenician colonists tried to duplicate familiar ways of life from the old country. In contrast, the Israelites who settled in Canaan and, at a later time, emigrated to the Diaspora underwent significant political, social, and cultural transformations as they adapted to new zones of settlement.

It is no accident that several of the peoples featured in this and the previous chapters who settled outside their places of origin had long and distinguished destinies ahead of them. Diasporas proved to be fertile sources of innovation and helped preserve culture. The Carthaginian enterprise eventually was cut short by the Romans, but Jews and Greeks survive into our own time. Ironically, the Assyrians, the most powerful of all these societies, suffered the most complete termination of their way of life. Because Assyrians did not settle outside their homeland in significant numbers, when their state was toppled in the late seventh century B.C.E. their culture all but perished.

The Neo-Babylonian kingdom that arose on the ashes of the Neo-Assyrian Empire would be the last revival of the ancient Sumerian and Semitic cultural legacy in western Asia. The next chapter relates how the destinies of the peoples of the Mediterranean and the Middle East became enmeshed in the new forms of political and social organization emerging from Iran and Greece.

■ Key Terms

Iron Age	mass deportation
Hittites	Library of Ashurbanipal
Hatshepsut	Israel
Akhenaten	Hebrew Bible
Ramesses II	First Temple
Minoan	monotheism
Mycenae	Diaspora
shaft graves	Phoenicians
Linear B	Carthage
Neo-Assyrian Empire	Neo-Babylonian kingdom

■ Suggested Reading

Fundamental for all periods in the ancient Middle East is Jack M. Sasson, ed., *Civilizations of the Ancient Near East*, 4 vols. (1995), containing nearly two hundred articles by contemporary experts and bibliography on a wide range of topics. John Boardman, I. E. S. Edwards, N. G. L. Hammond, and E. Sollberger, *The Cambridge Ancient History*, 2d ed., vols. 3.1–3.3 (1982–1991), provides extremely detailed historical coverage of the entire Mediterranean and western Asia. Barbara Lesko, ed., *Women's Earliest Records: From Ancient Egypt and Western Asia* (1989), is a collection of papers on the experiences of women in the ancient Middle East.

Many of the books recommended in the Suggested Reading list for Chapter 2 are useful for Mesopotamia, Syria, and Egypt in the Late Bronze Age. In addition see Miriam Lichtheim, *Ancient Egyptian Literature: A Book of Readings*, vol. 2, *The New Kingdom* (1978); Donald B. Redford, *Egypt, Canaan, and Israel in Ancient Times* (1992), which explores the relations of Egypt with the Syria-Palestine region in this period; Erik Hornung, *Akhenaten and the Religion of Light* (1999), which, while focusing on the religious innovations, deals with many facets of the reign of Akhenaten; Karol Mysliwiec, *The Twilight of Ancient Egypt: First Millennium B.C.E.* (2000), which traces the story of Egyptian civilization after the New Kingdom; and H. W. F. Saggs, *Babylonians* (1995), which devotes several chapters to this more thinly documented epoch in the history of southern Mesopotamia. The most up-to-date treatment of the Hittites can be found in Trevor Boyce, *The Kingdom of the Hittites* (1998) and *Life and Society in the Hittite World* (2002). Also useful are O. R. Gurney, *The Hittites*, 2d ed., rev. (1990), and J. G. Macqueen, *The Hittites and Their Contemporaries in Asia Minor* (1975).

R. A. Higgins, *The Archaeology of Minoan Crete* (1973) and *Minoan and Mycenaean Art*, new rev. ed. (1997); Rodney Castleden, *Minoans: Life in Bronze Age Crete* (1990); J. Walter Graham, *The Palaces of Crete* (1987); O. Krzyszkowska and L. Nixon, *Minoan Society* (1983); and N. Marinatos, *Minoan Religion* (1993), examine the archaeological evidence for the Minoan civilization. The brief discussion of M. I. Finley, *Early Greece: The Bronze and Archaic Ages* (1970), and the much fuller accounts of Emily Vermeule, *Greece in the Bronze Age* (1972), and J. T. Hooker, *Mycenaean Greece* (1976), are still useful treatments of Mycenaean Greece, based primarily on archaeological evidence. Robert Drews, *The Coming of the Greeks: Indo-European Conquests in the Aegean and the Near East* (1988), examines the evidence for the earliest Greeks. For the Linear B tablets see John Chadwick, *Linear B and Related Scripts* (1987) and *The Mycenaean World* (1976). J. V. Luce, *Homer and the Heroic Age* (1975), and Carol G. Thomas, *Myth Becomes History: Pre-Classical Greece* (1993), examine the usefulness of the Homeric poems for reconstructing the Greek past. For the disruptions and destructions of the Late Bronze Age in the eastern Mediterranean, see N. K. Sandars, *The Sea Peoples: Warriors of the Ancient Mediterranean* (1978), and Trude Dothan and Moshe Dothan, *People of the Sea: The Search for the Philistines* (1992).

For general history and cultural information about the Neo-Assyrian Empire, Mesopotamia, and western Asia in the first half of the first millennium B.C.E. see Michael Roaf, *Cultural Atlas of Mesopotamia and the Ancient Near East* (1990); Amelie Kuhrt, *The Ancient Near East, c. 3000–300 B.C.* (1995); H. W. F. Saggs, *Civilization Before Greece and Rome* (1989); and A. Bernard Knapp, *The History and Culture of Ancient Western Asia and Egypt* (1988). H. W. F. Saggs, *Babylonians* (1995), has coverage of the fate of the old centers in southern Mesopotamia during this era in which the north attained dominance. Primary texts in translation for Assyria and other parts of western Asia can be found in James B. Pritchard, ed., *Ancient Near Eastern Texts Relating to the Old Testament*, 3d ed. (1969). Jeremy Black and Anthony Green, *Gods, Demons and Symbols of Ancient Mesopotamia: An Illustrated Dictionary* (1992), is valuable for religious concepts, institutions, and mythology. Julian Reade, *Assyrian Sculpture* (1983), provides a succinct introduction to the informative relief sculptures from the Assyrian palaces. J. E. Curtis and J. E. Reade, eds., *Art and Empire: Treasures from Assyria in the British Museum* (1995), relates the art to many facets of Assyrian life. Andre Parrot, *The Arts of Assyria* (1961), provides full coverage of all artistic media.

For general historical introductions to ancient Israel see Michael Grant, *The History of Israel* (1984); J. Maxwell Miller and John H. Hayes, *A History of Ancient Israel and Judah* (1986); and

J. Alberto Soggin, *A History of Israel: From the Beginnings to the Bar Kochba Revolt, A.D. 135* (1984). Amnon Ben-Tor, *The Archaeology of Ancient Israel* (1991), and Amihai Mazar, *Archaeology of the Land of the Bible, 10,000–586 B.C.E.* (1990), provide overviews of the discoveries of archaeological excavation in Israel. William G. Dever, *What Did the Biblical Writers Know, and When Did They Know It? What Archaeology Can Tell Us About the Reality of Ancient Israel* (2001), and B. J. S. Isserlin, *The Israelites* (2001), both review the archaeological evidence and take moderate positions in the heated debate about the value of the biblical text for reconstructing the history of Israel. Hershel Shanks, *Jerusalem, an Archaeological Biography* (1995), explores the long and colorful history of the city. For social and economic issues see Shunya Bendor, *The Social Structure of Ancient Israel: The Institution of the Family (beit 'ab) from the Settlement to the End of the Monarchy* (1996), and Moses Aberbach, *Labor, Crafts and Commerce in Ancient Israel* (1994). Carol Meyers, *Discovering Eve: Ancient Israelite Women in Context* (1998), carefully sifts through literary and archaeological evidence to reach a balanced assessment of the position of women in the period before the monarchy. Victor H. Matthews, *The Social World of the Hebrew Prophets* (2001), provides social and historical contexts for all the prophets. For the Philistines see Trude Dothan, *The Philistines and Their Material Culture* (1982).

Glenn Markoe, *Phoenicians* (2000), Sabatino Moscati, *The Phoenicians* (1988), and Gerhard Herm, *The Phoenicians: The Purple Empire of the Ancient World* (1975), are general introductions to the Phoenicians in their homeland. Maria Eugenia Aubet, *The Phoenicians and the West: Politics, Colonies and Trade* (2001), is an insightful investigation of the dynamics of Phoenician expansion into the western Mediterranean. Lionel Casson, *The Ancient Mariners: Seafarers and Sea Fighters of the Mediterranean in Ancient Times*, 2d ed. (1991), 75–79, discusses the design of warships and merchant vessels. For Carthage see Serge Lancel, *Carthage: A History* (1995), and David Soren, Aicha Ben Abed Ben Khader, and Hedi Slim, *Carthage: Uncovering the Mysteries and Splendors of Ancient Tunisia* (1990). Aicha Ben Abed Ben Khader and David Soren, *Carthage: A Mosaic of Ancient Tunisia* (1987), includes articles by American and Tunisian scholars as well as the catalog of a museum exhibition. R. C. C. Law, "North Africa in the Period of Phoenician and Greek Colonization, c. 800 to 323 B.C.," Chapter 2 in *The Cambridge History of Africa*, vol. 2 (1978), places the history of Carthage in an African perspective.

Elizabeth Wayland Barber, *Women's Work: The First 20,000 Years: Women, Cloth, and Society in Early Times* (1994), is an intriguing account of textile manufacture in antiquity, with emphasis on the social implications and primary role of women. I. Irving Ziderman, "Seashells and Ancient Purple Dyeing," *Biblical Archaeologist* 53 (June 1990): 98–101, is a convenient summary of Phoenician purple-dyeing technology.

■ Notes

1. Plutarch, *Moralia*, 799 D, trans. B. H. Warmington, *Carthage* (Harmondsworth, England: Penguin 1960), 163.

Animal Domestication

The earliest domestication of plants and animals took place long before the existence of written records. For this reason, we cannot be sure how and when humans first learned to plant crops and certain animals became tame enough to live among humans. Anthropologists and historians usually link the two processes as part of a Neolithic Revolution, but they were not necessarily connected.

The domestication of plants is much better understood than the domestication of animals. Foraging bands of preagricultural humans gained much of their sustenance from seeds, fruits, and tubers collected from wild plants. Humans may have planted seeds and tubers many times without lasting effect. In a few instances, however, their plantings accidentally included a higher proportion of one naturally occurring variety of a wild species. After repeated planting cycles, this variety, which was rare in the wild, became common. When a new variety suited human needs, usually by having more food value or being easier to grow or process, people stopped collecting the wild types and relied on farming and further developing their new domestic type. In some seemingly wild forest areas of Southeast Asia and Central America, a higher than normal frequency of certain fruit trees indicates that people deliberately planted them sometime in the distant past.

In the case of animals, the question of selection to suit human needs is hard to judge. Archaeologists and anthropologists looking at ancient bones and images interpret changes in hair color, horn shape, and other visible features as indicators of domestication. But these visible changes did not generally serve human purposes. As for the uses that are most commonly associated with domestic animals, some of the most important, such as milking cows, shearing sheep, and harnessing oxen and horses to plows and vehicles, first appeared hundreds and even thousands of years after domestication.

Anthropologists and archaeologists usually assume that animals were domesticated as meat producers, but even this is questionable. Dogs, which became domestic tens of thousands of years before any other species, seem not to have been eaten in most cultures, and cats, which became domestic much later, were eaten even less often.

Cattle, sheep, and goats became domestic around ten thousand years ago in the Middle East and North Africa. Coincidentally, wheat and barley were being domesticated at roughly the same time in the same general area. This is the main reason historians generally conclude that plant and animal domestication are closely related. Yet other major meat animals, such as chickens, which originated as jungle fowl in Southeast Asia, and pigs, which probably became domestic separately in several parts of North Africa, Europe, and Asia, have no agreed-upon association with early plant domestication. Nor is plant domestication connected with the horses and camels that became domestic in western Asia and the donkeys that became domestic in the Sahara region around six thousand years ago. Though the wild forebears of these species were probably eaten, the domestic forms were usually not used for meat.

In the Middle East humans may have originally kept wild sheep, goats, and cattle for food, though wild cattle were large and dangerous and must have been hard to control. It is questionable whether keeping these or other wild animals captive for food would have been more productive, in the earliest stages, than hunting. It is even more questionable whether the humans who kept animals for this purpose had any reason to anticipate that life in captivity would cause them to become domestic.

The human motivations for the domestication of animals can be better assessed after a consideration of the physical changes involved in going from wild to domestic. Genetically transmitted tameness, defined as the ability to live with and accept handling by humans, lies at the core of the domestication process. In separate experiments with wild rats and foxes in the twentieth century, scientists found that wild individuals with strong fight-or-flight tendencies reproduce poorly in captivity. Individual animals with the lowest adrenaline levels have the most offspring in captivity. In the wild, the same low level of excitability would have made these individuals vulnerable to predators and kept their reproduction rate down. Human selection probably reinforced the natural tendency for the least excitable animals to reproduce best in captivity. In other words, humans probably preferred the animals that seemed the tamest, and destroyed those that were most wild. In the rat and fox experiments, after twenty generations or so, the surviving animals were born with much smaller adrenal glands and greatly reduced fight-or-flight reactions. Since adrenaline production normally increases in the transition to adulthood, many of the low-adrenaline animals also retained juvenile characteristics, such as floppy ears and pushed-in snouts, both indicators of domestication. This tendency of certain domestic species to preserve immature characteristics is called *neoteny*.

It is quite probable that animal domestication was not a deliberate process but rather the unanticipated outcome of keeping animals for other purposes. Since a twenty-generation time span for wild cattle and other large quadrupeds would have amounted to several human lifetimes, it is highly unlikely that the people who ended up with domestic cows had any recollection of how the process started. This seems to rule out the possibility that people who had unwittingly domesticated one species would have attempted to repeat the process with other species. Since they probably did not know what they had done to produce genetically transmitted tameness, they would not have known how to duplicate the process.

Historians disagree on this matter. Some assume that domestication was an understood and reproducible process and conclude that through a series of domestication attempts, humans domesticated every species that could be domesticated. This is unlikely. It is probable that more species could be domesticated over time. Twentieth-century efforts to domesticate bison, eland, and elk have not fully succeeded, but they have generally not been maintained for as long as twenty generations. Rats and foxes have more rapid reproduction rates, and the experiments with them succeeded. In looking at the impact of animal domestication on different parts of the world, it is unwarranted to assume that some regions were luckier than others in being home to species that were ripe for domestication, or that some human societies were cleverer than others in figuring out how to make animals genetically tame.

Rather than being treated as a process once known to early human societies and subsequently forgotten, animal domestication is best studied on a case-by-case basis as an unintended result of other processes. In some instances, sacrifice probably played a key role. Religious traditions of animal sacrifice rarely utilize, and sometimes prohibit, the ritual killing of wild animals. It is reasonable to suppose that the practice of capturing wild animals and holding them for sacrifice sometimes eventually led to the appearance of genetically transmitted tameness as an unplanned result.

Horses and camels were domesticated relatively late, and most likely not for meat consumption. The societies within which these animals first appeared as domestic species already had domestic sheep, goats, and cattle and used oxen to carry loads and pull plows and carts. Horses, camels, and later reindeer may represent successful experiments with substituting one draft animal for another, with genetically transmitted tameness an unexpected consequence of separating animals trained for riding or pulling carts from their wilder kin.

Once human societies had developed the full range of uses of domestic animals—meat, eggs, milk, fiber, labor, transport—the likelihood of domesticating more species diminished. In the absence of concrete knowledge of how domestication had occurred, it was usually easier for people to move domestic livestock to new locations than to attempt to develop new domestic species. Domestic animals accompanied human groups wherever they ventured, and this practice triggered enormous environmental changes as domestic animals, and their human keepers, competed with wild species for food and living space.

PART TWO

The Formation of New Cultural Communities, 1000 B.C.E.–400 C.E.

The fourteen centuries from 1000 B.C.E. to 400 C.E. mark a new chapter in the story of humanity. Important changes in the ways of life established in the river-valley civilizations in the two previous millennia occurred, and the scale of human institutions and activities increased.

The political and social structure of the earliest river-valley centers reflected the importance of irrigation for agriculture. Powerful kings, hereditary priesthoods, dependent laborers, limited availability of metals, and very restricted literacy are hallmarks of the complex societies described in Part One. In the first millennium B.C.E., new centers arose, in lands watered by rainfall and worked by a free peasantry, on the shores of the Mediterranean, in Iran, India, Southeast Asia, and in Central and South America. Shaped by the natural environments in which they arose, they developed new patterns of political and social organization and economic activity, and moved in new intellectual, artistic, and spiritual directions, though under the influence of the older centers.

The rulers of the empires of this era took steps intended to control and tax their subjects: they constructed extensive networks of roads and promoted urbanization. These measures brought incidental benefits: more rapid

115

communication, the transport of trade goods over greater distances, and the broad diffusion of religious ideas, artistic styles, and technologies. Large cultural zones unified by common traditions emerged. A number of these cultural traditions—Iranian, Hellenistic, Roman—were to exercise substantial influence on subsequent ages. The influence of some—Hindu and Chinese—persists into our own time.

The expansion of agriculture and trade and improvements in technology led to population increases, the spread of cities, and the growth of a comfortable middle class. In many parts of the world iron replaced bronze as the preferred metal for weapons, tools, and utensils. People using iron tools cleared extensive forests around the Mediterranean, in India, and in eastern China. Iron weapons gave an advantage to the armies of Greece, Rome, and imperial China. Metal, still an important item of long-distance trade, was available to more people than it had been in the preceding age. Metal coinage, which originated in Anatolia, was adopted by many peoples. Metal coins facilitated commercial transactions and the acquisition of wealth.

New systems of writing also developed. Because these systems were more easily and rapidly learned, writing moved out of the control of specialists. The vast majority of people remained illiterate, but writing became an increasingly important medium for preserving and transmitting cultural knowledge. The spread of literacy gave birth to new ways of thinking, new genres of literature, and new types of scientific endeavor.

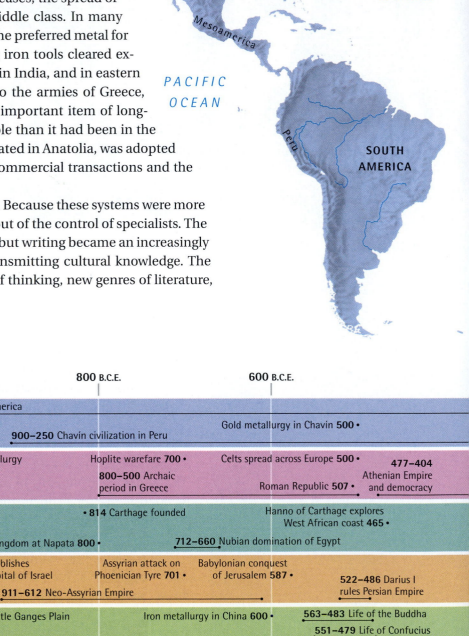

	1000 B.C.E.	800 B.C.E.	600 B.C.E.
Americas	1200–400 Olmec civilization in Mesoamerica		Gold metallurgy in Chavín 500 •
		900–250 Chavín civilization in Peru	
Europe	• 1000 Iron metallurgy	Hoplite warefare 700 • 800–500 Archaic period in Greece	Celts spread across Europe 500 • Roman Republic 507 •	477–404 Athenian Empire and democracy
Africa		• 814 Carthage founded	Hanno of Carthage explores West African coast 465 •
	Rise of Nubian kingdom at Napata 800 •	712–660 Nubian domination of Egypt	
Middle East	• 1000 David establishes Jerusalem as capital of Israel	Assyrian attack on Phoenician Tyre 701 • 911–612 Neo-Assyrian Empire	Babylonian conquest of Jerusalem 587 •	522–486 Darius I rules Persian Empire
Asia and Oceania	• 1000 Aryans settle Ganges Plain 1027–221 Zhou kingdom in China	Iron metallurgy in China 600 •	563–483 Life of the Buddha 551–479 Life of Confucius

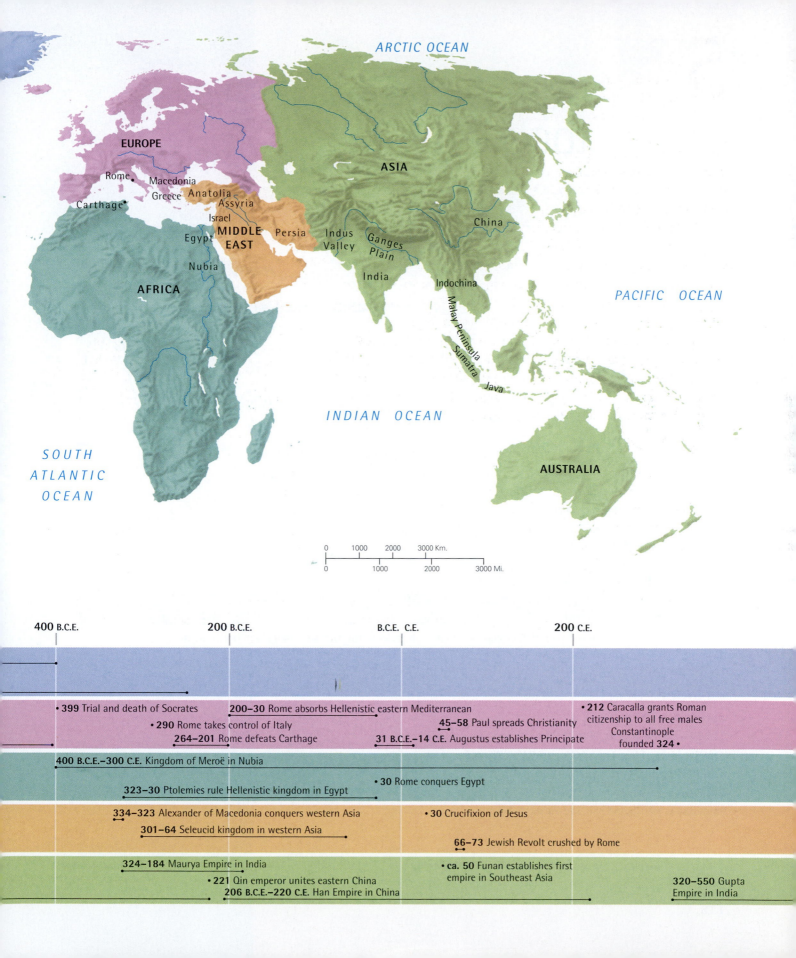

ARCTIC OCEAN

EUROPE

Rome
Macedonia
Greece
Anatolia
Assyria
Israel
MIDDLE
Egypt
EAST
Persia
Nubia

Carthage

AFRICA

ASIA

China

Indus
Valley
Ganges
Plain
India
Indochina

Malay Peninsula
Sumatra
Java

PACIFIC OCEAN

INDIAN OCEAN

AUSTRALIA

SOUTH
ATLANTIC
OCEAN

| 0 | 1000 | 2000 | 3000 Km. |
| 0 | 1000 | 2000 | 3000 Mi. |

400 B.C.E.　　200 B.C.E.　　B.C.E. C.E.　　200 C.E.

• 399 Trial and death of Socrates　　200–30 Rome absorbs Hellenistic eastern Mediterranean　　• 212 Caracalla grants Roman citizenship to all free males
• 290 Rome takes control of Italy　　45–58 Paul spreads Christianity
264–201 Rome defeats Carthage　　31 B.C.E.–14 C.E. Augustus establishes Principate　　Constantinople founded 324 •

400 B.C.E.–300 C.E. Kingdom of Meroë in Nubia
323–30 Ptolemies rule Hellenistic kingdom in Egypt　　• 30 Rome conquers Egypt

334–323 Alexander of Macedonia conquers western Asia　　• 30 Crucifixion of Jesus
301–64 Seleucid kingdom in western Asia　　66–73 Jewish Revolt crushed by Rome

324–184 Maurya Empire in India　　• ca. 50 Funan establishes first empire in Southeast Asia
• 221 Qin emperor unites eastern China　　320–550 Gupta Empire in India
206 B.C.E.–220 C.E. Han Empire in China

5

Greece and Iran, 1000–30 B.C.E.

Painted Cup of Arcesilas of Cyrene   The ruler of this Greek community in North Africa supervises the weighing and export of silphium, a valuable medicinal plant.

The Greek historian Herodotus° (ca. 485–425 B.C.E.), chronicler of the struggles of the city-states of Greece with the Persian Empire in the sixth and fifth centuries B.C.E., teaches a lesson about cultural differences. The Persian king Darius° I, whose vast empire stretched from eastern Europe to Pakistan, summoned the Greek and Indian wise men who served him at court. He first asked the Greeks whether under any circumstances they would be willing to eat the bodies of their deceased fathers. The Greeks, who cremated their dead, recoiled at the impiety of such an act. Darius then asked the Indians whether they would be prepared to burn the bodies of their dead parents. The Indians were repulsed; their practice was to ritually partake of the bodies of the dead. The point, as Herodotus noted, was that different peoples have very different practices, but each regards its own way as "natural" and superior.

Distinguishing between what was natural and what was cultural convention created much discomfort among Greeks in Herodotus's lifetime, for it called into question the validity of their fundamental beliefs. Herodotus's story also reminds us that the Persian Empire (and the Hellenistic Greek kingdoms that succeeded it) brought together, in eastern Europe, western Asia, and northwest Africa, peoples and cultural systems that previously had known little direct contact, and that this new cross-cultural interaction could be alarming even while it stimulated new and exciting cultural syntheses.

In this chapter we look at the eastern Mediterranean and western Asia in the first millennium B.C.E., emphasizing the experiences of the Persians and Greeks. The rivalry and wars of Greeks and Persians from the sixth to fourth centuries B.C.E. are traditionally seen as the first act of a drama that has continued intermittently ever since: the clash of the civilizations of East and West, of two peoples and two ways of life that were fundamentally different and thus almost certain to come into conflict. Some see recent tensions between the United States and Middle Eastern

Herodotus (heh-ROD-uh-tuhs)   Darius (duh-RIE-uhs)

states such as Iran and Iraq as the latest manifestation of this age-old conflict.

Ironically, Greeks and Persians had far more in common than they realized. Both spoke in tongues belonging to the same Indo-European family of languages found throughout Europe and western and southern Asia. Many scholars believe that all the ancient peoples who spoke languages belonging to this family inherited fundamental cultural traits, forms of social organization, and religious outlooks from their shared past.

As you read this chapter, ask yourself the following questions:

- How did geography, environment, and contacts with other peoples shape the institutions and values of Persians and Greeks?

- What brought the Greek city-states and the Persian Empire into conflict, and which factors dictated the outcome of their rivalry?

- In what ways were the lands and peoples of the eastern Mediterranean and western Asia influenced—culturally, economically, and politically—by the domination of the Persian Empire and the Greek kingdoms that succeeded it?

ANCIENT IRAN 1000–500 B.C.E.

Iran, the "land of the Aryans," links western Asia and southern and Central Asia, and its history has been marked by this mediating position (see Map 5.1). In the sixth century B.C.E. the vigorous Persians of southwest Iran created the largest empire the world had yet seen. Heirs to the long legacy of Mesopotamian history and culture, they introduced distinctly Iranian elements and developed new forms of political and economic organization in western Asia.

Relatively little written material from within the Persian Empire has survived, so we are forced to view it mostly through the eyes of the ancient Greeks—outsiders who were ignorant at best, usually hostile, and interested primarily in events that affected themselves. (Iranian groups and individuals are known in the western world by Greek approximations of their names; thus these familiar forms are used here, with the original Iranian

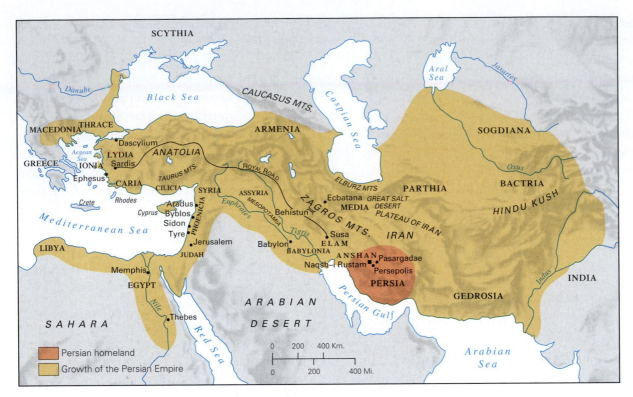

Map 5.1   The Persian Empire   Between 550 and 522 B.C.E., the Persians of southwest Iran, under their first two kings, Cyrus and Cambyses, conquered each of the major states of western Asia—Media, Babylonia, Lydia, and Egypt. The third king, Darius I, extended the boundaries as far as the Indus Valley to the east and the European shore of the Black Sea to the west. The first major setback came when the fourth king, Xerxes, failed in his invasion of Greece in 480 B.C.E. The Persian Empire was considerably larger than its recent predecessor, the Assyrian Empire. For their empire, the Persian rulers developed a system of provinces, governors, regular tribute, and communication by means of royal roads and couriers that allowed for efficient operations for almost two centuries.

names given in parentheses.) This Greek perspective leaves us unaware of developments in the central and eastern portions of the Persian Empire. Nevertheless, recent archaeological discoveries and close analysis of the limited written material from within the empire can supplement and correct the perspective of the Greek sources.

Geography and Resources

Iran is bounded by the Zagros° Mountains to the west, the Caucasus° Mountains and Caspian Sea to the northwest and north, the mountains of Afghanistan and the desert of Baluchistan° to the east and southeast, and the Persian Gulf to the southwest. The northeast is less protected by

Zagros (ZUHG-roes)   **Caucasus** (KAW-kuh-suhs)
Baluchistan (buh-loo-chi-STAN)

natural boundaries, and from that direction Iran was open to attacks by the nomads of Central Asia.

The fundamental topographical features of Iran are high mountains at the edges, salt deserts in the interior depressions, and mountain streams crossing a sloping plateau and draining into seas or interior salt lakes and marshes. Humans trying to survive in these harsh lands had to find ways to exploit limited water resources. Unlike the valleys of the Nile, Tigris-Euphrates, Ganges, and Yellow Rivers, ancient Iran never had a dense population. The best-watered and most populous parts of the country lie to the north and west; aridity increases and population decreases as one moves south and east. On the interior plateau, oasis settlements sprang up beside streams or springs. The Great Salt Desert, which covers most of eastern Iran, and Baluchistan in the southeast corner were extremely inhospitable. Scattered settlements in the narrow plains beside the Persian Gulf were cut off from the interior plateau by mountain barriers.

C H R O N O L O G Y

	Greece and the Hellenistic World	Persian Empire
1000 B.C.E.	1150–800 B.C.E. Greece's "Dark Age"	ca. 1000 B.C.E. Persians settle in southwest Iran
800 B.C.E.	ca. 800 B.C.E. Resumption of Greek contact with eastern Mediterranean 800–480 B.C.E. Greece's Archaic Period ca. 750–550 B.C.E. Era of colonization ca. 700 B.C.E. Beginning of hoplite warfare ca. 650–500 B.C.E. Era of tyrants	
600 B.C.E.	594 B.C.E. Solon reforms laws at Athens	
	546–510 B.C.E. Pisistratus and sons hold tyranny at Athens	550 B.C.E. Cyrus overthrows Medes 550–530 B.C.E. Reign of Cyrus 546 B.C.E. Cyrus conquers Lydia 539 B.C.E. Cyrus takes control of Babylonia 530–522 B.C.E. Reign of Cambyses; Conquest of Egypt 522–486 B.C.E. Reign of Darius
500 B.C.E.	499–494 B.C.E. Ionian Greeks rebel against Persia 490 B.C.E. Athenians check Persian punitive expedition at Marathon 480–323 B.C.E. Greece's classical period 477 B.C.E. Athens becomes leader of Delian League 461–429 B.C.E. Pericles dominant at Athens; Athens completes evolution to democracy	480–479 B.C.E. Xerxes' invasion of Greece
400 B.C.E.	431–404 B.C.E. Peloponnesian War 399 B.C.E. Trial and execution of Socrates 359 B.C.E. Philip II becomes king of Macedonia 338 B.C.E. Philip takes control of Greece 317 B.C.E. End of democracy in Athens	387 B.C.E. King's Peace makes Persia arbiter of Greek affairs 334–323 B.C.E. Alexander the Great defeats Persia and creates huge empire 323–30 B.C.E. Hellenistic period
300 B.C.E.	ca. 300 B.C.E. Foundation of the Museum in Alexandria	
100 B.C.E.	200 B.C.E. First Roman intervention in the Hellenistic East 30 B.C.E. Roman annexation of Egypt, the last Hellenistic kingdom	

In the first millennium B.C.E. irrigation enabled people to move down from the mountain valleys and open the plains to agriculture. To prevent evaporation of precious water in the hot, dry climate, they devised underground irrigation channels. Constructing and maintaining these subterranean channels and the vertical shafts that provided access to them was labor-intensive. Normally, local leaders oversaw the expansion of the network in each district. Activity accelerated when a strong central authority was able to organize large numbers of laborers. The connection between royal authority and prosperity is evident in the ideology of the first Persian Empire (discussed below). Even so, human survival depended on a delicate ecological balance, and a buildup of salt in the soil or a falling water table sometimes forced the abandonment of settlements.

Iran's mineral resources—copper, tin, iron, gold, and silver—were exploited on a limited scale in antiquity. Mountain slopes, more heavily wooded than they are now, provided fuel and materials for building and crafts. Because this austere land could not generate much of an agricultural surplus, objects of trade tended to be minerals and crafted goods such as textiles and carpets.

The Rise of the Persian Empire

In antiquity many groups of people, whom historians refer to collectively as "Iranians" because they spoke related languages and shared certain cultural features, spread out across western and Central Asia—an area comprising not only the modern state of Iran but also Turkmenistan, Afghanistan, and Pakistan. Several of these groups arrived in western Iran near the end of the second millennium B.C.E. The first to achieve a complex level of political organization was the Medes (Mada in Iranian). They settled in the northwest and came under the influence of the ancient centers in Mesopotamia and Urartu (modern Armenia and northeast Turkey). The Medes played a major role in the destruction of the Assyrian Empire in the late seventh century B.C.E. and extended their control westward across Assyria into Anatolia (modern Turkey). They also projected their power southeast toward the Persian Gulf, a region occupied by another Iranian people, the Persians (Parsa).

The Persian rulers—now called Achaemenids° because they traced their lineage back to an ancestor named Achaemenes—cemented their relationship with the Median court through marriage. **Cyrus** (Kurush), the son of a Persian chieftain and a Median princess, united the various Persian tribes and overthrew the Median monarch sometime around 550 B.C.E. His victory should perhaps be seen less as a conquest than as an alteration of the relations between groups, for Cyrus placed both Medes and Persians in positions of responsibility and retained the framework of Median rule. The differences

Achaemenid (a-KEY-muh-nid)

Gold Plaque from the Eastern Achaemenid Empire, fifth–fourth century B.C.E.   Part of the Oxus Treasure, a cache of gold and silver objects discovered in Tajikistan. A Median magus (religious expert), armed with a short sword and wearing pants, boots, tunic, and cloth headdress, holds a sheaf of twigs for use in a sacrificial ceremony.   (Courtesy of the Trustees of the British Museum)

between these two Iranian peoples—principally differences in the dialects they spoke and the way they dressed—were not great. The Greeks could not readily tell the two apart.

Like most Indo-European peoples, the early inhabitants of western Iran had a patriarchal family organization: the male head of the household had nearly absolute authority over family members. Society was divided into three social and occupational classes: warriors, priests, and peasants. Warriors were the dominant element. A landowning aristocracy, they took pleasure in hunting, fighting, and gardening. The king was the most illustrious member of this group. The priests, or Magi (*magush*), were ritual specialists who supervised the proper performance of sacrifices. The common people—peasants—were primarily village-based farmers and shepherds.

Over the course of two decades the energetic Cyrus (r. 550–530 B.C.E.) redrew the map of western Asia. In 546 B.C.E. he prevailed in a cavalry battle outside the gates of Sardis, the capital of the kingdom of Lydia in western Anatolia, reportedly because the smell of his camels caused a panic among his opponents' horses. All Anatolia, including the Greek city-states on the western coast, came under Persian control. In 539 B.C.E. he swept into Mesopotamia, where the Neo-Babylonian dynasty had ruled since the collapse of Assyrian power (see Chapter 4). Cyrus made a deal with disaffected elements within Babylon, and when he and his army approached, the gates of the city were thrown open to him without a struggle. A skillful propagandist, Cyrus showed respect to the Babylonian priesthood and had his son crowned king in accordance with native traditions.

After Cyrus lost his life in 530 B.C.E. while campaigning against a coalition of nomadic Iranians in the northeast, his son Cambyses° (Kambujiya, r. 530–522 B.C.E.) set his sights on Egypt, the last of the great ancient kingdoms of the Middle East. The Persians prevailed over the Egyptians in a series of bloody battles; then they sent exploratory expeditions south to Nubia and west to Libya. Greek sources depict Cambyses as a cruel and impious madman, but contemporary documents from Egypt show him operating in the same practical vein as his father, cultivating local priests and notables and respecting native traditions.

When Cambyses died in 522 B.C.E., **Darius I** (Darayavaush) seized the throne. His success in crushing many early challenges to his rule was a testimony to his skill, energy, and ruthlessness. From this reign forward, Medes played a lesser role, and the most important posts went to members of leading Persian families. Darius (r. 522–486 B.C.E.) extended Persian control eastward as far as the Indus Valley and westward into Europe, where he bridged the Danube River and chased the nomadic Scythian° peoples north of the Black Sea. The Persians erected a string of forts in Thrace (modern-day northeast Greece and Bulgaria) and by 500 B.C.E. were on the doorstep of Greece. Darius also promoted the development of maritime routes. He dispatched a fleet to explore the waters from the Indus Delta to the Red Sea, and he completed a canal linking the Red Sea with the Nile.

Imperial Organization and Ideology

The empire of Darius I was the largest the world had yet seen (see Map 5.1). Stretching from eastern Europe to Pakistan, from southern Russia to Sudan, it encompassed a multitude of ethnic groups and many forms of social and political organization, from nomadic kinship group to subordinate kingdom to city-state. Darius can rightly be considered a second founder of the Persian Empire, after Cyrus, because he created a new organizational structure that was maintained throughout the remaining two centuries of the empire's existence.

Darius divided the empire into twenty provinces. Each was under the supervision of a Persian **satrap°**, or governor, who was likely to be related or connected by marriage to the royal family. The satrap's court was a miniature version of the royal court. The tendency for the position of satrap to become hereditary meant that satraps' families lived in the province governed by their head, acquired a fund of knowledge about local conditions, and formed connections with the local native elite. The farther a province was from the center of the empire, the more autonomy the satrap had, because slow communications made it impractical to refer most matters to the central administration. This system of administration brought significant numbers of Persians and other peoples from the center of the empire to the provinces, resulting in intermarriage and cultural and technological exchanges. For example, recent archaeological work at a site in the western desert of Egypt has shown the use of underground water channels of Iranian design to serve a new agricultural settlement.

One of the satrap's most important duties was to collect and send tribute to the king. Darius prescribed how much precious metal each province was to contribute annually. This amount was forwarded to the central treasury. Some of it was disbursed for necessary expenditures, but most was hoarded. As more and more precious metal was taken out of circulation, the price of gold and silver rose, and provinces found it increasingly difficult to meet their quotas. Evidence from Babylonia indicates a gradual economic decline setting in by the fourth century B.C.E. The increasing burden of taxation and official corruption may have inadvertently caused the economic downturn.

Well-maintained and patrolled royal roads connected the outlying provinces to the heart of the empire. Way stations were built at intervals to receive important travelers and couriers carrying official correspondence. At

---

Cambyses (kam-BIE-sees)   **Scythian** (SITH-ee-uhn)   **satrap** (SAY-trap)

strategic points, such as mountain passes, river crossings, and important urban centers, garrisons controlled people's movements. The administrative center of the empire was Susa, the ancient capital of Elam, in southwest Iran near the present-day border with Iraq. It was to Susa that Greeks and others went with requests and messages for the king. It took a party of Greek ambassadors at least three months to make the journey. Altogether, travel time, time spent waiting for an audience with the Persian king, delays due to weather, and the duration of the return trip probably kept the ambassadors away from home a year or more.

The king lived and traveled with his numerous wives and children. The little information that we have about the lives of Persian royal women comes from foreign sources and is thus suspect. The Book of Esther in the Hebrew Bible tells a romantic story of how King Ahasuerus° (Xerxes° to the Greeks) picked the beautiful Jewish woman Esther to be one of his wives and how the courageous and clever queen later saved the Jewish people from a plot to massacre them. Greek sources show women of the royal family being used as pawns in the struggle for power. Darius strengthened his claim to the throne by marrying a daughter of Cyrus, and later the Greek conqueror Alexander the Great married a daughter of the last Persian king. Greek sources portray Persian queens as vicious intriguers, poisoning rival wives and plotting to win the throne for their sons. However, a recent study suggests that the Greek stereotype misrepresents the important role played by Persian women in protecting family members and mediating conflicts. Both Greek sources and documents within the empire reveal that Persian elite women were politically influential, possessed substantial property, traveled, and were prominent on public occasions.

Besides the royal family, the king's large entourage included several other groups: (1) the sons of Persian aristocrats, who were educated at court and also served as hostages for their parents' good behavior; (2) many noblemen, who were expected to attend the king when they were not otherwise engaged; (3) the central administration, including officials and employees of the treasury, secretariat, and archives; (4) the royal bodyguard; and (5) countless courtiers and slaves. Long gone were the simple days when the king hunted and caroused with his warrior companions. Inspired by Mesopotamian conceptions of monarchy, the king of Persia had become an aloof figure of majesty and splendor: "The Great King, King of Kings, King in Persia, King of countries." He referred to everyone, even the Persian nobility,

as "my slaves," and anyone who approached him had to bow down before him.

The king owned vast tracts of land throughout the empire. Some of it he gave to his supporters. Donations called "bow land," "horse land," and "chariot land" in Babylonian documents obliged the recipient to provide military service. Scattered around the empire were gardens, orchards, and hunting preserves belonging to the king and the high nobility. The *paradayadam* (meaning "walled enclosure"—the term has come into English as *paradise*), a green oasis in an arid landscape, advertised the prosperity that the king could bring to those who loyally served him.

Surviving administrative records from the Persian homeland give us a glimpse of how the complex tasks of administration were managed. The **Persepolis**° Treasury and Fortification Texts, inscribed in Elamite cuneiform on baked clay tablets, show that government officials distributed food and other essential commodities to large numbers of workers of many different nationalities. Some of these workers may have been prisoners of war brought to the center of the empire to work on construction projects, maintain and expand the irrigation network, and farm the royal estates. Workers were divided into groups of men, women, and children. Women received less than men of equivalent status, but pregnant women and women with babies received more. Men and women performing skilled jobs received more than their unskilled counterparts.

Tradition remembered Darius as a lawgiver who created a body of "laws of the King" and a system of royal judges operating throughout the empire, as well as encouraging the codification and publication of the laws of the various subject peoples. In a manner that typifies the decentralized character of the Persian Empire, he allowed each people to live in accordance with its own traditions and ordinances.

The central administration was based not in the Persian homeland (present-day Fars, directly north of the Persian Gulf) but farther west in Elam and Mesopotamia. Closer to the geographical center of the empire, this location allowed the kings to employ the trained administrators and scribes of those ancient civilizations. However, on certain occasions the kings returned to one special place back in the homeland. Darius began construction of a ceremonial capital at Persepolis (Parsa). An artificial platform was erected, and on it were built a series of palaces, audience halls, treasury buildings, and barracks. Here, too, Darius and his son Xerxes, who completed the project, were inspired by Mesopotamian

---

Ahasuerus (uh-HAZZ-yoo-ear-uhs)   **Xerxes** (ZERK-sees)

Persepolis (Per-SEH-poe-lis)

View of the East Front of the Apadana (Audience Hall) at Persepolis, ca. 500 B.C.E.   To the right lies the Gateway of Xerxes. Persepolis, in the Persian homeland, was built by Darius I and his son Xerxes, and it was used for ceremonies of special importance to the Persian king and people—coronations, royal weddings, funerals, and the New Year's festival. The stone foundations, walls, and stairways of Persepolis are filled with sculpted images of members of the court and embassies bringing gifts, offering a vision of the grandeur and harmony of the Persian Empire.   (Courtesy of the Oriental Institute, University of Chicago)

traditions, for the great Assyrian kings had created new fortress-cities as advertisements of wealth and power.

Darius's approach to governing can be seen in the luxuriant relief sculpture that covers the foundations, walls, and stairwells of the buildings at Persepolis. Representatives of all the peoples of the empire—recognizable by their distinctive hair, beards, dress, hats, and footwear—are depicted in the act of bringing gifts to the king. Historians used to think that the sculpture represented a real event that transpired each year at Persepolis, but now they see it as an exercise in what today we would call public relations or propaganda. It is Darius's carefully crafted vision of an empire of vast extent and abundant resources in which all the subject peoples willingly cooperate. In one telling sculptural example, Darius subtly contrasted the character of his rule with that of the Assyrian Empire, the Persians' predecessors in these lands (see Chapter 4). Where Assyrian kings had gloried in their power and depicted subjects staggering under the weight of a giant platform that supported the throne, Darius's artists showed erect subjects shouldering the burden willingly and without strain.

What actually took place at Persepolis? This opulent retreat in the homeland probably was the scene of events of special significance for the king and his people: the New Year's Festival, coronation, marriage, death, and burial. The kings from Darius on were buried in elaborate tombs cut into the cliffs at nearby Naqsh-i Rustam°.

Another perspective on what the Persian monarchy claimed to stand for is provided by the several dozen inscriptions that have survived (see Diversity and Dominance: The Persian Idea of Kingship). At Naqsh-i Rustam, Darius makes the following claim:

> Ahuramazda° [a Persian deity], when he saw this earth in commotion, thereafter bestowed it upon me, made me king. . . . By the favor of Ahuramazda I put it down in its place. . . . I am of such a sort that I am a friend to right, I am not a friend to wrong. It is not my desire that the weak man should have wrong done to him by the mighty; nor is that my desire, that the mighty man should have wrong done to him by the weak.[1]

Naqsh-i Rustam (NUHK-shee ROOS-tuhm)
Ahuramazda (ah-HOOR-uh-MAZZ-duh)

DIVERSITY AND DOMINANCE

THE PERSIAN IDEA OF KINGSHIP

Our most important internal source of information about the Persian Empire is a group of inscriptions commissioned by several kings. The most extensive and informative of these is the inscription that Darius had carved into a cliff face at Behistun (Beh-HISS-toon), high above the road leading from Mesopotamia to northwest Iran through a pass in the Zagros mountain range. It is written in three versions—Old Persian, the language of the ruling people (quite possibly being put into written form for the first time); Elamite, the language native to the ancient kingdom lying between southern Mesopotamia and the Persian homeland and used in Persia for local administrative documents; and Akkadian, the language of Babylonia, widely used for administrative purposes throughout western Asia. The multilingual inscription accompanied a monumental relief representing Darius looming over a line of bound prisoners, the leaders of the many forces he had to defeat in order to secure the throne after the death of Cambyses in 522 B.C.E.

I am Darius, the great king, king of kings, the king of Persia, the king of countries, the son of Hystaspes, the grandson of Arsames, the Achaemenid . . . from antiquity we have been noble; from antiquity has our dynasty been royal . . .

King Darius says: By the grace of Ahuramazda am I king; Ahuramazda has granted me the kingdom.

King Darius says: These are the countries which are subject unto me, and by the grace of Ahuramazda I became king of them: Persia, Elam, Babylonia, Assyria, Arabia, Egypt, the countries by the Sea, Lydia, the Greeks, Media, Armenia, Cappadocia, Parthia, Drangiana, Aria, Chorasmia, Bactria, Sogdiana, Gandara, Scythia, Sattagydia, Arachosia and Maka; twenty-three lands in all.

King Darius says: These are the countries which are subject to me; by the grace of Ahuramazda they became subject to me; they brought tribute unto me. Whatsoever commands have been laid on them by me, by night or by day, have been performed by them.

King Darius says: Within these lands, whosoever was a friend, him have I surely protected; whosoever was hostile, him have I utterly destroyed. By the grace of Ahuramazda these lands have conformed to my decrees; as it was commanded unto them by me, so was it done.

King Darius says: Ahuramazda has granted unto me this empire. Ahuramazda brought me help, until I gained this empire; by the grace of Ahuramazda do I hold this empire.

King Darius says: The following is what was done by me after I became king.

A lengthy description of the many battles Darius and his supporters fought against a series of other claimants to power follows.

King Darius says: This is what I have done. By the grace of Ahuramazda have I always acted. After I became king, I fought nineteen battles in a single year and by the grace of Ahuramazda I overthrew nine kings and I made them captive . . .

King Darius Says: As to these provinces which revolted, lies made them revolt, so that they deceived the people. Then Ahuramazda delivered them into my hand; and I did unto them according to my will.

King Darius says: You who shall be king hereafter, protect yourself vigorously from lies; punish the liars well, if thus you shall think, 'May my country be secure!' . . .

King Darius says: On this account Ahuramazda brought me help, and all the other gods, all that there are, because I was not wicked, nor was I a liar, nor was I a tyrant, neither I nor any of my family. I have ruled according to righteousness. Neither to the weak nor to the powerful did I do wrong. Whosoever helped by house, him I favored; he who was hostile, him I destroyed . . .

King Darius says: By the grace of Ahuramazda this is the inscription which I have made. Besides, it was in Aryan script, and it was composed on clay tablets and on parchment. Besides, a sculptured figure of myself I made. Besides, I made my lineage. And it was inscribed and was read off before me. Afterwards this inscription I sent off everywhere among the provinces. The people unitedly worked upon it.

This is an extremely important historical document. For all practical purposes, it is the only version we have of the circumstances by which Darius, who was not a member of the family of Cyrus, took over the Persian throne and established a new dynasty. The account of these events given by the Greek historian Herodotus, for all its additional (and often suspect) detail, is clearly based, however indirectly, on Darius' own account. While scholars have doubted the truthfulness of Darius's claims, the inscription is a resounding example of how the victors often get to impose their version of events on the historical record.

The Behistun inscription is certainly propaganda, but that does not mean that it lacks value. To be effective propaganda must be predicated on the moral values, political principles, and religious beliefs that are familiar and acceptable in a society, and thus it can provide us with a window on those views. The Behistun inscription also allows us to glimpse something of the personality of Darius and how he wished to be perceived.

Another document, found at Persepolis, the magnificent ceremonial center built by Darius and his son Xerxes, expands on the qualities of an exemplary ruler. While it purports to be the words of Xerxes, it is almost an exact copy of an inscription of Darius from nearby Naqsh-i Rustam, where Darius and subsequent kings were buried in monumental tombs carved into the sheer cliff. This shows the continuity of concepts through several reigns.

A great god is Ahuramazda, who created this excellent thing which is seen, who created happiness for man, who set wisdom and capability down upon King Xerxes.

Proclaims Xerxes the King: By the will of Ahuramazda I am of such a sort, I am a friend of the right, of wrong I am not a friend. It is not my wish that the weak should have harm done him by the strong, nor is it my wish that the strong should have harm done him by the weak.

The right, that is my desire. To the man who is a follower of the lie I am no friend. I am not hot-tempered. Whatever befalls me in battle, I hold firmly. I am ruling firmly my own will.

The man who is cooperative, according to his cooperation thus I reward him. Who does harm, him according to the harm I punish. It is not my wish that a man should do harm; nor indeed is it my wish that if he does harm he should not be punished.

What a man says against a man, that does not persuade me, until I hear the sworn statements of both.

What a man does or performs, according to his ability, by that I become satisfied with him, and it is much to my desire, and I am well pleased, and I give much to loyal men.

Of such a sort are my understanding and my judgment: if what has been done by me you see or hear of, both in the palace and in the expeditionary camp, this is my capability over will and understanding.

This indeed my capability: that my body is strong. As a fighter of battles I am a good fighter of battles. When ever with my judgment in a place I determine whether I behold or do not behold an enemy, both with understanding and with judgment, then I think prior to panic, when I see an enemy as when I do not see one.

I am skilled both in hands and in feet. A horseman, I am a good horseman. A bowman, I am a good bowman, both on foot and on horseback. A spearman, I am a good spearman, both on foot and on horseback.

These skills that Ahuramazada set down upon me, and which I am strong enough to bear, by the will of Ahuramazda, what was done by me, with these skills I did, which Ahuramazda set down upon me.

May Ahuramazda protect me and what was done by me.

QUESTIONS FOR ANALYSIS

1. How does Darius justify his assumption of power in the Behistun inscription? What is his relationship to Ahuramazda, the Zoroastrian god, and what role does divinity play in human affairs?

2. How does Darius conceptualize his empire (look at a map and follow the order in which he lists the provinces) and what are the expectations and obligations that he places on his subjects? What does his characterization of his opponents as "Lie-followers" tell us about his view of human nature?

3. Looking at the document of Xerxes from Persepolis, what qualities (physical, mental, and moral) are desirable in a ruler? What is the Persian concept of justice?

4. To what audiences are Darius and Xerxes directing their messages, and in what media are they being disseminated? Given that Darius himself is, in all likelihood, illiterate, and that so are most of his subjects, what is the effect of the often repeated phrase: "Darius the King says"?

Sources: Behistun inscription translated by L. W. King and R. C. Thompson, *The Sculptures and Inscription of Darius the Great on the Rock of Behistun in Persia*, London, 1907 (http://www.livius.org/be-bm/behistun03.html); document from Nagsh-i Rustam (http://www.livius.org/x/xerxes/xerxes_texts.htm#daeva)

As this inscription makes clear, behind Darius and the empire stands the will of god. Ahuramazda made Darius king and gave him a mandate to bring order to a world in turmoil, and, despite his reasonable and just disposition, the king will brook no opposition. Ahuramazda is the great god of a religion called **Zoroastrianism°**, and it is nearly certain that Darius and his successors were Zoroastrians.

The origins of this religion are shrouded in uncertainty. The Gathas, hymns in an archaic Iranian dialect, are said to be the work of Zoroaster° (Zarathushtra). The dialect and physical setting of the hymns indicate that Zoroaster lived in eastern Iran. Scholarly guesses about when he lived range from 1700 to 500 B.C.E. He revealed that the world had been created by Ahuramazda, "the wise lord," and was threatened by Angra Mainyu°, "the hostile spirit," backed by a host of demons. In this dualistic universe, the struggle between good and evil plays out over twelve thousand years, after which good is destined to prevail, and the world will return to the pure state of creation. In the meantime, humanity is a participant in the cosmic struggle, and individuals are rewarded or punished in the afterlife for their actions.

In addition to Zoroastrianism, the Persians drew on moral and metaphysical conceptions with deep roots in the Iranian past. They were sensitive to the beauties of nature and venerated beneficent elements, such as water, which was not to be sullied, and fire, which was worshiped at fire altars. They were greatly concerned about the purity of the body. Corpses were exposed to wild beasts and the elements to prevent them from putrefying in the earth or tainting the sanctity of fire. The Persians still revered major deities from the polytheist past, such as Mithra, associated with the sun and defender of oaths and compacts. They were expected to keep promises and tell the truth. In his inscriptions at Persepolis, Darius castigated evildoers as followers of "the Lie."

Zoroastrianism was one of the great religions of the ancient world. It preached belief in one supreme deity, held humans to a high ethical standard, and promised salvation. It traveled across western Asia with the advance of the Persian Empire, and it may have exerted a major influence on Judaism and thus, indirectly, on Christianity. God and the Devil, Heaven and Hell, reward and punishment, the Messiah and the End of Time all appear to be legacies of this profound belief system. Because of the accidents of history—the fall of the Achaemenid Persian Empire in the later fourth century B.C.E. and the Islamic conquest of Iran

in the seventh century C.E. (see Chapter 9)—Zoroastrianism has all but disappeared (except among a relatively small number of Parsees, as Zoroastrians are now called, in Iran and India).

THE RISE OF THE GREEKS, 1000–500 B.C.E.

Because Greece was a relatively resource-poor region, the cultural features that emerged there in the first millennium B.C.E. came into being only because the Greeks had access to foreign sources of raw materials and to markets abroad. Greeks were in contact with other peoples, and Greek merchants and mercenaries brought home not only raw materials and crafted goods but also ideas. Under the pressure of population, poverty, war, or political crisis, Greeks moved to other parts of the Mediterranean and western Asia, bringing their language and culture and exerting a powerful influence on other societies. Encounters with the different practices and beliefs of other peoples stimulated the formation of a Greek identity and sparked interest in geography, ethnography, and history. A two-century-long rivalry with the Persian Empire also played a large part in shaping the destinies of the Greek city-states.

Geography and Resources

Greece is part of a large ecological zone that encompasses the Mediterranean Sea and the lands surrounding it (see Map 4.5). This zone is bounded by the Atlantic Ocean to the west, the several ranges of the Alps to the north, the Syrian desert to the east, and the Sahara to the south. The lands lying within this zone have a roughly uniform climate, experience a similar sequence of seasons, and are home to similar plants and animals. In the summer a weather front stalls near the entrance of the Mediterranean, impeding the passage of storms from the Atlantic and allowing hot, dry air from the Sahara to creep up over the region. In winter the front dissolves and the ocean storms roll in, bringing waves, wind, and cold. It was relatively easy for people to migrate to new homes within this ecological zone without having to alter familiar cultural practices and means of livelihood.

Greek civilization arose in the lands bordering the Aegean Sea: the Greek mainland, the islands of the Aegean, and the western coast of Anatolia (see Map 5.2). As we saw in Chapter 4, southern Greece is a dry and

---

Zoroastrianism (zo-roe-ASS-tree-uh-niz-uhm)
Zoroaster (zo-roe-ASS-ter)
Angra Mainyu (ANG-ruh MINE-yoo)

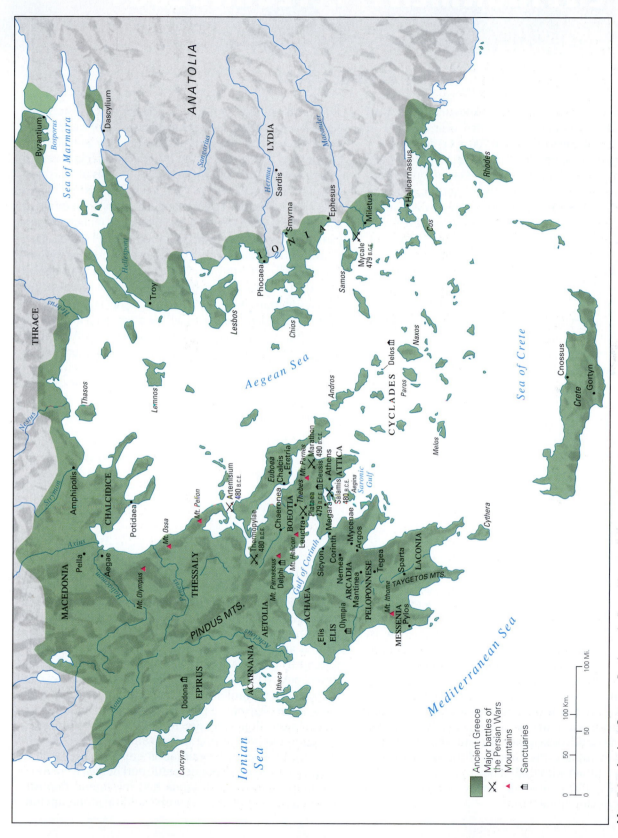

Map 5.2 Ancient Greece By the early first millennium B.C.E. Greek-speaking peoples were dispersed throughout the Aegean region, occupying the Greek mainland, most of the islands, and the western coast of Anatolia. The rough landscape of central and southern Greece, with small plains separated by ranges of mountains, and the many islands in the Aegean favored the rise of hundreds of small, independent communities. The presence of adequate rainfall meant that agriculture was organized on the basis of self-sufficient family farms. As a result of the limited natural resources of this region, the Greeks had to resort to sea travel and trade with other lands in the Mediterranean to acquire metals and other vital raw materials.

The Farmer's Year

Perhaps the first Greek we can get to know as an individual is Hesiod (HEE-see-uhd). Hesiod lived near a village in Boeotia, in central Greece, around 700 B.C.E. In his poem *Works and Days*, we learn about his work as a farmer and about his relationships with family members and neighbors. The poem is presented as advice to his good-for-nothing brother, stressing the necessity of hard and perpetual work in order to survive. Much of the poem is a kind of farmer's almanac, describing the annual cycle of tasks on a Greek farm.

As Hesiod makes clear, it was very important for farmers to perform work at the right time. How did Greeks of the Archaic period, with no clocks, calendars, or newspapers, know where they were in the cycle of the year? They oriented themselves by acute observation of natural phenomena such as the flowering of plants and trees and the behavior of animals, the migration of birds and changes in the weather, and the movements of planets, stars, and constellations in the night sky.

Hesiod gives the following advice for determining the proper times for planting and harvesting grain:

> Pleiades rising in the dawning sky,
> Harvest is nigh.
> Pleiades setting in the waning night,
> Plowing is right.

The Pleiades (PLEE-uh-dees) is a cluster of seven stars visible to the naked eye. In Greek mythology, the Pleiades were seven sisters whom the gods placed in the sky to help them escape from the hunter Orion. The ancient Greeks observed that individual stars and constellations (groups of stars perceived by the human eye to form images in the sky) moved from east to west during the night and appeared in different parts of the sky at different times of the year. (In fact, the apparent movement of the stars is due to the earth's rotation on its axis and orbit around the sun against a background of unmoving stars. To earthly observers, however, the stars appear to move.) Hesiod is telling his audience that, when the Pleiades appear above the eastern horizon just before the light of the rising sun makes all the other stars invisible (in May on the modern calendar), a sensible farmer will cut down his grain crop. Some months later (in our September), when the Pleiades dip below the western horizon just before sunrise, it is time to plow the fields and plant seeds for the next year's harvest.

Other events in nature provide similar indicators:

> Mind now, when you hear the call of the crane
> Coming from the clouds, as it does year by year:
> That's the sign for plowing . . .

---

rocky land with small plains carved up by low mountain ranges. No navigable rivers ease travel or the transport of commodities across this difficult terrain. The small islands dotting the Aegean were inhabited from early times. People could cross the water from Greece to Anatolia almost without losing sight of land. From about 1000 B.C.E. Greeks began to settle on the western edge of Anatolia. Rivers that formed broad and fertile plains near the coast made Ionia, as the ancient Greeks called this region, a comfortable place. The interior of Anatolia is rugged plateau, and the Greeks of the coast were in much closer contact with their fellows across the Aegean than with the native peoples of the interior. The sea was always a connector, not a barrier.

Without large rivers, Greek farmers on the mainland depended entirely on rainfall to water their crops (see Environment and Technology: The Farmer's Year). The limited arable land, thin topsoil, and sparse rainfall in the south could not sustain large populations. In the historical period farmers usually planted grain (mostly barley, which was hardier than wheat) in the flat plain, olive trees at the edge of the plain, and grapevines on the terraced lower slopes of the foothills. Sheep and goats grazed in the hills during the growing season. In northern Greece, where the rainfall is greater and the land opens out into broad plains, cattle and horses were more abundant. These Greek lands had few metal deposits and little timber, although both building stone, includ-

And even the stern Hesiod allows himself a break at the height of summer:

But when the thistle's in bloom, and the cicada
Chirps from its perch in a branch, pouring down
Shrill song from its wings in the withering heat,
Then goats are plumpest, wine at its best, women
Most lustful, but men at their feeblest, since Sirius
Scorches head and knees, and skin shrivels up. . . .
*   Time to drink sparkling wine*
Sitting in the shade, heart satisfied with food,
Face turned toward the cooling West Wind . . .

Sirius (SIH-ree-uhs), the brightest star in the sky, rose with the sun in late July. The ancients believed that the addition of its heat to the heat already provided by the sun accounted for sizzling temperatures at this time of year. (The ancient Egyptians connected the rising of Sirius with the beginning of the Nile flood.)

It is clear to any reader of Hesiod's poem that he and his fellow Greek farmers were intimately attuned to their environment. Their extensive knowledge of the natural world provided them with information vital for survival.

Black-Figure Vase from Athens, Late Sixth Century B.C.E. In this rare depiction of the activities of the working class, one man is up in an olive tree shaking the branches, two others knock olives down with sticks, while a fourth picks them off the ground. Olives were an important agricultural product, not only for eating, but also for the oil that was used for lamps, cooking, and cleaning and moisturizing the skin. Olive oil was a major export product at Athens. (Courtesy of the Trustees of the British Museum)

Source: From *Hesiod: Works and Days and Theogony,* translated by Stanley Lombardo (Indianapolis/Cambridge: Hackett Publishing, 1993) Reprinted by permission of Hacket Publishing Company, Inc. All rights reserved.

ing some fine marble, and clay for the potter were abundant.

A glance at a map of Greece reveals a deeply pitted coastline with many natural harbors. A combination of circumstances—the difficulty of overland transport, the availability of good anchorages, and the need to import metals, timber, and grain—drew the Greeks to the sea. They obtained timber from the northern Aegean, gold and iron from Anatolia, copper from Cyprus, tin from the western Mediterranean, and grain from the Black Sea, Egypt, and Sicily. Sea transport was much cheaper and faster than overland transport. Thus, though never comfortable with "the wine-dark sea," as the poet Homer called it, the Greeks had no choice but to embark upon it in their small, frail ships, hugging the coastline or island-hopping where possible.

The Emergence of the Polis

The first flowering of Greek culture in the Mycenaean civilization of the second millennium B.C.E. is described in Chapter 4. This was largely an adaptation of the imported institutions of Middle Eastern palace-dominated states to the Greek terrain. For several centuries after the destruction of the Mycenaean palace-states, Greece lapsed into a "Dark Age" (ca. 1150–800 B.C.E.): for those who lived through it, dark because of depopulation, poverty, and backwardness; for us, dark because it left few traces in the archaeological record. During the Dark Age, Greece and the whole Aegean region were largely isolated from the rest of the world. The importation of raw materials, especially metals, had been the chief source of Mycenaean prosperity. Lack of access to vital resources lay behind the poverty of the Dark Age.

Within Greece, regions that had little contact with one another developed distinctive local styles in pottery and other crafts. With fewer people to feed, the land was largely given over to grazing flocks of sheep, goats, and cattle. While there was continuity of language, religion, and other aspects of culture, there was a sharp break with the authoritarian Mycenaean political structure and centralized control of the economy. This would open the way for the development of new political, social, and economic forms rooted in the Greek environment.

The isolation of Greece ended around 800 B.C.E. when Phoenician ships began to visit the Aegean (see Chapter 4). The Phoenician city-states were dominated by a merchant class that was making ever more distant voyages west in search of valuable commodities and trading partners. By reestablishing contact between the Aegean and the Middle East, the Phoenicians gave Greek civilization an important push and inaugurated what scholars now term the "Archaic" period of Greek history (ca. 800–480 B.C.E.). Soon Greek ships were also plying the waters of the Mediterranean in search of raw materials, trade opportunities, and fertile farmland.

Various evidence reveals the influx of new ideas from the east, such as the appearance of naturalistic human and animal figures and imaginative mythical beasts on painted Greek pottery. The most auspicious gift of the Phoenicians was a writing system. The Phoenicians used a set of twenty-two symbols to represent the consonants in their language, leaving the vowel sounds to be inferred by the reader. To represent Greek vowel sounds, the Greeks utilized some of the Phoenician symbols for which there were no equivalent sounds in the Greek language. This was the first true alphabet, a system of writing that fully represents the sounds of spoken language. An alphabet offers tremendous advantages over systems of writing such as cuneiform and hieroglyphics, whose signs represent entire words or syllables. Because cuneiform and hieroglyphics required years of training and the memorization of several hundred signs, they remained the preserve of a scribal class whose elevated social position stemmed from their mastery of the technology. An alphabet opens the door for more widespread literacy. Because only a few dozen signs are required to represent all the possible statements in a language, people can learn an alphabet in a relatively short period of time.

There is controversy about the earliest uses of the Greek alphabet. Some scholars maintain that the Greeks first used it for economic purposes, such as to keep inventories of a merchant's wares. Others propose that it originated as a vehicle for preserving the oral poetic epics so important to the Greeks. Whatever its first use, the Greeks soon came to employ the new technology to produce new forms of literature, law codes, religious dedications, and epitaphs on gravestones. This does not mean, however, that Greek society immediately became literate in the modern sense. For many centuries, Greece remained a primarily oral culture: people used story-telling, rituals, and performances to preserve and transmit information. Many of the distinctive intellectual and artistic creations of Greek civilization, such as theatrical drama, philosophical dialogues, and political and court-room oratory, are products of the dynamic interaction of speaking and writing.

One indicator of the powerful new forces at work in the Archaic period was a veritable explosion of population. Studies of cemeteries in the vicinity of Athens show that there was a dramatic population increase (perhaps as much as fivefold or sevenfold) during the eighth century B.C.E. Its causes are not fully understood but probably include the more intensive use of land as farming replaced herding and independent farmers and their families began to work previously unused land on the margins of the plains. The accompanying shift to a diet based on bread and vegetables rather than meat may have increased fertility and life span. A second factor was increasing prosperity based on the importation of food and raw materials. Rising population density led villages to merge and become urban centers. It also created the potential for specialization of labor: freed from agricultural tasks, some members of the society were able to develop skills in other areas, such as crafts and commerce.

Greece at this time consisted of hundreds of independent political entities, reflecting the facts of Greek geography—small plains separated from each other by mountain barriers. The Greek **polis**° (usually translated "city-state") consisted of an urban center and the rural territory that it controlled. City-states came in various sizes, with populations as small as several thousand or as large as several hundred thousand in the case of Athens.

Most urban centers had certain characteristic features. A hilltop *acropolis*° ("top of the city") offered a place of refuge in an emergency. The town spread out around the base of this fortified high point. An *agora*° ("gathering place") was an open area where citizens came together to ratify the decisions of their leaders or to line up with their weapons before military ventures.

---

polis (POE-lis) **acropolis** (uh-KRAW-poe-lis) **agora** (ah-go-RAH)

The Acropolis at Athens This steep, defensible plateau jutting up from the Attic Plain served as a Mycenaean fortress in the second millennium B.C.E., and the site of Athens has been continuously occupied since that time. In the mid-sixth century B.C.E. the tyrant Pisistratus built a temple to Athena, the patron goddess of the community. It was destroyed by the Persians when they invaded Greece in 480 B.C.E. The Acropolis was left in ruins for three decades as a reminder of what the Athenians sacrificed in defense of Greek freedom, but in the 440s B.C.E. Pericles initiated a building program, using funds from the naval empire that Athens headed. These construction projects, including a new temple to Athena—the Parthenon—brought glory to the city and popularity to Pericles and to the new democracy that he championed. (Robert Harding Picture Library)

Government buildings were located there, but the agora soon developed into a marketplace as well (vendors everywhere are eager to set out their wares wherever crowds gather). Fortified walls surrounded the urban center; but as the population expanded, new buildings went up beyond the perimeter.

City and country were not as sharply distinguished as they are today. The urban center depended on its agricultural hinterland to provide food, and many of the people living within the walls of the city went out to work on nearby farms during the day. Unlike the dependent workers on the estates of early Mesopotamia, the rural populations of the Greek city-states were free members of the community.

Each polis was fiercely jealous of its independence and suspicious of its neighbors, and this state of mind led to frequent conflict. By the early seventh century B.C.E. the Greeks had developed a new kind of warfare, waged by **hoplites**°—heavily armored infantrymen who

fought in close formation. Protected by a helmet, a breastplate, and leg guards, each hoplite held a round shield over his own left side and the right side of the man next to him and brandished a thrusting spear, keeping a sword in reserve. In this style of combat, the key to victory was maintaining the cohesion of one's own formation while breaking open the enemy's line. Most of the casualties were suffered by the defeated army in flight.

Recent studies have emphasized the close relationship of hoplite warfare to the agricultural basis of Greek society. Greek states were defended by armies of private citizens—mostly farmers—called up for brief periods of crisis, rather than by a professional class of soldiers. Although this kind of fighting called for strength to bear the weapons and armor, and courage to stand one's ground in battle, no special training was needed by the citizen-soldiers. Campaigns took place when farmers were available, in the windows of time between major tasks in the agricultural cycle. When a hoplite army marched into the fields of another community, the enraged farmers of that community, who had expended a

hoplite (HAWP-lite)

lot of hard labor on their land and buildings, could not fail to meet the challenge. Though brutal and terrifying, the clash of two hoplite lines did offer a quick decision. Battles rarely lasted more than a few hours, and the survivors could promptly return home to tend their farms.

The expanding population soon surpassed the capacity of the small plains, and many communities sent excess population abroad to establish independent "colonies" in distant lands. Not every colonist left willingly. Sources tell of people being chosen by lot and forbidden to return on pain of death. Others, seeing an opportunity to escape from poverty, avoid the constraints of family, or find adventure, voluntarily set out to seek their fortunes on the frontier. After obtaining the approval of the god Apollo from his sanctuary at Delphi, the colonists departed, carrying fire from the communal hearth of the "mother-city," a symbol of the kinship and religious ties that would connect the two communities. They settled by the sea in the vicinity of a hill or other natural refuge. The "founder," a prominent member of the mother-city, allotted parcels of land and drafted laws for the new community. In some cases the indigenous population was driven away or reduced to a semiservile status; in other cases there was intermarriage and mixing between colonists and natives.

A wave of colonization from the mid-eighth through mid-sixth centuries B.C.E. spread Greek culture far beyond the land of its origins. New settlements sprang up in the northern Aegean area, around the Black Sea, and on the Libyan coast of North Africa. In southern Italy and on the island of Sicily (see Map 4.5) another Greek core area was established. Although the creation of new homes, farms, and communities undoubtedly posed many challenges for the Greek settlers, they were able to transplant their entire way of life, mostly because of the general similarity in climate and ecology in the Mediterranean lands.

Greeks began to use the term *Hellenes°* (*Graeci* is what the Romans later called them) to distinguish themselves from *barbaroi* (the root of the English word *barbarian*). Interaction with new peoples and exposure to their different practices made the Greeks aware of the factors that bound them together: their language, religion, and lifestyle. It also introduced them to new ideas and technologies. Developments first appearing in the colonial world traveled back to the Greek homeland— urban planning, new forms of political organization, and, as we shall see shortly, new intellectual currents.

Another significant development was the invention of coins in the early sixth century B.C.E., probably in Lydia

Hellenes (HELL-leans)

(western Anatolia). They soon spread throughout the Greek world and beyond. In the ancient world a coin was a piece of metal whose weight and purity, and thus value, were guaranteed by the state. Silver, gold, bronze, and other metals were attractive choices for a medium of exchange: sufficiently rare to be valuable, relatively lightweight and portable (at least in the quantities available to most individuals), seemingly indestructible and therefore permanent, yet easily divided. (Other items with similar qualities have been used as money in various historical societies, including beads, hard-shelled beans, and cowrie shells.) Prior to the invention of coinage, people in the lands of the eastern Mediterranean and western Asia weighed out quantities of gold, silver, or bronze in exchange for the items they wanted to buy. Coinage allowed for more rapid exchanges of goods as well as for more efficient recordkeeping and storage of wealth. It stimulated trade and increased the total wealth of the society. Even so, international commerce could still be confusing because different states used different weight standards that had to be reconciled, just as people have to exchange currencies when traveling today.

By reducing surplus population, colonization helped relieve pressures within the Archaic Greek world. Nevertheless, this was an era of political instability. Kings ruled the Dark Age societies depicted in Homer's *Iliad* and *Odyssey*, but at some point councils composed of the heads of noble families superseded the kings. This aristocracy derived its wealth and power from ownership of large tracts of land. Peasant families worked this land; they were allowed to occupy a plot and keep a portion of what they grew. Debt-slaves, too, worked the land. They were people who had borrowed money or seed from the lord and lost their freedom when they were unable to repay the loan. Also living in a typical community were free peasants, who owned small farms, and urban-based craftsmen and merchants, who began to constitute a "middle class."

In the mid-seventh and sixth centuries B.C.E. in one city-state after another, an individual **tyrant**—a person who seized and held power in violation of the normal political institutions and traditions of the community— gained control. Greek tyrants were often disgruntled or ambitious members of the aristocracy, backed by the emerging middle class. New opportunities for economic advancement and the declining cost of metals meant that more and more men could acquire arms. These individuals, who already played an important role as hoplite soldiers in the local militias, must have demanded some political rights as the price of their support for their local tyrant.

Ultimately, the tyrants of this age were unwitting catalysts in an evolving political process. Some were able

Vase Painting Depicting a Sacrifice to the God Apollo, ca. 440 B.C.E. For the Greeks, who believed in a multitude of gods who looked and behaved like humans, the central act of worship was the sacrifice, the ritualized offering of a gift. Sacrifice created a relationship between the human worshiper and the deity and raised expectations that the god would bestow favors in return. Here we see a number of male devotees, wearing their finest clothing and garlands in their hair, near a sacred outdoor altar and statue of Apollo. The god is shown at the far right, standing on a pedestal and holding his characteristic bow and laurel branch. The first worshiper offers the god bones wrapped in fat. All of the worshipers will feast on the meat carried by the boy. (Museum für Vor-und. Frühgeschichte, Frankfurt)

to pass their positions on to their sons, but eventually the tyrant-family was ejected. Authority in the community developed along one of two lines: toward oligarchy°, the exercise of political privilege by the wealthier members of society, or toward **democracy,** the exercise of political power by all free adult males. In any case, the absence of a professional military class in the early Greek states was essential to broadening the base of political participation.

Greek religion encompassed a wide range of cults and beliefs. The ancestors of the Greeks brought a collection of sky-gods with them when they entered the Greek peninsula at the end of the third millennium B.C.E. Male gods predominated, but several female deities had important roles. Some of the gods represented forces in nature: for example, Zeus sent storms and lightning, and Poseidon was master of the sea and earthquakes. The two great epic poems, the *Iliad* and *Odyssey*, which Greek schoolboys memorized and professional performers recited, put a distinctive stamp on the personalities and characters of these deities. The gods that Homer portrayed were anthropomorphic°—that is, conceived as humanlike in appearance (though they were taller, more beautiful, and more powerful than mere mortals and had a supernatural radiance) and humanlike in their displays of emotion. Indeed, the chief difference between them and human beings was humans' mortality.

The worship of the gods at state-sponsored festivals was as much an expression of civic identity as of personal piety. **Sacrifice,** the central ritual of Greek religion,

was performed at altars in front of the temples that the Greeks built to be the gods' places of residence. Greeks gave their gods gifts, often as humble as a small cake or a cup of wine poured on the ground, in the hope that the gods would favor and protect them. In more spectacular forms of sacrifice, a group of people would kill one or more animals, spray the altar with the victim's blood, burn parts of its body so that the aroma would ascend to the gods on high, and enjoy a rare feast of meat. In this way the Greeks created a sense of community out of shared participation in the taking of life.

Greek individuals and communities sought information, advice, or predictions about the future from oracles—sacred sites where they believed the gods communicated with humans. Especially prestigious was the oracle of Apollo at Delphi in central Greece. Petitioners left gifts in the treasuries, and the god responded to their questions through his priestess, the Pythia°, who gave forth obscure, ecstatic utterances. Because most Greeks were farmers, fertility cults, whose members worshiped and sought to enhance the productive forces in nature (usually conceived as female), were popular, though often hidden from modern view because of our dependence on literary texts expressing the values of an educated, urban elite.

New Intellectual Currents

The material changes taking place in Greece in the Archaic period—new technologies, increasing prosperity, and social

oligarchy (OLL-ih-gahr-key)
anthropomorphic (an-thruh-puh-MORE-fik)

Pythia (PITH-ee-uh)

and political development—led to innovations in intellectual outlook and artistic expression. One distinctive feature of the Archaic period was a growing emphasis on the individual. In early Greek communities the family enveloped the individual, and land belonged collectively to the family, including ancestors and descendants. Ripped out of this communal network and forced to establish new lives on a distant frontier, the colonist became a model of rugged individualism, as did the tyrant who seized power for himself alone. These new patterns led toward the concept of humanism—a valuing of the uniqueness, talents, and rights of the individual—which remains a central tenet of Western civilization.

We see clear signs of individualism in the new lyric poetry—short verses in which the subject matter is intensely personal, drawn from the experience of the poet and expressing his or her feelings and views. Archilochus°, a soldier and poet living in the first half of the seventh century B.C.E., made a surprising admission:

> Some barbarian is waving my shield, since I was
>   obliged to
> leave that perfectly good piece of equipment behind
> under a bush. But I got away, so what does it matter?
> Let the shield go; I can buy another one equally good.[2]

Here Archilochus is poking fun at the heroic ideal that scorned a soldier who ran away from the enemy. In challenging traditional values and exploiting the medium to express personal feeling and opinion, lyric poets paved the way for the modern Western conception of poetry.

There were also challenges to traditional religion from thinkers now known as pre-Socratic philosophers (the term *pre-Socratic* refers to philosophers before Socrates, who in the later fifth century B.C.E. shifted the focus of philosophy to ethical questions). In the sixth century B.C.E. Xenophanes° called into question the kind of gods that Homer had popularized.

> But if cattle and horses or lions had hands, or were
> able to draw with their hands and do the works that
> men can do, horses would draw the forms of the gods
> like horses, and cattle like cattle, and they would make
> their bodies such as they each had themselves.[3]

The pre-Socratic philosophers rejected traditional religious explanations of the origins and nature of the world and sought rational explanations. They were primarily concerned with learning how the world was created, what it is made of, and why changes occur. Some pre-Socratic thinkers postulated various combinations of earth, air, fire, and water as the primal elements that combine or dissolve to form the numerous substances found in nature. One advanced the theory that the world is composed of microscopic *atoms* (from a Greek word meaning "indivisible") that move through the void of space, colliding randomly and combining in various ways to form the many substances of the natural world. In some respects startlingly similar to modern atomic theory, this model was essentially a lucky intuition, but it is a testament to the sophistication of these thinkers. It is probably no coincidence that most of them came from Ionia and southern Italy, two zones in which Greeks were in close contact with non-Greek peoples. The shock of encountering people with very different ideas may have stimulated new lines of inquiry.

Another important intellectual development also took place in Ionia in the sixth century B.C.E. A group of men later referred to as logographers° ("writers of prose accounts"), taking full advantage of the nearly infinite capacity of writing to store information, began gathering data on a wide range of topics, including ethnography (description of a people's physical characteristics and cultural practices), the geography of Mediterranean lands, the foundation stories of important cities, and the origins of famous Greek families. They were the first to write in prose—the language of everyday speech—rather than poetry, which had long facilitated the memorization essential to an oral society. *Historia*, "investigation/research," was the name they gave to the method they used to collect, sort, and select information. In the mid-fifth century B.C.E. **Herodotus** (ca. 485–425 B.C.E.), from Halicarnassus in southwest Anatolia, published his *Histories*. Early parts of the work are filled with the geographic and ethnographic reports, legends, folktales, and marvels dear to the logographers, but in later sections Herodotus focuses on the great event of the previous generation: the wars between the Greeks and the Persian Empire.

Herodotus declared his new conception of his mission in the first lines of the book:

> I, Herodotus of Halicarnassus, am here setting forth
> my history, that time may not draw the color from
> what man has brought into being, nor those great and
> wonderful deeds, manifested by both Greeks and
> barbarians, fail of their report, and, together with all
> this, the reason why they fought one another.[4]

In stating that he wants to find out *why* Greeks and Persians came to blows, he reveals that he has become a historian seeking the causes behind historical events.

Archilochus (ahr-KIL-uh-kuhs)
Xenophanes (zeh-NOFF-uh-nees)

logographer (loe-GOG-ruff-er)

Herodotus directed the all-purpose techniques of *historia* to the service of *history* in the modern sense of the term, thereby narrowing the meaning of the word. For this achievement he is known as the "father of history."

Athens and Sparta

The two preeminent Greek city-states of the late Archaic and Classical periods were Athens and Sparta. The different character of these two communities underscores the potential for diversity in the evolution of human societies, even those arising in similar environmental and cultural contexts.

The ancestors of the Spartans migrated into the Peloponnese°, the southernmost part of the Greek mainland, around 1000 B.C.E. For a time Sparta followed a typical path of development, participating in trade and fostering the arts. Then in the seventh century B.C.E. something happened to alter the destiny of the Spartan state. Like many other parts of Greece, the Spartan community was feeling the effects of increasing population and a shortage of arable land. However, instead of sending out colonists, the Spartans crossed their mountainous western frontier and invaded the fertile plain of Messenia (see Map 5.2). Hoplite tactics may have given the Spartans the edge they needed to prevail over fierce Messenian resistance. The result was the takeover of Messenia and the domination of the native population, who descended to the status of helots°, the most abused and exploited population on the Greek mainland.

Fear of a helot uprising led to the evolution of the unique Spartan way of life. The Spartan state became a military camp in a permanent state of preparedness. Territory in Messenia and Laconia (the Spartan homeland) was divided into several thousand lots, which were assigned to Spartan citizens. Helots worked the land and turned over a portion of what they grew to their Spartan masters, who were thereby freed from food production and able to spend their lives in military training and service.

The professional Spartan soldier was the best in Greece, and the Spartan army was superior to all others, since the other Greek states relied on citizen militias called out only in time of crisis. The Spartans, however, paid a huge personal price for their military readiness. At age seven, boys were taken from their families and put into barracks, where they were toughened by a severe regimen of discipline, beatings, and deprivation. A Spartan male's whole life was subordinated to the demands of the state. Sparta essentially stopped the clock, declining to participate in the economic, political, and cultural renaissance taking place in the Archaic Greek world. There were no longer any poets or artists at Sparta. In an attempt to maintain equality among citizens, precious metals and coinage were banned, and Spartans were forbidden to engage in commerce. The fifth-century B.C.E. historian Thucydides°, a native of Athens, remarked that in his day Sparta appeared to be little more than a large village and that no future observer of the ruins of the site would be able to guess its power.

The Spartans purposefully cultivated a mystique by rarely putting their reputation to the test, practicing a foreign policy that was cautious and isolationist. Reluctant to march far from home for fear of a helot uprising, the Spartans sought to maintain peace in the Peloponnese through the Peloponnesian League, a system of alliances between Sparta and its neighbors.

Athens followed a different path. In comparison with other Greek city-states, it possessed an unusually large and populous territory: the entire region of Attica. Attica contained a number of moderately fertile plains and was ideally suited for cultivation of olive trees. In addition to the urban center of Athens, located some 5 miles (8 kilometers) from the sea where the sheer-sided Acropolis towered above the Attic Plain, the peninsula was dotted with villages and a few larger towns.

Attica's large land area provided a buffer against the initial stresses of the Archaic period, but by the early sixth century B.C.E. things had reached a critical point. In 594 B.C.E. Solon was appointed lawgiver and was granted extraordinary powers to avert a civil war. He divided Athenian citizens into four classes based on the annual yield of their farms. Those in the top three classes could hold state offices. Members of the lowest class, who had little or no property, could not hold office but were allowed to participate in meetings of the Assembly. This arrangement, which made rights and privileges a function of wealth, was far from democratic. But it broke the absolute monopoly on power of a small circle of aristocratic families, and it allowed for social and political mobility. By abolishing the practice of enslaving individuals for failure to repay their debts, Solon guaranteed the freedom of Athenian citizens.

Despite Solon's efforts to defuse the crisis, political turmoil continued until 546 B.C.E., when an aristocrat named Pisistratus° seized power. To strengthen his position and weaken the aristocracy, the tyrant Pisistratus tried to shift the allegiance of the still largely rural population to the urban center of Athens, where he was the dominant figure. He undertook a number of monumental

---

Peloponnese (PELL-uh-puh-neze)   **helot** (HELL-ut)

Thucydides (thoo-SID-ih-dees)   **Pisistratus** (pie-SIS-truh-tuhs)

building projects, including a Temple of Athena on the Acropolis. He also instituted or expanded several major festivals that drew people to Athens for religious processions, performances of plays, and athletic and poetic competitions.

Pisistratus passed the tyranny on to his sons, but with Spartan assistance the Athenians turned the tyrant-family out in the last decade of the sixth century B.C.E. In the 460s and 450s B.C.E. **Pericles°** and his political allies took the last steps in the evolution of Athenian democracy, transferring all power to popular organs of government: the Assembly, Council of 500, and People's Courts. From that time on, men of moderate or little means could hold office and participate in the political process. Men were selected by lot to fill even the highest offices, and they were paid for public service so they could afford to take time off from their work. The focal point of Athenian political life became the Assembly of all citizens. Several times a month proposals were debated there; decisions were openly made, and any citizen could speak to the issues of the day.

During this century and a half of internal political evolution, Athens's economic clout and international reputation rose steadily. From the time of Pisistratus, Athenian pottery is increasingly prominent in the archaeological record at sites all around the Mediterranean, crowding out the products of former Greek commercial powerhouses such as Corinth and Aegina (see Map 5.2). These pots often contained olive oil, Athens's chief export, but elegant painted vases were desirable luxury commodities in their own right. Extensive trade increased the numbers and wealth of the middle class and helps explain why Athens took the path of increasing democratization.

THE STRUGGLE OF PERSIA AND GREECE, 546–323 B.C.E.

For the Greeks of the fifth and fourth centuries B.C.E., Persia was the great enemy and the wars with Persia were the decisive historical event. The Persians probably were more concerned about developments farther east and did not regard the wars with the Greeks as so consequential. Nevertheless, the encounter with the Greeks over a period of two centuries was of profound importance for the history of the eastern Mediterranean and western Asia.

Early Encounters

Cyrus's conquest of Lydia in 546 B.C.E. led to the subjugation of the Greek cities on the Anatolian seacoast. In the years that followed, these cities were ruled by local groups or individuals who collaborated with the Persian government so as to maintain themselves in power and allow their cities to operate with minimal Persian interference. All this changed when the Ionian Revolt, a great uprising of Greeks and other subject peoples on the western frontier, broke out in 499 B.C.E. The Persians needed five years and a massive infusion of troops and resources to stamp out the insurrection.

The failed revolt led to the **Persian Wars**—two Persian attacks on Greece in the early fifth century B.C.E. In 490 B.C.E. Darius dispatched a naval fleet to punish Eretria° and Athens, two states on the Greek mainland that had given assistance to the Ionian rebels, and to warn others about the foolhardiness of crossing the Persian king. Eretria was betrayed to the Persians by several of its own citizens, and the survivors were marched off to permanent exile in southwest Iran. In this, as in many things, the Persians took over the practices of their Assyrian predecessors, although they resorted to mass deportation less often and were more reticent about advertising it. Next on the Persians' list were the Athenians, who probably would have suffered a similar fate if their hoplites had not defeated the lighter-armed Persian troops in a short, sharp engagement at Marathon, 26 miles (42 kilometers) from Athens.

Xerxes (Khshayarsha, r. 486–465 B.C.E.) succeeded his father on the Persian throne and soon turned his attention to the troublesome Greeks. In 480 B.C.E. he set out with a huge invasionary force consisting of the Persian army, contingents summoned from all the peoples of the Persian Empire, and a large fleet of ships drawn from maritime subjects. Crossing the Hellespont (the narrow strait at the edge of the Aegean separating Europe and Asia), Persian forces descended into central and southern Greece (see Map 5.2). Xerxes sent messengers ahead to most of the Greek states, bidding them to offer up "earth and water"—tokens of submission.

Many Greek communities acknowledged Persian overlordship. But in southern Greece an alliance of states bent on resistance was formed under the leadership of the Spartans. This Hellenic League, as modern historians call it, initially failed to halt the Persian advance. At the pass of Thermopylae° in central Greece, three hundred Spartans and their king gave their lives to buy time for their fellows to escape. However, after seizing and sacking the city of Athens in 480 B.C.E., the Persians allowed their navy to be lured into the narrow straits of nearby

---

Pericles (PER-eh-kleez)

Eretria (er-EH-tree-uh)   **Thermopylae** (thuhr-MOP-uh-lee)

Salamis°, where they lost their advantage in numbers and maneuverability and suffered a devastating defeat. The following spring (479 B.C.E.), the Persian land army was routed at Plataea°, and the immediate threat to Greece receded. A number of factors account for the outcome: the Persians' difficulty in supplying their very large army in a distant land; the Persian high command's tactical error in allowing naval forces to be drawn into the narrow waters off Salamis; and the superiority of heavily armed Greek hoplite soldiers over lighter-armed Asiatic infantry.

The collapse of the threat to the Greek mainland did not mean an end to war. The Greeks went on the offensive. Athens's stubborn refusal to submit to the Persian king, even after the city was sacked twice in two successive years, and the vital role played by the Athenian navy, which made up fully half of the allied Greek fleet, earned the city a large measure of respect. The next phase of the war, designed to drive the Persians away from the Aegean and liberate Greek states still under Persian control, was naval. Thus Athens replaced land-based, isolationist Sparta as leader of the campaign against Persia.

In 477 B.C.E. the Delian° League was formed. It was initially a voluntary alliance of Greek states eager to prosecute the war against Persia. In less than twenty years, League forces led by Athenian generals swept the Persians from the waters of the eastern Mediterranean and freed all Greek communities except those in distant Cyprus (see Map 4.5).

The Height of Athenian Power

By scholarly convention, the Classical period of Greek history (480–323 B.C.E.) begins with the successful defense of the Greek homeland against the forces of the Persian Empire. Ironically, the Athenians, who had played such a crucial role, exploited these events to become an imperial power. A string of successful campaigns and the passage of time led many of their Greek allies to grow complacent and contribute money instead of military forces. The Athenians used the money to build up and staff their navy. Eventually they saw the other members of the Delian League as their subjects and demanded annual contributions and other signs of submission from them. States that tried to leave the League were brought back by force, stripped of their defenses, and rendered subordinate to Athens.

Athens's mastery of naval technology transformed Greek warfare and politics and brought power and wealth to Athens itself. Unlike commercial ships, whose stable, round-bodied hulls were propelled by a single square sail, military vessels could not risk depending on the wind. By the late sixth century B.C.E. the **trireme**°, a sleek, fast vessel powered by 170 rowers, had become the premier warship. The design of the trireme has long been a puzzle, but the unearthing of the slips where these vessels were moored at Athens and recent experiments with a full-scale replica manned by international volunteers have revealed much about the trireme's design and the battle tactics it made possible. Rowers using oars of different lengths and carefully positioned on three levels so as not to run afoul of one another were able to achieve short bursts of speed of up to 7 knots. Athenian crews, by constant practice, became the best in the eastern Mediterranean.

The effectiveness of the new Athenian navy had significant consequences both at home and abroad. The emergence at Athens of a democratic system in which each male citizen had, at least in principle, an equal voice is connected to the new primacy of the fleet. Hoplites were members of the middle and upper classes (they had to provide their own protective gear and weapons). Rowers, in contrast, came from the lower classes, but because they were providing the chief protection for the community and were the source of its power, they could insist on full rights.

Possession of a navy allowed Athens to project its power farther than it could have done with a citizen militia (which could be kept in arms for only short periods of time). In previous Greek wars, the victorious state had little capability to occupy a defeated neighbor permanently (with the exception, as we have seen, of Sparta's takeover of Messenia). Usually the victor was satisfied with booty and, perhaps, minor adjustments to boundary lines. Athens was able to continually dominate and exploit other, weaker communities in an unprecedented way.

Athens did not hesitate to use military and political power to promote its commercial interests. Athens's port, Piraeus°, grew into the most important commercial center in the eastern Mediterranean. The money collected each year from the subject states helped subsidize the increasingly expensive Athenian democracy as well as underwrite the construction costs of the beautiful buildings on the Acropolis, including the majestic new temple of Athena, the Parthenon. Many Athenians worked on the construction and decoration of these monuments. Indeed, the building program was a means by which the Athenian leader Pericles redistributed the profits of em-

---

Salamis (SAH-lah-miss) Plataea (pluh-TEE-uh)
Delian (DEE-lih-yuhn)

trireme (TRY-reem) Piraeus (pih-RAY-uhs)

Replica of Ancient Greek Trireme   Greek warships had a metal-tipped ram in front to pierce the hulls of enemy vessels and a pair of steering rudders in the rear. Though equipped with masts and sails, in battle these warships were propelled by 170 rowers. This modern, full-size replica represents one solution to the puzzle of how three tiers of oars could operate simultaneously without becoming entangled. Volunteer crews are helping scholars to determine attainable speeds and maneuvering techniques.   (Courtesy, the Trireme Trust)

pire to the Athenian people and gained extraordinary popularity.

In other ways as well, Athens's cultural achievements were dependent on the profits of empire. The economic advantages that empire brought to Athens indirectly subsidized the festivals at which the great dramatic tragedies of Aeschylus, Sophocles, and Euripides and the comedies of Aristophanes° were performed. Money is a prerequisite for support of the arts and sciences, and the brightest and most creative artists and thinkers in the Greek world were drawn to Athens. Traveling teachers called Sophists ("wise men") provided instruction in logic and public speaking to pupils who could afford their fees. The new discipline of rhetoric—the construction of attractive and persuasive arguments—gave those with training and quick wits a great advantage in politics and the courts. The Greek masses became connoisseurs of oratory, eagerly listening for each innovation, yet so aware of the power of words that *sophist* came to mean one who uses cleverness to distort and manipulate reality.

Aristophanes (ah-ruh-STOFF-eh-neze)

These new intellectual currents came together in 399 B.C.E. when the philosopher **Socrates** (ca. 470–399 B.C.E.) was brought to trial. A sculptor by trade, Socrates spent most of his time in the company of young men who enjoyed conversing with him and observing him deflate the pretensions of those who thought themselves wise. He wryly commented that he knew one more thing than everyone else: that he knew nothing. At his trial, Socrates was easily able to dispose of the charges of corrupting the youth of Athens and not believing in the gods of the city. He argued that the real basis of the hostility he faced was twofold: (1) He was being held responsible for the actions of several of his aristocratic students who had tried to overthrow the Athenian democracy. (2) He was being blamed unfairly for the controversial teachings of the Sophists, which were widely believed to be contrary to traditional religious beliefs and to undermine morality. In Athenian trials, juries of hundreds of citizens decided guilt and punishment, often motivated more by emotion than by legal principles. The vote that found Socrates guilty was fairly close. But his lack of contrition in the penalty phase—he proposed that he be rewarded for his services to the state—led the jury to condemn him to death by drinking hemlock. Socrates' disciples regarded his execution as a martyrdom, and smart young men such as Plato withdrew from public life and dedicated themselves to the philosophical pursuit of knowledge and truth.

This period encompasses the last stage in Greece of the transition from orality to literacy. Socrates himself wrote nothing, preferring to converse with people he met in the street. His disciple Plato (ca. 428–347 B.C.E.) may represent the first generation to be truly literate. He gained much of his knowledge from books and habitually wrote down his thoughts. On the outskirts of Athens, Plato founded the Academy, a school where young men could pursue a course of higher education. Yet even Plato retained traces of the orality of the world in which he had grown up. He wrote dialogues—an oral form—in which his protagonist, Socrates, uses the "Socratic method" of question and answer to reach a deeper understanding of the meaning of values such as justice, excellence, and wisdom. Plato refused to write down the most advanced stages of the philosophical and spiritual training that took place at his Academy. He believed that full apprehension of a higher reality, of which our own sensible world is but a pale reflection, could be entrusted only to "initiates" who had completed the earlier stages.

The third of the great classical philosophers, Aristotle (384–322 B.C.E.), came from Stagira, a community on the Thracian coast. After several decades of study at Plato's Academy in Athens, he was chosen by the king of Macedonia, Philip II, who had a high regard for Greek culture, to be the tutor of his son Alexander. Later, Aristotle returned to Athens to found his own school, the Lyceum. Of a very different temperament than Plato, who had been drawn to mysticism and metaphysical speculation, Aristotle sought to collect and categorize a vast array of knowledge. He lectured and wrote about politics, philosophy, ethics, logic, poetry, rhetoric, physics, astronomy, meteorology, zoology, and psychology, laying the foundations for many modern disciplines.

Vase Painting Depicting Women at an Athenian Fountain House, ca. 520 B.C.E.   Paintings on Greek vases provide the most vivid pictorial record of ancient Greek life. The subject matter usually reflects the interests of the aristocratic males who purchased the vases—warfare, athletics, mythology, drinking parties—but sometimes we are given glimpses into the lives of women and the working classes. These women are presumably domestic servants sent to fetch water for the household from the public fountain. The large water jars they are filling are like the one on which this scene is depicted.   (William Francis Warden Fund, Courtesy, Museum of Fine Arts Boston)

Inequality in Classical Greece

Athenian democracy, the inspiration for the concept of democracy in the Western tradition, was a democracy only for the relatively small percentage of the inhabitants of Attica who were truly citizens—free adult males of pure Athenian ancestry. Excluding women, children, slaves, and foreigners, this group amounted to 30,000 or 40,000 people out of a total population of approximately 300,000—only 10 or 15 percent.

Slaves, mostly of foreign origin, constituted perhaps one-third of the population of Attica in the fifth and fourth centuries B.C.E., and the average Athenian family owned one or more. Slaves were needed to run the shop or work on the farm while the master was attending meetings of the Assembly or serving on one of the boards that oversaw the day-to-day activities of the state. The slave was a "living piece of property," required to do any work, submit to any sexual acts, and receive any punishments that the owner ordained. In the absence of huge estates, there were no rural slave gangs, and most Greek slaves were domestic servants, often working on the same tasks as the master or mistress. Close daily contact between owners and slaves meant, in many cases, that a relationship developed, making it hard for Greek slave owners to deny the essential humanity of their slaves. Still, Greek thinkers rationalized the institution of slavery by arguing that barbaroi (non-Greeks) lacked the capacity to reason and thus were better off under the direction of rational Greek owners.

The position of women varied across Greek communities. The women of Sparta, who were expected to bear and raise strong children, were encouraged to exercise, and they enjoyed a level of public visibility and outspokenness that shocked other Greeks. Athens may have been at the opposite extreme as regards the confinement and suppression of women. Ironically, the exploitation of women in Athens, as of slaves, is linked to the high degree of freedom enjoyed by Athenian men in the democratic state.

Athenian marriages were unequal affairs. A new husband might be thirty, reasonably well educated, a veteran of war, and experienced in business and politics. Under law he had nearly absolute authority over the members of his household. He arranged his marriage with the parents of his prospective wife, who was likely to be a teenager brought up with no formal education and only minimal training in weaving, cooking, and household management. Coming into the home of a husband she hardly knew, she had no political rights and limited legal protection. Given the differences in age, social experience, and authority, the relationship between husband and wife was in many ways similar to that of father and daughter.

The primary function of marriage was to produce children, preferably male. It is impossible to prove the extent of infanticide—the killing through exposure of unwanted children—because the ancients were sufficiently ashamed to say little about it. But it is likely that more girls than boys were abandoned.

Husbands and wives had limited daily contact. The man spent the day outdoors attending to work or political responsibilities; he dined with male friends at night; and usually he slept alone in the men's quarters. The woman stayed home to cook, clean, raise the children, and supervise the servants. The closest relationship in the family was likely to be between the wife and her slave attendant. These women, often roughly the same age, spent enormous amounts of time together. The servant could be sent into town on errands. The wife stayed in the house, except to attend funerals and certain festivals and to make discreet visits to the houses of female relatives. Greek men justified the confinement of women by claiming that they were naturally promiscuous and likely to introduce other men's children into the household—an action that would threaten the family property and violate the strict regulation of citizenship rights.

Without any documents written by women in this period, we cannot tell the extent to which Athenian women resented their situation or accepted it because they knew little else. Women's festivals provided rare opportunities for women to get out. During the three-day Thesmophoria° festival, the women of Athens lived together and managed their own affairs in a great encampment, carrying out mysterious rituals meant to enhance the fertility of the land. The appearance of bold and self-assertive women on the Athenian stage is also suggestive: the defiant Antigone° of Sophocles' play who buried her brother despite the prohibition of the king; and the wives in Aristophanes' comedy *Lysistrata*° who refused to have sex with their husbands until the men ended a war. Although these plays were written by men and probably reflect a male fear of strong women, the playwrights must have had models in their mothers, sisters, and wives.

The inequality of men and women posed obstacles to creating a "meaningful" relationship between the sexes. To find his intellectual and emotional equal, a man often looked to other men. Bisexuality was common in ancient Greece, as much a product of the social structure as of biological inclinations. A common pattern was that of an older man serving as admirer, pursuer, and mentor of a youth. Bisexuality became part of a system by which young men were educated and initiated into the community of adult males. At least this was true of the elite intellectual groups that loom large in the written sources. It is hard to say how prevalent bisexuality and the confinement of women were among the Athenian masses.

Failure of the City-State and Triumph of the Macedonians

The emergence of Athens as an imperial power in the half-century after the Persian invasion aroused the suspicions of other Greek states and led to open hostilities between former allies. In 431 B.C.E. the **Peloponnesian War** broke out. This nightmarish struggle for survival between the Athenian and Spartan alliance systems encompassed most of the Greek world. It was a war unlike any previous Greek war because the Athenians used their naval power to insulate themselves from the dangers of an attack by land. In midcentury they had built three long walls connecting the city with the port of Piraeus and the adjacent shoreline. At the start of the war, Pericles formulated an unprecedented strategy, refusing to engage the Spartan-

---

Thesmophoria (thes-moe-FOE-ree-uh)
Antigone (an-TIG-uh-nee)   **Lysistrata** (lis-uh-STRAH-tuh)

led armies that invaded Attica each year. Pericles knew that, as long as Athens controlled the sea lanes and was able to provision itself, the enemy hoplites must soon return to their farms and the city could not be starved into submission by a land-based siege. Thus, instead of culminating in a short, decisive battle like most Greek hoplite warfare, the Peloponnesian War dragged on for nearly three decades with great loss of life and squandering of resources. It sapped the morale of all of Greece and ended only with the defeat of Athens in a naval battle in 404 B.C.E. The Persian Empire had bankrolled the construction of ships by the Spartan alliance, so Sparta finally was able to take the conflict into Athens's own element, the sea.

The victorious Spartans, who had entered the war championing "the freedom of the Greeks," took over Athens's overseas empire until their own increasingly highhanded behavior aroused the opposition of other city-states. Indeed, the fourth century B.C.E. was a time of nearly continuous skirmishing among Greek states. One can make the case that the independent polis, from one point of view the glory of Greek culture, was also the fundamental structural flaw because it fostered rivalry, fear, and mistrust among neighboring communities.

Internal conflict in the Greek world allowed the Persians to recoup old losses. By the terms of the King's Peace of 387 B.C.E., to which most of the states of war-weary Greece subscribed, all of western Asia, including the Greek communities of the Anatolian seacoast, were conceded to Persia. The Persian king became the guarantor of a status quo that kept the Greeks divided and weak. Luckily for the Greeks, rebellions in Egypt, Cyprus, and Phoenicia as well as trouble with some of the satraps in the western provinces diverted Persian attention from thoughts of another Greek invasion.

Meanwhile, in northern Greece developments were taking place that would irrevocably alter the balance of power in the eastern Mediterranean and western Asia. Philip II (r. 359–336 B.C.E.) was transforming his previously backward kingdom of Macedonia into the premier military power in the Greek world. (Although southern Greeks had long doubted the "Greekness" of the rough and rowdy Macedonians, modern scholarship is inclined to regard their language and culture as Greek at base, though much influenced by contact with non-Greek neighbors.) Philip had made a number of improvements to the traditional hoplite formation. He increased the striking power and mobility of his force by equipping soldiers with longer thrusting spears and less armor. Because horses thrived in the broad, grassy plains of the north, he experimented with the coordinated use of infantry and cavalry. His engineers had also developed new kinds of siege equipment, including the first catapults—machines using the power of twisted cords

that, when released, hurled arrows or stones great distances. For the first time it became possible to storm a fortified city rather than wait for starvation to take effect.

In 338 B.C.E. Philip defeated a coalition of southern states and established the Confederacy of Corinth as an instrument for controlling the Greek city-states. Philip had himself appointed military commander for a planned all-Greek campaign against Persia, and his generals established a bridgehead on the Asiatic side of the Hellespont. It appears that Philip was following the advice of Greek thinkers who had pondered the lessons of the Persian Wars of the fifth century B.C.E. and had urged a crusade against the national enemy as a means of unifying their quarrelsome countrymen.

We will never know how far Philip's ambitions extended, for an assassin killed him in 336 B.C.E. When **Alexander** (356–323 B.C.E.), his son and heir, crossed over into Asia in 334 B.C.E., his avowed purpose was to exact revenge for Xerxes' invasion a century and half before. He defeated the Persian forces of King Darius III (r. 336–330 B.C.E.) in three pitched battles in Anatolia and Mesopotamia, and ultimately campaigned as far as the Punjab region of modern Pakistan.

Alexander the Great, as he came to be called, maintained the framework of Persian administration in the lands he conquered. He realized that it was well adapted to local circumstances and familiar to the subject peoples. At first, however, he replaced Persian officials with his own Macedonian and Greek comrades. To control strategic points in his expanding empire, he established a series of Greek-style cities, beginning with Alexandria in Egypt, and he settled wounded and aged former soldiers in them. After his decisive victory at Gaugamela in northern Mesopotamia (331 B.C.E.), he began to experiment with leaving cooperative Persian officials in place. He also admitted some Persians and other Iranians into his army and into the circle of his courtiers, and he adopted elements of Persian dress and court ceremonial. Finally, he married several Iranian women who had useful royal or aristocratic connections, and he pressed his leading subordinates to do the same.

Scholars have reached widely varying conclusions about why Alexander adopted these policies, which were unexpected and fiercely resented by the Macedonian nobility. It is probably wisest to see Alexander as operating from a combination of motives, both pragmatic and idealistic. He set off on his Asian campaign with visions of glory, booty, and revenge. But the farther east he traveled, the more he began to see himself as the legitimate successor of the Persian king (a claim facilitated by the death of Darius III at the hands of subordinates). Alexander may have recognized that he had responsibilities to all the diverse peoples who fell under his control. He also

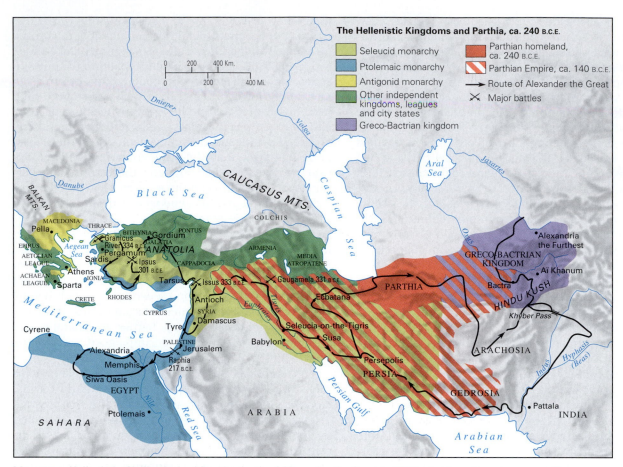

The Hellenistic Kingdoms and Parthia, ca. 240 B.C.E.

- Seleucid monarchy
- Ptolemaic monarchy
- Antigonid monarchy
- Other independent kingdoms, leagues and city states
- Greco-Bactrian kingdom
- Parthian homeland, ca. 240 B.C.E.
- Parthian Empire, ca. 140 B.C.E.
- → Route of Alexander the Great
- ✕ Major battles

Map 5.3 Hellenistic Civilization After the death of Alexander the Great in 323 B.C.E., his vast empire soon split apart into a number of large and small political entities. A Macedonian dynasty was established on each continent: the Antigonids ruled the Macedonian homeland and tried with varying success to extend their control over southern Greece: the Ptolemies ruled Egypt; and the Seleucids inherited the majority of Alexander's conquests in Asia, though they lost control of the eastern portions because of the rise of the Parthians of Iran in the second century B.C.E. This period saw Greeks migrating in large numbers from their overcrowded homeland to serve as a privileged class of soldiers and administrators on the new frontiers, where they replicated the lifestyle of the city-state.

may have realized the difficulty of holding down so vast an empire by brute force and without the cooperation of important elements among the conquered peoples. In this, he was following the example of the Achaemenids.

THE HELLENISTIC SYNTHESIS, 323–30 B.C.E.

At the time of his sudden death in 323 B.C.E. at the age of thirty-two, Alexander apparently had made no plans for the succession. Thus his death ushered in a half-century of chaos as the most ambitious and ruthless

of his officers struggled for control of the vast empire. When the dust cleared, the empire had been broken up into three major kingdoms, each ruled by a Macedonian dynasty—the Seleucid°, Ptolemaic°, and Antigonid° kingdoms (see Map 5.3). Each major kingdom faced a unique set of problems, and although the three frequently were at odds with one another, a rough balance of power prevented any one from gaining the upper hand and enabled smaller states to survive by playing off the great powers.

Historians call the epoch ushered in by the conquests of Alexander the **"Hellenistic Age"** (323–30 B.C.E.)

Seleucid (sih-LOO-sid) Ptolemaic (tawl-uh-MAY-ik)
Antigonid (an-TIG-uh-nid)

Hellenistic Cameo, Second Century B.C.E.
This sardonyx cameo is an allegory of the prosperity of Ptolemaic Egypt. At left, the bearded river-god Nile holds a horn of plenty while his wife, seated on a sphinx and dressed like the Egyptian goddess Isis, raises a stalk of grain. Their son, at center, carries a seed bag and the shaft of a plow. The Seasons are seated at right. Two wind-gods float overhead. The style is entirely Greek, but the motifs are a blending of Greek and Egyptian elements.
(G. Dagli-Orti, Paris)

because the lands in northeastern Africa and western Asia that came under Greek rule tended to be "Hell-enized"—that is, powerfully influenced by Greek culture. This was a period of large kingdoms with heterogeneous populations, great cities, powerful rulers, pervasive bureaucracies, and vast disparities in wealth—a far cry from the small, homogeneous, independent city-states of Archaic and Classical Greece. It was a cosmopolitan age of long-distance trade and communications, which saw the rise of new institutions like libraries and universities, new kinds of scholarship and science, and the cultivation of sophisticated tastes in art and literature. In many respects, in comparison with the preceding Classical era, it was a world much more like our own.

Of all the successor states, the kingdom of the Seleucids, who took over the bulk of Alexander's conquests, faced the greatest challenges. The Indus Valley and Afghanistan soon split off, and over the course of the third and second centuries B.C.E. Iran was lost to the Parthians. What remained for the Seleucids was a core in Mesopotamia, Syria, and parts of Anatolia, which the Seleucid monarchs ruled from their capital at Syrian Antioch°. Their sprawling territories were open to attack from many directions, and, like the Persians before them, they had to administer lands inhabited by many different ethnic groups organized under various political

and social forms. In the countryside, where most of the native peoples resided, the Seleucids maintained an administrative structure modeled on the Persian system. They also continued Alexander's policy of founding Greek-style cities throughout their domains. These cities served as administrative centers and were also the lure that the Seleucids used to attract colonists from Greece. The Seleucids desperately needed Greek soldiers, engineers, administrators, and other professionals.

The dynasty of the **Ptolemies**° ruled Egypt and sometimes laid claim to adjacent Syria-Palestine. The people of Egypt belonged to only one ethnic group and were fairly easily controlled because the vast majority of them were farmers living in villages alongside the Nile. The Ptolemies were able to take over much of the administrative structure of the pharaohs and to extract the surplus wealth of this populous and productive land. The Egyptian economy was centrally planned and highly controlled. Vast revenues poured into the royal treasury from rents (the king owned most of the land), taxes of all sorts, and royal monopolies on olive oil, salt, papyrus, and other key commodities.

The Ptolemies ruled from **Alexandria,** the first of the new cities laid out by Alexander himself. The orientation and status of this city says much about Ptolemaic policies and attitudes. Memphis and Thebes, the capitals of

---

Antioch (AN-tee-awk)

Ptolemies (TAWL-uh-meze)

ancient Egypt, had been located upriver. Alexandria was situated near to where the westernmost branch of the Nile runs into the Mediterranean Sea and clearly was meant to be a link between Egypt and the Mediterranean world. In the language of the Ptolemaic bureaucracy, Alexandria was technically "beside Egypt" rather than in it, as if to emphasize the gulf between rulers and subjects.

Like the Seleucids, the Ptolemies actively encouraged the immigration of Greeks from the homeland and, in return for their skills and collaboration in the military or civil administration, gave them land and a privileged position in the new society. But the Ptolemies did not seek to plant Greek-style cities throughout the Egyptian countryside, and they made no effort to encourage the native population to adopt the Greek language or ways. In fact, so separate was the Greek ruling class from the subject population that only the last Ptolemy, Queen Cleopatra (r. 51–30 B.C.E.), even bothered to learn the language of the Egyptians. For the Egyptian peasant population laboring on the land, life was little changed by the advent of new masters. Yet from the early second century B.C.E., periodic native insurrections in the countryside, which government forces in cooperation with Greek and Hellenized settlers quickly stamped out, were signs of Egyptians' growing resentment of the Greeks' exploitation and arrogance.

In Europe, the Antigonid dynasty ruled the Macedonian homeland and adjacent parts of northern Greece. This was a compact and ethnically homogeneous kingdom, so there was little of the hostility and occasional resistance that the Seleucid and Ptolemaic ruling classes faced. Macedonian garrisons at strongpoints gave the Antigonids a toehold in central and southern Greece, and the shadow of Macedonian intervention always hung over the south. The southern states met the threat by banding together into confederations, such as the Achaean° League in the Peloponnese, in which the member-states maintained local autonomy but pooled resources and military power.

Athens and Sparta, the two leading cities of the Classical period, stood out from these confederations. The Spartans never quite abandoned the myth of their own invincibility and made a number of heroic but futile stands against Macedonian armies. Athens, which held a special place in the hearts of all Greeks because of the artistic and literary accomplishments of the fifth century B.C.E., pursued a policy of neutrality. The city became a large museum, filled with the relics and memories of a glorious past, as well as a university town that attracted

the children of the well-to-do from all over the Mediterranean and western Asia.

In an age of cities, the greatest city of all was Alexandria, with a population of nearly half a million. At the heart of this city was the royal compound, containing the palace and administrative buildings for the ruling dynasty and its massive bureaucracy. The centerpiece was the magnificent Mausoleum of Alexander. The first Ptolemy had stolen the body of Alexander while it was being brought back to Macedonia for burial. The theft was aimed at gaining legitimacy for Ptolemaic rule by claiming the blessing of the great conqueror, who was declared to be a god. Two harbors served the needs of the many trading ventures that linked the commerce of the Mediterranean with the Red Sea and Indian Ocean. A great lighthouse—the first of its kind, a multistory tower with a fiery beacon visible at a distance of 30 miles (48 kilometers)—was one of the wonders of the ancient world.

Alexandria gained further luster from its famous Library, which had several hundred thousand volumes, and from its Museum, or "House of the Muses" (divinities who presided over the arts and sciences), a research institution that supported the work of the greatest poets, philosophers, doctors, and scientists of the day. The existence of such well-funded institutions made possible significant advances in science, both in the systematization and extension of earlier work. Some of the greatest achievements were in mathematics and astronomy. The mathematical writings of Euclid° (ca. 276–194 B.C.E.) and the astronomical text of Claudius Ptolemy (second century C.E.), each a grand synthesis of Greek accomplishments in these areas, were highly influential in Europe and the Islamic world into early modern times. Aristarchus° (ca. 310–230 B.C.E.) calculated the distances and relative sizes of the moon and sun. He also argued against the prevailing notion that the earth was the center of the universe, asserting that the earth and other planets revolved around the sun, a view that would not be accepted for another 1,800 years. Eratosthenes° (ca. 276–194 B.C.E.) made a surprisingly accurate calculation of the circumference of the earth. While the claim is often made that the Greeks had a strong predilection for abstract theorizing rather than experimental verification and practical application, experience was put to use in some fields. Archimedes° (ca. 287–211 B.C.E.) invented many mechanical devices, including the screw pump for extracting underground water, and developed a tech-

---

Achaean (uh-KEY-uhn)

Euclid (YOO-klid)   **Aristarchus** (ah-ris-TAWR-kiss)
Eratosthenes (eh-ruh-TOSS-thih-nees)
Archimedes (ahr-kih-MEE-dees)

nique for determining the volume of an object. Galen° (ca. 129–210 C.E.), a Greek physician of the Roman era, conveyed the legacy of Greek medical knowledge to subsequent ages.

Greek residents of Alexandria enjoyed citizenship in a Greek-style polis with an Assembly, a Council, and officials who dealt with purely local affairs, and they took advantage of public works and institutions that signified the Greek way of life. Public baths and shaded arcades were places to relax and socialize with friends. Ancient plays were revived in the theaters, and musical performances and demonstrations of oratory took place in the concert halls. Gymnasiums offered facilities for exercise and fitness and were places where young men of the privileged classes were schooled in athletics, music, and literature. Jews had their own civic corporation, officials, and courts and predominated in two of the five main residential districts. Other quarters were filled with the sights, sounds, and smells of ethnic groups from Syria, Anatolia, and the Egyptian countryside.

In all the Hellenistic states, ambitious members of the indigenous populations learned the Greek language and adopted elements of the Greek way of life, because doing so put them in a position to become part of the privileged and wealthy ruling class. For the ancient Greeks, to be Greek was primarily a matter of language and lifestyle rather than physical traits. In the Hellenistic Age there was a spontaneous synthesis of Greek and indigenous ways. Egyptians migrated to Alexandria, and Greeks and Egyptians intermarried in the villages of the countryside. Greeks living amid the monuments and descendants of the ancient civilizations of Egypt and western Asia were exposed to the mathematical and astronomical wisdom of Mesopotamia, the elaborate mortuary rituals of Egypt, and the many attractions of foreign religious cults. With little official planning or blessing, stemming for the most part from the day-to-day experiences and actions of ordinary people, a great multicultural experiment unfolded as Greek and Middle Eastern cultural traits clashed and merged.

CONCLUSION

Profound changes took place in the lands of the eastern Mediterranean and western Asia in the first millennium B.C.E. Persians and Greeks played pivotal roles. Let us compare the impacts of these two peoples and assess the broad significance of these centuries.

Galen (GAY-luhn)

The empire of the Achaemenid Persians was the largest empire yet to appear in the world. It was also a new kind of empire because it encompassed such a wide variety of landscapes, peoples, and social, political, and economic systems. How did the Persians manage to hold together this diverse collection of lands for more than two centuries?

The answer did not lie entirely in brute force. The Persians lacked the manpower to install garrisons everywhere, and communication between the central administration and provincial officials was sporadic and slow. They managed to co-opt leaders among the subject peoples who were willing to collaborate in return for being allowed to retain their power and influence. The Persian government demonstrated flexibility and tolerance in its handling of the laws, customs, and beliefs of subject peoples. Persian administration, superimposed on top of local structures, left a considerable role for local institutions.

The Persians also displayed a flair for public relations. The Zoroastrian religion underlined the authority of the king as the appointee of god and upholder of world order. In their art and inscriptions, the Persian kings broadcast an image of a benevolent empire in which the dependent peoples contributed to the welfare of the realm. Certain peoples with long and proud traditions, such as the Egyptians and Babylonians, revolted from time to time. But most subjects found the Persians to be decent enough masters and a great improvement over earlier Middle Eastern empires such as that of the Assyrians.

Western Asia underwent significant changes in the period of Persian supremacy. First, the early Persian kings put an end to the ancient centers of power in Mesopotamia, Anatolia, and Egypt. Then, by imposing a uniform system of law and administration and by providing security and stability, the Persian government fostered commerce and prosperity, at least for some. Some historians have argued that this period was a turning point in the economic history of western Asia. The Achaemenid government possessed an unprecedented capacity to organize labor on a large scale to construct an expanded water distribution network and work the extensive estates of the Persian royal family and nobility. The Persian "paradise" was not only the symbol but also the proof of the connection between political authority and the productivity of the earth.

Most difficult to assess is the cultural impact of Persian rule. The long-dominant culture of Mesopotamia fused with some Iranian elements. The resulting new synthesis is most visible in the art, architecture, and inscriptions of the Persian monarchs. The lands east of the Zagros Mountains as far as northwest India were brought within this cultural sphere. It has been suggested that the Zoroastrian religion spread across the empire and influenced other religious traditions, such as Judaism, but Zoroastrianism does not appear to have had broad, popular appeal. The Persian administration relied heavily on the scribes and written languages of its Mesopotamian, Syrian, and Egyptian subjects, and literacy remained the preserve of a small, professional class. Thus the Persian language does not seem to have been widely adopted by inhabitants of the empire. Even if there was a greater degree of Persianization in the provinces than is suggested by the extant evidence, it was so thoroughly swamped by Hellenism in the succeeding era that few traces are left.

Nearly two centuries of trouble with the Greeks on their western frontier vexed the Persians but was probably not their first priority. It appears that Persian kings were always more concerned about the security of their eastern and northeastern frontiers, where they were vulnerable to attack by the nomads of Central Asia. The technological differences between Greece and Persia were not great. The only difference that seems to have been of significance was a set of arms and a military formation used by the Greeks that often allowed them to prevail over the Persians. The Persian king's response in the later fifth and fourth centuries B.C.E. was to hire Greek mercenaries to use hoplite tactics for his benefit. The claim is sometimes made that the Persian Empire was weak and crumbling by the time Alexander invaded, but there is little evidence to support this, and no one could have anticipated the charismatic leadership and boundless ambition of Alexander of Macedonia.

The shadow of Persia loomed large over the affairs of the Greek city-states for more than two centuries, and even after the repulse of Xerxes' great expeditionary force there was perpetual fear of another Persian invasion. The victories in 480 and 479 B.C.E. did allow the Greek city-states to continue to evolve politically and culturally at a critical time. Athens, in particular, vaulted into power, wealth, and intense cultural creativity as a result of its role in the Greek victory. It evolved into a new kind of Greek state, upsetting the rough equilibrium of the Archaic period by threatening the autonomy of other city-states and changing the rules of war. The result was the Peloponnesian War, which squandered lives and resources for a generation, raised serious doubts about the viability of the city-state, and diminished many people's allegiance to it.

Alexander's conquests brought changes to the Greek world almost as radical as those suffered by the Persians. Greeks spilled out into the sprawling new frontiers in northeastern Africa and western Asia, and the independent city-state became inconsequential in a world of large

kingdoms. The centuries of Greek domination had a far more pervasive cultural impact on the Middle East than did the Persian period. Alexander had been inclined to preserve the Persian administrative apparatus, leaving native institutions and personnel in place. His successors relied almost exclusively on a privileged class of Greek soldiers, officers, and administrators.

Equally significant were the foundation of Greek-style cities, which exerted a powerful cultural influence on important elements of the native populations, and a system of easily learned alphabetic Greek writing, which led to more widespread literacy and far more effective dissemination of information. The result was that the Greeks had a profound impact on the peoples and lands of the Middle East, and Hellenism persisted as a cultural force for a thousand years. As we shall see in the next chapter, the Romans who arrived in the eastern Mediterranean in the second century B.C.E. were greatly influenced by the cultural and political practices of the Hellenistic kingdoms.

■ Key Terms

Cyrus	Herodotus
Darius I	Pericles
satrap	Persian Wars
Persepolis	trireme
Zoroastrianism	Socrates
polis	Peloponnesian War
hoplite	Alexander
tyrant	Hellenistic Age
democracy	Ptolemies
sacrifice	Alexandria

■ Suggested Reading

The most up-to-date treatment of ancient Persia is Pierre Briant, *From Cyrus to Alexander: A History of the Persian Empire* (2002). Also useful is J. M. Cook, *The Persian Empire* (1983). Josef Wiesehofer, *Ancient Persia: From 550 B.C. to 650 A.D.* (1996); Richard N. Frye, *The History of Ancient Iran* (1984); and volume 2 of *The Cambridge History of Iran*, ed. Ilya Gershevitch (1985), are written by Iranian specialists and have abundant bibliographies. John Curtis, *Ancient Persia* (1989), emphasizes the archaeological record. Roland G. Kent, *Old Persian: Grammar, Texts, Lexicon*, 2d ed. (1953), contains translations of the royal inscriptions.

Maria Brosius, *Women in Ancient Persia, 559–331 B.C.* (1996), gathers and evaluates the scattered evidence. William W. Malandra, *An Introduction to Ancient Iranian Religion: Readings from the Avesta and Achaemenid Inscriptions* (1983), contains documents in translation pertaining to religious subjects. Vesta

Sarkhosh Curtis, *Persian Myths* (1993), is a concise, illustrated introduction to Iranian myths and legends. John Boardman, *Persia and the West: An Archaeological Investigation of the Genesis of Achaemenid Persian Art* (2000), explores the complex question of Greek influence on Persian art and architecture.

The fullest treatment of Greek history and civilization in this period is in *The Cambridge Ancient History*, 3d ed., vols. 3–7 (1970–). Sarah B. Pomeroy, Stanley M. Burstein, Walter Donlan, and Jennifer Tolbert Roberts, *Ancient Greece: A Political, Social, and Cultural History* (1999), is a fine one-volume treatment of Greek civilization. Bella Vivante, ed., *Events That Changed Ancient* Greece (2002), contains an overview, interpretative essay, and up-to-date bibliography for each period of Greek history. Other general treatments include J. B. Bury and Russell Meiggs, *A History of Greece* (1975), and Nancy Demand, *A History of Ancient Greece (*1996*)*. For the Archaic period see Oswyn Murray, *Early Greece*, 2d ed. (1993), and Robin Osborne, *Greece in the Making, 1200–479 B.C.* (1996).

Social history is emphasized by Frank J. Frost, *Greek Society*, 3d ed. (1987). Robert Morkot, *The Penguin Historical Atlas of Ancient Greece* (1996), and Peter Levi, *Atlas of the Greek World* (1980), are filled with maps, pictures, and general information about Greek civilization, as is Lesley Adkins and Roy A. Adkins, *Handbook to Life in Ancient Greece* (1997). Michael Grant and Rachel Kitzinger, eds., *Civilization of the Ancient Mediterranean* (1987), is a three-volume collection of essays by contemporary experts on nearly every aspect of ancient Greco-Roman civilization and includes select bibliographies.

We are fortunate to have an abundant written literature from ancient Greece, and the testimony of the ancients themselves should be the starting point for any inquiry. Herodotus, Thucydides, and Xenophon chronicled the history of the Greeks and their Middle Eastern neighbors from the sixth through fourth centuries B.C.E. Arrian, who lived in the second century C.E., provides the most useful account of the career of Alexander the Great. Among the many collections of documents in translation, see Michael Crawford and David Whitehead, eds., *Archaic and Classical Greece: A Selection of Ancient Sources in Translation* (1983). David G. Rice and John E. Stambaugh, eds., *Sources for the Study of Greek Religion* (1979); Mary R. Lefkowitz and Maureen B. Fant, eds., *Women's Life in Greece and Rome: A Source Book in Translation* (1982); Thomas Wiedemann, ed., *Greek and Roman Slavery* (1981); Michael M. Sage, *Warfare in Ancient Greece: A Sourcebook* (1996), and Michael Gagarin and Paul Woodruff, *Early Greek Political Thought from Homer to the Sophists* (1995), are specialized collections. The Perseus Project (*www.perseus.tufts.edu*) is a remarkable internet site containing hundreds of ancient texts, thousands of photographs of artifacts and sites, maps, encyclopedias, dictionaries, and other resources for the study of Greek (and Roman) civilization.

Victor Davis Hanson, *The Other Greeks: The Family Farm and the Agrarian Roots of Western Civilization* (1995), emphasizes the centrality of farming to the development of Greek institutions and values. Eric A. Havelock, *The Muse Learns to Write: Reflections on Orality and Literacy from Antiquity to the Present* (1986), and Rosalind Thomas, *Literacy and Orality in Ancient* Greece (1992), explore the profound effects of alphabetic literacy on the Greek mind.

Valuable treatments of other key topics include Elaine Fantham, Helene Peet Foley, Natalie Boymel Kampen, Sarah B. Pomeroy, and H. Alan Shapiro, *Women in the Classical World* (1994); Cynthia Patterson, *The Family in Greek History* (1998); Yvon Garlan, *Slavery in Ancient Greece* (1988); Walter Burkert, *Greek Religion* (1985); Victor Davis Hanson, *The Western Way of War: Infantry Battle in Classical Greece* (1989); Lionel Casson, *The Ancient Mariners: Seafarers and Sea Fighters of the Mediterranean in Ancient Times*, 2d ed. (1991); Michail Yu Treister, *The Role of Metals in Ancient Greek History* (1996); Joint Association of Classical Teachers, *The World of Athens: An Introduction to Classical Athenian Culture* (1984); N. G. L. Hammond, *The Macedonian State: The Origins, Institutions and History* (1989); Joseph Roisman, ed., *Alexander the Great: Ancient and Modern Perspectives* (1995); and William R. Biers, *The Archaeology of Greece: An Introduction* (1990). Mary R. Lefkowitz and Guy MacLean Rogers, *Black Athena Revisited* (1996), explores the controversies surrounding the Greek cultural obligation to Egypt and western Asia. For the Hellenistic world see F. W. Walbank, *The Hellenistic World*, rev. ed. (1993), and Michael Grant, *From Alexander to Cleopatra: The Hellenistic World* (1982). M. M. Austin, ed., *The Hellenistic World from Alexander to the Roman Conquest: A Selection of Ancient Sources in Translation* (1981), provides sources in translation. Jean-Yves Empereur, *Alexandria Rediscovered* (1998), summarizes exciting new finds from the palace precinct in the waters off Alexandria.

◼ Notes

1. Quoted in Roland G. Kent, *Old Persian: Grammar, Texts, Lexicon*, 2d ed. (New Haven, CT: American Oriental Society, 1953), 138, 140.
2. Richmond Lattimore, *Greek Lyrics*, 2d ed. (Chicago: University of Chicago Press, 1960), 2.
3. G. S. Kirk and J. E. Raven, *The Presocratic Philosophers: A Critical History with a Selection of Texts* (Cambridge, England: Cambridge University Press, 1957), 169.
4. Herodotus, *The History*, trans. David Grene (Chicago: University of Chicago Press, 1988), 33. (Herodotus 1.1)

6 An Age of Empires: Rome and Han China, 753 B.C.E.–330 C.E.

Terracotta Soldiers from the Tomb of Shi Huangdi, "First Emperor" of China   Thousands of these life-size, baked-clay figures—each with distinctive features—have been unearthed.

CHAPTER OUTLINE

According to Chinese sources, in the year 166 C.E. a group of travelers identifying themselves as delegates from Andun, the king of distant Da Qin, arrived at the court of the Chinese emperor Huan, one of the Han rulers. Andun was Marcus Aurelius Antoninus, the emperor of Rome. As far as we know, these travelers were the first "Romans" to reach China, although they probably were residents of one of the eastern provinces of the Roman Empire, perhaps Egypt or Syria, and they may have stretched the truth in claiming to be official representatives of the Roman emperor. More likely they were merchants hoping to set up a profitable trading arrangement at the source of the silk so highly prized in the West. Chinese officials, however, were in no position to disprove their claim, since there was no direct contact between the Roman and Chinese Empires.

We do not know what became of these travelers, and their mission apparently did not lead to more direct or regular contact between the empires. Even so, the episode raises some interesting points. First, in the early centuries C.E. Rome and China were linked by far-flung international trading networks encompassing the entire Eastern Hemisphere, and were dimly aware of each other's existence. Second, the last centuries B.C.E. and the first centuries C.E. saw the emergence of two manifestations of a new kind of empire.

The Roman Empire encompassed all the lands surrounding the Mediterranean Sea as well as substantial portions of continental Europe and the Middle East. The Han Empire stretched from the Pacific Ocean to the oases of Central Asia. The largest empires the world had yet seen, they managed to centralize control to a greater degree than earlier empires; their cultural impact on the lands and peoples they dominated was more pervasive; and they were remarkably stable and lasted for many centuries.

Thousands of miles separated Rome and Han China; neither influenced the other. Why did two such unprecedented political entities flourish at the same time? Historians have put forth theories stressing supposedly common factors—such as climate change and the pressure of nomadic peoples from Central Asia on the Roman and Chinese frontiers—but no theory has won the support of most scholars.

As you read this chapter, ask yourself the following questions:

- How did the Roman and Han Empires come into being?

- What were the sources of their stability or instability?

- What benefits and liabilities did these empires bring to the rulers and their subjects?

- What were the most important similarities and differences between these two empires, and what do the similarities and differences tell us about the circumstances and the character of each?

ROME'S CREATION OF A MEDITERRANEAN EMPIRE, 753 B.C.E.–330 C.E.

Rome's central location contributed to its success in unifying Italy and then all the lands ringing the Mediterranean Sea (see Map 6.1). The middle of three peninsulas that jut from the European landmass into the Mediterranean, the boot-shaped Italian peninsula and the large island of Sicily constitute a natural bridge almost linking Europe and North Africa. Italy was a crossroads in the Mediterranean, and Rome was a crossroads within Italy. Rome lay at the midpoint of the peninsula, about 15 miles (24 kilometers) from the western coast, where a north-south road intersected an east-west river route. The Tiber River on one side and a double ring of seven hills on the other afforded natural protection to the site.

Italy is a land of hills and mountains. The Apennine range runs along its length like a spine, separating the eastern and western coastal plains, while the arc of the Alps shields it on the north. Many of Italy's rivers are navigable, and passes through the Apennines and through the snowcapped Alps allowed merchants and armies to travel overland. The mild Mediterranean climate affords a long growing season and conditions suitable for a wide variety of crops. The hillsides, largely denuded of cover today, were well forested in ancient times, providing tim-

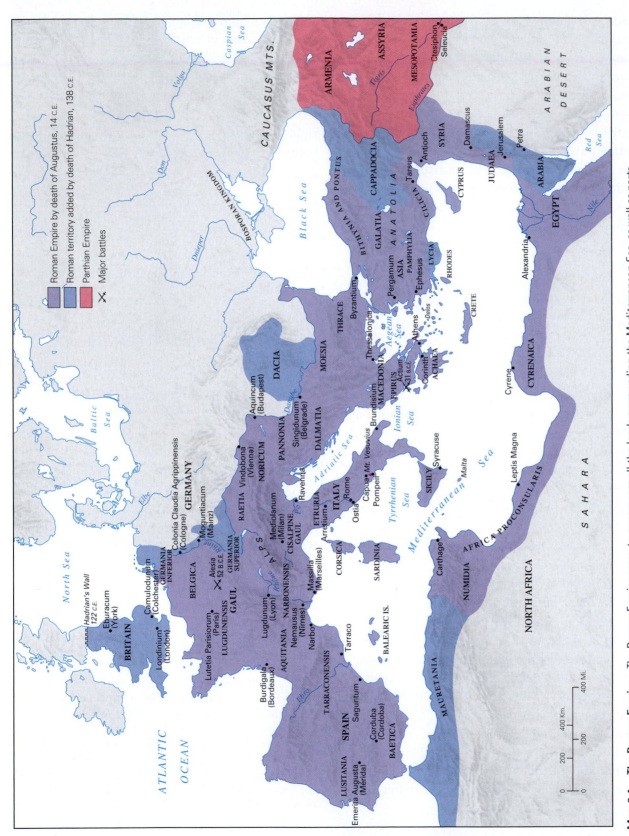

Map 6.1   The Roman Empire   The Roman Empire came to encompass all the lands surrounding the Mediterranean Sea, as well as parts of continental Europe. When Augustus died in 14 C.E., he left instructions to his successors not to expand beyond the limits he had set, but Claudius invaded southern Britain in the mid-first century and the soldier-emperor Trajan added Romania early in the second century. Deserts and seas provided solid natural boundaries, but the long and vulnerable river border in central and eastern Europe would eventually prove expensive to defend and vulnerable to invasion by Germanic and Central Asian peoples.

C H R O N O L O G Y

	Rome	China
1000 B.C.E.	**1000 B.C.E.** First settlement on site of Rome	
500 B.C.E.	**507 B.C.E.** Establishment of the Republic	
		480–221 B.C.E. Warring States Period
300 B.C.E.		
	290 B.C.E. Defeat of tribes of Samnium gives Romans control of Italy	
	264–202 B.C.E. Wars against Carthage guarantee Roman control of western Mediterranean	**221 B.C.E.** Qin emperor unites eastern China
		206 B.C.E. Han dynasty succeeds Qin
200 B.C.E.	**200–146 B.C.E.** Wars against Hellenistic kingdoms lead to control of eastern Mediterranean	
		140–87 B.C.E. Emperor Wu expands the Han Empire
100 B.C.E.		
	88–31 B.C.E. Civil wars and failure of the Republic	
	31 B.C.E.–14 C.E. Augustus establishes the Principate	
50 C.E.		**23 C.E.** Han capital transfered from Chang'an to Luoyang
	45–58 C.E. Paul spreads Christianity in the eastern Mediterranean	
200 C.E.		
		220 C.E. Fall of Han Empire
	235–284 C.E. Third-century crisis	
300 C.E.		
	324 C.E. Constantine moves capital to Constantinople	

ber for construction and fuel. The region of Etruria in the northwest was rich in iron and other metals.

Even though as much as 75 percent of the total area of the Italian peninsula is hilly, there is still ample arable land in the coastal plains and river valleys. Much of this land has extremely fertile volcanic soil and sustained a much larger population than was possible in Greece. While expanding within Italy, the Roman state created effective mechanisms for tapping the human resources of the countryside.

A Republic of Farmers, 753–31 B.C.E.

According to popular legend, Romulus, who was cast adrift on the Tiber River as a baby and was nursed by a she-wolf, founded the city of Rome in 753 B.C.E. Archaeological research, however, shows that the Palatine Hill—one of the seven hills on the site of Rome—was occupied as early as 1000 B.C.E. The merging of several hilltop communities to form an urban nucleus, made possible by the draining of a swamp on the

Statue of a Roman Carrying Busts of His Ancestors, First Century B.C.E.   Roman society was extremely conscious of status, and the status of an elite Roman family was determined in large part by the public achievements of ancestors and living members. A visitor to a Roman home found portraits of distinguished ancestors in the entry hall, along with labels listing the offices they held. Portrait heads were carried in funeral processions. (Alinari/Art Resource, NY)

site of the future Roman Forum (civic center), took place shortly before 600 B.C.E. The Latin speech and cultural patterns of the original inhabitants of the site were typical of the indigenous population of most of the peninsula. However, tradition remembered Etruscan immigrants arriving in the seventh century B.C.E., and Rome came to pride itself on offering hospitality to exiles and outcasts.

Agriculture was the essential economic activity in the early Roman state, and land was the basis of wealth. As a consequence, social status, political privilege, and fundamental values were related to landownership. The vast majority of early Romans were self-sufficient independent farmers who owned small plots of land. A relatively small number of families managed to acquire large tracts of land. The heads of these wealthy families were members of the Senate—a "Council of Elders" that played a dominant role in the politics of the Roman state. According to tradition, there were seven kings of Rome between 753 and 507 B.C.E. The first was Romulus; the last was the tyrannical Tarquinius Superbus. In 507 B.C.E. members of the senatorial class, led by Brutus "the Liberator," deposed Tarquinius Superbus and instituted a *res publica*, a "public possession," or republic.

The **Roman Republic,** which lasted from 507 to 31 B.C.E., was not a democracy. Sovereign power resided in several assemblies, and while male citizens were eligible to attend, the votes of the wealthy classes counted for more than the votes of poor citizens. A slate of civic officials was elected each year, and a hierarchy of state offices evolved. The culmination of a political career was to be selected as one of the two consuls who presided over meetings of the Senate and assemblies and commanded the army on military campaigns.

The real center of power was the **Roman Senate.** Technically an advisory council, first to the kings and later to the annually changing Republican officials, the Senate increasingly made policy and governed. Senators nominated their sons for public offices and filled Senate vacancies from the ranks of former officials. This self-perpetuating body, whose members served for life, brought together the state's wealth, influence, and political and military experience.

The inequalities in Roman society led to periodic unrest and conflict between the elite (called 'patricians°') and the majority of the population (called 'plebeians°'), a struggle known as the Conflict of the Orders. On a number of occasions the plebeians refused to work or fight, and even physically withdrew from the city, in order to pressure the elite to make political concessions. One result was publication of the laws on twelve stone tablets ca. 450 B.C.E., a check on arbitrary decisions by judicial officials. Another important reform was the creation of new officials, the tribunes°, who were drawn from and elected by the lower classes, and who had the power to veto, or block, any action of the Assembly or patrician officials that they deemed to be against the inter-

patrician (puh-TRISH-uhn)   **plebeian** (pluh-BEE-uhn)
tribune (TRIH-byoon)

ests of the lower orders. The elite, though forced to give in on key points, found ways to blunt the reforms, in large part by bringing the plebeian leadership into an expanded elite.

The basic unit of Roman society was the family, made up of several generations of family members plus domestic slaves. The oldest living male, the *paterfamilias*, exercised absolute authority over other family members. The important male members of the society possessed *auctoritas*, the quality that enabled them to inspire and demand obedience from their inferiors.

Complex ties of obligation, such as the **patron/client relationship,** bound together individuals and families. Clients sought the help and protection of patrons, men of wealth and influence. A senator might have dozens or even hundreds of clients, to whom he provided legal advice and representation, physical protection, and loans of money in tough times. In turn, the client was expected to follow his patron into battle, support him in the political arena, work on his land, and even contribute toward the dowry of his daughter. Throngs of clients awaited their patrons in the morning and accompanied them to the Forum for the day's business. Especially large retinues brought great prestige. Middle-class clients of aristocrats might be patrons of poorer men. In Rome inequality was accepted, institutionalized, and turned into a system of mutual benefits and obligations.

Historical sources do not often report on the activities of Roman women, largely because they played no public role. Nearly all our information about Roman women pertains to those in the upper classes. In early Rome, a woman never ceased to be a child in the eyes of the law. She started out under the absolute authority of her paterfamilias. When she married, she came under the jurisdiction of the paterfamilias of her husband's family. Unable to own property or represent herself in legal proceedings, she had to depend on a male guardian to advocate her interests.

Despite the limitations put on them, Roman women seem to have been less constrained than their counterparts in the Greek world (see Chapter 5). Over time they gained greater personal protection and economic freedom: for instance, some took advantage of a form of marriage that left a woman under the jurisdiction of her father and independent after his death. There are many stories of strong women who had great influence on their husbands or sons and thereby helped shape Roman history. Roman poets confess their love for women who appear to have been educated and outspoken, and the accounts of the careers of the early emperors are filled with tales of self-assured and assertive queen-mothers and consorts.

Like other Italian peoples, early Romans believed in invisible, shapeless forces known as *numina*. Vesta, the living, pulsating energy of fire, dwelled in the hearth. Janus guarded the door. The Penates watched over food stored in the cupboard. Other deities resided in nearby hills, caves, grottoes, and springs. Romans made small offerings of cakes and liquids to win the favor of these spirits. Certain gods had larger spheres of operation—for example, Jupiter was the god of the sky, and Mars initially was a god of agriculture as well as of war.

The Romans tried to maintain the *pax deorum* ("peace of the gods"), a covenant between the gods and the Roman state. Boards of priests drawn from the aristocracy performed sacrifices and other rituals to win the gods' favor. In return, the gods were expected to bring success to the undertakings of the Roman state. When the Romans came into contact with the Greeks of southern Italy (see Chapter 5), they equated their major deities with gods from the Greek pantheon, such as Zeus (Jupiter) and Ares (Mars), and they took over the myths attached to those gods.

Expansion in Italy and the Mediterranean

At the dawn of the Roman Republic, around 500 B.C.E., Rome was a relatively insignificant city-state among many in the region of central Italy called Latium. Three-and-a-half centuries later, Rome was the center of a huge empire encompassing virtually all the lands surrounding the Mediterranean Sea. Expansion began slowly, then picked up momentum, reaching a peak in the third and second centuries B.C.E. Some scholars attribute this expansion to the greed and aggressiveness of a people fond of war. Others observe that the structure of the Roman state encouraged war, because the two consuls had only one year in office in which to gain military glory. The Romans invariably claimed that they were only defending themselves. It is possible that, as fear drove the Romans to expand the territory under their control in order to provide a buffer against attack, each new conquest became vulnerable and a sense of insecurity led to further expansion. Yet the Romans were also quick to seize opportunities as they appeared.

The chief instrument of Roman expansion was the army. All male citizens who owned a specified amount of land were subject to service. The Roman soldiers' equipment—body armor, shield, spear, and sword—was not far different from that of Greek hoplites, but the Roman battle line was more flexible than the phalanx, being subdivided into units that could maneuver independently. Roman armies were famous for their training and discipline. One observer noted that, whereas a Greek army would minimize its exertions by finding a hill or some other naturally defended location to camp for the night, a Roman army would go to the trouble of fortifying an identical camp in the plain on every occasion.

Rome's conquest of Italy was sparked by ongoing friction between the pastoral hill tribes of the Apennines, whose livelihood depended on driving their herds to seasonal grazing grounds, and the farmers of the coastal plains. In the fifth century B.C.E. Rome rose to a position of leadership within a league of central Italian cities organized for defense against the hill tribes. On several occasions in the fourth century B.C.E. the Romans were asked to defend the wealthy and sophisticated cities of Campania, the region on the Bay of Naples possessing the richest farmland in the peninsula. By 290 B.C.E., in the course of three wars with the tribes of Samnium in central Italy, the Romans had extended their "protection" over nearly the entire peninsula.

Unlike the Greeks, who were reluctant to share the privileges of citizenship with outsiders (see Chapter 5), the Romans granted the political, legal, and economic privileges of Roman citizenship to conquered populations. In essence, they co-opted the most influential elements within the conquered communities and made Rome's interests their interests. Rome demanded soldiers from its Italian subjects, and a seemingly inexhaustible reservoir of manpower was a key element of its military success. In a number of crucial wars, Rome was able to endure higher casualties than the enemy and to prevail by sheer numbers.

Between 264 and 202 B.C.E. Rome fought two protracted and bloody wars against the Carthaginians, those energetic descendants of Phoenicians from Lebanon who had settled in present-day Tunisia and dominated the commerce of the western Mediterranean (see Chapter 4). The Roman state emerged as the unchallenged master of the western Mediterranean and acquired its first overseas provinces in Sicily, Sardinia, and Spain (see Map 6.1). Between 200 and 146 B.C.E. a series of wars pitted the Roman state against the major Hellenistic kingdoms in the eastern Mediterranean. The Romans were at first reluctant to occupy such distant territories and withdrew their troops at the conclusion of several wars. But when the settlements that they imposed failed to take root, the frustrated Roman government took over direct administration of the turbulent lands. The conquest of the Celtic peoples of Gaul (modern France; see Chapter 3) by Rome's most brilliant general, Gaius Julius Caesar, between 59 and 51 B.C.E. led to its first territorial acquisitions in Europe's heartland.

At first the Romans resisted extending their system of governance and citizenship rights to the distant provinces. Indigenous elite groups willing to collaborate with the Roman authorities were given considerable autonomy, including responsibility for local administration and tax collection. Every year a senator, usually someone who recently had held a high public post, was dispatched to each province to serve as governor. The governor, accompanied by a surprisingly small retinue of friends and relations who served as advisers and deputies, was primarily responsible for defending the province against outside attack and internal disruption, overseeing the collection of taxes and other revenues due Rome, and deciding legal cases.

Over time, this system of provincial administration proved inadequate. Officials were chosen because of their political connections and often lacked competence or experience. Yearly changes of governor meant that incumbents had little time to gain experience or make local contacts. Although many governors were honest, some were notoriously unscrupulous and extorted huge sums of money from the provincial populace. While governing an ever-larger Mediterranean empire, the Romans were still relying on the institutions and attitudes that had developed when Rome was merely a city-state.

The Failure of the Republic

Rome's success in creating a vast empire unleashed forces that eventually destroyed the Republican system of government. As a result of the frequent wars and territorial expansion of the third and second centuries B.C.E., profound changes were taking place in the Italian landscape. Italian peasant farmers were away from home on military service for long periods of time, and while they were away, it was easy for investors to take possession of their farms by purchase, deception, or intimidation. Most of the wealth generated by the conquest and control of new provinces ended up in the hands of the upper classes, who used it to purchase Italian land. As a result, the small, self-sufficient farms of the Italian countryside, whose peasant owners had been the backbone of the Roman legions (units of 6,000 soldiers), were replaced by *latifundia*, literally "broad estates," or ranches.

The owners of these large estates found it more lucrative to graze herds of cattle or to grow crops—such as grapes for wine—that brought in big profits than to grow wheat, the staple food of ancient Italy. Large segments of the population of Italy, especially in the burgeoning cities, became dependent on expensive imported grain. Meanwhile, the cheap slave labor provided by prisoners of war (see Diversity and Dominance: The Treatment of Slaves in Rome and China) made it hard for peasants who had lost their farms to find work in the countryside. When they moved to Rome and other cities, they found

Scene from Trajan's Column, Rome, ca. 113 C.E.   The Roman emperor Trajan erected a marble column 125 feet (38 meters) in height to commemorate his triumphant campaign in Dacia (modern Romania). The relief carving, which snakes around the column for 656 feet (200 meters), illustrates numerous episodes of the conquest and provides a detailed pictorial record of the equipment and practices of the Roman army in the field. This panel depicts soldiers building a fort.   (Peter Rockwell, Rome)

no work there either, and they lived in dire poverty. The growing urban masses, idle and prone to riot, would play a major role in the political struggles of the late Republic.

One consequence of the decline of peasant farmers in Italy was a shortage of men who owned the minimum amount of property required for military service. During a war in North Africa at the end of the second century B.C.E. Gaius Marius—a "new man," as the Romans called politically active individuals who did not belong to the traditional ruling class—achieved political prominence by accepting into the Roman legions poor, propertyless men to whom he promised farms upon retirement from military service. These troops became devoted to Marius and helped him get elected to an unprecedented (and illegal) six consulships.

Between 88 and 31 B.C.E., a series of ambitious individuals—Sulla, Pompey, Julius Caesar, Mark Antony, and Octavian—commanded armies that were more loyal to them than to the state. Their use of Roman troops to increase their personal power and influence led to bloody civil wars between military factions. The city of Rome itself was taken by force on several occasions, and victorious commanders executed political opponents and exercised dictatorial control of the state.

The Roman Principate, 31 B.C.E.–330 C.E.

Julius Caesar's grandnephew and heir, Octavian (63 B.C.E.–14 C.E.), eliminated all rivals by 31 B.C.E. and painstakingly set about refashioning the Roman system of government. He was careful to maintain the forms of the Republic—the offices, honors, and social prerogatives of the senatorial class—but fundamentally altered the realities of power. A military dictator in fact, he never called himself king or emperor, claiming merely to be *princeps,* "first among equals," in a restored Republic. For this reason, the period following the Roman Republic is called the **Roman Principate.**

Augustus, one of the many honorific titles that the Roman Senate gave Octavian, connotes prosperity and piety, and it became the name by which he is best known to posterity. Augustus's ruthlessness, patience, and intuitive grasp of psychology enabled him to manipulate all the groups that made up Roman society. When he died in 14 C.E., after forty-five years of carefully veiled rule, almost no one could remember the Republic. During his reign Egypt and parts of the Middle East and Central Europe were added to the empire, leaving only the southern half of Britain and modern Romania to be added later.

Augustus had allied himself with the *equites,*° the class of well-to-do Italian merchants and landowners second in wealth and social status only to the senatorial class. This body of competent and self-assured individuals became the core of a new civil service that helped run the Roman Empire. At last Rome had an administrative bureaucracy up to the task of managing a large empire with considerable honesty, consistency, and efficiency.

So popular was Augustus when he died that four members of his family succeeded to the position of "emperor" (as we call it) despite their serious personal and political shortcomings. However, due to Augustus's calculated ambiguity about his role, the position of emperor was never automatically regarded as hereditary, and after the mid-first century C.E. other families obtained the post. In theory the early emperors were affirmed by the Senate; in reality they were chosen by the armies. By the second century C.E. a series of very capable emperors instituted a

equites (EH-kwee-tays)

령이 대중 앞에 나타나거나 애국심
을 고취하는 노래만을 내보내던 방
송마저 중단됐다.

라크 전후 대책
의에서는 전쟁
영국 주도로

DIVERSITY AND DOMINANCE

THE TREATMENT OF SLAVES IN ROME AND CHINA

Although slaves were found in most ancient societies, Rome was one of the few in which slave labor became the indispensable foundation of the economy. In the course of the frequent wars of the second century B.C.E., large numbers of prisoners were carried into slavery. The prices of such slaves were low, and landowners and manufacturers found they could compel slaves to work longer and harder than hired laborers. Periodically, the harsh working and living conditions resulted in slave revolts.

The following excerpt, from one of several surviving manuals on agriculture, gives advice about controlling and efficiently exploiting slaves:

When the head of a household arrives at his estate, after he has prayed to the family god, he must go round his farm on a tour of inspection on the very same day, if that is possible, if not, then on the next day. When he has found out how his farm has been cultivated and which jobs have been done and which have not been done, then on the next day after that he must call in his manager and ask him which are the jobs that have been done and which remain, and whether they were done on time, and whether what still has to be done can be done, and how much wine and grain and anything else has been produced. When he has found this out, he must make a calculation of the labor and the time taken. If the work doesn't seem to him to be sufficient, and the manager starts to say how hard he tried, but the slaves weren't any good, and the weather was awful, and the slaves ran away, and he was required to carry out some public works, then when he has finished mentioning these and all sorts of other excuses, you must draw his attention to your calculation of the labor employed and time taken. If he claims that it rained all the time, there are all sorts of jobs that can be done in rainy weather—washing wine-jars, coating them with pitch, cleaning the house, storing grain, shifting muck, digging a manure pit, cleaning seed, mending ropes or making new ones; the slaves ought to have been mending their patchwork cloaks and their hoods. On festival days they would have been able to clean out old ditches, work on the public highway, prune back brambles,

dig up the garden, clear a meadow, tie up bundles of sticks, remove thorns, grind barley and get on with cleaning. If he claims that the slaves have been ill, they needn't have been given such large rations. When you have found out about all these things to your satisfaction, make sure that all the work that remains to be done will be carried out. . . The head of the household [on his tour of inspection] should examine his herds and arrange a sale; he should sell the oil if the price makes it worthwhile, and any wine and rain that is surplus to needs; he should sell any old oxen, cattle or sheep that are not up to standard, wool and hides, an old cart or old tools, an old slave, a sick slave—anything else that is surplus to requirements. The head of a household ought to sell, and not to buy. (Cato the Elder, *Concerning Agriculture*, bk. 2, second century B.C.E.)

Cato, the Roman author of that excerpt, was notorious for his stern manner and hard-edged traditionalism, and he expresses a point of view that Roman society found acceptable. In reality, the treatment of slaves by Roman masters varied widely.

Slavery was far less prominent in ancient China. During the Warring States Period, dependent peasants as well as slaves worked the large holdings of the landowning aristocracy. The Qin government sought to abolish slavery, but the institution persisted into the Han period, although it involved only a small fraction of the population and was not a central component of the economy. The relatives of criminals could be seized and enslaved, and poor families sometimes sold unwanted children into slavery. In China slaves, whether they belonged to the state or to individuals, generally performed domestic tasks, as can be seen in the following text:

Wang Ziyuan of Shu Commandery went to the Jian River on business, and went up to the home of the widow Yang Hui, who had a male slave named Bianliao. Wang Ziyuan requested him to go and buy some wine. Picking up a big stick, Bianliao climbed to the top of the grave mound and said: "When my master bought me, Bianliao, he only contracted for me to care for the grave and did not contract for me to buy wine for some other gentleman."

Wang Ziyuan was furious and said to the widow: "Wouldn't you prefer to sell this slave?"

Yang Hui said: "The slave's father offered him to people, but no one wanted him."

Wang Ziyuan immediately settled on the sale contract.

The slave again said: "Enter in the contract everything you wish to order me to do. I, Bianliao, will not do anything not in the contract."

Wang Ziyuan said: "Agreed."

The text of the contract said:

Third year of Shenjiao , the first month, the fifteenth day, the gentleman Wang Ziyuan, of Zizhong, purchases from the lady Yang Hui of Anzhi village in Zhengdu, the bearded male slave, Bianliao, of her husband's household. The fixed sale [price] is 15,000 [cash]. The slave shall obey orders about all kinds of work and may not argue.

He shall rise at dawn and do an early sweeping. After eating he shall wash up. Ordinarily he should pound the grain mortar, tie up broom straws, carve bowls and bore wells, scoop out ditches, tie up fallen fences, hoe the garden, trim up paths and dike up plots of land, cut big flails, bend bamboos to make rakes, and scrape and fix the well pulley. In going and coming he may not ride horseback or in the cart, [nor may he] sit crosslegged or make a hubbub. When he gets out of bed he shall shake his head [to wake up], fish, cut forage, plait reeds and card hemp, draw water for gruel, and help in making zumo [drink]. He shall weave shoes and make [other] coarse things . . .

In the second month at the vernal equinox he shall bank the dikes and repair the boundary walls [of the fields]; prune the mulberry trees, skin the palm trees, plant melons to make gourd [utensils], select eggplant [seeds for planting], and transplant onion sets; burn plant remains to generate the fields, pile up refuse and break up lumps [in the soil]. At midday he shall dry out things in the sun. At cockcrow he shall rise and pound grain in the mortar, exercise and curry the horses, the donkeys, and likewise the mules . . . [The list of tasks continues for two-and-a-half pages.]

He shall be industrious and quick-working, and he may not idle and loaf. When the slave is old and his strength spent, he shall plant marsh grass and weave mats. When his work is over and he wishes to rest he should pound a picul [of grain]. Late at night when there is no work he shall wash clothes really white. If he has private savings they shall be the master's gift, or from guests. The slave may not have evil secrets; affairs should be open and reported. If the slave does not heed instructions, he shall be whipped a hundred strokes.

The reading of the text of the contract came to an end.

The slave was speechless and his lips were tied. Wildly he beat his head on the ground, and beat himself with his hands; from his eyes the tears streamed down, and the drivel from his nose hung a foot long.

He said: "If it is to be exactly as master Wang says, I would rather return soon along the yellow-soil road, with the grave worms boring through my head. Had I known before I would have bought the wine for master Wang. I would not have dared to do that wrong." (Wang Bao, first century B.C.E.)

This story shows that Chinese slaves could be forced to work hard and engaged in many of the same menial tasks as their Roman counterparts. However, it is hard to imagine a Roman slave daring to refuse a request and arguing publicly with a nobleman, for fear of severe punishment. It also appears that slaves in China had legal protections provided by contracts specifying and limiting what could be demanded of them.

QUESTIONS FOR ANALYSIS

1. Why might slavery have been less important in Han China than in the Roman Empire? Why would the treatment of slaves have been less harsh in China than in Rome?

2. In what ways were slaves treated like other forms of property, such as animals and tools? In what ways was a slave's "humanity" taken into account?

3. What are some of the passive-resistance tactics that slaves resorted to, and what did they achieve by these actions?

Source: First selection from Thomas Wiedemann, *Greek and Roman Slavery,* (Baltimore: Johns Hopkins University Press (1981), 183–184. Reprinted with the permission of Thomas Publishing Services. Second selection reprinted with permission of Scribner, an imprint of Simon and Schuster Adult Publishing Group, from *Slavery in China During the Former Han Dynasty, 206 B.C.–A.D. 25* by Clarence Martin Wilbur (New York: Russell & Russell, 1967).

new mechanism of succession: each adopted a mature man of proven ability as his son, designated him as his successor, and shared offices and privileges with him.

While Augustus had felt it important to appeal to Republican traditions and conceal the source and extent of his power, this became less necessary over time, and later emperors exercised their authority more overtly. In imitation of Alexander the Great and the Hellenistic kings, many Roman emperors were officially deified (regarded as gods) after death. A cult of worship of the living emperor developed as a useful way to commemorate and increase the loyalty of subjects.

During the Republic a body of laws had developed, starting with the terse Law of the Twelve Tables ca. 450 B.C.E., supplemented by decrees of the Senate, bills passed in the Assembly, and the annual proclamations of the praetors,° elected public officials responsible for hearing cases and administering the law. In the later Republic a relatively small group of legal experts began to emerge who analyzed laws and legal procedures to determine the underlying principles, then applied these principles to the creation of new laws required by a changing society. These experts were less lawyers in the modern sense than teachers, though they were sometimes consulted by magistrates or the parties to legal actions.

During the Principate the emperor became a major source of new laws. In this period the law was studied and codified with a new intensity by the class of legal experts, and their opinions and interpretations often were given the force of law. The basic divisions of Roman law—persons, things, and actions—reveal the importance of property and the rights of individuals in Roman eyes. The separation of the class of jurists from the government, at least before the later second century C.E., gave Roman Law a unique independence and flexibility. The culmination of this long process of development and interpretation of the law was the sixth-century C.E. Digest of Justinian. Roman law has remained the foundation of European law to this day.

An Urban Empire

The Roman Empire of the first three centuries C.E. was an "urban" empire. This does not mean that most people were living in cities and towns. Perhaps 80 percent of the 50 to 60 million people living within the borders of the empire engaged in agriculture and lived in villages or on isolated farms in the countryside. The empire, however, was administered through a network of towns and cities, and the urban populace benefited most.

Numerous towns had several thousand inhabitants. A handful of major cities—Alexandria in Egypt, Antioch in Syria, and Carthage—had populations of several hundred thousand. Rome itself had approximately a million residents. The largest cities strained the limited technological capabilities of the ancients; providing adequate food and water and removing sewage were always problems.

In Rome the upper classes lived in elegant townhouses on one or another of the seven hills. Such a house was centered around an *atrium*, a rectangular courtyard with an open skylight that let in light and rainwater for drinking and washing. Surrounding the atrium were a large dining room for dinner and drinking parties, an interior garden, a kitchen, and possibly a private bath. Bedrooms were on the upper level. The floors were decorated with pebble mosaics, and the walls and ceilings were covered with frescoes (paintings done directly on wet plaster) of mythological scenes or outdoor vistas, giving a sense of openness in the absence of windows. The typical aristocrat also owned a number of villas in the Italian countryside to which the family could retreat to escape the pressures of city life.

The poor lived in crowded slums in the low-lying parts of the city. Damp, dark, and smelly, with few furnishings, their wooden tenements were susceptible to frequent fires. Fortunately, Romans could spend much of the year outdoors.

The cities, towns, and even the ramshackle settlements that sprang up on the edge of frontier forts were miniature replicas of the capital city in political organization, physical layout, and appearance. A town council and two annually elected officials drawn from prosperous members of the community maintained law and order and collected both urban and rural taxes. In return for the privilege of running local affairs with considerable autonomy and in appreciation of the state's protection of their wealth and position, this "municipal aristocracy" served Rome loyally. In their desire to imitate the manners and values of Roman senators, they endowed cities and towns, which had very little revenue of their own, with attractive elements of Roman urban life—a forum (an open plaza that served as a civic center), government buildings, temples, gardens, baths, theaters, amphitheaters, and games and public entertainments of all sorts. These amenities made the situation of the urban poor superior to that of the rural poor. Poor people living in a city could pass time at the baths, seek refuge from the elements amid the colonnades, and attend the games.

In the countryside hard work and drudgery were relieved by occasional holidays and village festivals and by the everyday pleasures of sex, family, and social exchange. Rural people had to fend for themselves in deal-

---

praetor (PRAY-tuhr)

Roman Shop Selling Food and Drink
The bustling town of Pompeii on the Bay of Naples was buried in ash by the eruption of Mt. Vesuvius in 79 C.E. Archaeologists have unearthed the streets, stores, and houses of this typical Roman town. Shops such as this sold hot food and drink served from clay vessels set into the counter. Shelves and niches behind the counter contained other items. In the background can be seen a well-paved street and a public fountain where the inhabitants could fetch water. (Courtesy, Leo C. Curran)

ing with bandits, wild animals, and other hazards of country life. People living away from urban centers had little direct contact with the Roman government other than occasional run-ins with bullying soldiers and the dreaded arrival of the tax collector.

The concentration of ownership of the land in ever fewer hands was temporarily reversed during the civil wars that brought an end to the Roman Republic, but it resumed in the era of the emperors. However, after the era of conquest ended in the early second century C.E., slaves were no longer plentiful or inexpensive, and landowners needed a new source of labor. Over time, the independent farmers were replaced by "tenant farmers" who were allowed to live on and cultivate plots of land in return for a portion of their crops. The landowners still lived in the cities and hired foremen to manage their estates. Thus wealth was concentrated in the cities but was based on the productivity of rural agricultural laborers.

Some urban dwellers got rich from manufacture and trade. Commerce was greatly enhanced by the ***pax romana*** ("Roman peace"), the safety and stability guaranteed by Roman might. Grain, meat, vegetables, and other bulk foodstuffs usually could be exchanged only locally because transportation was expensive and many products spoiled quickly. However, the city of Rome depended on the import of massive quantities of grain from Sicily and Egypt to feed its huge population, and special naval squadrons performed this vital task.

Glass, metalwork, delicate pottery, and other fine manufactured products were exported throughout the empire. The centers of production, first located in Italy, moved into the provinces as knowledge of the necessary skills spread. Roman armies stationed on the frontiers were a large market, and their presence promoted the prosperity of border provinces. Other merchants traded in luxury items from far beyond the boundaries of the empire, especially silk from China and spices from India and Arabia.

The system of taxes and other revenues collected by the central government produced a transfer of wealth. Funds from the rich interior provinces like Gaul (France) and Egypt flowed to Rome to support the emperor and the central government, then were dispatched to the frontier provinces to subsidize the armies.

Romanization—the spread of the Latin language and Roman way of life—was one of the most enduring consequences of empire, primarily in the western provinces. Greek language and culture, a legacy of the Hellenistic kingdoms, continued to dominate the eastern Mediterranean (see Chapter 5). Portuguese, Spanish, French, Italian, and Romanian evolved from the Latin language, proving that the language of the conquerors spread among the common people as well as the elite.

The Roman government did not force Romanization. The inhabitants of the provinces chose to switch to Latin and adopt the cultural habits that went with it. There were advantages to speaking Latin and wearing a *toga* (the traditional cloak worn by Roman male citizens), just as people in today's developing nations see advantages in moving to the city, learning English, and putting on a suit and tie. Latin facilitated dealings with the Roman administration and helped merchants get contracts to supply the military. Many also must have been drawn to the aura of success surrounding the language and culture of a people who had created so vast an empire.

As towns sprang up and acquired the features of Roman urban life, they served as magnets for ambitious members of the indigenous populations. The empire gradually and reluctantly granted Roman citizenship, with its attendant privileges, legal protections, and exemptions from some types of taxation, to people living outside Italy. Men who completed a twenty-six-year term of service in the native military units that backed up the Roman legions were granted citizenship and could pass this coveted status on to their descendants. Emperors made grants of citizenship to individuals or entire communities as rewards for good service. In 212 C.E. the emperor Caracalla granted citizenship to all free, adult, male inhabitants of the empire.

The gradual extension of citizenship mirrored the empire's transformation from an Italian dominion over Mediterranean lands into a commonwealth of peoples. As early as the first century C.E. some of the leading literary and intellectual figures came from the provinces. By the second century even the emperors hailed from Spain, Gaul, and North Africa.

The Rise of Christianity

During this same period of general peace and prosperity, at the eastern end of the Mediterranean events were taking place that, though little noted at the moment, would prove to be of great historical significance. The Jewish homeland of Judaea (see Chapter 4), roughly equivalent to present-day Israel, was put under direct Roman rule in 6 C.E. Over the next half-century Roman governors insensitive to the Jewish belief in one god managed to increase tensions, and various kinds of opposition to Roman rule sprang up. Many waited for the arrival of the Messiah, the "Anointed One," presumed to be a military leader who would liberate the Jewish people and drive the Romans out of the land.

It is in this context that we must see the career of **Jesus,** a young carpenter from the Galilee region in northern Israel. While scholars largely agree that the portrait of Jesus found in the New Testament reflects the viewpoint of followers a half-century after his death, it is difficult to determine the motives and teachings of the

historical Jesus. Some experts believe that he was essentially a rabbi, or teacher, and that, offended by what he perceived as Jewish religious and political leaders' excessive concern with money and power and by the perfunctory nature of mainstream Jewish religious practice in his time, he prescribed a return to the personal faith and spirituality of an earlier age. Others stress his connections to the apocalyptic fervor found in certain circles of Judaism, such as John the Baptist and the community that authored the Dead Sea Scrolls. They view Jesus as a fiery prophet who urged people to prepare themselves for the imminent end of the world and God's ushering in of a blessed new age. Still others see him as a political revolutionary, upset by the downtrodden condition of the peasants in the countryside and the poor in the cities, who determined to drive out the Roman occupiers and their collaborators among the Jewish elite. Whatever the real nature of his mission may have been, the charismatic Jesus eventually attracted the attention of the Jewish authorities in Jerusalem, who regarded popular reformers as potential troublemakers. They turned him over to the Roman governor, Pontius Pilate. Jesus was imprisoned, condemned, and executed by crucifixion, a punishment usually reserved for common criminals. His followers, the Apostles, carried on after his death and sought to spread his teachings and their belief that he was the Messiah and had been resurrected (returned from death to life) among their fellow Jews.

Paul, a Jew from the Greek city of Tarsus in southeast Anatolia, converted to the new creed. Between 45 and 58 C.E. he threw his enormous talent and energy into spreading the word. Traveling throughout Syria-Palestine, Anatolia, and Greece, he became increasingly frustrated with the refusal of most Jews to accept his claim that Jesus was the Messiah and had ushered in a new age. Many Jews, on the other hand, were appalled by the failure of the followers of Jesus to maintain traditional Jewish practices. Discovering a spiritual hunger among many non-Jews (sometimes called "gentiles"), Paul redirected his efforts toward them and set up a string of Christian (from the Greek name *christos*, meaning "anointed one," given to Jesus by his followers) communities in the eastern Mediterranean. Paul's career exemplifies the cosmopolitan nature of the Roman Empire. Speaking both Greek and Aramaic, he moved comfortably between the Greco-Roman and Jewish worlds. He used Roman roads, depended on the peace guaranteed by Roman arms, called on his Roman citizenship to protect him from the arbitrary action of local authorities, and moved from city to city in his quest for converts. In 66 C.E. long-building tensions in Roman Judaea erupted into a full-scale revolt that lasted until 73. One of the casualties of the Roman reconquest of Judaea was the Jerusalem-based Christian community, which focused on converting the Jews. This left the field clear for Paul's non-Jewish converts, and Christianity began to diverge more and more from its Jewish roots.

For more than two centuries, the sect grew slowly but steadily. Many of the first converts were from disenfranchised groups—women, slaves, the urban poor. They hoped to receive respect not accorded them in the larger society and to obtain positions of responsibility when the members of early Christian communities democratically elected their leaders. However, as the religious movement grew and prospered, it developed a hierarchy of priests and bishops and became subject to bitter disputes over theological doctrine (see Chapter 10).

As monotheists forbidden to worship other gods, early Christians were persecuted by Roman officials who regarded their refusal to worship the emperor as a sign of disloyalty. Despite occasional government-sponsored attempts at suppression and spontaneous mob attacks, or perhaps because of them, the young Christian movement continued to gain strength and attract converts. By the late third century C.E. its adherents were a sizable minority within the Roman Empire and included many educated and prosperous people with posts in the local and imperial governments.

The expansion of Christianity should be seen as part of a broader religious tendency. By the Greek Classical period a number of "mystery" cults had gained popularity by claiming to provide secret information about the nature of life and death and promising a blessed afterlife to their adherents. In the Hellenistic and Roman periods, a number of cults making similar promises arose in the eastern Mediterranean and spread throughout the Greco-Roman lands, presumably in response to a growing spiritual and intellectual hunger not satisfied by traditional pagan practices. These included the worship of the mother-goddess Cybele in Anatolia, the Egyptian goddess Isis, and the Iranian sun-god Mithra. As we shall see, the ultimate victory of Christianity over these rivals had as much to do with historical circumstances as with its spiritual appeal.

Technology and Transformation

The relative ease and safety of travel brought by Roman arms and engineering enabled merchants to sell their wares and helped the early Christians spread their faith. Surviving remnants of roads, fortification walls, aqueducts, and buildings testify to the engineering expertise of the ancient Romans. Some of the best engineers served with the army, building bridges, siege works, and ballistic weapons that hurled stones and shafts. In peacetime soldiers were often put to work on construction projects. **Aqueducts**—long elevated or underground conduits—carried water from a source to an urban center, using only the force of gravity (see Environment and Technology: Water Engineering in Rome and China). The Romans were pioneers in the use of arches, which allow the even distribution of great weights without thick supporting walls. The invention of concrete—a mixture of lime powder, sand, and water that could be poured into molds—allowed the Romans to create vast vaulted and domed interior spaces unlike the rectilinear pillar-and-post designs of the Greeks.

Defending borders that stretched for thousands of miles was a great challenge. In a document released after his death, Augustus advised against expanding the empire because the costs of administering and defending subsequent acquisitions would be greater than the revenues. The Roman army was reorganized and redeployed to reflect the shift from an offensive to a defensive strategy. At most points the empire was protected by mountains, deserts, and seas. But the lengthy Rhine and Danube river frontiers in Germany and Central Europe were vulnerable. They were guarded by a string of forts with relatively small garrisons adequate for dealing with raiders. On particularly desolate frontiers, such as in Britain and North Africa, the Romans built long walls to keep out the peoples who lived beyond.

Most of Rome's neighbors were less technologically advanced and more loosely organized, and they did not pose a serious threat to the security of the empire. The one exception was the Parthian kingdom, heir to the Mesopotamian and Persian Empires, which controlled the lands on the eastern frontier (today's Iran and Iraq). For centuries Rome and Parthia engaged in a rivalry that sapped both sides without any significant territorial gain by either party.

The Roman state prospered for two-and-a-half centuries after Augustus stabilized the internal political situation and addressed the needs of the empire with an ambitious program of reforms. In the third century C.E. cracks in the edifice became visible. Historians use the expression **"third-century crisis"** to refer to the period from 235 to 284 C.E., when political, military, and economic problems beset and nearly destroyed the Roman Empire. The most visible symptom of the crisis was the frequent change of rulers. Twenty or more men claimed the office of emperor during this period. Most reigned for only a few months or years before being overthrown by rivals or killed by their own troops. Germanic tribesmen on the Rhine/Danube frontier took advantage of the frequent civil wars and periods of anarchy to raid deep into the empire. For the first time in centuries, Roman cities began to erect walls for protection. Several regions, feeling that the central government was not adequately protecting them, turned power over to a man on the spot who promised to put their interests first.

The political and military emergencies had a devastating impact on the empire's economy. Buying the loyalty of the army and paying to defend the increasingly permeable frontiers drained the treasury. The unending demands of the central government for more tax revenues from the provinces, as well as the interruption of commerce by fighting, eroded the towns' prosperity. Shortsighted emperors, desperate for cash, secretly reduced the amount of precious metal in Roman coins and pocketed the excess. The public quickly caught on, and the devalued coinage became less and less acceptable in the marketplace. The empire reverted to a barter economy, a far less efficient system that further curtailed large-scale and long-distance commerce.

The municipal aristocracy, once the most vital and public-spirited class in the empire, was slowly crushed out of existence. As town councilors, its members were personally liable for shortfalls in taxes owed to the state. The decline in trade eroded their wealth, which often was based on manufacture and commerce, and many began to evade their civic duties and even went into hiding.

Population shifted out of the cities and into the countryside. Many people sought employment and protection from both raiders and government officials on the estates of wealthy and powerful country landowners. The shrinking of cities and movement of the population to the country estates were the first steps in a demographic shift toward the social and economic structures of the European Middle Ages—roughly seven hundred years during which wealthy rural lords dominated a peasant population tied to the land (see Chapter 10).

Roman Aqueduct Near Tarragona, Spain   How to provide an adequate supply of water was a problem posed by the growth of Roman towns and cities. Aqueducts channeled water from a source, sometimes many miles away, to an urban complex, using only the force of gravity. To bring an aqueduct from high ground into the city, Roman engineers designed long, continuous rows of arches that maintained a steady downhill slope. Roman troops were often used in such large-scale construction projects. Scholars sometimes can roughly estimate the population of an ancient city by calculating the amount of water that was available to it.   (Robert Frerck/Woodfin Camp & Associates)

ENVIRONMENT + TECHNOLOGY

Water Engineering in Rome and China

People needed water to drink; it was vital for agriculture; and it provided a rapid and economical means for transporting people and goods. Some of the most impressive technological achievements of ancient Rome and China involved hydraulic (water) engineering.

Roman cities, with their large populations, required abundant and reliable sources of water. One way to obtain it was to build aqueducts—stone channels to bring water from distant lakes and streams to the cities. The water flowing in these conduits was moved only by the force of gravity. Surveyors measured the land's elevation and plotted a course that very gradually moved downhill.

Some conduits were elevated atop walls or bridges, which made it difficult for unauthorized parties to tap the water line for their own use. Portions of some aqueducts were built underground. Still-standing aboveground segments indicate that the Roman aqueducts were well-built structures made of large cut stones closely fitted and held together by a cement-like mortar. Construction of the aqueducts was labor-intensive, and often both design and construction were carried out by military personnel. This was one of the ways in which the Roman government could keep large numbers of soldiers busy in peacetime.

Sections of aqueduct that crossed rivers presented the same construction challenges as bridges. Roman engineers lowered prefabricated wooden cofferdams—large, hollow cylinders—into the riverbed and pumped out the water so workers could descend and construct cement piers to support the arched segments of the bridge and the water channel itself. This technique is still used for construction in water.

When an aqueduct reached the outskirts of a city, the water flowed into a reservoir, where it was stored. Pipes connected the reservoir to different parts of the city. Even within the city, gravity provided the motive force until the water reached the public fountains used by the poor and the private storage tanks of individuals wealthy enough to have plumbing in their houses.

In ancient China, rivers running generally in an east-west direction were the main thoroughfares. The earliest development of complex societies centered on the Yellow River Valley, but by the beginning of the Qin Empire the Yangzi River Valley and regions farther south were becoming increasingly important to China's political and economic vitality. In this era the Chinese began to build canals connecting the northern and southern zones, at first for military purposes but eventually for transporting commercial goods as well. In later periods, with the acquisition of more advanced engineering skills, an extensive network of canals was built, including the 1,100-mile-long (1,771-kilometer-long) Grand Canal.

One of the earliest efforts was the construction of the Magic Canal. A Chinese historian tells us that the Qin emperor Shi Huangdi ordered his engineers to join two rivers by a 20-mile-long (32.2-kilometer-long) canal so that he could more easily supply his armies of conquest in the south. Construction of the canal posed a difficult engineering challenge, because the rivers Hsiang and Li, though coming within 3 miles (4.8 kilometers) of one another, flowed in opposite directions and with a strong current.

The engineers took advantage of a low point in the chain of hills between the rivers to maintain a relatively level grade. The final element of the solution was to build a snout-shaped mound to divide the waters of the Hsiang, funneling part of that river into an artificial channel. Several spillways further reduced the volume of water flowing into the canal, which was 15 feet wide and 3 feet deep (about 4.5 meters wide and 1 meter deep). The joining of the two rivers completed a network of waterways that permitted continuous inland water transport of goods between the latitudes of Beijing and Guangzhou (Canton), a distance of 1,250 miles (2,012 kilometers). Modifications were made in later centuries, but the Magic Canal is still in use.

The Magic Canal Engineers of Shi Huangdi, "First Emperor" of China, exploited the contours of the landscape to connect the river systems of northern and southern China. (From Robert Temple, *The Genius of China* [1986]. Photographer: Robert Temple)

Just when things looked bleakest, one man pulled the empire back from the brink of self-destruction. Like many of the rulers of that age, Diocletian came from one of the eastern European provinces most vulnerable to invasion. A commoner by birth, he had risen through the ranks of the army and gained power in 284. His success is indicated by the fact that he ruled for more than twenty years and died in bed.

Diocletian implemented radical reforms that saved the Roman state by transforming it. To halt inflation (the process by which prices rise as money becomes worth less), Diocletian issued an edict that specified the maximum prices that could be charged for various commodities and services. To ensure an adequate supply of workers in vital services, he froze many people into their professions and required them to train their sons to succeed them. This unprecedented government regulation of prices and vocations had unforeseen consequences. A "black market" arose among buyers and sellers who chose to ignore the government's price controls and establish their own prices for goods and services. Many inhabitants of the empire began to see the government as an oppressive entity that no longer deserved their loyalty.

When Diocletian resigned in 305, the old divisiveness reemerged as various claimants battled for the throne. The eventual winner was **Constantine** (r. 306–337), who reunited the entire empire under his sole rule by 324.

In 312 Constantine won a key battle at the Milvian Bridge over the Tiber River near Rome. He later claimed that he had seen a cross (the sign of the Christian God) superimposed on the sun before this battle. Believing that the Christian God had helped him achieve the victory, in the following year Constantine issued the so-called Edict of Milan, ending the persecution of Christianity and guaranteeing freedom of worship to Christians and all others. Throughout his reign he supported the Christian church, although he tolerated other beliefs as well. Historians disagree about whether Constantine was spiritually motivated or was pragmatically seeking to unify the peoples of the empire under a single religion. In either case his embrace of Christianity was of tremendous historical significance. Large numbers of people began to convert when they saw that Christians seeking political office or favors from the government had clear advantages over non-Christians.

In 324 Constantine transferred the imperial capital from Rome to Byzantium, an ancient Greek city on the Bosporus° strait leading from the Mediterranean into the Black Sea. The city was renamed Constantinople°,

"City of Constantine." This move both reflected and accelerated changes already taking place. Constantinople was closer than Rome to the most-threatened borders in eastern Europe (see Map 6.1). The urban centers and prosperous middle class in the eastern half of the empire had better withstood the third-century crisis than had those in the western half. In addition, more educated people and more Christians were living in the eastern provinces (see Chapter 10).

The conversion of Constantine and the transfer of the imperial capital away from Rome often have been seen as marking the end of Roman history. But many of the important changes that culminated during Constantine's reign had their roots in events of the previous two centuries, and the Roman Empire as a whole survived for at least another century. The eastern, or Byzantine, portion of the empire (discussed in Chapter 10) survived Constantine by more than a thousand years. Nevertheless, the Roman Empire of the fourth century was fundamentally different from the earlier empire, and for that reason it is convenient to see Constantine's reign as the beginning of a new epoch.

THE ORIGINS OF IMPERIAL CHINA, 221 B.C.E.–220 C.E.

The early history of China (described in Chapter 3) was characterized by the fragmentation that geography seemed to dictate. The Shang (ca. 1750–1027 B.C.E.) and Zhou (1027–221 B.C.E.) dynasties ruled over a relatively compact zone in northeastern China. The last few centuries of nominal Zhou rule—the Warring States Period—saw rivalry and belligerence among a group of small states with somewhat different languages and cultures. As in the contemporary Greek city-states (see Chapter 5), competition and conflict gave rise to many distinctive elements of a national culture.

In the second half of the third century B.C.E. one of the warring states—the **Qin**° state of the Wei° Valley—rapidly conquered its rivals and created China's first empire (221–206 B.C.E.). Built at a great cost in human lives and labor, the Qin Empire barely survived the death of its founder, **Shi Huangdi**°. Power soon passed to a new dynasty, the **Han,** which ruled China from 206 B.C.E. to 220 C.E. (see Map 6.2). Thus began the long history of imperial China—a tradition of political and cultural unity and continuity that lasted into the early twentieth century

---

Bosporus (BAHS-puhr-uhs)
Constantinople (cahn-stan-tih-NO-pul)

Qin (chin)   **Wei** (way)   **Shi Huangdi** (Shee wahng-dee)

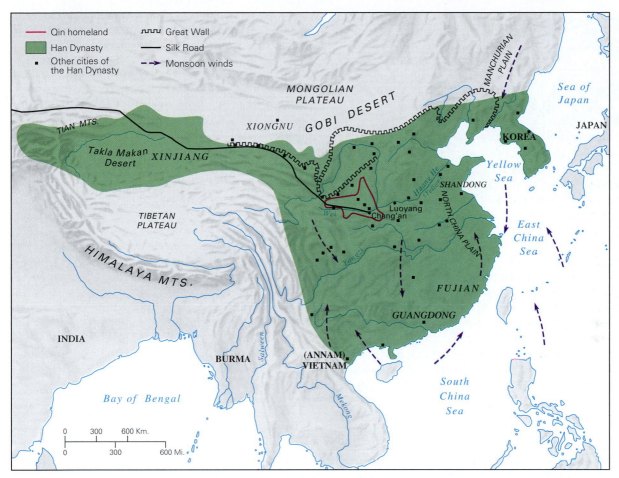

Map 6.2   Han China   The Qin and Han rulers of northeast China extended their control over all of eastern China and extensive territories to the west. A series of walls in the north and northwest, built to check the incursions of nomadic peoples from the steppes, were joined together to form the ancestor of the present-day Great Wall of China. An extensive network of roads connecting towns, cities, and frontier forts promoted rapid communication and facilitated trade. The Silk Road carried China's most treasured product to Central, South, and West Asia and the Mediterranean lands.

and still has meaning for the very different China of our own time.

Resources and Population

An imperial state in East Asia controlling lands of extremely diverse topography, climate, plant and animal life, and human population faced greater obstacles to long-distance communications and to a uniform way of life than did the Roman Empire. The climates and agricultural potentials of Rome's territories were, for the most part, roughly similar, and the Mediterranean Sea facilitated relatively rapid and inexpensive travel and transport of commodities. What resources, technologies, institutions, and val-ues made possible the creation and maintenance of a Chinese empire?

Agriculture produced the wealth and taxes that sup-ported the institutions of imperial China. The main tax, a percentage of the annual harvest, funded government activities ranging from the luxurious lifestyle of the royal court to the daily tasks of officials and military units throughout the country and on the frontiers. Large pop-ulations in China's capital cities, first Chang'an° and later Luoyang°, had to be fed. As intensive agriculture spread in the Yangzi River Valley, the need to transport southern crops to the north spurred the construction of canals to connect the Yangzi with the Yellow River (see

Chang'an (chahng-ahn)   **Luoyang** (LWOE-yahng)

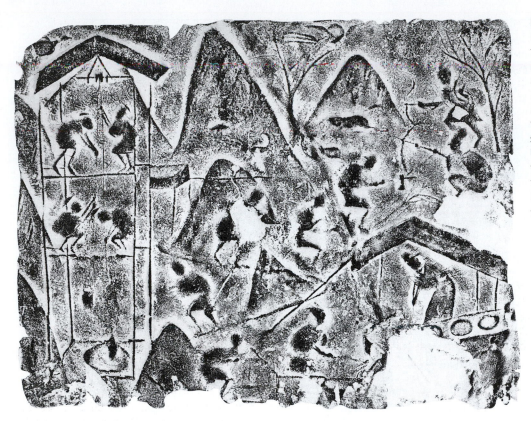

Rubbing of Salt Mining Found in a Chinese tomb of the first century C.E., this rubbing illustrates a procedure for mining salt. The tower on the left originally served as a derrick for drilling a deep hole through dirt and rock. In this scene workers are hauling up buckets full of brine (saltwater) from underground deposits. In the background are hunters in the mountains. (Courtesy of the Trustees of the British Museum)

Environment and Technology: Water Engineering in Rome and China). During prosperous times, the government also collected and stored surplus grain that could be sold at reasonable prices in times of shortage.

Human labor was the other fundamental commodity. The government periodically conducted a census of inhabitants, and the results for 2 C.E. and 140 C.E. are available today. The earlier survey counted approximately 12 million households and 60 million people; the later, not quite 10 million households and 49 million people. The average household contained 5 persons. Then, as now, the vast majority of the people lived in the eastern portion of the country, the river-valley regions where intensive agriculture could support a dense population. At first the largest concentration was in the Yellow River Valley and North China Plain, but by early Han times the demographic center had begun to shift to the Yangzi River Valley.

In the intervals between seasonal agricultural tasks, every able-bodied man donated one month of labor a year to public works projects—building palaces, temples, fortifications, and roads; transporting goods; excavating and maintaining canal channels; laboring on imperial estates; or working in the mines. The state also required two years of military service. On the frontiers, young conscripts built walls and forts, kept an eye on barbarian neighbors, fought when necessary, and grew crops to support themselves. Annually updated registers of land and households enabled imperial officials to keep track of money and services due. Like the Romans, the Chinese government depended on a large population of free peasants to contribute taxes and services to the state.

The Han Chinese gradually but persistently expanded at the expense of other ethnic groups. Population growth in the core regions and a shortage of good, arable land spurred pioneers to push into new areas. Sometimes the government organized new settlements, at militarily strategic sites and on the frontiers, for example. Neighboring kingdoms also invited Chinese settlers so as to exploit their skills and learn their technologies.

Han people preferred regions suitable for the kind of agriculture they had practiced in the eastern river valleys. They took over land on the northern frontier, pushing back nomadic populations. They also expanded into the tropical forests of southern China and settled in the western oases. In places not suitable for their preferred kind of agriculture, particularly the steppe and the desert, Han Chinese did not displace other groups.

Hierarchy, Obedience, and Belief

As the Han Chinese expanded into new regions, they took along their social organization, values, language, and other cultural practices. The basic unit of Chinese society was the family, which included not only the living generations but also all the previous generations—the ancestors. The Chinese believed that their ancestors maintained an ongoing interest in the fortunes of living family members, so they consulted, appeased, and venerated them in order to maintain their favor. The family was viewed as a living, self-renewing organism, and each generation was required to have sons to perpetuate the family and maintain the ancestor cult that provided a kind of immortality to the deceased.

The doctrine of Confucius (Kongzi), which had its origins in the sixth century B.C.E. (see Chapter 3) became very influential in the imperial period. Confucianism regarded hierarchy as a natural aspect of human society and laid down rules of appropriate conduct. People saw themselves as part of an interdependent unit rather than as individual agents. Each person had a place and responsibilities within the family hierarchy, based on his or her gender, age, and relationship to other family members. Absolute authority rested with the father, who was an intermediary between the living members and the ancestors, presiding over the rituals of ancestor worship.

The same concepts operated in society as a whole. Peasants, soldiers, administrators, and rulers all made distinctive and necessary contributions to the welfare of society. Confucianism optimistically maintained that people could be guided to the right path through education, imitation of proper role models, and self-improvement. The family inculcated the basic values of Chinese society: loyalty, obedience to authority, respect for elders and ancestors, and concern for honor and appropriate conduct. Because the hierarchy in the state mirrored the hierarchy in the family, these same attitudes carried over into the relationship between individuals and the state.

The experiences of women in ancient Chinese society are hard to pinpoint because, as elsewhere, contemporary written sources are largely silent on the subject. Confucian ethics stressed the impropriety of women participating in public life. Traditional wisdom about conduct appropriate for women is preserved in an account of the life of the mother of the Confucian philosopher Mencius (Mengzi):

A woman's duties are to cook the five grains, heat the wine, look after her parents-in-law, make clothes, and that is all! . . . [She] has no ambition to manage affairs outside the house. . . . She must follow the "three submissions." When she is young, she must submit to her parents. After her marriage, she must submit to her husband. When she is widowed, she must submit to her son.[1]

That is an ideal perpetuated by males of the upper classes, the social stratum that is the source of most of the written texts. Upper-class females were under considerable pressure to conform to those expectations. Women of the lower classes, less affected by Confucian ways of thinking, may have been less constrained than their more "privileged" counterparts.

After her parents arranged her marriage, a young bride went to live with her husband's family, where she was a stranger who had to prove herself. Ability and force of personality—as well as the capacity to produce sons—could make a difference. Dissension between the wife and her mother-in-law and sisters-in-law grew out of competition for influence with husbands, sons, and brothers and for a larger share of the family's economic resources.

Like the early Romans, the ancient Chinese believed that divinity resided within nature rather than outside and above it, and they worshiped and tried to appease the forces of nature. The state erected and maintained shrines to the lords of rain and winds as well as to certain great rivers and high mountains. Gathering at mounds or altars where the local spirit of the soil was thought to reside, people sacrificed sheep and pigs and beat drums loudly to promote the fertility of the earth. Strange or disastrous natural phenomena, such as eclipses or heavy rains, called for symbolic restraint of the deity by tying a red cord around the sacred spot. Because it was believed that supernatural forces flowed through the landscape, bringing good and evil fortune, experts in *feng shui*, meaning "earth divination," were consulted to determine the most favorable location and orientation for buildings and graves. The faithful learned to adapt their lives to the complex rhythms they perceived in nature.

Some people tried to cheat death by taking life-enhancing drugs or building ostentatious tombs flanked by towers or covered by mounds of earth and filled with things they believed would allow them to maintain the quality of life they had enjoyed on earth. The objects in these tombs have provided archaeologists with a wealth of knowledge about Han society.

The First Chinese Empire, 221–207 B.C.E.

For centuries eastern China was divided among rival states whose frequent hostilities gave rise to the label "Warring States Period" (480–221 B.C.E.). In the second half of the third century B.C.E. the state of the Qin suddenly burst forth and took over the other states one by one. By 221 B.C.E., the first emperor had united the northern plain and the Yangzi River Valley under one rule, marking the creation of China and the inauguration of the imperial age. Many scholars maintain that the name "China," by which this land has been known in the Western world, is derived from "Qin."

Several factors account for the meteoric rise of the Qin. The Qin ruler, who took the title *Shi Huangdi* ("First Emperor"), and his adviser and prime minister Li Si° were able and ruthless men who exploited the exhaustion resulting from the long centuries of interstate rivalry. The Qin homeland in the valley of the Wei, a tributary of the Yellow River, was less urbanized and commercialized than the kingdoms farther east, with a large pool of sturdy peasants to serve in the army. Moreover, long experience in mobilizing manpower for the construction of irrigation and flood-control works had strengthened the authority of the Qin king at the expense of the nobles and endowed his government with superior organizational skills.

Shi Huangdi and Li Si created a totalitarian structure that subordinated the individual to the needs of the state. By publicly burning large numbers of books, they symbolically expressed a radical break with the past. They cracked down on Confucianism, regarding its demands for benevolent and nonviolent conduct from rulers to be a check on the absolute power they sought. They instead drew from a stream of political thought known as Legalism (see Chapter 3). Developing earlier Legalist thinking, Li Si insisted that the will of the ruler was supreme, and that it was necessary to impose discipline and obedience on the subjects through the rigid application of rewards and punishments.

The new regime was determined to eliminate rival centers of authority. Its first target was the landowning aristocracy of the conquered rival states and the system on which aristocratic wealth and power had been based. Because primogeniture—the right of the eldest son to inherit all the landed property—allowed a small number of individuals to accumulate vast tracts of land, the Qin government abolished it, instead requiring estates to be broken up and passed on to several heirs.

The large estates of the aristocracy had been worked by slaves (see Diversity and Dominance: The Treatment of Slaves in Rome and China) and peasant serfs, who gave their landlords a substantial portion of their harvest. The Qin abolished slavery and took steps to create a free peasantry who paid taxes and provided labor, as well as military service, to the state.

The Qin government's commitment to standardization helped create a unified Chinese civilization. During the Warring States Period, small states found many ways to emphasize their independence. For example, states had their own forms of music, with different scales, systems of notation, and instruments. The Qin imposed standard weights, measures, and coinage, a uniform law code, a common system of writing, and even regulations governing the axle length of carts so as to leave just one set of ruts on the roads.

The Qin built thousands of miles of roads—comparable in scale to the roads of the Roman Empire—to connect the parts of the empire and to move Qin armies quickly. They also built canals connecting the river systems of northern and southern China (see Environment and Technology: Water Engineering in Rome and China). The frontier walls of the old states began to be linked into a continuous barricade, the precursor of the Great Wall (see Chapter 11), to protect cultivated lands from raids by northern nomads. Large numbers of people were forced to donate their labor and often their lives to build the walls and roads. So oppressive were the financial exploitation and demands for forced labor that a series of rebellions broke out when Shi Huangdi died in 210 B.C.E., bringing down the Qin dynasty.

The Long Reign of the Han, 206 B.C.E.–220 C.E.

When the dust cleared, Liu Bang°, who may have been born a peasant, had outlasted his rivals and established a new dynasty, the Han (206 B.C.E.–220 C.E.). The new emperor promised to reject the excesses and mistakes of the Qin and to restore the institutions of a venerable past. To sustain and protect a large empire, however, the Han administration maintained much of Qin's structure and Legalist ideology, though with less fanatical zeal. The Han tempered Legalist government with a Confucianism revised to serve a large, centralized political entity. This Confucianism emphasized the government's benevolence and the appropriateness of particular rituals and behaviors in a manifestly hierarchical society. The Han system of administration became the standard for later ages, and the Chinese people today refer to themselves ethnically as "Han."

After eighty years of imperial consolidation, Emperor Wu (r. 140–87 B.C.E.) launched a period of military expansion, south into Fujian, Guangdong, and present-day north Vietnam, and north into Manchuria and present-day North Korea. Han armies also went west to inner Mongolia and Xinjiang° to secure the lucrative Silk

---

Li Si (luh suh)

Lui Bang (le-oo bahng)   **Xinjiang** (SHIN-jyahng)

Road (see Chapter 8). Controlling the newly acquired territories was expensive, however, so Wu's successors curtailed further expansion.

The Han Empire endured, with a brief interruption between 9 and 23 C.E., for more than four hundred years. From 202 B.C.E. to 8 C.E.—the period of the Early, or Western, Han—the capital was at Chang'an, in the Wei Valley, an ancient seat of power from which the Zhou and Qin dynasties had emerged. From 23 to 220 C.E. the Later, or Eastern, Han established its base farther east, in the more centrally located Luoyang.

Protected by a ring of hills but with ready access to the fertile plain, **Chang'an** was surrounded by a wall of pounded earth and brick 15 miles (24 kilometers) in circumference. Contemporaries described it as a bustling place, filled with courtiers, officials, soldiers, merchants, craftsmen, and foreign visitors. In 2 C.E. its population was 246,000. Part of the city was carefully planned. Broad thoroughfares running north and south intersected with others running east and west. High walls protected the palaces, administrative offices, barracks, and storehouses of the imperial compound, and access was restricted. Temples and marketplaces were scattered about the civic center. Chang'an became a model of urban planning, and its main features were imitated in the cities and towns that sprang up throughout the Han Empire.

Moralizing writers who criticized the elite provide glimpses of their private lives. Living in multistory houses, wearing fine silks, traveling about Chang'an in ornate horse-drawn carriages, well-to-do officials and merchants devoted their leisure time to art and literature, occult religious practices, elegant banquets, and various entertainments—music and dance, juggling and acrobatics, dog and horse races, cock and tiger fights. In stark contrast, the common people inhabited a sprawling warren of alleys, living in dwellings packed "as closely as the teeth of a comb," as one poet put it.

As in the Zhou monarchy (see Chapter 3), the emperor was the "Son of Heaven," chosen to rule in accordance with the Mandate of Heaven. He stood at the center of government and society. As the father held authority in the family and was a link between the living generations and the ancestors, so was the emperor supreme in the state. He brought the support of powerful imperial ancestors and guaranteed the harmonious interaction of heaven and earth. To a much greater degree than his Roman counterpart, he was regarded as a divinity and his word was law.

Living in seclusion within the walled palace compound, surrounded by his many wives, children, servants, courtiers, and officials, the emperor presided over unceasing pomp and ritual emphasizing the worship of Heaven and imperial ancestors as well as the practical

Clay Figurine of a Storyteller   Found in a tomb of the later Han period, this performer, who has bare feet and a bare chest and is holding a drum and stick, clearly relates his tales in a dramatic and humorous manner. Storytelling was a popular form of entertainment in this era.   (The National Museum of Chinese History)

business of government. The royal compound was also a hive of intrigue, no more so than when the emperor died and his chief widow chose his heir from among the male members of the ruling clan.

The central government was run by a prime minister, a civil service director, and nine ministers with military, economic, legal, and religious responsibilities. Like the imperial Romans, the Han depended on local officials for day-to-day administration of their far-flung territories. Local people collected taxes and dispatched revenues to the central government, regulated conscription for the army and for labor projects, provided protection, and settled disputes. The remote central government rarely impinged on the lives of most citizens.

As part of their strategy to weaken the rural aristocrats and exclude them from political posts, the Qin and Han emperors allied themselves with the **gentry**—the class next in wealth below the aristocrats. To serve as local officials the central government chose members of this class of moderately prosperous landowners, usually men with education and valued expertise who resembled the Roman equites favored by Augustus and his successors. These officials were a privileged and respected group within Chinese society, and they made the government more efficient and responsive than it had been in the past.

The guiding philosophy of the new gentry class of officials was a modified Confucianism that provided a system for training officials to be intellectually capable and morally worthy of their role and set forth a code of conduct for measuring their performance. According to Chinese tradition, an imperial university with as many as thirty thousand students was located outside Chang'an, and provincial centers of learning were established. (Some scholars doubt that such a complex institution existed this early.) Students from these centers were chosen to enter various levels of government service.

In theory, young men from any class could rise in the state hierarchy. In practice, sons of the gentry had an advantage because they were most likely to receive the necessary training in the Confucian classics. As civil servants advanced in the bureaucracy, they received distinctive emblems and privileges of rank, including preferential treatment in the legal system and exemption from military service. Over time, the gentry became a new aristocracy of sorts, banding together in cliques and family alliances that had considerable clout and worked to advance the careers of group members.

Daoism, which also had its origins in the Warring States Period (see Chapter 3), took deeper root, becoming popular with the common people. Daoism emphasized the search for the *Dao*, or "path," of nature and the value of harmonizing with the cycles and patterns of the natural world. Enlightenment was achieved not so much by education as by solitary contemplation and physical and mental discipline. Daoism was skeptical, questioning age-old beliefs and values and rejecting the hierarchy, rules, and rituals of the Confucianism of the elite classes. It urged passive acceptance of the disorder of the world, denial of ambition, contentment with simple pleasures, and trusting one's own instincts.

Technology and Trade

China was the home of many important inventions, and what the Chinese did not invent they improved. Chinese tradition seems to have recognized the importance of technology for the success and spread of Chinese civilization,

Han-Era (First Century B.C.E.) Stone Rubbing of a Horse-Drawn Carriage The "trace harness," a strap running across the horse's chest, was a Chinese invention that allowed horses to pull far heavier loads than were possible with the constricting throat harness used in Europe. In the Han period, officials, professionals, and soldiers who served the regime enjoyed a lifestyle made pleasant by fine clothing, comfortable transportation, servants, and delightful pastimes, but at the same time they were guided by a Confucian emphasis on duty, honesty, and appropriate behavior. (From Wu family shrine, Jiaxiang, Shantung. From *Chin-shih-so* [Jinshisuo])

crediting legendary rulers of the distant past with the introduction of major new technologies.

The advent of bronze tools around 1500 B.C.E. helped clear the forests and open land for agriculture on the North China Plain. Almost a thousand years later iron arrived. The Qin may have been among the first to take full advantage of the new iron technology. Chinese metallurgists employed more advanced techniques than did their counterparts elsewhere in the hemisphere. Whereas Roman blacksmiths produced wrought-iron tools and weapons by hammering heated iron, the Chinese hammered ores with a higher carbon content to produce steel, and they mastered the technique of liquefying iron and pouring it into molds. The resulting steel and cast-iron tools and weapons were considerably stronger.

In the succeeding centuries, the crossbow and use of cavalry helped the Chinese military repel nomads from the steppe regions. The watermill, which harnessed the power of running water to turn a grindstone, was used in China long before it appeared in Europe. The development of a horse collar that did not constrict the animal's breathing allowed Chinese horses to pull much heavier loads than European horses could. The Chinese also were the first to make paper, perhaps as early as the second century B.C.E. They pounded soaked plant fibers and bark with a mallet, then poured the mixture through a porous mat. Once the residue left on the mat surface dried out, it provided a relatively smooth, lightweight medium for writing on with ink.

The Qin began and the Han rulers continued an extensive program of road building. Roads enabled rapid movement of military forces and supplies. The network of couriers that carried messages to and from the central administration used horses, boats, and even footpaths, and they found food and shelter at relay stations. The network of navigable rivers was improved and connected by canals (see Environment and Technology: Water Engineering in Rome and China).

Population growth and increasing trade gave rise to local market centers. These thriving towns grew to become county seats from which imperial officials operated. Between 10 and 30 percent of the population lived in Han towns and cities.

China's most important export commodity was silk. For a long time the fact that silk cocoons are secreted onto the leaves of mulberry trees by silkworms was a closely guarded secret that gave the Chinese a monopoly on the manufacture of silk. As silk was carried on a perilous journey westward through the Central Asian oases to the Middle East, India, and the Mediterranean, it passed through the hands of middlemen who raised the price to make a profit. The value of a beautiful textile may have increased a hundredfold by the time it reached its destination. The Chinese government sought to control the Silk Road by launching periodic campaigns into Central Asia. Garrisons were installed, and colonies of Chinese settlers were sent out to occupy the oases.

Decline of the Han Empire

For the Han government, as for the Romans, maintaining the security of the frontiers—particularly the north and northwest frontiers—was a primary concern. In general, the Han Empire successfully controlled lands occupied by farming peoples, but met resistance from nomadic groups whose livelihood depended on their horses and herds. The different ways of life of farmers and herders gave rise to insulting stereotypes on both sides. The settled Chinese thought of nomads as "barbarians"—rough, uncivilized peoples—much as the inhabitants of the Roman Empire looked down on the Germanic tribes living beyond their frontier.

Along the boundary, the closeness of the herders and farmers often led to significant commercial activity. The nomadic herders sought the food and crafted goods produced by the farmers and townsfolk, and the settled farmers depended on the nomads for horses and other herd animals and products. Sometimes, however, nomads raided the settled lands and took what they needed or wanted. Tough and warlike because of the demands of their way of life, mounted nomads could strike swiftly and just as swiftly disappear.

Although nomadic groups tended to be relatively small and often fought with one another, from time to time circumstances and a charismatic leader could create a large coalition. The major external threat to Chinese civilization in the Han period came from the **Xiongnu°**, a great confederacy of Turkic peoples. For centuries the Chinese succeeded in containing the Xiongnu. In order to mount periodic campaigns onto the steppe, they developed cavalry forces that could match the mobility of the nomads, and access to good stocks of horses and pasturing of herds on northern grasslands became a state priority. Other strategies included maintaining colonies of soldier-farmers and garrisons on the frontier; settling compliant nomadic groups inside the borders to serve as a buffer against warlike groups; paying bribes to promote dissension among the nomad leadership; and paying protection money. One frequently successful approach was a "tributary system" in which nomad rulers nominally accepted Chinese su-

Xiongnu (SHE-OONG-noo)

premacy and paid tribute, for which they were rewarded with marriages to Chinese princesses, dazzling receptions at court, and gifts from the Han emperor that exceeded the value of the tribute.

In the end, continuous military vigilance along the frontier burdened Han finances and worsened the economic troubles of later Han times. Despite the earnest efforts of Qin and Early Han emperors to reduce the power and wealth of the aristocracy and to turn land over to a free peasantry, by the end of the first century B.C.E. nobles and successful merchants again controlled huge tracts of land, and many peasants sought their protection against the demands of the imperial government. Over the next two centuries strongmen who were largely independent of imperial control emerged, and the central government was deprived of tax revenues and manpower. The system of military conscription broke down, forcing the government to hire more and more foreign soldiers and officers. These men were willing to serve for pay, but they were not very loyal to the Han state.

Several factors contributed to the fall of the Han dynasty in 220 C.E.: factional intrigues within the ruling clan, official corruption and inefficiency, uprisings of desperate and hungry peasants, the spread of banditry, attacks by nomadic groups on the northwest frontier, and the ambitions of rural warlords. China entered a period of political fragmentation and economic and cultural regression that lasted until the rise of the Sui° and Tang° dynasties in the late sixth and early seventh centuries C.E., a story we take up in Chapter 11.

IMPERIAL PARALLELS

The similarities between the Roman and Han Empires begin at the level of the family. In both cultures the family comprised the living generations and was headed by an all-powerful patriarch. Strong loyalties and obligations bound family members. Values first learned in the family—obedience, respect for superiors, piety, and a strong sense of duty and honor—created a pervasive social cohesion.

Agriculture was the fundamental economic activity and source of wealth in both civilizations. Government revenues were primarily derived from a percentage of the annual harvest. Both empires depended on free peasantry—sturdy farmers who could be pressed into

military service or other forms of compulsory labor. Conflicts over who owned the land and how it was to be used were at the heart of the political and social turmoil in both places. The autocratic rulers of the Roman and Chinese states secured their positions by breaking the power of the old aristocratic families, seizing their excess land, and giving land to small farmers (as well as keeping extensive tracts for themselves). They veiled the revolutionary nature of these changes by claiming to restore the institutions of a venerable past. The later reversal of this process, when wealthy noblemen once again gained control of vast tracts of land and reduced the peasants to dependent tenant farmers, signaled the erosion of the authority of the state.

Both empires spread out from an ethnically homogeneous core to encompass widespread territories containing diverse ecosystems, populations, and ways of life. Both brought those regions a cultural unity that has persisted, at least in part, to the present day. This development involved far more than military conquest and political domination. The skill of Roman and Chinese farmers and the high yields that they produced led to a dynamic expansion of population. As the population of the core areas outstripped the available resources, Italian and Han settlers moved into new regions, bringing their languages, beliefs, customs, and technologies with them. Many people in the conquered lands were attracted to the culture of the ruler nation and chose to adopt these practices and attach themselves to a "winning cause." Both empires found similar solutions to the problems of administering far-flung territories and large populations in an age when men on horseback or on foot carried messages. The central government had to delegate considerable autonomy to local officials. These local elites identified their own interests with the central government they loyally served. In both empires a kind of civil service developed, staffed by educated and capable members of a prosperous middle class.

Technologies that facilitated imperial control also fostered cultural unification and improvements in the general standard of living. Roads built to expedite the movement of troops became the highways of commerce and the thoroughfares by which imperial culture spread. A network of cities and towns served as the nerve center of each empire, providing local administrative bases, further promoting commerce, and radiating imperial culture out into the surrounding countryside.

Cities and towns modeled themselves on the capital cities of Rome and Chang'an. Travelers could find the same types and styles of buildings and public spaces, as well as other attractive features of urban life, in outlying

Sui (sway)   **Tang** (tahng)

regions that they had seen in the capital. The majority of the population still resided in the countryside, but most of the advantages of empire were enjoyed by people living in urban centers.

The empires of Rome and Han China faced similar problems of defense: long borders located far from the administrative center and aggressive neighbors who coveted the prosperity of the empire. Both empires had to build walls and maintain a chain of forts and garrisons to protect against incursions. The cost of frontier defense was staggering and eventually eroded the economic prosperity of the two empires. Rough neighbors gradually learned the skills that had given the empires an initial advantage and were able to close the "technology gap." As the imperial governments became ever more beholden to the military and demanded more taxes and services from the hard-pressed civilian population, they lost the loyalty of their own people, many of whom sought protection on the estates of powerful rural landowners. Eventually, both empires were so weakened that their borders were overrun and their central governments collapsed. Ironically, the newly dominant immigrant groups had been so deeply influenced by imperial culture that they maintained it to the best of their abilities.

In referring to the eventual failure of these two empires, we are brought up against the different long-term consequences of their respective demises. In China the imperial model was revived in subsequent eras, but the lands of the Roman Empire never again achieved the same level of unification. Several interrelated factors help account for the different outcomes.

First, these cultures had different attitudes about the relationship of individuals to the state. In China the individual was deeply embedded in the larger social group. The Chinese family, with its emphasis on a precisely defined hierarchy, unquestioning obedience, and solemn rituals of deference to elders and ancestors, served as the model for society and the state. Respect for authority was (and remains) deeply seated. The architects of Qin Legalism largely got their way, and the emperor's word was regarded as law. Moreover, Confucianism, which sanctified hierarchy and provided a code of conduct for professionals and public officials, had arisen long before the imperial system and could be revived and tailored to fit subsequent political circumstances. Although the Roman family had its own hierarchy and traditions of obedience, the cult of ancestors was not as strong as among the Chinese, and the family was not the organizational model for Roman society and the Roman state. Also, there was no Roman equivalent of Confucianism—no ideology of political organi-

zation and social conduct that could survive the dissolution of the Roman state.

It is probably also fair to say that economic and social mobility, which allows some people to rise dramatically in wealth and status, enhances a society's sense of the significance of the individual. Opportunities for individuals to improve their economic status were more limited in ancient China than in the Roman Empire, and the merchant class in China was frequently disparaged and constrained by the government. The greater importance of commerce in the Roman Empire and the absence of government interference resulted in greater economic mobility. Roman law gave great weight to the sanctity of property and the rights of the individual. To a much greater extent than the Chinese emperor, the Roman emperor had to resort to persuasion, threats, and promises in order to forge a consensus for his initiatives.

Although Roman emperors tried to create an ideology to bolster their position, they were hampered by the persistence of Republican traditions and the ambiguities about the position of emperor deliberately cultivated by Augustus. As a result, Roman rulers were likely to be chosen by the army or by the Senate; the dynastic principle never took deep root; and the cult of the emperor had little spiritual content. This stands in sharp contrast to the clear-cut Chinese belief that the emperor was the divine Son of Heaven with privileged access to the beneficent power of the royal ancestors. Thus, in the lands that had once comprised the western part of the Roman Empire, there was no compelling basis for reviving the position of emperor and the territorial claims of empire in later ages.

Finally, Christianity, with its insistence on monotheism and one doctrine of truth, negated the Roman emperor's pretensions to divinity and was essentially unwilling to come to terms with pagan beliefs. The spread of Christianity through the provinces during the Late Roman Empire, and the decline of the western half of the empire in the fifth century C.E. (see Chapter 10), constituted an irreversible break with the past. On the other hand, Buddhism, which came to China in the early centuries C.E. and flourished in the post-Han era (see Chapter 11), was more easily reconciled with traditional Chinese values and beliefs.

CONCLUSION

Both the Roman Empire and the first Chinese empire arose from relatively small states that, because of their discipline and military toughness, were initially able to subdue small and quarreling neighbors. Ultimately they unified widespread territories under strong central governments.

In China the Qin Empire emerged rapidly, in the reign of a single ruler, because many of the elements for unification were already in place. The "First Emperor" looked back to the precedents of the Shang and Zhou states, which had controlled large core areas in the North China Plain. He drew upon the preexisting concept of the Mandate of Heaven, a claim to divine backing for the ruler who was himself the Son of Heaven; and the Legalist political philosophy justified authoritarian measures. The harshness of the new order generated discontent and resistance that soon brought down the Qin dynasty, but Han successors were able to moderate and build on Qin structures to create a durable imperial regime.

The early Roman state had no such precedents to draw upon. The creation of the Roman Empire was a much slower process in which solutions were discovered by trial and error. The Republican form of government, developed to meet the needs of an Italian city-state, proved inadequate to the demands of empire, and Rome's military success led to social and economic disruption and an acute political struggle. Out of this crisis emerged the Principate, which persevered for several centuries. Even so, the Roman emperors were never able to develop an effective ideology of rule.

In both empires, large and efficient professional armies maintained social order and defended the frontiers. An administrative bureaucracy staffed by educated civil servants kept records and collected taxes to support the military and government. Roads, cities, standardized systems of money and measurement, and widely understood languages facilitated travel, commerce, and communication. The culture of the imperial center spread throughout the lands under its control, and this shared culture, as well as shared self-interest, bonded local elites to the empire's ruling class.

For long periods these stabilizing forces, which brought peace, prosperity, and an improved standard of living to many, were stronger than the weaknesses inherent in these two great empires. Over time, however, the costs of defending lengthy frontiers drained imperial treasuries and imposed greater burdens of taxation on the subjects. As hard-pressed subjects sought the protection of rural landowners, cities became depopulated, commerce was disrupted, and the central government was less able to compel payment of taxes and find recruits for the armed forces.

In the end, both empires succumbed to a combination of external pressures and internal divisions. In China the imperial tradition and the class structure and value system that maintained it were eventually revived (see Chapters 11 and 14), and they survived with remarkable continuity into the twentieth century C.E. In Europe, North Africa, and the Middle East, in contrast, there was no restoration of the Roman Empire, and the later history of those lands was marked by great political changes and cultural diversity.

■ Key Terms

Roman Republic	aqueduct
Roman Senate	third-century crisis
patron/client relationship	Constantine
Roman Principate	Qin
Augustus	Shi Huangdi
equites	Han
pax romana	Chang'an
Romanization	gentry
Jesus	Xiongnu
Paul	

■ Suggested Reading

Tim Cornell and John Matthews, *Atlas of the Roman World* (1982), offers a general introduction, pictures, and maps to illustrate many aspects of Roman civilization. Michael Grant and Rachel Kitzinger, eds., *Civilization of the Ancient Mediterranean*, 3 vols. (1988), is an invaluable collection of essays with bibliographies by specialists on every major facet of life in the Greek and Roman worlds. Among the many good surveys of Roman history are Michael Grant, *History of Rome* (1978), and M. Cary and H. H. Scullard, *A History of Rome Down to the Reign of Constantine* (1975). Naphtali Lewis and Meyer Reinhold, eds., *Roman Civilization*, 2 vols. (1951), contains extensive ancient sources in translation.

For Roman political and legal institutions, attitudes, and values see J. A. Crook, *Law and Life of Rome: 90 B.C.–A.D. 212* (1967). Michael Crawford, *The Roman Republic*, 2d ed. (1993), and Chester G. Starr, *The Roman Empire, 27 B.C.–A.D. 476: A Study in Survival* (1982), assess the evolution of the Roman state during the Republic and Principate. Fergus Millar, *The Emperor in the Roman World (31 B.C.–A.D. 337)* (1977), is a comprehensive study of the position of the princeps. Barbara Levick, *The Government of the Roman Empire: A Sourcebook* (2000), presents original texts in translation.

For Roman military expansion and defense of the frontiers see W. V. Harris, *War and Imperialism in Republican Rome* (1979), and Stephen L. Dyson, *The Creation of the Roman Frontier* (1985). For military technology see M. C. Bishop, *Roman Military Equipment: From the Punic Wars to the Fall of Rome* (1993). David Macaulay, *City: A Story of Roman Planning and Construction* (1974), uses copious illustrations to reveal the wonders of Roman engineering; more depth and detail are found in K. D.

White, *Greek and Roman Technology* (1984). The characteristics of Roman urban centers are highlighted in John E. Stambaugh, *The Ancient Roman City* (1988).

Kevin Greene, *The Archaeology of the Roman Economy* (1986), showcases new approaches to social and economic history. Suzanne Dickson, *The Roman Family* (1992) explores this most basic social group. Lionel Casson, *Everyday Life in Ancient Rome* (1998), and U. E. Paoli, *Rome: Its People, Life and Customs* (1983), look at the features that typified daily life. Jo-Ann Shelton, ed., *As the Romans Did: A Sourcebook in Roman Social History* (1998), offers a selection of translated ancient sources. Elaine Fantham, Helene Peet Foley, Natalie Boymel Kampen, Sarah B. Pomeroy, and H. Alan Shapiro, *Women in the Classical World: Image and Text* (1994), provides an up-to-date discussion of women in the Roman world. Many of the ancient sources on Roman women can be found in Mary R. Lefkowitz and Maureen B. Fant, eds., *Women's Life in Greece and Rome: A Source Book in Translation* (1982). Thomas Wiedemann, ed., *Greek and Roman Slavery* (1981), contains the ancient sources in translation. Donald G. Kyle, *Spectacles of Death in Ancient Rome* (1998), explores the nature and significance of blood sports in the arena.

A number of the chapters in John Boardman, Jasper Griffin, and Oswyn Murray, eds., *The Roman World* (1988), survey the intellectual and literary achievements of the Romans. Ronald Mellor, ed., *The Historians of Ancient Rome* (1998), provides context for reading the historical sources. Michael von Albrecht, *History of Roman Literature: From Livius Andronicus to Boethius: With Special Regard to Its Influence on World Literature* (1997), Michael Grant, *Art in the Roman Empire* (1995), and Nancy H. Ramage and Andrew Ramage, *The Cambridge Illustrated History of Roman Art* (1991) are surveys of Roman creative arts. Robert Turcan, *The Gods of Ancient Rome: Religion in Everyday Life from Archaic to Imperial Times* (2000), and R. M. Ogilvie, *The Romans and Their Gods in the Age of Augustus* (1969), are accessible introductions to Roman religion in its public and private manifestations. Michael Grant, *The Jews in the Roman World* (1973), and Erich S. Gruen, *Diaspora: Jews Amidst Greeks and Romans* (2002), explore the complicated situation of Jews in the Roman Empire. Joseph F. Kelly, *The World of the Early Christians* (1997), W. H. C. Frend, *The Rise of Christianity* (1984), and R. A. Markus, *Christianity in the Roman World* (1974), investigate the rise of Christianity. Everett Ferguson, ed., *Encyclopedia of Early Christianity* (2d ed., 1998), contains articles and bibliographies on a wide range of topics.

For the geography and demography of China see the well-illustrated *Cultural Atlas of China* (1983) by Caroline Blunden and Mark Elvin. Valerie Hansen, *The Open Empire: A History of China to 1600* (2000), emphasizes social history and China's interactions with other societies. Other basic surveys of Chinese history include Jacques Gernet, *A History of Chinese Civilization* (1982), and John K. Fairbank, *China: A New History* (1992). In greater depth for the ancient period is Edward L. Shaughnessy and Michael Loewe, eds., *The Cambridge History of Ancient China* (1998); Denis Twitchett and Michael Loewe, eds., *The Cambridge History of China*, vol. 1, *The Ch'in and Han Empires, 221 B.C.–A.D. 220* (1986); and Michele Pirazzoli-t'Serstevens, *The Han Dynasty* (1982). Nicola Di Cosmo, *Ancient China and Its Enemies: The Rise of Nomadic Power in East Asian History* (2002), explores the interactions of Chinese and nomads on the northern frontier. Kwang-chih Chang, *The Archaeology of Ancient China*, 4th ed. (1986), emphasizes the archaeological record. Patricia Buckley Ebrey, *Chinese Civilization: A Sourcebook* (2d ed., 1993), and W. de Bary, W. Chan, and B. Watson, eds., *Sources of Chinese Tradition* (1960), are collections of sources in translation. Sima Qian, *Historical Records* (1994), translated by Raymond Dawson, provides a very readable selection of varied material pertaining to the Qin dynasty compiled by the premier historian of the Han period.

For social history see Michael Loewe, *Everyday Life in Early Imperial China During the Han Period, 202 B.C.–A.D. 220* (1988), and Anne Behnke Kinney, "Women in Ancient China," in Bella Vivante, ed., *Women's Roles in Ancient Civilizations: A Reference Guide* (1999). For economic history and foreign relations see Xinru Liu, *Ancient India and Ancient China: Trade and Religious Exchanges, A.D. 1–600* (1994), and Ying-shih Yu, *Trade and Expansion in Han China* (1967). For scientific and technological achievements see Robert Temple, *The Genius of China: 3,000 Years of Science, Discovery, and Invention* (1986).

Benjamin I. Schwartz addresses intellectual history in *The World of Thought in Ancient China* (1985). Spiritual matters are taken up by Laurence G. Thompson, *Chinese Religion: An Introduction*, 3d ed. (1979). For art see Michael Sullivan, *A Short History of Chinese Art*, rev. ed. (1970), and Jessica Rawson, *Ancient China: Art and Archaeology* (1980).

For a stimulating comparison of the Roman and Han Empires that emphasizes the differences, see the first chapter of S. A. M. Adshead, *China in World History*, 2d ed. (1995).

■ Notes

1. Patricia Buckley Ebrey, ed., *Chinese Civilization and Society: A Sourcebook* (New York: Free Press, 1981), 33–34.

7 India and Southeast Asia, 1500 B.C.E.–1025 C.E.

The Thousand Pillared Hall in the Temple of Minakshi at Madurai
At the annual Chittarai Festival, the citizens of this city in south India
celebrate the wedding of their patron goddess, Minakshi, to Shiva.

CHAPTER OUTLINE

Foundations of Indian Civilization, 1500 B.C.E.–300 C.E.

Imperial Expansion and Collapse, 324 B.C.E.–650 C.E.

Southeast Asia, 50–1025 C.E.

ENVIRONMENT AND TECHNOLOGY: Indian Mathematics

DIVERSITY AND DOMINANCE: The Situation of Women in the *Kama Sutra*

In the *Bhagavad-Gita°*, the most renowned of all Indian sacred texts, Arjuna°, the greatest warrior of Indian legend, rides out in his chariot to the open space between two armies preparing for battle. Torn between his social duty to fight for his family's claim to the throne and his conscience, which balks at the prospect of killing the relatives, friends, and former teachers who are in the enemy camp, Arjuna slumps down in his chariot and refuses to fight. But his chariot driver, the god Krishna° in disguise, persuades him, in a carefully structured dialogue, both of the necessity to fulfill his duty as a warrior and of the proper frame of mind for performing these acts. In the climactic moment of the dialogue Krishna endows Arjuna with a "divine eye" and permits him to see the true appearance of god:

> It was a multiform, wondrous vision,
> with countless mouths and eyes
> and celestial ornaments,
> Everywhere was boundless divinity
> containing all astonishing things,
> wearing divine garlands and garments,
> anointed with divine perfume.
> If the light of a thousand suns
> were to rise in the sky at once,
> it would be like the light
> of that great spirit.
> Arjuna saw all the universe
> in its many ways and parts,
> standing as one in the body
> of the god of gods.[1]

In all of world literature, this is one of the most compelling attempts to depict the nature of deity. Graphic images emphasize the vastness, diversity, and multiplicity of the god, but in the end we learn that Krishna is the organizing principle behind all creation, that behind diversity and multiplicity lies a higher unity.

This is an apt metaphor for Indian civilization. If one word can characterize India in both ancient and modern times, it is *diversity*. The enormous variety of the Indian landscape is mirrored in the patchwork of ethnic and linguistic groups that occupy it, the political fragmentation that has marked most of Indian history, the elaborate hierarchy of social groups into which the Indian population is divided, and the thousands of deities who are worshiped at the innumerable holy places that dot the subcontinent. Yet, in the end, one can speak of an Indian civilization that is united by a set of shared views and values.

In this chapter we survey the history of South and Southeast Asia from approximately 1500 B.C.E. to 1025 C.E., focusing on the evolution of defining features of Indian civilization. Considerable attention is given to Indian religious conceptions. This coverage is due, in part, to religion's profound role in shaping Indian society. It is also a consequence of the sources of information available to historians. Lengthy epic poems, such as the *Mahabharata°* and *Ramayana°*, preserve useful information about early Indian society, but most of the earliest texts are religious documents—such as the *Vedas°*, *Upanishads°*, and Buddhist dialogues and stories—that were preserved and transmitted orally long before they were written down. In addition, Indian civilization held a conception of vast expanses of time during which creatures were repeatedly reincarnated and lived many lives. This belief may be why ancient Indians did not develop a historical consciousness like that of their Israelite and Greek contemporaries and took little interest in recording specific historical events: such events seemed relatively insignificant when set against the long cycles of time and lives.

As you read this chapter, ask yourself the following questions:

- What historical forces led to the development of complex social groupings in ancient India?
- Why did Indian civilization develop religious traditions with such distinctive conceptions of space, time, gods, and the life cycle, and how did these beliefs shape nearly every aspect of South Asian culture?

Bhagavad-Gita (BUH-guh-vahd GEE-tuh)
Arjuna (AHR-joo-nuh)   **Krishna** (KRISH-nuh)

Mahabharata (muh-huh-BAH-ruh-tuh)
Ramayana (ruh-muh-YAH-nuh)   *Vedas* (VAY-duhs)
Upanishads (oo-PAHN-ih-shahds)

- How, in the face of powerful forces that tended to keep India fragmented, did two great empires—the Mauryan° Empire of the fourth to second centuries B.C.E. and the Gupta° Empire of the fourth to sixth centuries C.E.—succeed in unifying much of India?

- How did a number of states in Southeast Asia become wealthy and powerful by exploiting their position on the trade routes between China and India?

FOUNDATIONS OF INDIAN CIVILIZATION, 1500 B.C.E.–300 C.E.

India is called a *subcontinent* because it is a large—roughly 2,000 miles (3,200 kilometers) in both length and breadth—and physically isolated landmass within the continent of Asia. It is set off from the rest of Asia by the Himalayas°, the highest mountains on the planet, to the north, and by the Indian Ocean on its eastern, southern, and western sides (see Map 7.1). The most permeable frontier, and the one used by a long series of invaders and migrating peoples, lies to the northwest. But people using this corridor must cross over the mountain barrier of the Hindu Kush° (via the Khyber° Pass) and the Thar° Desert east of the Indus River.

The Indian Subcontinent

The subcontinent—which encompasses the modern nations of Pakistan, Nepal, Bhutan, Bangladesh, India, and the adjacent island of Sri Lanka—can be divided into three distinct topographical zones. The mountainous northern zone takes in the heavily forested foothills and high meadows on the edge of the Hindu Kush and Himalaya ranges. Next come the great basins of the Indus and Ganges° Rivers. Originating in the ice of the Tibetan mountains to the north, these rivers have repeatedly overflowed their banks and deposited layer on layer of silt, creating large alluvial plains. Northern India is divided from the third zone, the peninsula proper, by the Vindhya range and the Deccan°, an arid, rocky plateau that brings to mind parts of the American southwest. The tropical coastal strip of Kerala (Malabar) in the west, the Coromandel Coast in the east with its web of rivers

descending from the central plateau, the flatlands of Tamil Nadu on the southern tip of the peninsula, and the island of Sri Lanka often have followed paths of political and cultural development separate from those of northern India.

The rim of mountains looming above India's northern frontier shelters the subcontinent from cold Arctic winds and gives it a subtropical climate. The most dramatic source of moisture is the **monsoon** (seasonal wind). The Indian Ocean is slow to warm or cool, and the vast landmass of Asia swings rapidly between seasonal extremes of heat and cold. The temperature difference between the water and the land acts like a bellows, producing a great wind in this and adjoining parts of the globe. The southwest monsoon begins in June. It picks up huge amounts of moisture from the Indian Ocean and drops it over a swath of India that encompasses the rain-forest belt on the western coast and the Ganges Basin. Three harvests a year are possible in some places. Rice is grown in the moist, flat Ganges Delta (the modern region of Bengal). Elsewhere the staples are wheat, barley, and millet. The Indus Valley, in contrast, gets little precipitation (see Chapter 2). In this arid region agriculture depends on extensive irrigation. Moreover, the volume of water in the Indus is irregular, and the river has changed course from time to time.

Although invasions and migrations usually came by land through the northwest corridor, the ocean surrounding the peninsula has not been a barrier to travel and trade. Indian Ocean mariners learned to ride the monsoon winds across open waters from northeast to southwest in January and to make the return voyage in July. Ships made their way west across the Arabian Sea to the Persian Gulf, the southern coast of Arabia, and East Africa, and east across the Bay of Bengal to Indochina and Indonesia (see Chapter 8).

It is tempting to trace many of the characteristic features of later Indian civilization back to the Indus Valley civilization of the third and early second millennia B.C.E., but proof is hard to come by because the writing from that period has not yet been deciphered. That society, which responded to the challenge of an arid terrain by developing high levels of social organization and technology, seems to have succumbed around 1900 B.C.E. to some kind of environmental crisis (see Chapter 2).

The Vedic Age

Historians call the period from 1500 to 500 B.C.E. the "Vedic Age," after the *Vedas,* religious texts that are our main source of information about the period. The foundations for Indian civilization were laid

---

Mauryan (MORE-yuhn)   **Gupta** (GOOP-tuh)
Himalayas (him-uh-LAY-uhs)   **Hindu Kush** (HIHN-doo KOOSH)
Khyber (KIE-ber)   **Thar** (tahr)   **Ganges** (GAHN-jeez)
Deccan (de-KAN)

C H R O N O L O G Y

	India	Southeast Asia
2000 B.C.E.		**ca. 2000 B.C.E.** Swidden agriculture
		ca. 1600 B.C.E. Beginning of migrations from mainland Southeast Asia to islands in Pacific and Indian Oceans
1500 B.C.E.	**ca. 1500 B.C.E.** Migration of Indo-European peoples into northwest India	
1000 B.C.E.	**ca. 1000 B.C.E.** Indo-European groups move into the Ganges Plain	
500 B.C.E.	**ca. 500 B.C.E.** Siddhartha Gautama founds Buddhism; Mahavira founds Jainism	
	324 B.C.E. Chandragupta Maurya becomes king of Magadha and lays foundation for Mauryan Empire	
1 C.E.	**184 B.C.E.** Fall of Mauryan Empire	
	320 C.E. Chandra Gupta establishes Gupta Empire	**ca. 50–560 B.C.E.** Funan dominates southern Indochina and the Isthmus of Kra
500 C.E.		
	550 C.E. Collapse of Gupta Empire	**ca. 500 B.C.E.** Trade route develops through Strait of Malacca
	606–647 B.C.E. Reign of Harsha Vardhana	
		683 C.E. Rise of Srivijaya in Sumatra
		770–825 C.E. Construction of Borobodur in Java
1000 C.E.		**1025 C.E.** Chola attack on Palembang and decline of Srivijaya

in the Vedic Age. Most historians believe that new groups of people—nomadic warriors speaking Indo-European languages—migrated into northwest India around 1500 B.C.E. Some argue for a much earlier Indo-European presence in this region in conjunction with the spread of agriculture. In any case, in the mid-second millennium B.C.E. northern India entered a new historical period associated with the dominance of Indo-European groups.

After the collapse of the Indus Valley civilization there was no central authority to direct irrigation efforts. The region became home to kinship groups that depended mostly on their herds of cattle for sustenance and perhaps supplemented their diet by doing some gardening. These societies, like those of other Indo-European peoples—Celts, Greeks, Iranians, Romans—were patriarchal. The father dominated the family as the king ruled the tribe. Members of the warrior class boasted of their martial skill and courage, relished combat, celebrated with lavish feasts of beef and rounds of heavy drinking, and filled their leisure time with chariot racing and gambling.

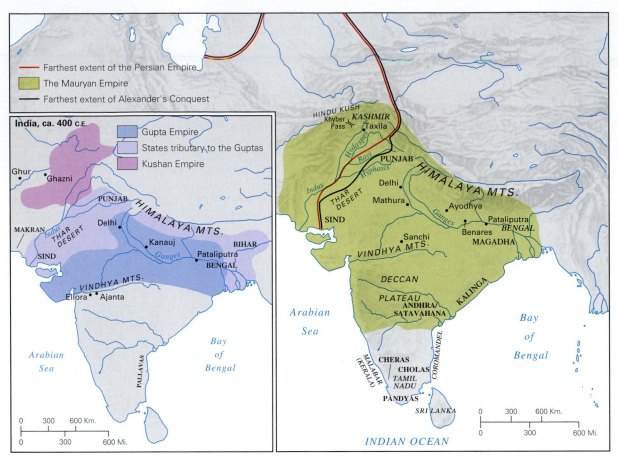

Map 7.1 Ancient India Mountains and ocean largely separate the Indian subcontinent from the rest of Asia. Migrations and invasions usually came through the Khyber Pass in the northwest. Seaborne commerce with western Asia, Southeast Asia, and East Asia often flourished. Peoples speaking Indo-European languages migrated into the broad valleys of the Indus and Ganges Rivers in the north. Dravidian-speaking peoples remained the dominant population in the south. The diversity of the Indian landscape, the multiplicity of ethnic groups, and the primary identification of people with their class and caste lie behind the division into many small states that has characterized much of Indian political history.

After 1000 B.C.E. some of these groups began to push east into the Ganges Plain. New technologies made this advance possible. Iron tools—harder than bronze and able to hold a sharper edge—allowed settlers to fell trees and work the newly cleared land with plows pulled by oxen. The soil of the Ganges Plain was fertile, well watered by the annual monsoon, and able to sustain two or three crops a year. As in Greece at roughly the same time (see Chapter 5), the use of iron tools to open new land for agriculture must have led to a significant increase in population.

Stories about this era, not written down until much later but long preserved by memorization and oral recitation, speak of bitter rivalry and warfare between two groups of people: the Aryas, relatively light-skinned speakers of Indo-European languages, and the Dasas, dark-skinned speakers of Dravidian languages. Some scholars contend that some Dasas were absorbed into Arya populations and elites from both groups merged. For the most part, however, Aryas pushed the Dasas south into central and southern India, where their descendants still live. Signaling the ultimate success of the Aryas is the fact that Indo-European languages are primarily spoken in northern India today. Dravidian speech prevails in the south.

Skin color has been a persistent concern of Indian society and is one of the bases for its historically sharp internal divisions. Over time there evolved a system of **varna**—literally "color," though the word came to indicate something akin to "class." Individuals were born into one of four classes: *Brahmin,* the group comprising priests and scholars; *Kshatriya°,* warriors and officials; *Vaishya°,* merchants, artisans, and landowners; or *Shudra°,* peasants and laborers. The designation *Shudra* originally may have been reserved for Dasas, who were given the menial jobs in society. Indeed, the very term *dasa* came to mean "slave." Eventually a fifth group was marked off: the Untouchables. They were excluded from the class system, and members of the other groups literally avoided them because of the demeaning or polluting work to which they were relegated—such as leather tanning, which involved touching dead animals, and sweeping away ashes after cremations.

People at the top of the social pyramid in ancient India could explain why this hierarchy existed. According to one creation myth, a primordial creature named Purusha allowed itself to be sacrificed. From its mouth sprang the class of Brahmin priests, the embodiment of intellect and knowledge. From its arms came the Kshatriya warrior class, from its thighs the Vaishya landowners and merchants, and from its feet the Shudra workers.

The varna system was just one of the mechanisms that Indian society developed to regulate relations between different groups. Within the broad class divisions, the population was further subdivided into numerous **jati,** or birth groups (sometimes called *castes,* from a Portuguese term meaning "breed"). Each jati had its proper occupation, duties, and rituals. Individuals who belonged to a given jati lived with members of their group, married within the group, and ate only with members of the group. Elaborate rules governed their interactions with members of other groups. Members of higher-status groups feared pollution from contact with lower-caste individuals and had to undergo elaborate rituals of purification to remove any taint.

The class and caste systems came to be connected to a widespread belief in reincarnation. The Brahmin priests taught that every living creature had an immortal essence: the *atman,* or "breath." Separated from the body at death, the atman was later reborn in another body. Whether the new body was that of an insect, an animal, or a human depended on the **karma,** or deeds, of the atman in its previous incarnations. People who lived exemplary lives would be reborn into the higher classes. Those who misbehaved would be punished in the next life by being relegated to a lower class or even a lower life form. The underlying message was: You are where you deserve to be, and the only way to improve your lot in the

next cycle of existence is to accept your current station and its attendant duties.

The dominant deities in Vedic religion were male and were associated with the heavens. To release the dawn, Indra, god of war and master of the thunderbolt, daily slew the demon encasing the universe. Varuna, lord of the sky, maintained universal order and dispensed justice. Agni, the force of fire, consumed the sacrifice and bridged the spheres of gods and humans.

Sacrifice—the dedication to a god of a valued possession, often a living creature—was the essential ritual. The purpose of these offerings was to invigorate the gods and thereby sustain their creative powers and promote stability in the world.

Brahmin priests controlled the technology of sacrifice, for only they knew the rituals and prayers. The *Rig Veda,* a collection of more than a thousand poetic hymns to various deities, and the *Brahmanas,* detailed prose descriptions of procedures for ritual and sacrifice, were collections of priestly lore couched in the Sanskrit language of the Arya upper classes. This information was handed down orally from one generation of priests to the next. Some scholars have hypothesized that the Brahmins opposed the introduction of writing. Such opposition would explain why this technology did not come into widespread use in India until the Gupta period (320–550 C.E.), long after it had begun to play a conspicuous role in other societies of equivalent complexity. The priests' "knowledge" (the term *veda* means just that) was the basis of their economic well-being. They were amply rewarded for officiating at sacrifices, and their knowledge gave them social and political power because they were the indispensable intermediaries between gods and humans.

As in nearly all ancient societies, it is difficult to uncover the experiences of women in ancient India. Limited evidence indicates that women in the Vedic period studied sacred lore, composed religious hymns, and participated in the sacrificial ritual. They had the opportunity to own property and usually were not married until they reached their middle or late teens. A number of strong and resourceful women appear in the epic poem *Mahabharata.* One of them, the beautiful and educated Draupadi, married—by her own choice—the five royal Pandava brothers. This probably should not be taken as evidence of the regular practice of polyandry (having more than one husband). In India, as in Greece, legendary figures had their own rules.

The sharp internal divisions of Indian society, the complex hierarchy of groups, and the claims of some to superior virtue and purity served important social functions. They provided each individual with a clear identity

---

Kshatriya (kshuh-TREE-yuh) **Vaishya** (VIESH-yuh)
Shudra (SHOOD-ra)

Carved Stone Gateway Leading to the Great Stupa at Sanchi   Pilgrims traveled long distances to visit stupas, mounds containing relics of the Buddha. The complex at Sanchi, in central India, was begun by Ashoka in the third century B.C.E., though the gates probably date to the first century C.E. This relief shows a royal procession bringing the remains of the Buddha to the city of Kushinagara.   (Dinodia Photo Library)

and role and offered the benefits of group solidarity and support. There is evidence that groups sometimes were able to upgrade their status. Thus the elaborate system of divisions was not static and provided a mechanism for working out social tensions. Many of these features persisted into modern times.

Challenges to the Old Order: Jainism and Buddhism

After 700 B.C.E. various forms of reaction against Brahmin power and privilege emerged. People who objected to the rigid hierarchy of classes and castes or the community's demands on the individual could retreat to the forest. Despite the clearing of extensive tracts of land for agriculture, much of ancient India was covered with forest. Never very far from civilized areas, these wild places served as a refuge and symbolized freedom from societal constraints.

Certain charismatic individuals who abandoned their town or village and moved to the forest attracted bands of followers. Calling into question the priests' exclusive claims to wisdom and the necessity of Vedic chants and sacrifices, they offered an alternate path to salvation: the individual pursuit of insight into the nature of the self and the universe through physical and mental discipline (*yoga*), special dietary practices, and meditation. They taught that by distancing oneself from desire for the things of this world, one could achieve **moksha,** or "liberation." This release from the cycle of reincarnations and union with the divine force that animates the universe sometimes was likened to "a deep, dreamless sleep." The *Upanishads*—a collection of more than one hundred mystical dialogues between teachers

and disciples—reflect this questioning of the foundations of Vedic religion.

The most serious threat to Vedic religion and to the prerogatives of the Brahmin priestly class came from two new religions that emerged around this time: Jainism° and Buddhism. Mahavira (540–468 B.C.E.) was known to his followers as Jina, "the Conqueror," from which is derived *Jainism,* the name of the belief system that he established. Emphasizing the holiness of the life force that animates all living creatures, Mahavira and his followers practiced strict nonviolence. They wore masks to prevent themselves from accidentally inhaling small insects, and they carefully brushed off a seat before sitting down. Those who gave themselves over completely to Jainism practiced extreme asceticism and nudity, ate only what they were given by others, and eventually starved themselves to death. Less zealous Jainists, restricted from agricultural work by the injunction against killing, tended to be city dwellers engaged in commerce and banking.

Of far greater significance for Indian and world history was the rise of Buddhism. So many stories have been told about Siddhartha Gautama (563–483 B.C.E.), known as the **Buddha,** "the Enlightened One," that it is difficult to separate fact from legend. He came from a Kshatriya family of the Sakyas, a people in the foothills of the Himalayas. As a young man he enjoyed the princely lifestyle to which he had been born, but at some point he experienced a change of heart and gave up family and privilege to become a wandering ascetic. After six years of self-deprivation, he came to regard asceticism as no more likely than the luxury of his previous life to produce spiritual insight, and he decided to adhere to a "Middle

---

Jainism (JINE-iz-uhm)

Sculpture of the Buddha, Second or Third Century C.E. This depiction of the Buddha, showing the effects of a protracted fast before he abandoned asceticism for the path of moderation, is from Gandhara in the northwest. It displays the influence of Greek artistic styles emanating from Greek settlements established in that region by Alexander the Great in the late fourth century B.C.E. (Robert Fisher)

Path" of moderation. Sitting under a tree in a deer park near Benares on the Ganges River, he gained a sudden and profound insight into the true nature of reality, which he set forth as "Four Noble Truths": (1) life is suffering; (2) suffering arises from desire; (3) the solution to suffering lies in curbing desire; and (4) desire can be curbed if a person follows the "Eightfold Path" of right views, aspirations, speech, conduct, livelihood, effort, mindfulness, and meditation. Rising up, the Buddha preached his First Sermon, a central text of Buddhism, and set into motion the "Wheel of the Law." He soon attracted followers, some of whom took vows of celibacy, nonviolence, and poverty.

In its original form, Buddhism centered on the individual. Although it did not quite reject the existence of gods, it denied their usefulness to a person seeking enlightenment. What mattered was living one's life with moderation, in order to minimize desire and suffering, and searching for spiritual truth through self-discipline

and meditation. The ultimate reward was *nirvana,* literally "snuffing out the flame." With nirvana came release from the cycle of reincarnations and achievement of a state of perpetual tranquility. The Vedic tradition emphasized the eternal survival of the atman, the "breath" or nonmaterial essence of the individual. In contrast, Buddhism regarded the individual as a composite without any soul-like component that survived upon entering nirvana.

When the Buddha died, he left no final instructions, instead urging his disciples to "be their own lamp." As the Buddha's message—contained in philosophical discourses memorized by his followers—spread throughout India and into Central, Southeast, and East Asia, its very success began to subvert the individualistic and essentially atheistic tenets of the founder. Buddhist monasteries were established, and a hierarchy of Buddhist monks and nuns came into being. Worshipers erected *stupas*° (large earthen mounds that symbolized the universe) over relics of the cremated founder and walked around them in a clockwise direction. Believers began to worship the Buddha himself as a god. Many Buddhists also revered *bodhisattvas*°, men and women who had achieved enlightenment and were on the threshold of nirvana but chose to be reborn into mortal bodies to help others along the path to salvation.

The makers of early pictorial images had refused to show the Buddha as a living person and represented him only indirectly, through symbols such as his footprints, his begging bowl, or the tree under which he achieved enlightenment, as if to emphasize his achievement of a state of nonexistence. From the second century C.E., however, statues of the Buddha and bodhisattvas began to proliferate, done in native sculptural styles and in a style that showed the influence of the Greek settlements established in Bactria (modern Afghanistan) by Alexander the Great (see Chapter 5). A schism emerged within Buddhism. Devotees of **Mahayana**° ("Great Vehicle") **Buddhism** embraced the popular new features, while practitioners of **Theravada**° ("Teachings of the Elders") **Buddhism** followed most of the original teachings of the founder.

The Rise of Hinduism

Challenged by new, spiritually satisfying, and egalitarian movements, Vedic religion made important adjustments, evolving into **Hinduism,** the religion of hundreds of millions of people in South Asia today. (The term *Hinduism,* how-

---

stupa (STOO-puh)   bodhisattva (boe-dih-SUT-vuh)
Mahayana (mah-huh-YAH-nuh)   Theravada (there-uh-VAH-duh)

Hindu Temple at Khajuraho   This sandstone temple of the Hindu deity Shiva, representing the celestial mountain of the gods, was erected at Khajuraho, in central India, around 1000 C.E., but it reflects the architectural symbolism of Hindu temples developed in the Gupta period. Worshipers made their way through several rooms to the image of the deity, located in the innermost "womb-chamber" directly beneath the tallest tower.   (Jean-Louis Nou)

ever, was imposed from outside. Islamic invaders who reached India in the eleventh century C.E. labeled the diverse range of practices they saw there as Hinduism: "what the Indians do.") The foundation of Hinduism is the Vedic religion of the Arya peoples of northern India. But Hinduism also incorporated elements drawn from the Dravidian cultures of the south, such as an emphasis on intense devotion to the deity and the prominence of fertility rituals and symbolism. Also present are elements of Buddhism.

The process by which Vedic religion was transformed into Hinduism by the fourth century C.E. is largely hidden from us. The Brahmin priests maintained their high social status and influence. But sacrifice, though still part of traditional worship, was less central, and there was much more opportunity for direct contact between gods and individual worshipers.

The gods were altered, both in identity and in their relationships with humanity. Two formerly minor deities, Vishnu° and Shiva°, assumed preeminent positions in the Hindu pantheon. Hinduism emphasized the wor-

shiper's personal devotion to a particular deity, usually Vishnu, Shiva, or Devi° ("the Goddess"). Both Shiva and Devi appear to be derived from the Dravidian tradition, in which a fertility cult and female deities played a prominent role. Their Dravidian origin is a telling example of how Arya and non-Arya cultures fused to form classic Hindu civilization. It is interesting to note that Vishnu, who has a clear Arya pedigree, remains more popular in northern India, while Shiva is dominant in the Dravidian south. These gods can appear in many guises. They are identified by various cult names and are represented by a complex symbolism of stories, companion animals, birds, and objects.

Vishnu, the preserver, is a benevolent deity who helps his devotees in time of need. Hindus believe that whenever demonic forces threaten the cosmic order, Vishnu appears on earth in one of a series of *avataras*, or incarnations. Among his incarnations are the legendary hero Rama, the popular cowherd-god Krishna, and the Buddha (a clear attempt to co-opt the rival religion's founder). Shiva, who lives in ascetic isolation on Mount Kailasa in

---

Vishnu (VIHSH-noo)   **Shiva** (SHEE-vuh)   **Devi** (DEH-vee)

the Himalayas, is a more ambivalent figure. He represents both creation and destruction, for both are part of a single, cyclical process. He often is represented performing dance steps that symbolize the acts of creation and destruction. Devi manifests herself in various ways—as a full-bodied mother-goddess who promotes fertility and procreation, as the docile and loving wife Parvati, and as the frightening deity who, under the name Kali or Durga, lets loose a torrent of violence and destruction.

The multiplicity of gods (330 million according to one tradition), sects, and local practices within Hinduism is dazzling, reflecting the ethnic, linguistic, and cultural diversity of India. Yet within this variety there is unity. A worshiper's devotion to one god or goddess does not entail denial of the other main deities or the host of lesser divinities and spirits. Ultimately, all are seen as manifestations of a single divine force that pervades the universe. This sense of underlying unity is expressed in texts, such as the passage from the Bhagavad-Gita quoted at the beginning of this chapter; in the different potentials of women represented in the various manifestations of Devi; and in composite statues that are split down the middle—half Shiva, half Vishnu—as if to say that they are complementary aspects of one cosmic principle.

Hinduism offers the worshiper a variety of ways to approach god and obtain divine favor—through special knowledge of sacred truths, mental and physical discipline, or extraordinary devotion to the deity. Worship centers on the temples, which range from humble village shrines to magnificent, richly decorated stone edifices built under royal patronage. Beautifully proportioned statues beckon the deity to take up temporary residence within the image, to be reached and beseeched by eager worshipers. A common form of worship is *puja,* service to the deity, which can take the form of bathing, clothing, or feeding the statue. Potent blessings are conferred on the man or woman who glimpses the divine image.

Pilgrimage to famous shrines and attendance at festivals offer worshipers additional opportunities to show devotion. The entire Indian subcontinent is dotted with sacred places where a worshiper can directly sense and benefit from the inherent power of divinity. Mountains, caves, and certain trees, plants, and rocks are enveloped in an aura of mystery and sanctity. The literal meaning of *tirthayatra,* the term for a pilgrimage site, is "journey to a river-crossing," pointing out the frequent association of Hindu sacred places with flowing water. Hindus consider the Ganges River to be especially sacred, and each year millions of devoted worshipers travel to its banks to bathe and receive the restorative and purifying power of its waters. The habit of pilgrimage to the major shrines has promoted contact and the exchange of ideas among people from different parts of India and has helped create

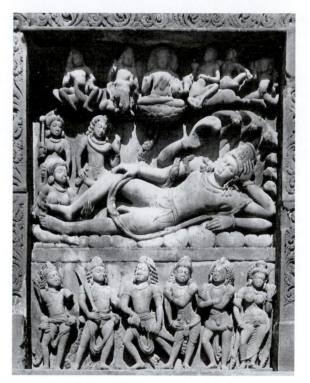

Stone Relief Depicting Vishnu Asleep and Dreaming on the Ocean Floor, Fifth Century c.e.   In this relief from a temple at Deogarh, in central India, Vishnu reclines on the coiled body of a giant multiheaded serpent that he subdued. The beneficent god of preservation, Vishnu appears in a new incarnation whenever demonic forces threaten the world. The Indian view of the vastness of time is embodied in this mythic image, which conceives of Vishnu as creating and destroying universes as he exhales and inhales.   (John C. Huntington)

a broad Hindu identity and the concept of India as a single civilization, despite enduring political fragmentation.

Religious duties may vary, depending not only on the worshiper's social standing and gender but also on his or her stage of life. A young man from one of the three highest classes (Brahmin, Kshatriya, or Vaishya) undergoes a ritual rebirth through the ceremony of the sacred thread, marking the attainment of manhood and readiness to receive religious knowledge. From this point, the ideal life cycle passes through four stages: (1) the young man becomes a student and studies the sacred texts; (2) he then becomes a householder, marries, has children, and acquires material wealth; (3) when his grandchildren are born, he gives up home and family and becomes a forest dweller, meditating on the nature and meaning of existence; (4) he abandons his personal identity altogether and becomes a wandering ascetic awaiting death. In the course of a virtuous life he has fulfilled first his duties to society and then his duties to himself, so that by the end of his life he is so disconnected from the world that he can achieve moksha (liberation).

The successful transformation of a religion based on Vedic antecedents and the ultimate victory of Hinduism over Buddhism—Buddhism was driven from the land of its birth, though it maintains deep roots in Central, East, and Southeast Asia (see Chapters 8 and 11)—are remarkable phenomena. Hinduism responded to the needs of people for personal deities with whom they could establish direct connections. The austerity of Buddhism in its most authentic form, its denial of the importance of gods, and its expectation that individuals find their own path to enlightenment may have demanded too much of ordinary people. The very features that made Mahayana Buddhism more accessible to the populace—gods, saints, and myths—also made it more easily absorbed into the vast social and cultural fabric of Hinduism.

IMPERIAL EXPANSION AND COLLAPSE, 324 B.C.E.–650 C.E.

Political unity in India, on those rare occasions when it has been achieved, has not lasted long. A number of factors have contributed to India's habitual political fragmentation. Different terrains—mountains, foothills, plains, forests, steppes, deserts—called forth different forms of organization and economic activity, and peoples occupying topographically diverse zones differed from one another in language and cultural practices. Perhaps the most significant barrier to political unity lay in the complex social hierarchy. Individuals identified themselves primarily in terms of their class and caste (birth group); allegiance to a higher political authority was of secondary concern.

Despite these divisive factors, two empires arose in the Ganges Plain: the Mauryan Empire of the fourth to second centuries B.C.E. and the Gupta Empire of the fourth to sixth centuries C.E. Each extended political control over a substantial portion of the subcontinent and fostered the formation of a common Indian civilization.

The Mauryan Empire, 324–184 B.C.E.

Around 600 B.C.E. separate kinship groups and independent states dotted the landscape of north India. The kingdom of Magadha, in eastern India south of the Ganges (see Map 7.1), began to play an increasingly influential role, however, thanks to wealth based on agriculture, iron mines, and its strategic location astride the trade routes of the eastern Ganges Basin.

In the late fourth century B.C.E. Chandragupta Maurya°, a young man who may have belonged to the Vaishya or Shudra class, gained control of the kingdom of Magadha and expanded it into the **Mauryan Empire**—India's first centralized empire. He may have been inspired by the example of Alexander the Great, who had followed up his conquest of the Persian Empire with a foray into the Punjab (northern Pakistan) in 326 B.C.E. (see Chapter 5). Indeed, Greek tradition claimed that Alexander met a young Indian native by the name of "Sandracottus," an apparent corruption of "Chandragupta."

The collapse of Greek rule in the Punjab after the death of Alexander created a power vacuum in the northwest. Chandragupta (r. 324–301 B.C.E.) and his successors Bindusara (r. 301–269 B.C.E.) and Ashoka (r. 269–232 B.C.E.) extended Mauryan control over the entire subcontinent except for the southern tip of the peninsula. Not until the height of the Mughal Empire of the seventeenth century C.E. and then the advent of British rule in the nineteenth century was so much of India again under the control of a single government.

Tradition holds that Kautilya, a crafty elderly Brahmin, guided Chandragupta in his conquests and consolidation of power. Kautilya is said to have written a surviving treatise on government, the *Arthashastra*°. Although recent studies have shown that the *Arthashastra* in its present form is a product of the third century C.E., its core text may well go back to Kautilya. This coldly pragmatic guide to political success and survival advocates the so-called *mandala*° (circle) theory of foreign policy: "My enemy's enemy is my friend." It also relates a long list of schemes for enforcing and increasing the collection of tax revenues, and it prescribes the use of spies to keep watch on everyone in the kingdom.

A tax equivalent to one-fourth the value of the harvest supported the Mauryan kings and government. Close relatives and associates of the king governed administrative districts based on traditional ethnic boundaries. A large imperial army—with infantry, cavalry, chariot, and elephant divisions—and royal control of mines, shipbuilding, and the manufacture of armaments further secured power. Standard coinage issued throughout the empire fostered support for the government and military and promoted trade.

The Mauryan capital was at Pataliputra (modern Patna), where five tributaries join the Ganges. Several extant descriptions of the city composed by foreign visitors provide valuable information and testify to the international connections of the Indian monarchs. Surrounded

---

Maurya (MORE-yuh)   **Arthashastra** (ahr-thuh-SHAHS-truh)
mandala (man-DAH-luh)

by a timber wall and moat, the city extended along the river for 8 miles (13 kilometers). It was governed by six committees with responsibility for features of urban life such as manufacturing, trade, sales, taxes, the welfare of foreigners, and the registration of births and deaths.

Ashoka, Chandragupta's grandson, is an outstanding figure in early Indian history. At the beginning of his reign he engaged in military campaigns that extended the boundaries of the empire. During his conquest of Kalinga (modern Orissa, a coastal region southeast of Magadha), hundreds of thousands of people were killed, wounded, or deported. Overwhelmed by the brutality of this victory, the young monarch became a convert to Buddhism and preached nonviolence, morality, moderation, and religious tolerance in both government and private life.

Ashoka publicized this program by inscribing edicts on great rocks and polished pillars of sandstone scattered throughout his enormous empire. Among the inscriptions that have survived—they constitute the earliest decipherable Indian writing—is the following:

> For a long time in the past, for many hundreds of years have increased the sacrificial slaughter of animals, violence toward creatures, unfilial conduct toward kinsmen, improper conduct toward Brahmins and ascetics. Now with the practice of morality by King [Ashoka], the sound of war drums has become the call to morality . . . You [government officials] are appointed to rule over thousands of human beings in the expectation that you will win the affection of all men. All men are my children. Just as I desire that my children will fare well and be happy in this world and the next, I desire the same for all men . . . King [Ashoka] . . . desires that there should be the growth of the essential spirit of morality or holiness among all sects . . . There should not be glorification of one's own sect and denunciation of the sect of others for little or no reason. For all the sects are worthy of reverence for one reason or another.[2]

Ashoka, however, was not naive. Despite his commitment to employing peaceful means whenever possible, he hastened to remind potential transgressors that "the king, remorseful as he is, has the strength to punish the wrongdoers who do not repent."

Commerce and Culture in an Era of Political Fragmentation

The Mauryan Empire prospered for a time after Ashoka's death in 232 B.C.E. Then, weakened by dynastic disputes, it collapsed from the pressure of attacks in the northwest in 184 B.C.E. Five hundred years passed before another indigenous state was able to extend its control over northern India.

In the meantime, a series of foreign powers dominated the northwest, present-day Afghanistan and Pakistan, and extended their influence east and south. The first was the Greco-Bactrian kingdom (180–50 B.C.E.), descended from troops and settlers left in Afghanistan by Alexander the Great. Greek influence is especially evident in the art of this period and in the designs of coins. Occupation by two nomadic peoples from Central Asia followed, resulting from large-scale movements of peoples set off by the pressure of Han Chinese forces on the Xiongnu (see Chapter 6). The Shakas, an Iranian people known as Scythians in the Mediterranean world, driven southwest along the edge of the mountain barrier of the Pamirs and Himalayas, were dominant from 50 B.C.E. to 50 C.E. They were followed by the Kushans°, originally from Xinjiang in northwest China, who were preeminent from 50 to 240 C.E. At its height the Kushan kingdom controlled much of present-day Uzbekistan, Afghanistan, Pakistan, and northwest India, fostering trade and prosperity by connecting to both the overland Silk Road and Arabian seaports (see Chapter 8). Several foreign kings—most notably the Greco-Bactrian Milinda (Menander in Greek) and the Kushan Kanishka—were converts to Buddhism, a logical choice because of the lack of an easy mechanism for working foreigners into the Hindu system of class and caste. The eastern Ganges region reverted to a patchwork of small principalities, as it had been before the Mauryan era.

Despite the political fragmentation of India in the five centuries after the collapse of the Mauryan Empire, there were many signs of economic, cultural, and intellectual development. The network of roads and towns that had sprung up under the Mauryans fostered lively commerce within the subcontinent, and India was at the heart of international land and sea trade routes that linked China, Southeast Asia, Central Asia, the Middle East, East Africa, and the lands of the Mediterranean. In the absence of a strong central authority, guilds of merchants and artisans became politically powerful in the Indian towns. Their wealth enabled them to serve as patrons of culture and to endow the religious sects to which they adhered—particularly Buddhism and Jainism—with richly decorated temples and monuments.

During the last centuries B.C.E. and first centuries C.E. the two greatest Indian epics, the *Ramayana* and the *Mahabharata,* based on oral predecessors dating back many centuries, achieved their final form. The events that both epics describe are said to have occurred several million years in the past, but the political forms, social organization, and other elements of cultural context—proud kings,

Kushan (KOO-shahn)

beautiful queens, wars among kinship groups, heroic conduct, and chivalric values—seem to reflect the conditions of the early Vedic period, when Arya warrior societies were moving onto the Ganges Plain.

The *Ramayana* relates the exploits of Rama, a heroic prince, who is an incarnation of the god Vishnu. When his beautiful wife is kidnapped, aided by his loyal brother and the king of the monkeys, he defeats and destroys the chief of the demons and his evil horde. The vast pageant of the **Mahabharata** (it is eight times the length of the Greek *Iliad* and *Odyssey* combined) tells the story of two sets of cousins, the Pandavas and Kauravas, whose quarrel over succession to the throne leads them to a cataclysmic battle at the field of Kurukshetra. The battle is so destructive on all sides that the eventual winner, Yudhishthira, is reluctant to accept the fruits of so tragic a victory.

The **Bhagavad-Gita,** quoted at the beginning of this chapter, is a self-contained (and perhaps originally separate) episode set in the midst of those events. The great hero Arjuna, at first reluctant to fight his own kinsmen, is tutored by the god Krishna and learns the necessity of fulfilling his duty as a warrior. Death means nothing in a universe in which souls will be reborn again and again. The climactic moment comes when Krishna reveals his true appearance—awesome and overwhelmingly powerful—and his identity as time itself, the force behind all creation and destruction. The Bhagavad-Gita offers an attractive resolution to the tension in Indian civilization between duty to society and duty to one's own soul. Disciplined action—that is, action taken without regard for any personal benefits that might derive from it—is a form of service to the gods and will be rewarded by release from the cycle of rebirths.

This era also saw significant advances in science and technology. Indian doctors had a wide knowledge of herbal remedies and were in demand in the courts of western and southern Asia. Indian scholars made impressive strides in linguistics. Panini (late fourth century B.C.E.) undertook a detailed analysis of Sanskrit word forms and grammar. The work of Panini and later linguists led to the standardization of Sanskrit, which arrested its natural development and turned it into a formal, literary language. Prakrits—popular dialects—emerged to become the ancestors of the modern Indo-European languages of northern and central India.

This period of political fragmentation in the north also saw the rise of important states in central India, particularly the Andhra dynasty in the Deccan Plateau (from the second century B.C.E. to the second century C.E.), and the three **Tamil kingdoms** of Cholas, Pandyas, and Cheras in southern India (see Map 7.1). The three Tamil kingdoms were in frequent conflict with one another

and experienced periods of ascendancy and decline, but they persisted in one form or another for over two thousand years. Historians regard the period from the third century B.C.E. to the third century C.E. as a "classical" period of great literary and artistic productivity in Tamil society. Under the patronage of the Pandya kings and the intellectual leadership of an academy of five hundred authors, works of literature on a wide range of topics—grammatical treatises, collections of ethical proverbs, epics, and short poems about love, war, wealth, and the beauty of nature—were produced, and music, dance, and drama were performed.

The Gupta Empire, 320–550 C.E.

In the early fourth century C.E. a new imperial entity took shape in northern India. Like its Mauryan predecessor, the **Gupta Empire** grew out of the kingdom of Magadha on the Ganges Plain and had its capital at Pataliputra. Clear proof that the founder of this empire consciously modeled himself on the Mauryans is the fact that he called himself Chandra Gupta (r. 320–335), borrowing the very name of the Mauryan founder. A claim to wide dominion was embodied in the title that the monarchs of this dynasty assumed—"Great King of Kings"—although they never controlled territories as extensive as those of the Mauryans. Nevertheless, over the fifteen-year reign of Chandra Gupta and the forty-year reigns of his three successors—Samudra Gupta, Chandra Gupta II, and Kumara Gupta—Gupta power and influence reached across northern and central India, west to Punjab and east to Bengal, north to Kashmir, and south into the Deccan Plateau (see Map 7.1).

This new empire enjoyed the same strategic advantages as its Mauryan predecessor, sitting astride important trade routes, exploiting the agricultural productivity of the Ganges Plain, and controlling nearby iron deposits. It adopted similar methods for raising revenue and administering broad territories. The chief source of revenue was a 25 percent tax on agriculture. Those who used the irrigation network also had to pay for the service, and there were special taxes on particular commodities. The state maintained monopolies in key areas such as the mining of metals and salt. The state also owned extensive tracts of farmland and demanded a specified number of days of labor annually from the subjects for the construction and upkeep of roads, wells, and the irrigation network.

Gupta control, however, was never as effectively centralized as Mauryan authority. The Gupta administrative bureaucracy and intelligence network were smaller and less pervasive. A powerful army maintained tight control and taxation in the core of the empire, but governors had a free hand in organizing the outlying areas. The position of governor offered tempting opportunities to exploit the populace. It often was hereditary, passed from father to son in families of high-ranking members of the civil and military administrations. Distant subordinate kingdoms and areas inhabited by kinship groups were expected to make annual donations of tribute, and garrisons were stationed at certain key frontier points to keep open the lines of trade and expedite the collection of customs duties.

Limited in its ability to enforce its will on outlying areas, the empire found ways to "persuade" others to follow its lead. One medium of persuasion was the splendor, beauty, and orderliness of life at the capital and royal court. A constant round of solemn rituals, dramatic ceremonies, and exciting cultural events were such a potent advertisement for the benefits of association with the empire that modern historians point to the Gupta Empire as a good example of a **"theater-state."** The relationship of ruler and subjects in a theater-state also has an economic base. The center collects luxury goods and profits from trade and redistributes them to its dependents through the exchange of gifts and other means. Subordinate princes gained prestige by emulating the Gupta center on whatever scale they could manage, and maintained close ties through visits, gifts, and marriages to the Gupta royal family.

Astronomers, mathematicians, and other scientists received royal Gupta support. Indian mathematicians invented the concept of zero and developed the "Arabic" numerals and system of place-value notation that are in use in most parts of the world today (see Environment and Technology: Indian Mathematics).

Because the moist climate of the Ganges Plain does not favor the preservation of buildings and artifacts, there is relatively little archaeological data for the Gupta era. An eyewitness account, however, provides valuable information about the Gupta kingdom and Pataliputra, its capital city. A Chinese Buddhist monk named Faxian° made a pilgrimage to the homeland of his faith around 400 C.E. and left a record of his journey:

> The royal palace and halls in the midst of the city, which exist now as of old, were all made by spirits which [King Ashoka] employed, and which piled up the stones, reared the walls and gates, and executed the elegant carving and inlaid sculpture-work—in a way which no human hands of this world could accomplish . . . By the side of the stupa of Ashoka, there has been made a Mahayana [Buddhist] monastery, very grand and beautiful; there is also a Hinayana [Theravada] one; the two together containing six hun-

dred or seven hundred monks. The rules of demeanor and the scholastic arrangements in them are worthy of observation . . . The cities and towns of this country are the greatest of all in the Middle Kingdom. The inhabitants are rich and prosperous, and vie with one another in the practice of benevolence and righteousness . . . The heads of the Vaishya families in them establish in the cities houses for dispensing charity and medicines. All the poor and destitute in the country, orphans, widowers, and childless men, maimed people and cripples, and all who are diseased, go to those houses, and are provided with every kind of help.[3]

Various kinds of evidence point to a decline in the status of women in this period (see Diversity and Dominance: The Situation of Women in the *Kama Sutra*). In all likelihood, this was similar to developments in Mesopotamia from the second millennium B.C.E., in Archaic and Classical Greece, and in China from the first millennium B.C.E. In those civilizations, several factors—urbanization, the formation of increasingly complex political and social structures, and the emergence of a nonagricultural middle class that placed high value on the acquisition and inheritance of property—led to a loss of women's rights and an increase in male control over women's behavior.

Over time, women in India lost the right to own or inherit property. They were barred from studying sacred texts and participating in the sacrificial ritual. In many respects, they were treated as equivalent to the lowest class, the Shudra. As in Confucian China, a woman was expected to obey first her father, then her husband, and finally her sons (see Chapter 6). Indian girls were married at an increasingly early age, sometimes as young as six or seven. This practice meant that the prospective husband could be sure of his wife's virginity and, by bringing her up in his own household, could train and shape her to suit his purposes. The most extreme form of control of women's conduct took place in parts of India where a widow was expected to cremate herself on her husband's funeral pyre. This ritual, called *sati*°, was seen as a way of keeping a woman "pure." Women who declined to make this ultimate gesture of devotion were forbidden to remarry, shunned socially, and given little opportunity to earn a living.

Some women escaped these instruments of male control. One way to do so was by entering a Jainist or Buddhist religious community. Status also gave women more freedom. Women who belonged to powerful families and courtesans who were trained in poetry and music as well as in ways of providing sexual pleasure had high social standing and sometimes gave money for the erection of Buddhist stupas and other shrines.

Faxian (fah-shee-en)

sati (suh-TEE)

Indian Mathematics

The so-called Arabic numerals used in most parts of the world today were developed in India. The Indian system of place-value notation was far more efficient than the unwieldy numerical systems of Egyptians, Greeks, and Romans, and the invention of zero was a profound intellectual achievement. Indeed, it has to be ranked as one of the most important and influential discoveries in human history. This system is used even more widely than the alphabet derived from the Phoenicians (see Chapter 4) and is, in one sense, the only truly global language.

In its fully developed form the Indian method of arithmetic notation employed a base-10 system. It had separate columns for ones, tens, hundreds, and so forth, as well as a zero sign to indicate the absence of units in a given column. This system makes possible the economical expression of even very large numbers. And it allows for the performance of calculations not possible in a system like the numerals of the Romans, where any real calculation had to be done mentally or on a counting board.

A series of early Indian inscriptions using the numerals from 1 to 9 are deeds of property given to religious institutions by kings or other wealthy individuals. They were incised in the Sanskrit language on copper plates (see below). The earliest known example has a date equivalent to 595 C.E. A sign for zero is attested by the eighth century. Other textual evidence leads to the inference that a place-value system and the zero concept were already known in the fifth century.

This Indian system spread to the Middle East, Southeast Asia, and East Asia by the seventh century. Other peoples quickly recognized its capabilities and adopted it, sometimes using indigenous symbols. Europe received the new technology somewhat later. Gerbert of Aurillac, a French Christian monk, spent time in Spain between 967 and 970, where he was exposed to the mathematics of the Arabs. A great scholar and teacher who eventually became Pope Sylvester II (r. 999–1003), he spread word of the "Arabic" system in the Christian West.

Knowledge of the Indian system of mathematical notation eventually spread throughout Europe, in part through the use of a mechanical calculating device—an improved version of the Roman counting board, with counters inscribed with variants of the Indian numeral forms. Because the counters could be turned sideways or upside down, at first there was considerable variation in the forms. But by the twelfth century they had become standardized into forms close to those in use today. As the capabilities of the place-value system for written calculations became clear, the counting board fell into disuse. The abandonment of this device led to the adoption of the zero sign—not necessary on the counting board, where a column could be left empty—by the twelfth century. Leonardo Fibonacci, a thirteenth century C.E. Italian who learned algebra in Muslim North Africa and employed the Arabic numeral system in his mathematical treatise, gave additional impetus to the movement to discard the traditional system of Roman numerals.

Why was this marvelous system of mathematical notation invented in ancient India? The answer may lie in the way in which its range and versatility correspond to elements of Indian cosmology. The Indians conceived of immense spans of time—trillions of years (far exceeding current scientific estimates of the age of the universe as approximately 14 billion years old)—during which innumerable universes like our own were created, existed for a finite time, then were destroyed. In one popular creation myth, Vishnu is slumbering on the coils of a giant serpent at the bottom of the ocean, and worlds are being created and destroyed as he exhales and inhales. In Indian thought our world, like others, has existed for a series of epochs lasting more than 4 million years, yet the period of its existence is but a brief and insignificant moment in the vast sweep of time. The Indians developed a number system that allowed them to express concepts of this magnitude.

Copper Plate with Indian Numerals
This property deed from western India shows an early form of the symbol system for numbers that spread to the Middle East and Europe, and today is used all over the world. (Facsimile by Georges Ifrah. Reproduced by permission of Georges Ifrah.)

Wall Painting from the Caves at Ajanta, Fifth or Sixth Century C.E During and after the Gupta period, natural caves in the Deccan were turned into complexes of shrines decorated with sculpture and painting. This painting depicts one of the earlier lives of the Buddha, a king named Mahajanaka who lost and regained his kingdom, here listening to his queen, Sivali. While representing scenes from the earlier lives of the Buddha, the artists also give us a glimpse of life at the royal court in their own times.   (Benoy K. Behl)

The Mauryans had been Buddhists, but the Gupta monarchs were Hindus. They revived ancient Vedic practices to bring an aura of sanctity to their position. This period also saw a reassertion of the importance of class and caste and the influence of Brahmin priests. Nevertheless, it was an era of religious tolerance. The Gupta kings were patrons for Hindu, Buddhist, and Jain endeavors. Buddhist monasteries with hundreds or even thousands of monks and nuns in residence flourished in the cities. Northern India was the destination of Buddhist pilgrims from Southeast and East Asia, traveling to visit the birthplace of their faith.

The classic form of the Hindu temple evolved during the Gupta era. Sitting atop a raised platform surmounted by high towers, the temple was patterned on the sacred mountain or palace in which the gods of mythology resided, and it represented the inherent order of the universe. From an exterior courtyard worshipers approached the central shrine, where the statue of the deity stood. Paintings or sculptured depictions of gods and mythical events covered the walls of the best-endowed sanctuaries. Cave-temples carved out of rock were also richly adorned with frescoes or with sculpture.

During the period of political fragmentation between the eclipse of the Mauryan Empire and the rise of the Guptas, extensive networks of trade within India, as well as land and sea routes to foreign lands, developed. This vibrant commerce continued into the Gupta pe-

riod. Coined money served as the medium of exchange, and artisan guilds played an influential role in the economic, political, and religious life of the towns. The Guptas sought control of the ports on the Arabian Sea but saw a decline in trade with the weakened Roman Empire. In compensation, trade with Southeast and East Asia was on the rise. Adventurous merchants from the ports of eastern and southern India made the sea voyage to the Malay° Peninsula and islands of Indonesia in order to exchange Indian cotton cloth, ivory, metalwork, and exotic animals for Chinese silk or Indonesian spices. The overland Silk Road from China was also in operation but was vulnerable to disruption by Central Asian nomads (see Chapter 8).

By the later fifth century C.E. the Gupta Empire was coming under pressure from the Huns. These nomadic invaders from the steppes of Central Asia poured into the northwest corridor. Defense of this distant frontier region eventually exhausted the imperial treasury, and the empire collapsed by 550.

The early seventh century saw a brief but glorious revival of imperial unity. Harsha Vardhana (r. 606–647), ruler of the region around Delhi, extended his power over the northern plain and moved his capital to Kanauj on the Ganges River. We have an account of the life and long reign of this fervent Buddhist, poet, patron of artists,

Malay (muh-LAY)

우세인 은신처 망

운드폭탄 4발 투하··· 두 아들과 함께 사망 가

점심진지 구축··· 이틀째 시가戰

령이 대중 앞에 나타나거나 애국심
을 고취하는 노래만을 내보내던 방
송마저 중단됐다.

라크 전후 대책
의에서는 전후
영국 주도로

DIVERSITY AND DOMINANCE

THE SITUATION OF WOMEN IN THE *KAMA SUTRA*

The ancient Indians articulated three broad areas of human concern: Dharma—the realm of religious and moral behavior; Artha—the acquisition of wealth and property; and Kama—the pursuit of pleasure. The Kama Sutra, *which means "Treatise on Pleasure," while best known in the West for its detailed descriptions of erotic activities, is actually far more than a sex manual. It addresses, in a very broad sense, the relations between women and men in ancient Indian society, providing valuable information about the character and activities of men and women, the psychology of relationships, the forms of courtship and marriage, the household responsibilities of married women, appropriate behavior, and much more. The author of this text, Vatsyayana, lived in the third century C.E. He claims to be abridging and sharpening a series of earlier texts on the subject.*

When a girl of the same caste, and a virgin, is married in accordance with the precepts of Holy Writ, the results of such a union are the acquisition of Dharma and Artha, offspring, affinity, increase of friends, and untarnished love. For this reason a man should fix his affections upon a girl who is of good family, whose parents are alive, and who is three years or more younger than himself. She should be born of a highly respectable family, possessed of wealth, well connected, and with many relations and friends. She should also be beautiful, of a good disposition, with lucky marks on her body, and with good hair, nails, teeth, ears, eyes and breasts, neither more nor less than they ought to be, and no one of them entirely wanting, and not troubled with a sickly body. The man should, of course, also possess these qualities himself. But at all events, says Ghotakamukha [an earlier writer], a girl who has been already joined with others (i.e. no longer a maiden) should never be loved, for it would be reproachable to do such a thing.

Now in order to bring about a marriage with such a girl as described above, the parents and relations of the man should exert themselves, as also such friends on both sides as may be desired to assist in the matter. These friends should bring to the notice of the girl's parents the faults, both present and future, of all the other men that may wish to marry her, and should at the same time extol even to exaggeration all the excellencies, ancestral, and paternal, of their friend, so as to endear him to them, and particularly to those that may be liked by the girl's mother. One of the friends should also disguise himself as an astrologer, and declare the future good fortune and wealth of his friend by showing the existence of all the lucky omens and signs, the good influence of planets, the auspicious entrance of the sun into a sign of the Zodiac, propitious stars and fortunate marks on his body. Others again should rouse the jealousy of the girl's mother by telling her that their friend has a chance of getting from some other quarter even a better girl than hers.

A girl should be taken as a wife, as also given in marriage, when fortune, signs, omens, and the words of others are favourable, for, says Ghotakamukha, a man should not marry at any time he likes. A girl who is asleep, crying, or gone out of the house when sought in marriage, or who is betrothed to another, should not be married. The following also should be avoided:

- One who is kept concealed
- One who has an ill-sounding name
- One who has her nose depressed
- One who has her nostril turned up
- One who is formed like a male
- One who is bent down
- One who has crooked thighs
- One who has a projecting forehead
- One who has a bald head
- One who does not like purity
- One who has been polluted by another
- One who is affected with the Gulma [glandular enlargement]
- One who is disfigured in any way
- One who has fully arrived at puberty
- One who is a friend
- One who is a younger sister
- One who is a Varshakari [prone to extreme perspiration]

In the same way a girl who is called by the name of one of the twenty-seven stars, or by the name of a tree, or of a river, is considered worthless, as also a girl whose name ends in "r" or "l." But some authors say that prosperity is gained only by marrying that girl to whom one becomes attached, and that therefore no other girl but the one who is loved should be married by anyone.

194

When a girl becomes marriageable her parents should dress her smartly, and should place her where she can be easily seen by all. Every afternoon, having dressed her and decorated her in a becoming manner, they should send her with her female companions to sports, sacrifices, and marriage ceremonies, and thus show her to advantage in society, because she is a kind of merchandise. They should also receive with kind words and signs of friendliness those of an auspicious appearance who may come accompanied by their friends and relations for the purpose of marrying their daughter, and under some pretext or other having first dressed her becomingly, should then present her to them. . . .

When a girl, possessed of good qualities and well-bred, though born in a humble family, or destitute of wealth, and not therefore desired by her equals, or an orphan girl, or one deprived of her parents, but observing the rules of her family and caste, should wish to bring about her own marriage when she comes of age, such a girl should endeavour to gain over a strong and good looking young man, or a person whom she thinks would marry her on account of the weakness of his mind, and even without the consent of his parents. She should do this by such means as would endear her to the said person, as well as by frequently seeing and meeting him. Her mother also should constantly cause them to meet by means of her female friends, and the daughter of her nurse. The girl herself should try to get alone with her beloved in some quiet place, and at odd times should give him flowers, betel nut, betel leaves and perfumes. She should also show her skill in the practice of the arts, in shampooing, in scratching and in pressing with the nails. She should also talk to him on the subjects he likes best, and discuss with him the ways and means of gaining over and winning the affections of a girl . . .

To the girl also she [the daughter of the girl's nurse, essentially a friend of the same age serving as a go-between] should speak about the excellent qualities of the man, especially of those qualities which she knows are pleasing to the girl. She should, moreover, speak with disparagement of the other lovers of the girl, and talk about the avarice and indiscretion of their parents, and the fickleness of their relations. She should also quote samples of many girls of ancient times, such as Sakoontala and others, who, having united themselves with lovers of their own caste and their own choice, were ever happy afterwards in their society. And she should also tell of other girls who married into great families, and being troubled by rival wives, became wretched and miserable, and were finally abandoned. She should further speak of the good fortune, the continual happiness, the chastity, obedience, and affection of the man, and if the girl gets amorous about him, she should endeavour to allay her shame and her fear as well as her suspicions about any disaster that might result from her marriage. In a word, she should act the whole part of a female messenger by telling the girl all about the man's affection for her, the places he frequented, and the endeavours he made to meet her, and by frequently repeating, "It will be all right if the man will take you away forcibly and unexpectedly." . . .

A virtuous woman, who has affection for her husband, should act in conformity with his wishes as if he were a divine being, and with his consent should take upon herself the whole care of his family. She should keep the whole house well cleaned, and arrange flowers of various kinds in different parts of it, and make the floor smooth and polished so as to give the whole a neat and becoming appearance. She should surround the house with a garden, and place ready in it all the materials required for the morning, noon and evening sacrifices. Moreover she should herself revere the sanctuary of the Household Gods, for, says Gonardiya [another earlier writer], "nothing so much attracts the heart of a householder to his wife as a careful observance of the things mentioned above." . . .

The wife should always avoid the company of female beggars, female Buddhist mendicants, unchaste and roguish women, female fortune tellers and witches. As regards meals, she should always consider what her husband likes and dislikes and what things are good for him, and what are injurious to him. When she hears the sounds of his footsteps coming home she should at once get up and be ready to do whatever he may command her, and either order her female servant to wash his feet, or wash them herself. When going anywhere with her husband, she should put on her ornaments, and without his consent she should not either give or accept invitations, or attend marriages and sacrifices, or sit in the company of female friends, or visit the temples of the Gods. And if she wants to engage in any kind of games or sports, she should not do it against his will. In the same way she should always sit down after him, and get up before him, and should never awaken him when he is asleep.

QUESTIONS FOR ANALYSIS

1. In what ways are women given essentially equal treatment to men in these excerpts? In what ways are they treated unequally?

2. On what bases do men and women choose spouses and lovers?

3. What were the most important household responsibilities of ancient Indian women? What social, intellectual, and cultural activities did they engage in?

4. In light of the treatise's prescriptions for how a married woman should treat her husband, what do you think was the nature of the emotional relationship of husband and wife? How might this differ from marriages in our society?

Source: Sir Richard Burton and F. F. Arbuthnot, *The Kama Sutra of Vatsyayana* (1883), sections III.1, III.4, III.5, IV.1, found at http://www.sacred-texts.com/sex/kama/index.htm.

and dynamic warrior, written by the courtier Bana. In addition, the Chinese Buddhist pilgrim Xuanzang° (600–664) left an account of his travels in India during Harsha's reign. After Harsha's death, northern India reverted to its customary state of political fragmentation and remained divided until the Islamic invasions of the eleventh and twelfth centuries (see Chapter 14).

During the centuries of Gupta ascendancy and decline in the north, the Deccan Plateau and the southern part of the peninsula followed an independent path. In this region, where the landscape is segmented by mountains, rocky plateaus, tropical forests, and sharply cut river courses, there were many small centers of power. Later, from the seventh to twelfth centuries, the Pallavas, Cholas, and other warrior dynasties collected tribute and plundered as far as their strength permitted, storing their wealth in urban fortresses. These rulers sought legitimacy and fame as patrons of religion and culture, and much of the distinguished art and architecture of the period was produced in the kingdoms of the south. These kingdoms served as the conduit through which Indian religion and culture reached Southeast Asia.

SOUTHEAST ASIA, 50–1025 C.E.

Southeast Asia consists of three geographical zones: the Indochina mainland, the Malay Peninsula, and thousands of islands extending on an east-west axis far out into the Pacific Ocean (see Map 7.2). Encompassing a vast area of land and water, this region is now occupied by the countries of Myanmar° (Burma), Thailand, Laos, Cambodia, Vietnam, Malaysia, Singapore, Indonesia, Brunei°, and the Philippines. Poised between the ancient centers of China and India, Southeast Asia has been influenced by the cultures of both civilizations. The region first rose to prominence and prosperity because of its intermediate role in the trade exchanges between southern and eastern Asia.

The strategic importance of Southeast Asia is enhanced by the region's natural resources. This is a geologically active zone; the islands are the tops of a chain of volcanoes. Lying along the equator, Southeast Asia has a tropical climate. The temperature hovers around 80 degrees Fahrenheit (30 degrees Celsius), and the monsoon winds provide dependable rainfall throughout the year. Thanks to several growing cycles each year, the region is capable of supporting a large human popula-

tion. The most fertile agricultural lands lie along the floodplains of the largest silt-bearing rivers or contain rich volcanic soil deposited by ancient eruptions.

Early Civilization

Rain forest covers much of Southeast Asia. Rain-forest ecosystems are particularly fragile because of the great local variation of plant forms within them and because of the vulnerability of their soil to loss of fertility if the protective forest canopy is removed. As early as 2000 b.c.e. people in this region were clearing land for farming by cutting and burning the vegetation growing on it. The cleared land, known as swidden, was farmed for several growing seasons. When the soil was exhausted, the farmers abandoned the patch, allowing the forest to reclaim it before they cleared it again for agriculture. In the meantime, they cleared and cultivated other nearby fields in similar fashion.

A number of plant and animal species spread from Southeast Asia to other regions. Among them were wet rice (rice cultivated in deliberately flooded fields), soybeans, sugar cane, yams, bananas, coconuts, cocoyams, chickens, and pigs. Rice was the staple food product, for even though rice cultivation is labor-intensive (see Chapter 3), it can support a large population.

Historians believe that the **Malay peoples** who became the dominant population in this region were the product of several waves of migration from southern China beginning around 3000 b.c.e. In some cases the indigenous peoples merged with the Malay newcomers; in other cases they retreated to remote mountain and forest zones. Subsequently, rising population and disputes within communities prompted streams of people to leave the Southeast Asian mainland in the longest-lasting colonization movement in human history. By the first millennium b.c.e. the inhabitants of Southeast Asia had developed impressive navigational skills. They knew how to ride the monsoon winds and interpret the patterns of swells, winds, clouds, and bird and sea life. Over a period of several thousand years groups of Malay peoples in large, double outrigger canoes spread out across the Pacific and Indian Oceans—half the circumference of the earth—to settle thousands of islands.

The inhabitants of Southeast Asia tended to cluster along riverbanks or in fertile volcanic plains. Their fields and villages were never far from the rain forest, with its wild animals and numerous plant species. Forest trees provided fruit, wood, and spices. The shallow waters surrounding the islands teemed with fish. This region was also an early center of metallurgy, particularly bronze. Metalsmiths heated copper and tin ore to the right tem-

---

Xuanzang (shoo-wen-zahng) **Myanmar** (myahn-MAH)
Brunei (broo-NIE)

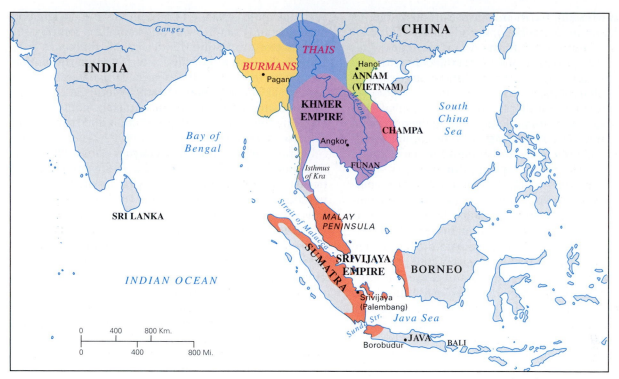

Map 7.2   Southeast Asia   Southeast Asia's position between the ancient centers of civilization in India and China had a major impact on its history. In the first millennium C.E. a series of powerful and wealthy states arose in the region by gaining control of major trade routes: first Funan, based in southern Vietnam, Cambodia, and the Malay Peninsula, then Srivijaya on the island of Sumatra, then smaller states on the island of Java. Shifting trade routes led to the demise of one and the rise of others.

perature for producing and shaping bronze implements by using hollow bamboo tubes to funnel a stream of oxygen to the furnace.

The first political units were small. The size of the fundamental unit reflected the number of people who drew water from the same source. Water resource "boards," whose members were representatives of the leading families of the different villages involved, met periodically to allocate and schedule the use of this critical resource.

Northern Indochina, by its geographic proximity, was particularly vulnerable to Chinese pressure and cultural influences, and was under Chinese political control for a thousand years (111 B.C.E.–939 C.E.). Farther south, larger states emerged in the early centuries C.E. in response to two powerful forces: commerce and Hindu-Buddhist culture. Southeast Asia was strategically situated along a new trade route that merchants used to carry Chinese silk westward to India and the Mediterranean. The movements of nomadic peoples had disrupted the old land route across Central Asia. But in India demand for silk

was increasing—both for domestic use and for transshipment to the Arabian Gulf and Red Sea to satisfy the fast-growing luxury market in the Roman Empire. At first, a route developed across the South China Sea, by land over the Isthmus of Kra on the Malay peninsula, and across the Bay of Bengal to India (see Map 7.2). Over time, merchants extended this exchange network to include not only silk but also goods from Southeast Asia, such as aromatic woods, resins, and cinnamon, pepper, cloves, nutmeg, and other spices. By serving this trade network and controlling key points, Southeast Asian centers rose to prominence.

The other force leading to the rise of larger political entities was the influence of Hindu-Buddhist culture imported from India. Commerce brought Indian merchants and sailors into the ports of Southeast Asia. As Buddhism spread, Southeast Asia became a way station for Indian missionaries and East Asian pilgrims going to and coming from the birthplace of their faith. Indian cosmology, rituals, art, and statecraft constituted a rich treasury of knowledge and a source of prestige and legitimacy for local rulers who adopted them. The use of Sanskrit terms such as *maharaja*° (great king), the adaptation of Indian ceremonial practices and forms of artistic representation, and the employment of scribes skilled in writing all proved invaluable to the most ambitious and capable Southeast Asian rulers.

The first major Southeast Asian center, called **"Funan°"** by Chinese visitors, flourished between the first and sixth centuries C.E. (see Map 7.2). Its capital was at the modern site of Oc-Eo in southern Vietnam. Funan occupied the delta of the Mekong° River, a "rice bowl" capable of supporting a large population. The rulers mobilized large numbers of laborers to dig irrigation channels and prevent destructive floods. By extending its control over most of southern Indochina and the Malay Peninsula, Funan was able to dominate the Isthmus of Kra—a key point on the trade route from India to China. Seaborne merchants from the ports of northeast India found that offloading their goods from ships and carrying them across the narrow strip of land was safer than making the 1,000-mile (1,600-kilometer) voyage around the Malay Peninsula—a dangerous trip marked by treacherous currents, rocky shoals, and pirates. Once the portage across the isthmus was finished, the merchants needed food and lodging while they waited for the monsoon winds to shift so that they could make the last leg of the voyage to China by sea. Funan stockpiled food and provided security for those engaged in this trade—in return, most probably, for customs duties and other fees.

According to one legend (a sure indicator of the influence of Indian culture in this region), the kingdom of Funan arose out of the marriage of an Indian Brahmin and a local princess. Chinese observers have left reports of the prosperity and sophistication of Funan, emphasizing the presence of walled cities, palaces, archives, systems of taxation, and state-organized agriculture. Nevertheless, for reasons not yet clear to modern historians, Funan declined in the sixth century. The most likely explanation is that international trade routes changed and Funan no longer held a strategic position.

The Srivijayan Kingdom

By the sixth century a new, all-sea route had developed. Merchants and travelers from south India and Sri Lanka sailed through the Strait of Malacca (lying between the west side of the Malay Peninsula and the northeast coast of the large island of Sumatra) and into the South China Sea. This route presented both human and navigational hazards, but it significantly shortened the journey. Another factor promoting the use of this route was a decline in the demand of the Eastern Roman (Byzantine) Empire for imported Chinese silk. Christian monks had hidden silkworms in bamboo stalks, smuggled them out of China, and brought them to Constantinople, thereby exposing the secret of silk production and breaking the Chinese monopoly.

A new center of power, **Srivijaya°**—Sanskrit for "Great Conquest"—was dominating the new southerly route by 683 C.E. The capital of the Srivijayan kingdom was at modern-day Palembang, 50 miles (80 kilometers) up the Musi River from the southeastern coast of Sumatra. Srivijaya had a good natural harbor on a broad and navigable river and a productive agricultural hinterland. The kingdom was well situated to control the southern part of the Malay Peninsula, Sumatra, parts of Java and Borneo, and the Malacca° and Sunda straits—vital passageways for shipping (see Map 7.2).

The Srivijayan capital, one of several thriving Sumatran river ports, gained ascendancy over its rivals and assumed control of the international trade route by fusing four distinct ecological zones into an interdependent network. The core area was the productive agricultural plain along the Musi River. The king and his clerks, scribes, judges, and tax collectors controlled this zone directly. Less direct was the king's control of the second zone, the upland regions of Sumatra's interior, which were the source of commercially valuable forest products. The local rulers of this area were bound to the center in a dependent relationship held together by oaths of loyalty, elaborate court ceremonies, and the sharing of profits from trade. The third zone consisted of river ports that had been Srivijaya's main rivals. They were conquered and controlled thanks to an alliance between Srivijaya and neighboring sea nomads, pirates who served as a Srivijayan navy as long as the king guaranteed them a steady income.

The fourth zone was a fertile "rice bowl" on the central plain of the nearby island of Java—a region so productive, because of its volcanic soil, that it houses and feeds the majority of the population of present-day Indonesia. Srivijayan monarchs maintained alliances with several ruling dynasties that controlled this region. The alliances were cemented by intermarriage, and the Srivijayan kings even claimed descent from the main Javanese dynasty. These arrangements gave Srivijaya easy access to the large quantities of foodstuffs that people living in the capital and merchants and sailors visiting the various ports needed.

---

maharaja (mah-huh-RAH-juh)   **Funan** (FOO-nahn)
Mekong (MAY-kawng)

Srivijava (sree-vih-JUH-yuh)   **Malacca** (muh-LAH-kuh)

The kings of Srivijaya who constructed and maintained this complex network of social, political, and economic relationships were men of extraordinary energy and skill. Although their authority depended in part on force, it owed more to diplomatic and even theatrical talents. Like the Gupta monarchy, Srivijaya should be seen as a theater-state, securing its position of prominence and binding dependents by its sheer splendor and its ability to attract labor, talent, and luxury products. According to one tradition, the Srivijayan monarch was so wealthy that he deposited bricks of gold in the river estuary to appease the local gods, and a hillside near town was said to be covered with silver and gold images of the Buddha to which devotees brought lotus-shaped vessels of gold. The gold originated in East or West Africa and came to Southeast Asia through trade with the Muslim world (see Chapter 8).

The Srivijayan king drew upon Buddhist conceptions to present himself as a bodhisattva, one who had achieved enlightenment and sought to share his precious insights for the betterment of his subjects. The king was believed to have great magical powers. He mediated between the spiritually potent realms of the mountains and the sea, and he embodied powerful forces of fertility associated with the rivers in flood. His capital and court were the scene of ceremonies designed to dazzle observers and reinforce his image of wealth, power, and sanctity. Subjects and visitors wanted to be associated with his success. Subordinate rulers took oaths of loyalty that carried dire threats of punishment for violations, and in their own home locales they imitated the splendid ceremonials of the capital.

The kings built and patronized Buddhist monasteries and schools. In central Java local dynasties allied with Srivijaya built magnificent temple complexes to advertise their glory. The most famous of these, **Borobodur°**, built between 770 C.E. and 825 C.E., was the largest human construction in the Southern Hemisphere. The winding ascent through the ten tiers of this mountain of volcanic stone is a Buddhist allegory for the progressive stages of enlightenment. Numerous sculptured reliefs depicting Buddhist legends provide modern viewers with glimpses of daily life in early Java.

In all of this, the cultural influence of India was paramount. Shrewd Malay rulers looked to Indian traditions to supply conceptual rationales for kingship and social order. They utilized Indian models of bureaucracy and the Sanskrit system of writing to expedite government business. Their special connection to powerful gods and higher knowledge raised them above their rivals. Southeast Asia's central position on long-distance trade and

Borobodur (booh-roe-boe-DOOR)

Stone Image of Durga, a Fierce Manifestation of the Goddess, Slaying the Buffalo–Demon, from Java, Thirteenth Century C.E. The Goddess, one of the three major Hindu divinities, appeared in a number of complementary manifestations. The most dramatic is Durga, a murderous warrior equipped with multiple divine weapons. That the same divine figure could, in its other manifestations, represent life-bringing fertility and docile wifely duties in the household shows how attuned Indian thought was to the interconnectedness of different aspects of life. (Eliot Elisofon Collection, Harry Ransom Humanities Center, University of Texas, Austin)

pilgrimage routes guaranteed the presence of foreigners with useful skills to serve as priests, scribes, and administrators. Hindu beliefs and social structures have survived to this day on the island of Bali, east of Java. Even more influential was Buddhism because of the flow of Buddhist pilgrims and missionaries between East Asia and India. (Islam, the dominant religion in modern-day Indonesia, was not introduced until the thirteenth century.)

The Southeast Asian kingdoms, however, were not just passive recipients of Indian culture. They took what was useful to them and synthesized it with indigenous beliefs, values, and institutions—for example, local concepts of chiefship, ancestor worship, and forms of oaths. Moreover, they trained their own people in the new ways, so that the bureaucracy contained both foreign experts and native disciples. The whole process amounted

View of the Buddhist Monument at Borobodur, Java   The great monument was more than 300 feet (90 meters) in length and over 100 feet (30 meters) high. Pilgrims made a three-mile-long (nearly 5-kilometer-long) winding ascent through ten levels intended to represent the ideal Buddhist journey from ignorance to enlightenment.   (Josephine Powell, Rome)

to a cultural dialogue between India and Southeast Asia, in which both were active participants.

The kings of Srivijaya carried out this marvelous balancing act for centuries. But the system they erected was vulnerable to shifts in the pattern of international trade. Some such change must have contributed to the decline of Srivijaya in the eleventh century, even though the immediate cause was a destructive raid on the Srivijayan capital by forces of the Chola kingdom of southeast India in 1025 C.E.

After the decline of Srivijaya, the leading role passed to new, vigorous kingdoms on the eastern end of Java, and the maritime realm of Southeast Asia remained prosperous and connected to the international network of trade. A few Europeans were aware of this region as a source of spices and other luxury items. Some four centuries after the decline of Srivijaya, an Italian navigator serving under the flag of Spain—Christopher Columbus—embarked on a westward course across the Atlantic Ocean, seeking to establish a direct route to the fabled "Indies" from which the spices came.

CONCLUSION

This chapter traces the emergence of complex societies in India and Southeast Asia between the second millennium B.C.E. and the first millennium C.E. Because of migrations, trade, and the spread of belief systems, an Indian style of civilization spread throughout the subcontinent and adjoining regions and eventually made its way to the mainland and island chains of Southeast Asia. In this period were laid cultural foundations that in large measure still endure.

The development and spread of belief systems—Vedism, Buddhism, Jainism, and Hinduism—have a central place in this chapter because nearly all the sources are religious. A visitor to a museum who examines artifacts from ancient Mesopotamia, Egypt, the Greco-Roman Mediterranean, China, and India will find that a prominent part of the collection consists of objects from religious shrines or with cultic function. Only the Indian artifacts, however, will be almost exclusively from the religious sphere.

The prolific use of writing came later to India than to other parts of the Eastern Hemisphere, for reasons particular to the Indian situation. Like Indian artifacts, most of the ancient Indian texts are of a religious nature. Ancient Indians did not generate historiographic texts of the kind written elsewhere in the ancient world, primarily because they held a strikingly different view of time. Mesopotamian scribes compiled lists of political and military events and the strange celestial and earthly phenomena that coincided with them. They were inspired by a cyclical conception of time and believed that the recurrence of an omen at some future date potentially signaled a repetition of the historical event associated with it. Greek and Roman historians described and analyzed the progress of wars and the character of rulers. They believed that these accounts would prove useful because of the essential constancy of human nature and the value of understanding the past as a sequence of causally linked events. Chinese annalists set down the deeds and conduct of rulers as inspirational models of right conduct and cautionary tales of the consequences of impropriety. In contrast, the distinctive Indian view of time—as vast epochs in which universes are created and destroyed again and again and the essential spirit of living creatures is reincarnated repeatedly—made the particulars of any brief moment seem relatively unilluminating.

The tension between divisive and unifying forces can be seen in many aspects of Indian life. Political and social division has been the norm throughout much of the history of India. It is a consequence of the topographical and environmental diversity of the subcontinent and the complex mix of ethnic and linguistic groups inhabiting it. The elaborate structure of classes and castes was a response to this diversity—an attempt to organize the population and position individuals within an accepted hierarchy, as well as to regulate group interactions. Strong central governments, such as those of the Mauryan and Gupta kings, gained ascendancy for a time and promoted prosperity and development. They rose to dominance by gaining control of metal resources and important trade routes, developing effective military and administrative institutions, and creating cultural forms that inspired admiration and emulation. However, as in Archaic Greece and Warring States China, the periods of fragmentation and multiple small centers of power seemed as economically and intellectually fertile and dynamic as the periods of unity.

India possessed many of the advanced technologies available elsewhere in the ancient world—agriculture, irrigation, metallurgy, textile manufacture, monumental construction, military technology, writing, and systems of administration. But of all the ancient societies, India made the most profound contribution to mathematics, devising the so-called Arabic numerals and place-value notation.

Many distinctive social and intellectual features of Indian civilization—the class and caste system, models of kingship and statecraft, and Vedic, Jainist, and Buddhist belief systems—originated in the great river valleys of the north, where descendants of Indo-European immigrants came to dominate. Hinduism embraced elements drawn from the Dravidian cultures of the south as well as from Buddhism. Hindu beliefs and practices are less fixed and circumscribed than the beliefs and practices of Judaism, Christianity, and Islam, which rely on clearly defined textual and organizational sources of authority. The capacity of the Hindu tradition to assimilate a wide range of popular beliefs facilitated the spread of elements of a common Indian civilization across the subcontinent, although there was, and is, considerable variation from one region to another.

This same malleable quality also came into play as the pace of international commerce quickened in the first millennium C.E. and Indian merchants embarking by sea for East Asia passed through Funan, Srivijaya, and other commercial centers in Southeast Asia. Indigenous elites in Southeast Asia came into contact with Indian merchants, sailors, and pilgrims. Involvement in the lucrative long-distance commerce and adoption of Indian political and religious ideas and methods brought wealth, power, and prestige to able and ambitious leaders. Finding elements of Indian civilization attractive and useful, they fused it with their own traditions to create a culture unique to Southeast Asia. Chapter 8 describes how the networks of long-distance trade and communication established in the Eastern Hemisphere in antiquity continued to expand and foster technological and cultural development in the subsequent era.

■ Key Terms

monsoon	Ashoka
Vedas	*Mahabharata*
varna	*Bhagavad-Gita*
jati	Tamil kingdoms
karma	Gupta Empire
moksha	theater-state
Buddha	Malay peoples
Mahayana Buddhism	Funan
Theravada Buddhism	Srivijaya
Hinduism	Borobodur
Mauryan Empire	

■ Suggested Reading

A useful starting point for the Indian subcontinent is Karl J. Schmidt, *An Atlas and Survey of South Asian History* (1995), with maps and facing text illustrating geographic, environmental, cultural, and historical features of South Asian civilization. Concise discussions of the history of ancient India can be found in Stanley Wolpert, *A New History of India*, 3d ed. (1989), and Romila Thapar, *A History of India*, vol. 1 (1966). D. D. Kosambi, *Ancient India: A History of Its Culture and Civilization* (1965), and Paul Masson-Oursel, *Ancient India and Indian Civilization* (1998), are fuller presentations.

Ainslie T. Embree, *Sources of Indian Tradition*, vol. 1, 2d ed. (1988), contains translations of primary texts, with the emphasis almost entirely on religion and few materials from southern India. Barbara Stoler Miller, *The Bhagavad-Gita: Krishna's Counsel in Time of War* (1986), is a readable translation of this ancient classic with a useful introduction and notes. An abbreviated version of the greatest Indian epic can be found in R. K. Narayan, *The Mahabharata: A Shortened Modern Prose Version of the Indian Epic* (1978). The filmed version of Peter Brook's stage production of *The Mahabharata* (3 videos, 1989) generated much controversy because of its British director and multicultural cast, but it is a painless introduction to the plot and main characters. Robert Goldman, *The Ramayana of Valmiki: An Epic of Ancient India* (1984), makes available the other Indian epic. To sample the fascinating document on state building supposedly composed by the adviser to the founder of the Mauryan Empire, see T. N. Ramaswamy, *Essentials of Indian Statecraft: Kautilya's Arthasastra for Contemporary Readers* (1962). James Legge, *The Travels of Fa-hien [Faxian]: Fa-hien's Record of Buddhistic Kingdoms* (1971), and John W. McCrindle, *Ancient India as Described by Megasthenes and Arrian* (1877), provide translations of reports of foreign visitors to ancient India.

A number of works explore political institutions and ideas in ancient India: Charles Drekmeier, *Kingship and Community in Early India* (1962); John W. Spellman, *Political Theory of Ancient India: A Study of Kingship from the Earliest Times to Circa A.D. 300* (1964); and R. S. Sharma, *Aspects of Political Ideas and Institutions in Ancient India*, 2d ed. (1968). Romila Thapar, *Asoka and the Decline of the Mauryas* (1963), is a detailed study of the most interesting and important Maurya king.

For fundamental Indian social and religious conceptions see David R. Kinsley, *Hinduism: A Cultural Perspective* (1982). See also David G. Mandelbaum, *Society in India*, 2 vols. (1970), who provides essential insights into the complex relationship of class and caste. Kevin Trainor, ed., *Buddhism: The Illustrated Guide* (2001), devotes several chapters to Buddhism in Ancient India. Jacob Pandian, *The Making of India and Indian Tradition* (1995), contains much revealing historical material, with particular attention to often neglected regions such as southern India, in its effort to explain the diversity of contemporary India. The chapter on ancient India by Karen Lang in Bella Vi-

vante, ed., *Women's Roles in Ancient Civilizations: A Reference Guide* (1999), provides an up-to-date overview and bibliography. Stephanie W. Jamison, *Sacrificed Wife/Sacrificer's Wife: Women, Ritual, and Hospitality in Ancient India* (1996), deals with the roles early Indian women filled in ritual practices and the creation and maintenance of social relations, including several forms of marriage. Stella Kramrisch, *The Hindu Temple*, 2 vols. (1946), and Surinder M. Bhardwaj, *Hindu Places of Pilgrimage in India: A Study in Cultural Geography* (1973), examine important elements of worship in the Hindu tradition.

Roy C. Craven, *Indian Art* (1976), is a clear, historically organized treatment of its subject. Mario Bussagli and Calembus Sivaramamurti, *5000 Years of the Art of India* (1971), is lavishly illustrated. For the uniqueness and decisive historical impact of Indian mathematics see Georges Ifrah, *From One to Zero: A Universal History of Numbers* (1985).

Kameshwar Prasad, *Cities, Crafts, and Commerce under the Kusanas* (1984), discusses the dynamic, multicultural domain of the Kushans. Jean W. Sedlar, *India and the Greek World: A Study in the Transmission of Culture* (1980), relates the interaction of Greek and Indian civilizations. Lionel Casson, *The Periplus Maris Erythraei: Text with Introduction, Translation and Commentary* (1989), explicates a fascinating mariner's guide to the ports, trade goods, and human and navigational hazards of Indian Ocean commerce in the Roman era. Xinru Liu, *Ancient India and Ancient China: Trade and Religious Exchanges, A.D. 1–600* (1994), covers interactions with East Asia.

Richard Ulack and Gyula Pauer, *Atlas of Southeast Asia* (1989), provides a very brief introduction and maps for the environment and early history of Southeast Asia. Nicholas Tarling, ed., *The Cambridge History of Southeast Asia*, vol. 1 (1999); D. R. SarDeSai, *Southeast Asia: Past and Present*, 3d ed. (1994); and Milton E. Osborne, *Southeast Asia: An Introductory History* (1995), provide general accounts of Southeast Asian history. Lynda Shaffer, *Maritime Southeast Asia to 1500* (1996), focuses on early Southeast Asian history in a world historical context. Also useful is Kenneth R. Hall, *Maritime Trade and State Development in Early Southeast Asia* (1985).

The art of Southeast Asia is taken up by M. C. S. Diskul, *The Art of Srivijaya* (1980); Maud Girard-Geslan et al., *Art of Southeast Asia* (1998); and Daigoro Chihara, *Hindu-Buddhist Architecture in Southeast Asia* (1996).

■ Notes

1. Barbara Stoler Miller, *The Bhagavad-Gita: Krishna's Counsel in Time of War* (New York: Bantam, 1986), 98–99.
2. B. G. Gokhale, *Asoka Maurya* (New York: Twayne, 1966), 152–153, 156–157, 160.
3. James Legge, *The Travels of Fa-hien: Fa-hien's Record of Buddhistic Kingdoms* (Delhi: Oriental Publishers, 1971), 77–79.

Oral Societies and the Consequences of Literacy

The availability of written documents is one of the key factors historians use to divide human prehistory from history. When we can read what the people of the past thought and said about their lives, we can begin to understand their cultures, institutions, values, and beliefs in ways that are not possible based only on the material remains unearthed by archaeologists.

There are profound differences between nonliterate and literate societies. However, literacy and nonliteracy are not absolute alternatives. Personal literacy ranges from illiteracy through many shades of partial literacy (the ability to write one's name or to read simple texts with difficulty) to the fluent ability to read that is possessed by anyone reading this textbook. And there are degrees of societal literacy, ranging from nonliteracy through so-called craft literacy—in which a small specialized elite uses writing for limited purposes, such as administrative record-keeping—and a spectrum of conditions in which more and more people use writing for more and more purposes, up to the near-universal literacy and the use of writing for innumerable purposes that is the norm in the developed world in our times.

The vast majority of human beings of the last five to six thousand years living in societies that possessed the technology of writing were not themselves literate. If most people in a society rely on the spoken word and memory, that culture is essentially "oral" even if some members know how to write. The differences between oral and literate cultures are immense, affecting not only the kinds of knowledge that are valued and the forms in which information is preserved, but the very use of language, the categories for conceptualizing the world, and ultimately the hard-wiring of the individual human brain (now recognized by neuroscientists to be strongly influenced by individual experience and mental activity).

Ancient Greece of the Archaic and Classical periods (ca. 800–323 B.C.E.) offers a particularly instructive case study because we can observe the process by which writing was introduced into an oral society as well as the far-reaching consequences. The Greeks of the Dark Age and early Archaic Period lived in a purely oral society; all knowledge was preserved in human memory and passed on by telling it to others. The *Iliad* and the *Odyssey* (ca. 700 B.C.E.), Homer's epic poems, reflect this state of affairs. Scholars recognize that the creator of these poems was an oral poet, almost certainly not literate, who had heard and memorized the poems of predecessors and retold them his own way. The poems are treasuries of information that this society regarded as useful—events of the past; the conduct expected of warriors, kings, noblewomen, and servants; how to perform a sacrifice, build a raft, put on armor, and entertain guests; and much more.

Embedding this information in a story and using the colorful language, fixed phrases, and predictable rhythm of poetry made it easier for poet and audience to remember vast amounts of material. The early Greek poets, drawing on their strong memories, skill with words, and talent for dramatic performance, developed highly specialized techniques to assist them in memorizing and presenting their tales. They played a vital role in the preservation and transmission of information and thus enjoyed a relatively high social standing and comfortable standard of living. Analogous groups can be found in many other oral cultures of the past, including the bards of medieval Celtic lands, Norse *skalds,* west African *griots,* and the tribal historians of Native American peoples.

Nevertheless, human memory, however cleverly trained and well-practiced, can only do so much. Oral societies must be extremely selective about what information to preserve in the limited storage medium of human memory, and they are slow to give up old information to make way for new.

Sometime in the eighth century B.C.E. the Greeks borrowed the system of writing used by the Phoenicians of Lebanon and, in adapting it to their language, created the first purely alphabetic writing, employing several dozen symbols to express the sounds of speech. The Greek alphabet, although relatively simple to learn as compared to the large and cumbersome sets of symbols in such craft-literacy systems as cuneiform, hieroglyphics, or Linear B, was probably known at first only to a small number of people and used for restricted purposes. Scholars believe that it may have taken three or four centuries for knowledge of reading and writing to spread to large numbers of Greeks and for the written word to became the primary storage medium for the accumulated knowledge of Greek civilization. Throughout that time Greece was still primarily an oral society, even though some Greeks, mostly highly educated members of the upper classes, were beginning to write down poems, scientific speculations, stories about the past, philosophic musings, and the laws of their communities.

It is no accident that some of the most important intellectual and artistic achievements of the Greeks, including early science, history, drama, and rhetoric, developed in the period when oral and literate ways existed side-by-side. Scholars have persuasively argued that writing, by opening up a virtually limitless capacity to store information, released the human mind from the hard discipline of memorization and ended the need to be so painfully selective about what was preserved. This made previously unimaginable innovation and experimentation possible. The Greeks began to organize and categorize information in linear ways, perhaps inspired by the linear sequence of the alphabet; and they began to engage in abstract thinking now that it was no longer necessary to put everything in a story format. We can observe changes in the Greek language as it developed a vocabulary full of abstract nouns, accompanied by increasing complex sentence structure now that the reader had time to go back over the text.

Nevertheless, all the developments associated with literacy were shaped by the deeply rooted oral habits of Greek culture. It is often said that Plato (ca. 429–347 B.C.E.) and his contemporaries of the later Classical period may have been the first generation of Greeks who learned much of what they knew from books. Even so, Plato was a disciple of the philosopher Socrates, who wrote nothing, and Plato employed the oral form of the dialogue, a dramatized sequence of questions and answers, to convey his ideas in written form.

The transition from orality to literacy met stiff resistance in some quarters. Groups whose position in the oral culture was based on the special knowledge only they possessed—members of the elite who judged disputes, priests who knew the time-honored formulas and rituals for appeasing the gods, oral poets who preserved and performed the stories of a heroic past—resented the consequences of literacy. They did what they could to inflame the common people's suspicions of the impiety of literate men who sought scientific explanations for phenomena, such as lightning and eclipses, that had traditionally been attributed to the will and action of the gods. They attacked the so-called Sophists, or "wise men," who charged fees to teach what they claimed were the skills necessary for success, accusing them of subverting traditional morals and corrupting the young.

Other societies, ancient and modern, offer parallel examples of these processes. Oral "specialists" in antiquity, including the Brahmin priests of India and the Celtic Druids, preserved in memory valuable religious information about how to win the favor of the gods. These groups jealously guarded their knowledge because it was the basis of their livelihood and social standing. They resisted committing it to writing even after that technology was available, in their determination to select and to maintain control over those who received it from them. The ways in which oral authorities feel threatened by writing and resist it can be seen in the following quotation from a twentieth century C.E. "griot," an oral rememberer and teller of the past in Mali in West Africa:

> We griots are depositories of the knowledge of the past . . . Other peoples use writing to record the past, but this invention has killed the faculty of memory among them. They do not feel the past anymore, for writing lacks the warmth of the human voice. With them everybody thinks he knows, whereas learning should be a secret . . . What paltry learning is that which is congealed in dumb books! . . . For generations we have passed on the history of kings from father to son. The narrative was passed on to me without alteration, for I received it free from all untruth.[1]

This point of view is hard for us to grasp, living as we do in an intensely literate society in which the written word is often felt to be more authoritative and objective than the spoken word. It is important, in striving to understand societies of the past, not to superimpose our assumptions on them, and to appreciate the complex interplay of oral and literate patterns in many of them.

◼ Notes

1. D. T. Niane, *Sundiata: An Epic of Old Mali.* (Harlow U.K.: Longman, 1986), 41.

PART THREE

Growth and Interaction of Cultural Communities, 300 B.C.E.–1200 C.E.

In 300 B.C.E., societies still had only limited contacts beyond their frontiers. Fifteen centuries later, by 1200 C.E., this situation had changed dramatically. Trade, folk migrations, and religious missionary work had created a world of pervasive interconnections among peoples. Three long-distance trade routes fostered the exchange of products and technologies: the Silk Road across Inner Asia, trans-Saharan caravan routes linking northern and sub-Saharan Africa, and a variety of maritime routes connecting the coastal lands of the Indian Ocean.

In Africa, the spread of the Bantu peoples from West Africa brought iron implements and new techniques of food production to most of sub-Saharan Africa and helped foster a distinctive African cultural pattern. In the Middle East, the Arabs of the Arabian peninsula, under the inspiration of the Prophet Muhammad, conquered an empire that stretched from Spain to India, implanting their faith, their cultural values, and an urban-based style of life.

In Asia, Buddhism drew on the energies of missionaries and pilgrims as it spread by land and sea from India to Sri Lanka, Tibet, Southeast Asia, China, Korea, and Japan. In each of these lands, the new faith interacted with older philosophies and religious outlooks to produce distinctive patterns of social interaction. At about the same time, the expansion of the Tang Empire resulted in the dissemination of Chinese culture and technologies throughout Inner and East Asia.

In Europe, monks and missionaries labored to convert the Celtic, Germanic, and Slavic peoples to Christianity. Christian beliefs became wedded to new political and social structures: a struggle between royal and church authority in western Europe; a combining of religious and imperial authority in the Byzantine East; and distinctive Christian kingdoms in Armenia, Kievan Russia, and Ethiopia. The Crusades opened new contacts between western Europe and lands to the east after centuries of near isolation.

Unexplored seas still separated the Eastern and Western Hemispheres, but the development of urban, agricultural civilizations in the Andes, the Yucatán lowlands, and the central plateau of Mexico climaxed during this period in the Aztec and Inca Empires and, somewhat earlier, in the flourishing of the Maya. All of the aspects of long-distance cultural exchange and interaction that mark this era in Eurasia and Africa have their counterparts in the Western Hemisphere.

	300 B.C.E.	B.C.E. C.E.	300 C.E.
Americas	• 300 Migrants from Mesoamerica bring irrigation farming to Arizona	• 100 Teotihuacan founded	250–900 Classic period of Maya civilization • 200–700 Moche culture in coastal Peru
Europe		• 146 Rome destroys Carthage, begins direct control of territories ouside Europe	Council of Nicaea 325 • Fall of Roman Empire in West 476 • Reign of Roman emperor Diocletian 284–305
Africa	Bananas and yams reach Africa from Southeast Asia ca. 100 • 500 B.C.E.–1000 C.E. Bantu migrations		First Christian bishop in Ethiopia ca. 330 • • ca. 300 Camel use spreads in southern Sahara
Middle East	• 300 Petra flourishes as caravan city in Jordan 248 B.C.E–226 C.E Kingdom of Parthia in Iran		• 276 Prophet Mani martyred 226–650 Sasanid Empire in Iraq and Iran
Asia and Oceania	• 128 Chinese general Zhang Jian explores Silk Road 206 B.C.E–220 C.E Han Empire in China	• ca. 100 Stirrup developed in Afghanistan 200–400 Rice introduced to Japan from Korea	

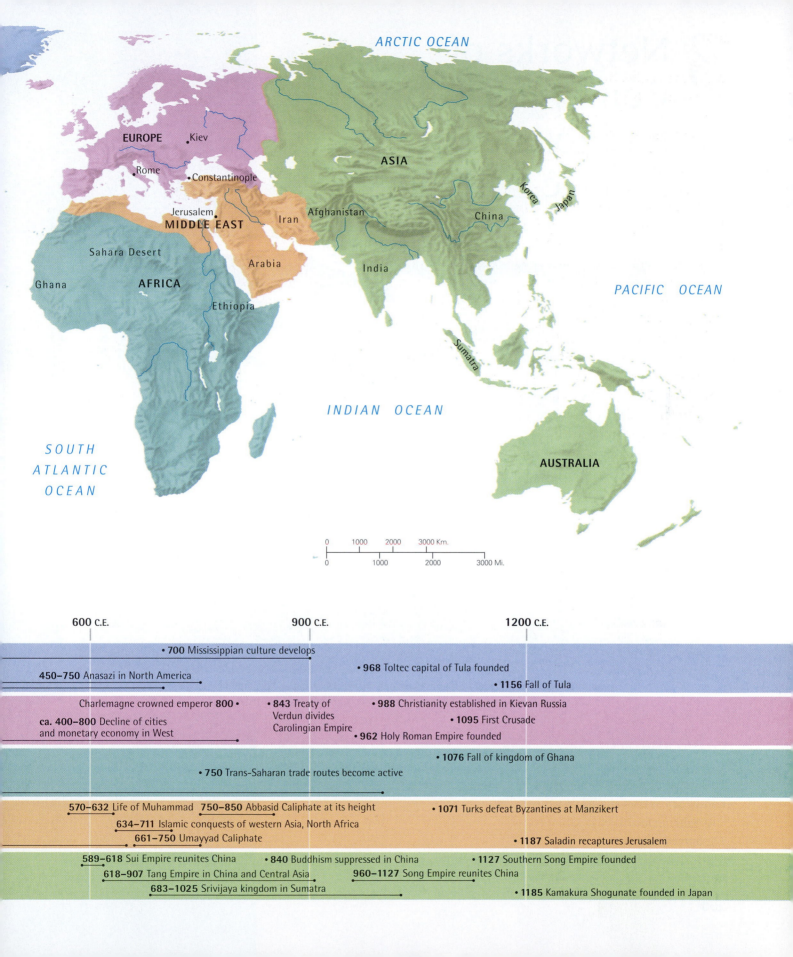

ARCTIC OCEAN

EUROPE
Kiev
Rome
Constantinople
Jerusalem
MIDDLE EAST
Iran
Afghanistan
ASIA
China
Korea
Japan
Sahara Desert
Arabia
Ghana
AFRICA
India
Ethiopia
Sumatra
INDIAN OCEAN
PACIFIC OCEAN
SOUTH
ATLANTIC
OCEAN
AUSTRALIA

0   1000   2000   3000 Km.
0   1000   2000   3000 Mi.

600 C.E.   **900** C.E.   **1200** C.E.

• **700** Mississippian culture develops

968 Toltec capital of Tula founded

450–750 Anasazi in North America

• **1156** Fall of Tula

Charlemagne crowned emperor **800** •   • **843** Treaty of
Verdun divides
Carolingian Empire

• **988** Christianity established in Kievan Russia

ca. 400–800 Decline of cities
and monetary economy in West

• **1095** First Crusade

• **962** Holy Roman Empire founded

• **1076** Fall of kingdom of Ghana

• **750** Trans-Saharan trade routes become active

570–632 Life of Muhammad   **750–850** Abbasid Caliphate at its height

• **1071** Turks defeat Byzantines at Manzikert

634–711 Islamic conquests of western Asia, North Africa

661–750 Umayyad Caliphate

• **1187** Saladin recaptures Jerusalem

589–618 Sui Empire reunites China   • **840** Buddhism suppressed in China

• **1127** Southern Song Empire founded

618–907 Tang Empire in China and Central Asia   **960–1127** Song Empire reunites China

683–1025 Srivijaya kingdom in Sumatra

• **1185** Kamakura Shogunate founded in Japan

8 Networks of Communication and Exchange, 300 B.C.E.–1100 C.E.

Indian Ocean Sailing Vessel   Ships like this one, in a rock carving on the Buddhist temple of Borobodur in Java, probably carried colonists from Indonesia to Madagascar.

Around the year 800 C.E., a Chinese poet named Po Zhuyi° nostalgically wrote:

> Iranian whirling girl, Iranian whirling girl—
> Her heart answers to the strings,
> Her hands answer to the drums.
> At the sound of the strings and drums, she raises
>   her arms,
> Like whirling snowflakes tossed about, she turns
>   in her twirling dance.
> Iranian whirling girl,
> You came from Sogdiana°.
> In vain did you labor to come east more than ten
>   thousand tricents.
> For in the central plains there were already some
>   who could do the Iranian whirl,
> And in a contest of wonderful abilities, you
>   would not be their equal.[1]

The western part of Central Asia, the region around Samarkand° and Bukhara° known in the eighth century C.E. as Sogdiana, was 2,500 miles (4,000 kilometers) from the Chinese capital of Chang'an°. Caravans took more than four months to trek across the mostly unsettled deserts, mountains, and grasslands.

The Silk Road connecting China and the Middle East across Central Asia fostered the exchange of agricultural goods, manufactured products, and ideas. Musicians and dancing girls traveled, too—as did camel pullers, merchants, monks, and pilgrims. The Silk Road was not just a means of bringing peoples and parts of the world into contact; it was a social system. This and similar trading networks that have had a deep impact on world history deserve special scrutiny.

With every expansion of territory, the growing wealth of temples, kings, and emperors enticed traders to venture ever farther afield for precious goods. For the most part, the customers were wealthy elites. But the new products, agricultural and industrial processes, and foreign ideas and customs these long-distance traders brought with them sometimes affected an entire society.

Travelers and traders seldom owned much land or wielded political power. Socially isolated (some-times by law) and secretive because any talk about markets, products, routes, and travel conditions could help their competitors, they nevertheless contributed more to drawing the world together than did all but a few kings and emperors.

This chapter examines the social systems and historical impact of exchange networks that developed between 300 B.C.E. and 1100 C.E. in Europe, Asia, and Africa. The Silk Road, the Indian Ocean maritime system, and the trans-Saharan caravan routes in Africa illustrate the nature of long-distance trade in this era.

Trading networks were not the only medium for the spread of new ideas, products, and customs. Chapter 3 discussed the migration into Europe of people speaking Celtic languages. This chapter compares folk migration with developments along trade routes by looking at the rise of trans-Saharan caravan commerce and the simultaneous spread of Bantu-speaking peoples within sub-Saharan Africa. Chapter 6 discussed a third pattern of cultural contact and exchange, that taking place with the beginning of Christian missionary activity in Europe. This chapter further explores the process by examining the spread of Buddhism in Asia and Christianity in Africa and Asia.

As you read this chapter, ask yourself the following questions:

- What role does technology play in long-distance trade?

- How does geography affect trade patterns?

- How do human groups affect communication between regions?

- Why do some goods and ideas travel more easily than others?

- How do the three modes of cultural contact and exchange affect patterns of dominance and diversity?

THE SILK ROAD

Archaeology and linguistic studies show that the peoples of Central Asia engaged in long-distance movement and exchange from at least 1500 B.C.E. In Roman times Europeans became captivated by the idea of a trade route linking the lands of the Mediterranean with China by way of Mesopotamia, Iran, and Central Asia. The **Silk Road,** as it came to be called in modern times,

---

Po Zhuyi (boh joo-yee)   Sogdiana (sog-dee-A-nuh)
Samarkand (SAM-mar-kand)   Bukhara (boo-CAR-ruh)
Chang'an (chahng-ahn)

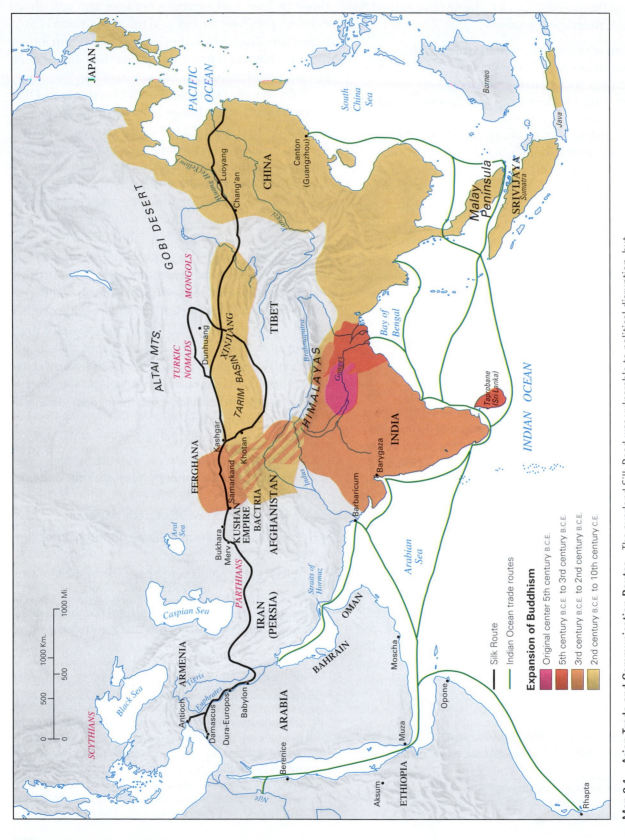

Map 8.1 Asian Trade and Communication Routes The overland Silk Road was vulnerable to political disruption, but was much shorter than the maritime route from the South China Sea to the Red Sea, and ships were more expensive than pack animals. Moreover, China's political centers were in the north.

CHRONOLOGY

	Silk Road	Indian Ocean Trade	Saharan Trade
300 B.C.E.			**500 B.C.E.–ca. 1000 C.E.** Bantu migrations
	247 B.C.E. Parthian rule begins in Iran		
	128 B.C.E. General Zhang Jian reaches Ferghana		**ca. 200 B.C.E.** Camel nomads in southern Sahara
			46 B.C.E. First mention of camels in northern Sahara
1 C.E.	**100 B.C.E.–300 C.E.** Kushans rule northern Afghanistan and Sogdiana	**1st cent. C.E.** *Periplus of the Erythraean Sea;* Indonesian migration to Madagascar	
300 C.E.			**ca. 300** Beginning of camel nomadism in northern Sahara
	ca. 400 Buddhist pilgrim Faxian travels Silk Road		
600 C.E.			**6th cent.** Kingdom of Ghana begins
	ca. 630 Buddhist pilgrim Xuanzang travels Silk Road		**639–42** Arabs conquer Egypt
		683–1025 Srivijaya trading kingdom in Southeast Asia	
		711 Arabs conquer lower Indus Valley partially by sea	**711** Berbers and Arabs conquer Spain
			740 Berber revolts; independent states in North Africa; trade develops across Sahara
900 C.E.	**907** Collapse of Tang Empire	**ca. 900** Arab and Persian merchants in Canton	
			1076 Almoravids defeat ruler of Ghana

experienced several periods of heavy use (see Map 8.1). The first extended from approximately 100 B.C.E. to 907 C.E., when the collapse of the Tang° Empire in China led to disruption at its eastern end (see Chapter 11). Another period of heavy use began with the Mongol invasions in the thirteenth century C.E. and lasted until the seventeenth century (see Chapter 13).

Origins and Operations

The Seleucid kings who succeeded to the eastern parts of Alexander the Great's empire in the third century B.C.E. focused their energies on Mesopotamia and Syria, their most prosperous and densely populated provinces, al-

lowing an Iranian nomadic leader to establish an independent kingdom in northeastern Iran. The **Parthians,** named after their homeland east of the Caspian Sea, had become a major force by 247 B.C.E. They left few written sources, and recurring wars between the Parthians and the Seleucids, and later between the Parthians and the Romans, prevented travelers from the Mediterranean region from gaining firm knowledge of the Parthian kingdom. It seems likely, however, that their place of origin on the threshold of Central Asia and the lifestyle they had in common with nomadic pastoral groups farther to the east helped foster the Silk Road.

In 128 B.C.E. a Chinese general named Zhang Jian° made his first exploratory journey westward across the trackless deserts and mountains of Central Asia on be-

Tang (tahng)

Zhang Jian (jahng jee-en)

Hybrid Camel Breeding This small breeding herd is one of the last remnants of the once widespread practice of crossing one-humped and two-humped camels to produce very strong and cold resistant animals for Silk Road caravans. The two-humped male is accompanied by several one-humped females. The two animals on the left have the depressed area toward the front of the long hump and the long neck wool that marks them as bukhts, or hybrids. (Courtesy, Mike Bonine, photographer)

half of Emperor Wu of the Han dynasty. After crossing the broad and desolate Tarim Basin north of Tibet, he reached the fertile valley of Ferghana° and for the first time encountered westward-flowing rivers. There he found horse breeders whose animals far outclassed any horses he had seen.

Later Chinese historians looked on General Zhang, who ultimately led eighteen expeditions, as the originator of overland trade with the western lands, and they credited him with personally introducing a whole garden of new plants and trees to China. Zhang's own account, however, proves that the people of Ferghana were already familiar with goods produced in China, though they probably learned of them by way of India.

Long-distance travel was more familiar to the Central Asians than to the Chinese. Kin to the trouser-wearing, horse-riding Parthians in language and customs, the populations of Ferghana and neighboring regions included many nomads who followed their herds. Their migrations had little to do with trade. The trading demands that brought the Silk Road into being were Chinese eagerness for western products, especially horses, and on the western end, the organized Parthian state, which controlled the flourishing markets of Mesopotamia and linked them culturally to the pastoralists of

Central Asia. These nomads provided pack animals and controlled transit across their lands. Caravan cities that supported the trade and organized relations with the nomads were an equally important intermediate factor.

Once the route was fully functioning, around 100 B.C.E., Greeks could buy Chinese silk from Parthian traders in Mesopotamian border entrepôts. Yet caravans also bought and sold goods along the way in prosperous Central Asian cities like Samarkand and Bukhara. These cities grew and flourished, often under the rule of local princes.

General Zhang definitely seems to have brought two plants to China: alfalfa and wine grapes. The former provided the best fodder for the growing Chinese herds of Ferghana horses. In addition, Chinese farmers adopted pistachios, walnuts, pomegranates, sesame, coriander, spinach, and other new crops. Chinese artisans and physicians made good use of other trade products, such as jasmine oil, oak galls (used in tanning animal hides, dyeing, and making ink), sal ammoniac (for medicines), copper oxides, zinc, and precious stones.

Caravan traders going west from China carried new fruits such as peaches and apricots, which the Romans mistakenly attributed to other eastern lands, calling them Persian plums and Armenia plums, respectively. They also carried cinnamon, ginger, and other spices that could not be grown in the West. Manufactured goods—particularly silk, pottery, and paper—were eventually adopted or imitated in western lands, starting with Iran.

Ferghana (fer-GAH-nuh)

Iranian Musicians from Silk Road   This three-color glazed pottery figurine, 23 inches (58.4 centimeters) high, comes from a northern Chinese tomb of the Tang era (sixth to ninth centuries C.E.) The musicians playing Iranian instruments confirm the migration of Iranian culture across the Silk Road. At the same time, dishes decorated by the Chinese three-color glaze technique were in vogue in northern Iran.   (The National Museum of Chinese History)

chants and landholders wearing Chinese silks and Iranian brocades and riding on richly outfitted horses and camels. They also give evidence of an avid interest in Buddhism, which competed with Christianity, Manichaeism, Zoroastrianism, and—eventually—Islam in a lively and inquiring intellectual milieu.

Religion (discussed later in this chapter) exemplifies the impact of foreign customs and beliefs on the Central Asian peoples, but Central Asian practices in turn affected surrounding areas. For example, Central Asian military techniques had a profound impact on both East and West. Chariot warfare and the use of mounted bowmen originated in Central Asia and spread eastward and westward through military campaigns and folk migrations that began in the second millennium B.C.E. and recurred throughout the period of the Silk Road.

Evidence of the **stirrup,** one of the most important inventions, comes first from the Kushan people who ruled northern Afghanistan in approximately the first century C.E. At first a solid bar, then a loop of leather to support the rider's big toe, and finally a device of leather and metal or wood supporting the instep, the stirrup gave riders far greater stability in the saddle—which itself was in all likelihood an earlier Central Asian invention.

Using stirrups, a mounted warrior could supplement his bow and arrow with a long lance and charge his enemy at a gallop without fear that the impact of his attack would push him off his mount. Far to the west, the stirrup made possible the armored knights who dominated the battlefields of Europe (see Chapter 10), and it contributed to the superiority of the Tang cavalry in China (see Chapter 11).

The Impact of the Silk Road

As trade became a more important part of Central Asian life, the Iranian-speaking peoples increasingly settled in trading cities, which remained comparatively small, and surrounding farm villages. This allowed nomads originally from the Altai Mountains farther east to spread across the steppes and become the dominant pastoral group. These peoples, who spoke Turkic languages unrelated to the Iranian tongues, were well in evidence by the sixth century C.E. The prosperity that trade created affected not only the ethnic mix of the region but also its cultural values. The nomads continued to live in the round, portable felt huts called yurts that can still occasionally be seen in Central Asia, but prosperous merchants and landholders built stately homes decorated with brightly colored wall paintings. The paintings show the mer-

THE INDIAN OCEAN MARITIME SYSTEM

A multilingual, multiethnic society of seafarers established the **Indian Ocean Maritime System,** a trade network across the Indian Ocean and the South China Sea. These people left few records and seldom played a visible part in the rise and fall of kingdoms and empires, but they forged increasingly strong economic and social ties between the coastal lands of East Africa, southern Arabia, the Persian Gulf, India, Southeast Asia, and southern China.

This trade took place in three distinct regions: (1) In the South China Sea, Chinese and Malays (including Indonesians) dominated trade. (2) From the east coast of India to the islands of Southeast Asia, Indians and Malays were the main traders. (3) From the west coast of India to the Persian Gulf and the east coast of Africa, merchants and sailors were predominantly Persians and Arabs. However, Chinese and Malay sailors could and did voyage to East Africa, and Arab and Persian traders reached southern China.

From the time of Herodotus in the fifth century B.C.E., Greek writers regaled their readers with stories of marvelous voyages down the Red Sea into the Indian Ocean and around Africa from the west. Most often, they attributed such trips to the Phoenicians, the most fearless of Mediterranean seafarers. Occasionally a Greek appears. One such was Hippalus, a Greek ship's pilot who was said to have discovered the seasonal monsoon winds that facilitate sailing across the Indian Ocean (see Diversity and Dominance: The Indian Ocean Trading World).

Of course, the regular, seasonal alternation of steady winds could not have remained unnoticed for thousands of years, waiting for an alert Greek to happen along. The great voyages and discoveries made before written records became common should surely be attributed to the peoples who lived around the Indian Ocean rather than to interlopers from the Mediterranean Sea. The story of Hippalus resembles the Chinese story of General Zhang Jian, whose role in opening trade with Central Asia overshadows the anonymous contributions made by the indigenous peoples. The Chinese may indeed have learned from General Zhang and the Greeks from Hippalus, but other people played important roles anonymously.

Mediterranean sailors of the time of Alexander used square sails and long banks of oars to maneuver among the sea's many islands and small harbors. Indian Ocean vessels relied on roughly triangular lateen sails and normally did without oars in running before the wind on long ocean stretches. Mediterranean shipbuilders nailed their vessels together. The planks of Indian Ocean ships were pierced, tied together with palm fiber, and caulked with bitumen. Mediterranean sailors rarely ventured out of sight of land. Indian Ocean sailors, thanks to the monsoon winds, could cover long reaches entirely at sea.

These technological differences prove that the world of the Indian Ocean developed differently from the world of the Mediterranean Sea, where the Phoenicians and Greeks established colonies that maintained contact with their home cities (see Chapters 4 and 5). The traders of the Indian Ocean, where distances were greater and contacts less frequent, seldom retained political ties with their homelands. The colonies they established were sometimes socially distinctive but rarely independent of the local political powers. War, so common in the Mediterranean, seldom beset the Indian Ocean maritime system prior to the arrival of European explorers at the end of the fifteenth century C.E.

Origins of Contact and Trade

By 2000 B.C.E. Sumerian records indicate regular trade between Mesopotamia, the islands of the Persian Gulf, Oman, and the Indus Valley. However, this early trading contact broke off, and later Mesopotamian trade references mention East Africa more often than India.

A similarly early chapter in Indian Ocean history concerns migrations from Southeast Asia to Madagascar, the world's fourth largest island, situated off the southeastern coast of Africa. About two thousand years ago, people from one of the many Indonesian islands of Southeast Asia established themselves in that forested, mountainous land 6,000 miles (9,500 kilometers) from home. They could not possibly have carried enough supplies for a direct voyage across the Indian Ocean, so their route must have touched the coasts of India and southern Arabia. No physical remains of their journeys have been discovered, however.

Apparently, the sailing canoes of these people plied the seas along the increasingly familiar route for several hundred years. Settlers farmed the new land and entered into relations with Africans who found their way across the 250-mile-wide (400-kilometer-wide) Mozambique° Channel around the fifth century C.E. Descendants of the seafarers preserved the language of their homeland and some of its culture, such as the cultivation of bananas, yams, and other native Southeast Asian plants. These food crops spread to mainland Africa. But the memory of their distant origins gradually faded, not to be recovered until modern times, when scholars established the linguistic link between the two lands.

The Impact of Indian Ocean Trade

The only extensive written account of trade in the Indian Ocean before the rise of Islam in the seventh century C.E. is an anonymous work by a Greco-Egyptian of the first century C.E. *The Periplus of the Erythraean° Sea* (that is, the Indian Ocean). It describes ports of call along the Red Sea and down the East African coast to somewhere south of the island of Zanzibar. Then it describes the ports of southern Arabia and the Persian Gulf before continuing eastward to India, mentioning ports all the way around the subcontinent to the mouth of the Ganges River. Though the geographer Ptolemy, who lived slightly later, had heard of ports as far away as Southeast Asia, the author of the *Periplus* had obviously voyaged to the places he mentions. What he describes is unquestionably a trading *system* and is clear evidence of

---

Mozambique (moe-zam-BEEK)   **Erythraean** (eh-RITH-ree-an)

Asklepios, the Greek God of Medicine   This representation, found in the sea off the coast of Bahrain in the Persian Gulf, reflects the extension of Greek culture along sea routes into distant lands. Greek medical knowledge and principles became known as far away as India. The crude craftsmanship of this effigy indicates that it was locally made and not imported from Greece. (Courtesy, Bahrain National Museum)

the steady growth of interconnections during the preceding centuries.

The demand for products from the coastal lands inspired mariners to persist in their long ocean voyages. Africa produced exotic animals, wood, and ivory. Since ivory also came from India, Mesopotamia, and North Africa, the extent of African ivory exports cannot be determined. The highlands of northern Somalia and southern Arabia grew the scrubby trees whose aromatic resins were valued as frankincense and myrrh. Pearls abounded in the Persian Gulf, and evidence of ancient copper mines has been found in Oman in southeastern Arabia. India shipped spices and manufactured goods, and more spices came from Southeast Asia, along with manufactured items, particularly pottery, obtained in trade with China. In sum, the Indian Ocean trading region had a great variety of highly valued products. Given the long distances and the comparative lack of islands, however, the volume of trade there was undoubtedly much lower than in the Mediterranean Sea.

Furthermore, the culture of the Indian Ocean ports was often isolated from the hinterlands, particularly in the west. The coasts of the Arabian peninsula, the African

side of the Red Sea, southern Iran, and northern India (today's Pakistan) were mostly barren desert. Ports in all these areas tended to be small, and many suffered from meager supplies of fresh water. Farther south in India, the monsoon provided ample water, but steep mountains cut off the coastal plain from the interior of the country. Thus few ports between Zanzibar and Sri Lanka had substantial inland populations within easy reach. The head of the Persian Gulf was one exception: shipborne trade was possible from the port of Apologus (later called Ubulla, the precursor of modern Basra) as far north as Babylon and, from the eighth century C.E., nearby Baghdad.

By contrast, eastern India, the Malay Peninsula, and Indonesia afforded more hospitable and densely populated shores with easier access to inland populations. Though the fishers, sailors, and traders of the western Indian Ocean system supplied a long series of kingdoms and empires, none of these consumer societies became primarily maritime in orientation, as the Greeks and Phoenicians did in the Mediterranean. In the east, in contrast, sea-borne trade and influence seem to have been important even to the earliest states of Southeast Asia (see Chapter 7).

In coastal areas throughout the Indian Ocean system, small groups of seafarers sometimes had a significant social impact despite their usual lack of political power. Women seldom accompanied the men on long sea voyages, so sailors and merchants often married local women in port cities. The families thus established were bilingual and bicultural. As in many other situations in world history, women played a crucial though not well-documented role as mediators between cultures. Not only did they raise their children to be more cosmopolitan than children from inland regions, but they also introduced the men to customs and attitudes that they carried with them when they returned to sea. As a consequence, the designation of specific seafarers as Persian, Arab, Indian, or Malay often conceals mixed heritages and a rich cultural diversity.

ROUTES ACROSS THE SAHARA

The windswept Sahara, a desert stretching from the Red Sea to the Atlantic Ocean and broken only by the Nile River, isolates sub-Saharan Africa from the Mediterranean world (see Map 8.2). The current dryness of the Sahara dates only to about 2500 B.C.E. The period of drying out that preceded that date lasted twenty-five centuries and encompassed several cultural changes. During that time, travel between a slowly shrinking number of

DIVERSITY AND DOMINANCE

THE INDIAN OCEAN TRADING WORLD

The most revealing description of ancient trade in the Indian Ocean and of the diversity and economic forces shaping the Indian Ocean trading system, "The Periplus of the Erythraean Sea," a sailing itinerary (periplus in Greek), was composed in the first century C.E. by an unknown Greco-Egyptian merchant. It highlights the diversity of peoples and products from the Red Sea to the Bay of Bengal and illustrates the comparative absence of a dominating political force in the Indian Ocean trading system. Historians believe that the descriptions of market towns were based on first-hand experience. Information on more remote regions was probably hearsay (see Map 8.1).

Of the designated ports on the Erythraean Sea [Indian Ocean], and the market-towns around it, the first is the Egyptian port of Mussel Harbor. To those sailing down from that place, on the right hand . . . there is Berenice. The harbors of both are at the boundary of Egypt. . . .

On the right-hand coast next below Berenice is the country of the Berbers. Along the shore are the Fish-Eaters, living in scattered caves in the narrow valleys. Further inland are the Berbers, and beyond them the Wild-flesh-Eaters and Calf-Eaters, each tribe governed by its chief; and behind them, further inland, in the country towards the west, there lies a city called Meroe.

Below the Calf-Eaters there is a little market-town on the shore . . . called Ptolemais of the Hunts, from which the hunters started for the interior under the dynasty of the Ptolemies . . . But the place has no harbor and is reached only by small boats . . . .

Beyond this place, the coast trending toward the south, there is the Market and Cape of Spices, an abrupt promontory, at the very end of the Berber coast toward the east. . . . A sign of an approaching storm . . . is that the deep water becomes more turbid and changes its color. When this happens they all run to a large promontory called Tabae, which offers safe shelter. . . .

Beyond Tabae [lies] . . . another market-town called Opone . . . [I]n it the greatest quantity of cinnamon is produced . . . and slaves of the better sort, which are brought to Egypt in increasing numbers. . . .

[Ships also come] from the places across this sea, from . . . Barygaza, bringing to these . . . market-towns the products of their own places; wheat, rice, clarified butter, sesame oil, cotton cloth . . . and honey from the reed called sacchari [sugar cane]. Some make the voyage especially to these market-towns, and others exchange their cargoes while sailing along the coast. This country is not subject to a King, but each market-town is ruled by its separate chief.

Beyond Opone, the shore trending more toward the south . . . this coast [the Somali region of Azania, or East Africa] is destitute of harbors . . . until the Pyralax islands [Zanzibar] . . . . [A] little to the south of south-west . . . is the island Menuthias [Madagascar], about three hundred stadia from the mainland, low and wooded, in which there are rivers and many kinds of birds and the mountain-tortoise. There are no wild beasts except the crocodiles; but there they do not attack men. In this place there are sewed boats, and canoes hollowed from single logs. . . .

Two days' sail beyond, there lies the very last market-town of the continent of Azania, which is called Rhapta [Dar es-Salaam]; which has its name from the sewed boats (*rhapton ploiarion*) . . . ; in which there is ivory in great quantity, and tortoise-shell. Along this coast live men of piratical habits, very great in stature, and under separate chiefs for each place. [One] chief governs it under some ancient right that subjects it to the sovereignty of the state that is become first in Arabia. And the people of Muza [Mocha in Yemen] now hold it under his authority, and send thither many large ships; using Arab captains and agents, who are familiar with the natives and intermarry with them, and who know the whole coast and understand the language.

There are imported into these markets the lances made at Muza especially for this trade, and hatchets and daggers and awls, and various kinds of glass; and at some places a little wine, and wheat, not for trade, but to serve for getting the good-will of the savages. There are exported from these places a great quantity of ivory . . . and rhinoceros-horn. . . .

And these markets of Azania are the very last of the continent that stretches down on the right hand from Berenice; for beyond these places the unexplored ocean curves around toward the west, and running along by the regions to the south of Aethiopia and Libya and Africa, it mingles with the western sea. . . .

Beyond the harbor of Moscha [Musqat in Oman] . . . a mountain range runs along the shore; at the end of which, in a row, lie seven islands. . . . Beyond these there is a barbarous region which is no longer of the same Kingdom, but now belongs to Persia. Sailing along this coast well out at sea . . . there meets you an island called Sarapis. . . . It is about two hundred stadia wide and six hundred long, inhabited by three settlements of Fish-Eaters, a villainous lot, who use the Arabian language and wear girdles of palm-leaves. . . .

[T]here follows not far beyond, the mouth of the Persian Gulf, where there is much diving for the pearl-mussel. . . . At the upper end of this Gulf there is a market-town designated by law called Apologus, situated near . . . the River Euphrates.

Sailing [southeast] through the mouth of the Gulf, after a six-days' course there is another market-town of Persia called Ommana . . . . [L]arge vessels are regularly sent from Barygaza, loaded with copper and sandalwood and timbers of teakwood and logs of blackwood and ebony. . . .

Beyond this region . . . there follows the coast district of Scythia, which lies above toward the north; the whole marshy; from which flows down the river Sinthus [Indus], the greatest of all the rivers that flow into the Erythraean Sea, bringing down an enormous volume of water. . . . This river has seven mouths, very shallow and marshy, so that they are not navigable, except the one in the middle; at which by the shore, is the market-town, Barbaricum. . . . [I]nland behind it is the metropolis of Scythia . . . it is subject to Parthian princes who are constantly driving each other out.

Now the whole country of India has very many rivers, and very great ebb and flow of the tides. . . . But about Barygaza [Broach] it is much greater, so that the bottom is suddenly seen, and now parts of the dry land are sea, and now it is dry where ships were sailing just before; and the rivers, under the inrush of the flood tide, when the whole force of the sea is directed against them, are driven upwards more strongly against their natural current. . . .

The country inland from Barygaza is inhabited by numerous tribes. . . . Above these is the very warlike nation of the Bactrians, who are under their own king. And Alexander, setting out from these parts, penetrated to the Ganges. . . . [T]o the present day ancient drachmae are current in Barygaza, coming from this country, bearing inscriptions in Greek letters, and the devices of those who reigned after Alexander. . . .

Inland from this place and to the east, is the city called Ozene [Ujjain]. . . . [F]rom this place are brought down all things needed for the welfare of the country about Barygaza, and many things for our trade: agate and carnelian, Indian muslins . . . .

There are imported into this market-town, wine, Italian preferred, also Laodicean and Arabian; copper, tin, and lead; coral and topaz; thin clothing and inferior sorts of all kinds . . . gold and silver coin, on which there is a profit when exchanged for the money of the country. . . . And for the King there are brought into those places very costly vessels of silver, singing boys, beautiful maidens for the harem, fine wines, thin clothing of the finest weaves, and the choicest ointments. There are exported from these places [spices], ivory, agate and carnelian . . . cotton cloth of all kinds, silk cloth. . . .

Beyond Barygaza the adjoining coast extends in a straight line from north to south. . . . The inland country back from the coast toward the east comprises many desert regions and great mountains; and all kinds of wild beasts—leopards, tigers, elephants, enormous serpents, hyenas, and baboons of many sorts; and many populous nations, as far as the Ganges. . . .

This whole voyage as above described . . . they used to make in small vessels, sailing close around the shores of the gulfs; and Hippalus was the pilot who by observing the location of the ports and the conditions of the sea, first discovered how to lay his course straight across the ocean. . . .

About the following region, the course trending toward the east, lying out at sea toward the west is the island Palaesimundu, called by the ancients Taprobane [Sri Lanka]. . . . It produces pearls, transparent stones, muslins, and tortoise-shell. . . .

Beyond this, the course trending toward the north, there are many barbarous tribes, among whom are the Cirrhadae, a race of men with flattened noses, very savage; another tribe, the Bargysi; and the Horse-faces and the Long-faces, who are said to be cannibals.

After these, the course turns toward the east again, and sailing with the ocean to the right and the shore remaining beyond to the left, Ganges comes into view. . . . And just opposite this river there is an island in the ocean, the last part of the inhabited world toward the east, under the rising sun itself; it is called Chryse; and it has the best tortoise-shell of all the places on the Erythraean Sea.

After this region under the very north, the sea outside ending in a land called This, there is a very great inland city called Thinae, from which raw silk and silk yarn and silk cloth are brought on foot. . . . But the land of This is not easy of access; few men come from there, and seldom.

QUESTIONS FOR ANALYSIS

1. Of what importance were political organization and ethnicity to a traveling merchant?
2. How might a manual like this have been used?
3. To what extent can the observations of a Greco-Egyptian merchant be taken as evidence for understanding how merchants from other lands saw the trade in the Indian Ocean?

Source: Excerpts from W. H. Schoff (tr. & ed.), *The Periplus of the Erythraean Sea: Travel and Trade in the Indian Ocean by a Merchant of the First Century* (London, Bombay & Calcutta, 1912).

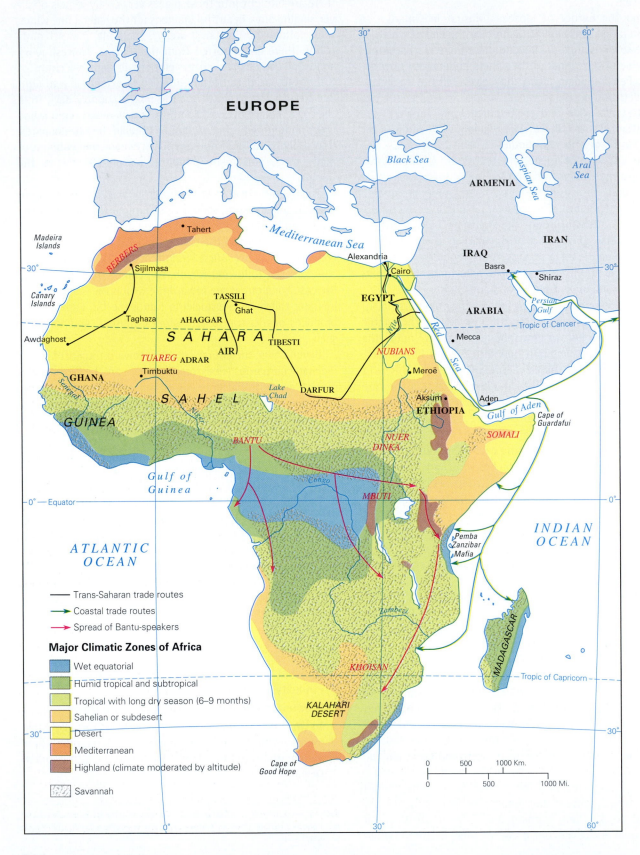

EUROPE

*Madeira
Islands*

•Tahert

BERBERS

•Sijilmasa

*Canary
Islands*

Taghaza•

Awdaghost•

GHANA

Senegal

GUINEA

SAHARA

AHAGGAR

Ghat

TASSILI

AIR

TIBESTI

TUAREG ADRAR

•Timbuktu

SAHEL

Niger

Lake
Chad

DARFUR

Mediterranean Sea

Alexandria•
•Cairo

EGYPT

Nile

NUBIANS

•Meroë

Black Sea

ARMENIA

Caspian Sea

*Aral
Sea*

IRAN

IRAQ

Basra•

•Shiraz

*Persian
Gulf*

ARABIA

•Mecca

Red Sea

Aksum•

ETHIOPIA

Aden• *Gulf of Aden*

*Cape of
Guardafui*

SOMALI

Tropic of Cancer

BANTU

NUER
DINKA

*Gulf of
Guinea*

Congo

MBUTI

*ATLANTIC
OCEAN*

Equator

Pemba
Zanzibar
Mafia

*INDIAN
OCEAN*

Zambezi

KHOISAN

MADAGASCAR

Tropic of Capricorn

KALAHARI
DESERT

*Cape of
Good Hope*

—— Trans-Saharan trade routes

→ Coastal trade routes

→ Spread of Bantu-speakers

Major Climatic Zones of Africa

Wet equatorial

Humid tropical and subtropical

Tropical with long dry season (6–9 months)

Sahelian or subdesert

Desert

Mediterranean

Highland (climate moderated by altitude)

Savannah

| 0 | 500 | 1000 Km. |
| 0 | 500 | 1000 Mi. |

Cattle Herders in Saharan Rock Art These paintings represent the most artistically accomplished type of Saharan art. Herding societies of modern times living in the Sahel region south of the Sahara strongly resemble the society depicted here. (Henri Lhote)

grassy areas was comparatively easy. However, by 300 B.C.E., scarcity of water was restricting travel to a few difficult routes initially known only to desert nomads. Trade over **trans-Saharan caravan routes,** at first only a trickle, eventually expanded into a significant stream.

Early Saharan Cultures

Sprawling sand dunes, sandy plains, and vast expanses of exposed rock make up most of the great desert. Stark and rugged mountain and highland areas separate its northern and southern portions. The cliffs and caves of these highlands, the last spots where water and grassland could be found as the climate changed, preserve rock paintings and engravings that constitute the primary evidence for early Saharan history.

Though dating is difficult, what appear to be the earliest images, left by hunters in much wetter times, include elephants, giraffes, rhinoceros, crocodiles, and other animals that have long been extinct in the region. Overlaps in the artwork indicate that the hunting societies were gradually joined by new cultures based on cat-

Map 8.2 Africa and the Trans–Saharan Trade Routes The Sahara and the surrounding oceans isolated most of Africa from foreign contact before 1000 C.E. The Nile Valley, a few trading points on the east coast, and limited transdesert trade provided exceptions to this rule; but the dominant forms of sub-Saharan African culture originated far to the west, north of the Gulf of Guinea.

tle breeding and well adapted to the sparse grazing that remained. Domestic cattle may have originated in western Asia or in North Africa. They certainly reached the Sahara before it became completely dry. The beautiful paintings of cattle and scenes of daily life seen in the Saharan rock art depict pastoral societies that bear little similarity to any in western Asia. The people seem physically akin to today's West Africans, and the customs depicted, such as dancing and wearing masks, as well as the breeds of cattle, particularly those with piebald coloring (splotches of black and white), strongly suggest later societies to the south of the Sahara. These factors support the hypothesis that some southern cultural patterns originated in the Sahara.

Overlaps in artwork also show that horse herders succeeded the cattle herders. The rock art changes dramatically in style, from the superb realism of the cattle pictures to sketchier images that are often strongly geometric. Moreover, the horses are frequently shown drawing light chariots. According to the most common theory, intrepid charioteers from the Mediterranean shore drove their flimsy vehicles across the desert and established societies in the few remaining grassy areas of the central Saharan highlands. Some scholars suggest possible chariot routes that refugees from the collapse of the Mycenaean and Minoan civilizations of Greece and Crete (see Chapter 4) might have followed deep into the desert around the twelfth century B.C.E. However, no archaeological evidence of actual chariot use in the Sahara has been discovered, and it is difficult to imagine large numbers of refugees from the politically chaotic Mediterranean region driving chariots into a waterless, trackless desert in search of a new homeland somewhere to the south.

As with the cattle herders, therefore, the identity of the Saharan horse breeders and the source of their passion for drawing chariots remain a mystery. Only with the coming of the camel is it possible to make firm connections with the Saharan nomads of today through the depiction of objects and geometric patterns still used by the veiled, blue-robed Tuareg° people of the highlands in southern Algeria, Niger, and Mali.

Some historians maintain that the Romans inaugurated an important trans-Saharan trade, but they lack firm archaeological evidence. More plausibly, Saharan trade relates to the spread of camel domestication. Supporting evidence comes from rock art, where overlaps of images imply that camel riders in desert costume constitute the latest Saharan population. The camel-oriented images are decidedly the crudest to be found in the region.

First mention of camels in North Africa comes in a Latin text of 46 B.C.E. Since the native camels of Africa probably died out before the era of domestication, the domestic animals probably reached the Sahara from Arabia, probably by way of Egypt in the first millennium B.C.E. They could have been adopted by peoples farther and farther to the west, from one central Saharan highland to the next, only much later spreading northward and coming to the attention of the Romans (see Environment and Technology: Camel Saddles). Camel herding made it easier for people to move away from the Saharan highlands and roam the deep desert. Through contacts made by far-ranging camel herders, the people north of the Sahara finally gained access to the camel, though they exploited it primarily as a work animal, even developing harnesses for attaching camels to plows and carts. These practices, entirely unknown in the southern Sahara, persist in Tunisia° today.

Trade Across the Sahara

Linkage between two different trading systems, one in the south, the other in the north, developed slowly. Southern traders concentrated on supplying salt from large deposits in the southern desert to the peoples of sub-Saharan Africa. Traders from the equatorial forest zone brought forest products, such as kola nuts (a condiment and source of caffeine) and edible palm oil, to trading centers near the desert's southern fringe. Each received the products they needed in their homelands from the other, or from the farming peoples of the **Sahel°**—literally "the coast" in Arabic, the southern borderlands of the Sahara (see Map 8.2). Middlemen who were native to the Sahel played an important role in this trade, but precise historical details are lacking.

In the north, Roman colonists supplied Italy with agricultural products, primarily wheat and olives. Surviving mosaic pavements depicting scenes from daily life show that people living on the farms and in the towns of the interior consumed Roman manufactured goods and shared Roman styles. This northern pattern began to change in the third century C.E. with the decline of the Roman Empire, the abandonment of many Roman farms, the growth of nomadism, and a lessening of trade across the Mediterranean. After the Arabs invaded North Africa in the middle of the seventh century C.E., the direction of trade shifted to the Middle East, the center of Arab rule. Since the Arab conquests were inspired by the new religion of Islam (see Chapter 9) and the Christian lands of Europe constituted enemy territory, trans-Mediterranean trade diminished still further. The Arabs, many of them from camel-breeding societies, felt a cultural kinship with those Berber-speakers who had taken up camel pastoralism during the preceding centuries. Like the Parthians involved in opening the Silk Road, they related better to the peoples of the interior than had the previous Carthaginian and Roman regimes.

A series of Berber revolts against Arab rule from 740 onward led to the appearance of several small principalities on the northern fringe of the Sahara. The Islamic beliefs of their rulers, which differed somewhat from those of the Arab rulers to the east, may have interfered with their east-west overland trade and led them to look for new possibilities elsewhere. It appears that these city-states, Sijilmasa° and Tahert°, developed the first significant and regular trading contact with the south in the ninth century. Most of their populations being Berber, they already knew that nomads speaking closely related languages inhabited the central and southern reaches of the desert.

Once traders looked south, they discovered that the already existing trade in the south sometimes involved exchanging gold dust for salt. The gold came from deposits along the Niger and other West African rivers (see Map 8.2). The people who panned for the gold did not value it nearly as highly as did the traders from Sijilmasa. They readily provided the nomads of the southern desert, who controlled the salt sources but had little use for gold, with products not available from the south, such as copper and certain manufactured goods. Thus everyone benefited from the creation of the new trade

---

Tuareg (TWAH-reg)   **Tunisia** (too-NEE-zhee-uh)

Sahel (SAH-hel)   **Sijilmasa** (sih-jil-MAS-suh)   **Tahert** (TAH-hert)

Camel Saddles

As seemingly simple a technology as saddle design can indicate a society's economic structure. The South Arabian saddle, a Tunisian example of which is shown to the right, was good for riding, and baggage could easily be tied to the wooden arches at its front. It was militarily inefficient, however, because the rider knelt on the cushion behind the camel's hump, which made it difficult to use weapons.

The North Arabian saddle was a significant improvement that came into use in the first centuries B.C.E. The two arches anchoring the front end of the South Arabian saddle were separated and greatly enlarged, one arch going in front of the hump and the other behind. This formed a solid wooden framework to which loads could easily be attached, but the placement of the prominent front and back arches seated the rider on top of the camel's hump instead of behind it and thereby gave warriors a solid seat and the advantage of height over enemy horsemen. Arabs in northern Arabia used these saddles to take control of the caravan trade through their lands.

The lightest and most efficient riding saddles, shown below, come from the southern Sahara, where personal travel and warfare took priority over trade. These excellent war saddles could not be used for baggage because they did not offer a convenient place to tie bundles.

Camel Saddles   The militarily inefficient south Arabian saddle (above) seats the rider behind the animal's hump atop its hindquarters. The rider controls his mount by tapping its neck with a long camelstick. The Tuareg saddle (below) seats the rider over the animal's withers, leaving his hands free to wield a sword and letting him control his mount with his toes.   (above: Private collection; below: Fred Bavendam/Peter Arnold, Inc.)

---

link. Sijilmasa and Tahert became wealthy cities, the former minting gold coins that circulated as far away as Egypt and Syria.

The Kingdom of Ghana

The earliest known sub-Saharan beneficiary of the new exchange system was the kingdom of **Ghana°**. Its first appearance is in an Arabic text of the late eighth century as the "land of gold." Few details survive about the early years of this realm, which was established by the Soninke° people and covered parts of Mali, Mauritania, and Senegal. In the mid-eleventh century the Arab geographer al-Bakri (d. 1094) described it as follows:

> The city of Ghana consists of two towns situated on a plain. One of these towns is inhabited by Muslims. It is large and possesses a dozen mosques, one being for the Friday prayer, and each having imams [prayer leaders], muezzins [people to make the call to prayer], and salaried reciters of the Quran. There are jurisconsults [legal specialists] and scholars. Around the town

---

Ghana (GAH-nuh)

Soninke (soh-NIN-kay)

are sweet wells, which they use for drinking and for cultivating vegetables. The royal city, called al-Ghaba ["the grove"], is six miles away, and the area between the two towns is covered with habitations. Their houses are constructed of stone and acacia wood. The king has a palace with conical huts, surrounded by a fence like a wall. In the king's town, not far from the royal court, is a mosque for the use of Muslims who visit the king on missions. . . . The interpreters of the king are Muslims, as are his treasurer and the majority of his ministers.

Their religion is paganism, and the worship of idols. . . . Around the royal town are domed dwellings, woods and copses where live their sorcerers, those in charge of their religious cults. There are also their idols and their kings' tombs.[2]

The king of Ghana required the sons of vassal kings to attend his court. He meted out justice and controlled trade, collecting taxes on the salt and copper coming from the north. His large army of bowmen and cavalry made Ghana the dominant power in the entire region. By the end of the tenth century, the king's sway extended even to Awdaghost°, the Arab and Berber trade entrepôt in the desert at the southern end of the track to Sijilmasa.

After 1076 Ghana fell prey to a new state formed by Muslim desert nomads known as Almoravids°. Later Muslim historians assert that many people in Ghana converted to Islam during the decade of nomad domination before the Almoravids withdrew to concentrate their attentions on Morocco and Spain. Although Ghana regained its independence, many former provinces had fallen away, and it never recovered its greatness.

Prior to the arrival of the religiously zealous Almoravids, the traders who had reached Ghana from the north had not been overly insistent on propagating Islam. Over the three centuries separating al-Bakri's account in the eleventh century from the earliest mention of Ghana, Muslims had come to hold high economic positions, and the kings tolerated their religious practices. But in general, the people of Ghana had not converted to Islam. Widespread adoption of the Islamic religion, with consequent impact on the way of life of the Sahel peoples, came under later kingdoms.

SUB-SAHARAN AFRICA

The Indian Ocean network and later trade across the Sahara provided **sub-Saharan Africa,** the portion of Africa south of the Sahara, with a few external contacts.

The most important African network of cultural exchange from 300 B.C.E. to 1100 C.E., however, arose within the region and took the form of folk migration. These migrations and exchanges put in place enduring characteristics of African culture.

A Challenging Geography

Many geographic obstacles impede access to and movement within sub-Saharan Africa (see Map 8.2). The Sahara, the Atlantic and Indian Oceans, and the Red Sea form the boundaries of the region. With the exception of the Nile, a ribbon of green traversing the Sahara from south to north, the major river systems empty into the Atlantic, in the case of the Senegal, Niger, and Zaire° Rivers, or into the Mozambique Channel of the Indian Ocean, in the case of the Zambezi. Rapids limit the use of these rivers for navigation.

Stretching over 50 degrees of latitude, sub-Saharan Africa encompasses dramatically different environments. A 4,000-mile (6,500-kilometer) trek from the southern edge of the Sahara to the Cape of Good Hope would take a traveler from the flat, semiarid **steppes** of the Sahel region to tropical **savanna** covered by long grasses and scattered forest, and then to **tropical rain forest** on the lower Niger and in the Zaire Basin. The rain forest gives way to another broad expanse of savanna, followed by more steppe and desert, and finally by a region of temperate highlands at the southern extremity, located as far south of the equator as Greece and Sicily are to its north. East-west travel is comparatively easy in the steppe and savanna regions—a caravan from Senegal to the Red Sea would have traversed a distance comparable to that of the Silk Road—but difficult in the equatorial rain-forest belt and across the mountains and deep rift valleys that abut the rain forest to the east and separate East from West Africa.

The Development of Cultural Unity

Cultural heritages shared by the educated elites within each region—heritages that some anthropologists call "**great traditions**"—typically include a written language, common legal and belief systems, ethical codes, and other intellectual attitudes. They loom large in written records as traditions that rise above the diversity of local customs and beliefs commonly distinguished as "**small traditions.**"

By the year 1 C.E. sub-Saharan Africa had become a distinct cultural region, though one not shaped by impe-

Awdaghost (OW-duh-gost) **Almoravid** (al-moe-RAH-vid)   **Zaire** (zah-EER)

rial conquest or characterized by a shared elite culture, a "great tradition." The cultural unity of sub-Saharan Africa rested on similar characteristics shared to varying degrees by many popular cultures, or "small traditions." These had developed during the region's long period of isolation from the rest of the world and had been refined, renewed, and interwoven by repeated episodes of migration and social interaction. Historians know little about this complex prehistory. Thus, to a greater degree than in other regions, they call on anthropological descriptions, oral history, and comparatively late records of various "small traditions" to reconstruct the broad outlines of cultural formation.

Sub-Saharan Africa's cultural unity is less immediately apparent than its diversity. By one estimate, Africa is home to two thousand distinct languages, many corresponding to social and belief systems endowed with distinctive rituals and cosmologies. There are likewise numerous food production systems, ranging from hunting and gathering—very differently carried out by the Mbuti° Pygmies of the equatorial rain forest and the Khoisan° peoples of the southwestern deserts—to the cultivation of bananas, yams, and other root crops in forest clearings and of sorghum and other grains in the savanna lands. Pastoral societies, particularly those depending on cattle, display somewhat less diversity across the Sahel and savanna belt from Senegal to Kenya.

Sub-Saharan Africa covered a larger and more diverse area than any other cultural region of the first millennium C.E. and had a lower overall population density. Thus societies and polities had ample room to form and reform, and a substantial amount of space separated different groups. The contacts that did occur did not last long enough to produce rigid cultural uniformity.

In addition, for centuries external conquerors could not penetrate the region's natural barriers and impose a uniform culture. The Egyptians occupied Nubia, and some traces of Egyptian influence appear in Saharan rock art farther west, but the Nile cataracts and the vast swampland in the Nile's upper reaches blocked movement farther south. The Romans sent expeditions against pastoral peoples living in the Libyan Sahara but could not incorporate them into the Roman world. Not until the nineteenth century did outsiders gain control of the continent and begin the process of establishing an elite culture—that of European imperialism.

African Cultural Characteristics

European travelers who got to know the sub-Saharan region well in the nineteenth and twentieth centuries observed broad commonalties underlying African life and culture. In agriculture, the common technique was cultivation by hoe and digging stick. Musically, different groups of Africans played many instruments, especially types of drums, but common features, particularly in rhythm, gave African music as a whole a distinctive character. Music played an important role in social rituals, as did dancing and wearing masks, which often showed great artistry in their design.

African kingdoms varied, but kingship displayed common features, most notably the ritual isolation of the king himself (see Diversity and Dominance: Personal Styles of Rule in India and Mali in Chapter 14). Fixed social categories—age groupings, kinship divisions, distinct gender roles and relations, and occupational groupings—also show resemblances from one region to another, even in societies too small to organize themselves into kingdoms. Though not hierarchical, these categories played a role similar to the divisions between noble, commoner, and slave prevalent where kings ruled. Such indications of underlying cultural unity have led modern observers to identify a common African quality throughout most of the region, even though most sub-Saharan Africans themselves did not perceive it. An eminent Belgian anthropologist, Jacques Maquet, has called this quality "Africanity."

Some historians hypothesize that this cultural unity emanated from the peoples who once occupied the southern Sahara. In Paleolithic times, periods of dryness alternated with periods of wetness as the Ice Age that locked up much of the world's fresh water in glaciers and icecaps came and went. When European glaciers receded with the waning of the Ice Age, a storm belt brought increased wetness to the Saharan region. Rushing rivers scoured deep canyons. Now filled with fine sand, those canyons are easily visible on flights over the southern parts of the desert. As the glaciers receded farther, the storm belt moved northward to Europe, and dryness set in after 5000 B.C.E. As a consequence, runs the hypothesis, the region's population migrated southward, becoming increasingly concentrated in the Sahel, which may have been the initial incubation center for Pan-African cultural patterns.

Increasing dryness and the resulting difficulty in supporting the population would have driven some people out of this core into more sparsely settled lands to the east, west, and south. In a parallel development farther to the east, migration away from the growing aridity of the desert seems to have contributed to the settling of the Nile Valley and the emergence of the Old Kingdom of Egypt (see Chapter 2).

Mbuti (m-BOO-tee)　**Khoisan** (KOI-sahn)

The Advent of Iron and the Bantu Migrations

Archaeology confirms that agriculture had become common between the equator and the Sahara by the early second millennium B.C.E. It then spread southward, displacing hunting and gathering as a way of life. Moreover, botanical evidence indicates that banana trees, probably introduced to southeastern Africa from Southeast Asia, made their way north and west, retracing in the opposite direction the presumed migration routes of the first agriculturists.

Archaeology has also uncovered traces of copper mining in the Sahara from the early first millennium B.C.E. Copper appears in the Niger Valley somewhat later, and in the Central African copper belt between 400 and 900 C.E. Gold was mined in Zimbabwe by the eighth and ninth centuries C.E. Most important of all, iron smelting began in northern sub-Saharan Africa in the early first millennium C.E. and spread southward from there, becoming firmly established in southern Africa by 800.

Many historians believe that the secret of smelting iron, which requires very high temperatures, was discovered only once, by the Hittites of Anatolia (modern Turkey) around 1500 B.C.E. (see Chapter 4). If that is the case, it is hard to explain how iron smelting reached sub-Saharan Africa. The earliest evidence of ironworking from the kingdom of Meroë, situated on the upper Nile and in cultural contact with Egypt, is no earlier than the evidence from West Africa (northern Nigeria). Even less plausible than the Nile Valley as a route of technological diffusion is the idea of a spread southward from Phoenician settlements in North Africa, since archaeological evidence has failed to substantiate the vague Greek and Latin accounts of Phoenician excursions to the south.

A more plausible scenario focuses on Africans' discovering for themselves how to smelt iron. Some historians suggest that they might have done so while firing pottery in kilns. No firm evidence exists to prove or disprove this theory.

Linguistic analysis provides the strongest evidence of extensive contacts among sub-Saharan Africans in the first millennium C.E.—and offers suggestions about the spread of iron. More than three hundred languages spoken south of the equator belong to the branch of the Niger-Congo family known as **Bantu,** after the word meaning "people" in most of the languages.

The distribution of the Bantu languages both north and south of the equator is consistent with a divergence beginning in the first millennium B.C.E. By comparing core words common to most of the languages, linguists have drawn some conclusions about the original Bantu-speakers, whom they call "proto-Bantu." These people engaged in fishing, using canoes, nets, lines, and hooks.

They lived in permanent villages on the edge of the rain forest, where they grew yams and grains and harvested wild palm nuts from which they pressed oil. They possessed domesticated goats, dogs, and perhaps other animals. They made pottery and cloth. Linguists surmise that the proto-Bantu homeland was near the modern boundary of Nigeria and Cameroon. Although dates for their dispersal are scarce, Bantu-speaking people appear in East Africa by the eighth century C.E.

Because the presumed home of the proto-Bantu lies near the known sites of early iron smelting, migration by Bantu-speakers seems a likely mechanism for the southward spread of iron. The migrants probably used iron axes and hoes to hack out forest clearings and plant crops. According to this scenario, their actions would have established an economic basis for new societies capable of sustaining much denser populations than could earlier societies dependent on hunting and gathering alone. Thus the period from 500 B.C.E. to 1000 C.E. saw a massive transfer of Bantu traditions and practices southward, eastward, and westward and their transformation, through intermingling with preexisting societies, into Pan-African traditions and practices.

THE SPREAD OF IDEAS

Ideas, like social customs, religious attitudes, and artistic styles, can spread along trade routes and through folk migrations. In both cases, documenting the dissemination of ideas, particularly in preliterate societies, poses a difficult historical problem.

Ideas and Material Evidence

Historians know about some ideas only through the survival of written sources. Other ideas do not depend on writing but are inherent in material objects studied by archaeologists and anthropologists. Customs surrounding the eating of pork are a case in point. Scholars disagree about whether pigs became domestic in only one place, from which the practice of pig keeping spread elsewhere, or whether several peoples hit on the same idea at different times and in different places.

Southeast Asia was an important early center of pig domestication. Anthropological studies tell us that the eating of pork became highly ritualized in this area and that it was sometimes allowed only on ceremonial occasions. On the other side of the Indian Ocean, wild swine were common in the Nile swamps of ancient Egypt. There, too, pigs took on a sacred role, being associated with the evil god Set, and eating them was prohibited. The biblical prohibition on the Israelites' eating pork, echoed later by the Muslims, probably came from Egypt in the second millennium B.C.E.

In a third locale in eastern Iran, an archaeological site dating from the third millennium B.C.E. provides evidence of another religious taboo relating to pork. Although the area around the site was swampy and home to many wild pigs, not a single pig bone has been found. Yet small pig figurines seem to have been used as symbolic religious offerings, and the later Iranian religion associates the boar with an important god.

What accounts for the apparent connection between domestic pigs and religion in these far-flung areas? There is no way of knowing. It has been hypothesized that pigs were first domesticated in Southeast Asia by people who had no herd animals—sheep, goats, cattle, or horses—and who relied on fish for most of their animal protein. The pig therefore became a special animal to them. The practice of pig herding, along with religious beliefs and rituals associated with the consumption of pork, could conceivably have spread from Southeast Asia along the maritime routes of the Indian Ocean, eventually reaching Iran and Egypt. But no evidence survives to support this hypothesis. In this case, therefore, material evidence can only hint at the spread of religious ideas, leaving the door open for other explanations.

A more certain example of objects' indicating the spread of an idea is the practice of hammering a carved die onto a piece of precious metal and using the resulting coin as a medium of exchange. From its origin in the Lydian kingdom in Anatolia in the first millennium B.C.E. (see Chapter 5), the idea of trading by means of struck coinage spread rapidly to Europe, North Africa, and India. Was the low-value copper coinage of China, made by pouring molten metal into a mold, also inspired by this practice from far away? It may have been, but it might also derive from indigenous Chinese metalworking. There is no way to be sure. Theoretically, all that is needed for an idea to spread is a single returning traveler telling about some wonder that he or she saw abroad.

Statue of a Bodhisattva at Bamian   This is one of two monumental Buddhist sculptures near the top of a high mountain pass connecting Kabul, Afghanistan, with the northern parts of the country. Carved into the side of a cliff in the sixth or seventh century, C.E., the sculptures were surrounded by cave dwellings of monks and rock sanctuaries, some dating to the first century B.C.E. This statue and the one alongside it were blown to pieces by the intolerant Taliban regime in Afghanistan in 2001.   (Ian Griffiths/ Robert Harding Picture Library)

The Spread of Buddhism

While material objects associated with religious beliefs and rituals are important indicators of the spread of spiritual ideas, written sources deal with the spread of today's major religions. Buddhism grew to become, with Christianity and Islam (see Chapter 9), one of the most popular and widespread religions in the world. In all three cases, the religious ideas spread without dependency on a single ethnic or kinship group.

King Ashoka, the Maurya ruler of India, and Kanishka, the greatest king of the Kushans of northern Afghanistan, promoted Buddhism between the third century B.C.E. and the second century C.E. However, monks, missionaries, and pilgrims who crisscrossed India, followed the Silk Road, or took ships on the Indian Ocean brought the Buddha's teachings to Southeast Asia, China, Korea, and ultimately Japan (see Map 8.1).

The Chinese pilgrims Faxian° (died between 418 and 423 C.E.) and Xuanzang° (600–664 C.E.) left written accounts of their travels. Both followed the Silk Road, through which Buddhism had arrived in China. Along the way they encountered Buddhist communities and monasteries that previous generations of missionaries and pilgrims had established.

Faxian began his trip in the company of a Chinese envoy to an unspecified ruler or people in Central Asia. After traveling from one Buddhist site to another across Afghanistan and India, he reached Sri Lanka, a Buddhist land, where he lived for two years. He then embarked for China on a merchant ship with two hundred men aboard. A storm drove the ship to Java, which he chose not to describe since it was Hindu rather than Buddhist. After five months ashore, Faxian finally reached China on another ship. The narrative of Xuanzang's journey two centuries later is quite similar, though he returned to China the way he had come, along the Silk Road.

Less reliable accounts make reference to missionaries traveling to Syria, Egypt, and Macedonia, as well as to Southeast Asia. One of Ashoka's sons allegedly led a band of missionaries to Sri Lanka. Later, his sister brought a company of nuns there, along with a branch of the sacred Bo tree under which the Buddha had received enlightenment. At the same time, there are reports of other monks traveling to Burma, Thailand, and Sumatra. Ashoka's missionaries may also have reached Tibet by way of trade routes across the Himalayas. A firmer tradition maintains that in 622 C.E. a minister of the Tibetan king traveled to India to study Buddhism and on his return introduced writing to his homeland.

The different lands that received the story and teachings of the Buddha preserved or adapted them in different ways. Theravada Buddhism, "Teachings of the Elder," was centered in Sri Lanka. Holding closely to the Buddha's earliest teachings, it maintained that the goal of religion, available only to monks, is *nirvana*, the total absence of suffering and the end of the cycle of rebirth (see Chapter 7). This teaching contrasted with Mahayana, or "Great Vehicle" Buddhism, which stressed the goal of becoming a *bodhisattva*, a person who attains nirvana but chooses to remain in human company to help and guide others.

An offshoot of Mahayana Buddhism stressing ritual prayer and personal guidance by "perfected ones" became dominant in Tibet after the eighth century C.E. In China another offshoot, Chan (called Zen in its Japanese form), focused on meditation and sudden enlightenment. It became one of the dominant sects in China, Korea, and Japan (see Chapter 11).

The Spread of Christianity

The post-Roman development of Christianity in Europe is discussed in Chapter 10. The Christian faith enjoyed an earlier spread in Asia and Africa before its confrontation with Islam (described in Chapter 9). Jerusalem in Palestine, Antioch in Syria, and Alexandria in Egypt became centers of Christian authority soon after the crucifixion, but the spread of Christianity to Armenia and Ethiopia illustrates the connections between religion, trade, and imperial politics.

Situated in eastern Anatolia (modern Turkey), **Armenia** served recurrently as a battleground between Iranian states to the south and east and Mediterranean states to the west. Each imperial power wanted to control this region so close to the frontier where Silk Road traders met their Mediterranean counterparts. In Parthian times, Armenia's kings favored Zoroastrianism. Armenian not then being a written language, Christianity was known to "only those who were to some degree acquainted with Greek or Syriac learning" and thus able to obtain "some partial inkling of it."[3]

The invention of an Armenian alphabet in the early fifth century opened the way to a wider spread of Christianity. The Iranians did not give up domination easily, but within a century the Armenian Apostolic Church had become the center of Armenian cultural life.

Far to the south Christians similarly sought to outflank Iran. The Christian emperors in Constantinople (see Chapter 10) sent missionaries along the Red Sea trade route to seek converts in Yemen and **Ethiopia.** In the fourth century C.E. a Syrian philosopher traveling with two young relatives sailed to India. On the way back the ship docked at a Red Sea port occupied by Ethiopians from the prosperous kingdom of Aksum. Being then at odds with the Romans, the Ethiopians killed everyone on board except the two boys, Aedisius—who later narrated this story—and Frumentius. Impressed by their learning, the king made the former his cupbearer and the latter his treasurer and secretary.

When the king died, his wife urged Frumentius to govern Aksum on her behalf and that of her infant son, Ezana. As regent Frumentius sought out Roman Christians among the merchants who visited the country and helped them establish Christian communities. When he became king, Ezana, who may have become a Christian, permitted Aedisius and Frumentius to return to Syria. The patriarch of Alexandria, on learning about the progress of Christianity in Aksum, elevated Frumentius to the rank of bishop, though he had not previously been a clergyman, and sent him back to Ethiopia as the first leader of its church.

Faxian (fah-shee-en)   **Xuanzang** (shoo-wen-zahng)

Stele of Aksum   This 70-foot (21-meter) stone is the tallest remnant of a field of stelae, or standing stones, marking the tombs of Aksumite kings. The carvings of doors, windows, and beam ends imitate common features of Aksumite architecture, suggesting that each stele symbolized a multistory royal palace. The largest stelae date from the fourth century C.E.   (J. Allan Cash)

The patriarch of Alexandria continues today to appoint the head of the Ethiopian Church, but the spread of Christianity into Nubia, the land south of Egypt along the Nile River, proceeded from Ethiopia rather than Egypt. Politically and economically, Ethiopia became a power at the western end of the Indian Ocean trading system, occasionally even extending its influence across the Red Sea and asserting itself in Yemen (see Map 8.2).

Ethiopian Christianity developed its own unique features. One popular belief, perhaps deriving from the Ethiopian Jewish community, was that the Ark of the Covenant, the most sacred object of the ancient Hebrews (see Chapter 4), had been transferred from Jerusalem to the Ethiopian church of Our Lady of Zion. Another tradition maintains that Christ miraculously dried up a lake to serve as the site for this church, which became the place of coronation for Ethiopia's rulers.

CONCLUSION

Exchange facilitated by the early long-distance trading systems differed in many ways from the ebb and flow of culture, language, and custom that folk migrations brought about. Transportable goods and livestock and ideas about new technologies and agricultural products sometimes worked great changes on the landscape and in people's lives. But nothing resembling the Africanity observed south of the Sahara can be attributed to the societies involved in the Silk Road, Indian Ocean, or trans-Saharan exchanges. Not only were few people directly involved in these complex social systems of travel and trade compared with the populations with whom they were brought into contact, but their lifestyles as pastoral nomads or seafarers isolated them still more. Communities of traders contributed to this isolation by their reluctance to share knowledge with people who might become commercial competitors.

The Bantu, however, if current theories are correct, spread far and wide in sub-Saharan Africa with the deliberate intent of settling and implanting a lifestyle based on iron implements and agriculture. The metallurgical skills and agricultural techniques they brought with them permitted much denser habitation and helped ensure that the languages of the immigrants would supplant those of their hunting and gathering predecessors. Where the trading systems encouraged diversity by introducing new products and ideas, the Bantu migrations brought a degree of cultural dominance that strongly affected later African history.

An apparent exception to the generalization that trading systems have less impact than folk migrations on patterns of dominance lies in the intangible area of ideas. Christianity, Buddhism, and Islam all spread along trade routes, at least to some degree. Each instance of spread, however, gave rise to new forms of cultural diversity even as overall doctrinal unity made these religions dominant. As "great traditions," the new faiths based on conversion linked priests, monks, nuns, and religious scholars across vast distances. The masses of believers, however, seldom considered their spiritual lives in such broad contexts. Missionary religions imported through long-distance trading networks merged with myriad "small traditions" to provide for the social and spiritual needs of peoples living in many lands under widely varying circumstances.

■ Key Terms

Silk Road	steppes
Parthians	savanna
stirrup	tropical rain forest
Indian Ocean Maritime System	"great traditions"
trans-Saharan caravan routes	"small traditions"
Sahel	Bantu
Ghana	Armenia
sub-Saharan Africa	Ethiopia

■ Suggested Reading

For broad and suggestive overviews on cross-cultural exchange see Philip D. Curtin, *Cross-Cultural Trade in World History* (1985), and C. G. F. Simkin, *The Traditional Trade of Asia* (1968).

Readable overviews of the Silk Road include Luce Boulnois, *The Silk Road* (1966), and Irene M. Franck and David M. Brownstone, *The Silk Road: A History* (1986). For products traded across Central Asia based on an eighth-century Japanese collection, see Ryoichi Hayashi, *The Silk Road and the Shoso-in* (1975). Xinru Liu, *Silk and Religion* (1996), covers one specific product. Owen Lattimore gives a first-person account of traveling by camel caravan in *The Desert Road to Turkestan* (1928). More generally on Central Asia, see Denis Sinor, *Inner Asia, History-Civilization-Languages: A Syllabus* (1987), and Karl Jettmar, *Art of the Steppes,* rev. ed. (1967). Richard Foltz, *Religions of the Silk Road* (1999), is an excellent brief introduction.

For a readable but sketchy historical overview see August Toussaint, *History of the Indian Ocean* (1966). Alan Villiers recounts what it was like to sail dhows between East Africa and the Persian Gulf in *Sons of Sinbad* (1940).

On a more scholarly plane, see K. N. Chaudhuri's *Trade and Civilization in the Indian Ocean: An Economic History from the Rise of Islam to 1750* (1985). Archaeologist Pierre Vérin treats the special problem of Madagascar in *The History of Civilisation in North Madagascar* (1986). For Rome and India see E. H. Warmington's *The Commerce Between the Roman Empire and India* (1974); J. Innes Miller's *The Spice Trade of the Roman Empire, 29 B.C. to A.D. 641* (1969); and Vimala Begley and Richard Daniel De Puma's edited collection of articles, *Rome and India: The Ancient Sea Trade* (1991), along with the primary source *The Periplus Maris Erythraei: Text with Introduction, Translation, and Commentary* (1989) edited and translated by Lionel Casson. George F. Hourani's brief *Arab Seafaring in the Indian Ocean in Ancient and Early Medieval Times* (1975) covers materials in Arabic sources.

Nicholas Tarling, ed., *The Cambridge History of Southeast Asia,* vol. 1 (1992); D. R. SarDesai, *Southeast Asia: Past and Present,* 3d ed. (1994); and Milton E. Osborne, *Southeast Asia: An Introductory History* (1995), provide general accounts of Southeast Asian history. Lynda Shaffer, *Maritime Southeast Asia to 1500* (1996), focuses on the world historical context. Also useful is Kenneth R. Hall, *Maritime Trade and State Development in Early Southeast Asia* (1985).

On art see M. C. S. Diskul, *The Art of Srivijaya* (1980); Maud Girard-Geslan et al., *Art of Southeast Asia* (1998); and Daigoro Chihara, *Hindu-Buddhist Architecture in Southeast Asia* (1996).

Richard W. Bulliet's *The Camel and the Wheel* (1975) deals with camel use in the Middle East, along the Silk Road, and in North Africa and the Sahara. For a well-illustrated account of Saharan rock art see Henri Lhote, *The Search for the Tassili Frescoes: The Story of the Prehistoric Rock-Paintings of the Sahara* (1959). Additional views on Saharan trade and politics appear in E. Ann McDougall, "The Sahara Reconsidered: Pastoralism, Politics and Salt from the Ninth Through the Twelfth Centuries," *History in Africa 12* (1983): 263–286, and Nehemia Levtzion, *Ancient Ghana and Mali,* 2d ed. (1980). For translated texts see J. F. P. Hopkins and Nehemia Levtzion, eds., *Corpus of Early Arabic Sources for West African History* (1981).

J. F. A. Ajayi and Michael Crowder, *A History of West Africa,* vol. 1 (1976), and G. Mokhtar, ed., *General History of Africa II: Ancient Civilizations of Africa* (1981), include many articles by numerous authors; the latter work specifically treats ironworking and the Bantu migrations. On African cultural unity see Jacques Maquet, *Africanity: The Cultural Unity of Black Africa* (1972).

Of special importance on Christianity in Asia and Africa is Garth Fowden, *Empire to Commonwealth: Consequences of Monotheism in Late Antiquity* (1993). For specific topics treated in this chapter see Stuart Munro-Hay, *Aksum: An African Civilisation of Late Antiquity* (1991); Xinru Liu, *Ancient India and Ancient China: Trade and Religious Exchanges, A.D. 1–600* (1998); Rolf A. Stein, *Tibetan Civilization* (1972); Tilak Hettiarachchy, *History of Kingship in Ceylon up to the Fourth Century A.D.* (1972); and Yoneo Ishii, *Sangha, State, and Society: Thai Buddhism in History* (1986). The Chinese travelers' accounts cited are Fa-hsien [Faxian], *The Travels of Fahsien (399–414 A.D.), or, Record of the Buddhistic Kingdoms,* trans. H. A. Giles (1923; reprint, 1981), and Hiuen Tsiang [Xuanzang], *Si-Yu-Ki: Buddhist Records of the Western World,* trans. Samuel Beal (1884; reprint, 1981).

■ Notes

1. Victor H. Mair, ed., *The Columbia Anthology of Traditional Chinese Literature* (New York: Columbia University Press, 1994), 485; translated by Victor H. Mair.
2. J. F. A. Ajayi and Michael Crowder, eds., *History of West Africa,* vol. 1 (New York: Columbia University Press, 1976), 120–121.
3. Pawstos Busand, *Epic Histories* (late fifth century), quoted in Garth Fowden, *Empire to Commonwealth* (Princeton NJ: Princeton University Press, 1993), 105.

The Sasanid Empire and the Rise of Islam, 200–1200

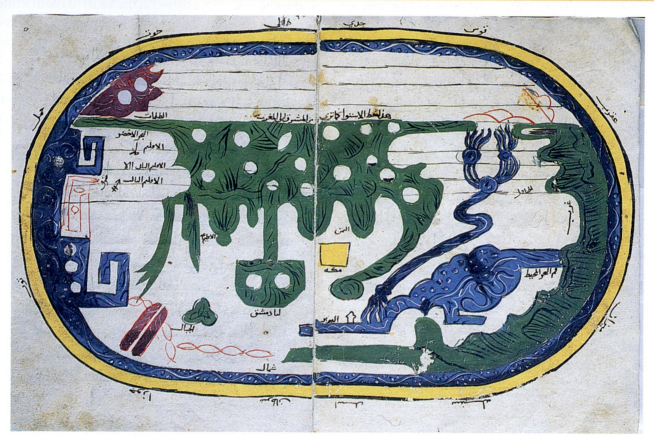

9

Islamic World Map   Oriented with south at the top, this copy of a tenth-century original was probably made in the fourteenth century.

CHAPTER OUTLINE

The Sasanid Empire, 224–651

The Origins of Islam

The Rise and Fall of the Caliphate, 632–1258

Islamic Civilization

DIVERSITY AND DOMINANCE: Beggars, Con Men, and Singing-girls

ENVIRONMENT AND TECHNOLOGY: Automata

The story is told that in the early days of Islam, at the time of the Prophet Muhammad's last pilgrimage to Mecca in 630, a dispute over distribution of booty arose between his daughter's husband, Ali, who was also Muhammad's first cousin, and some troops Ali commanded. Muhammad quelled the grumbling and later on the same journey, at a place named Ghadir al-Khumm°, drew his followers together, took Ali's hand, and declared: "Am I not nearer to the believers than their own selves? Whomever I am nearest to, so likewise is Ali. O God, be the friend of him who is his friend, and the foe of him who is his foe."

Written narratives of Muhammad's praise of Ali, like all stories of Muhammad's life, date to well over a century after the event. By that time, Ali had served as leader of Muhammad's community for a brief time and had then been defeated in a civil war and assassinated. Subsequently, his son Husayn, along with his family, died in a hopelessly lopsided battle while trying to claim leadership as the Prophet's grandson.

Out of these events grew a division in the Islamic community: some believers, called **Shi'ites°,** from the Arabic term *Shi'at Ali* ("Party of Ali"), thought that religious leadership rightfully belonged to Ali and his descendants; others, eventually called **Sunnis°,** followers of the sunna, or "tradition" of the community, felt that the community should choose its leaders more broadly. Sunnis and Shi'ites agreed that Muhammad commended Ali at Ghadir al-Khumm. But the Sunnis considered his remarks to relate only to the distribution of the booty, and the Shi'ites understood them to be Muhammad's formal and public declaration of Ali's special and elevated position, and hence of his right to rule.

Shi'ite rulers rarely achieved power, but those who ruled from Cairo between 969 and 1171 made the commemoration of Ghadir al-Khumm a major festival. At the beginning of every year, Shi'ites everywhere also engaged in public mourning over the deaths of Husayn and his family. Sunni rulers, in contrast, sometimes ordered that Ali be cursed in public prayers.

Muhammad's Arab followers conquered an enormous territory in the seventh century. In the name of Islam, they created an empire that encompassed many peoples speaking many languages and worshiping in many ways. Its immediate forerunners, the realms of the Byzantine emperors (see Chapter 10) and Iran's Sasanid° shahs, closely linked religion with imperial politics.

Although urbanism, science, manufacturing, trade, and architecture flourished in the lands of Islam while medieval Europe was enduring hardship and economic contraction, religion shaped both societies. Just as the medieval Christian calendar revolved around Easter and Christmas, Islamic fasts, pilgrimages, and political religious observances like Ghadir al-Khumm marked the yearly cycle in the lands of Muhammad's followers.

As you read this chapter, ask yourself the following questions:

- How did social and political developments under the Sasanid Empire pave the way for the spread of Islam?

- How did the Arab conquests grow out of the career of Muhammad?

- Why did the caliphate break up?

- How did Muslim societies differ from region to region?

- What was the relationship between urbanization and the development of Islamic culture?

THE SASANID EMPIRE, 224–651

The rise in the third century of a new Iranian state, the **Sasanid Empire,** continued the old rivalry between Rome and the Parthians along the Euphrates frontier. However, behind this façade of continuity, a social and economic transformation took place that set the stage for a new and powerful religio-political movement: Islam.

Ghadir al-Khumm (ga-DEER al-KUM)   Shi'ite (SHE-ite)
Sunni (SUN-nee)

Sasanid (SAH-suh-nid)

C H R O N O L O G Y

	The Arab Lands	Iran and Central Asia
200		**224–651** Sasanid Empire
600	**570–632** Life of the Prophet Muhammad	
	634 Conquests of Iraq and Syria commence	
	639–42 Conquest of Egypt by Arabs	
	656–61 Ali caliph; first civil war	
	661–750 Umayyad Caliphate rules from Damascus	
700	**711** Berbers and Arabs invade Spain from North Africa	**711** Arabs capture Sind in India
	750 Beginning of Abbasid Caliphate	**747** Abbasid revolt begins in Khurasan
	755 Umayyad state established in Spain	
	776–809 Caliphate of Hurun al-Rashid	
800	**835–92** Abbasid capital moved from Baghdad to Samarra	
900	**909** Fatimids seize North Africa, found Shi'ite Caliphate	**875** Independent Samanid state founded in Bukhara
	929 Abd al-Rahman III declares himself caliph in Cordoba	
	945 Shi'ite Buyids take control in Baghdad	**945** Buyids from northern Iran take control of Abbasid Caliphate
	969 Fatimids conquer Egypt	
1000	**1055** Seljuk Turks take control in Baghdad	**1036** Beginning of Turkish Seljuk rule in Khurasan
	1099 First Crusade captures Jerusalem	
	1171 Fall of Fatimid Egypt	
	1187 Saladin recaptures Jerusalem	
	1250 Mamluks control Egypt	
	1258 Mongols sack Baghdad and end Abbasid Caliphate	
	1260 Mamluks defeat Mongols at Ain Jalut	

Politics and Society

Ardashir, whose dynasty takes its name from an ancestor named Sasan, defeated the Parthians around 224 and established the Sasanid kingdom. To the west, the new rulers confronted the Romans, whom later historians frequently refer to as the Byzantines after about 330.

Along their desert Euphrates frontier, the Sasanids subsidized nomadic Arab chieftains to protect their empire from invasion (the Byzantines did the same with Arabs on their Jordanian desert frontier). Arab pastoralists farther to the south remained isolated and independent. The rival empires launched numerous attacks on each other across that frontier between the 340s and 628. In

The mountains and plateaus of Iran proper formed the Sasanids' political hinterland, often ruled by the cousins of the shah (king) or by powerful nobles. Cities there were small walled communities that served more as military strongpoints than as centers of population and production. Society revolved around a local aristocracy that lived on rural estates and cultivated the arts of hunting, feasting, and war just like the noble warriors described in the sagas of ancient kings and heroes sung at their banquets.

Despite the dominance of powerful aristocratic families, long-lasting political fragmentation of the medieval European variety did not develop (see Chapter 10). Also, although many nomads lived in the mountain and desert regions, no folk migration took place comparable to that of the Germanic peoples who defeated Roman armies and established kingdoms in formerly Roman territory from about the third century C.E. onward. The Sasanid and Byzantine Empires successfully maintained central control of imperial finances and military power and found effective ways of integrating frontier peoples as mercenaries or caravaneers.

The Silk Road brought new products to Mesopotamia, some of which became part of the agricultural landscape. Sasanid farmers pioneered in planting cotton, sugar cane, rice, citrus trees, eggplants, and other crops adopted from India and China. Although the acreage devoted to new crops increased slowly, these products became important consumption and trade items during the succeeding Islamic period.

Sasanid Silver Vase   The Sasanid aristocracy, based in the countryside, invested part of its wealth in silver plates and vessels. The image is of the fertility goddess Anahita, a deity acceptable to the Zoroastrian faith. One inscription in Pahlavi (a Middle Persian language) gives the weight, 116.9 grams in modern terms, while another in Sogdian, a language common along the Silk Road, gives the owner's name, Mithrak.   (The State Heritage Museum, St Petersburg)

times of peace, however, exchange between the empires flourished, allowing goods transported over the Silk Road to enter the zone of Mediterranean trade.

The Arab pastoralists inhabiting the desert between Syria and Mesopotamia supplied camels and guides and played a significant role as merchants and organizers of caravans. The militarily efficient North Arabian camel saddle (see Chapter 8, Environment and Technology: Camel Saddles), developed around the third century B.C.E., provided another key to Arab prosperity. The Arabs used it to take control of the caravan trade in their territories and thereby became so important as suppliers of animal power even in agricultural districts that wheeled vehicles—mostly ox carts and horse-drawn chariots—had all but disappeared by the sixth century C.E.

Religion and Empire

The Sasanids established their Zoroastrian faith (see Chapter 5), which the Parthians had not particularly stressed, as a state religion similar to Christianity in the Byzantine Empire (see Chapter 10). The proclamation of Christianity and Zoroastrianism as official faiths marked the fresh emergence of religion as an instrument of politics both within and between the empires, setting a precedent for the subsequent rise of Islam as the focus of a political empire.

Both Zoroastrianism and Christianity practiced intolerance. A late-third-century inscription in Iran boasts of the persecutions of Christians, Jews, and Buddhists carried out by the Zoroastrian high priest. Yet sizable Christian and Jewish communities remained, especially in Mesopotamia. Similarly, from the fourth century onward, councils of Christian bishops declared many theological beliefs heretical—so unacceptable that they were un-Christian.

Christians became pawns in the political rivalry with the Byzantines and were sometimes persecuted, sometimes patronized by the Sasanid kings. In 431 a council of bishops called by the Byzantine emperor declared the Nestorian Christians heretics for overemphasizing the humanness of Christ. The Nestorians believed that human characteristics and divinity coexisted in Jesus and that Mary was not the mother of God, as many other Christians maintained, but the mother of the human Jesus. After the bishops' ruling, the Nestorians sought refuge under the Sasanid shah and eventually extended their missionary activities along the Central Asian trade routes.

In the third century a preacher named Mani had founded a new religion in Mesopotamia: Manichaeism. He preached a dualist faith—a struggle between Good and Evil—theologically derived from Zoroastrianism. Although at first Mani enjoyed the favor of the shah, he and many of his followers were martyred in 276. His religion survived and spread widely. Nestorian missionaries in Central Asia competed with Manichaean missionaries for converts. In later centuries, the term *Manichaean* was applied to all sorts of beliefs about a cosmic struggle between Good and Evil.

The Arabs became enmeshed in this web of religious conflict. The border protectors subsidized by the Byzantines adopted a Monophysite theology, which emphasized Christ's divine nature; the allies of the Sasanids, the Nestorian faith. Through them, knowledge of Christianity penetrated deeper into the Arabian peninsula during the fifth and sixth centuries.

Religion permeated all aspects of community life. Most subjects of the Byzantine emperors and Sasanid shahs identified themselves first and foremost as members of a religious community. Their schools and law courts were religious. They looked on priests, monks, rabbis, and the Zoroastrian mobads as moral guides in daily life. Most books discussed religious subjects. In some areas, religious leaders represented their flocks even in such secular matters as tax collection.

THE ORIGINS OF ISLAM

The Arabs who lived beyond the frontiers of the Sasanid Empire seldom interested the Sasanid rulers. But it was precisely in the interior of Arabia, far from the gaze and political reach of the Sasanid and Byzantine Empires, that the religion of Islam took form and inspired a movement that would humble the proud emperors.

The Arabian Peninsula Before Muhammad

Throughout history more people living on the Arabian peninsula have lived in settled communities than as pastoral nomads. The highlands of Yemen, fertile and abundantly watered by the spring monsoon, and the interior mountains farther east in southern Arabia have supported farming and village life. Small inlets along the southern coast favored occasional fishing or trading communities. However, the enormous sea of sand known as the "Empty Quarter" isolated these southern regions from the Arabian interior. In the seventh century, most people in southern Arabia knew more about Africa, India, and the Persian Gulf (see Chapter 8, Diversity and Dominance: "The Indian Ocean Trading World") than about the forbidding interior and the scattered camel- and sheep-herding nomads who lived there.

Exceptions to this pattern mostly involved caravan trading. Several kingdoms rose and fell in Yemen, leaving stone ruins and stone-cut inscriptions to testify to their bygone prosperity. From these commercial entrepôts came the aromatic resins frankincense and myrrh. Nomads derived income from providing camels, guides, and safe passage to merchants wanting to transport incense northward, where the fragrant substances had long been burned in religious rituals. Return caravans brought manufactured products from Mesopotamia and the Mediterranean.

Just as the Silk Road enabled small towns in Central Asia to become major trading centers, so the trans-Arabian trade gave rise to desert caravan cities. The earliest and most prosperous, Petra in southern Jordan and Palmyra in northern Syria, were swallowed up by Rome. This, coupled with an early Christian distaste for incense, which seemed too much a feature of pagan worship, contributed to a slackening of trade in Sasanid times. Nevertheless, trade across the desert did not lapse altogether. Camels, leather, and gold and other minerals mined in the mountains of western Arabia took the place of frankincense and myrrh as exports. This reduced trade kept alive the relations between the Arabs and the settled farming regions to the north, and it familiarized the Arabs who accompanied the caravans with the cultures and lifestyles of the Sasanid and Byzantine Empires.

In the desert, Semitic polytheism, with its worship of natural forces and celestial bodies, began to encounter other religions. Christianity, as practiced by Arabs in Jordan and southern Mesopotamia, and Judaism, possibly carried by refugees from the Roman expulsion of the Jews from their homeland in the first century C.E., made inroads on polytheism.

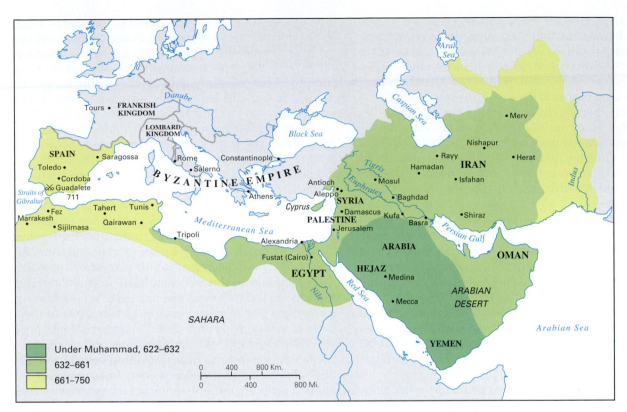

Map 9.1   Early Expansion of Muslim Rule   Arab conquests of the first Islamic century brought vast territory under Muslim rule, but conversion to Islam proceeded slowly. In most areas outside the Arabian peninsula, the only region where Arabic was then spoken, conversion did not accelerate until the third century after the conquest.

Mecca, a late-blooming caravan city, lies in a barren mountain valley halfway between Yemen and Syria and a short way inland from the Red Sea coast of Arabia (see Map 9.1). A nomadic kin group known as the Quraysh° settled in Mecca in the fifth century and assumed control of trade. Mecca rapidly achieved a measure of prosperity, partly because it was too far from Byzantine Syria, Sasanid Iraq, and Ethiopian-controlled Yemen for them to attack it.

A cubical shrine called the Ka'ba°, containing idols, a holy well called Zamzam, and a sacred precinct surrounding the two wherein killing was prohibited, contributed to the emergence of Mecca as a pilgrimage site. Some Meccans associated the shrine with stories known to Jews and Christians. They regarded Abraham (Ibrahim in Arabic) as the builder of the Ka'ba, and they identified a site outside Mecca as the location where God asked Abraham to sacrifice his son. The son was not Isaac

(Ishaq in Arabic), the son of Sarah, but Ishmael (Isma'il in Arabic), the son of Hagar, cited in the Bible as the forefather of the Arabs.

Muhammad in Mecca

Born in Mecca in 570, **Muhammad** grew up an orphan in the house of his uncle. He engaged in trade and married a Quraysh widow named Khadija°, whose caravan interests he superintended. Their son died in childhood, but several daughters survived. Around 610 Muhammad began meditating at night in the mountainous terrain around Mecca. During one night vigil, known to later tradition as the "Night of Power and Excellence," a being whom Muhammad later understood to be the angel Gabriel (Jibra'il in Arabic) spoke to him:

Quraysh (koo-RYYSH)   **Ka'ba** (KAH-buh)

Khadija (kah-DEE-juh)

Proclaim! In the name of your Lord who created.
Created man from a clot of congealed blood.
Proclaim! And your Lord is the Most Bountiful.
He who has taught by the pen.
Taught man that which he knew not.[1]

For three years he shared this and subsequent revelations only with close friends and family members. This period culminated in Muhammad's conviction that he was hearing the words of God (Allah° in Arabic). Khadija, his uncle's son Ali, his friend Abu Bakr°, and others close to him shared this conviction. The revelations continued until Muhammad's death in 632.

Like most people of the time, including Christians and Jews, the Arabs believed in unseen spirits: gods, desert spirits called *jinns*, demonic *shaitans*, and others. They further believed that certain individuals had contact with the spirit world, notably seers and poets, who were thought to be possessed by jinns. Therefore, when Muhammad began to recite his rhymed revelations in public, many people believed he was inspired by an unseen spirit even if it was not, as Muhammad asserted, the one true god.

Muhammad's earliest revelations called on people to witness that one god had created the universe and everything in it, including themselves. At the end of time, their souls would be judged, their sins balanced against their good deeds. The blameless would go to paradise; the sinful would taste hellfire:

By the night as it conceals the light;
By the day as it appears in glory;
By the mystery of the creation of male and female;
Verily, the ends ye strive for are diverse.
So he who gives in charity and fears God,
And in all sincerity testifies to the best,
We will indeed make smooth for him the path to Bliss.
But he who is a greedy miser and thinks himself
  self-sufficient,
And gives the lie to the best,
We will indeed make smooth for him the path to
  misery.[2]

The revelation called all people to submit to God and accept Muhammad as the last of his messengers. Doing so made one a **muslim,** meaning one who makes "submission," **Islam,** to the will of God.

Because earlier messengers mentioned in the revelations included Noah, Moses, and Jesus, Muhammad's hearers felt that his message resembled the Judaism and Christianity they were already somewhat familiar with. Yet his revelations charged the Jews and Christians with being negligent in preserving God's revealed word. Thus, even though they identified Abraham/Ibrahim, whom Muslims consider the first Muslim, as the builder of the Ka'ba, which superseded Jerusalem as the focus of Muslim prayer in 624, Muhammad's followers considered his revelation more perfect than the Bible because it had not gone through an editing process.

Some non-Muslim scholars maintain that Muhammad's revelations appealed especially to people distressed over wealth replacing kinship as the most important aspect of social relations. They see verses criticizing taking pride in money and neglecting obligations to orphans and other powerless people as conveying a message of social reform. Other scholars, along with most Muslims, put less emphasis on a social message and stress the power and beauty of Muhammad's revelations. Forceful rhetoric and poetic vision, coming in the Muslim view directly from God, go far to explain Muhammad's early success.

The Formation of the Umma

Mecca's leaders feared that accepting Muhammad as the sole agent of the one true God would threaten their power and prosperity. They pressured his kin to disavow him and persecuted the weakest of his followers. Stymied by this hostility, Muhammad and his followers fled Mecca in 622 to take up residence in the agricultural community of **Medina** 215 miles (346 kilometers) to the north. This hijra° marks the beginning of the Muslim calendar.

Prior to the hijra, Medinan representatives had met with Muhammad and agreed to accept and protect him and his followers because they saw him as an inspired leader who could calm their perpetual feuding. Together, the Meccan migrants and major groups in Medina bound themselves into a single **umma°,** a community defined solely by acceptance of Islam and of Muhammad as the "Messenger of God," his most common title. Three Jewish kin groups chose to retain their own faith, thus contributing to the Muslims' changing the direction of their prayer toward the Ka'ba, now thought of as the "House of God."

During the last decade of his life, Muhammad took active responsibility for his umma. Having left their Meccan kin groups, the immigrants in Medina felt vulnerable. Fresh revelations provided a framework for regulating social and legal affairs and stirred the Muslims to fight against the still-unbelieving city of Mecca. Sporadic war, largely conducted by raiding and negotiation with

---

Allah (AH-luh)   **Abu Bakr** (ah-boo BAK-uhr)

hijra (HIJ-ruh)   **umma** (UM-muh)

desert nomads, sapped Mecca's strength and convinced many Meccans that God favored Muhammad. In 630 Mecca surrendered. Muhammad and his followers made the pilgrimage to the Ka'ba unhindered.

Muhammad did not return to Mecca again. Medina had grown into a bustling city-state. He had charged the Jewish kin groups with disloyalty at various points during the war and had expelled or eliminated them. Delegations from all over Arabia came to meet Muhammad, and he sent emissaries back with them to teach about Islam and collect their alms. Muhammad's mission to bring God's message to humanity had brought him unchallenged control of a state that was coming to dominate the Arabian peninsula. But the supremacy of the Medinan state, unlike preceding short-lived nomadic kingdoms, depended not on kinship but on a common faith in a single god.

In 632, after a brief illness, Muhammad died. Within twenty-four hours a group of Medinan leaders, along with three of Muhammad's close friends, determined that Abu Bakr, one of the earliest believers and the father of Muhammad's favorite wife A'isha°, should succeed him. They called him the *khalifa*°, or "successor," the English version of which is *caliph*. But calling Abu Bakr a successor did not clarify his powers. Everyone knew that neither Abu Bakr nor anyone else could receive revelations, and they likewise knew that Muhammad's revelations made no provision for succession or for any government purpose beyond maintaining the umma. Indeed, some people thought the world would soon end because God's last messenger was dead.

Abu Bakr continued and confirmed Muhammad's religious practices, notably the so-called Five Pillars of Islam: (1) avowal that there is only one god and Muhammad is his messenger, (2) prayer five times a day, (3) fasting during the lunar month of Ramadan, (4) paying alms, and (5) making the pilgrimage to Mecca at least once during one's lifetime. He also reestablished and expanded Muslim authority over Arabia's nomadic and settled communities. After Muhammad's death, some had abandoned their allegiance to Medina or followed various would-be prophets. Muslim armies fought hard to confirm the authority of the newborn **caliphate.** In the process, some fighting spilled over into non-Arab areas in Iraq.

Abu Bakr ordered those who had acted as secretaries for Muhammad to organize the Prophet's revelations into a book. Hitherto written haphazardly on pieces of leather or bone, the verses of revelation became a single document gathered into chapters. This resulting book, which Muslims believe acquired its final form around the year 650, was called the **Quran°,** or the Recitation. Muslims regard it not as the words of Muhammad but as the unalterable word of God. As such, it compares not so much to the Bible, a book written by many hands over many centuries, as to the person of Jesus Christ, whom Christians consider a human manifestation of God.

Though united in its acceptance of God's will, the umma soon disagreed over the succession to the caliphate. The first civil war in Islam followed the assassination of the third caliph, Uthman°, in 656. To succeed him, his assassins, rebels from the army, nominated Ali, Muhammad's first cousin and the husband of his daughter Fatima. Ali had been passed over three times previously, even though many people considered him to be the Prophet's natural heir. As mentioned previously, Ali and his supporters felt that Muhammad had indicated as much at Ghadir al-Khumm.

When Ali accepted the nomination to be caliph, two of Muhammad's close companions and his favorite wife A'isha challenged him. Ali defeated them in the Battle of the Camel (656), so called because the fighting raged around the camel on which A'isha was seated in an enclosed woman's saddle.

After the battle, the governor of Syria, Mu'awiya°, a kinsman of the slain Uthman from the Umayya clan of the Quraysh, renewed the challenge. Inconclusive battle gave way to arbitration. The arbitrators decided that Uthman, whom his assassins considered corrupt, had not deserved death and that Ali had erred in accepting the nomination. Ali rejected the arbitrators' findings, but before he could resume fighting, one of his own supporters killed him for agreeing to the arbitration. Mu'awiya then offered Ali's son Hasan a dignified retirement and thus emerged as caliph in 661.

Mu'awiya chose his own son, Yazid, to succeed him, thereby instituting the **Umayyad° Caliphate.** When Hasan's brother Husayn revolted in 680 to reestablish the right of Ali's family to rule, Yazid ordered Husayn and his family killed. Sympathy for Husayn's martyrdom helped transform Shi'ism from a political movement into a religious sect.

Several variations in Shi'ite belief developed, but Shi'ites have always agreed that Ali was the rightful successor to Muhammad and that God's choice as Imam, leader of the Muslim community, has always been one or another of Ali's descendants. They see the office of caliph as more secular than religious. Because the Shi'ites seldom held power, their religious feelings came to focus on

---

A'isha (AH-ee-shah)   khalifa (kah-LEE-fuh)

Quran (kuh-RAHN)   **Uthman** (ooth-MAHN)
Mu'awiya (moo-AH-we-yuh)   **Umayyad** (oo-MY-ad)

outpourings of sympathy for Husayn and other martyrs and on messianic dreams that one of their Imams would someday triumph.

Those Muslims who supported the first three caliphs gradually came to be called "People of Tradition and Community"—in Arabic, *Ahl al-Sunna wa'l-Jama'a*, Sunnis for short. Sunnis consider the caliphs to be Imams. As for Ali's followers who had abhorred his acceptance of arbitration, they evolved into small and rebellious Kharijite sects (from *kharaja* meaning "to secede or rebel") claiming righteousness for themselves alone. These three divisions of Islam, the last now quite minor, still survive. Today the umma numbers more than a billion people.

THE RISE AND FALL OF THE CALIPHATE, 632–1258

The Islamic caliphate built on the conquests the Arabs carried out after Muhammad's death gave birth to a dynamic and creative religious society. By the late 800s, however, one piece after another of this huge realm broke away. Yet the idea of a caliphate, however unrealistic it became, remained a touchstone of Sunni belief in the unity of the umma.

Sunni Islam never gave a single person the power to define true belief, expel heretics, and discipline clergy. Thus, unlike Christian popes and patriarchs, the caliphs had little basis for reestablishing their universal authority once they lost political and military power.

The Islamic Conquests, 634–711

Arab conquests outside Arabia began under the second caliph, Umar (r. 634–644), possibly prompted by earlier forays into Iraq. Arab armies wrenched Syria (636) and Egypt (639–642) away from the Byzantine Empire and defeated the last Sasanid shah, Yazdigird III (r. 632–651) (see Map 9.1). After a decade-long lull, expansion began again. Tunisia fell and became the governing center from which was organized, in 711, the conquest of Spain by an Arab-led army mostly composed of Berbers from North Africa. In the same year, Sind—the southern Indus Valley and westernmost region of India—succumbed to partially seaborne invaders from Iraq. The Muslim dominion remained roughly stable for the next three centuries. In the eleventh century, conquest began anew in India, Anatolia, and sub-Saharan Africa. Islam also expanded peacefully by trade in these and other areas both before and after the year 1000.

The speed and political cohesiveness of the Arab campaigns distinguishes them from the piecemeal incursions of the Germanic peoples into the Roman Empire (see Chapter 10). The close Meccan companions of the Prophet, men of political and economic sophistication inspired by his charisma, guided the conquests. The social structure and hardy nature of Arab society lent itself to flexible military operations; and the authority of Medina, reconfirmed during the caliphate of Abu Bakr, ensured obedience.

The decision made during Umar's caliphate to prohibit Arabs from taking over conquered territory for their own use proved important. Umar tied army service, with its regular pay and occasional windfalls of booty, to residence in large military camps—two in Iraq (Kufa and Basra), one in Egypt (Fustat), and one in Tunisia (Qairawan). East of Iraq, Arabs settled around small garrison towns at strategic locations and in one large garrison at Marv in present-day Turkmenistan. Down to the early eighth century, this policy kept the armies together and ready for action and preserved life in the countryside, where some three-fourths of the population lived, virtually unchanged. Most people who became subjects of the caliphate by conquest probably never saw an Arab, and only a tiny proportion in Syria, Egypt, and Iraq understood the Arabic language.

The million or so Arabs who participated in the conquests over several generations constituted a small, self-isolated ruling minority living on the taxes paid by a vastly larger non-Arab, non-Muslim subject population. The Arabs had little material incentive to encourage conversion, and there is no evidence of coherent missionary efforts to spread Islam during the conquest period.

The Umayyad and Early Abbasid Caliphates, 661–850

The Umayyad caliphs presided over an ethnically defined Arab realm rather than a religious empire. Ruling from Damascus, their armies consisted almost entirely of Muslim Arabs. They adopted and adapted the administrative practices of their Sasanid and Byzantine predecessors, as had the caliphs who preceded them. Only gradually did they replace non-Muslim secretaries and tax officials with Muslims and introduce Arabic as the language of government. The introduction of distinctively Muslim silver and gold coins early in the eighth century symbolized the new order. From that time on, silver dirhams and gold dinars bearing Arabic religious phrases circulated in monetary exchanges from Morocco to the frontiers of China.

The Umayyad dynasty fell in 750 after a decade of growing unrest. Converts to Islam, by that date no more than 10 percent of the indigenous population, were numerically significant because of the comparatively small number of Arab warriors. They resented not achieving equal status with the Arabs. The Arabs of Iraq and elsewhere envied the Syrian Arab influence in caliphal affairs. Pious Muslims looked askance at the secular and even irreligious behavior of the caliphs. Shi'ites and Kharijites attacked the Umayyad family's legitimacy as rulers, launching a number of rebellions.

In 750 one such rebellion, in the region of Khurasan° in what is today northeastern Iran, Turkmenistan, and northwestern Afghanistan, overthrew the last Umayyad caliph, though one family member escaped to Spain and founded an Umayyad principality there in 755. Many Shi'ites supported the rebellion, thinking they were fighting for the family of Ali. As it turned out, the family of Abbas, one of Muhammad's uncles, controlled the secret organization that coordinated the revolt. Upon victory they established the **Abbasid° Caliphate.** Some of the Abbasid caliphs who ruled after 750 befriended their relatives in Ali's family, and one even flirted with transferring the caliphate to them. The Abbasid family, however, held on to the caliphate until 1258, when Mongol invaders killed the last of them in Baghdad (see Chapter 13).

At its outset the Abbasid dynasty made a fine show of leadership and concern for Islam. Theology and religious law became preoccupations at court and among a growing community of scholars, along with interpretation of the Quran, collecting the sayings of the Prophet, and Arabic grammar. (In recent years, some western scholars have maintained that the Quran, the sayings of the Prophet, and the biography of the Prophet were all composed around this time and do not reflect historical fact. This radical reinterpretation of Islamic origins has not been generally accepted in either the scholarly community or among Muslims.) Some caliphs fought on the Byzantine frontier to extend Islam. Others sponsored ambitious projects to translate the great works of Greek, Persian, and Indian thought into Arabic.

At the same time, the new dynasty, with its roots among the semi-Persianized Arabs of Khurasan, gradually adopted the ceremonies and customs of the Sasanid shahs. Government grew increasingly complex in Baghdad, the newly built capital city on the Tigris River. As more and more non-Arabs converted to Islam, the ruling elite became more cosmopolitan. Greek, Iranian, Central Asian, and African cultural currents met in the capital and gave rise to an abundance of literary works, a process facilitated by the introduction of papermaking from China. Arab poets neglected the traditional odes extolling life in the desert and wrote instead wine songs (despite Islam's prohibition of alcohol) or poems in praise of their patrons.

The translation of Aristotle into Arabic, the founding of the main currents of theology and law, and the splendor of the Abbasid court—reflected in stories of *The Arabian Nights* set in the time of the caliph Harun al-Rashid° (r. 776–809)—in some respects warrant calling the early Abbasid period a "golden age." Yet the refinement of Baghdad culture only slowly made its way into the provinces. Egypt remained predominantly Christian and Coptic-speaking in the early Abbasid period. Iran never adopted Arabic as a spoken tongue. Berber-speaking North Africa freed itself almost entirely of caliphal rule: Morocco and Algeria through Kharijite revolts in 740, Tunisia after 800 by agreeing to pay regular tribute to Baghdad.

Gradual conversion to Islam among the conquered population accelerated in the second quarter of the ninth century. Social discrimination against non-Arab converts gradually faded, and the Arabs themselves—at least those living in cosmopolitan urban settings—lost their previously strong attachment to kinship and ethnic identity.

Political Fragmentation, 850–1050

Abbasid decline became evident in the second half of the ninth century as the conversion to Islam accelerated (see Map 9.2). No government ruling an empire stretching almost a quarter of the way around the world could hold power easily. Caravans traveled only 20 miles (32 kilometers) a day, and the couriers of the caliphal post system usually did not exceed 100 miles (160 kilometers) a day. News of frontier revolts took weeks to reach Baghdad. Military responses might take months. Administrators struggled to centralize tax payments, often made in grain or other produce rather than cash, and ensure that provincial governors forwarded the proper amounts to Baghdad.

The first Arab garrisons had been strung like beads across territory populated mostly by non-Muslims; revolts against Arab rule had been a concern. Members of the Muslim umma had had every reason to cling together, despite the long distances. But with the growing conversion of the population to Islam, the idea that Islam might disappear faded. Muslims became an over-

---

Khurasan (kor-uh-SAHN) **Abbasid** (ah-BASS-id)

Harun al-Rashid (hah-ROON al–rah-SHEED)

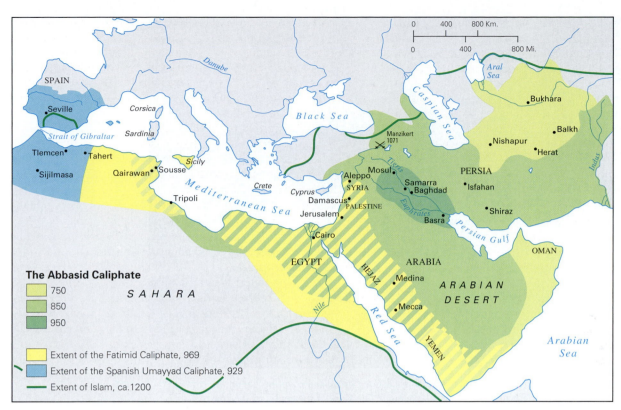

Map 9.2   Rise and Fall of the Abbasid Caliphate   Though Abbasid rulers occupied the caliphal seat in Iraq from 750 to 1258, when Mongol armies destroyed Baghdad, real political power waned sharply and steadily after 850. The rival caliphates of the Fatimids (909–1171) and Spanish Umayyads (929–976) were comparatively short-lived.

whelming majority and gradually realized that a highly centralized empire with a rich and splendid capital did not necessarily serve the interests of all the people.

Eighth-century revolts had often targeted Arab or Muslim domination. By the middle of the ninth century, this type of rebellion gave way to movements within the Islamic community that concentrated on seizure of territory and formation of principalities. None of the states carved out of the Abbasid Caliphate after 850 repudiated or even threatened Islam. They did, however, prevent tax revenues from flowing to Baghdad, thereby increasing local prosperity. Local Muslim communities either supported such rebels or remained neutral.

Increasingly starved for funds by breakaway provinces and by an unexplained fall in revenues from Iraq itself, the caliphate experienced a crisis in the late ninth century. Distrusting generals and troops from outlying areas, the caliphs purchased Turkic slaves, **mamluks°,** from Cen-

tral Asia and established them as a standing army. Well trained and hardy, the Turks proved an effective but expensive military force. When the government could not pay them, the mamluks took it on themselves to seat and unseat caliphs, a process made easier by the construction of a new capital at Samarra, north of Baghdad on the Tigris River.

The Turks dominated Samarra without interference from an unruly Baghdad populace that regarded them as rude and highhanded. However, the money and effort that went into the huge city, which was occupied only from 835 to 892, further sapped the caliphs' financial strength and deflected labor from more productive pursuits.

In 945, after several attempts to find a strongman to reform government administration and restore military power, the Abbasid Caliphate fell under the control of rude mountain warriors from the province of Daylam in northern Iran. Led by the Shi'ite Buyid° family, they

---

mamluk (MAM-luke)

Buyid (BOO-yid)

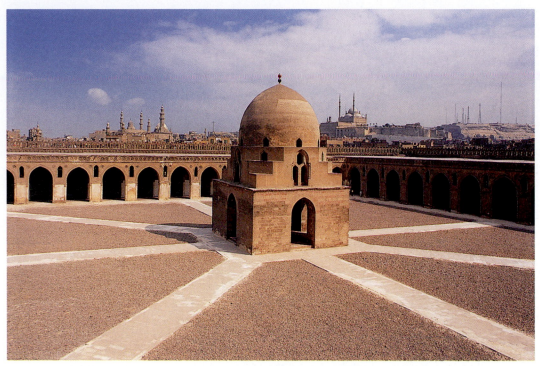

Mosque of Ibn Tulun in Fustat   Completed in 877, this mosque symbolized Egypt becoming for the first time a quasi-independent province under its governor. The kiosk in the center of the court-yard contains fountains for washing before prayer. Before its restoration in the thirteenth century, the mosque had a spiral minaret and a door to an adjoining governor's palace. (Ellen Rooney/Robert Harding Picture Library)

conquered western Iran as well as Iraq. Each Buyid commander ruled his own principality. After almost two centuries of glory, the sun began to set on Baghdad. The Abbasid caliph remained, but the Buyid princes controlled him. Being Shi'ites, the Buyids had no special reverence for the Sunni caliph. According to their particular Shi'ite sect, the twelfth and last divinely appointed Imam had disappeared around 873 and would return as a messiah only at the end of the world. Thus they had no Shi'ite Imam to defer to and retained the caliph only to help control their predominantly Sunni subjects.

Dynamic growth in outlying provinces paralleled the caliphate's gradual loss of temporal power. In the east in 875, the dynasty of the Samanids°, one of several Iranian families to achieve independence, established a glittering court in Bukhara, a major city on the Silk Road (see Map 9.2). Samanid princes patronized literature and learning, but the language they favored was Persian

written in Arabic letters. For the first time, a non-Arabic literature rose to challenge the eminence of Arabic within the Islamic world. The new Persian poetry and prose foreshadowed the situation today, in which Iran sharply distinguishes itself from the Arab world.

In Egypt a Shi'ite ruler established himself as a rival caliph in 969, culminating a sixty-year struggle by his family, the Fatimids°, to extend their power beyond an initial base in Tunisia. His governing complex outside the old conquest-era garrison city of Fustat° was named Cairo. For the first time Egypt became a major cultural, intellectual, and political center of Islam (see Map 9.2). The al-Azhar Mosque built at this time remains a paramount religious and educational center to this day. Shi'ite religious influence in Sunni Egypt remained slight even after two centuries of Fatimid rule. Nevertheless, the abundance of Fatimid gold coinage, derived from West African sources, made them an economic power in the Mediterranean.

Samanid (sah-MAN-id)

Fatimid (FAT-uh-mid)   **Fustat** (fuss-TAHT)

Cut off from the rest of the Islamic world by the Strait of Gibraltar and, from 740 onward, by independent city-states in Morocco and Algeria, Umayyad Spain developed a distinctive Islamic culture blending Roman, Germanic, and Jewish traditions with those of the Arabs and Berbers (see Map 9.1). Historians disagree on how rapidly and completely the Spanish population converted to Islam. If we assume a process similar to that in the eastern regions, it seems likely that the most rapid surge in Islamization occurred in the middle of the tenth century.

As in the east, governing cities symbolized the Islamic presence in al-Andalus, as the Muslims called their Iberian territories. Cordoba, Seville, Toledo, and other cities grew substantially, becoming much larger and richer than contemporary cities in neighboring France. Converts to Islam and their descendants, unconverted Arabic-speaking Christians, and Jews joined with the comparatively few descendants of Arab settlers to create new architectural and literary styles. In the countryside, where the Berbers preferred to settle, a fusion of pre-existing agricultural technologies with new crops, notably citrus fruits, and irrigation techniques from the east gave Spain the most diverse and sophisticated agricultural economy in Europe.

The rulers of al-Andalus took the title *caliph* only in 929, when Abd al-Rahman° III (r. 912–961) did so in response to a similar declaration by the newly established (909) Fatimid ruler in Tunisia. By the century's end, however, this caliphate encountered challenges from breakaway movements that eventually splintered al-Andalus into a number of small states. Political decay did not impede cultural growth. Some of the greatest writers and thinkers in Jewish history worked in Muslim Spain in the eleventh and twelfth centuries, sometimes writing in Arabic, sometimes in Hebrew. Judah Halevi (1075–1141) composed exquisite poetry and explored questions of religious philosophy. Maimonides (1135–1204) made a major compilation of Judaic law and expounded on Aristotelian philosophy. At the same time, Islamic thought in Spain attained its loftiest peaks in Ibn Hazm's (994–1064) treatises on love and other subjects, the Aristotelian philosophical writings of Ibn Rushd° (1126–1198, known in Latin as Averroës°) and Ibn Tufayl° (d. 1185), and the mystic speculations of Ibn al-Arabi° (1165–1240). Christians, too, shared in the intellectual and cultural dynamism of al-Andalus. Translations from Arabic to Latin made during this period

Tomb of the Samanids in Bukhara   This early-tenth-century structure has the basic layout of a Zoroastrian fire temple: a dome on top of a cube. However, geometic ornamentation in baked brick marks it as an early masterpiece of Islamic architecture. The Samanid family achieved independence as rulers of northeastern Iran and western Central Asia in the tenth century. (Art Resource, NY)

had a profound effect on the later intellectual development of western Europe (see Chapter 10).

The Samanids, Fatimids, and Spanish Umayyads, three of many regional principalities, represent the political diversity and awakening of local awareness that coincided with Abbasid decline. Yet drawing and redrawing political boundaries did not result in the rigid division of the Islamic world into kingdoms, as was then occurring in Europe. Religious and cultural developments, particularly the rise in cities of a social group of religious scholars known as the **ulama**°—Arabic for "people with (religious) knowledge"—worked against any permanent division of the Islamic umma.

Assault from Within and Without, 1050–1258

The role played by Turkish mamluks in the decline of Abbasid power established an enduring stereotype of the Turk as a ferocious warrior little interested in religion or urban

---

Abd al-Rahman (AHB-d al–ruh-MAHN)   **Ibn Rushd** (IB-uhn RUSHED)   **Averroës** (uh-VERR-oh-eez)   **Ibn Tufayl** (IB-uhn too-FILE)   **Ibn al-Arabi** (IB-uhn ahl-AH-rah-bee)

ulama (oo-leh-MAH)

Spanish Muslim Textile of the Twelfth Century   This fragment of woven silk, featuring peacocks and Arabic writing, is one of the finest examples of Islamic weaving. The cotton industry flourished in the early Islamic centuries, but silk remained a highly valued product. Some fabrics were treasured in Christian Europe. (Victoria & Albert Museum)

sophistication. This image gained strength in the 1030s when the Seljuk° family established a Turkish Muslim state based on nomadic power. Taking the Arabic title *Sultan,* meaning "power," and the revived Persian title *Shahan-shah,* or King of Kings, the Seljuk ruler Tughril° Beg created a kingdom that stretched from northern Afghanistan to Baghdad, which he occupied in 1055. After a century under the thumb of the Shi'ite Buyids, the Abbasid caliph breathed easier under the slightly lighter thumb of the Sunni Turks. The Seljuks pressed on into Syria and Anatolia, administering a lethal blow to Byzantine power at the Battle of Manzikert° in 1071. The

Seljuk (sel-JOOK)   Tughril (TUUG-ruhl)
Manzikert (MANZ-ih-kuhrt)

Byzantine army fell back on Constantinople, leaving Anatolia open to Turkish occupation.

Under Turkish rule, cities shrank as pastoralists overran their agricultural hinterlands, already short on labor because of migration to the cities. Irrigation works suffered from lack of maintenance in the unsettled countryside. Tax revenues fell. Twelfth-century Seljuk princes contesting for power fought over cities, but few Turks participated in urban cultural and religious life. The gulf between a religiously based urban society and the culture and personnel of the government deepened. When factional riots broke out between Sunnis and Shi'ites, or between rival schools of Sunni law, rulers generally remained aloof, even as destruction and loss of life mounted. Similarly, when princes fought for the title *sultan,* religious leaders advised citizens to remain neutral.

By the early twelfth century, unrepaired damage from floods, fires, and civil disorder had reduced old Baghdad on the west side of the Tigris to ruins. The caliphs took advantage of fighting among the Seljuks to regain some power locally and built a wall around the palace precinct on the east side of the river. Nevertheless, the heart of the city died, not to regain prosperity until the twentieth century. The withering of Baghdad reflected a broader environmental problem: the collapse of the canal system on which agriculture in the Tigris and Euphrates Valley depended. For millennia a center of world civilization, Mesopotamia underwent substantial population loss and never again regained its geographical importance.

The Turks alone cannot be blamed for the demographic and economic misfortunes of Iran and Iraq. Too-robust urbanization had strained food resources, and political fragmentation had dissipated revenues. The growing practice of using land grants to pay soldiers and courtiers also played a role. When absentee grant holders used agents to collect taxes, the agents tended to gouge villagers and take little interest in improving production, all of which weakened the agricultural base of the economy.

The Seljuk Empire was beset by internal quarrels when the first crusading armies of Christians reached the Holy Land. The First Crusade captured Jerusalem in 1099 (see Chapter 10). Though charged with the stuff of romance, the Crusades had little lasting impact on the Islamic lands. The four crusader principalities of Edessa, Antioch, Tripoli, and Jerusalem simply became pawns in the shifting pattern of politics already in place. Newly arrived knights eagerly attacked the Muslim enemy, whom they called "Saracens°;" but veteran crusaders, including

Saracen (SAR-uh-suhn)

the religious orders of the Knights of the Temple (Templars) and the Knights of the Hospital of St. John (Hospitallers), recognized that diplomacy and seeking partners of convenience among rival Muslim princes offered a sounder strategy.

The Muslims finally unified to face the European enemy in the mid-twelfth century. Nur al-Din ibn Zangi° established a strong state based in Damascus and sent an army to terminate the Fatimid Caliphate in Egypt. A nephew of the Kurdish commander of that expedition, Salah-al-Din, known in the West as Saladin, took advantage of Nur al-Din's timely death to seize power and unify Egypt and Syria. The Fatimid dynasty fell in 1171. In 1187 Saladin recaptured Jerusalem from the Europeans.

Saladin's descendants fought off subsequent Crusades. After one such battle, however, in 1250, Turkish mamluk troops seized control of the government in Cairo, ending Saladin's dynasty. In 1260 these mamluks rode east to confront a new invading force. At the Battle of Ain Jalut° (Spring of Goliath) in Syria, they met and defeated an army of Mongols from Central Asia (see Chapter 13), thus stemming an invasion that had begun several decades before and legitimizing their claim to dominion over Egypt and Syria.

A succession of Mamluk sultans ruled Egypt and Syria until 1517. In Abbasid times, *mamluk* was a term used for military slaves; the Mamluks who established an empire in Egypt and Syria in 1250 used the name "Mamluk" for their regime and their ruling class. Fear of new Mongol attacks receded after 1300, but by then the new ruling system had become fixed. Young Turkish or Circassian slaves, the latter from Georgia and other parts of the Caucasus region, were imported from non-Muslim lands, raised in military training barracks, and converted to Islam. Owing loyalty to the Mamluk officers who purchased them and also to their barracks mates, they formed a military ruling class that was socially disconnected from the Arabic-speaking native population.

The Mongol invasions, especially their destruction of the Abbasid Caliphate in Baghdad in 1258, shocked the world of Islam. The Mamluk sultan placed a relative of the last Baghdad caliph on a caliphal throne in Cairo, but the Egyptian Abbasids were never more than puppets serving Mamluk interests. In the Muslim lands from Iraq eastward, non-Muslim rule lasted for much of the thirteenth century. Although the Mongols left few ethnic or linguistic traces in these lands, their initial destruction of cities and slaughter of civilian populations, their diversion of Silk Road trade from the traditional route

terminating in Baghdad to more northerly routes ending at ports on the Black Sea, and their casual disregard, even after their conversion to Islam, of Muslim religious life and urban culture, hastened currents of change already under way.

ISLAMIC CIVILIZATION

Though increasingly unsettled in its political dimension and subject to economic disruptions caused by war, the ever-expanding Islamic world underwent a fruitful evolution in law, social structure, and religious expression. Religious conversion and urbanization reinforced each other to create a distinct Islamic civilization. The immense geographical and human diversity of the Muslim lands allowed many "small traditions" to coexist with the developing "great tradition" of Islam.

Law and Dogma

The Shari'a, the law of Islam, provides the foundation of Islamic civilization. Yet aside from certain Quranic verses conveying specific divine ordinances—most pertaining to personal and family matters—Islam had no legal system in the time of Muhammad. Arab custom and the Prophet's own authority offered the only guidance. After Muhammad died, the umma tried to follow his example. This became harder and harder to do, however, as those who knew Muhammad best passed away, and many Arabs found themselves living in far-off lands. Non-Arab converts to Islam, who at first tried to follow Arab customs they had little familiarity with, had an even harder time.

Islam slowly developed laws to govern social and religious life. The full sense of Islamic civilization, however, goes well beyond the basic Five Pillars mentioned earlier. Some Muslim thinkers felt that the reasoned consideration of a mature man—women had little voice in religious matters—offered the best resolution of issues not covered by Quranic revelation. Others argued for the sunna, or tradition, of the Prophet as the best guide. To understand that sunna they collected and studied the thousands of reports, called **hadith°**, purporting to convey the precise words or deeds of Muhammad. It gradually became customary to precede each hadith with a statement indicating whom the speaker had heard it from, whom that person had heard it from, and so on, back to the Prophet personally.

Nur al-Din ibn Zangi (NOOR-al-DEEN ib-uhn ZAN-gee)
Ain Jalut (ine jah-LOOT)

hadith (hah-DEETH)

Scholarly Life in Medieval Islam   Books being scarce and expensive, teachers dictated to their students, as shown on the right. Notice that the student is writing on a single sheet of paper while the scholar in the center holds an entire book. On the left, an author presents his work to a wealthy patron. (Bibliothèque nationale de France)

Many hadith dealt with ritual matters, such as how to wash before prayer. Others provided answers to legal questions not covered by Quranic revelation or suggested principles for deciding such matters. By the eleventh century most legal thinkers had accepted the idea that Muhammad's personal behavior provided the best model for Muslim behavior, and that the hadith constituted the most authoritative basis for Islamic law after the Quran itself.

Yet the hadith themselves posed a problem because the tens of thousands of anecdotes included not only genuine reports about the Prophet but also invented ones, politically motivated ones, and stories derived from non-Muslim religious traditions. Only a specialist could hope to separate a sound from a weak tradition. As the hadith grew in importance, so did the branch of learning devoted to their analysis. Scholars discarded thousands for having weak chains of authority. The most reliable they collected into books that gradually achieved authoritative status. Sunnis placed six books in this category; Shi'ites, four. The Shari'a grew over centuries, incorporating the ideas of many legal scholars as well as the implications of thousands of hadith.

The Shari'a embodies a vision of an umma in which all Muslims subscribe to the same moral values. In this vision, political or ethnic divisions lose importance, for the Shari'a expects every Muslim ruler to abide by and enforce the religious law. In practice, this expectation often lost out in the hurly-burly of political life. Even so, it proved an important basis for an urban lifestyle that varied surprisingly little from Morocco to India.

Converts and Cities

Conversion to Islam, more the outcome of people's learning about the new rulers' religion than an escape from the tax on non-Muslims, as some scholars have suggested, helped spur urbanization. Conversion did not require extensive knowledge of the faith. To become a Muslim, a person recited, in the presence of a Muslim, the profession of faith in Arabic: "There is no God but God, and Muhammad is the Messenger of God."

Few converts knew Arabic, and fewer could read the Quran. Many converts knew no more of the Quran than the verses necessary for their daily prayers. Muhammad had established no priesthood to define and spread the faith. Thus new converts, whether Arab or non-Arab, faced the problem of finding out for themselves what Islam was about and how they should act as Muslims.

Spending time with Muslims, learning their language, and imitating their behavior proved the best way to solve this problem. In many areas, this meant migrating to an Arab governing center. The alternative, converting to Is-

lam but remaining in one's home community, posed a problem. Before the emergence of Islam, religion had developed into the main component of social identity in the Byzantine and Sasanid Empires. Converts to Islam thus encountered discrimination if they went on living within their Christian, Jewish, or Zoroastrian communities. Again, migration afforded a solution, and the economic opportunities opened up by tax revenues flowing into the Arab governing centers made it more attractive.

The large Arab military settlements of Kufa and Basra in Iraq blossomed into cities and became important centers for Muslim cultural activities. As conversion rapidly spread in the mid-ninth century, urbanization also increased in other regions, most visibly in Iran, where most cities previously had been quite small. Nishapur in the northeast grew from fewer than 10,000 pre-Islamic inhabitants to between 100,000 and 200,000 by the year 1000. Other Iranian cities experienced similar growth. In Iraq, Baghdad and Mosul joined Kufa and Basra as major cities. In Syria, Aleppo and Damascus flourished under Muslim rule. New districts added to Fustat—the final one in 969 named Cairo—created one of the largest and greatest of the Islamic cities. The primarily Christian patriarchal cities of Jerusalem, Antioch, and Alexandria, not being Muslim governing centers, shrank and stagnated.

The cities became heavily Muslim before the countryside. Muhammad and his first followers had lived in a commercial city, and Islam acquired a peculiarly urban character very different from that of medieval European Christendom. Mosques in large cities served both as ritual centers and as places for learning and social activities.

Islam colored all aspects of urban social life (see Diversity and Dominance: Beggars, Con Men, and Singing-girls). Without religious officials to instruct them, the new Muslims imitated Arab dress and customs and emulated people they regarded as particularly pious. Inevitably, in the absence of a central religious authority comparable to a pope, local variations developed in the way people practiced Islam and in the hadith they attributed to the Prophet. This gave the rapidly growing religion the flexibility to accommodate many different social situations. Since the profession of faith called only for the acknowledgment of God's unity and Muhammad's prophethood, Islam escaped most of the severe conflicts over heresy that beset Christianity at a comparable stage of development.

By the tenth century, urban growth was affecting the countryside by expanding the consumer market. Citrus fruits, rice, and sugar cane increased in acreage and spread to new areas. Cotton became a major crop in Iran and elsewhere and supplied a diverse and profitable textile industry. Irrigation works expanded. Diet diversified. Abundant coinage made for a lively economy. Intercity and long-distance trade flourished, providing regular links between isolated districts and integrating the pastoral nomads, who provided pack animals, into the region's economy. Manufacturing expanded as well, particularly the production of cloth, metal goods, and pottery. Urban economies grew under the strong influence of Islamic ethics and law, overseen by religiously sanctioned market inspectors.

Science and technology also flourished (see Environment and Technology: Automata). Building on Hellenistic traditions and their own observations and experience, Muslim doctors and astronomers developed skills and theories far in advance of their European counterparts. Working in Egypt in the eleventh century, the mathematician and physicist Ibn al-Haytham° wrote more than a hundred works. Among other things, he determined that the Milky Way lies far beyond earth's atmosphere, proved that light travels from a seen object to the eye and not the reverse, and explained why the sun and moon appear larger on the horizon than overhead.

Islam, Women, and Slaves

Women seldom traveled. Those living in rural areas worked in the fields and tended animals. Urban women, particularly members of the elite, lived in seclusion and did not leave their homes without covering themselves completely. Seclusion of women in their houses and veiling in public already existed in Byzantine and Sasanid times. Through interpretation of specific verses from the Quran, these practices now became fixtures of Muslim social life. Although women sometimes studied and became literate, they did so away from the gaze of men who were not related to them. Although women played influential roles within the family, any public role had to be indirect, through their husbands. Only slave women could perform before unrelated men as musicians and dancers. A man could have sexual relations with as many slave concubines as he pleased, in addition to marrying as many as four wives.

Muslim women fared better legally under Islamic law than did Christian and Jewish women under their respective religious codes. Muslim women could own property and retain it in marriage. They could remarry if their husbands divorced them, and they received a cash payment upon divorce. Although a man could divorce his wife without stating a cause, a woman could initiate

Ibn al-Haytham (IB-uhn al–HY-tham)

령이 대중 앞에 나타나거나 애국심
을 고취하는 노래만을 내보내던 방
송마저 중단됐다.

라크 전후 대
의에서는 전
영국 주도로

DIVERSITY AND DOMINANCE

BEGGARS, CON MEN, AND SINGING-GIRLS

Though rulers, warriors, and religious scholars dominate the traditional narratives, the society that developed over the early centuries of Islam was remarkably diverse. Beggars, tricksters, and street performers belonged to a single loose fraternity: the Banu Sasan, or Tribe of Sasan. Tales of their tricks and exploits amused staid, pious Muslims, who often encountered them in cities and on their scholarly travels. The tenth-century poet Abu Dulaf al-Khazraji, who lived in Iran, studied the jargon of the Banu Sasan and their way of life and composed a long poem in which he cast himself as one of the group. However, he added a commentary to each verse to explain the jargon words that his sophisticated court audience would have found unfamiliar.

We are the beggars' brotherhood, and no one can deny
     us our lofty pride . . .
And of our number if the feigned madman and mad
     woman, with metal charms strung from their [sic] necks.
And the ones with ornaments drooping from their ears,
     and with collars of leather or brass round their necks . . .
And the one who simulates a festering internal wound,
     and the people with false bandages round their heads
     and sickly, jaundiced faces.
And the one who slashes himself, alleging that he has
     been mutilated by assailants, or the one who darkens
     his skin artificially pretending that he has been
     beaten up and wounded . . .
And the one who practices as a manipulator and quack
     dentist, or who escapes from chains wound round his
     body, or the one who uses almost invisible silk thread
     mysteriously to draw off rings . . .
And of our number are those who claim to be refugees
     from the Byzantine frontier regions, those who go
     round begging on pretext of having left behind cap-
     tive families . . .
And the one who feigns an internal discharge, or who
     showers the passers-by with his urine, or who farts in
     the mosque and makes a nuisance of himself, thus
     wheedling money out of people . . .
And of our number are the ones who purvey objects of
     veneration made from clay, and those who have their
     beards smeared with red dye.

And the one who brings up secret writing by immersing it
     in what looks like water, and the one who similarly
     brings up the writing by exposing it to burning embers.

One of the greatest masters of Arabic prose, Jahiz (776–869), was a famously ugly man—his name means "Pop-eyed"—of Abyssinian family origin. Spending part of his life in his native Basra, in southern Iraq, and part in Baghdad, the Abbasid capital, he wrote voluminously on subjects ranging from theology to zoology to miserliness. These excerpts come from his book devoted to the business of training slave girls as musicians, a lucrative practice of suspect morality but great popularity among men of wealth. He pretends that he is not the author, but merely writing down the views of the owners of singing-girls.

Now I will describe for you the definition of the passion of love, so that you may understand what exactly it is. It is a malady which smites the spirit, and affects the body as well by contagion: just as physical weakness impairs the spirit and low spirits in a man make him emaciated . . . The stronger the constituent causes of the malady are, the more inveterate it is, and the slower to clear up . . .

Passion for singing-girls is dangerous, in view of their manifold excellences and the satisfaction one's soul finds in them. . . . The singing-girl is hardly ever sincere in her passion, or wholehearted in her affection. For both by training and by innate instinct her nature is to set up snares and traps for the victims, in order that they may fall into her toils. As soon as the observer notices her, she exchanges provocative glances with him, gives him playful smiles, dallies with him in verses set to music, falls in with his suggestions, is eager to drink when he drinks, expresses her fervent desire for him to stay a long while, her yearning for his prompt return, and her sorrow at his departure. Then when she perceives that her sorcery has worked on him and that he has become entangled in the net, she redoubles the wiles she had used at first, and leads him to suppose that she is more in love than he is . . .

But it sometimes happens that this pretence leads her on to turning it into reality, and she in fact shares her lover's

torments . . . Sometimes she may renounce her craft, in order for her to be cheaper for him [to buy], and makes a show of illness and is sullen towards her guardians and asks the owners to sell her . . . specially if she finds [her lover] to be sweet-tempered, clever in expressing himself, pleasant-tongued, with a fine apprehension and delicate sensibility, and light-hearted; while if he can compose and quote poetry or warble a tune, that gives him all the more favour in her eyes . . .

How indeed could a singing-girl be saved from falling prey to temptation, and how is it possible for her to be chaste? It is in the very place where she is brought up that she acquires unbridled desires, and learns her modes of speech and behaviour. From cradle to grave she is nourished by such idle talk, and all sorts of frivolous and impure conversation, as must hinder her from recollection of God; among abandoned and dissolute persons, who never utter a serious word, from whom she could never look for any trustworthiness, religion, or safe-guarding of decent standards.

An accomplished singing-girl has a repertoire of upwards of four thousands songs, each of them two to four verses long, so that the total amount . . . comes to ten thousand verses, in which there is not one mention of God (except by inadvertence). . . . They are all founded on references to fornication, pimping, passion, yearning, desire, and lust. Later on she continues to study her profession assiduously, learning from music teachers whose lessons are all flirting and whose directives are a seduction . . .

Among the advantages enjoyed by each man among us [i.e., speaking as a keeper of singing-girls] is that other men seek him out eagerly in his abode, just as one eagerly seeks out caliphs and great folk; is visited without having the trouble of visiting; receives gifts and is not compelled to give; has presents made to him and none required from him. Eyes remain wakeful, tears flow, minds are agitated, emotions lacerated, and hopes fixed—all on the property which he has under his control: which is something that does not occur with anything [else] that is sold or bought. . . . [F]or who could reach anything like the price fetched by an Abyssinian girl, the slave of Awn, namely 120,000 dinars [i.e., gold coins]?

The owner of singing-girls . . . takes the substance and gives the appearance, gets the real thing and gives the shadow, and sells the gusty wind for solid ore and pieces of silver and gold. Between the suitors and what they desire lies the thorniest of obstacles. For the owner, were he not to abstain from granting the dupe his desire for motives of purity and decency, would at any rate do so out of sharp-wittedness and wiliness, and to safeguard his trade and defend the sanctity of his estate. For when the lover once possesses himself of the beloved, nine-tenths of his ardour disappear, and his liberality and contributions [to the owner] diminish on the same scale. What is there, consequently, to induce the owner of the singing-girls to give you his girl, spiting his own face and causing himself to be no longer sought after?

If he were not a past-master in this splendid and noble profession, why is it that he abandons jealous surveillance of the girls (though choosing his spies well), accepts the room rent, pretends to doze off before supper, takes no notice of winkings, is indulgent to a kiss, ignores signs [passing between the pair of lovers], turns a blind eye to the exchange of billets-doux, affects to forget all about the girl on the day of the visit, does not scold her for retiring to a private place, does not pry into her secrets or cross-examine her about how she passed the night, and does not bother to lock the doors and draw close the curtains? He reckons up each victim's income separately, and knows how much money he is good for; just as the trader sorts out his various kinds of merchandise and prices them according to their value . . . When he has an influential customer, he takes advantage of his influence and makes requests from him; if the customer is rich but not influential, he borrows money from him without interest. If he is a person connected with the authorities, such a one can be used as a shield against the unfriendly attentions of the police; and when such a one comes on a visit, drums and hautbois [i.e., double-reed pipes] are sounded.

Both of these passages fall into the category of Arabic literature known as adab, *or belles-lettres. The purpose of adab was to entertain and instruct through a succession of short anecdotes, verses, and expository discussions. It attracted the finest writers of the Abbasid era and affords one of the richest sources for looking at everyday life, always keeping in mind that the intended readers were a restricted class of educated men, including merchants, court and government officials, and even men of religion.*

QUESTIONS FOR ANALYSIS

1. What do the authors' portrayals of beggars, con men, singing-girls, and keepers of singing-girls indicate about the diversity of life in the city?

2. Taken together, what do these passages indicate about the conventional portrayal of religious laws and moral teachings dominating everyday life?

3. In the discussion of singing-girls, what do you see as the importance of the practices of veiling and seclusion among urban, free-born, Muslim women?

4. In evaluating these as historical sources, is it necessary to take the tastes of the intended audience into account?

Sources: First selection excerpts from Clifford Edmund Bosworth, *The Mediaeval Islamic Underworld: The Banu Sasan in Arabic Society and Literature* (Leiden: E. I. Brill, 1976), 191–199. Copyright © 1976. With kind permission of Koninklijke Brill N.V. Leiden, the Netherlands. Second selection excerpts from Jahiz, *The Epistle on Singing-Girls,* tr. and ed. A. F. L. Beeston (Warminster: Aris and Phillips, 1980), 28–37. Reprinted with permission of Oxbow Books, Ltd.

Automata

Model of a Water-Lifting Device The artist's effort to render a three-dimensional construction in two dimensions shows a talent for schematic drawing. (Widener Library Photographic Services)

Muslim scientists made discoveries and advances in almost every field, from mathematics and astronomy to chemistry and optics. Many worked under the patronage of rulers who paid for translations from Greek and other languages into Arabic and built libraries and observatories to facilitate their work. Fascination with science and technology also manifested itself in designs for elaborate mechanical devices—automata—intended for the entertainment of rulers and amazement of court visitors. In this example, a conventional-looking device for drawing water from a well, known as a saqiya (suh-KEY-yuh) and still in use from Morocco to Afghanistan, appears to be powered by a wooden cow that actually is moved by the force of the beam it is attached to rather than providing the motion itself.

A saqiya is a chain of buckets descending to a water source from a spoked drum attached to interlocking gears. In real life, an animal walks in a circle turning the first gear above it and thereby setting the drum in motion by way of a connecting gear that turns horizontal rotation into vertical rotation. In this automaton, real power comes from a water wheel with cups on its arms and hidden beneath the pool of water and connected by gears to the platform the wooden cow is standing on. The water flowing into the pond at left and right provides the hydraulic pressure needed to keep the apparatus in motion, causing the gears above to operate the chain of buckets lifting water to the outlet trough on the upper left.

divorce under specified conditions. Women could practice birth control. They could testify in court, although their testimony counted as half that of a man. They could go on pilgrimage. Nevertheless, a misogynistic tone sometimes appears in Islamic writings. One saying attributed to the Prophet observed: "I was raised up to heaven and saw that most of its denizens were poor people; I was raised into the hellfire and saw that most of its denizens were women."[3]

In the absence of writings by women about women from this period, the status of women must be deduced from the writings of men. Two episodes involving the Prophet's wife A'isha, the daughter of Abu Bakr, provide examples of how Muslim men appraised women in soci-

ety. Only eighteen when Muhammad died, A'isha lived for another fifty years. Early reports stress her status as Muhammad's favorite, the only virgin he married and the only wife to see the angel Gabriel. These reports emanate from A'isha herself, who was an abundant source of hadith. As a fourteen-year-old she had become separated from a caravan and rejoined it only after traveling through the night with a man who found her alone in the desert. Gossips accused her of being untrue to the Prophet, but a revelation from God proved her innocence. The second event was her participation in the Battle of the Camel, fought to derail Ali's caliphate. These two episodes came to epitomize what Muslim men feared most about women: sexual infidelity and med-

Women Playing Chess in Muslim Spain As shown in this thirteenth-century miniature, women in their own quarters, without men present, wore whatever clothes and jewels they liked. Notice the henna decorating the hands of the woman in the middle. The woman on the left, probably a slave, plays an oud. (Institute Amatller d'Art Hispanic. © Patrimonio Nacional, Madrid)

dling in politics. Even though the earliest literature dealing with A'isha stresses her position as Muhammad's favorite, his first wife, Khadija, and his daughter, Ali's wife Fatima, eventually surpassed A'isha as ideal women. Both appear as model wives and mothers with no suspicion of sexual irregularity or political manipulation.

As the seclusion of women became commonplace in urban Muslim society, some writers extolled homosexual relationships, partly because a male lover could appear in public or go on a journey. Although Islam deplored homosexuality, one ruler wrote a book advising his son to follow moderation in all things and thus share his affections equally between men and women. Another ruler and his slave-boy became models of perfect love in the verses of mystic poets.

Islam allowed slavery but forbade Muslims from enslaving other Muslims or so-called People of the Book—Jews, Christians, and Zoroastrians, who revered holy books respected by the Muslims—who were living under Muslim protection. Being enslaved as a prisoner of war constituted an exception. Later centuries saw a constant flow of slaves into Islamic territory from Africa and Central Asia. A hereditary slave society, however, did not develop. Usually slaves converted to Islam, and many masters then freed them as an act of piety. The offspring of slave women and Muslim men were born free.

The Recentering of Islam

Early Islam centered on the caliphate, the political expression of the unity of the umma. No formal organization or hierarchy, however, directed the process of conversion. Thus there emerged a multitude of local Islamic communities so disconnected from each other that numerous competing interpretations of the developing religion arose. Inevitably, the centrality of the caliphate diminished (see Map 9.2). The appearance of rival caliphates in Tunisia and Cordoba accentuated the problem of decentralization just as Abbasid temporal power waned.

The rise of the ulama as community leaders did not prevent growing fragmentation because the ulama themselves divided into contentious factions. During the twelfth century factionalism began to abate, and new socioreligious institutions emerged to provide the umma with a different sort of religious center. These new developments stemmed in part from an exodus of religious scholars from Iran in response to economic and political disintegration during the late eleventh and twelfth centuries.

The flow of Iranians to the Arab lands and to newly conquered territories in India and Anatolia increased after the Mongol invasion. Fully versed in Arabic as well as their native Persian, immigrant scholars were warmly received. They brought with them a view of religion devel-

Quran Page Printed from a Woodblock   Printing from woodblocks or tin plates existed in Islamic lands between approximately 800 and 1400. Most prints were narrow amulets designed to be rolled and worn around the neck in cylindrical cases. Less valued than handwritten amulets, many prints came from Banu Sasan con men. Why blockprinting had so little effect on society in general and eventually disappeared is unknown.   (Cambridge University Library)

oped in Iran's urban centers. A type of religious college, the *madrasa*°, gained sudden popularity outside Iran, where madrasas had been known since the tenth century. Scores of madrasas, many founded by local rulers, appeared throughout the Islamic world.

Iranians also contributed to the growth of mystic groups known as *Sufi* brotherhoods in the twelfth and thirteenth centuries. The doctrines and rituals of certain Sufis spread from city to city, giving rise to the first geographically extensive Islamic religious organizations.

---

madrasa (MAH-dras-uh)

Sufi doctrines varied, but a quest for a sense of union with God through rituals and training was a common denominator. Sufism had begun in early Islamic times and had doubtless benefited from the ideas and beliefs of people from religions with mystic traditions who converted to Islam.

The early Sufis had been saintly individuals given to ecstatic and poetic utterances and wonderworking. They attracted disciples but did not try to organize them. The growth of brotherhoods, a less ecstatic form of Sufism, set a tone for society in general. It soon became common for most Muslim men, particularly in the cities, to belong to at least one brotherhood.

A sense of the social climate the Sufi brotherhoods fostered can be gained from a twelfth-century manual:

> Every limb has its own special ethics. . . . The ethics of the tongue. The tongue should always be busy in reciting God's names (*dhikr*) and in saying good things of the brethren, praying for them, and giving them counsel. . . . The ethics of hearing. One should not listen to indecencies and slander. . . . The ethics of sight. One should lower one's eyes in order not to see forbidden things. . . . The ethics of the hands: to give charity and serve the brethren and not use them in acts of disobedience.[4]

Special dispensations allowed people who merely wanted to emulate the Sufis and enjoy their company to follow less demanding rules:

> It is allowed by way of dispensation to possess an estate or to rely on a regular income. The Sufis' rule in this matter is that one should not use all of it for himself, but should dedicate this to public charities and should take from it only enough for one year for himself and his family. . . .
>
> There is a dispensation allowing one to be occupied in business; this dispensation is granted to him who has to support a family. But this should not keep him away from the regular performance of prayers. . . .
>
> There is a dispensation allowing one to watch all kinds of amusement. This is, however, limited by the rule: What you are forbidden from doing, you are also forbidden from watching.[5]

Some Sufi brotherhoods spread in the countryside. Local shrines and pilgrimages to the tombs of Muhammad's descendants and saintly Sufis became popular. The pilgrimage to Mecca, too, received new prominence as a religious duty. The end of the Abbasid Caliphate enhanced the religious centrality of Mecca, which eventually became an important center of madrasa education.

CONCLUSION

The Sasanid empire that held sway in Iran and Iraq from the third to the seventh century strongly resembled the contemporary realm of the eastern Roman emperors ruling from Constantinople. Both states forged strong relations between the ruler and the dominant religion, Zoroastrianism in the former empire, Christianity in the latter. Priestly hierarchies paralleled state administrative structures, and the citizenry came to think of themselves more as members of a faith community than as subjects of a ruler. This gave rise to conflict among religious sects and also raised the possibility of the founder of a new religion commanding both political and religious loyalty on an unprecedented scale. This possibility was realized in the career of the prophet Muhammad in the seventh century.

Islam culminated the trend toward identity based on religion. The concept of the umma united all Muslims in a universal community embracing enormous diversity of language, appearance, and social custom. Though Muslim communities adapted to local "small traditions," by the twelfth century a religious scholar could travel anywhere in the Islamic world and blend easily into the local Muslim community.

By the ninth century, the forces of conversion and urbanization fostered social and religious experimentation in urban settings. From the eleventh century onward, political disruption and the spread of pastoral nomadism slowed this early economic and technological dynamism. The Muslim community then turned to new religious institutions, such as the madrasas and Sufi brotherhoods, to create the flexible and durable community structures that carried Islam into new regions and protected ordinary believers from capricious political rule.

■ Key Terms

Shi'ites	umma
Sunnis	caliphate
Sasanid Empire	Quran
Mecca	Umayyad Caliphate
Muhammad	Abbasid Caliphate
muslim	mamluks
Islam	ulama
Medina	hadith

■ Suggested Reading

For Sasanid history see Josef Wiesehöfer, *Ancient Persia* (2001). Ehsan Yarshater, ed., *The Cambridge History of Iran*, vol. 3 (pts. 1–2), *The Seleucid, Parthian and Sasanian Periods* (1983) contains up-to-date articles on Iranian history just prior to Islam.

Ira M. Lapidus, *A History of Islamic Societies* (1988), focuses on social developments and includes the histories of Islam in India, Southeast Asia, sub-Saharan Africa, and other parts of the world. Marshall G. S. Hodgson, *The Venture of Islam*, 3 vols. (1974), critiques traditional ways of studying the Islamic Middle East while offering an alternative interpretation. Bernard Lewis's *The Middle East: A Brief History of the Last 2,000 Years* (1995) provides a lively narration from the time of Christ.

For a shorter survey see J. J. Saunders, *History of Medieval Islam* (1965; reprint, 1990). Richard W. Bulliet, *Islam: The View from the Edge* (1993), offers, in brief form, an approach that concentrates on the lives of converts to Islam and local religious notables.

Muslims regard the Quran as untranslatable because they consider the Arabic in which it is couched to be inseparable from God's message. Most "interpretations" in English adhere reasonably closely to the Arabic text.

Martin Lings, *Muhammad: His Life Based on the Earliest Sources*, rev. ed. (1991), offers a readable biography reflecting Muslim viewpoints. Standard Western treatments include W. Montgomery Watt's *Muhammad at Mecca* (1953) and *Muhammad at Medina* (1956; reprint, 1981); and the one-volume summary: *Muhammad, Prophet and Statesman* (1974). Michael A. Cook, *Muhammad* (1983), intelligently discusses historiographical problems and source difficulties. Karen Armstrong's *Muhammad: A Biography of the Prophet* (1993) achieves a sympathetic balance.

For information on the new school of thought that rejects the traditional accounts of Muhammad's life and of the origins of the Quran, see Patricia Crone and Michael Cook, *Hagarism* (1977), Patricia Crone, *Meccan Trade and the Rise of Islam* (1987), and Fred Donner, *Narratives of Islamic Origins* (1998).

Wilfred Madelung's *The Succession to Muhammad: A Study of the Early Caliphate* (1997) gives an interpretation unusually sympathetic to Shi'ite viewpoints. G. R. Hawting, *The First Dynasty of Islam: The Umayyad Caliphate, A.D. 661–750* (1987), offers a more conventional and easily readable history of a crucial century.

Western historians have debated the beginnings of the Abbasid Caliphate. Moshe Sharon, *Black Banners from the East: The Establishment of the 'Abbasid State—Incubation of a Revolt* (1983), and Jacob Lassner, *Islamic Revolution and Historical Memory: An Inquiry into the Art of Abbasid Apologetics* (1987), give differing accounts based on newly utilized sources. For a broader history that puts the first three centuries of Abbasid rule into the context of the earlier periods, see Hugh N. Kennedy, *The Prophet and the Age of the Caliphates: The Islamic Near East from the Sixth to the Eleventh Century* (1986). Harold

Bowen, *The Life and Times of Ali ibn Isa "The Good Vizier"* (1928; reprint, 1975), supplements Kennedy's narrative superbly with a detailed study of corrupt caliphal politics in the tumultuous early tenth century.

Articles in Michael Gervers and Ramzi Jibran Bikhazi, eds., *Conversion and Continuity: Indigenous Christian Communities in Islamic Lands, Eighth to Eighteenth Centuries* (1990), detail Christian responses to Islam. For a Zoroastrian perspective see Jamsheed K. Choksy, *Conflict and Cooperation: Zoroastrian Subalterns and Muslim Elites in Medieval Iranian Society* (1997). Jacob Lassner summarizes S. D. Goitein's definitive multivolume study of the Jews of medieval Egypt in *A Mediterranean Society: An Abridgement in One Volume* (1999). On the process of conversion see the work in quantitative history of Richard W. Bulliet, *Conversion to Islam in the Medieval Period* (1979).

With the fragmentation of the Abbasid Caliphate beginning in the ninth century, studies of separate areas become more useful than general histories. Richard N. Frye, *The Golden Age of Persia: The Arabs in the East* (1975), skillfully evokes the complicated world of early Islamic Iran and the survival and revival of Persian national identity. Thomas F. Glick, *Islamic and Christian Spain in the Early Middle Ages* (1979) and *From Muslim Fortress to Christian Castle: Social and Cultural Change in Medieval Spain* (1995), questions standard ideas about Christians and Muslims in Spain from a geographical and technological standpoint. For North Africa, Charles-André Julien, *History of North Africa: Tunisia, Algeria, Morocco, from the Arab Conquest to 1830* (1970), summarizes a literature primarily written in French. This same French historiographical tradition is challenged and revised by Abdallah Laroui, *The History of the Maghrib: An Interpretive Essay* (1977). For a detailed primary source, see the English translation of the most important chronicle of early Islamic history, *The History of al-Tabari,* published in thirty-eight volumes under the general editorship of Ehsan Yarshater.

Roy P. Mottahedeh, *Loyalty and Leadership in an Early Islamic Society* (1980); Richard W. Bulliet, *The Patricians of Nishapur* (1972); and Ira Marvin Lapidus, *Muslim Cities in the Later Middle Ages* (1984), discuss social history in tenth-century Iran, eleventh-century Iran, and fourteenth-century Syria, respectively. Jonathan Berkey, *The Transmission of Knowledge in Medieval Cairo: A Social History of Islamic Education* (1992), and Michael Chamberlain, *Knowledge and Social Practice in Medieval Damascus, 1190–1350* (1994), put forward competing assessments of education and the ulama. For urban geography see Paul Wheatley, *The Places Where Men Pray Together* (2001).

Ahmad Y. al-Hassan and Donald R. Hill, *Islamic Technology: An Illustrated History* (1986), introduces a little-studied field. For a more crafts-oriented look see Hans E. Wulff, *The Traditional Crafts of Persia: Their Development, Technology, and Influence on Eastern and Western Civilizations* (1966). Jonathan Bloom's *Paper Before Print* (2001) details the great impact of papermaking in many cultural areas.

Denise Spellberg, *Politics, Gender, and the Islamic Past: The Legacy of A'isha bint Abi Bakr* (1994), provides pathbreaking guidance on women's history. Basim Musallam, *Sex and Society in Islamic Civilization* (1983), treats the social, medical, and legal history of birth control. On race and slavery see Bernard Lewis, *Race and Slavery in the Middle East: A Historical Enquiry* (1992).

Among the numerous introductory books on Islam as a religion, a reliable starting point is David Waines, *An Introduction to Islam* (1995). For more advanced work, Fazlur Rahman, *Islam,* 2d ed. (1979), skillfully discusses some of the subject's difficulties. Islamic law is well covered in Noel J. Coulson, *A History of Islamic Law* (1979). For Sufism see Annemarie Schimmel, *Mystical Dimensions of Islam* (1975).

Two religious texts available in translation are Abu Hamid al-Ghazali, *The Faith and Practice of al-Ghazali,* trans. W. Montgomery Watt (1967; reprint, 1982), and Abu al-Najib al-Suhrawardi, *A Sufi Rule for Novices,* trans. Menaham Milson (1975).

For detailed and abundant maps see William C. Brice, ed., *An Historical Atlas of Islam* (1981). The most complete reference work for people working in Islamic studies is *The Encyclopedia of Islam,* new ed. (Leiden: E. J. Brill, 1960–), now available in CD-ROM format. For encyclopedia-type articles on pre-Islamic topics see G. W. Bowersock, Peter Brown, and Oleg Grabar *Late Antiquity: A Guide to the Postclassical World* (1999). On Iran see the excellent but still unfinished *Encyclopedia Iranica,* edited by Ehsan Yarshater.

■ Notes

1. Quran. Sura 96, verses 1–5.
2. Quran. Sura 92, verses 1–10.
3. Richard W. Bulliet, *Islam: The View from the Edge* (New York: Columbia University Press, 1994), 87.
4. Abu Najib al-Suhrawardi, *A Sufi Rule for Novices,* trans. Menaham Milson (Cambridge, MA: Harvard University Press, 1975), 45–58.
5. Ibid., 73–82.

10

Christian Europe Emerges, 300–1200

Boatbuilding Scene from the Bayeaux Tapestry Eleventh-century shipwrights prepare vessels for William of Normandy's invasion of England.

253

Christmas Day in 800 found Charles, king of the Franks, in Rome instead of at his palace at Aachen in northwestern Germany. At six-foot-three, Charles towered over the average man of his time, and his royal career had been equally gargantuan. Crowned king in his mid-twenties in 768, he had crisscrossed Europe for three decades, waging war on Muslim invaders from Spain, Avar° invaders from Hungary, and a number of German princes.

Charles had subdued many enemies and had become protector of the papacy. So not all historians believe the eyewitness report of his secretary and biographer that Charles was surprised when, as the king rose from his prayers, Pope Leo III placed a new crown on his head. "Life and victory to Charles the August, crowned by God the great and pacific Emperor of the Romans," proclaimed the pope.[1] Then, amid the cheers of the crowd, he humbly knelt before the new emperor.

Charlemagne° (from Latin *Carolus magnus*, "Charles the Great") was the first in western Europe to bear the title *emperor* in over three hundred years. Rome's decline and Charlemagne's rise marked a shift of focus for Europe—away from the Mediterranean and toward the north and west. German custom and Christian piety transformed the Roman heritage to create a new civilization. Irish monks preaching in Latin became important intellectual influences in some parts of Europe, while the memory of Greek and Roman philosophy faded. Urban life continued the decline that began in the later days of the Roman Empire. Historians originally called this era "**medieval,**" literally "middle age," because it comes between the era of Greco-Roman civilization and the intellectual, artistic, and economic changes of the Renaissance in the fourteenth century; but research has uncovered many aspects of medieval culture that are as rich and creative as those that came earlier and later.

Charlemagne was not the only ruler in Europe to claim the title emperor. Another emperor held sway in the Greek-speaking east, where Rome's political and legal heritage continued. The Eastern Roman Empire was often called the **Byzantine Empire** after the seventh century, and was known to the Muslims as Rum. Western Europeans lived amid the ruins of empire, while the Byzantines maintained and reinterpreted Roman traditions. The authority of the Byzantine emperors blended with the influence of the Christian church to form a cultural synthesis that helped shape the emerging kingdom of **Kievan Russia.** Byzantium's centuries-long conflict with Islam helped spur the crusading passion that overtook western Europe in the eleventh century.

The comparison between western and eastern Europe appears paradoxical. Byzantium inherited a robust and self-confident late Roman society and economy, while western Europe could not achieve political unity and suffered severe economic decline. Yet by 1200 western Europe was showing renewed vitality and flexing its military muscles, while Byzantium was showing signs of decline and military weakness. As we explore the causes and consequences of these different historical paths, we must remember that the emergence of Christian Europe included both developments.

As you read this chapter, ask yourself the following questions:

- What role did Christianity play in reshaping European society in east and west?

- How did the Roman heritage differently affect the east and the west?

- How can one compare Kievan Russia's resemblances to western Europe and to the Byzantine Empire?

- How did Mediterranean trade and the Crusades help revive western Europe?

THE BYZANTINE EMPIRE, 300–1200

The Byzantine emperors established Christianity as their official religion, but they also represented a continuation of Roman imperial rule and tradition that was largely absent in the kingdoms that succeeded Rome in the west. They inherited imperial law intact; only provincial forms of Roman law survived in the west. Combining the imperial role with political oversight over the Christian church, they made a comfortable transition into the role of all-powerful Christian monarchs. The Byzantine drama, however, played on a steadily shrinking stage. Territorial losses and almost constant military pressure from north and south deprived the empire of long periods of peace.

Avar (ah-vahr)   Charlemagne (SHAHR-leh-mane)

C H R O N O L O G Y

	Western Europe	Eastern Europe
300		**325** Constantine convenes Council of Nicaea; Arian heresy condemned
		392 Emperor Theodosius bans paganism in Byzantine Empire
	432 Saint Patrick begins missionary work in Ireland	
	476 Deposing of the last Roman emperor in the West	
500		
	ca. 547 Death of Saint Benedict	**527–565** Justinian and Theodora rule Byzantine Empire; imperial edicts collected in single law code
		634–650 Muslims conquer Byzantine provinces of Syria, Egypt, and Tunisia
	711 Muslim conquest of Spain	
	732 Battle of Tours	
800	**800** Coronation of Charlemagne	
	843 Treaty of Verdun divides Carolingian Empire among Charlemagne's grandsons	
	910 Monastery of Cluny founded	**882** Varangians take control of Kiev
	962 Beginning of Holy Roman Empire	
1000		**980** Vladimir becomes grand prince of Kievan Russia
	1054 Formal schism between Latin and Orthodox Churches	
	1066 Normans under William the Conqueror invade England	
	1077 Climax of investiture controversy	**1081–1118** Alexius Comnenus rules Byzantine Empire, calls for western military aid against Muslims
	1095 Pope Urban II preaches First Crusade	
1200		**1204** Western knights sack Constantinople in Fourth Crusade

Church and State In 324, in the nineteenth year of his reign, the emperor Constantine (r. 306–337) led a procession marking the expanded limits of the city he had selected as his new capital: the millennium-old Greek city of Byzantium, located on a long, narrow inlet at the entrance to the Bosporus strait (see Chapter 6). In the forum of the new Constantinople°, he erected a 120-foot-tall (36-meter) column topped with a statue of Apollo, and he retained the old Roman title *pontifex maximus*° (chief priest). Nevertheless, he leaned toward Christianity—historians disagree on when he embraced it fully—and he and his mother studded both his capital and the Christian centers of Jerusalem and Rome with important churches.

Constantinople (cahn-stan-tih-NO-pul)

pontifex maximus (PAHN-tih-fex MAX-ih-muhs)

Constantine appointed the patriarch of Constantinople and involved himself in doctrinal disputes over which beliefs constituted heresy. In 325 he called hundreds of bishops to a council at the city of Nicaea° (modern Iznik in northwestern Turkey) to resolve disputes over religious doctrine. The bishops rejected the views of a priest from Alexandria named Arius, who maintained that Jesus was of lesser importance than God the Father. The Arian doctrine enjoyed greatest popularity among the Germanic peoples then migrating along the Danube frontier and into the western Roman lands. An Arian bishop named Ulfilas (ca. 311–383), himself belonging to the Germanic people known as Goths, translated the Bible into Gothic, reportedly using an alphabet of his own devising. This set the Arians apart from Christians who relied on scriptures written in Latin or Greek.

Following the Arian controversy, disputes over theology and quarrels among the patriarchs of Constantinople, Alexandria, and Antioch continued to tear at the Byzantine Empire. Literature of the period shows widespread concern for religious affairs, which deeply permeated society. A fourth-century bishop reported: "Everything is full of those who are speaking of unintelligible things. . . . I wish to know the price of bread; one answers, 'The Father is greater than the Son.' I inquire whether my bath is ready; one says, 'The Son has been made out of nothing.' "[2]

Early Christians had established communities in many cities (see Map 10.1). The most prominent were in Jerusalem, Antioch, Alexandria, and Rome, and their bishops became recognized as patriarchs and paramount leaders. Other important theologians, like St. Augustine (354–430), the bishop of Hippo in North Africa, were not patriarchs. Constantine made Constantinople a fifth patriarchate°. The patriarchs appointed bishops throughout their regions, and each bishop consecrated priests within his area of jurisdiction, called a diocese. Church rules set by the patriarch or by councils of bishops guided priests in serving ordinary believers.

Priests commemorated Christ's sacrifice on the cross in the consumption of bread and wine in the Mass, or church service, and performed ceremonies relating to birth, marriage, and death. But church leaders differed on the precise form of rituals and on which should be considered sacred mysteries, or sacraments. Before baptism became standardized as a ritual for newborns, for example, it was sometimes postponed until late in life so that the person could benefit from the forgiveness of sin that it conveyed.

The church hierarchy strove for consistency in Christian belief throughout the Christian community, but disagreement arose here as well. One area of disagreement centered on Jesus' relationship to God the Father and to the Holy Spirit. The bishops gathered for the Council of Nicaea agreed that, contrary to the view of the Arians, the three formed a divine Trinity in which three aspects or manifestations of God somehow came together. But they did not all understand the Trinity in the same way. They also disagreed on whether Mary was the mother of God, or the mother of a man named Jesus. Some Christians thought that images of God or Jesus or Mary, called icons, were proper objects to pray before because they stimulated pious thoughts; others, known as iconoclasts, or image-breakers, condemned the practice as too much like praying to pagan statues.

For some four centuries after 300, disagreements like these led to charges and countercharges of heresy, beliefs or practices so unacceptable as to be un-Christian. Charges of heresy touched ordinary people, even when they involved hard-to-understand theological issues, because they involved salvation. They also threatened the unity of the Christian church at a time of rapidly increasing political fragmentation.

The most severe disagreements arose in North Africa and the lands of the eastern Mediterranean and resulted in **schism**°—a formal division resulting from disagreements about doctrine. Monophysite° (Greek for "one nature") doctrine, for example, emphasized the divinity of Jesus Christ and minimized his human characteristics. Finding abhorrent the idea that Christ suffered like an ordinary human on the cross, some Monophysites maintained that another man had been substituted for him. Versions of Monophysitism persist to this day in Egyptian, Ethiopian, and Armenian churches. Commonly, a council of bishops, like that at Nicaea, deliberated and declared a particular doctrine true or false. In the east, the Byzantine emperor claimed the authority to call such conferences.

In the Byzantine world, as in the western Roman lands, Christianity progressed most rapidly in urban centers. Though the country folk (Latin *pagani*, whence the word *pagan* used as a negative label for polytheists) long retained customs deriving from worship of the old gods, the emperor Julian (r. 361–363) tried in vain to restore the old polytheism as the state cult. When a blind Christian addressed Julian by the pejorative term "apostate" (renegade from Christianity), which later historians commonly attached to his name, calling him Julian the Apostate, the emperor said, "You are blind, and your God will not cure you." To this the Christian replied, "I thank God for my blindness, since it prevents me from behold-

---

Nicaea (nye-SEE-uh)   **patriarchate** (PAY-tree-ar-kayt)

schism (SKIZ-uhm)   **Monophysite** (muh-NAH-fi-site)

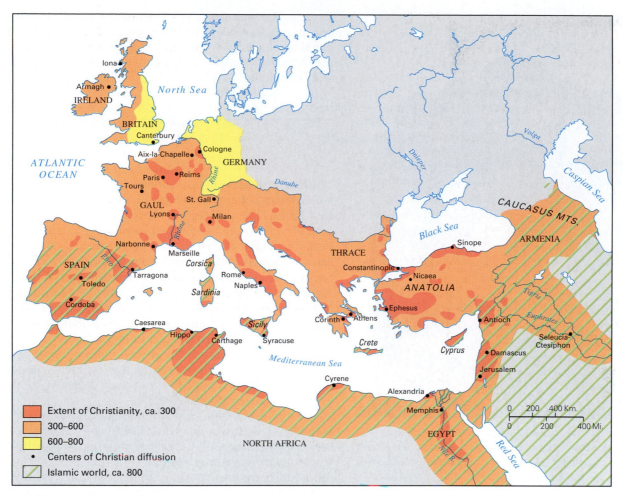

Map 10.1 The Spread of Christianity By the early eighth century, Christian areas around the southern Mediterranean from northern Syria to northern Spain, accounting for most of the Christian population, had fallen under Muslim rule; the slow process of conversion to Islam had begun. This accentuated the importance of the patriarchs of Constantinople, the popes in Rome, and the later converting regions of northern and eastern Europe.

ing your impiety."[3] In 392 the emperor Theodosius banned all pagan ceremonies. The following year he terminated the eleven-hundred-year-old tradition of the Olympic Games, which had originated as religious rites but had become increasingly professionalized in Roman times.

Having a single ruler endowed with supreme legal and religious authority prevented the breakup of the Eastern Empire into petty principalities, but a series of territorial losses sapped the empire's strength. A strong emperor might temporarily recover lost ground, as Justinian (r. 527–565) did in seizing Tunisia from Germanic Vandal rulers and reasserting Byzantine control along the east coast of Italy, but military pressures seldom

abated. A new Iranian empire ruled by the Sasanid family (see Chapter 9) threatened from the east in the fourth century. Various enemies including the Germanic Goths and the nomadic Huns of Central Asia threatened from the north at different periods. Bribes, diplomacy, and occasional military victories usually persuaded the Goths and Huns to settle peacefully or move on and attack western Europe. War with the Sasanids, however, flared up repeatedly for almost three hundred years. Finally, a new enemy appeared from the Arabian peninsula: followers of the Arab prophet Muhammad. Between 634 and 650, Arab armies destroyed the Sasanid Empire and captured Byzantine Egypt, Syria, and Tunisia. By the end of the twelfth century, at least

Byzantine Church from a Twelfth-Century Manuscript
The upper portion shows the church façade and domes. The lower portion shows the interior with a mosaic of Christ enthroned at the altar end. (Bibliothèque nationale de France)

two-thirds of the Christians in these former Byzantine territories had adopted the Muslim faith.

The loss of such populous and prosperous provinces shook the empire and reduced its power. Although the empire had largely recovered and reorganized militarily by the tenth century, it never regained the lost lands and eventually succumbed to Muslim conquest in 1453. The later Byzantine emperors faced new enemies in the north and south. Following the wave of Germanic migrations, Slavic and Turkic peoples appeared on the northern frontiers as part of centuries-long and poorly understood population migrations in Eurasian steppe lands. Other Turks led by the Seljuk family became the primary foe in the south (see Chapter 9).

At the same time, relations with the popes and princes of western Europe steadily worsened. In the mid-ninth century the patriarchs of Constantinople had challenged the territorial jurisdiction of the popes of

Rome and some of the practices of the Latin Church. These arguments worsened over time and in 1054 culminated in a formal schism between the Latin Church and the Orthodox Church—a break that has been only partially mended.

Society and Urban Life

Imperial authority and urban prosperity in the eastern provinces of the old Roman Empire initially sheltered Byzantium from many of the economic reverses and population losses suffered by western Europe from the third century on. The two regions shared a common demographic crisis during a sixth-century epidemic of bubonic plague known as "the plague of Justinian." A similar though gradual and less pronounced social transformation set in around the seventh century, possibly sparked by the loss of Egypt and Syria to the Muslims. Narrative histories tell us little, but popular narratives of saints' lives show a transition from stories about educated saints hailing from cities to stories about saints who originated as peasants. In many areas, barter replaced money transactions; some cities declined in population and wealth; and the traditional class of local urban notables nearly disappeared.

As the urban elite class shrank, the importance of high-ranking aristocrats at the imperial court and of rural landowners increased. Power organized by family began to rival power from class-based officeholding. By the end of the eleventh century, a family-based military aristocracy had emerged. Of Byzantine emperor Alexius Comnenus° (r. 1081–1118) it was said: "He considered himself not a ruler, but a lord, conceiving and calling the empire his own house."[4]

The situation of women changed, too. Although earlier Roman family life was centered on a legally all-powerful father, women enjoyed comparative freedom in public. After the seventh century women increasingly found themselves confined to the home. Some sources indicate that when they went out, they concealed their faces behind veils. The only men they socialized with were family members. Paradoxically, however, from 1028 to 1056 women ruled the Byzantine Empire alongside their husbands. These social changes and the apparent increase in the seclusion of women resemble simultaneous developments in neighboring Islamic countries, but historians have not uncovered any firm linkage between them.

Alexius Comnenus (uh-LEX-see-uhs kom-NAY-nuhs)

Economically, the Byzantine emperors continued the Late Roman inclination to set prices, organize grain shipments to the capital, and monopolize trade in luxury goods like Tyrian purple cloth. Such government intervention may have slowed technological development and economic innovation. So long as merchants and pilgrims hastened to Constantinople from all points of the compass, aristocrats could buy rare and costly goods. Just as the provisioning and physical improvement of Rome overshadowed the development of other cities at the height of the Roman Empire, so other Byzantine cities suffered from the intense focus on Constantinople. In the countryside, Byzantine farmers continued to use slow oxcarts and light scratch plows, which were efficient for many, but not all, soil types, long after farmers in western Europe had begun to adopt more efficient techniques (see below).

Because Byzantium's Roman inheritance remained so much more intact than western Europe's, few people recognized the slow deterioration. Gradually, however, pilgrims and visitors from the west saw the reality beyond the awe-inspiring, incense-filled domes of cathedrals and beneath the glitter and silken garments of the royal court. An eleventh-century French visitor wrote:

> The city itself [Constantinople] is squalid and fetid and in many places harmed by permanent darkness, for the wealthy overshadow the streets with buildings and leave these dirty, dark places to the poor and to travelers; there murders and robberies and other crimes which love the darkness are committed. Moreover, since people live lawlessly in this city, which has as many lords as rich men and almost as many thieves as poor men, a criminal knows neither fear nor shame, because crime is not punished by law and never entirely comes to light. In every respect she exceeds moderation; for, just as she surpasses other cities in wealth, so too, does she surpass them in vice.[5]

A Byzantine contemporary, Anna Comnena, the brilliant daughter of Emperor Alexius Comnenus, expressed the view from the other side. She scornfully described a prominent churchman and philosopher who happened to be from Italy: "Italos . . . was unable with his barbaric, stupid temperament to grasp the profound truths of philosophy; even in the act of learning he utterly rejected the teacher's guiding hand, and full of temerity and barbaric folly, [believed] even before study that he excelled all others."[6]

Cultural Achievements

Justinian's collection of Roman laws endured far longer than his restoration of Byzantine rule in Italy and North Africa. At his command a team of seventeen legal scholars made a systematic compilation, in Latin, of a thousand years of Roman legal tradition. The *Corpus Juris Civilis (Body of Civil Law)*, as it has been called since the sixteenth century, consisted of four sections: a general introduction and survey, a digest for lawyers and judges containing specific laws and quotations from well-known commentaries, a collection of imperial decrees since the time of the emperor Hadrian (r. 117–138), and another collection of recent decrees not previously collected. In the eleventh century a legal scholar named Irnerius (ca. 1055–ca. 1130) revived the study of this code (see below) at the University of Bologna° in Italy, and it subsequently became the basis of most modern European legal systems.

Constantinople's cathedral, the Hagia Sophia° ("Sacred Wisdom"), also dates in its present form to the reign of Justinian and his influential wife, the empress Theodora. Its great dome became a hallmark of Byzantine architecture. Artistic creativity appeared in the design and ornamentation of other churches and monasteries as well. Byzantine religious art, featuring stiff but arresting images of holy figures against gold backgrounds, strongly influenced painting in western Europe down to the thirteenth century, and Byzantine musical traditions strongly affected the chanting employed in medieval Latin churches.

Other important Byzantine achievements date to the empire's long period of political decline. In the ninth century brothers named Cyril and Methodius embarked on a highly successful mission to the Slavs of Moravia (part of the modern Czech Republic). Like the Gothic bishop Ulfilas in the fourth century, they preached in the local language, and their followers perfected a writing system, called Cyrillic°, that came to be used by Slavic Christians adhering to the Orthodox—that is, Byzantine—rite. Their careers also mark the beginning of a competition between the Greek and Latin forms of Christianity for the allegiance of the Slavs. The use today of the Cyrillic alphabet among the Russians and other Slavic peoples of Orthodox Christian faith, and of the Roman alphabet among the Poles, Czechs, and Croatians, testifies to this competition (see the section below on Kievan Russia).

Bologna (boe-LOAN-yuh) **Hagia Sophia** (AH-yah SOH-fee-uh)
Cyrillic (sih-RIL-ik)

EARLY MEDIEVAL EUROPE, 300–1000

Constantine kept the Roman Empire under his sole rule (see Chapter 6) even as he was building his new capital of Constantinople, but union did not last. Divisions between east and west that had appeared earlier became permanent in 395. Germanic peoples fleeing the Huns, a new invader from Asia, put pressure on both halves. Byzantine armies and diplomats warded off most assaults on the comparatively short Danube River frontier, persuading the bands of warriors to keep moving westward. But the Roman legions in the west could not hold. Gaul, Britain, Spain, and North Africa fell to various Germanic peoples in the early fifth century. Visigoths sacked Rome itself in 410, and the last Roman emperor was deposed in 476.

The disappearance of the imperial legal framework that had persisted to the final days of the Western Roman Empire and the rise of various kings, nobles, and chieftains changed the legal and political landscape of western Europe. In region after region, the family-based traditions of the Germanic peoples, which often fit local conditions better than previous practices, supplanted the edicts of the Roman emperors.

Fear and physical insecurity led communities to seek the protection of local strongmen. In places where looters and pillagers might appear at any moment, a local lord with a castle at which peasants could take refuge counted for more than a distant king. Dependency of weak people on strong people became a hallmark of the post-Roman period in western Europe.

From Roman Empire to Germanic Kingdoms

By 530 the Western Roman Empire had fragmented into a handful of kingdoms under Germanic rulers. The Franks held much of Gaul; the Visigoths ruled in Spain and the Ostrogoths in Italy and present-day Austria and Hungary. Saxons, Angles, and Jutes made raids across the North Sea and eventually took over most of Britain (see Map 10.2). By 600 the Lombards had replaced the Ostrogoths in northern Italy, and the Byzantine Empire had regained footholds in the south and around Ravenna along the east coast. The city of Rome had lost its political importance but retained prominence as the seat of the most influential Western churchman, the bishop of Rome. Local noble families competed for control of this position, which over several centuries acquired the title *Pope* along with supreme power in the Latin-speaking church. Greek, which had once been common in Rome and had become the religious language of the Byzantine church, became rare.

The educated few, increasingly only Christian priests and monks, still spoke and wrote a somewhat simplified form of Latin. But the Latin of the uneducated masses who had lived under Roman rule rapidly evolved into the Romance dialects that eventually became modern Portuguese, Spanish, French, Italian, and Romanian. In the north and east of the Rhine River, where Roman culture had scarcely penetrated, people spoke Germanic and related Scandinavian languages. East of the Elbe River speakers of Slavic languages formed a third major group.

In 711 a frontier raiding party of Arabs and Berbers, acting under the authority of the Umayyad caliph in

Saxon Belt Buckle from Eastern England   This fine specimen of the German jeweler's art was found in the excavation of a buried ship at the site known as Sutton Hoo. The find dates from ca. 660 and shows the fascination of the Germanic peoples with patterns of interlaced animal figures. This interlace style reappears in Christian manuscripts such as the Book of Kells shown on page 268.   (Courtesy of the Trustees of the Bristish Museum)

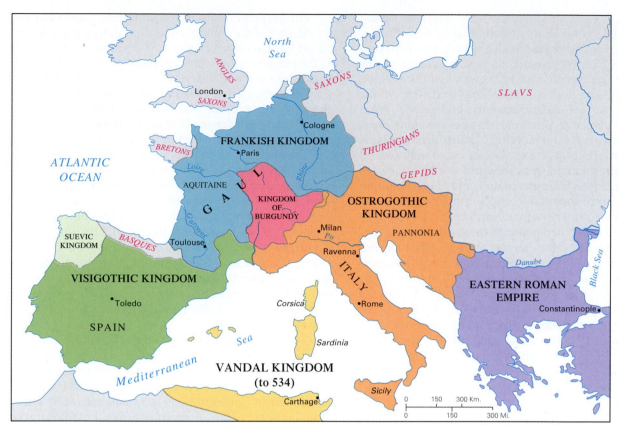

Map 10.2   Germanic Kingdoms   Though German kings asserted authority over most of western Europe, German-speaking peoples were most numerous east of the Rhine River. In most other areas, Celtic languages, for example, Breton on this map, or languages derived from Latin predominated. Though the Germanic Anglo-Saxon tongue increasingly supplanted Welsh and Scottish in Britain, the absolute number of Germanic settlers seems to have been fairly limited.

Syria, crossed the Strait of Gibraltar and overturned the kingdom of the Visigoths in Spain (see Chapter 9). The disunited Europeans could not stop them from consolidating their hold on the Iberian Peninsula. After pushing the remaining Christian chieftains into the northern mountains, the Muslims moved on to France. They occupied much of the southern coast and penetrated as far north as Tours, less than 150 miles (240 kilometers) from the English Channel, before Charlemagne's grandfather, Charles Martel, stopped their most advanced raiding party in 732.

Military effectiveness was the key element in the rise of the Carolingian° family (from Latin *Carolus*, "Charles") first as protectors of the Frankish kings, then as kings themselves under Charlemagne's father Pepin (r. 751–768), and finally, under Charlemagne, as emperors. At the peak of Charlemagne's power, the Carolingian Em-

pire encompassed all of Gaul and parts of Germany and Italy, with the pope ruling part of the latter. When Charlemagne's son, Louis the Pious, died, the Germanic tradition of splitting property among sons led to the Treaty of Verdun (843), which split the empire into three parts. French-speaking in the west (France) and middle (Burgundy), and German-speaking in the east (Germany), the three regions never reunited. Nevertheless, the Carolingian economic system based on landed wealth and a brief intellectual revival sponsored personally by Charlemagne—though he himself was illiterate—provided a common heritage.

A new threat to western Europe appeared in 793, when the Vikings, sea raiders from Scandinavia, attacked and plundered a monastery on the English coast, the first of hundreds of such raids. Local sources from France, the British Isles, and Muslim Spain attest to widespread dread of Viking warriors descending from multi-oared, dragon-prowed boats to pillage monasteries, villages,

Carolingian (kah-roe-LIN-gee-uhn)

and towns. Viking shipbuilders made versatile vessels that could brave the stormy North Atlantic and also maneuver up rivers to attack inland towns. In the ninth century raiders from Denmark and Norway harried the British and French coasts (see Diversity and Dominance: Archbishop Adalbert of Hamburg and the Christianization of the Scandinavians and Slavs) while Varangians° (Swedes) pursued raiding and trading interests, and eventually the building of kingdoms, along the rivers of eastern Europe and Russia, as we shall see. Although many Viking raiders sought booty and slaves, in the 800s and 900s Viking captains organized the settlement of Iceland, Greenland, and, around the year 1000, Vinland on the northern tip of Newfoundland.

Vikings long settled on lands they had seized in Normandy (in northwestern France) organized the most important and ambitious expeditions in terms of numbers of men and horses and long-lasting impact. William the Conqueror, the duke of Normandy, invaded England in 1066 and brought Anglo-Saxon domination of the island to an end. Other Normans (from "north men") attacked Muslim Sicily in the 1060s and, after thirty years of fighting, permanently severed it from the Muslim world.

A Self-Sufficient Economy

Archaeology and records kept by Christian monasteries and convents reveal a profound economic transformation that accompanied the new Germanic political order. The new rulers cared little for the urban-based civilization of the Romans, which accordingly shrank in importance. Though the pace of change differed from region to region, most cities lost population, in some cases becoming villages. Roman roads fell into disuse and disrepair. Small thatched houses sprang up beside abandoned villas, and public buildings made of marble became dilapidated in the absence of the laborers, money, and civic leadership needed to maintain them. Paying for purchases in coin largely gave way to bartering goods and services.

The level of trade diminished. Egyptian wheat that had once fed the multitudes of Rome went to Constantinople and after the seventh century to Mecca and Medina. In 439 an invasion by Germanic Vandals from Spain cut off Tunisia, another of Rome's breadbaskets. Trade across the Mediterranean did not entirely stop; occasional shipments from Egypt and Syria continued to reach western ports. But most of western Europe came to rely on meager local resources. These resources, moreover, underwent redistribution.

Roman centralization had channeled the wealth and production of the empire to the capital, which in turn radiated Roman cultural styles and tastes to the provinces. As Roman governors were replaced by Germanic territorial lords who found the riches of their own culture more appealing than those of Rome, local self-sufficiency became more important. The decline of literacy and other aspects of Roman life made room for the growth of Celtic and Germanic cultural traditions.

The diet in the northern countries featured beer, lard or butter, and bread made of barley, rye, or wheat, all supplemented by pork from herds of swine fed on forest acorns and beechnuts, and by game from the same forests. Nobles ate better than peasants, but even the peasant diet was reasonably balanced. The Roman diet based on wheat, wine, and olive oil persisted in the south. The average western European of the ninth century was probably better nourished than his or her descendants three hundred years later, when population was increasing and the nobility monopolized the resources of the forests.

In both north and south, self-sufficient farming estates known as **manors** became the primary centers of agricultural production. Wealthy Romans had commonly built country houses on their lands. From the fourth century onward, fear of attack led many common farmers in the most vulnerable regions to give their lands to large landowners in return for political and physical protection. The warfare and instability of the post-Roman centuries made unprotected country houses especially vulnerable to pillaging. Isolated by poor communications and lack of organized government, landowners depended on their own resources for survival. Many became warriors or maintained a force of armed men. Others swore allegiance to landowners who had armed forces to protect them.

A well-appointed manor possessed fields, gardens, grazing lands, fish ponds, a mill, a church, workshops for making farm and household implements, and a village where the farmers dependent on the lord of the manor lived. Depending on local conditions, protection ranged from a ditch and wooden stockade to a stone wall surrounding a fortified keep (a stone building). Fortification tended to increase until the twelfth century, when stronger monarchies made it less necessary.

Manor life reflected personal status. Nobles and their families exercised almost unlimited power over the **serfs**—agricultural workers who belonged to the manor, tilled its fields, and owed other dues and obligations. Serfs could not leave the manor where they were born and attach themselves to another lord. Most peasants in England, France, and western Germany

---

Varangians (va-RAN-gee-anz)

were unfree serfs in the tenth and eleventh centuries. In Bordeaux°, Saxony, and a few other regions free peasantry survived based on the egalitarian social structure of the Germanic peoples during their period of migration. Outright slavery, the mainstay of the Roman economy (see Chapter 6), diminished as more and more peasants became serfs in return for a lord's protection. The enslavement of prisoners to serve as laborers became less important as an object of warfare.

Early Medieval Society in the West

Europe's reversion to a self-sufficient economy limited the freedom and potential for personal achievement of most people, but an emerging class of nobles reaped great benefits. During the Germanic migrations and later among the Vikings of Scandinavia, men regularly answered the call to arms issued by war chiefs, to whom they swore allegiance. All warriors shared in the booty gained from raiding. As settlement enhanced the importance of agricultural tasks, laying down the plow and picking up the sword at the chieftain's call became harder.

Those who, out of loyalty or desire for adventure, continued to join the war parties included a growing number of horsemen. Mounted warriors became the central force of the Carolingian army. At first, fighting from horseback did not make a person either a nobleman or a landowner. By the tenth century, however, nearly constant warfare to protect land rights or support the claims of a lord brought about a gradual transformation in the status of the mounted warrior, which led, at different rates in different areas, to landholding becoming almost inseparable from military service.

In trying to understand long-standing traditions of landholding and obligation, lawyers in the sixteenth century and later simplified thousands of individual agreements into a neat system they called "feudalism," from Latin *feodum* meaning a land awarded for military service. It became common to refer to medieval Europe as a "feudal society" in which kings and lords gave land to "vassals" in return for sworn military support. By analyzing original records, more recent historians have discovered this to be an oversimplification. Relations between landholders and serfs and between lords and vassals differed too much from one place to another, and from one time to another, to fit together in anything resembling a system.

The German foes of the Roman legions had equipped themselves with helmets, shields, and swords, spears, or throwing axes. Some rode horses, but most fought on foot. Before the invention of the stirrup by Central Asian pastoralists in approximately the first century C.E., horsemen had gripped their mounts with their legs and fought with bows and arrows, throwing javelins, stabbing spears, and swords. Stirrups allowed a rider to stand in the saddle and absorb the impact when his lance struck an enemy at full gallop. This type of warfare required grain-fed horses that were larger and heavier than the small, grass-fed animals of the Central Asian nomads, though smaller and lighter than the draft horses bred in later times for hauling heavy loads. Thus agricultural Europe rather than the grassy steppes produced the charges of armored knights that came to dominate the battlefield.

By the eleventh century, the knight, called by different terms in different places, had emerged as the central figure in medieval warfare. He wore an open-faced helmet and a long linen shirt, or hauberk°, studded with small metal disks. A century later, knightly equipment commonly included a visored helmet that covered the head and neck and a hauberk of chain mail.

Each increase in armor for knight and horse entailed a greater financial outlay. Since land was the basis of wealth, a knight needed financial support from land revenues. Accordingly, kings began to reward armed service with grants of land from their own property. Lesser nobles with extensive properties built their own military retinues the same way.

A grant of land in return for a pledge to provide military service was often called a **fief.** At first, kings granted fiefs to their noble followers, known as **vassals,** on a temporary basis. By the tenth century, most fiefs could be inherited as long as the specified military service continued to be provided. Though patterns varied greatly, the association of landholding with military service made the medieval society of western Europe quite different from the contemporary city-based societies of the Islamic world.

Kings and lords might be able to command the service of their vassals for only part of the year. Vassals could hold land from several different lords and owe loyalty to each one. Moreover, the allegiance that a vassal owed to one lord could entail military service to that lord's master in time of need.

A "typical" medieval realm—actual practices varied between and within realms—consisted of lands directly owned by a king or a count and administered by his royal

---

Bordeaux (bore-DOE)

hauberk (HAW-berk)

DIVERSITY AND DOMINANCE

ARCHBISHOP ADALBERT OF HAMBURG AND THE CHRISTIANIZATION OF THE SCANDINAVIANS AND SLAVS

Adam of Bremen's History of the Archbishops of Hamburg-Bremen, *consists of four sections. The third is devoted to the Archbishop Adalbert, whose death in 1072 stirred Adam to write. References to classical poets, the lives of saints, and royal documents show that Adam, a churchman, had a solid education and access to many sources. He also drew on living informants, in particular the Danish king Svein Estrithson, a nephew of Canute, king of England from 1015 to 1035, and father-in-law of Gottschalk, a lord over the Slavs mentioned below. The excerpts below illustrate the close connection between political and religious institutions in establishing a structure of domination in lands on the European frontier.*

Archbishop Adalbert held the see for twenty-nine years. He received the pastoral staff from the [Holy Roman] Emperor Henry, the son of Conrad, who was, counting from Caesar Augustus, the ninetieth Roman emperor to sit upon the throne . . . The archiepiscopal pallium [i.e., bishop's cloak] was brought to him . . . by legates from the Pope Benedict . . . [who] was the one hundred and forty-seventh after the Apostles in the succession of Roman pontiffs. His consecration took place in Aachen in the presence of Caesar and of the princes of the realm. Twelve bishops assisted and laid their hands on him . . .

This remarkable man may for all that be extolled with praise of every kind in that he was noble, handsome, wise, eloquent, chaste, temperate. All these qualities he comprised in himself and others besides, such as one is wont to attach to the outer man: that he was rich, that he was successful, that he was glorious, that he was influential. All these things were his in abundance. Moreover, in respect of the mission to the heathen, which is the first duty of the Church at Hamburg, no one so vigorous could ever be found . . . Although he was such in the beginning, he seemed to fail toward the end. Not being well on his guard against any defect in his virtue, the man met with ruin as much through his own negligence as through the driving malice of others . . .

Keen and well trained of mind, he was skillful in many arts. In things divine and human he was possessed of great prudence and was well known for retaining in memory and setting forth with matchless eloquence what he had acquired by hearing or by study. Then, besides, although handsome in physical form, he was a lover of chastity. His generosity was of a kind that made him regard asking favors as unworthy, that made him slow and humble in accepting them but prompt and cheerful in giving, often generously, to those who had not asked. His humility appears doubtful in that he exhibited it only in respect of the servants of God, the poor, and pilgrims, and it went to such lengths that before retiring he often would on bended knees personally wash the feet of thirty or more beggars. To the princes of the world, however, and to his peers he would in no way stoop. Toward them he even broke out at times with a vehemence that at last spared no one he thought outstanding. Some he upbraided for luxury, others for greed, still others for infidelity . . .

On seeing that the basilica [i.e., cathedral] which had lately been started was an immense structure requiring very great resources, he with too precipitate judgment immediately had the city wall, begun by his predecessors, pulled down, as if it were not at all necessary, and ordered its stones built into the temple. Even the beautiful tower, . . . fitted out with seven chambers, was then razed to its foundations . . . Alebrand before him had begun [the cathedral] in the style of the church at Cologne [in western Germany], but he planned to carry it out in the manner of the cathedral at Benevento [in southern Italy] . . .

And because the great prelate saw that his Church and bishopric . . . was troubled again by the iniquitous might of the dukes, he made a supreme effort to restore to that Church its former freedom, that thus neither the duke nor the count nor any person of judicial position would have any right or power in his diocese. But this objective could not be attained without incurring hatred, since the wrath of the princes, rebuked for their wickedness, would be further inflamed. And they say that Duke Bernhard, who held the archbishop under suspicion because of his nobility and wisdom, often said that Adalbert had been stationed in this country like a spy, to betray the weaknesses of the land to the aliens and to Caesar. Consequently the duke declared that as long as he or any of his sons lived, the bishop should not have a happy day in the bishopric . . .

As soon as the metropolitan [i.e., Archbishop Adalbert] had entered upon his episcopate, he sent legates to the kings of the north in the interest of friendship. There were also dispersed throughout all Denmark and Norway and Sweden and to the ends of the earth admonitory letters in which he exhorted the bishops and priests living in those parts . . . fearlessly to forward the conversion of the pagans . . . [Svein, the Danish king who died after invading England in 1013 and left his throne to his son Canute] forgot the heavenly King as things prospered with him and married a blood relative from Sweden. This mightily displeased the lord archbishop, who sent legates to the rash king, rebuking him severely for his sin, and who stated finally that if he did not come to his senses, he would have to be cut off with the sword of excommunication. Beside himself with rage, the king then threatened to ravage and destroy the whole diocese of Hamburg. Unperturbed by these threats, our archbishop, reproving and entreating, remained firm, until at length the Danish tyrant was prevailed upon by letters from the pope to give his cousin a bill of divorce. Still the king would not give ear to the admonitions of the priests. Soon after he had put aside his cousin he took to himself other wives and concubines, and again still others . . .

While these events were taking place there, the most Christian king of the Swedes, James, departed this world, and his brother, Edmund the Bad, succeeded him. He was born of a concubine by Olaf [the Lapp King] and, although he had been baptized, took little heed of our religion. He had with him a certain bishop named Osmund, of irregular status, whom the bishop of the Norwegians, Sigefrid, had once commended to the school at Bremen for instruction. But later he forgot these kindnesses and went to Rome for consecration. When he was rejected there, he wandered about through many parts and so finally secured consecration from a Polish archbishop. Going to Sweden then, he boasted that he had been consecrated archbishop for those parts. But when our archbishop sent his legates to King [Edmund], they found this same vagabond Osmund there, having the cross borne before him after the manner of an archbishop. They also heard that he had by his unsound teaching of our faith corrupted the barbarians, who were still neophytes [i.e., beginners] . . .

In Norway . . . King Harold surpassed all the madness of tyrants in his savage wildness. Many churches were destroyed by that man; many Christians were tortured to death by him. But he was a mighty man and renowned for the victories he had previously won in many wars with barbarians in Greece and in the Scythian regions [i.e., while assisting the Byzantine empress Zoë fight the Seljuk Turks]. After he came into his fatherland, however, he never ceased from warfare;

he was the thunderbolt of the north . . . And so, as he ruled over many nations, he was odious to all on account of his greed and cruelty. He also gave himself up to the magic arts and, wretched man that he was, did not heed the fact that his most saintly brother [i.e., Saint Olaf, one of Harold's predecessors] had eradicated such illusions from the realm and striven even unto death for the adoption of the precepts of Christianity . . .

Across the Elbe [i.e., east of the river Hamburg is on] and in Slavia our affairs were still meeting with great success. For Gottschalk . . . married a daughter of the Danish king and so thoroughly subdued the Slavs that they feared him like a king, offered to pay tribute, and asked for peace with subjection. Under these circumstances our Church at Hamburg enjoyed peace, and Slavia abounded in priests and churches . . . Gottschalk is said to have been inflamed with such ardent zeal for the faith that, forgetting his station, he frequently made discourse in church in exhortation of the people—in church because he wished to make clearer in the Slavic speech what was abstrusely preached by the bishops or priests. Countless was the number of those who were converted every day; so much so that he sent into every province for priests. In the several cities were then also founded monasteries for holy men who lived according to canonical rule . . .

I have also heard the most veracious king of the Danes say . . . that the Slavic peoples without doubt could easily have been converted to Christianity long ago but for the avarice of the Saxons. "They are," he said, "more intent on the payment of tribute than on the conversion of the heathen." Nor do these wretched people realize with what great danger they will have to atone for their cupidity, they who through their avarice in the first place threw Christianity in Slavia into disorder, in the second place have by their cruelty forced their subjects to rebel, and who now by their desire only for money hold in contempt the salvation of a people who wish to believe" . . .

QUESTIONS FOR ANALYSIS

1. Using this work as a historical source, what would you consider the main concerns of the church in northern Germany?

2. How does Adam distinguish Christians from pagans in his descriptive passages?

3. What appears to be the relationship between ecclesiastical lords like the archbishop and the secular kings and dukes?

Source: Excerpts from *History of the Archbishops of Hamburg-Bremen*, tr. Francis J. Tschan (New York: Columbia University Press, 1959 [new ed. 2002]), 114–133. Reprinted with the permission of the publisher.

Noblewoman Directing Construction of a Church   This picture of Berthe, wife of Girat de Rouissillion, acting as mistress of the works comes from a tenth-century manuscript that shows a scene from the ninth century. Wheelbarrows rarely appear in medieval building scenes.   (Copyright Brussels, Royal Library of Belgium)

officers. The king's or count's major vassals held and administered other lands, often the greater portion, in return for military service. These vassals, in turn, granted land to their own vassals.

The lord of a manor provided governance and justice, direct royal government being quite limited. The king had few financial resources and seldom exercised legal jurisdiction at a local level. Members of the clergy, as well as the extensive agricultural lands owned by monasteries and nunneries, fell under the jurisdiction of the church, which further limited the reach and authority of the monarch.

Noblewomen became enmeshed in this tangle of obligations as heiresses and as candidates for marriage. A man who married the widow or daughter of a lord with no sons could gain control of that lord's property. Marriage alliances affected entire kingdoms. Noble daughters and sons had little say in marriage matters; issues of land, power, and military service took precedence. Noblemen guarded the women in their families as closely as their other valuables.

Nevertheless, women could own land. A noblewoman sometimes administered her husband's estates when he was away at war. Nonnoble women usually worked alongside their menfolk, performing agricultural tasks such as raking and stacking hay, shearing sheep, and picking vegetables. As artisans, women spun, wove, and sewed clothing. The Bayeux° Tapestry, a piece of embroidery 230 feet (70 meters) long and 20 inches (51 centimeters) wide depicting William the Conqueror's invasion of England in 1066, was designed and executed entirely by women, though historians do not agree on who those women were.

THE WESTERN CHURCH

Just as the Christian populations in eastern Europe followed the religious guidance of the patriarch of Constantinople appointed by the Byzantine emperor, so the pope commanded similar authority over church affairs in western Europe. And just as missionaries in the east spread Christianity among the Slavs, so missionaries in

Bayeux (bay-YUH)

the west added territory to Christendom with forays into the British Isles and the lands of the Germans. Throughout the period covered by this chapter Christian society was emerging and changing in both areas.

In the west Roman nobles lost control of the **papacy**— the office of the pope—and it became a more powerful international office after the tenth century. Councils of bishops—which normally set rules, called canons, to regulate the priests and laypeople (men and women who were not members of the clergy) under their jurisdiction—became increasingly responsive to papal direction.

Nevertheless, regional disagreements over church regulations, shortages of educated and trained clergy, difficult communications, political disorder, and the general insecurity of the period posed formidable obstacles to unifying church standards and practices. Clerics in some parts of western Europe were still issuing prohibitions against the worship of rivers, trees, and mountains as late as the eleventh century. Church problems included lingering polytheism, lax enforcement of prohibitions against marriage of clergy, nepotism (giving preferment to one's close kin), and simony (selling ecclesiastical appointments, often to people who were not members of the clergy). The persistence of the papacy in asserting its legal jurisdiction over clergy, combating polytheism and heretical beliefs, and calling on secular rulers to recognize the pope's authority, including unpopular rulings like a ban on first-cousin marriage, constituted a rare force for unity and order in a time of disunity and chaos.

Politics and the Church

In politically fragmented western Europe, the pope needed allies. Like his son, Charlemagne's father Pepin was a strong supporter of the papacy. The relationship between kings and popes was tense, however, since both thought of themselves as ultimate authorities. In 962 the pope crowned the first "Holy Roman Emperor" (Charlemagne never held this full title). This designation of a secular political authority as the guardian of general Christian interests proved more apparent then real. Essentially a loose confederation of German princes who named one of their own to the highest office, the **Holy Roman Empire** had little influence west of the Rhine River.

Although the pope crowned the early Holy Roman emperors, this did not signify political superiority. The law of the church (known as canon law because each law was called a canon) gave the pope exclusive legal jurisdiction over all clergy and church property wherever located. But bishops who held land as vassals owed military support or other services and dues to kings and princes. The secular rulers argued that they should have the power to appoint those bishops because that was the only way to guarantee fulfillment of their duties as vassals. The popes disagreed.

In the eleventh century, this conflict over the control of ecclesiastical appointments came to a head. Hildebrand°, an Italian monk, capped a career of reorganizing church finances when the cardinals (a group of senior bishops) meeting in Rome selected him to be Pope Gregory VII in 1073. His personal notion of the papacy (preserved among his letters) represented an extreme position, stating among other claims, that

§ The pope can be judged by no one;
§ The Roman church has never erred and never will err till the end of time;
§ The pope alone can depose and restore bishops;
§ He alone can call general councils and authorize canon law;
§ He can depose emperors;
§ He can absolve subjects from their allegiance;
§ All princes should kiss his feet.[7]

Such claims antagonized lords and monarchs, who had become accustomed to *investing*—that is, conferring a ring and a staff as symbols of authority on bishops and abbots in their domains. Historians apply the term **investiture controversy** to the medieval struggle between the church and the lay lords to control ecclesiastical appointments; the term also refers to the broader conflict of popes versus emperors and kings. When Holy Roman Emperor Henry IV defied Gregory's reforms, Gregory excommunicated him in 1076, thereby cutting him off from church rituals. Stung by the resulting decline in his influence, Henry stood barefoot in the snow for three days outside a castle in northern Italy waiting for Gregory, a guest there, to receive him. Henry's formal act of penance induced Gregory to forgive him and restore him to the church; but the reconciliation, an apparent victory for the pope, did not last. In 1078 Gregory declared Henry deposed. The emperor then forced Gregory to flee from Rome to Salerno, where he died two years later.

The struggle between the popes and emperors continued until 1122, when a compromise was reached at Worms, a town in Germany. In the Concordat of Worms, Emperor Henry V renounced his right to choose bishops and abbots or bestow spiritual symbols upon them. In return, Pope Calixtus II permitted the emperor to invest papally appointed bishops and abbots with any lay rights or obligations before their spiritual consecration.

Hildebrand (HILL-de-brand)

Such compromises did not fully solve the problem, but they reduced tensions between the two sides.

Assertions of royal authority triggered other conflicts as well. Though barely twenty when he became king of England in 1154, Henry II, a great-grandson of William the Conqueror, instituted reforms designed to strengthen the power of the Crown and weaken the nobility. He appointed traveling justices to enforce his laws. He made juries, a holdover from traditional Germanic law, into powerful legal instruments. He established the principle that criminal acts violated the "king's peace" and should be tried and punished in accordance with charges brought by the Crown instead of in response to charges brought by victims.

Henry had a harder time controlling the church. His closest friend and chancellor, or chief administrator, Thomas à Becket (ca. 1118–1170), lived the grand and luxurious life of a courtier. In 1162 Henry persuaded Becket to become a priest and assume the position of archbishop of Canterbury, the highest church office in England. Becket agreed but cautioned that from then on he would act solely in the interest of the church if it came into conflict with the Crown. When Henry sought to try clerics accused of crimes in royal instead of ecclesiastical courts, Archbishop Thomas, now leading an austere and pious life, resisted.

In 1170 four of Henry's knights, knowing that the king desired Becket's death, murdered the archbishop in Canterbury Cathedral. Their crime backfired, and an outpouring of sympathy caused Canterbury to become a major pilgrimage center. In 1173 the pope declared the martyred Becket a saint. Henry allowed himself to be publicly whipped twice in penance for the crime, but his authority had been badly damaged.

Henry II's conflict with Thomas à Becket, like the Concordat of Worms, yielded no clear victor. The problem of competing legal traditions made political life in western Europe more complicated than in Byzantium or the lands of Islam (see Chapter 9). Feudal law, rooted in Germanic custom, gave supreme power to the king. Canon law, based on Roman precedent, visualized a single hierarchical legal institution with jurisdiction over all of Western Christendom. In the eleventh century Roman civil law, contained in the *Corpus Juris Civilis*, added a third tradition.

Monasticism

Monasticism featured prominently in the religious life of almost all medieval Christian lands. The origins of group monasticism lay in the eastern lands of the Roman Empire. Pre-Christian practices such as celibacy, continual devotion to prayer, and living

Illuminated Manuscript from Monastic Library   This page from the Book of Kells, written around 800 in Ireland, contains the Greek letters chi and rho, or CR, a monogram for Jesus Christ. The intricate interwoven forms that fill the background derive from pagan design traditions that featured intertangled dragons, snakes, and other beasts.   (The Board of Trinity College, Dublin)

apart from society (alone or in small groups) came together in Christian form in Egypt. A fourth-century account portrays Anthony, the most important solitary monk, as a pious desert hermit continually tempted by Satan. On one occasion, "when he was weaving palm leaves . . . that he might make baskets to give as gifts to people who were continually coming to visit him . . . he saw an animal which had the following form: from its head to its side it was like a man, and its legs and feet were those of an ass."[8] As was his custom, Anthony prayed to God upon seeing this sight, and Satan left him alone. Exaggerated stories like these are common in the popular accounts of saints' lives. In reality, saintly hermits gave strong moral leadership to their pious admirers.

The most important form of monasticism in western Europe involved groups of monks or nuns living together in a single community. An Egyptian monk named Pachomius had begun this practice in Egypt, but the person most responsible for introducing it in the Latin west was Benedict of Nursia (ca. 480–547) in Italy. Benedict began his pious career as a hermit in a cave but eventually organized several monasteries, each headed by an abbot. The Rule he wrote to govern the monks' behavior envisions a balanced life of devotion and work, along with obligations of celibacy, poverty, and obedience to the abbot. Those who lived by this or other monastic rules became *regular clergy,* in contrast to *secular clergy,* priests who lived in society instead of in seclusion and did not follow a formal code of regulations. The Rule of Benedict was the starting point for most forms of western European monastic life and remains in force today in Benedictine monasteries.

Though monks and nuns, women who lived by monastic rules in convents, made up a small percentage of the total population, their secluded way of life reinforced the separation of religious affairs from ordinary politics and economics. Monasteries followed Jesus' axiom to "render unto Caesar what is Caesar's and unto God what is God's" better than the many town-based bishops who behaved like lords.

Monasteries preserved literacy and learning in the early medieval period, although some rulers, like Charlemagne, encouraged scholarship at court. Many illiterate lay nobles interested themselves only in warfare and hunting. Monks (but seldom nuns) saw copying manuscripts and even writing books as a religious calling. Monastic scribes preserved many ancient Latin works that would otherwise have disappeared. The survival of Greek works depended more on Byzantine and Muslim scribes in the east.

Monasteries and convents served other functions as well (see Environment and Technology: Cathedral Organs). A few planted Christianity in new lands, as Irish monks did in parts of Germany. Most serviced the needs of travelers, organized agricultural production on their lands, and took in infants abandoned by their parents. Convents provided refuge for widows and other women who lacked male protection in the harsh medieval world or who desired a spiritual life. These religious houses presented problems of oversight to the church, however. A bishop might have authority over an abbot or abbess (head of a convent), but he could not exercise constant vigilance over what went on behind monastery walls.

The failure of some abbots to maintain monastic discipline led to the growth of a reform movement centered on the Benedictine abbey of Cluny° in eastern France. Founded in 910 by William the Pious, the first

Cluny (KLOO-nee)

duke of Aquitaine, who completely freed it of lay authority, Cluny gained similar freedom from the local bishop a century later. Its abbots pursued a vigorous campaign, eventually in alliance with reforming popes like Gregory VII, to improve monastic discipline and administration. A magnificent new abbey church symbolized Cluny's claims to eminence. With later additions, it became the largest church in the world.

At the peak of Cluny's influence, nearly a thousand Benedictine abbeys and priories (lower-level monastic houses) in various countries accepted the authority of its abbot. The Benedictine Rule had presumed that each monastery would be independent; the Cluniac reformers stipulated that every abbot and every prior (head of a priory) be appointed by the abbot of Cluny and have personal experience of the religious life of Cluny. Monastic reform gained new impetus in the second half of the twelfth century with the rapid rise of the Cistercian order, which emphasized a life of asceticism and poverty. These movements set the pattern for the monasteries, cathedral clergy, and preaching friars that would dominate ecclesiastical life in the thirteenth century.

KIEVAN RUSSIA, 900–1200

Though Latin and Orthodox Christendom followed different paths in later centuries, which had a more promising future was not apparent in 900. The Poles and other Slavic peoples living in the north eventually accepted the Christianity of Rome as taught by German priests and missionaries (see Diversity and Dominance: Archbishop Adalbert of Hamburg and the Christianization of Scandinavians and Slavs). The Serbs and other southern Slavs took their faith from Constantinople.

The conversion of Kievan Russia, farther to the east, shows how economics, politics, and religious life were closely intertwined. The choice of orthodoxy over Catholicism had important consequences for later European history.

The Rise of the Kievan State

The territory between the Black and Caspian Seas in the south and the Baltic and White Seas in the north divides into a series of east-west zones. Frozen tundra in the far north gives way to a cold forest zone, then to a more temperate forest, then to a mix of forest and steppe grasslands, and

Cathedral Organs

The Christian church directly encouraged musical development. Pope Gregory I (d. 604) is traditionally credited with making a standard collection of chants then in use. Later, a special school in Rome trained choir directors who were sent out to teach the chants in cathedrals and monasteries. Organ accompaniment, initially in the form of long, sustained bass notes, came into common use by the end of the seventh century. The organ worked by directing a current of air to a set of pipes of different lengths that could be opened or closed at one end. Each pipe sounded a tone as long as the air was flowing past its open end.

A monk named Wulstan (d. 963) described the organ installed in Winchester Cathedral in England:

> Twice six bellows above are ranged in a row, and fourteen lie below. These, by alternate blasts, supply an immense quantity of wind, and are worked by 70 strong men, laboring with their arms, covered with perspiration, each inciting his companions to drive the wind up with all his strength, that the full-bosomed box may speak with its 400 pipes, which the hand of the organist governs. Some when closed he opens, others when open he closes, as the individual nature of the varied sound requires. Two brethren of concordant spirit sit at the instrument . . . Like thunder their tones batter the ear, so that it may receive no sound but that alone. To such an amount does it reverberate, echoing in every direction, that everyone stops with his hand his gaping ears, being in no wise able to draw near and bear the sound, which so many combinations produce.

A century later huge levers or keys came into use for opening and closing the pipes. Each was several inches in width, one or two inches thick, and up to three feet in length. So much muscle was required to operate the keys that organists were called "organ pounders." Over time, organs became smaller and capable of playing magnificent music.

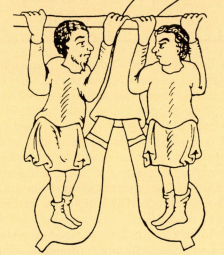

Cathedral Organ   Note the unhappy faces on the men assigned the dreary and noisy job of pumping the bellows for an organ. Note also the ping-pong paddle shaped keys that are more appropriate to pounding with a fist than pressing with a finger.
(St. John's College Library, Cambridge Manuscript, B.18)

Source: Alexander Russell, "Organ," *The International Cyclopedia of Music and Musicians*, ed. Oscar Thompson (New York: Dodd, Mead, 1943), 1315.

---

finally to grassland only. Several navigable rivers, including the Volga, the Dnieper°, and the Don, run from north to south across these zones.

Early historical sources reflect repeated linguistic and territorial changes, seemingly under pressure from poorly understood population migrations. Most of the Germanic peoples, along with some Iranian and west Slavic peoples, migrated into eastern Europe from Ukraine and Russia in Roman times. The peoples who remained behind spoke eastern Slavic languages, except in the far north and south: Finns and related peoples lived in the former region, Turkic-speakers in the latter.

Forest dwellers, farmers, and steppe nomads complemented each other economically. Nomads traded an-

Dnieper (d-NYEP-er)

Cathedral of Saint Dmitry in Vladimir
Built between 1193 and 1197, this Russian Orthodox cathedral shows Byzantine influence. The three-arch façade, small dome, and symmetrical Greek-cross floor plan strongly resemble features of the Byzantine church shown on page 258.   (Sovfoto)

imals for the farmers' grain; and honey, wax, and furs from the forest became important exchange items. Traders could travel east and west by steppe caravan (see Chapters 8 and 13), or they could use boats on the rivers to move north and south.

Hoards containing thousands of Byzantine and Islamic coins buried in Poland and on islands in the Baltic Sea where fairs were held attest to the trading activity of Varangians (Swedish Vikings) who sailed across the Baltic and down Russia's rivers. They exchanged forest products and slaves for manufactured goods and coins, which they may have used as jewelry rather than as money, at markets controlled by the Khazar Turks. The powerful Khazar kingdom centered around the mouth of the Volga River.

Historians debate the early meaning of the word *Rus* (from which *Russia* is derived), but at some point it came to refer to Slavic-speaking peoples ruled by Varangians. Unlike western European lords, the Varangian princes and their *druzhina* (military retainers) lived in cities, while the Slavs farmed. The princes occupied themselves with trade and fending off enemies. The Rus of the city of Kiev° controlled trade on the Dnieper River and dealt more with Byzantium than with the Muslim world because the Dnieper flows into the Black Sea. The Rus of Novgorod° played the same role on the Volga. The semi-legendary account of the Kievan Rus conversion to Christianity must be seen against this background.

In 980 Vladimir° I, a ruler of Novgorod who had fallen from power, returned from exile to Kiev with a band of

Kiev (KEE-yev)   **Novgorod** (NOHV-goh-rod)
Vladimir (VLAD-ih-mir)

Varangians and made himself the grand prince of Kievan Russia (see Map 10.3). Though his grandmother Olga had been a Christian, Vladimir built a temple on Kiev's heights and placed there the statues of the six gods his Slavic subjects worshipped. The earliest Russian chronicle reports that Vladimir and his advisers decided against Islam as the official religion because of its ban on alcohol, rejected Judaism (the religion to which the Khazars had converted) because they thought that a truly powerful god would not have let the ancient Jewish kingdom be destroyed, and even spoke with German emissaries advocating Latin Christianity. Why Vladimir chose Orthodox Christianity over the Latin version is not precisely known. The magnificence of Constantinople seems to have been a consideration. After visiting Byzantine churches, his agents reported: "We knew not whether we were in heaven or on earth, for on earth there is no such splendor of [sic] such beauty, and we are at a loss how to describe it. We know only that God dwells there among men, and their service is finer than the ceremonies of other nations."[9]

After choosing a reluctant bride from the Byzantine imperial family, Vladimir converted to Orthodox Christianity, probably in 988, and opened his lands to Orthodox clerics and missionaries. The patriarch of Constantinople appointed a metropolitan (chief bishop) at Kiev to govern ecclesiastical affairs. Churches arose in Kiev, one of them on the ruins of Vladimir's earlier hilltop temple. Writing was introduced, using the Cyrillic alphabet devised earlier for the western Slavs. This extension of Orthodox Christendom northward provided a barrier against the eastward expansion of Latin Christianity. Kiev became firmly oriented toward trade with Byzantium and turned its back on the Muslim world, though the Volga trade continued through Novgorod.

Struggles within the ruling family and with other enemies, most notably the steppe peoples of the south, marked the later political history of Kievan Russia. But down to the time of the Mongols in the thirteenth century (see Chapter 13), the state remained and served as an instrument for the Christianization of the eastern Slavs.

Society and Culture

In Kievan Russia political power derived from trade rather than from landholding, so the manorial agricultural system of western Europe never developed. Farmers practiced shifting cultivation of their own lands. They would burn a section of forest, then lightly scratch the ash-strewn surface with a plow. When fertility waned, they would move to another section of forest. Poor land and a short growing season in the most northerly latitudes made food scarce. Living on their own estates, the druzhina evolved from infantry into cavalry and focused their efforts more on horse breeding than on agriculture.

Large cities like Kiev and Novgorod may have reached thirty thousand or fifty thousand people—roughly the size of contemporary London or Paris, but far smaller than Constantinople or major Muslim metropolises like Baghdad and Nishapur. Many cities amounted to little more than fortified trading posts. Yet they served as centers for the development of crafts, some, such as glassmaking, based on skills imported from Byzantium. Artisans enjoyed higher status in society than peasant farmers. Construction relied on wood from the forests, although Christianity brought the building of stone cathedrals and churches on the Byzantine model.

Christianity penetrated the general population slowly. Several polytheist uprisings occurred in the eleventh century, particularly in times of famine. Passive resistance led some groups to reject Christian burial and persist in cremating the dead and keeping the bones of the deceased in urns. Women continued to use polytheist designs on their clothing and bracelets, and as late as the twelfth century they were still turning to polytheist priests for charms to cure sick children. Traditional Slavic marriage practices involving casual and polygamous relations particularly scandalized the clergy.

Christianity eventually triumphed, and its success led to increasing church engagement in political and economic affairs. In the twelfth century, Christian clergy became involved in government administration, some of them collecting fees and taxes related to trade. Direct and indirect revenue from trade provided the rulers with the money they needed to pay their soldiers. The rule of law also spread as Kievan Russia experienced its peak of culture and prosperity in the century before the Mongol invasion of 1237.

Map 10.3 Kievan Russia and the Byzantine Empire in the Eleventh Century By the mid-eleventh century, the princes of Kievan Russia had brought all the eastern Slavs under their rule. The loss of Egypt, Syria, and Tunisia to Arab invaders in the seventh to eighth century had turned Byzantium from a far-flung empire into a fairly compact state. From then on the Byzantine rulers looked to the Balkans and Kievan Russia as the primary arena for extending their political and religious influence.

WESTERN EUROPE REVIVES, 1000–1200

Between 1000 and 1200 western Europe slowly emerged from nearly seven centuries of subsistence economy—in which most people who worked on the land could meet only their basic needs for food, clothing, and shelter. Population and agricultural production climbed, and a growing food surplus found its way to town markets, speeding the return of a money-based economy and providing support for larger numbers of craftspeople, construction workers, and traders.

Historians have attributed western Europe's revival to population growth spurred by new technologies and to the appearance in Italy and Flanders, on the coast of the North Sea, of self-governing cities devoted primarily to seaborne trade. For monarchs, the changes facilitated improvements in central administration, greater control over vassals, and consolidation of realms on the way to becoming stronger kingdoms.

The Role of Technology

A lack of concrete evidence confirming the spread of technological innovations frustrates efforts to relate the exact course of Europe's revival to technological change. Nevertheless, most historians agree that technology played a significant role in the near doubling of the population of western Europe between 1000 and 1200. The population of England seems to have risen from 1.1 million in 1086 to 1.9 million in 1200, and the population of the territory of modern France seems to have risen from 5.2 million to 9.2 million over the same period.

Examples that illustrate the difficulty of drawing historical conclusions from scattered evidence of technological change were a new type of plow and the use of efficient draft harnesses for pulling wagons. The Roman plow, which farmers in southern Europe and Byzantium continued to use, scratched shallow grooves, as was appropriate for loose, dry Mediterranean soils. The new plow cut deep into the soil with a knife-like blade, while a curved board mounted behind the blade lifted the cut layer and turned it over. This made it possible to farm the heavy, wet clays of the northern river valleys. Pulling the new plow took more energy, which could mean harnessing several teams of oxen or horses.

Horses plowed faster than oxen but were more delicate. Iron horseshoes, which were widely adopted in this period, helped protect their feet, but like the plow itself, they added to the farmer's expenses. Roman horse harnesses, inefficiently modeled on the yoke used for oxen, put such pressure on the animal's neck that a horse pulling a heavy load risked strangulation. A mystery surrounds the adoption of more efficient designs. The **horse collar,** which moves the point of traction from the animal's throat to its shoulders, first appeared around 800 in a miniature painting, and it is shown clearly as a harness for plow horses in the Bayeux Tapestry, embroidered after 1066. The breast-strap harness, which is not as well adapted for the heaviest work but was preferred in southern Europe, seems to have appeared around 500. In both cases, linguists have tried to trace key technical terms to Chinese or Turko-Mongol words and have argued for technological diffusion across Eurasia. Yet third-century Roman farmers in Tunisia and Libya used both types of harness to hitch horses and camels to plows and carts. This technology, which is still employed in Tunisia, appears clearly on Roman bas-reliefs and lamps; but there is no more evidence of its movement northward into Europe than there is of similar harnessing moving across Asia. Thus the question of where efficient harnessing came from and whether it began in 500 or in 800, or was known even earlier but not extensively used, cannot be easily resolved.

Hinging on this problem is the question of when and why landowners in northern Europe began to use teams of horses to pull plows through moist, fertile river-valley soils that were too heavy for teams of oxen. Stronger and faster than oxen, horses increased productivity by reducing the time needed for plowing, but they cost more to feed and equip. Thus, while agricultural surpluses did grow and better plowing did play a role in this growth, areas that continued to use oxen and even old-style plows seem to have shared in the general population growth of the period.

Cities and the Rebirth of Trade

Independent cities governed and defended by communes appeared first in Italy and Flanders and then elsewhere. Communes were groups of leading citizens who banded together to defend their cities and demand the privilege of self-government from their lay or ecclesiastical lord. Lords who granted such privileges benefited from the commune's economic dynamism. Lacking extensive farmlands, these cities turned to manufacturing and trade, which they encouraged through the laws they enacted. Laws making serfs free once they came into the city, for example, attracted many workers from the countryside. Cities in Italy that had shrunk within walls built by the Romans now pressed against those walls, forcing the construction of new ones. Pisa built a new wall in 1000 and

Vertical Two-Beam Loom These women weavers set up their loom out-of-doors. The vertical strands are the warp threads around which the weft is interwoven. The pole across the bottom of the loom holds the warp threads taut. The kneeling weaver holds a beater to compact the weft at the loom's bottom. In Europe, horizontal looms were more common and paved the way for the mechanization of weaving. (Courtesy, Master and Fellows of Trinity College, Cambridge, Ms. R17.I.f.260 [detail])

expanded it in 1156. Other twelfth-century cities that built new walls include Florence, Brescia°, Pavia, and Siena°.

Settlers on a group of islands at the northern end of the Adriatic Sea that had been largely uninhabited in Roman times organized themselves into the city of Venice. In the eleventh century it became the dominant sea power in the Adriatic. Venice competed with Pisa and Genoa, its rivals on the western side of Italy, for leadership in the trade with Muslim ports in North Africa and the eastern Mediterranean. A somewhat later merchant's list mentions trade in some three thousand "spices" (including dyestuffs, textile fibers, and raw materials), some of them products of Muslim lands and some coming via the Silk Road or the Indian Ocean trading system (see Chapter 8). Among them were eleven types of alum (for dyeing), eleven types of wax, eight types of cotton, four types of indigo, five types of ginger, four types of paper, and fifteen types of sugar, along with cloves, caraway, tamarind, and fresh oranges. By the time of the Crusades (see below), maritime commerce throughout the Mediterranean had come to depend heavily on ships from Genoa, Venice, and Pisa.

Ghent, Bruges°, and Ypres° in Flanders rivaled the Italian cities in prosperity, trade, and industry. Enjoying comparable independence based on privileges granted by the counts of Flanders, these cities centralized the fishing and wool trades of the North Sea region. Around

Brescia (BREH-shee-uh) **Siena** (see-EN-uh) **Bruges** (broozh)
Ypres (EEP-r)

1200 raw wool from England began to be woven into woolen cloth for a very large market.

More abundant coinage also signaled the upturn in economic activity. In the ninth and tenth centuries most gold coins had come from Muslim lands and the Byzantine Empire. Being worth too much for most trading purposes, they seldom reached Germany, France, and England. The widely imitated Carolingian silver penny sufficed. With the economic revival of the twelfth century, minting of silver coins began in Scandinavia, Poland, and other outlying regions. In the following century the reinvigoration of Mediterranean trade made possible a new and abundant gold coinage.

THE CRUSADES, 1095–1204

Western European revival coincided with and contributed to the **Crusades,** a series of religiously inspired Christian military campaigns against Muslims in the eastern Mediterranean that dominated the politics of Europe from 1095 to 1204 (see Chapter 9 and Map 10.4). Four great expeditions, the last redirected against the Byzantines and resulting in the Latin capture of Constantinople, constituted the region's largest military undertakings since the fall of Rome. The cultural impact of the Crusades upon western Europe resulted in noble courts and burgeoning cities consuming more goods from the east. This set the stage for the later adoption of

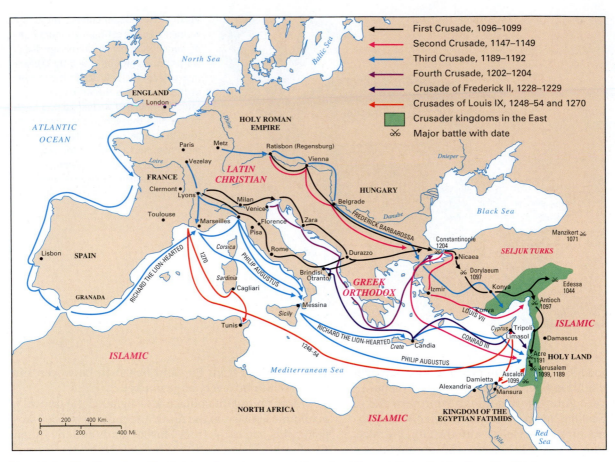

Map 10.4   The Crusades   The first two Crusades proceeded overland through Byzantine territory. The Third Crusade included contingents under the French and English kings, Philip Augustus and Richard the Lion-Hearted, that traveled by sea, and a contingent under the Holy Roman Emperor Frederick Barbarossa that took the overland route. Frederick died in southern Anatolia. Later Crusades were mostly seaborne, with Sicily, Crete, and Cyprus playing important roles.

ideas, artistic styles, and industrial processes from Byzantium and the lands of Islam.

The Roots of the Crusades

Several social and economic currents of the eleventh century contributed to the Crusades. First, reforming leaders of the Latin Church, seeking to soften the warlike tone of society, popularized the Truce of God. This movement limited fighting between Christian lords by specifying times of truce, such as during Lent (the forty days before Easter) and on Sundays. Many knights welcomed a religiously approved alternative to fighting other Christians. Second, ambitious rulers, like the Norman chieftains who invaded England and Sicily, were looking for new lands to conquer. Nobles, particularly younger sons in ar-

eas where the oldest son inherited everything, were hungry for land and titles to maintain their status. Third, Italian merchants wanted to increase trade in the eastern Mediterranean and acquire trading posts in Muslim territory. However, without the rivalry between popes and kings already discussed, and without the desire of the church to demonstrate political authority over western Christendom, the Crusades might never have occurred.

Several factors focused attention on the Holy Land, which had been under Muslim rule for four centuries. **Pilgrimages** played an important role in European religious life. In western Europe, pilgrims traveled under royal protection, a few actually being tramps, thieves, beggars, peddlers, and merchants for whom pilgrimage was a safe way of traveling. Genuinely pious pilgrims often journeyed to visit the old churches and sacred relics preserved in Rome or Constantinople. The most intrepid went to Jerusalem, Antioch, and other cities under Muslim control to fulfill a vow or to atone for a sin.

Knights who followed a popular pilgrimage route across northern Spain to pray at the shrine of Santiago de Compostela learned of the expanding efforts of Christian kings to dislodge the Muslims. The Umayyad Caliphate in al-Andalus had broken up in the eleventh century, leaving its smaller successor states prey to Christian attacks from the north (see Chapter 9). This was the beginning of a movement of reconquest that culminated in 1492 with the surrender of the last Muslim kingdom. The word *crusade*, taken from Latin *crux* for "cross," was first used in Spain. Stories also circulated of the war conducted by seafaring Normans against the Muslims in Sicily, whom they finally defeated in the 1090s after thirty years of fighting.

The tales of pilgrims returning from Palestine further induced both churchmen and nobles to consider the Muslims a proper target for Christian militancy. Muslim rulers, who had controlled Jerusalem, Antioch, and Alexandria since the seventh century, generally tolerated and protected Christian pilgrims. But after 1071, when a Seljuk army defeated the Byzantine emperor at the Battle of Manzikert (see Chapter 9), Turkish nomads spread throughout the region, and security along the pilgrimage route through Anatolia, already none too good, deteriorated further. The decline of Byzantine power threatened ancient centers of Christianity, such as Ephesus in Anatolia, previously under imperial control.

Despite the theological differences between the Orthodox and Roman churches, the Byzantine emperor Alexius Comnenus asked the pope and western European rulers to help him confront the Muslim threat and reconquer what the Christians termed the Holy Land, the early centers of Christianity in Palestine and Syria. Pope Urban II responded at the Council of Clermont in 1095. He addressed a huge crowd of people gathered in a field and called on them, as Christians, to stop fighting one another and go to the Holy Land to fight Muslims.

"God wills it!" exclaimed voices in the crowd. People cut cloth into crosses and sewed them on their shirts to symbolize their willingness to march on Jerusalem. Thus began the holy war now known as the "First Crusade." People at the time more often used the word *peregrinatio*, "pilgrimage." Urban promised to free crusaders who had committed sins from their normal penance, or acts of atonement, the usual reward for peaceful pilgrims to Jerusalem.

The First Crusade captured Jerusalem in 1099 and established four crusader principalities, the most important being the Latin Kingdom of Jerusalem. The next two expeditions strove with diminishing success to protect these gains. Muslim forces retook Jerusalem in 1187. By the time of the Fourth Crusade in 1204, the original religious ardor

Armored Knights in Battle   This painting from around 1135 shows the armament of knights at the time of the Crusades. Chain mail, a helmet, and a shield carried on the left side protect the rider. The lance carried underarm and the sword are the primary weapons. Notice that riders about to make contact with lances have their legs straight and braced in the stirrups, while riders with swords and in flight have bent legs.   (Pierpont Morgan Library/ Art Resource, NY)

had so diminished that the commanders agreed, at the urging of the Venetians, to sack Constantinople first to help pay the cost of transporting the army by ship.

The Impact of the Crusades

Exposure to Muslim culture in Spain, Sicily, and the crusader principalities established in the Holy Land made many Europeans aware of things lacking in their own lives. Borrowings from Muslim society occurred gradually and are not always easy to date, but Europeans eventually learned how to manufacture hard soap, pasta, paper, refined sugar, colored glass, and many other items that had formerly been imported. Arabic translations of and commentaries on Greek philosophical and scientific works, and equally important original works by Arabs and Iranians, provided a vital stimulus to European thought.

Some works were brought directly into the Latin world through the conquests of Sicily, parts of Spain and the Holy Land, and Constantinople (for Greek texts). Others were rendered into Latin by translators who worked in parts of Spain that continued under Muslim rule. Generations passed before all these works were studied and understood, but they eventually transformed the intellectual world of the western Europeans, who previously had little familiarity with Greek writings. The works of Aristotle and the Muslim commentaries on them were of particular importance to theologians, but Muslim writers like Avicenna (980–1037) were of parallel importance in medicine.

Changes affecting the lifestyle of the nobles took place more quickly. Eleanor of Aquitaine (1122?–1204), one of the most influential women of the crusading era, accompanied her husband, King Louis VII of France, on the Second Crusade (1147–1149). The court life of her uncle Raymond, ruler of the crusader principality of Antioch, particularly appealed to her. After her return to France, a lack of male offspring led to an annulment of her marriage with Louis, and she married Henry of Anjou in 1151. He inherited the throne of England as Henry II three years later. Eleanor's sons Richard Lion-Heart, famed in romance as the chivalrous foe of Saladin during the Third Crusade (1189–1192), and John rebelled against their father but eventually succeeded him as kings of England.

In Aquitaine, a powerful duchy in southern France, Eleanor maintained her own court for a time. The poet-singers called troubadours who enjoyed her favor made her court a center for new music based on the idea of "courtly love," an idealization of feminine beauty and grace that influenced later European ideas of romance. Thousands of troubadour melodies survive in manuscripts, and some show the influence of the poetry styles then current in Muslim Spain. The favorite troubadour instrument, moreover, was the lute, a guitar-like instrument with a bulging shape whose design and name (Arabic *al-ud*) come from Muslim Spain. In centuries to come the lute would become the mainstay of Renaissance music in Italy.

CONCLUSION

The collapse of imperial Rome was not unique. China's Han dynasty (see Chapter 6) and the Abbasid Caliphate (see Chapter 9) both dissolved into successor states. Although western Europe endured chaos, disunity, and economic regression, cultural vitality emerged from the centuries of disorder. Similarly, the Tang Empire, which emerged in China in the seventh century C.E. (see Chapter 11), had a distinctive and lively culture based only in part on survivals from the Han era. In the Middle East the emergence of a distinctive society based on the Islamic religion largely followed the collapse of the central Islamic state in the tenth century (see Chapter 9). The dynamic development of Islam after this political collapse parallels the powerful influence gained by Christianity in western Europe by the end of the twelfth century.

However, the competition between the Orthodox and Catholic forms of Christianity complicated the role of religion in the emergence of medieval European society and culture. The Byzantine Empire, constructed on a Roman political and legal heritage that had largely passed away in the west, was more prosperous than the Germanic kingdoms of western Europe, and its arts and culture were initially more sophisticated. Furthermore, Byzantine society became deeply Christian well before a comparable degree of Christianization had been reached in western Europe. Yet despite their success in transmitting their versions of Christianity and imperial rule to Kievan Russia, and in the process erecting a barrier between the Russians and the Catholic Slavs to their west, the Byzantines failed to demonstrate the dynamism and ferment that characterized both the Europeans to their west and the Muslims to their south. Byzantine armies played only a supporting role in the Crusades, and the emperors lost their capital and at least temporarily lost their power to western crusaders in 1204.

Technology and commerce deepened the political and religious gulf between the two Christian zones. Changes in military techniques in western Europe increased battlefield effectiveness, while new agricultural technologies led to population increases that revitalized urban life and contributed to the crusading movement by making the nobility hunger for new lands. At the same time, the need to import food for growing urban populations contributed to the growth of maritime commerce in the Mediterranean and North Seas. Culture and manufacturing benefited greatly from the increased pace of communication and exchange. Lacking parallel developments of a similar scale, the Byzantine Empire steadily lost the dynamism of its early centuries and by the end of the period had clearly fallen behind western Europe in prosperity and cultural innovation.

■ Key Terms

Charlemagne	serf	investiture
medieval	fief	controversy
Byzantine Empire	vassal	monasticism
Kievan Russia	papacy	horse collar
schism	Holy Roman	Crusades
manor	Empire	pilgrimage

■ Suggested Reading

Standard Byzantine histories include Dimitri Obolensky, *The Byzantine Commonwealth* (1971); and Warren Treadgold, *A History of Byzantine State and Society* (1997). Cyril Mango's *Byzantium: The Empire of New Rome* (1980) emphasizes cultural matters. For later Byzantine history see A. P. Kazhdan and Ann Wharton Epstein in *Change in Byzantine Culture in the Eleventh and Twelfth Centuries* (1985), which stresses social and economic issues; and D. M. Nicol, *Byzantium and Venice* (1988).

Roger Collins's *Early Medieval Europe, 300–1000* (1991), surveys institutional and political developments, while Robert Merrill Bartlett, *The Making of Europe* (1994), emphasizes frontiers. For the later part of the period see Susan Reynolds, *Kingdoms and Communities in Western Europe, 900–1300,* 2d ed. (1997). Jacques Le Goff, *Medieval Civilization, 400–1500* (1989), stresses questions of social structure. Among many books on religious matters see Richard W. Southern, *Western Society and the Church in the Middle Ages* (1970) and Richard Fletcher, *The Barbarian Conversion* (1997). Susan Reynolds makes the case for avoiding the term *feudalism* in *Fiefs and Vassals* (1994).

More specialized economic and technological studies begin with the classic Lynn White, Jr., *Medieval Technology and Social Change* (1962). See also Michael McCormick, *Origins of the European Economy: Communications and Commerce, AD 300–900* (2002); C. M. Cipolla, *Money, Prices and Civilization in the Mediterranean World, Fifth to Seventeenth Century* (1956); and Georges Duby, *Rural Economy and Country Life in the Medieval West* (1990), which includes translated documents. J. C. Russell, *The Control of Late Ancient and Medieval Population* (1985), analyzes demographic history and the problems of data.

On France see the numerous works of Rosamond McKitterick, including *The Frankish Kingdoms Under the Carolingians, 751–987* (1983). On England see Peter Hunter Blair, *An Introduction to Anglo-Saxon England* (1977), and Christopher Brooke, *The Saxon and Norman Kings* 3d ed. (2001). On Italy see Chris Wickham, *Early Medieval Italy: Central Power and Local Society, 400–1000* (1981), and Edward Burman, *Emperor to Emperor: Italy Before the Renaissance* (1991). On Germany and the Holy Roman Empire see Timothy Reuter, *Germany in the Early Middle Ages, c. 800–1056* (1991). On Spain see J. F. O'Callaghan, *A History of Medieval Spain* (1975), and R. Collins, *Early Medieval Spain: Unity and Diversity 400–1000* (1983). On

Viking Scandinavia see John Haywood's illustrated *Encyclopaedia of the Viking age* (2000).

Amy Keller's popularly written *Eleanor of Aquitaine and the Four Kings* (1950), tells the story of an extraordinary woman. Dhuoda, *Handbook for William: A Carolingian Woman's Counsel for Her Son,* trans. Carol Neel (1991), offers a firsthand look at a Carolingian noblewoman. More general works include Margaret Wade's *A Small Sound of the Trumpet: Women in Medieval Life* (1986), and Bonnie S. Anderson and Judith P. Zinsser's *A History of Their Own: Women in Europe from Prehistory to the Present* (1989). In the area of religion, Caroline Bynum's *Jesus as Mother: Studies in the Spirituality of the High Middle Ages* (1982) illustrates new views about women.

On Kievan Russia see Janet Martin's *Medieval Russia, 980–1584* (1995); Simon Franklin and Jonathan Shepard, *The Emergence of Rus: 750–1200* (1996); and Thomas S. Noonan, *The Islamic World, Russia and the Vikings, 750–900: The Numismatic Evidence* (1998).

Jonathan Riley-Smith, *The Crusades: A Short History* (1987), is a standard work. He has also a more colorful version in *The Oxford Illustrated History of the Crusades* (1995). For other views see Jonathan Phillips, *The Crusades, 1095–1197* (2002), and Norman Housley, *Crusading and Warfare in Medieval and Renaissance Europe* (2001). For a masterful account with a Byzantine viewpoint, see Steven Runciman, *A History of the Crusades,* 3 vols. (1987). For accounts from the Muslim side see Carole Hillenbrand, *The Crusades: Islamic Perspectives* (1999).

Henri Pirenne, *Medieval Cities: Their Origins and the Revival of Trade* (1952), and Robert S. Lopez, *The Commercial Revolution of the Middle Ages, 950–1350* (1971), masterfully discuss the revival of trade. Lopez and Irving W. Raymond compile and translate primary documents in *Medieval Trade in the Mediterranean World: Illustrative Documents with Introductions and Notes* (1990).

■ Notes

1. Lewis G. M. Thorpe, *Two Lives of Charlemagne* (Harmondsworth, England: Penguin, 1969).
2. A. A. Vasiliev, *History of the Byzantine Empire, 324–1453,* vol. 1 (Madison: University of Wisconsin Press, 1978), 79–80.
3. Ibid., p 71.
4. A. P. Kazhdan and Ann Wharton Epstein, *Change in Byzantine Culture in the Eleventh and Twelfth Centuries* (Berkeley: University of California Press, 1985), 71.
5. Ibid., 248.
6. Ibid., 255.
7. R. W. Southern, *Western Society and the Church in the Middle Ages* (Harmondsworth, England: Penguin, 1970), 102.
8. Anne Fremantle, *A Treasury of Early Christianity* (New York: New American Library of World Literature, 1960), 400–401.
9. S. A. Zenkovsky, ed., *Medieval Russia's Epics, Chronicles, and Tales* (New York: New American Library, 1974), 67.

11

Inner and East Asia, 400–1200

Buddhism at a Distance   The Buddhist monk Xuanzang returns to the Tang capital Chang'an from Tibet in 645, his ponies laden with Sanskrit texts.

280

The powerful and expansive Tang° Empire (618–907) ended four centuries of rule by short-lived and competing states that had repeatedly brought turmoil to China after the fall of the Han Empire in 220 C.E. (see Chapter 6) but had also encouraged the spread of Buddhism. The Tang left an indelible mark on the Chinese imagination long after it too fell.

According to surviving memoirs, people could watch shadow plays and puppet shows, listen to music and scholarly lectures, or take in less edifying spectacles like wrestling and bear baiting in the entertainment quarters of the cities that flourished in southern China under the succeeding Song° Empire. Song-stories provided a novel and popular entertainment from the 1170s onward. Singer-storytellers spun long romantic narratives that alternated prose passages with sung verse.

Master Tung's *Western Chamber Romance* stood out for its literary quality. Little is known of Master Tung° beyond a report that he lived at the end of the twelfth century. In 184 prose passages and 5,263 lines of verse the narrator tells the story of a love affair between Chang, a young Confucian scholar, and Ying-ying, a ravishing damsel. Secondary characters include Ying-ying's shrewd and worldly mother, a general who practices just and efficient administration, and a fighting monk named Fa-ts'ung°. It is based on *The Story of Ying-ying* by the Tang period author Yüan Chen° (779–831).

As the tale begins, the abbot of a Buddhist monastery responds to Chang's request to rent him a study room, singing:

Sir, you're wrong to offer me rent.
We Buddhists and Confucians are of one family.
As things stand, I can't give you
A place in our dormitory,
But you're welcome to stay
In one of the guest apartments.

As soon as Chang spies Ying-ying, who lives there with her mother, thoughts of studying flee his mind.

The course of romance takes a detour, however, when bandits attack the monastery. A prose passage explains:

During the T'ang dynasty, troops were stationed in the P'u prefecture. The year of our story, the commander of the garrison, Marshal Hun, died. Because the second-in-command, Ting Wen-ya, did not have firm control of the troops, Flying Tiger Sun, a subordinate general, rebelled with five thousand soldiers. They pillaged and plundered the P'u area. How do I know this to be true? It is corroborated by *The Ballad of the True Story of Ying-ying*.

As the monks dither, one of them lifts his robe to reveal his "three-foot consecrated sword."

[Prose] Who was this monk? He was none other than Fa-ts'ung. Fa-ts'ung was a descendant of a tribesman from western Shensi. When he was young he took great pleasure in archery, fencing, hunting, and often sneaked into foreign states to steal. He was fierce and courageous. When his parents died, it suddenly became clear to him that the way of the world was frivolous and trivial, so he became a monk in the Temple of Universal Salvation . . .

[Song]   He didn't know how to read sutras;
He didn't know how to follow rituals;
He was neither pure nor chaste
But indomitably courageous . . . [1]

Amidst the love story, the ribaldry, and the derring-do, the author implants historical vignettes that mingle fact and fiction. Sophisticates of the Song era, living a life of ease, enjoyed these romanticized portrayals of Tang society.

As you read this chapter, ask yourself the following questions:

- What is the importance of Inner and Central Asia as a region of interchange during the Tang period?

- On what were new relationships among East Asian societies based after the fall of the Tang?

Tang (tahng)   **Song** (soong)   **Tung** (toong)   **Fa-ts'ung** (fa-soong)
Yüan Chen (you-ahn shen)

- Why do Buddhism and Confucianism play different political roles in Tang and Song China, and in Tibet, Korea, and Japan?

- What accounts for the scientific and economic advancement that contributed to the thriving urban life of Song China?

THE SUI AND TANG EMPIRES, 581–755

The reunification of China took place under the Sui° dynasty, father and son rulers who held sway from 581 until Turks from Inner Asia (the part of the Eurasian steppe east of the Pamir Mountains) defeated the son in 615. He was assassinated three years later, and the Tang filled the political vacuum.

The small kingdoms of northern China and Inner Asia that had come and gone during the centuries following the fall of the Han Empire had structured themselves around a variety of political ideas and institutions. Some favored the Chinese tradition, with an emperor, a bureaucracy using the Chinese language exclusively, and a Confucian state philosophy (see Chapter 3). Others reflected Tibetan, Turkic, or other regional cultures and depended on Buddhism to legitimate their rule. Throughout the period the relationship between northern China and the deserts and steppe of Inner Asia remained a central focus of political life, a key commercial linkage, and a source of new ideas and practices.

Reunification Under the Sui and Tang

In their brief time in power, the Sui rulers had not only reunified China but had also reestablished the Confucian system of examining candidates for bureaucratic office on the classic Confucian texts, a practice that the Tang continued. Yet Buddhism, which had gained many adherents and widespread respect during the centuries of disunity, exerted a strong political influence as well. Other religious and philosophical beliefs, including Daoism, Nestorian Christianity, and Islam, enjoyed some popularity, the latter two signaling the continuing cultural importance of communications along the Silk Road (see Chapter 8).

Sui (sway)

The Sui rulers called their new capital Chang'an° in honor of the old Han capital nearby in the Wei° River Valley (modern Shaanxi province). Though northern China constituted the Sui heartland, population centers along the Yangzi° River in the south grew steadily and pointed to what would be the future direction of Chinese expansion. To facilitate communication and trade with the south, the Sui built the 1,100-mile (1771 kilometers) **Grand Canal,** linking the Yellow River with the Yangzi, and constructed irrigation systems in the Yangzi valley. On their northern frontier, the Sui also improved the Great Wall, the barrier against nomadic incursions that had been gradually constructed by several earlier states.

Sui military ambition, which extended to Korea and Vietnam as well as Inner Asia, required high levels of organization and mustering of resources—manpower, livestock, wood, iron, and food supplies. The same is true of their massive public works projects. These burdens proved more than the Sui could sustain. Overextension compounded the political dilemma stemming from the military defeat and subsequent assassination of the second Sui emperor. This opened the way for another strong leader to establish a new state.

In 618 the powerful Li family took advantage of Sui disorder to carve out an empire of similar scale and ambition. They adopted the dynastic name Tang (Map 11.1). The brilliant emperor **Li Shimin°** (r. 627–649) extended his power primarily westward into Inner Asia. Though he and succeeding rulers of the **Tang Empire** retained many Sui governing practices, they avoided overcentralization by allowing local nobles, gentry, officials, and religious establishments to exercise significant power. (See Diversity and Dominance: Law and Society in Tang China).

The Tang emperors and nobility descended from the Turkic elites that built small states in northern China after the Han, and from Chinese officials and settlers who had settled there. They appreciated Turkic Inner Asian culture as well as Chinese traditions Some of the most impressive works of Tang ceramic sculpture, for example, are large figurines of the horses and two-humped camels used along the Silk Road, brilliantly colored with glazes devised by Chinese potters. In warfare, the Tang combined Chinese weapons—the crossbow and armored infantrymen—with Inner Asian expertise in horsemanship and the use of iron stirrups. At their peak, from about 650 to 751, when they were defeated in Central Asia (present-day Kirgizstan) by an Arab Muslim army at the Battle of the Talas River, the Tang armies were a formidable force.

Chang'an (chahng-ahn)   **Wei** (way)   **Yangzi** (yahng-zeh)
Li Shimin (lee shir-meen)

C H R O N O L O G Y

	Inner Asia	China	Northeast Asia	Japan
200		220–589 China disunited		
	552 Turkic Empire founded			
600		581–618 Sui unification		
	620–640 Tibetan Empire emerges under Songsam Gyampo	618 Tang Empire founded		
		627–649 Li Shimin reign		645–655 Taika era
			668 Silla victory in Korea	
	744 Uighur empire founded	690–705 Wu Zhao reign		710–784 Nara as capital
	751 Battle of Talas River			752 "Eye-Opening" ceremony
		755–757 An Lushan rebellion		794–1185 Heian era
800				
	ca. 850 Buddhist political power secured in Tibet	840 Suppression of Buddhism		
		879–881 Huang Chao rebellion		
		907 End of Tang Empire	916 Liao Empire founded	
		938 Liao capital at Beijing	918 Koryo founded	
		960 Song Empire Founded		ca. 950–1180 Fujiwara influence
1000				
		1127–1279 Southern Song period	1115 Jin Empire founded	ca. 1000 *The Tale of Genji*
				1185 Kamakura shogunate founded

Buddhism and the Tang Empire

The Tang rulers followed Inner Asian precedents in their political use of Buddhism. State cults based on Buddhism had flourished in Inner Asia and north China since the fall of the Han. Some interpretations of Buddhist doctrine accorded kings and emperors the spiritual function of welding humankind into a harmonious Buddhist society. Protecting spirits were to help the ruler govern and prevent harm from coming to his people.

Mahayana°, or "Great Vehicle," Buddhism predominated. Mahayana fostered faith in enlightened beings—bodhisattvas—who postpone nirvana (see Chapter 7) to help others achieve enlightenment. This permitted the absorption of local gods and goddesses into Mahayana sainthood and thereby made conversion more attractive to the common people. Mahayana also encouraged translating Buddhist scripture into local languages, and it accepted

Mahayana (mah-HAH-YAH-nah)

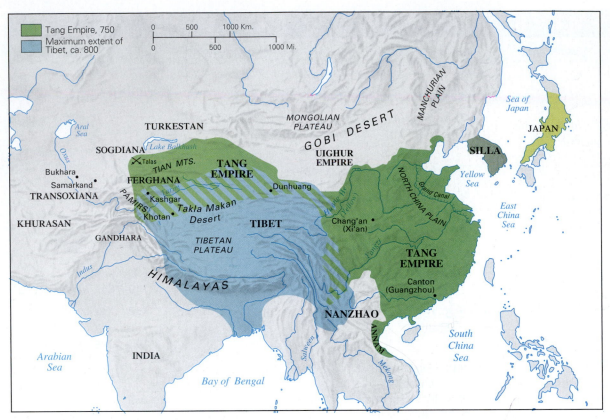

Map 11.1 The Tang Empire in Inner and Eastern Asia, 750 For over a century the Tang Empire controlled China and a very large part of Inner Asia. The defeat of Tang armies in 751 by a force of Arabs, Turks, and Tibetans at the Talas River in present-day Kirgizstan ended Tang westward expansion. To the east the Tang dominated Annam, and Japan and the Silla kingdom in Korea were leading tributary states of the Tang.

religious practices not based on written texts. The tremendous reach of Mahayana views, which proved adaptable to different societies and classes of people, invigorated travel, language learning, and cultural exchange.

Early Tang princes competing for political influence enlisted monastic leaders to pray for them, preach on their behalf, counsel aristocrats to support them, and—perhaps most important—contribute monastic wealth to their war chests. In return, the monasteries received tax exemptions, land privileges, and gifts.

As the Tang Empire expanded westward, contacts with Central Asia and India increased, and so did the complexity of Buddhist influence throughout China. Chang'an, the Tang capital, became the center of a continentwide system of communication. Central Asians, Tibetans, Vietnamese, Japanese, and Koreans regularly visited the capital and took away with them the most recent ideas and styles. Thus the Mahayana network connecting Inner Asia and China intersected a vigorous commercial world in which material goods and cultural

influences mixed. Though Buddhism and Confucianism proved attractive to many different peoples, regional cultures and identities remained strong, just as regional commitments to Tibetan, Uighur, and other languages and writing systems coexisted with the widespread use of written Chinese. Textiles reflected Persian, Korean, and Vietnamese styles, while influences from every part of Asia appeared in sports, music, and painting. Many historians characterize the Tang Empire as "cosmopolitan" because of its breadth and diversity.

To Chang'an by Land and Sea

Well-maintained roads and water transport connected Chang'an, the capital and hub of Tang communications, to the coastal towns of south China, most importantly Canton (Guangzhou°). Though the Grand Canal did not reach Chang'an, it was a key component of this trans-

Guangzhou (gwahng-jo)

Iron Stirrups   This bas-relief from the tomb of Li Shimin depicts the type of horse on which the Tang armies conquered China and Inner Asia. Saddles with high supports in front and back, breastplates, and cruppers (straps beneath the tail that help keep the saddle in place) point to the importance of high speeds and quick maneuvering. Central and Inner Asian horsemen had iron stirrups available from the time of the Huns (fifth century). Earlier stirrups were of leather or wood. Stirrups could support the weight of shielded and well-armed soldiers rising in the saddle to shoot arrows or use lances.   (University of Pennsylvania Museum, neg. #S8-62844)

portation network. Chang'an became the center of what is often called the **tributary system,** a type of political relationship dating from Han times by which independent countries acknowledged the Chinese emperor's supremacy. Each tributary state sent regular embassies to the capital to pay tribute (see Chapter 6). As symbols of China's political supremacy, these embassies sometimes meant more to the Chinese than to the tribute-payers, who might see them more as a means of accessing the Chinese trading system.

During the Tang period, Chang'an had something over a million people, only a minority of whom lived in the central city. Most people lived in suburbs that extended beyond the main gates. Others dwelt in separate outlying towns that had special responsibilities like maintaining nearby imperial tombs or operating the imperial resort, where aristocrats relaxed in sunken tile tubs while the steamy waters of natural springs swirled around them.

Foreigners, whether merchants, students, or ambassadors, resided in special compounds in Chang'an and other entrepôts. These included living accommodations and general stores. By the end of the Tang period, West Asians in Chang'an probably numbered over 100,000.

In the main parts of the city, restaurants, inns, temples, mosques, and street stalls along the main thoroughfares kept busy every evening. At curfew, generally between eight and ten o'clock, commoners returned to their neighborhoods, which were enclosed by brick walls and wooden gates that guards locked until dawn to control crime.

Of the many routes converging on Chang'an, the Grand Canal commanded special importance with its own army patrols, boat design, canal towns, and maintenance budget. It conveyed vital supplies and contributed to the economic and cultural development of eastern China, where later capitals were built within easier reach.

The Tang consolidated Chinese control of the southern coastal region, increasing access to the Indian Ocean and facilitating the spread of Islamic and Jewish influences. A legend credits an uncle of Muhammad with erecting the Red Mosque at Canton in the mid-seventh century.

Chinese mariners and shipwrights excelled in compass design and the construction of very large oceangoing vessels. The government took direct responsibility for outfitting grain transport vessels for the Chinese coastal cities and the Grand Canal. Commercial ships, built to sail from south China to the Philippines and Southeast Asia, carried twice as much as contemporary vessels in the Mediterranean Sea or the western parts of the Indian Ocean trading system (see Chapter 8).

The sea route linking the Red Sea and Persian Gulf with Canton also brought East Asia the **bubonic plague,** called the Justinian plague because it coincided with the reign of the Byzantine emperor Justinian. Historical sources mention plague in Canton and south China in the early 600s. As in certain other parts of the world, the plague bacillus became endemic among rodent populations in parts of southwestern China and thus lingered long after its disappearance in West Asia and Europe.

DIVERSITY AND DOMINANCE

LAW AND SOCIETY IN TANG CHINA

The Tang law code, compiled in the early seventh century, served as the basis for the Tang legal system and as a model for later dynastic law codes. It combined the centralized authority of the imperial government, as visualized in the legalist tradition dating back to Han times, with Confucian concern for status distinctions and personal relationships. Like contemporary approaches to law in Christian Europe and the Islamic world, it did not fully distinguish between government as a structure of domination and law as an echo of religious and moral values.

Following a Preface, 502 articles, each with several parts, are divided into twelve books: (1) General Principles, (2) Imperial Guard and Prohibitions, (3) Administrative Regulations, (4) Household and Marriage, (5) Public Stables and Granaries, (6) Unauthorized Levies, (7) Violence and Robberies, (8) Assaults and Accusations, (9) Fraud and Counterfeiting, (10) Miscellaneous Articles, (11) Arrest and Flight, and (12) Judgment and Imprisonment. Each article contained a basic ordinance with commentary, subcommentary, and sometimes additional questions. Excerpts from a single Article from Book 1 follow.

THE TEN ABOMINATIONS

Text: The first is called plotting rebellion.

Subcommentary: The *Gongyang* [GON-gwang] *Commentary* states: "The ruler or parent has no harborers [of plots]. If he does have such harborers, he must put them to death." This means that if there are those who harbor rebellious hearts that would harm the ruler or father, he must then put them to death.

The king occupies the most honorable position and receives Heaven's precious decrees. Like Heaven and Earth, he acts to shelter and support, thus serving as the father and mother of the masses. As his children, as his subjects, they must be loyal and filial. Should they dare to cherish wickedness and have rebellious hearts, however, they will run counter to Heaven's constancy and violate human principle. Therefore this is called plotting rebellion.

Text: The second is called plotting great sedition.

Subcommentary: This type of person breaks laws and destroys order, is against traditional norms, and goes contrary to virtue . . .

Commentary: Plotting great sedition means to plot to destroy the ancestral temples, tombs, or palaces of the reigning house.

Text: The third is called plotting treason.

Subcommentary: The kindness of father and mother is like "great heaven, illimitable" . . . Let one's heart be like the *xiao* bird or the *jing* beast, and then love and respect both cease. Those whose relationship is within the five degrees of mourning are the closest of kin. For them to kill each other is the extreme abomination and the utmost in rebellion, destroying and casting aside human principles. Therefore this is called contumacy.

Commentary: Contumacy means to beat or plot to kill [without actually killing] one's paternal grandparents or parents; or to kill one's paternal uncles or their wives, or one's elder brothers or sisters, or one's maternal grandparents, or one's husband, or one's husband's paternal grandparents, or his parents . . . .

Text: The fifth is called depravity.

Subcommentary: This article describes those who are cruel and malicious and who turn their backs on morality. Therefore it is called depravity.

Commentary: Depravity means to kill three members of a single household who have not committed a capital crime, or to dismember someone . . .

Commentary: The offense also includes the making or keeping of poison or sorcery.

Subcommentary: This means to prepare the poison oneself, or to keep it, or to give it to others in order to harm people. But if the preparation of the poison is not yet completed, this offense does not come under the ten abominations. As to sorcery, there are a great many methods, not all of which can be described.

Text: The sixth is called great irreverence . . .

Commentary: Great irreverence means to steal the objects of the great sacrifices to the spirits or the carriage or possessions of the emperor.

Text: The seventh is called lack of filiality.

Subcommentary: Serving one's parents well is called filiality. Disobeying them is called lack of filiality.

Text: The ninth is called what is not right . . .
Commentary: [This] means to kill one's department head, prefect, or magistrate, or the teacher from whom one has received one's education . . .

Text: The tenth is called incest.

Subcommentary: The *Zuo Commentary* states: "The woman has her husband's house; the man has his wife's chamber; and there must be no defilement on either side." If this is changed, then there is incest. If one behaves like birds and beasts and introduces licentious associates into one's family, the rules of morality are confused. Therefore this is called incest.

Commentary: This section includes having illicit sexual intercourse with relatives who are of the fourth degree of mourning or closer . . . .

The following are the titles of 26 of the 46 articles in Book 4 of the Code entitled "The Household and Marriage.

- Omitting to File a Household Register
- Unauthorized Ordainment as a Buddhist or Daoist Priest
- Sons and Grandsons in the Male Line Are Not Permitted to Have a Separate Household Register
- Having a Child During the Period of Mourning for Parents
- Adopted Sons Who Reject Their Adoptive Parents
- Falsely Combining Households
- Possession of More than the Permitted Amount of Land
- Illegal Cultivation of Public or Private Land
- Wrongfully Laying Claim to or Selling Public or Private Land
- Officials Who Encroach Upon Private Land
- Illegal Cultivation of Other Persons' Grave Plots
- Not Allowing Rightful Exemption from Taxes and Labor Services
- Betrothal of a Daughter and Announcement of the Marriage Contract
- Wrongful Substitution by the Bride's Family in a Marriage
- Taking a Second Wife
- Making the Wife a Concubine
- Marriage During the Period of Mourning for Parents or Husband
- Marriage While Parents Are in Prison
- Marriage by Those of the Same Surname
- Marrying a Runaway Wife
- Marriage of Officials with Women Within Their Area of Jurisdiction
- Marrying Another Man's Wife by Consent
- Divorcing a Wife Who Has Not Given Any of the Seven Causes for Repudiation
- Divorce
- Slaves Who Take Commoners as Wives
- General Bondsmen Are Not Permitted to Marry Commoners
- Marriages That Violate the Code

The day-to-day realities of country life appear in the following account by a scholar living during the late 700s.

Wealthy landowning families bought townhouses and engaged in conspicuous consumption while farmers, whose high rents and low pay contributed to the gentry's growing wealth, enjoyed few direct benefits.

When a farmer falls on bad times, he has to sell his field and his hut. If it is a good year, he might be able to pay his debts by selling out. But no sooner will the harvest be in than his storage bins will be empty again, and he will have to try to contract a new debt promising his labor for the next year. Each time he indentures himself he incurs higher interest rates, and soon will be destitute again.

If it is a bad year, and there is a famine, then the situation is hopeless. Families break up, parents separate, and all try to sell themselves into slavery. But in a bad year nobody will buy them.

In these circumstances land prices fall low enough that the rich buy up tens of thousands of acres, or simply seize the land of defaulted farmers. The poor then have no land, and try for places as servants, bodyguards, or enforcers for the rich families. If they manage to attach themselves to the organization of a gentry family, they can borrow seed and grain, and rent land as tenants. Then they will work themselves to death, all year round, without a day off. If they should manage to clear their debts, they live in constant anxiety about when the next bad patch will leave them destitute again.

The gentry, however, live off their rents, with no troubles and no cares. Wealth and poverty are very clearly divided.

This is how we have reached the situation where the rents from private land are much higher, and collected more ruthlessly, than the government's taxes. In areas around the capital, rents are twenty times higher than taxes. Even rents in more remote areas are ten times what the government collects in tax.

QUESTIONS FOR ANALYSIS

1. Comparing these historical documents, what would seem to have been the relationship between law and equity under the Tang?

2. Did the Confucian concern for family relations and social status manifested in the law code prevent injustice?

3. Does the law code appear more an expression of ideals and compilation of past philosophical ideas than a practical guide to a just society?

Sources: The first two selections are from Theodore de Bary and Irene Bloom, eds., *Sources of Chinese Tradition,* vol. 1, 2d ed. Copyright © 1999 by Columbia University Press. Reprinted with permission of the publisher. The third selection is adapted from Etienne Balazs, *Chinese Civilization and Bureaucracy: Variations on a Theme,* trans. by H. M. Wright, ed. by Arthur F. Wright. Copyright © 1964. Reprinted by permission of Yale University Press.

The disease followed trade and embassy routes to Korea, Japan, and Tibet, where initial outbreaks followed the establishment of diplomatic ties in the seventh century.

Trade and Cultural Exchange

Influences from Central Asia and the Islamic world introduced lively new motifs to ceramics, painting, and silk designs. At the other end of the Silk Road, Iranian potters imitated the glazes of Tang vessels. Clothing styles changed in north China; working people switched from robes to the pants favored by horse-riding Turks from Central Asia. Inexpensive cotton imported from Central Asia, where cotton production boomed in the early Islamic centuries, gradually replaced hemp in clothes worn by commoners. The Tang court promoted polo, a pastime from the steppes, and followed the Inner Asian tradition of allowing noblewomen to compete. Various stringed instruments reached China across the Silk Road, along with Turkic folk melodies. Grape wine from West Asia and tea, sugar, and spices from India and Southeast Asia transformed the Chinese diet.

Such changes reflected new economic and trade relationships. Silk had dominated the caravan trade across Central Asia in Han times (see Chapter 8). Now China's monopoly on silk disappeared as several centers in West Asia learned to compete. However, western Asia lost its monopoly in cotton; by the end of the Tang, China had begun to produce its own. This process of "import substitution"—the domestic production and sale of previously imported goods—also affected tea and sugar.

By about the year 1000 the magnitude of exports from Tang territories, facilitated by China's excellent transportation systems, dwarfed Chinese imports from Europe, West Asia, and South Asia. Stories of ships carrying Chinese exports outnumbering those laden with South Asian, West Asian, European, or African goods by a hundred to one cannot be relied on. Tang exports did, however, tilt the trade balance with both the Central Asia caravan cities and the lands of the Indian Ocean, causing precious metal to flow into China in return for export goods.

China remained the source of superior silks. Tang factories created more and more complex styles, partly to counter foreign competition. China became the sole supplier of porcelain—a fine, durable ceramic made from a special clay—to West Asia. As travel along the Silk Road and to the various ports of the Indian Ocean trading system increased, the economies of seaports and entrepôts involved in the trade—even distant ones—became increasingly commercialized, leading to networks of private traders devising new instruments of

Tang Women at Polo The Tang Empire, like the Sui, was strongly influenced by Inner Asian as well as Chinese traditions. As in many Inner Asian cultures, women in Tang China were likely to exercise greater influence in the management of property, in the arts, and in politics than women in Chinese society at later times. They were not excluded from public view, and noblewomen could even compete at polo. The game, widely known in various forms in Central and Inner Asia from a very early date, combined the Tang love of riding, military arts, and festive spectacles. (The Nelson-Atkins Museum of Art, Kansas City, Missouri)

credit and finance. As we shall see, these networks would later contribute to the prosperity of the Song era.

RIVALS FOR POWER IN INNER ASIA AND CHINA, 600–907

Li Bo, the most renowned Tang poet and one of the greatest ever to write in the Chinese language, wrote in 751 of the seemingly endless succession of wars:

> The beacons are always alight, fighting and marching never stop.
> Men die in the field, slashing sword to sword;
> The horses of the conquered neigh piteously to Heaven.
> Crows and hawks peck for human guts,
> Carry them in their beaks and hang them on the branches of withered trees.

Captains and soldiers are smeared on the bushes and
  grass;
The General schemed in vain.
Know therefore that the sword is a cursed thing
which the wise man uses only if he must.[2]

Between 600 and 751, when the Tang Empire was at
its height, the Turkic-speaking Uighurs° and the Tibetans built large rival states in Inner Asia. The power of the
former centered on the basin of the Tarim River, a largely
desert area north of Tibet that formed a vital link on the
Silk Road. The Tibetan empire at its peak stretched well
beyond modern Tibet into northeastern India, southwestern China, and the Tarim Basin. The contest between
these states and the Tang for control of the land routes
west of China reached a standoff by the end of the period. Mutually beneficial trade required diplomatic accommodation more than political unity. By the mid-800s
all three empires were experiencing political decay and
military decline. The problems of one aggravated those
of the others, since governmental collapse allowed soldiers, criminals, and freebooters to roam without hin-
drance into neighboring territories.

Centralization and integration being most extensively developed in Tang territory, the impact fell most
heavily there. Nothing remained of Tang power but pre-
tense by the early 800s, the period reflected in the original romance of Ying-ying described at the start of this
chapter. In the provinces military governors suppressed
the rebellion of General An Lushan°, a commander of
Sogdian (Central Asian) and Turkic origin, which raged
from 755 to 763, and then seized power for themselves.

The nomads of the steppe survived the social disorder and agricultural losses best. The caravan cities that
had prospered from overland trade, and that lay at the
heart of the Uighur state in the Tarim Basin, had as much
to lose as China itself. Eventually, the urban and agricultural economies of Inner Asia and China recovered. In
the short term, however, the debilitating contest for
power with the Inner Asian states prompted a strong cultural backlash, particularly in China, where disillusion-
ment with northern neighbors combined with social and
economic anxieties to fuel an antiforeign movement.

The Uighur and Tibetan Empires

The original homeland of the
Turks lay in the northern part
of modern Mongolia. After the
fall of the Han Empire, Turkic
peoples began moving south and west, through Mongolia, then west to Central Asia, on the long migration that

Uighur (WEE-ger)   An Lushan (ahn loo-shahn)

eventually brought them to what is today modern Turkey
(see Chapter 9). In 552 a unified Turkic state had emerged,
only to split internally a century later. It was this fissure
that allowed the Tang Empire under Li Shimin to establish control over the Tarim Basin. Yet within a century,
a new Turkic group, the **Uighurs,** had taken much of Inner Asia.

Under the Uighurs, caravan cities like Kashgar and
Khotan (see Map 11.1) displayed a literate culture with
strong ties to both the Islamic world and China. The
Uighurs excelled as merchants and as scribes able to
transact business in many languages. They adapted the
syllabic script of the Sogdians, who lived to the west of
them in Central Asia, to writing Turkic. Literacy made
possible several innovations in Uighur government,
such as changing from a tax paid in kind (with products
or services) to a money tax and, later, the minting of
coins. Their flourishing urban culture exhibited a cosmopolitan enthusiasm for Buddhist teachings, religious
art derived from northern India, and a mixture of East
Asian and Islamic tastes in dress.

Unified Uighur power collapsed after half a century,
leaving only Tibet as a rival to the Tang in Inner Asia. A
large, stable empire critically positioned where China,
Southeast Asia, South Asia, and Central Asia meet, **Tibet**

Women of Turfan Grinding Flour   Women throughout Inner
and East Asia were critical to all facets of economic life. In the
Turkic areas of Central and Inner Asia, women commonly headed
households, owned property, and managed businesses. These small
figurines, made to be placed in tombs, portray women of Turfan—
an Inner Asian area crossed by the Silk Road—performing tasks in
the preparation of wheat flour.   (Xinjiang Uighur Autonomous District
Museum)

experienced a variety of cultural influences. In the seventh century Chinese Buddhists on pilgrimage to India advanced contacts between India and Tibet. The Tibetans derived their alphabet from India, as well as a variety of artistic and architectural styles. India and China both contributed to Tibetan knowledge of mathematics, astronomy, divination, farming, and milling of grain. Islam and the monarchical traditions of Iran and Rome became familiar through Central Asian trading connections. The Tibetan royal family favored Greek medicine transmitted through Iran.

Under Li Shimin, cautious friendliness had prevailed between China and Tibet. A Tang princess, called Kongjo by the Tibetans, came to Tibet in 634 to marry the Tibetan king and cement an alliance. She brought Mahayana Buddhism, which combined with the native religion to create a distinctive form of Buddhism. Tibet sent ambassadors and students to the Tang imperial capital. Regular contact and Buddhist influences consolidated the Tang-Tibet relationship for a time. The Tibetan kings encouraged Buddhist religious establishments and prided themselves on being cultural intermediaries between India and China.

Tibet also excelled at war. Horses and armor, techniques borrowed from the Turks, raised Tibetan forces to a level that startled even the Tang. By the late 600s the Tang emperor and the Tibetan king were rivals for religious leadership and political dominance in Inner Asia, and Tibetan power reached into what are now Qinghai°, Sichuan°, and Xinjiang° provinces in China. War weariness affected both empires after 751, however.

In the 800s a new king in Tibet decided to follow the Tang lead and eliminate the political and social influence of the monasteries (see below). He was assassinated by Buddhist monks, and control of the Tibetan royal family passed into the hands of religious leaders. In the centuries that followed down to modern times, monastic domination isolated Tibet from surrounding regions.

Upheavals and Repression, 750–879

The Tang elites came to see Buddhism as undermining the Confucian idea of the family as the model for the state. The Confucian scholar Han Yu (768–824) spoke powerfully for a return to traditional Confucian practices. In "Memorial on the Bone of Buddha" written to the emperor in 819 on the occasion of ceremonies to receive a bone of the Buddha in the imperial palace, he scornfully disparages the Buddha and his followers:

> Now Buddha was a man of the barbarians who did not speak the language of China and wore clothes of a different fashion. His sayings did not concern the ways of our ancient kings, nor did his manner of dress conform to their laws. He understood neither the duties that bind sovereign and subject nor the affections of father and son. If he were still alive today and came to our court by order of his ruler, Your Majesty might condescend to receive him, but . . . he would then be escorted to the borders of the state, dismissed, and not allowed to delude the masses. How then, when he has long been dead, could his rotten bones, the foul and unlucky remains of his body, be rightly admitted to the palace? Confucius said, "Respect spiritual beings, while keeping at a distance from them."[3]

Buddhism was also attacked for encouraging women in politics. Wu Zhao°, a woman who had married into the imperial family, seized control of the government in 690 and declared herself emperor. She based her legitimacy on claiming to be a bodhisattva, an enlightened soul who had chosen to remain on earth to lead others to salvation. She also favored Buddhists and Daoists over Confucianists in her court and government.

Later Confucian writers expressed contempt for Wu Zhao and other powerful women, such as the concubine Yang Guifei°. Bo Zhuyi°, in his poem "Everlasting Remorse," lamented the influence of women at the Tang court, which had caused "the hearts of fathers and mothers everywhere not to value the birth of boys, but the birth of girls."[4] Confucian elites heaped every possible charge on prominent women who offended them, accusing Emperor Wu of grotesque tortures and murders, including tossing the dismembered but still living bodies of enemies into wine vats and cauldrons. They blamed Yang Guifei for the outbreak of the An Lushan rebellion in 755.

Serious historians dismiss the stories about Wu Zhao as stereotypical characterizations of "evil" rulers. Eunuchs (castrated palace servants) charged by historians with controlling Chang'an and the Tang court and publicly executing rival bureaucrats represent a similar stereotype. In fact Wu seems to have ruled effectively and was not deposed until 705, when extreme old age (eighty-plus) incapacitated her. Nevertheless, traditional Chinese historians commonly describe unorthodox rulers and all-powerful women as evil, and the truth about Wu will never be known.

Qinghai (CHING-hie)   **Sichuan** (SUH-chwahn)
Xinjiang (shin-jee-yahng)

Wu Zhao (woo jow)   **Yang Guifei** (yahng gway-fay)
Bo Zhuyi (baw joo-ee)

Buddhist Cave Painting at Dunhuang Hundreds of caves dating to the period when Buddhism enjoyed popularity and government favor in China survive in Gansu province, which was beyond the reach of the Tang rulers when they turned against Buddhism. This cave, dated to the year 538/9, contains elaborate wall decorations narrating the life of the Buddha and depicting scenes from the Western Paradise, where devotees of the Pure Land sect of Buddhism hoped to be reborn.   (NHK International, Inc.)

Even Chinese gentry living in safe and prosperous localities associated Buddhism with social ills. People who worried about "barbarians" ruining their society pointed to Buddhism as evidence of the foreign evil since it had such strong roots in Inner Asia and Tibet. They claimed that eradicating Buddhist influence would restore the ancient values of hierarchy and social harmony. Because Buddhism shunned earthly ties, monks and nuns severed relations with the secular world in search of enlightenment. They paid no taxes, served in no army. They deprived their families of advantageous marriage alliances and denied descendants to their ancestors. The Confucian elites saw all this as threatening to the family, and to the family estates that underlay the Tang economic and political structure.

In 840 (a year of disintegration on many fronts) the government moved to crush the monasteries. An imperial edict of 845 reports the demolition of 4,600 temples and the forcible conversion of 26,500 monks and nuns into ordinary workers. The tax exemption of monasteries had allowed them to purchase land and precious objects and to employ large numbers of serfs. Wealthy believers had given the monasteries large tracts of land, and poor people had flocked to the Buddhist institutions to work as artisans, fieldworkers, cooks, housekeepers, and guards. By the ninth century, hundreds of thousands of people had entered tax exempt Buddhist institutions.

Now an enormous amount of land and 150,000 workers were returned to the tax rolls.

Though some Buddhist cultural centers, such as the cave monasteries at Dunhuang, were protected by local warlords dependent on the favor of Buddhist rulers in Inner Asia, the dissolution of the monasteries was an incalculable loss to China's cultural heritage. Some sculptures and grottoes survived only in defaced form. Wooden temples and façades sheltering great stone carvings burned to the ground. Monasteries became legal again in later times, but Buddhism never recovered the social, political, and cultural influence of early Tang times.

The End of the Tang Empire, 879–907

The Tang order succumbed to the very forces that were essential to its creation and maintenance. The campaigns of expansion in the seventh century had left the empire dependent on local military commanders and a complex tax collection system. Such reverses as the Battle of the Talas River in 751, which halted the drive westward into Central Asia, led to military demoralization and underfunding. In 755 An Lushan, a Tang general appointed as regional commander on the northeast frontier, led about 200,000 soldiers in a rebellion that forced the emperor to flee Chang'an and execute his favorite concubine, Yang Guifei, whom some accused of being An Lushan's lover. Though he was killed by his own son in 757, An Lushan's rebellion lasted for eight years and resulted in new powers and greater independence for the provincial military governors who helped suppress it. The Uighurs also helped bring the disorder to an end.

Despite continuing prosperity, political disintegration and the elite's sense of cultural decay created an unsettled environment that encouraged aspiring dictators. A disgruntled member of the gentry, Huang Chao°, led the most devastating uprising between 879 and 881. Despite ruthless and violent domination of the villages he controlled, his rebellion attracted hundreds of thousands of poor farmers and tenants who could not protect themselves from local bosses, or who sought escape from oppressive landlords or taxes, or who simply did not know what else to do in the deepening chaos. The new hatred of "barbarians" spurred the rebels to murder thousands of foreign residents in Canton and Beijing°.

Local warlords finally wiped out the rebels, using the same violent tactics. But Tang society did not find peace. Refugees, migrant workers, and homeless people became common sights in both city and country. Residents of northern China fled to the southern frontiers as groups from Inner Asia took advantage of the flight of population to move into localities in the north. Though Tang emperors continued to rule in Chang'an until their line was terminated by one of the warlords in 907, they never regained effective power after Huang Chao's rebellion.

Silk Painting Depicting Khitan Hunters Resting Their Horses
The artist shows the Khitans' soft riding boots, leggings, and robes (much like those used by the Mongols) and the Khitans' patterned hairstyle, with part of the skull shaved and some of the hair worn long. Men in Inner and North Asia (including Japan) used patterned hairstyles to indicate their political allegiance. The custom was documented in the 400s (but is certainly much older) and continued up to the twentieth century.   (National Palace Museum, Taipai, Taiwan, Republic of China)

THE EMERGENCE OF EAST ASIA, TO 1200

In the aftermath of the Tang, three new states emerged and competed to inherit its legacy (see Map 11.2). The Liao° Empire of the Khitan° people, pastoral nomads related to the Mongols living on the northeastern frontier, established their rule in the north. They centered their government on several cities, but the emperors preferred to spend their time in their nomad encampments. In western China, the Minyak people (closely related to the Tibetans) established a second successor state. They called themselves "Tangguts°" to show their connection with the former empire. The third state, the Chinese-speaking **Song Empire,** came into being in 960 in central China.

Huang Chao (wang show)   **Beijing** (bay-jeeng)   **Liao** (lee-OW)
Khitan (kee-THAN)   **Tanggut** (TAHNG-gut)

Competition among these states was unavoidable. They embodied the political ambitions of peoples who spoke very different languages and subscribed to different religious and philosophical systems—Mahayana Buddhism among the Liao, Tibetan Buddhism among the Tangguts, and Confucianism among the Song. The Liao and especially the Tangguts maintained some continuing relationship with Inner and Central Asia, but the Song were cut off. Instead they developed their sea connections with other states in East Asia, West Asia, and Southeast Asia. This effort led to advanced seafaring and sailing technologies. The Song elite shared the late Tang dislike of "barbaric" or "foreign" influences as they tried to cope with multiple enemies that heavily taxed their military capacities. Meanwhile, Korea and Japan strengthened political and cultural ties with China, including an appreciation of Confucianism; and some Southeast Asian states, relieved of any Tang military threat, entered into friendly relations with the Song court.

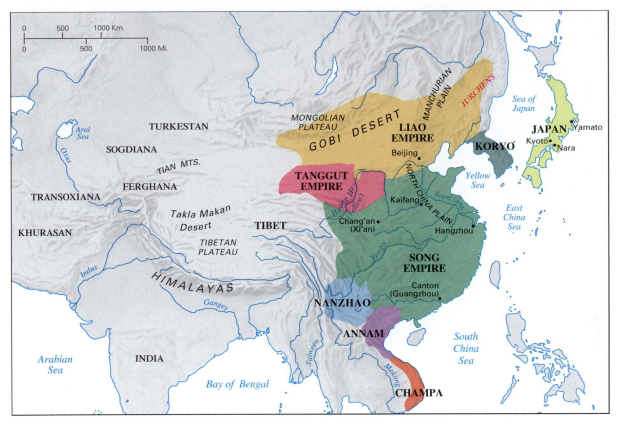

Map 11.2   Liao and Song Empires, ca. 1100   The states of Liao in the north and Song in the south generally ceased open hostilities after a treaty in 1005 stabilized the border and imposed an annual payment on Song China.

The Liao and Jin Challenge

The Liao Empire of the Khitan people extended from Siberia to Central Asia, connecting China with societies to the north and west. Variations on the Khitan name became the name for China in these distant regions: "Kitai" for the Mongols, "Khitai" for the Russians, and "Cathay" for those, like contemporaries of the Italian merchant Marco Polo, who reached China from Europe (see Chapter 13).

The Liao rulers prided themselves on their pastoral traditions, the continuing source of their military might, and made no attempt to create a single elite culture. They encouraged Chinese elites to use their own language, study their own classics, and see the emperor through Confucian eyes; and they encouraged other peoples to use their own languages and see the emperor as a champion of Buddhism or as a nomadic leader. On balance, Buddhism far outweighed Confucianism in this and other northern states, where rulers depended on

their roles as bodhisattvas or as Buddhist kings to legitimate power. Liao rule lasted from 916 to 1121.

Superb horsemen and archers, the Khitans added siege machines from China and Central Asia to their armory for challenging the Song. In 1005 the Song emperor agreed to a truce that included enormous annual payments in cash and silk to the Liao. This lasted for more than a century, but eventually the Song tired of paying the annual tribute and entered into a secret alliance with the Jurchens of northeastern Asia, who were also chafing under Liao rule. In 1125 the Jurchens destroyed the Liao capital in Mongolia and proclaimed their own empire—the Jin. Then they turned against their former Song ally (Map 11.2).

The Jurchens grew rice, millet, and wheat, but they also spent a good deal of time hunting, fishing, and tending livestock. Though their language was unrelated to that of the Khitan, the Jurchens nevertheless learned much from the Khitan about the military arts and politi-

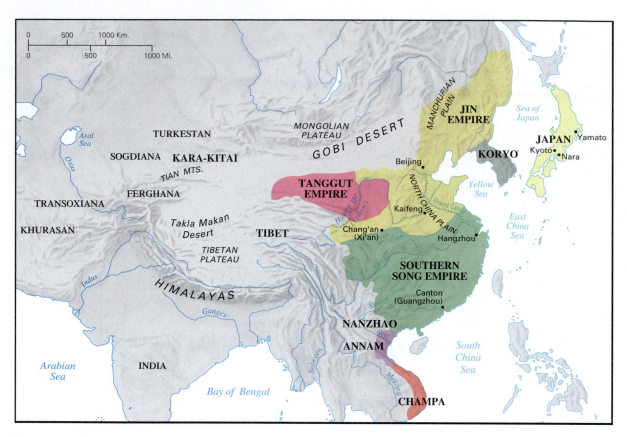

Map 11.3 Jin and Southern Song Empires, ca. 1200 After 1127 Song abandoned its northern territories to Jin. The Southern Song continued the policy of annual payments—to Jin rather than Liao—and maintained high military preparedness to prevent further invasions.

cal organization. This helped them become formidable enemies of the Song Empire, against whom they mounted an all-out campaign in 1127. They laid siege to the Song capital, Kaifeng°, and captured the Song emperor. Within a few years the Song withdrew south of the Yellow River and established a new capital at Hangzhou°, leaving central as well as northern China in Jurchen control (Map 11.3). The Song made annual payments to the Jin Empire to avoid open warfare. Historians generally refer to this period as the "Southern Song" (1127–1279).

Song Industries

Historians look upon the Southern Song as the premodern state and society that came closest to initiating an industrial revolution. Divided into three separate states from 907 to 1279, China did not exhibit the military expansionism and exploitation of

---

Kaifeng (kie-fuhng)   **Hangzhou** (hahng-jo)

far-flung networks of communication that had characterized the Tang at their height. Yet many of the advances in technology, medicine, astronomy, and mathematics for which the Song is famous derived from information that had come to China in Tang times, sometimes from very distant places. Song officials, scholars, and businessmen had the motivation and resources to adapt Tang information and technology to meet their needs, particularly in warfare, extension of agriculture, and the management of economic and social changes.

Chinese scholars made great strides in the arts of measurement and observation, drawing on the work of Indian and West Asian mathematicians and astronomers who had migrated to the Tang Empire in previous generations. Song mathematicians introduced the use of fractions, first employing them to describe the phases of the moon. From lunar observations, Song astronomers constructed a very precise calendar and, alone among the world's astronomers, noted the explosion of the Crab Nebula in 1054. Chinese scholars used their work in as-

Su Song's Astronomical Clock This gigantic clock built at Kaifeng between 1088 and 1092 combined mathematics, astronomy, and calendar-making with skillful engineering. The team overseen by Su Song placed an armillary sphere on the observation platform and linked it with chains to the water-driven central mechanism shown in the cutaway view. The water wheel also rotated the buddha statues in the multistory pagoda the spectators are looking at. Other devices displayed the time of the day, the month, and the year. (Courtesy, Joseph Needham, *Science and Civilization in China*)

tronomy and mathematics to make significant contributions to timekeeping and the development of the compass.

In 1088 the engineer Su Song constructed a gigantic mechanical celestial clock in Kaifeng. Escapement mechanisms for controlling the revolving wheels in water-powered clocks had appeared under the Tang, as had the application of water wheels to weaving and threshing. But this knowledge had not been widely applied. Su Song adapted the escapement and water wheel to his clock, which featured the first known chain-drive mechanism. The clock told the time of day and the day of the month, and it indicated the movement of the moon and certain stars and planets across the night sky. An observation deck and a mechanically rotated armillary sphere crowned the 80-foot (24-meter) structure. The clock exemplified the Song ability to integrate observational astronomy, applied mathematics, and engineering.

Song inventors drew on their knowledge of celestial coordinates, particularly the Pole Star, to refine the de-

sign of the compass. Long known in China, the magnetic compass shrank in size in Song times and gained a fixed pivot point for the needle, and sometimes even a small protective case with a glass covering. These changes made the compass suitable for seafaring, a use first attested in 1090. The Chinese compass and the Greek astrolabe, introduced later, improved navigation throughout Southeast Asia and the Indian Ocean.

Development of the seaworthy compass coincided with new techniques in building China's main ocean-going ship, the **junk.** A stern-mounted rudder improved the steering of the large ship in uneasy seas, and watertight bulkheads helped keep it afloat in emergencies. The shipwrights of the Persian Gulf soon copied these features in their ship designs.

Song innovation carried over into military affairs as well, though military pressure from the Liao and Jin Empires remained a serious challenge. The Song fielded an army four times as large as that of the Tang—about 1.25 million men (roughly the size of the present-day army of the United States)—though it occupied less than half the territory of the Tang. Song commanders were specially educated for the task, examined on military subjects, and paid regular salaries.

Because of the need for iron and steel to make weapons, the Song rulers fought their northern rivals for control of iron and coal mines in north China. The volume of Song mining and iron production, which again became a government monopoly in the eleventh century, soared. By the end of that century cast iron production reached about 125,000 tons (113,700 metric tons) annually, putting it on a par with the output of eighteenth-century Britain. Engineers became skilled at high-temperature metallurgy. They produced steel weapons of unprecedented strength by using enormous bellows, often driven by water wheels, to superheat the molten ore. Military engineers used iron to buttress defensive works because it was impervious to fire or concussion. Armorers used it in mass-produced body armor (in small, medium, and large sizes). Iron construction also appeared in bridges and small buildings. Mass-production techniques for bronze and ceramics in use in China for nearly two thousand years were adapted to iron casting and assembly.

To counter cavalry assaults, the Song experimented with **gunpowder,** which they initially used to propel clusters of flaming arrows. During the wars against the Jurchens in the 1100s the Song introduced a new and terrifying weapon. Shells launched from Song fortifications exploded in the midst of the enemy, blowing out shards of iron and dismembering men and horses. The short range of the shells limited them to defensive uses, and they had no major impact on the overall conduct of war.

Economy and Society in Song China

Despite the continuous military threats and the vigor of Song responses, Song elite culture idealized civil pursuits. Socially, the civil man outranked the military man. Private academies, designed to train young men for the official examinations and develop intellectual interests, became influential in culture and politics. New interpretations of Confucian teachings became so important and influential that the term **neo-Confucianism** is used for Song and later versions of Confucian thought.

Zhu Xi° (1130–1200), the most important early neo-Confucian thinker, wrote in reaction to the many centuries during which Buddhism and Daoism had often overshadowed the precepts of Confucius. He and others worked out a systematic approach to cosmology that focused on the central conception that human nature is moral, rational, and essentially good. To combat the Buddhist dismissal of worldly affairs as a transitory distraction, they reemphasized individual moral and social responsibility. Their human ideal was the sage, a person who could preserve mental stability and serenity while dealing conscientiously with troubling social problems. Where earlier Confucian thinkers had written about sage kings and political leaders, the neo-Confucians espoused the spiritual idea of universal sagehood, a state that could be achieved through proper study of the new Confucian principles and cosmology.

Despite the vigor and pervasiveness of neo-Confucianism, popular Buddhist sects persisted during the Song. The excerpt from a Song song-story quoted at the beginning of this chapter contained the line "We Buddhists and Confucians are of one family." While historically suitable for the time when the original version of the story of Ying-ying was written, before the Tang abolition of the Buddhist monasteries in 845, it is unlikely that the line would have pleased a Song audience if anti-Buddhist feelings had remained so ferocious. Some Buddhists elaborated upon Tang-era folk practices derived from India and Tibet. The best known, Chan Buddhism (known as **Zen** in Japan and as Son in Korea), asserted that mental discipline alone could win salvation.

Meditation, a key Chan practice, could be employed by Confucians as well as Buddhists. It could afford prospective officials relief from their preparation for civil service examinations, which continued into the Song from the Tang period. Dramatically different from the Han policy of hiring and promoting on the basis of recommendations, Song-style examinations persisted for nearly a thousand years. A large bureaucracy oversaw their design and administration. Test questions, which changed each time the examinations were given, even though they were always based on Confucian classics, often related to economic management or foreign policy.

The examinations had social implications, for hereditary class distinctions meant less than they had in Tang times, when noble lineages played a greater role in the structure of power. The new system recruited the most talented men for government service, whatever their origin. Men from wealthy families, however, succeeded most often. The tests required memorization of classics believed to date from the time of Confucius; preparation consumed so much time that peasant boys could rarely compete.

Success in the examinations brought good marriage prospects, the chance for a high salary, and enormous

---

Zhu Xi (jew she)

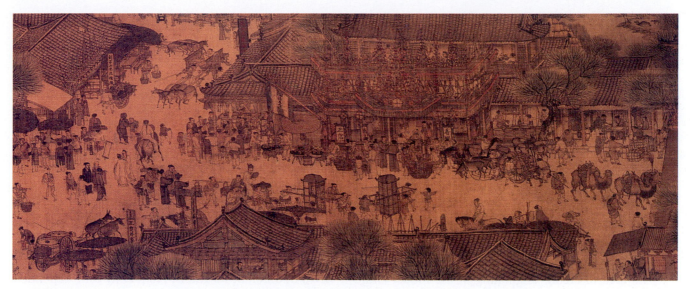

Going up the River   Song cities hummed with commercial and industrial activity, much of it concentrated on the rivers and canals linking the capital Kaifeng to the provinces. This detail from *Going Upriver at the Qingming [Spring] Festival* shows a tiny portion of the scroll painting's panorama. Painted by Zhang Zeduan sometime before 1125, its depiction of daily life makes it an important source of information on working people. Before open shop fronts and tea houses a camel caravan departs, donkey carts are unloaded, a scholar rides loftily (if gingerly) on horseback, and women of wealth go by in closed sedan-chairs.   (The Palace Museum, Beijing)

prestige. Failure could bankrupt a family and ruin a man both socially and psychologically. This put great pressure on candidates who spent days at a time in tiny, dim, airless examination cells, attempting to produce their answers—in beautiful calligraphy.

Changes in printing, from woodblock to an early form of **movable type,** allowed cheaper printing of many kinds of informative books and of test materials. The Song government realized that the examination system schooled millions of ambitious young men in Confucian ideals of state service—many times the number who eventually passed the tests. To promote its ideological goals, the government authorized the mass production of preparation books in the years before 1000. Though a man had to be literate to read the preparation books and basic education was still not common, some people of limited means were now able to take the examinations; and a moderate number of candidates entered the Song bureaucracy without noble, gentry, or elite backgrounds.

The availability of printed books changed country life as well, since landlords now had access to expert advice on planting and irrigation techniques, harvesting, tree cultivation, threshing, and weaving. Landlords frequently gathered their tenants and workers to show them illustrated texts and explain their meaning. This dissemination of knowledge, along with new technolo-

gies, furthered the development of new agricultural land south of the Yangzi River. Iron implements such as plows and rakes, first used in the Tang era, were adapted to wet-rice cultivation as the population moved south. Landowners and village leaders learned from books how to fight the mosquitoes that carried malaria. Control of the disease became one of the factors encouraging northerners to move south, which led to a sharp increase in population.

The increasing profitability of agriculture caught the attention of some ambitious members of the gentry. Still a frontier for Chinese settlers under the Tang, the south saw increasing concentration of land in the hands of a few wealthy families. In the process, the indigenous inhabitants of the region, related to the modern-day populations of Malaysia, Thailand, and Laos, retreated into the mountains or southward toward Vietnam.

During the 1100s the total population of the Chinese territories, spurred by prosperity, rose above 100 million. An increasing proportion lived in large towns and cities, though the leading Song cities had fewer than a million inhabitants. This still put them among the largest cities in the world.

Health and crowding posed problems in the Song capitals. Multistory wooden apartment houses fronted on narrow streets—sometimes only 4 or 5 feet (1.2 to 1.5

meters) wide—clogged by peddlers or families spending time outdoors. The crush of people called for new techniques in waste management, water supply, and fire-fighting. Controlling urban rodent and insect infestations improved health and usually kept the bubonic plague isolated in a few rural areas.

In Hangzhou engineers diverted the nearby river to flow through the city, flushing away waste and disease. Arab and European travelers who had firsthand experience with the Song capital, and who were sensitive to the urban crowding in their own societies, expressed amazement at the way Hangzhou city officials sheltered the densely packed population from danger so that they could enjoy the abundant pleasures of the city: restaurants, parks, bookstores, wine shops, tea houses, theaters, and the various entertainments mentioned at the start of this chapter.

The idea of credit, originating in the robust long-distance trade of the Tang period, spread widely under the Song. Intercity or interregional credit—what the Song called "flying money"—depended on the acceptance of guarantees that the paper could be redeemed for coinage at another location. The public accepted the practice because credit networks tended to be managed by families, so that brothers and cousins were usually honoring each other's certificates.

"Flying money" certificates differed from government-issued paper money, which the Song pioneered. In some years, military expenditures consumed 80 percent of the government budget. The state responded to this financial pressure by distributing paper money. But this made inflation so severe that by the beginning of the 1100s paper money was trading for only 1 percent of its face value. Eventually the government withdrew paper money and instead imposed new taxes, sold monopolies, and offered financial incentives to merchants. Privatization created opportunities for individuals with capital to engage in businesses that previously had been state monopolies.

Hard-pressed for the revenue needed to maintain the army, canals, roads, waterworks, and other state functions, the government finally resorted to tax farming, selling the rights to tax collection to private individuals. Tax farmers made their profit by collecting the maximum amount and sending an agreed upon smaller sum to the government. This meant exorbitant rates for taxable services, such as tolls, and much heavier tax burdens on the common people.

Rapid economic growth undermined the remaining government monopolies and the traditional strict regulation of business. Now merchants and artisans as well as gentry and officials could make fortunes. With land no longer the only source of wealth, the traditional social hierarchy common to an agricultural economy weakened, while cities, commerce, consumption, and the use of money and credit boomed. Urban life reflected the elite's growing taste for fine fabrics, porcelain, exotic foods, large houses, and exquisite paintings and books. Because the government and traditional elites did not control much of the new commercial and industrial development, historians sometimes describe Song China as "modern," using the term to refer to the era of private capitalism and the growth of an urban middle class in eighteenth-century Europe.

In conjunction with the backlash against Buddhism and revival of Confucianism that began under the Tang and intensified under the Song, women entered a long period of cultural subordination, legal disenfranchisement, and social restriction. Merchants spent long periods away from home, and many maintained several wives in different locations. Frequently they depended on wives to manage their homes and even their businesses in their absence. But though women took on responsibility for the management of their husbands' property, their own property rights suffered legal erosion. Under Song law, a woman's property automatically passed to her husband, and women could not remarry if their husbands divorced them or died.

The subordination of women proved compatible with Confucianism, and it became fashionable to educate girls just enough to read simplified versions of Confucian philosophy that emphasized the lowly role of women. Modest education made these young women more desirable as companions for the sons of gentry or noble families, and as literate mothers in lower ranking families aspiring to improve their status. Only rarely did a woman of extremely high station with unusual personal determination, as well as uncommon encouragement from father and husband, manage to acquire extensive education and freedom to pursue the literary arts. The poet Li Qingzhao° (1083–1141) acknowledged and made fun of her unusual status as a highly celebrated female writer:

> Although I've studied poetry for thirty years
> I try to keep my mouth shut and avoid reputation.
> Now who is this nosy gentleman talking about my
>   poetry
> Like Yang Ching-chih°
> Who spoke of Hsiang Ssu° everywhere he went. [5]

Her reference is to a hermit poet of the ninth century who was continually and extravagantly praised by a court official, Yang Ching-chih.

Li Qingzhao (lee CHING-jow)
Yang Ching-chih (yahng SHING-she)   **Hsiang Ssu** (sang sue)

The Players   Women—often enslaved—entertained at Chinese courts from early times. Tang art often depicts women with slender figures, but Tang taste also admired more robust physiques. Song women, usually pale with willowy figures, appear as here with bound feet. The practice appeared in Tang times but was not widespread until the Song, when the image of weak, housebound women unable to work became a status symbol and pushed aside the earlier enthusiasm for healthy women who participated in family business.   (The Palace Museum, Beijing)

NEW KINGDOMS IN EAST ASIA

With the rival states to the northeast and northwest strongly oriented toward Buddhism, the best possibilities for expanding the Confucian worldview of the Song lay with newly emerging kingdoms to the east and south. Korea, Japan, and Vietnam, like Song China, depended on agriculture. The cultivation of rice, an increasingly widespread crop, fit well with Confucian social ideas. Tending the young rice plants, irrigating the rice paddies, and managing the harvest required coordination among many village and kin groups and rewarded hierarchy, obedience, and self-discipline. Confucianism also justified using agricultural profits to support the education, safety, and comfort of the literate elite. In each of these new kingdoms Song civilization melded with indigenous cultural and historical traditions to create a distinctive synthesis.

Female footbinding first appeared among slave dancers at the Tang court, but it did not become widespread until the Song period. The bindings forced the toes under and toward the heel, so that the bones eventually broke and the woman could not walk on her own. In noble and gentry families, footbinding began between ages five and seven. In less wealthy families, girls worked until they were older, so footbinding began only in a girl's teens.

Many literate men condemned the maiming of innocent girls and the general uselessness of footbinding. Nevertheless, bound feet became a status symbol. By 1200 a woman with unbound feet had become undesirable in elite circles, and mothers of elite status, or aspiring to such status, almost without exception bound their daughters' feet. They knew that girls with unbound feet faced rejection by society, by prospective husbands, and ultimately by their own families. Working women and the indigenous peoples of the south, where northern practices took a longer time to penetrate, did not practice footbinding. As a consequence, they enjoyed considerably more mobility and economic independence than did elite Chinese women.

Chinese Influences

Since Han times Confucianism had spread through East Asia with the spread of the Chinese writing system. Political ideologies in Korea, Japan, and Vietnam varied somewhat from those of Song China, however. These three East Asian neighbors had first centralized power under ruling houses in the early Tang period, and their state ideologies continued to resemble that of the early Tang, when Buddhism and Confucianism were still seen as compatible.

Government offices in Korea, Japan, and Vietnam went to noble families and did not depend on passing an elaborate set of examinations on Confucian texts. Landowning and agriculture remained the major sources of income, and landowners did not face challenges to their status from a large merchant class or an urban elite.

Nevertheless, men in Korea, Japan, and Vietnam prized literacy in classical Chinese and a good knowledge of Confucian texts. Members of the ruling and landholding elite sought to instill Confucian ideals of hierarchy and harmony among the general population through teaching by example and formal education, which was available to only a small number of people. The elite in every country learned to read Chinese and the Confucian classics, and Chinese characters contributed to locally invented writing systems (see Environment and Technology: Writing in East Asia, 400–1200).

Writing in East Asia, 400–1200

An ideographic writing system that originated in China became a communications tool throughout East Asia. Variations on this system, based more on depictions of meanings than representations of sound, spread widely by the time of the Sui and Tang Empires. Many East Asian peoples adapted ideographic techniques to writing languages unrelated to Chinese in grammar or sound.

The Vietnamese, Koreans, and Japanese often simplified Chinese characters and associated them with the sounds of their own non-Chinese languages. For instance, the Chinese character *an,* meaning "peace" (Fig. 1), was pronounced "an" in Japanese and was familiar as a Chinese character to Confucian scholars in Japan's Heian (hay-ahn) period. However, nonscholars simplified the character and used it to write the Japanese sound "a" (Fig. 2). A set of more than thirty of these syllabic symbols adapted from Chinese characters could represent the inflected forms (forms with grammatical endings) of any Japanese word. Murasaki Shikibu used such a syllabic system when she wrote *The Tale of Genji.*

In Vietnam and later in northern Asia, phonetic and ideographic elements combined in new ways. The apparent circles in some *chu nom* writing from Vietnam (Fig. 3) derive from the Chinese character for "mouth" and indicate a primary sound association for the word. The Khitans, who spoke a language related to Mongolian, developed an ideographic system of their own, inspired by Chinese characters. The Chinese character *wang* (Fig. 4), meaning "king, prince, ruler," was changed to represent the Khitan word for "emperor" by adding an upward stroke representing a "superior" ruler (Fig. 5). Because the system was ideographic, we do not know the pronunciation of this Khitan word. The Khitan character for "God" or "Heaven" adds a top stroke representing the "supreme" ruler or power to the character meaning "ruler" (Fig. 6). Though inspired by Chinese characters, Khitan writings could not be read by anyone who was not specifically educated in them.

The Khitans developed another system to represent the sounds and grammar of their language. They used small, simplified elements arranged within an imaginary frame to indicate the sounds in any word. This idea might have come from the phonetic script used by the Uighurs. Here (Fig. 7) we see the word for horse in a Khitan inscription. Fitting sound elements within a frame also occurred later in *hangul,* the Korean phonetic system introduced in the 1400s. Here (Fig. 8) we see the two words making up the country name "Korea."

The Chinese writing system served the Chinese elite well. But peoples speaking unrelated languages continually experimented with the Chinese invention to produce new ways of expressing themselves. Some of the resulting sound-based writing systems remain in common use; others are still being deciphered.

  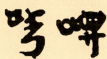

Figure 1   **Figure 2**   **Figure 3**   **Figure 4**   **Figure 5**   **Figure 6**   **Figure 7**   **Figure 8**

Korea

Written language arrived too late for these societies to record their earliest histories. Our first knowledge of Korea, Japan, and Vietnam comes from early Chinese officials and travelers. When the Qin Empire established its first colony in the Korean peninsula in the third century B.C.E., Chinese bureaucrats began documenting Korean history and customs. Han writers noted the horse breeding, strong hereditary elites, and **shamanism** (belief in the ability of certain individuals to contact ancestors and the invisible spirit world) of Korea's small kingdoms. But Korea quickly absorbed Confucianism and Buddhism.

A land of mountains, particularly in the east and north, Korea was largely covered by forest until modern times. Less than 20 percent of the land, mostly in the warmer south, is suitable for agriculture. In the early 500s the dominant landholding families made inherited status—the "bone ranks"—permanent in Silla°, a kingdom in the southeast of the peninsula. In 668 the larger Koguryo kingdom in the north came to an end after prolonged conflict with the Sui and Tang, and with Tang encouragement, Silla took control of much of the Korean peninsula. Silla could not stand by itself without Tang support, however, so after the fall of the Tang in the early 900s, the ruling house of **Koryo°,** from which the modern name "Korea" derives, united the peninsula. At constant threat from the Liao and then the Jin, Koryo pursued amicable relations with Song China. The Koryo kings supported Buddhism and made superb printed editions of Buddhist texts.

Woodblock printing exemplifies the technological exchanges that Korea enjoyed with China. The oldest surviving woodblock print in Chinese characters comes from Korea in the middle 700s. Commonly used during the Tang period, woodblock printing required great technical skill. A calligrapher would write the text on thin paper, which would then be pasted upside down on a block of wood. When the paper was wetted, the characters showed through from the back, and an artisan would carve away the wooden surface surrounding each character. A fresh block had to be carved for each printed page. Korean artisans developed their own advances in printing. By Song times, Korean experiments with movable type reached China, where further improvements led to metal or porcelain type from which texts could be cheaply printed.

Japan

Japan consists of four main islands and many smaller ones stretching in an arc from as far south as Georgia to as far north as Maine. The nearest point of contact with the Asian mainland lies 100 miles away in southern Korea. In early times Japan was even more mountainous and heavily forested than Korea, and only 11 percent of its land area was suitable for cultivation.

Japan's earliest history, like Korea's, comes from Chinese records. The first description, dating from the fourth century, tells of an island at the eastern edge of the world, divided into hundreds of small countries and ruled over by a shamaness named Himiko or Pimiko. This account describes the Japanese terrain, mountainous with small pockets and stretches of land suitable for agriculture, as influencing the social and political structures of the early period. The unification of central Japan came sometime in the fourth or fifth century C.E. How it

occurred remains a question, but horse-riding warriors from Korea may have united the small countries of Japan under a central government at Yamato, on the central plain of Honshu island.

In the mid-600s the rulers based at Yamato implemented the Taika° and other reforms, giving the Yamato regime the key features of Tang government, which they knew of through embassies to Chang'an: a legal code, an official variety of Confucianism, and an official reverence for Buddhism. Within a century a centralized government with a complex system of law had emerged, as attested by a massive history in the Confucian style. The Japanese mastered Chinese building techniques so well that Nara° and Kyoto, Japan's early capitals, provide invaluable evidence of the wooden architecture long since vanished from China. During the eighth century Japan in some ways surpassed China in Buddhist studies. In 752 dignitaries from all over Mahayana Buddhist Asia gathered at the enormous Todaiji temple, near Nara, to celebrate the "eye-opening" of the "Great Buddha" statue.

Japanese admiration of Chinese culture did not extend to everything, however. Though the Japanese adopted Chinese building styles and some street plans, Japanese cities were built without walls. Unlike China, central Japan was not plagued by constant warfare. Also, the Confucian Mandate of Heaven, which justified dynastic changes, played no role in legitimating Japanese government. The *tenno*—often called "emperor" in English—belonged to a family believed to have ruled Japan since the beginning of known history. The dynasty never changed. The royal family endured because the emperors seldom wielded political power. A prime minister and the leaders of the native religion, in later times called Shinto, the "way of the gods," exercised real control.

In 794 the central government moved to Kyoto, usually called by its ancient name, Heian. Legally centralized government lasted there until 1185, though power became decentralized toward the end. Members of the **Fujiwara°** family—an ancient family of priests, bureaucrats, and warriors—controlled power and protected the emperor. Fujiwara dominance favored men of Confucian learning over the generally illiterate warriors. Noblemen of the Fujiwara period read the Chinese classics, appreciated painting and poetry, and refined their sense of wardrobe and interior decoration.

Pursuit of an aesthetic way of life prompted the Fujiwara nobles to entrust responsibility for local government, policing, and tax collection to their warriors. Though often of humble origins, a small number of warriors had achieved wealth and power by the late

---

Silla (SILL-ah or SHILL-ah)   **Koryo** (KAW-ree-oh)

Taika (TIE-kah)   **Nara** (NAH-rah)   **Fujiwara** (foo-jee-WAH-rah)

1000s. By the middle 1100s the nobility had lost control, and civil war between rival warrior clans engulfed the capital.

Like other East Asian states influenced by Confucianism, the elite families of Fujiwara Japan did not encourage education for women. However, this did not prevent the exceptional woman from having a strong cultural impact. The hero of the celebrated Japanese novel *The Tale of Genji,* written around the year 1000 by the noblewoman Murasaki Shikibu, remarks: "Women should have a general knowledge of several subjects, but it gives a bad impression if they show themselves to be attached to a particular branch of learning."[6]

Fujiwara noblewomen lived in near-total isolation, generally spending their time on cultural pursuits and the study of Buddhism. To communicate with their families or among themselves, they depended on writing. The simplified syllabic script that they used represented the Japanese language in its fully inflected form (the Chinese classical script used by Fujiwara men could not do so). Loneliness, free time, and a ready instrument for expression produced an outpouring of poetry, diaries, and storytelling by women of the Fujiwara era. Their best-known achievement, however, remains Murasaki's portrait of Fujiwara court culture.

Military values acquired increasing importance during the period 1156–1185 when warfare between rival clans culminated in the establishment of the **Kamakura° shogunate,** the first of three decentralized military governments, in eastern Honshu, far from the old religious and political center at Kyoto. The standing of the Fujiwara family fell as nobles and the emperor hurried to accommodate the new warlords. *The Tale of the Heike,* an anonymously composed thirteenth-century epic account of the clan war, reflects an appreciation of the Buddhist doctrine of the impermanence of worldly things, a view that became common at that time among a new warrior class. This new class, in later times called *samurai,* eventually absorbed some of the Fujiwara aristocratic values, but the ascendancy of the nonmilitary civil elite had come to an end.

Vietnam

Vietnam had had contact with empires based in China since the third century B.C.E., but not until Tang times did the relationship become close enough for economic and cultural interchange to play an important cultural role. Occupying the coastal regions east of the mountainous spine of mainland South-

east Asia, Vietnam's economic and political life centered on two fertile river valleys, the Red River in the north and the Mekong° in the south. Agriculture was also possible in many smaller coastal areas where streams from the mountains—torrents during the monsoon season—flowed down to the sea. The rice-based agriculture of Vietnam made the region well suited for integration with southern China. As in southern China, the wet climate and hilly terrain of Vietnam demanded expertise in irrigation.

The ancestors of the Vietnamese may have preceded the Chinese in using draft animals in farming, working with metal, and making certain kinds of pots. But in Tang and Song times the elites of "Annam°"—as the Chinese called early Vietnam—adopted Confucian bureaucratic training, Mahayana Buddhism, and other aspects of Chinese culture. Annamese elites continued to rule in the Tang style after that dynasty's fall. Annam assumed the name Dai Viet° in 936 and maintained good relations with Song China as an independent country.

Champa, located largely in what is now southern Vietnam, rivaled the Dai Viet state. The cultures of India and Malaya strongly influenced Champa through the networks of trade and communication that encompassed the Indian Ocean. During the Tang period Champa had hostile relations with Dai Viet, but both kingdoms cooperated with the less threatening Song, the former as a voluntary tributary state. Among the tribute gifts brought to the Song court by Champa emissaries was **Champa rice** (originally from India). Chinese farmers soon made use of this fast-maturing variety to improve their yields of the essential crop.

Vietnam shared the Confucian interest in hierarchy that was also evident in Korea and Japan, but attitudes toward women, like those in the other two countries, differed from the Chinese model. None of the societies adopted the Chinese practice of footbinding. In Korea strong family alliances that functioned like political and economic organizations allowed women a role in negotiating and disposing of property. Before the adoption of Confucianism, Annamese women had enjoyed higher status than women in China, perhaps because both women and men participated in wet-rice cultivation. The Trung sisters of Vietnam, who lived in the second century C.E. and led local farmers in resistance against the Han Empire, still serve as national symbols in Vietnam and as local heroes in southern China. They recall a time when women played visible and active roles in community and political life.

Kamakura (kah-mah-KOO-rah)

Mekong (may-KONG)   Annam (ahn-nahm)
Dai Viet (die vee-yet)

CONCLUSION

The reunification of China under the Sui and Tang triggered major changes both within China and in neighboring lands. Connections across Inner Asia and Tibet facilitated the flow of cultural and economic influences into China. Diversity within the empire produced great wealth and new ideas, and the dominant position of the Tang in the entire region led neighboring peoples in Korea, Japan, and Vietnam to imitate their practices. In time, however, internal tensions and foreign military pressure from the Uighurs and Tibetans weakened the Tang political structure and touched off rebellions that eventually doomed the empire.

The post-Tang fragmentation reduced the degree of Chinese domination in East Asia. Combining indigenous traditions and ideas borrowed from the Tang, neighboring peoples experimented with and often improved upon Tang military, architectural, and scientific technologies. The Jin, Tangguts, and Jurchens pursued these refinements on the basis of Buddhism as the state ideology. But they were not averse to adopting bureaucratic practices based on Chinese traditions and military techniques combining nomadic horsemanship and strategies with Chinese armaments and weapons. Korea, Japan, and Vietnam became much more closely wedded to Confucian models of state and society.

In Song China the spread of Tang technological knowledge resulted in the privatization of commerce, major advances in technology and industry, increased productivity in agriculture, and deeper exploration of ideas relating to time, cosmology, and mathematics. The brilliant achievements of the Song period came from mutually reinforcing developments in economy and technology. Avoiding the Tang's discouragement of innovation and competition, the Song economy, though much smaller than its predecessor, showed great productivity, circulating goods and money throughout East Asia and stimulating the economies of neighboring states. In terms of industrial specialization Song China excelled in military technology, engineering of all kinds, and production of iron and coal.

All the East Asian societies made advances in agricultural technology and productivity. All raised their literacy rates after the improvement of printing. Building on knowledge derived from Tang and Song sources, Japan went beyond China in developing advanced techniques in steel making, and Korea excelled in textiles and agriculture and produced major innovations in printing.

In the long run Song China could not maintain the equilibrium necessary to sustain its own prosperity and that of the region. Constant military challenges from the north eventually overwhelmed Song finances, and the need to buy high-quality steel from Japan caused a drain of copper coinage. When historians compare Song China with eighteenth-century Great Britain, another society that achieved unprecedented industrial production and technological innovation, they speculate about the reasons China progressed to such high levels of achievement and then tapered off while developments in Britain interacted with those in other European countries to produce an industrial revolution. No one can answer such questions conclusively, but the complex character of interrelationships among the East Asian and Inner Asian states as a whole, and the differing views of the world presented by Buddhism and neo-Confucianism surely played important roles.

■ Key Terms

Grand Canal	gunpowder
Li Shimin	neo-Confucianism
Tang Empire	**Zen**
tributary system	**movable type**
bubonic plague	**shamanism**
Uighurs	**Koryo**
Tibet	**Fujiwara**
Song Empire	**Kamakura shogunate**
junk	**Champa rice**

■ Suggested Reading

On Inner Asia see the bibliography for Chapter 8 relating to the Silk Road. In addition, Denis Sinor, ed., *The Cambridge History of Early Inner Asia* (1990), and M. S. Asimov and C. E. Bosworth, eds., *History of Civilizations of Central Asia: Volume IV—The Age of Achievement, A.D. 750 to the End of the Fifteenth Century—Part Two, the Achievements* (2000), contain articles on many topics. Thomas Barfield, *The Perilous Frontier: Nomadic Empires and China* (1992), is an anthropologist's view of the broad relationship between pastoralists and agriculturists in the region. Susan Whitfield's *Life Along the Silk Road* (2001) uses fictional travelers as a narrative device but is solidly based on documentary research.

Arthur F. Wright, *The Sui Dynasty* (1978), is a very readable narrative of the reunification of China in the sixth century. The Tang Empire is the topic of a huge literature, but for a variety of enduring essays see Arthur F. Wright and David Twitchett, eds., *Perspectives on the T'ang* (1973). On Tang contacts with the cultures of Central, South, and Southeast Asia see Edward Schaeffer, *The Golden Peaches of Samarkand* (1963), *The Vermilion Bird* (1967), and *Pacing the Void* (1977). For an introduction to medieval Tibet see Rolf Stein, *Tibetan Civilization* (1972). On the Uighurs see Colin MacKarras, *The Uighur Empire* (1968).

There is comparatively little secondary work in English on the Inner and northern Asian empires that succeeded the Tang. But for a classic text see Karl Wittfogel and Chia-sheng Feng, *History of Chinese Society: Liao* (1949). On the Jurchen Jin, see Jin-sheng Tao, *The Jurchens in Twelfth Century China,* and on the Tang-guts see Ruth Dunnell, *The State of High and White: Buddhism and the State in Eleventh-Century Xia* (1996). Morris Rossabi, ed., *China Among Equals: The Middle Kingdom and Its Neighbors, 10th–14th Centuries* (1983), deals with post-Tang relationships more broadly.

On the Song there is a large volume of material, particularly relating to technological achievements. For an introduction to the monumental work of Joseph Needham see *Science in Traditional China* (1981). A classic thesis on Song advancement (and Ming backwardness) is Mark Elvin, *The Pattern of the Chinese Past* (1973), particularly Part II. Joel Mokyr, *The Lever of Riches* (1990), is a more-recent comparative treatment. Agriculture is the special concern of Francesca Bray, *The Rice Economies: Technology and Development in Asian Societies* (1994).

For neo-Confucianism and Buddhism see W. T. de Bary, W-T Chan, and B. Watson, compilers, *Sources of Chinese Tradition,* vol. 1, 2d ed. (1999), as well as Arthur F. Wright, *Buddhism in Chinese History* (1983). On religion more broadly see Robert P. Hymes, *Way and Byway: Taoism, Local Religion, and Models of Divinity in Sung China* (2002). On social and economic history see Miyazaki Ichisada, *China's Examination Hell* (1971); Richard von Glahn, *The Land of Streams and Grottoes* (1987); and Patricia Ebery, *The Inner Quarters: Marriage and the Lives of Chinese Women in the Sung Period* (1993). On the poet Li Qingzhao see Hu Pin-ch'ing, *Li Ch'ing-chao* (1966).

On the history of Korea see Andrew C. Nahm, *Introduction to Korean History and Culture* (1993), and Ki-Baik Kim, *A New History of Korea* (1984). Yongho Ch'oe et al., eds., include excerpts from many historical works in *Sources of Korean Tradition* (2000). An excellent introduction to Japanese history is Paul H. Varley, *Japanese Culture* (1984). Selections of relevant documents may be found in David John Lu, *Sources of Japanese History,* vol. 1 (1974), and R. Tsunoda, W. T. de Bary, and D. Keene, compilers, *Sources of Japanese Tradition,* vol. 1 (1964). Ivan Morris, *The World of the Shining Prince: Court Life in Ancient Japan* (1979), is a classic introduction to the literature and culture of Fujiwara Japan at the time of the composition of Murasaki Shikibu's *The Tale of Genji.* For Vietnam see Keith Weller Taylor, *The Birth of Vietnam* (1983).

■ Notes

1. *Master Tung's Western Chamber Romance,* tr. Li-li Ch'en (New York: Columbia University Press, 1994), 22, 42–43, 45–46.
2. Arthur Waley, *Poetry and Career of Li Po* (London: Unwin Hyman, 1954), 35.
3. Theodore de Bary, ed., *Sources of Chinese Tradition,* vol. 1, 2d ed. (New York: Columbia University Press, 1999), 584
4. Quoted in David Lattimore, "Allusion in T'ang Poetry," in *Perspectives on the T'ang,* ed. Arthur F. Wright and David Twitchett (New Haven, CT: Yale University Press, 1973), 436.
5. Quoted at "Women's Early Music, Art, Poetry," http://music.acu.edu/www/iawm/pages/reference/tzusongs.html.
6. Quoted in Ivan Morris, *The World of the Shining Prince: Court Life in Ancient Japan* (New York: Penguin Books, 1979), 221–222.

12

Peoples and Civilizations of the Americas, 200–1500

Maya Scribe   Mayan scribes used a complex writing system to record religious concepts and memorialize the actions of their kings. This picture of a scribe was painted on a ceramic plate.

In late August 682 C.E. the Maya° princess Lady Wac-Chanil-Ahau° walked down the steep steps from her family's residence and mounted a sedan chair decorated with rich textiles and animal skins. As the procession exited from the urban center of Dos Pilas°, her military escort spread out through the fields and woods along its path to prevent ambush by enemies. Lady Wac-Chanil-Ahau's destination was the Maya city of Naranjo°, where she was to marry a powerful nobleman. Her marriage had been arranged to re-establish the royal dynasty that had been eliminated when Caracol, the region's major military power, had defeated Naranjo. Lady Wac-Chanil-Ahau's passage to Naranjo symbolized her father's desire to forge a military alliance that could resist Caracol. For us, the story of Lady Wac-Chanil-Ahau illustrates the importance of marriage and lineage in the politics of the classic-period Maya.

Smoking Squirrel, the son of Lady Wac-Chanil-Ahau, ascended the throne of Naranjo as a five-year-old in 693 C.E. During his long reign he proved to be a careful diplomat and formidable warrior. He was also a prodigious builder, leaving behind an expanded and beautified capital as part of his legacy. Mindful of the importance of his mother and her lineage from Dos Pilas, he erected numerous stelae (carved stone monuments) that celebrated her life.[1]

When population increased and competition for resources grew more violent, warfare and dynastic crisis convulsed the world of Wac-Chanil-Ahau. The defeat of the city-states of Tikal and Naranjo by Caracol undermined long-standing commercial and political relations in much of southern Mesoamerica and led to more than a century of conflict. Caracol, in turn, was challenged by the dynasty created at Dos Pilas by the heirs of Lady Wac-Chanil-Ahau. Despite a shared culture and religion, the great Maya cities remained divided by the dynastic ambitions of their rulers and by the competition for resources.

As the story of Lady Wac-Chanil-Ahau's marriage and her role in the development of a Maya dynasty suggests, the peoples of the Americas were in constant competition for resources. Members of hereditary elites organized their societies to meet these challenges, even as their ambition for greater power predictably ignited new conflicts. No single set of political institutions or technologies worked in every environment, and enormous cultural diversity existed in the ancient Americas. In Mesoamerica (Mexico and northern Central America) and in the Andean region of South America, Amerindian peoples developed an extraordinarily productive and diversified agriculture.[2] They also built great cities that rivaled the capitals of the Chinese and Roman Empires in size and beauty. The Olmecs of Mesoamerica and Chavín° of the Andes were among the earliest civilizations of the Americas (see Chapter 3). In the rest of the hemisphere, indigenous peoples adapted combinations of hunting and agriculture to maintain a wide variety of settlement patterns, political forms, and cultural traditions. All the cultures and civilizations of the Americas experienced cycles of expansion and contraction as they struggled with the challenges of environmental changes, population growth, social conflict, and war.

As you read this chapter, ask yourself the following questions:

- How did differing environments influence the development of Mesoamerican, Andean, and northern peoples?

- What technologies were developed to meet the challenges of these environments?

- How were the civilizations of Mesoamerica and the Andean region similar? How did they differ?

- How did religious belief and practice influence political life in the ancient Americas?

Maya (MY-ah)   **Wac-Chanil-Ahau** (wac-cha-NEEL-ah-HOW)
Dos Pilas (dohs PEE-las)   **Naranjo** (na-ROHN-hoe)

Chavín (cha-VEEN)

C H R O N O L O G Y

	Mesoamerica	Northern peoples	Andes
100	**100** Teotihuacan founded	**100–400** Hopewell culture in Ohio River Valley	**100–600** Nazca culture
			200–700 Moche culture
400	**250** Maya early clasic period begins		
			500–1000 Tiwanaku and Wari control Peruvian highlands
700		**700–1200** Anasazi culture	
	ca. 750 Teotihuacan destroyed **800–900** Maya centers abandoned, end of classic period **968** Toltec capital of Tula founded	**919** Pueblo Bonito founded	
1000		**1050–1250** Cahokia reaches peak power	
	1156 Tula destroyed	**1150** Collapse of Anasazi centers begins	**1200** Chimu begin military expansion
1300	**1325** Aztec capital Tenochtitlan founded		
			1438 Inca expansion begins **1465** Inca conquer Chimu
1500	**1502** Moctezuma II crowned Aztec ruler	**1500** Mississippian culture declines	**1500–1525** Inca conquer Ecuador

CLASSIC-ERA CULTURE AND SOCIETY IN MESOAMERICA, 200–900

Between about 200 and 900 C.E. the peoples of Mesoamerica created a remarkable civilization. Despite enduring differences in language and the absence of regional political integration, Mesoamericans were unified by similarities in material culture, religious beliefs and practices, and social structures. Building on the earlier achievements of the Olmecs and others, the peoples of the area that is now Central America and south and central Mexico developed new forms of political organization, made great strides in astronomy and mathematics, and improved the productivity of their agriculture. This mix of achievements is called the classic period by archaeologists. During this period, population grew, a greater variety of products were traded over longer distances, and social hierarchies became more complex. Great cities were constructed, serving as centers of political life and as arenas of religious ritual and spiritual experience.

Classic-period civilizations built on the religious and political foundations established earlier in Olmec centers. The cities of the classic period continued to be

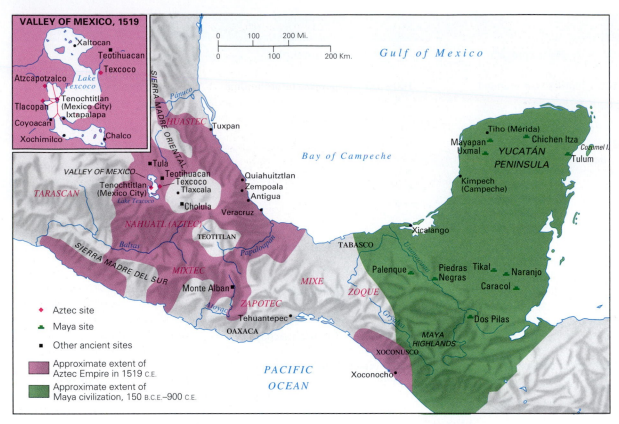

Map 12.1 **Major Mesoamerican Civilizations, 1000 B.C.E.–1519 C.E.** From their island capital of Tenochtitlan, the Aztecs militarily and commercially dominated a large region. Aztec achievements were built on the legacy of earlier civilizations such as the Olmecs and Maya.

dominated by platforms and pyramids devoted to religious functions, but they were more impressive and architecturally diversified. They had large full-time populations divided into classes and dominated by hereditary political and religious elites who controlled nearby towns and villages and imposed their will on the rural peasantry.

The political and cultural innovations of this period did not depend on the introduction of new technologies. The agricultural foundation of Mesoamerican civilization had been developed centuries earlier. Major innovations in agriculture such as irrigation, the draining of wetlands, and the terracing of hillsides had all been in place for more than a thousand years when great cities were developed after 200 C.E. Instead, the achievements of the classic era depended on the ability of increasingly powerful elites to organize and command growing numbers of laborers and soldiers. What had changed was the reach and power of religious and political leaders. The

scale and impressive architecture found at Teotihuacan° or at the great Maya cities illustrate both Mesoamerican aesthetic achievements and the development of powerful political institutions.

Teotihuacan

Located about 30 miles (48 kilometers) northeast of modern Mexico City, **Teotihuacan** (100 B.C.E.–750 C.E.) was one of Mesoamerica's most important classic-period civilizations (see Map 12.1). At the height of its power, from 450 to 600 C.E., it was the largest city in the Americas. With between 125,000 and 200,000 inhabitants, it was larger than all but a small number of contemporary European and Asian cities.

Religious architecture rose above a city center aligned with nearby sacred mountains and reflecting the

---

Teotihuacan (teh-o-tee-WAH-kahn)

Temple of Quetzalcoatl in Teotihuacan   This impressive temple was decorated with images of two gods, Quetzalcoatl and Tlaloc. Along both sides of the main temple steps are arrayed the serpent images associated with Quetzalcoatl, a culture god common to most of the Mesoamerican civilizations. Along the front of the temple the image of Quetzalcoatl is decorated with a feathered necklace. The image with the goggle-like decoration is Tlaloc, the rain or storm god.   (Jean Mazenod/Citadelles & Mazenod, Paris)

movement of the stars. Enormous pyramids dedicated to the Sun and Moon and more than twenty smaller temples devoted to other gods were arranged along a central avenue. The people recognized and worshiped many gods and lesser spirits. Among the gods were the Sun, the Moon, a storm-god, and Quetzalcoatl°, the feathered serpent. Quetzalcoatl was a culture-god believed to be the originator of agriculture and the arts. Like the earlier Olmecs, people living at Teotihuacan practiced human sacrifice. More than a hundred sacrificial victims were found during the excavation of the temple of Quetzalcoatl at Teotihuacan. Sacrifice was viewed as a sacred

duty toward the gods and as essential to the well-being of human society.

The rapid growth in urban population initially resulted from a series of volcanic eruptions that disrupted agriculture. Later, as the city elite increased its power, farm families from the smaller villages in the region were forced to relocate to the urban core. As a result, more than two-thirds of the city's residents retained their dependence on agriculture, walking out from urban residences to their fields. The elite of Teotihuacan used the city's growing labor resources to bring marginal lands into production. Swamps were drained, irrigation works were constructed, terraces were built into hillsides, and the use of chinampas was expanded. **Chinampas°,** sometimes called "floating gardens," were narrow artificial islands constructed along lakeshores or in marshes. They were created by heaping lake muck and waste material on beds of reeds that were then anchored to the shore by trees. Chinampas permitted year-round agriculture—because of subsurface irrigation and resistance to frost—and thus played a crucial role in sustaining the region's growing population. The productivity of the city's agriculture made possible its accomplishments in art, architecture, and trade.

As population grew, the housing of commoners underwent dramatic change. Apartment-like stone buildings were constructed for the first time. These apartment compounds were unique to Teotihuacan. They commonly housed members of a single kinship group, but some were used to house craftsmen working in the same trade. The two largest craft groups produced pottery and obsidian tools, the most important articles of long-distance trade. It appears that more than 2 percent of the urban population was engaged in making obsidian tools and weapons. The city's pottery and obsidian have been found throughout central Mexico and even in the Maya region of Guatemala.

The city's role as a religious center and commercial power provided both divine approval of and a material basis for the elite's increased wealth and status. Members of the elite controlled the state bureaucracy, tax collection, and commerce. Their prestige and wealth were reflected in their style of dress and diet and in the separate residence compounds built for aristocratic families. The central position and great prestige of the priestly class were evident in temple and palace murals. Teotihuacan's economy and religious influence drew pilgrims from as far away as Oaxaca and Veracruz. Some of them became permanent residents.

Unlike the other classic-period civilizations, the people of Teotihuacan did not concentrate power in the

Quetzalcoatl (kate-zahl-CO-ah-tal)

chinampas (chee-NAM-pahs)

hands of a single ruler. Although the ruins of their impressive housing compounds demonstrate the wealth and influence of the city's aristocracy, there is no clear evidence that individual rulers or a ruling dynasty gained overarching political power. In Teotihuacan the deeds of individual rulers were not featured in public art, nor were their images represented by statues or other monuments as in other Mesoamerican civilizations. In fact, some scholars suggest that Teotihuacan was ruled by alliances forged among elite families or by weak kings who were the puppets of these powerful families. Regardless of what form political decision making took, we know that this powerful classic-period civilization achieved regional preeminence without subordinating its political life to the personality of a powerful individual ruler or lineage.

Historians debate the role of the military in the development of Teotihuacan. The absence of walls or other defensive structures before 500 C.E. suggests that Teotihuacan enjoyed relative peace during its early development. Archaeological evidence, however, reveals that the city created a powerful military to protect long-distance trade and to compel peasant agriculturalists to transfer their surplus production to the city. The discovery of representations of soldiers in typical Teotihuacan dress in the Maya region of Guatemala suggests to some that Teotihuacan used its military to expand trade relations. Unlike later postclassic civilizations, however, Teotihuacan was not an imperial state controlled by a military elite.

It is unclear what forces brought about the collapse of Teotihuacan about 650 C.E. Weakness was evident as early as 500 C.E., when the urban population declined to about 40,000 and the city began to build defensive walls. These fortifications and pictorial evidence from murals suggest that the city's final decades were violent. Early scholars suggested that the city was overwhelmed militarily by a nearby rival city or by nomadic warrior peoples from the northern frontier. More recently, investigators have uncovered evidence of conflict within the ruling elite and the mismanagement of resources. This, they argue, led to class conflict and the breakdown of public order. As a result, most important temples in the city center were pulled down and religious images defaced. Elite palaces were also systematically burned and many of the residents killed. Regardless of the causes, the eclipse of Teotihuacan was felt throughout Mexico and into Central America.

The Maya

During Teotihuacan's ascendancy in the north, the **Maya** developed an impressive civilization in the region that today includes Guatemala, Honduras, Belize, and southern Mexico (see Map 12.1).

Given the difficulties imposed by a tropical climate and fragile soils, the cultural and architectural achievements of the Maya were remarkable. Although they shared a single culture, they were never unified politically. Instead, rival kingdoms led by hereditary rulers struggled with each other for regional dominance, much like the Mycenaean-era Greeks (see Chapter 4).

Today Maya farmers prepare their fields by cutting down small trees and brush and then burning the dead vegetation to fertilize the land. Swidden agriculture (also called shifting agriculture or slash and burn agriculture) can produce high yields for a few years. However, it uses up the soil's nutrients, eventually forcing people to move to more fertile land. The high population levels of the Maya classic period (250–900 C.E.) required more intensive forms of agriculture. Maya living near the major urban centers achieved high agricultural yields by draining swamps and building elevated fields. They used irrigation in areas with long dry seasons, and they terraced hillsides in the cooler highlands. Nearly every household planted a garden to provide condiments and fruits to supplement dietary staples. Maya agriculturists also managed nearby forests, favoring the growth of the trees and shrubs that were most useful to them, as well as promoting the conservation of deer and other animals hunted for food.

During the classic period, Maya city-states proliferated. The most powerful cities controlled groups of smaller dependent cities and a broad agricultural zone by building impressive religious temples and by creating rituals that linked the power of kings to the gods. Classic-period cities, unlike earlier sites, had dense central precincts that were visually dominated by monumental architecture. These political and ceremonial centers were commonly aligned with the movements of the sun and Venus. Open plazas were surrounded by high pyramids and by elaborately decorated palaces often built on high ground or on constructed mounds. The effect was to awe the masses drawn to the centers for religious and political rituals.

The Maya loved decoration. Nearly all of their public buildings were covered with bas-relief and painted in bright colors. Religious allegories, the genealogies of rulers, and important historical events were the most common motifs. Beautifully carved altars and stone monoliths were erected near major temples. This rich legacy of monumental architecture was constructed without the aid of wheels—no pulleys, wheelbarrows, or carts—or metal tools. Masses of men and women aided only by levers and stone tools cut and carried construction materials and lifted them into place.

The Maya cosmos was divided into three layers connected along a vertical axis that traced the course of the

The Great Plaza at Tikal   Still visible in the ruins of Tikal, in modern Guatemala, are the impressive architectural and artistic achievements of the classic-era Maya. Maya centers provided a dramatic setting for the rituals that dominated public life. Construction of Tikal began before 150 B.C.E.; the city was abandoned about 900 C.E. A ball court and residences for the elite were part of the Great Plaza.   (Martha Cooper/Peter Arnold, Inc.)

sun. The earthly arena of human existence held an intermediate position between the heavens, conceptualized by the Maya as a sky-monster, and a dark underworld. A sacred tree rose through the three layers; its roots were in the underworld, and its branches reached into the heavens. The temple precincts of Maya cities physically represented essential elements of this religious cosmology. The pyramids were sacred mountains reaching to the heavens. The doorways of the pyramids were portals to the underworld.

Rulers and other members of the elite served both priestly and political functions. They decorated their bodies with paint and tattoos and wore elaborate costumes of textiles, animal skins, and feathers to project both secular power and divine sanction. Kings communicated directly with the supernatural residents of the other worlds and with deified royal ancestors through bloodletting rituals and hallucinogenic trances. Scenes of rulers drawing blood from lips, ears, and penises are common in surviving frescoes and on painted pottery.

Warfare in particular was infused with religious meaning and attached to elaborate rituals. Battle scenes and the depiction of the torture and sacrifice of captives were frequent decorative themes. Typically, Maya military forces fought to secure captives rather than territory. Days of fasting, sacred ritual, and rites of purification preceded battle. The king, his kinsmen, and other ranking nobles actively participated in war. Elite captives were nearly always sacrificed; captured commoners were more likely to be forced to labor for their captors.

Only two women are known to have ruled Maya kingdoms. Maya women of the ruling lineages did play

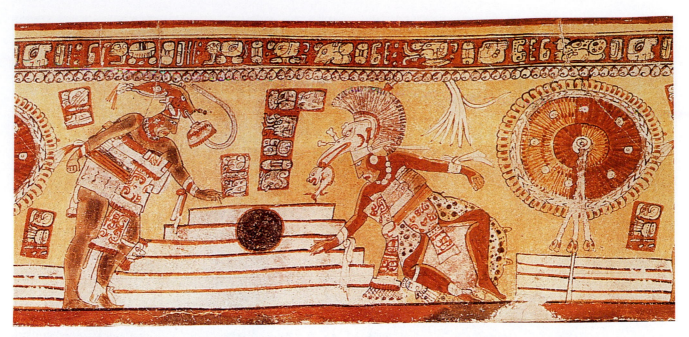

The Mesoamerican Ball Game From Guatemala to Arizona, archaeologists have found evidence of an ancient ball game played with a solid rubber ball on slope-sided courts shaped like a capital T. Among the Maya the game was associated with a creation myth and thus had deep religious meaning. There is evidence that some players were sacrificed. In this scene from a ceramic jar, players wearing elaborate ritual clothing—which includes heavy, protective pads around the chest and waist—play with a ball much larger than the ball actually used in such games. Some representations show balls drawn to suggest a human head. (Chrysler Museum of Art/Justin Kerr)

important political and religious roles, however. The consorts of male rulers participated in bloodletting rituals and in other important public ceremonies, and their noble blood helped legitimate the rule of their husbands. Although Maya society was patrilineal (tracing descent in the male line), there is evidence that some male rulers traced their lineages bilaterally (in both the male and the female lines). Like Lady Wac-Chanil-Ahau's son Smoking Squirrel, some rulers emphasized the female line if it held higher status. Much less is known about the lives of the women of the lower classes, but scholars believe that women played a central role in the religious rituals of the home. They were also healers and shamans. Women were essential to the household economy, maintaining essential garden plots and weaving, and in the management of family life.

Building on what the Olmecs had done, the Maya made important contributions to the development of the Mesoamerican calendar and to mathematics and writing. Their interest in time and in the cosmos was reflected in the complexity of their calendric system. Each day was identified by three separate dating systems. Like other peoples throughout Mesoamerica, the Maya had a calendar that tracked the ritual cycle (260 days divided into thirteen months of 20 days) as well as a solar calendar (365 days divided into eighteen months of 20 days, plus 5 unfavorable days at the end of the year). The concurrence of these two calendars every fifty-two years was believed to be especially ominous. Alone among Mesoamerican peoples, the Maya also maintained a continuous "long count" calendar, which began at a fixed date in the past that scholars have identified as 3114 B.C.E., a date that the Maya probably associated with creation.

Both the calendars and the astronomical observations on which they were based depended on Maya mathematics and writing. Their system of mathematics incorporated the concept of the zero and place value but had limited notational signs. Maya writing was a form of hieroglyphic inscription that signified whole words or concepts as well as phonetic cues or syllables. Aspects of public life, religious belief, and the biographies of rulers and their ancestors were recorded in deerskin and bark-paper books, on pottery, and on the stone columns and monumental buildings of the urban centers. In this sense every Maya city was a sacred text.

Between 800 and 900 C.E. many of the major urban centers of the Maya were abandoned or destroyed, although a small number of classic-period centers survived for centuries. This collapse was preceded in some areas by decades of urban population decline and increased warfare. Some scholars have proposed that epidemic disease and pestilence played a role in this catastrophe, although there is little evidence to support this argument. Other experts have contended that the earlier destruction of Teotihuacan around 650 C.E. disrupted trade, thus undermining the legitimacy of Maya rulers who had used the goods in rituals. There is growing consensus that the growing population led to environmental degradation and declining agricultural productivity. This environmental crisis, in turn, led to social conflict and increased levels of warfare as desperate elites sought to acquire additional agricultural land through conquest.

THE POSTCLASSIC PERIOD IN MESOAMERICA, 900–1500

The division between the classic and postclassic periods is somewhat arbitrary. Not only is there no single explanation for the collapse of Teotihuacan and many of the major Maya centers, but these events occurred over more than a century and a half. In fact, some important classic-period civilizations survived unscathed. Moreover, the essential cultural characteristics of the classic period were carried over to the postclassic. The two periods are linked by similarities in religious belief and practice, architecture, urban planning, and social organization.

There were, however, some important differences between the periods. There is evidence that the population of Mesoamerica expanded during the postclassic period. Resulting pressures led to an intensification of agricultural practices and to increased warfare. The governing elites of the major postclassic states—the Toltecs and the Aztecs—responded to these harsh realities by increasing the size of their armies and by developing political institutions that facilitated their control of large and culturally diverse territories acquired through conquest.

The Toltecs

Little is known about the **Toltecs**° prior to their arrival in central Mexico. Some scholars speculate that they were originally a satellite population that Teotihuacan had placed on the northern frontier to protect against the incursions of nomads. After their migration south, the Toltecs borrowed from the cultural legacy of Teotihuacan and created an important postclassic civilization. Memories of their military achievements and the violent imagery of their political and religious rituals dominated the Mesoamerican imagination in the late postclassic period. In the fourteenth century, the Aztecs and their contemporaries erroneously believed that the Toltecs were the source of nearly all the great cultural achievements of the Mesoamerican world. As one Aztec source later recalled:

> In truth [the Toltecs] invented all the precious and marvelous things. . . . All that now exists was their discovery. . . . And these Toltecs were very wise; they were thinkers, for they originated the year count, the day count. All their discoveries formed the book for interpreting dreams. . . . And so wise were they [that] they understood the stars which were in the heavens.[3]

In fact, all these contributions to Mesoamerican culture were in place long before the Toltecs gained control of central Mexico. The most important Toltec innovations were instead political and military.

The Toltecs created the first conquest state based largely on military power, and they extended their political influence from the area north of modern Mexico City to Central America. Established about 968 C.E., the Toltec capital of Tula° was constructed in a grand style (see Map 12.1). Its public architecture featured colonnaded patios and numerous temples. Although the population of Tula never reached the levels of classic-period Teotihuacan, the Toltec capital dominated central Mexico. Toltec decoration had a more warlike and violent character than did the decoration of earlier Mesoamerican cultures. Nearly all Toltec public buildings and temples were decorated with representations of warriors or with scenes suggesting human sacrifice.

Two chieftains or kings apparently ruled the Toltec state together. Evidence suggests that this division of responsibility eventually weakened Toltec power and led to the destruction of Tula. Sometime after 1000 C.E. a struggle between elite groups identified with rival religious cults undermined the Toltec state. According to legends that survived among the Aztecs, Topiltzin°—one of the two rulers and a priest of the cult of Quetzalcoatl—and his followers bitterly accepted exile in the east, "the land of the rising sun." These legendary events coincided with growing Toltec influence among the Maya of the Yucatán Peninsula. One of the ancient texts relates these events in the following manner:

Toltec (TOLL-tek)

Tula (TOO-la)   **Topilitzin** (tow-PEELT-zeen)

Thereupon he [Topiltzin] looked toward Tula, and then wept. . . . And when he had done these things . . . he went to reach the seacoast. Then he fashioned a raft of serpents. When he had arranged the raft, he placed himself as if it were his boat. Then he set off across the sea.[4]

After the exile of Topiltzin, the Toltec state began to decline, and around 1156 C.E. northern invaders overcame Tula itself. After its destruction, a centuries-long process of cultural and political assimilation produced a new Mesoamerican political order based on the urbanized culture and statecraft of the Toltecs. Like Semitic peoples of the third millennium B.C.E. interacting with Sumerian culture (see Chapter 2), the new Mesoamerican elites were drawn in part from the invading cultures. The Aztecs of the Valley of Mexico became the most important of these late postclassic peoples.

The Aztecs

The Mexica°, more commonly known as the **Aztecs,** were among the northern peoples who pushed into central Mexico in the wake of the collapse of Tula. At the time of their arrival they had a clan-based social organization. In their new environment they began to adopt the political and social practices that they found among the urbanized agriculturalists of the valley. At first, the Aztecs served their more powerful neighbors as serfs and mercenaries. As their strength grew, they relocated to small islands near the shore of Lake Texcoco, and around 1325 C.E. they began the construction of their twin capitals, **Tenochtitlan°** and Tlatelolco (together the foundation for modern Mexico City).

Military successes allowed the Aztecs to seize control of additional agricultural land along the lakeshore. With the increased economic independence and greater political security that resulted from this expansion, the Aztecs transformed their political organization by introducing a monarchical system similar to that found in more powerful neighboring states. The kinship-based organizations that had organized political life earlier survived to the era of Spanish conquest, but lost influence relative to monarchs and hereditary aristocrats. Aztec rulers did not have absolute power, and royal succession was not based on primogeniture. A council of powerful aristocrats selected new rulers from among male members of the ruling lineage. Once selected, the ruler was forced to renegotiate the submission of tribute dependencies and then demonstrate his divine mandate by undertaking a new round of military conquests. War was infused with religious meaning, providing the ruler with legitimacy and increasing the prestige of successful warriors.

With the growing power of the ruler and aristocracy, social divisions were accentuated. These alterations in social organization and political life were made possible by Aztec military expansion. Territorial conquest allowed the warrior elite of Aztec society to seize land and peasant labor as spoils of war (see Map 12.1). In time, the royal family and highest-ranking members of the aristocracy possessed extensive estates that were cultivated by slaves and landless commoners. The Aztec lower classes received some material rewards from imperial expansion but lost most of their ability to influence or control decisions. Some commoners were able to achieve some social mobility through success on the battlefield or by entering the priesthood, but the highest social ranks were always reserved for hereditary nobles.

The urban plan of Tenochtitlan and Tlatelolco continued to be organized around the clans, whose members maintained a common ritual life and accepted civic responsibilities such as caring for the sick and elderly. Clan members also fought together as military units. Nevertheless, the clans' historical control over common agricultural land and other scarce resources, such as fishing and hunting rights, declined. By 1500 C.E. great inequalities in wealth and privilege characterized Aztec society.

Aztec kings and aristocrats legitimated their ascendancy by creating elaborate rituals and ceremonies to distinguish themselves from commoners. One of the Spaniards who participated in the conquest of the Aztec Empire remembered his first meeting with the Aztec ruler Moctezuma° II (r. 1502–1520): "many great lords walked before the great Montezuma [Moctezuma II], sweeping the ground on which he was to tread and laying down cloaks so that his feet should not touch the earth. Not one of these chieftains dared look him in the face."[5] Commoners lived in small dwellings and ate a limited diet of staples, but members of the nobility lived in large, well-constructed two-story houses and consumed a diet rich in animal protein and flavored by condiments and expensive imports like chocolate from the Maya region to the south. Rich dress and jewelry also set apart the elite. Even in marriage customs the two groups were different. Commoners were monogamous, great nobles polygamous.

The Aztec state met the challenge of feeding an urban population of approximately 150,000 by efficiently

---

Mexica (meh-SHE-ca)   **Tenochtitlan** (teh-noch-TIT-lan)

Moctezuma (mock-teh-ZU-ma)

Costumes of Aztec Warriors
In Mesoamerican warfare individual warriors sought to gain prestige and improve their status by taking captives. This illustration from the sixteenth-century Codex Mendoza was drawn by an Amerindian artist. It shows the Aztecs' use of distinctive costumes to acknowledge the prowess of warriors. These costumes indicate the taking of two (top left) to six captives (bottom center). The individual on the bottom right shown without a weapon was a military leader. As was common in Mesoamerican illustrations of military conflict, the captives, held by their hair, are shown kneeling before the victors.   (The Bodleian Library, University of Oxford, Selder. A.I. fol. 64r)

organizing the labor of the clans and additional laborers sent by defeated peoples to expand agricultural land. The construction of a dike more than 5½ miles (9 kilometers) long by 23 feet (7 meters) wide to separate the freshwater and saltwater parts of Lake Texcoco was the Aztecs' most impressive land reclamation project. The dike allowed a significant extension of irrigated fields and the construction of additional chinampas. One expert has estimated that the project consumed 4 million person-days to complete. Aztec chinampas contributed maize, fruits, and vegetables to the markets of Tenochtitlan. The imposition of a **tribute system** on conquered peoples also helped relieve some of the pressure of Tenochtitlan's growing population. Unlike the tribute system of Tang China, where tribute had a more symbolic character (see Chapter 11), one-quarter of the Aztec capital's food requirements was satisfied by tribute payments of maize, beans, and other foods sent by nearby political dependencies. The Aztecs also demanded cotton cloth, military equipment, luxury goods like jade and feathers, and sacrificial victims as tribute. Trade supplemented these supplies.

A specialized class of merchants controlled long-distance trade. Given the absence of draft animals and wheeled vehicles, this commerce was dominated by lightweight and valuable products like gold, jewels, feathered garments, cacao, and animal skins. Merchants also provided essential political and military intelligence for the Aztec elite. Operating outside the protection of Aztec military power, merchant expeditions were armed and often had to defend themselves. Although merchants became wealthy and powerful as the Aztecs expanded their empire, they were denied the privileges of the high nobility, which was jealous of its power. As a result, the merchants feared to publicly display their affluence.

Like commerce throughout the Mesoamerican world, Aztec commerce was carried on without money and credit. Barter was facilitated by the use of cacao, quills filled with gold, and cotton cloth as standard units of value to compensate for differences in the value of bartered goods. Aztec expansion facilitated the integration of producers and consumers in the central Mexican economy. As a result, the markets of Tenochtitlan and

Tlatelolco offered a rich array of goods from as far away as Central America and what is now the southwestern border of the United States. Hernán Cortés (1485–1547), the Spanish adventurer who eventually conquered the Aztecs, expressed his admiration for the abundance of the Aztec marketplace:

> One square in particular is twice as big as that of Salamanca and completely surrounded by arcades where there are daily more than sixty thousand folk buying and selling. Every kind of merchandise such as may be met with in every land is for sale. . . . There is nothing to be found in all the land which is not sold in these markets, for over and above what I have mentioned there are so many and such various things that on account of their very number . . . I cannot detail them.[6]

The Aztecs succeeded in developing a remarkable urban landscape. The combined population of Tenochtitlan and Tlatelolco and the cities and hamlets of the surrounding lakeshore was approximately 500,000 by 1500 C.E. The island capital was designed so that canals and streets intersected at right angles. Three causeways connected the city to the lakeshore.

Religious rituals dominated public life in Tenochtitlan. Like the other cultures of the Mesoamerican world, the Aztecs worshiped a large number of gods. Most of these gods had a dual nature—both male and female. The major contribution of the Aztecs to the religious life of Mesoamerica was the cult of Huitzilopochtli°, the southern hummingbird. As the Aztec state grew in power and wealth, the importance of this cult grew as well. Huitzilopochtli was originally associated with war, but eventually the Aztecs identified this god with the Sun, worshiped as a divinity throughout Mesoamerica. Huitzilopochtli, they believed, required a diet of human hearts to sustain him in his daily struggle to bring the Sun's warmth to the world. Tenochtitlan was architecturally dominated by a great twin temple devoted to Huitzilopochtli and Tlaloc, the rain god, symbolizing the two bases of the Aztec economy: war and agriculture.

War captives were the preferred sacrificial victims, but large numbers of criminals, slaves, and people provided as tribute by dependent regions were also sacrificed. Although human sacrifice had been practiced since early times in Mesoamerica, the Aztecs and other societies of the late postclassic period transformed this religious ritual by dramatically increasing its scale. There are no reliable estimates for the total number of sacrifices, but the numbers clearly reached into the thousands each year. This form of violent public ritual had political consequences and was not simply the celebration of religious belief. Some scholars have emphasized the political nature of the rising tide of sacrifice, noting that sacrifices were carried out in front of large crowds that included leaders from enemy and subject states as well as the masses of Aztec society. The political subtext must have been clear: rebellion, deviancy, and opposition were extremely dangerous.

NORTHERN PEOPLES

By the end of the classic period in Mesoamerica, around 900 C.E., important cultural centers had appeared in the southwestern desert region and along the Ohio and Mississippi river valleys of what is now the United States. In both regions improved agricultural productivity and population growth led to increased urbanization and complex social and political structures. In the Ohio Valley Amerindian peoples who depended on locally domesticated seed crops as well as traditional hunting and gathering developed large villages with monumental earthworks. The introduction of maize, beans, and squash into this region from Mesoamerica after 1000 B.C.E. played an important role in the development of complex societies. Once established, these useful food crops were adopted throughout North America.

As growing populations came to depend on maize as a dietary staple, large-scale irrigation projects were undertaken in both the southwestern desert and the eastern river valleys. This development is a sign of increasingly centralized political power and growing social stratification. The two regions, however, evolved different political traditions. The Anasazi° and their neighbors in the southwest maintained a relatively egalitarian social structure and retained collective forms of political organization based on kinship and age. The mound builders of the eastern river valleys evolved more hierarchical political institutions: groups of small towns were subordinate to a political center ruled by a hereditary chief who wielded both secular and religious authority.

Southwestern Desert Cultures

Immigrants from Mexico introduced agriculture based on irrigation to present-day Arizona around 300 B.C.E. Because irrigation allowed the planting of two crops per year, the population grew and settled village life soon appeared.

Huitzilopochtli (wheat-zeel-oh-POSHT-lee)

Anasazi (ah-nah-SAH-zee)

Mesa Verde Cliff Dwelling   Located in southern Colorado, the Anasazi cliff dwellings of the Mesa Verde region hosted a population of about 7,000 in 1250 C.E. The construction of housing complexes and religious buildings in the area's large caves was probably prompted by increased warfare in the region.   (David Muench Photography)

Of all the southwestern cultures, the Hohokam of the Salt and Gila river valleys show the strongest Mexican influence. Hohokam sites have platform mounds and ball courts similar to those of Mesoamerica. Hohokam pottery, clay figurines, cast copper bells, and turquoise mosaics also reflect Mexican influence. By 1000 C.E. the Hohokam had constructed an elaborate irrigation system that included one canal more than 18 miles (30 kilometers) in length. Hohokam agricultural and ceramic technology spread over the centuries to neighboring peoples, but it was the Anasazi to the north who left the most vivid legacy of these desert cultures.

Archaeologists use **Anasazi,** a Navajo word meaning "ancient ones," to identify a number of dispersed, though similar, desert cultures located in what is now the Four Corners region of Arizona, New Mexico, Colorado, and Utah (see Map 12.2). Between 450 and 750 C.E. the Anasazi developed an economy based on maize, beans, and squash. Their successful adaptation of these crops permitted the formation of larger villages and led to an enriched cultural life centered in underground buildings called kivas. Evidence suggests that the Anasazi may have used kivas for weaving and pottery making, as well as religious rituals. They produced pottery decorated with geometric patterns, learned to weave cotton cloth, and, after 900 C.E., began to construct large multistory residential and ritual centers.

One of the largest Anasazi communities was located in Chaco Canyon in what is now northwestern Mexico. Eight large towns were built in the canyon and four more on surrounding mesas, suggesting a regional population of approximately 15,000. Many smaller villages were located nearby. Each town contained hundreds of rooms arranged in tiers around a central plaza. At Pueblo Bonito, the largest town, more than 650 rooms were arranged in a four-story block of residences and storage rooms. Pueblo Bonito had thirty-eight kivas, including a great kiva more than 65 feet (19 meters) in diameter. Social life and craft activities were concentrated in small open plazas or common rooms. Hunting, trade, and the need to maintain irrigation works often drew men away from the village. Women shared in agricultural tasks and were specialists in many crafts. They also were responsible for food preparation and childcare. If the practice of the modern Pueblos, cultural descendants of the Anasazi, is a guide, houses and furnishings may have belonged to the women, who formed extended families with their mothers and sisters.

At Chaco Canyon high-quality construction, the size and number of kivas, and the system of roads linking the canyon to outlying towns all suggest that Pueblo Bonito and its nearest neighbors exerted some kind of political or religious dominance over a large region. Some archaeologists have suggested that the Chaco Canyon culture originated as a colonial appendage of Mesoamerica, but the archaeological record provides little evidence for this theory. Merchants from Chaco provided Toltec-period peoples of northern Mexico with turquoise in exchange for shell jewelry, copper bells, macaws, and trumpets. But these exchanges occurred late in Chaco's development, and more important signs of Mesoamerican influence such as pyramid-shaped mounds and ball courts are not found at Chaco. Nor is there evidence from the excavation of burials and residences of clear class distinctions, a common feature of Mesoamerican culture. Instead, it appears that the Chaco Canyon culture developed from earlier societies in the region.

The abandonment of the major sites in Chaco Canyon in the twelfth century most likely resulted from a long drought that undermined the culture's fragile agricultural economy. Nevertheless, the Anasazi continued in the Four Corners region for more than a century after the abandonment of Chaco Canyon. There were major centers at Mesa Verde in present-day Colorado and at Canyon de Chelly and Kiet Siel in Arizona. Anasazi settlements on the Colorado Plateau and in Arizona were constructed in large natural caves high above valley floors. This hard-to-reach location suggests increased levels of warfare, probably provoked by population pressure on limited arable land. Elements of this cultural tradition survive today among the Pueblo peoples of the Rio Grande Valley and Arizona who still live in multistory villages and worship in kivas.

Mound Builders: The Adena, Hopewell, and Mississippian Cultures

The Adena people of the Ohio River Valley constructed large villages with monumental earthworks from about 500 B.C.E. This early mound-building culture was based on traditional hunting and gathering supplemented by limited cultivation of locally domesticated seed crops. Nearly all of the Adena mounds contained burials. Items found in these graves indicate a hierarchical society with an elite distinguished by its access to rare and valuable goods such as mica from North Carolina and copper from the Great Lakes region.

Around 100 C.E. the Adena culture blended into a successor culture now called Hopewell, also centered in the Ohio River Valley. The largest Hopewell centers appeared in present-day Ohio; but Hopewell influence, in the form of either colonies or trade dependencies, spread west to Illinois, Michigan, and Wisconsin, east to New York and Ontario, and south to Alabama, Louisiana, Mississippi, and even Florida (see Map 12.2). For the necessities of daily life Hopewell people were dependent on hunting and gathering and a limited agriculture inherited from the Adena.

Hopewell is an early example of a North American **chiefdom**—territory that had a population as large as 10,000 and was ruled by a chief, a hereditary leader with both religious and secular responsibilities. Chiefs organized periodic rituals of feasting and gift giving that established bonds among diverse kinship groups and guaranteed access to specialized crops and craft goods. They also managed long-distance trade, which provided luxury goods and additional food supplies.

The largest Hopewell towns in the Ohio River Valley served as ceremonial and political centers and had several thousand inhabitants. Villages had populations of a few hundred. Large mounds built to house elite burials and as platforms for temples and the residences of chiefs dominated major Hopewell centers. Chiefs and other members of the elite were buried in vaults surrounded by valuable goods such as river pearls, copper jewelry, and, in some cases, women and retainers who seem to have been sacrificed to accompany a dead chief into the afterlife. As was true of the earlier Olmec culture of Mexico, the abandonment of major Hopewell sites around 400 C.E. has no clear environmental or political explanation.

Map 12.2 Culture Areas of North America In each of the large ecological regions of North America, native peoples evolved distinctive cultures and technologies. Here the Anasazi of the arid southwest and the mound-building cultures of the Ohio and Mississippi river valleys are highlighted.

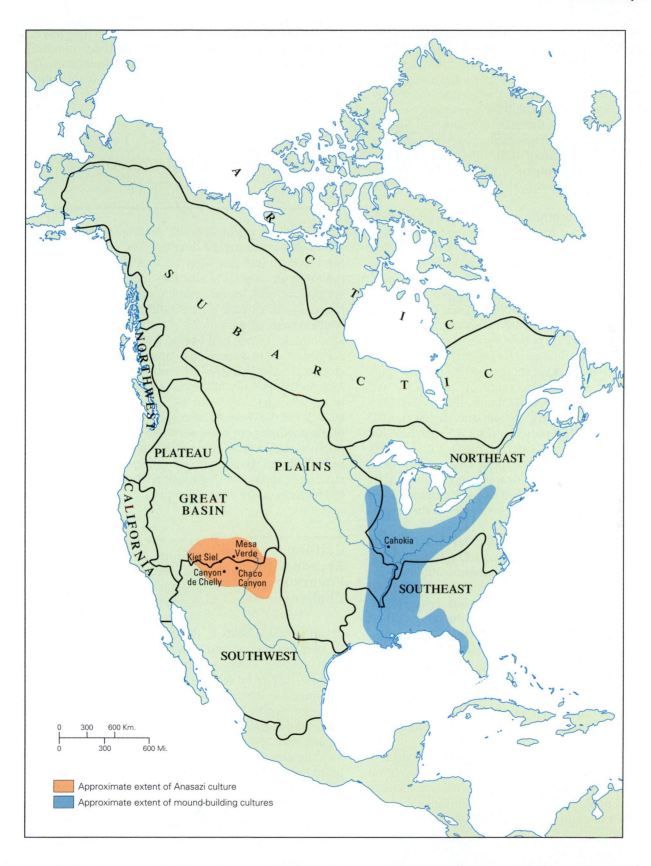

0 300 600 Km.

0 300 600 Mi.

Approximate extent of Anasazi culture
Approximate extent of mound-building cultures

Hopewell technology and mound building continued in smaller centers that have been linked to the development of Mississippian culture (700–1500 C.E.). As in the case of the Anasazi, some experts have suggested that contacts with Mesoamerica influenced Mississippian culture, but there is no convincing evidence to support this theory. It is true that maize, beans, and squash, all first domesticated in Mesoamerica, were closely associated with the development of the urbanized Mississippian culture. But these plants and related technologies were probably passed along through numerous intervening cultures.

The development of urbanized Mississippian chiefdoms resulted instead from the accumulated effects of small increases in agricultural productivity, the adoption of the bow and arrow, and the expansion of trade networks. An improved economy led to population growth, the building of cities, and social stratification. The largest towns shared a common urban plan based on a central plaza surrounded by large platform mounds. Major towns were trade centers where people bartered essential commodities, such as the flint used for weapons and tools.

The Mississippian culture reached its highest stage of evolution at the great urban center of Cahokia, located near the modern city of East St. Louis, Illinois (see Map 12.2). At the center of this site was the largest mound constructed in North America, a terraced structure 100 feet (30 meters) high and 1,037 by 790 feet (316 by 241 meters) at the base. Areas where commoners lived ringed the center area of elite housing and temples. At its height in about 1200 C.E., Cahokia had a population of about 20,000—about the same as some of the largest postclassic Maya cities.

Cahokia controlled surrounding agricultural lands and a number of secondary towns ruled by subchiefs. The urban center's political and economic influence depended on its location on the Missouri, Mississippi and Illinois Rivers. This location permitted canoe-based commercial exchanges as far away as the coasts of the Atlantic and the Gulf of Mexico. Sea shells, copper, mica, and flint were drawn to the city by trade and tribute from distant sources and converted into ritual goods and tools. Burial evidence suggests that the rulers of Cahokia enjoyed most of the benefits of this exalted position. In one burial more than fifty young women and retainers were apparently sacrificed to accompany a ruler on his travels after death.

As at Hopewell sites, no evidence links the decline and eventual abandonment of Cahokia, which occurred after 1250 C.E., with military defeat or civil war. Climate changes and population pressures undermined the center's vitality. Environmental degradation caused by deforestation, as more land was cleared to feed the growing population, and more intensive farming practices played roles as well. After the decline of Cahokia, smaller Mississippian centers continued to flourish in the southeast of the present-day United States until the arrival of Europeans.

ANDEAN CIVILIZATIONS, 200–1500

The Andean region of South America was an unlikely environment for the development of rich and powerful civilizations (see Map 12.3). Much of the region's mountainous zone is at altitudes that seem too high for agriculture and human habitation. Along the Pacific coast an arid climate posed a difficult challenge to the development of agriculture. To the east of the Andes Mountains, the hot and humid tropical environment of the Amazon headwaters also offered formidable obstacles to the organization of complex societies. Yet the Amerindian peoples of the Andean area produced some of the most socially complex and politically advanced societies of the Western Hemisphere. The very harshness of the environment compelled the development of productive and reliable agricultural technologies and attached them to a complex fabric of administrative structures and social relationships that became the central features of Andean civilization.

Cultural Response to Environmental Challenge

From the time of Chavín (see Chapter 3) all of the great Andean civilizations succeeded in connecting the distinctive resources of the coastal region with its abundant fisheries and irrigated maize fields to the mountainous interior with its herds of llamas and rich mix of grains and tubers. Both regions faced significant environmental challenges. The coastal region's fields were periodically overwhelmed by droughts or shifting sands that clogged irrigation works. The mountainous interior presented some of the greatest environmental challenges, averaging between 250 and 300 frosts per year.

The development of compensating technologies required an accurate calendar to time planting and harvests and the domestication of frost-resistant varieties of potatoes and grains. Native peoples learned to practice dispersed farming at different altitudes to reduce risks

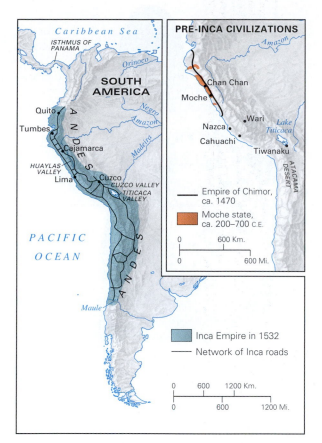

Map 12.3 Andean Civilizations, 200 B.C.E.–1532 C.E. In response to environmental challenges posed by an arid coastal plain and high interior mountain ranges, Andean peoples made complex social and technological adaptations. Irrigation systems, the domestication of the llama, metallurgy, and shared labor obligations helped provide a firm economic foundation for powerful, centralized states. In 1532 the Inca Empire's vast territory stretched from modern Chile in the south to Colombia in the north.

from frosts, and they terraced hillsides to create micro environments within a single area. They also discovered how to use the cold, dry climate to produce freeze-dried vegetable and meat products that prevented famine when crops failed. The domestication of the llama and alpaca also proved crucial, providing meat, wool, and long-distance transportation that linked coastal and mountain economies. Even though the Andean environment was harsher than that of Mesoamerica, the region's agriculture proved more dependable, and Andean peoples faced fewer famines.

The effective organization of human labor allowed the peoples of both the high mountain valleys and dry coastal plain to overcome the challenges posed by their environments. The remarkable collective achievements of Andean peoples were accomplished with a record-keeping system more limited than the one found in Mesoamerica. A system of knotted colored cords, **khipus°**, was used to aid administration and record population counts and tribute obligations. Large-scale drainage and irrigation works and the terracing of hillsides to control erosion and provide additional farmland led to an increase in agricultural production. Andean people also collectively undertook road building, urban construction, and even textile production.

The sharing of responsibilities began at the household level. But it was the clan, or **ayllu°**, that provided the foundation for Andean achievement. Members of an ayllu held land communally. Although they claimed descent from a common ancestor, they were not necessarily related. Ayllu members thought of each other as brothers and sisters and were obligated to aid each other in tasks that required more labor than a single household could provide. These reciprocal obligations provided the model for the organization of labor and the distribution of goods at every level of Andean society. Just as individuals and families were expected to provide labor to kinsmen, members of an ayllu were expected to provide labor and goods to their hereditary chief.

With the development of territorial states ruled by hereditary aristocracies and kings after 1000 B.C.E., these obligations were organized on a larger scale. The **mit'a°** was a rotational labor draft that organized members of ayllus to work the fields and care for the llama and alpaca herds owned by religious establishments, the royal court, and the aristocracy. Each ayllu contributed a set number of workers for specific tasks each year. Mit'a laborers built and maintained roads, bridges, temples, palaces, and large irrigation and drainage projects. They produced textiles and goods essential to ritual life, such as beer made from maize and coca (dried leaves chewed as a stimulant and now also the source of cocaine). The mit'a system was an essential part of the Andean world for more than a thousand years.

Work was divided along gender lines, but the work of men and women was interdependent. Hunting, military service, and government were largely reserved for men. Women had numerous responsibilities in textile production, agriculture, and the home. One early Spanish commentator described the responsibilities of Andean women in terms that sound very modern:

[T]hey did not just perform domestic tasks, but also [labored] in the fields, in the cultivation of their lands,

---

khipus (KEY-pooz) **ayllu** (aye-YOU) **mit'a** (MEET-ah) in building houses, and carrying burdens. . . . [A]nd more than once I heard that while women were carrying these burdens, they would feel labor pains, and giving birth, they would go to a place where there was water and wash the baby and themselves. Putting the baby on top of the load they were carrying, they would then continue walking as before they gave birth. In sum, there was nothing their husbands did where their wives did not help.[7]

The ayllu was intimately tied to a uniquely Andean system of production and exchange. Because the region's mountain ranges created a multitude of small ecological areas with specialized resources, each community sought to control a variety of environments so as to guarantee access to essential goods. Coastal regions produced maize, fish, and cotton. Mountain valleys contributed quinoa (the local grain) as well as potatoes and other tubers. Higher elevations contributed the wool and meat of llamas and alpacas, and the Amazonian region provided coca and fruits. Ayllus sent out colonists to exploit the resources of these ecological niches. Colonists remained linked to their original region and kin group by marriage and ritual. Historians commonly refer to this system of controlled exchange across ecological boundaries as vertical integration, or verticality.

The historical periodization of Andean history is similar to that of Mesoamerica. Both regions developed highly integrated political and economic systems long before 1500. The pace of agricultural development, urbanization, and state formation in the Andes also approximated that in Mesoamerica. Due to the unique environmental challenges in the Andean region, however, distinctive highland and coastal cultures appeared. In the Andes, more than in Mesoamerica, geography influenced regional cultural integration and state formation.

Moche Portrait Vase The Moche of ancient Peru were among the most accomplished ceramic artists of the Americas. Moche potters produced representations of gods and spirits, scenes of daily life, and portrait vases of important people. This man wears a headdress adorned by two birds and seashells. The stains next to the eyes of the birds represent tears. (Museo de Arqueologica y Antropologia, Lima/Lee Bolton Picture Library)

Moche and Chimu

Around 200 C.E., some four centuries after the collapse of Chavín (see Chapter 3), the **Moche°** developed cultural and political tools that allowed them to dominate the north coastal region of Peru. Moche identity was cultural in character. They did not establish a formal empire or create unified political structures. The most powerful of the Moche urban centers, such as Cerro Blanco located near the modern Peruvian city of Trujillo (see Map 12.3), did establish hegemony over smaller towns and villages. There is also evidence that the Moche extended political and economic control over their neighbors militarily.

Archaeological evidence indicates that the Moche cultivated maize, quinoa, beans, manioc, and sweet potatoes with the aid of massive irrigation works. At higher elevations they also produced coca, which they used ritually. Archaeological excavations reveal the existence of complex networks of canals and aqueducts that connected fields with water sources as far away as 75 miles (121 kilometers). These hydraulic works were maintained by mit'a labor imposed on Moche commoners or on subject peoples. The Moche maintained large herds of alpacas and llamas to transport goods across the region's difficult terrain. Their wool, along with cotton provided by farmers, provided the raw material for the thriving Moche textile production. Their meat provided an important part of the diet.

Evidence from surviving murals and decorated ceramics suggests that Moche society was highly stratified and theocratic. The need to organize large numbers of laborers to construct and maintain the irrigation system helped promote class divisions. Wealth and power among the Moche was concentrated, along with political control, in the hands of priests and military leaders. Hi-

Moche (MO-che)

erarchy was further reinforced by the military conquest of neighboring regions. The residences of the elite were constructed atop large platforms at Moche ceremonial centers. The elite literally lived above the commoners. Their power was also apparent in their rich clothing and jewelry, which confirmed their divine status and set them farther apart from commoners. Moche rulers and other members of the elite wore tall headdresses. They used gold and gold alloy jewelry to mark their social position: gold plates suspended from their noses concealed the lower portion of their faces, and large gold plugs decorated their ears.

These deep social distinctions also were reflected in Moche burial practices. A recent excavation in the Lambeyeque Valley discovered the tomb of a warrior-priest who was buried with a rich treasure of gold, silver, and copper jewelry, textiles, feather ornaments, and shells (see Diversity and Dominance: Burials as Historical Texts). Retainers and servants were also buried with this powerful man to serve him in the afterlife.

Most commoners, on the other hand, devoted their time to subsistence farming and to the payment of labor dues owed to their ayllu and to the elite. Both men and women were involved in agriculture, care of llama herds, and the household economy. They lived with their families in one-room buildings clustered in the outlying areas of cities and in surrounding agricultural zones.

The high quality of Moche textiles, ceramics, and metallurgy indicates the presence of numerous skilled artisans. As had been true centuries earlier in Chavín, women had a special role in the production of textiles; even elite women devoted time to weaving. Moche culture developed a brilliant representational art. Moche craftsmen produced highly individualized portrait vases that today adorn museum collections in nearly every city of the world. Ceramics were also decorated with line drawings representing myths and rituals. The most original Moche ceramic vessels were decorated with explicit sexual acts. The Moche were also accomplished metalsmiths, producing beautiful gold and silver religious and decorative objects and items for elite adornment. Metallurgy served more practical ends as well: artisans produced a range of tools made of heavy copper and copper alloy for agricultural and military purposes.

Since we have no written sources, a detailed history of the Moche can never be written. The archaeological record makes clear that the rapid decline of the major centers coincided with a succession of natural disasters in the sixth century and with the rise of a new military power in the Andean highlands. When an earthquake altered the course of the Moche River, major flooding seriously damaged urban centers. The Moche region also was threatened by long-term climate changes. A thirty-

year drought expanded the area of coastal sand dunes during the sixth century, and powerful winds pushed sand onto fragile agricultural lands, overwhelming the irrigation system. As the land dried, periodic heavy rains caused erosion that damaged fields and weakened the economy that had sustained ceremonial and residential centers. This succession of disasters undermined the authority of the religious and political leaders, whose privileges were based on their ability to control natural forces through rituals. Despite massive efforts to keep the irrigation canals open and despite the construction of new urban centers in less vulnerable valleys to the north, Moche civilization never recovered. In the eighth century, the rise of a new military power, the **Wari**°, also contributed to the disappearance of the Moche by putting pressure on trade routes that linked the coastal region with the highlands.

At the end of the Moche period the **Chimu**° developed a new and more powerful coastal civilization. Chan Chan, capital of the Empire of Chimor, was constructed around 800 C.E. near the earlier Moche cultural center. After 1200 C.E. Chimu began a period of aggressive military expansion. At the apex of its power, The Empire of Chimor controlled 625 miles (1,000 kilometers) of the Peruvian coast.

Within Chan Chan was a series of walled compounds, each one containing a burial pyramid. Scholars believe that each ruler built his own compound and was buried in it on death. Sacrifices and rich grave goods accompanied each royal burial. As did the Moche, Chimor's rulers separated themselves from the masses of society by their consumption of rare and beautiful textiles, ceramics, and precious metals as a way of suggesting the approval of the gods. Some scholars suggest that the Chimu dynasty practiced split inheritance: goods and lands of the deceased ruler went to secondary heirs or for religious sacrifices. The royal heir who inherited the throne was forced to construct his own residence compound and then undertake new conquests to fund his household. After the Inca conquered the northern coast in 1465, they borrowed from the rich rituals and court customs of the Chimu.

Tiwanaku and Wari

After 500 C.E. two powerful civilizations developed in the Andean highlands. At nearly 13,000 feet (3,962 meters) on the high treeless plain near Lake Titicaca in modern Bolivia stand the ruins of **Tiwanaku**° (see Map 12.3). Initial

---

Wari (WAH-ree)   **Chimu** (chee-MOO)
Tiwanaku (tee-wah-NA-coo)

DIVERSITY AND DOMINANCE

BURIALS AS HISTORICAL TEXTS

Efforts to reveal the history of the Americas before the arrival of Europeans depend on the work of archaeologists. The burials of rulers and other members of elites can be viewed as historical texts that describe how textiles, precious metals, beautifully decorated ceramics, and other commodities were used to reinforce the political and cultural power of ruling lineages. In public, members of the elite were always surrounded by the most desirable and rarest products as well as by elaborate rituals and ceremonies. The effect was to create an aura of godlike power. The material elements of political and cultural power were integrated into the experience of death and burial as members of the elite were sent into the afterlife.

The first photograph is of an excavated Moche tomb in Sipán, Peru. The Moche (100 C.E.–ca. 700 C.E.) were one of the most important of the pre-Inca civilizations of the Andean region. They were masters of metallurgy, ceramics, and textiles. The excavations at Sipán revealed a "warrior/priest" buried with an amazing array of gold ornaments, jewels, textiles, and ceramics. He was also buried with two women, perhaps wives or concubines, two male servants, and a warrior. The warrior, one woman, and one man are missing feet, as if this deformation would guarantee their continued faithfulness to the deceased ruler.

The second photograph shows the excavation of a Classic-Era (250 C.E.–ca. 800 C.E.) Maya burial at Río Azul in Guatemala. Here a member of the elite was laid out on a carved wooden platform and cotton mattress; his body painted with decorations. He was covered in beautifully woven textiles and surrounded by valuable goods. Among the discoveries were a necklace of individual stones carved in the shape of heads, perhaps a symbol of his prowess in battle, high-quality ceramics, some filled with foods consumed by the elite like cacao. The careful preparation of the burial chamber had required the work of numerous artisans and laborers, as was the case in the burial of the Moche warrior/priest. In death, as in life, these early American civilizations acknowledged the high status, political power, and religious authority of their elites.

QUESTIONS FOR ANALYSIS

1. If these burials are texts, what are stories?
2. Are there any visible differences in the two burials?
3. What questions might historians ask of these burials that cannot be answered?
4. Are modern burials texts in similar ways to these ancient practices?

occupation may have occurred as early as 400 B.C.E., but significant urbanization began only after 200 C.E. Tiwanaku's expansion depended on the adoption of technologies that increased agricultural productivity. Modern excavations provide the outline of vast drainage projects that reclaimed nearly 200,000 acres (8,000 hectares) of rich lakeside marshes for agriculture. This system of raised fields and ditches permitted intensive cultivation similar to that achieved by use of chinampas in Mesoamerica. Fish from the nearby lake and llamas added protein to a diet largely dependent on potatoes and grains. Llamas were also crucial for the maintenance of long-distance trade relationships that brought in corn, coca, tropical fruits, and medicinal plants.

The urban center of Tiwanaku was distinguished by the scale of its construction and by the high quality of its stone masonry. Large stones and quarried blocks were moved many miles to construct a large terraced pyramid, walled enclosures, and a reservoir—projects that probably required the mobilization of thousands of laborers over a period of years. Despite a limited metallurgy that produced only tools of copper alloy, Tiwanaku's artisans built large structures of finely cut stone that required little mortar to fit the blocks. They also produced gigantic human statuary. The largest example, a stern figure with a military bearing, is cut from a single block of stone that measures 24 feet (7 meters) high.

Burials Reveal Ancient Civilizations   (Left) Buried around 300 C.E., this Moche warrior-priest was buried amid rich tribute at Sipán in Peru. Also, buried were the bodies of retainers or kinsmen probably sacrificed to accompany this powerful man. The body lies with the head on the right and the feet on the left. (Right) Similarly, the burial of a member of the Maya elite at Río Azul in northern Guatemala indicates the care taken to surround the powerful with fine ceramics, jewelry and other valuable goods.   (*left:* Heinze Plenge/NGS Image Collection; *right:* George Mobley/NGS Image Collection)

Little is known of the social structure or daily life of this civilization. Neither surviving murals nor other decorative arts offer the suggestive guidance found in the burial goods of the Moche. Nevertheless, it is clear that Tiwanaku was a highly stratified society ruled by a hereditary elite. Most women and men devoted their time to agriculture and the care of llama herds. However, the presence of specialized artisans is evident in the high-quality construction in public buildings and in locally produced ceramics. The distribution of these ceramics to distant places suggests the presence of a specialized merchant class as well.

Many scholars portray Tiwanaku as the capital of a vast empire, a precursor to the later Inca state. It is clear that the elite controlled a large, disciplined labor force in the surrounding region. Military conquests and the establishment of colonial populations provided the highland capital with dependable supplies of products from ecologically distinct zones. Tiwanaku cultural influence extended eastward to the jungles and southward to the coastal regions and oases of the Atacama Desert in Chile. But archaeological evidence suggests that Tiwanaku, in comparison with contemporary Teotihuacan in central Mexico, had a relatively small full-time population of around 30,000. It was not a metropolis like the largest Mesoamerican cities; it was a ceremonial and political center for a large regional population.

Inca Roads

From the time of Chavín (900–250 B.C.E.), Andean peoples built roads to facilitate trade across ecological boundaries and to project political power over conquered peoples. In the fifteenth and sixteenth centuries, the Inca extended and improved the networks of roads constructed in earlier eras. Roads were crucially important to Inca efforts to collect and redistribute tribute paid in food, textiles, and chicha (corn liquor).

Two roads connected Cuzco, the Inca capital in southern Peru, to Quito, Ecudaor, in the north and to Chile farther south. One ran along the flat and arid coastal plain, the other through the mountainous interior. Shorter east-west roads connected important coastal and interior cities. Evidence suggests that administrative centers were sited along these routes to expedite rapid communication with the capital. Rest stops at convenient distances provided shelter and food to traveling officials and runners who carried messages between Cuzco and the empire's cities and towns. Warehouses were constructed along the roads to provide food and military supplies for passing Inca armies or to supply local laborers working on construction projects or cultivating the ruler's fields.

Because communication with regional administrative centers and the movement of troops were the central objectives of the Inca leadership, routes were selected to avoid natural obstacles and to reduce travel time. Mit'a laborers recruited from nearby towns and villages built and maintained the roads. Roads were commonly paved with stone or packed earth and often were bordered by stone or adobe walls to keep soldiers or pack trains of llamas from straying into farmers' fields. Whenever possible, roadbeds were made level. In mountainous terrain some roads were little more than improved paths, but in flat country three or four people could walk abreast. Care was always taken to repair damage caused by rain runoff or other drainage problems.

The achievement of Inca road builders is clearest in the mountainous terrain of the interior. They built suspension bridges across high gorges and cut roadbeds into the face of cliffs. A Spanish priest living in Peru in the seventeenth century commented that the Inca roads "were magnificent constructions, which could be compared favorably with the most superb roads of the Romans."

Source: Quotation from Father Bernabe Cobo, *History of the Inca Empire. An account of the Indians' customs and origin together with a treatise on Inca legends, history, and social institutions* (Austin: University of Texas Press, 1983), 223.

Inca Road The Inca built roads to connect distant parts of the empire to Cuzco, the Inca capital. These roads are still used in Peru. (Loren McIntyre/Woodfin Camp & Associates)

The contemporary site of Wari was located about 450 miles (751 kilometers) to the northwest of Tiwanaku, near the modern Peruvian city of Ayacucho. Wari clearly shared elements of the culture and technology of Tiwanaku, but the exact nature of this relationship remains unclear. Some scholars argue that Wari began as a dependency of Tiwanaku, while others suggest that they were joint capitals of a single empire. Recent archaeological discoveries indicate that Wari was also closely tied to Nazca, a powerful state located to the south. As was common throughout the history of the Andes, Wari benefited from its contacts and commercial exchanges with other powerful societies in the region.

Wari was larger than Tiwanaku, measuring nearly 4 square miles (10 square kilometers). The city center was surrounded by a massive wall and included a large temple. The center had numerous multifamily housing blocks. Less-concentrated housing for commoners was located in a sprawling suburban zone. Wari's development, unlike that of most other major urban centers in the Andes, appears to have occurred without central planning.

The small scale of its monumental architecture and the near absence of cut stone masonry in public and private buildings distinguish Wari from Tiwanaku. It is not clear that these characteristics resulted from the relative weakness of the elite or the absence of specialized construction crafts. There is a distinctive Wari ceramic style that has allowed experts to trace Wari's expanding power to the coastal area earlier controlled by the Moche and to the northern highlands. Wari's military expansion occurred at a time of increasing warfare throughout the Andes. As a result, roads were built to maintain communication with remote fortified dependencies. Perhaps as a consequence of military conflict, both Tiwanaku and Wari declined to insignificance by about 1000 C.E. The Inca inherited their political legacy.

The Inca

In little more than a hundred years, the **Inca** developed a vast imperial state, which they called "Land of Four Corners." By 1525 the empire had a population of more than 6 million and stretched from the Maule River in Chile to northern Ecuador and from the Pacific coast across the Andes to the upper Amazon and, in the south, into Argentina (see Map 12.3). In the early fifteenth century the Inca were one of many competing military powers in the southern highlands, an area of limited political significance after the collapse of Wari. Centered in the valley of Cuzco, the Inca were initially organized as a chiefdom based on reciprocal gift giving and the redistribution of food and textiles. Strong and resourceful leaders consolidated political authority in the 1430s and undertook an ambitious campaign of military expansion.

The Inca state, like earlier highland powers, was built on traditional Andean social customs and economic practices. Tiwanaku had relied in part on the use of colonists to provide supplies of resources from distant, ecologically distinct zones. The Inca built on this legacy by conquering additional distant territories and increasing the scale of forced exchanges. Crucial to this process was the development of a large, professional military. Unlike the peoples of Mesoamerica, who distributed specialized goods by developing markets and tribute relationships, Andean peoples used state power to broaden and expand the vertical exchange system that had permitted ayllus to exploit a range of ecological niches.

Like earlier highland civilizations, the Inca were pastoralists. Inca prosperity and military strength depended on vast herds of llamas and alpacas, which provided food and clothing as well as transport for goods. Both men and women were involved in the care of these herds. Women were primarily responsible for weaving; men were drivers in long-distance trade. This pastoral tradition provided the Inca with powerful metaphors that helped shape their political and religious beliefs. They believed that the gods and their ruler shared the obligations of the shepherd to his flock—an idea akin to references to "The Lord is my Shepherd."

Collective efforts by mit'a laborers made the Inca Empire possible. Cuzco, the imperial capital, and the provincial cities, the royal court, the imperial armies, and the state's religious cults all rested on this foundation. The mit'a system also created the material surplus that provided the bare necessities for the old, weak, and ill of Inca society. Each ayllu contributed approximately one-seventh of its adult male population to meet these collective obligations. These draft laborers served as soldiers, construction workers, craftsmen, and runners to carry messages along post roads. They also drained swamps, terraced mountainsides, filled in valley floors, built and maintained irrigation works, and built storage facilities and roads. Inca laborers constructed 13,000 miles (20,930 kilometers) of road, facilitating military troop movements, administration, and trade (see Environment and Technology: Inca Roads).

Imperial administration was similarly superimposed on existing political structures and established elite groups. The hereditary chiefs of ayllus carried out administrative and judicial functions. As the Inca expanded, they generally left local rulers in place. By leaving the rulers of defeated societies in place, the Inca risked rebellion, but they controlled these risks by means of a thinly veiled system of hostage taking and the

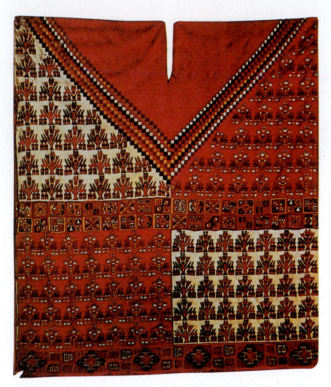

Inca Tunic   Andean weavers produced beautiful textiles from cotton and from the wool of llamas and alpacas. The Inca inherited this rich craft tradition and produced some of the world's most remarkable textiles. The quality and design of each garment indicated the weaver's rank and power in this society. This tunic was an outer garment for a powerful male.   (From *Textile Art of Peru*. Collection created and directed by Jose Antonio de Lavalle and Jose Alejandro Gonzalez Garcia [L. L. Editores, 1989])

use of military garrisons. The rulers of defeated regions were required to send their heirs to live at the Inca royal court in Cuzco. Inca leaders even required that representations of important local gods be brought to Cuzco and made part of the imperial pantheon. These measures promoted imperial integration while at the same time providing hostages to ensure the good behavior of subject peoples.

Conquests magnified the authority of the Inca ruler and led to the creation of an imperial bureaucracy drawn from among his kinsmen. The royal family claimed descent from the Sun, the primary Inca god. Members of the royal family lived in palaces maintained by armies of servants. The lives of the ruler and members of the royal family were dominated by political and religious rituals that helped legitimize their authority. Among the many obligations associated with kingship was the require-

ment to extend imperial boundaries by warfare. Thus each new ruler began his reign with conquest.

Tenochtitlan, the Aztec capital, had a population of about 150,000 in 1520. At the height of Inca power in 1530, Cuzco had a population of less than 30,000. Nevertheless, Cuzco was a remarkable place. The Inca were highly skilled stone craftsmen: their most impressive buildings were constructed of carefully cut stones fitted together without mortar. The city was laid out in the shape of a giant puma (a mountain lion). At the center were the palaces that each ruler built when he ascended to the throne, as well as the major temples. The richest was the Temple of the Sun. Its interior was lined with sheets of gold, and its patio was decorated with golden representations of llamas and corn. The ruler made every effort to awe and intimidate visitors and residents alike with a nearly continuous series of rituals, feasts, and sacrifices. Sacrifices of textiles, animals, and other goods sent as tribute dominated the city's calendar. The destruction of these valuable commodities, and a small number of human sacrifices, helped give the impression of splendor and sumptuous abundance that appeared to demonstrate the ruler's claimed descent from the Sun.

Inca cultural achievement rested on the strong foundation of earlier Andean civilizations. We know that astronomical observation was a central concern of the priestly class, as in Mesoamerica; the Inca calendar, however, is lost to us. All communication other than oral was transmitted by the khipus borrowed from earlier Andean civilizations. In weaving and metallurgy, Inca technology, building on earlier regional developments, was more advanced than in Mesoamerica. Inca craftsmen produced utilitarian tools and weapons of copper and bronze as well as decorative objects of gold and silver. Inca women produced textiles of extraordinary beauty from cotton and the wool of llamas and alpacas.

Although the Inca did not introduce new technologies, they increased economic output and added to the region's prosperity. The conquest of large populations in environmentally distinct regions allowed the Inca to multiply the yields produced by the traditional exchanges between distinct ecological niches. But the expansion of imperial economic and political power was purchased at the cost of reduced equality and diminished local autonomy. The imperial elite, living in richly decorated palaces in Cuzco and other urban centers, was increasingly cut off from the masses of Inca society. The royal court held members of the provincial nobility at arm's length, and commoners were subject to execution if they dared to look directly at the ruler's face.

After only a century of regional dominance, the Inca Empire faced a crisis in 1525. The death of the Inca ruler

Huayna Capac at the conclusion of the conquest of Ecuador initiated a bloody struggle for the throne. Powerful factions coalesced around two sons whose rivalry compelled both the professional military and the hereditary Inca elite to choose sides. Civil war was the result. The Inca state controlled a vast territory spread over more than 3,000 miles (4,830 kilometers) of mountainous terrain. Regionalism and ethnic diversity had always posed a threat to the empire. Civil war weakened imperial institutions and ignited the resentments of conquered peoples. On the eve of the arrival of Europeans, the destructive consequences of this violent conflict undermined the institutions and economy of Andean civilizations.

Conclusion

The indigenous societies of the Western Hemisphere developed unique technologies and cultural forms in mountainous regions, tropical rain forests, deserts, woodlands, and arctic regions. In Mesoamerica, North America, and the Andean region, the natural environment powerfully influenced cultural development. The Maya of southern Mexico, for example, developed agricultural technologies that compensated for the tropical cycle of heavy rains followed by long dry periods. On the coast of Peru the Moche used systems of trade and mutual labor obligation to meet the challenge of an arid climate and mountainous terrain, while the mound builders of North America expanded agricultural production by utilizing the rich floodplains of the Ohio and Mississippi Rivers. Across the Americas, hunting and gathering peoples and urbanized agricultural societies produced rich religious and aesthetic traditions as well as useful technologies and effective social institutions in response to local conditions. Once established, these cultural traditions proved very durable.

The Aztec and Inca Empires represented the culmination of a long developmental process that had begun before 1000 B.C.E. Each imperial state controlled extensive and diverse territories with populations that numbered in the millions. The capital cities of Tenochtitlan and Cuzco were great cultural and political centers that displayed some of the finest achievements of Amerindian technology, art, and architecture. Both states were based on conquests and were ruled by powerful hereditary elites who depended on the tribute of subject peoples. In both traditions religion met spiritual needs while also organizing collective life and legitimizing political authority.

The Aztec and Inca Empires were created militarily, their survival depending as much on the power of their armies as on the productivity of their economies or the wisdom of their rulers. Both empires were ethnically and environmentally diverse, but there were important differences. Elementary markets had been developed in Mesoamerica to distribute specialized regional production, although the forced payment of goods as tribute remained important. In the Andes reciprocal labor obligations and managed exchange relationships were used to allocate goods. The Aztecs used their military to force defeated peoples to provide food, textiles, and even sacrificial captives as tribute, but they left local hereditary elites in place. The Incas, in contrast, created a more centralized administrative structure managed by a trained bureaucracy.

As the Western Hemisphere's long isolation drew to a close in the late fifteenth century, both empires were challenged by powerful neighbors or by internal revolts. In earlier periods similar challenges had contributed to the decline of great civilizations in both Mesoamerica and the Andean region. In those cases, a long period of adjustment and the creation of new indigenous institutions followed the collapse of dominant powers such as the Toltecs in Mesoamerica and Tiwanaku in the Andes. With the arrival of Europeans, this cycle of crisis and adjustment would be transformed, and the future of Amerindian peoples would become linked to the cultures of the Old World.

■ Key Terms

Teotihuacan	khipu
chinampas	ayllu
Maya	mit'a
Toltecs	Moche
Aztecs	Wari
Tenochtitlan	Chimu
tribute system	Tiwanaku
Anasazi	Inca
chiefdom	

■ Suggested Reading

In *Prehistory of the Americas* (1987) Stuart Fiedel provides an excellent summary of the early history of the Western Hemisphere. Alvin M. Josephy, Jr., in *The Indian Heritage of America* (1968), also provides a thorough introduction to the topic. *Canada's First Nations* (1992) by Olive Patricia Dickason is a well-written survey that traces the history of Canada's Amerindian peoples to the modern era. *Early Man in the New World,* ed. Richard Shutler, Jr. (1983), provides a helpful addition to these works. *Atlas of Ancient America* (1986) by Michael Coe, Elizabeth P. Benson, and Dean R. Snow is a useful compendium of maps and information. George Kubler, *The Art and Architecture of Ancient America* (1962), is a valuable resource, though now dated.

Eric Wolf provides an enduring synthesis of Mesoamerican history in *Sons of the Shaking Earth* (1959). A good summary of recent research on Teotihuacan is found in Esther Pasztori, *Teotihuacan* (1997). Linda Schele and David Freidel summarize the most recent research on the classic-period Maya in their excellent *A Forest of Kings* (1990). See also David Drew, *The Lost Chronicles of the Maya Kings* (1999). The best summary of Aztec history is Nigel Davies, *The Aztec Empire: The Toltec Resurgence* (1987). Jacques Soustelle, *Daily Life of the Aztecs,* trans. Patrick O'Brian (1961), is a good introduction. Though controversial in some of its analysis, Inga Clendinnen's *Aztecs* (1991) is also an important contribution.

Chaco and Hohokam (1991), ed. Patricia L. Crown and W. James Judge, is a good summary of research issues. Robert Silverberg, *Mound Builders of Ancient America* (1968), supplies a good introduction to this topic. See also *Understanding Complexity in the Prehistoric Southwest,* ed. George J. Gumerman and Murray Gell-Mann (1994).

A helpful introduction to the scholarship on early Andean societies is provided by Karen Olsen Bruhns, *Ancient South America* (1994). For the Moche see Garth Bawden, *The Moche* (1996). *The History of the Incas* (1970) by Alfred Metraux is dated but offers a useful summary. The best recent modern synthesis is María Rostworowski de Diez Canseco, *History of the Inca*

Realm, trans. by Harry B. Iceland (1999). John Murra, *The Economic Organization of the Inca State* (1980), and Irene Silverblatt, *Moon, Sun, and Witches: Gender Ideologies and Class in Inca and Colonial Peru* (1987), are challenging, important works on Peru before the arrival of Columbus in the Western Hemisphere. Frederick Katz, *The Ancient Civilizations of the Americas* (1972), offers a useful comparative perspective on ancient American developments.

■ Notes

1. This summary closely follows the historical narrative and translation of names offered by Linda Schele and David Freidel in *A Forest of Kings: The Untold Story of the Ancient Maya* (New York: Morrow, 1990), 182–186.
2. From the Florentine Codex, quoted in Inga Clendinnen, *Aztecs* (New York: Cambridge University Press, 1991), 213.
3. Quoted in Nigel Davies, *The Toltec Heritage: From the Fall of Tula to the Rise of Tenochtitlán* (Norman: University of Oklahoma Press, 1980), 3.
4. Bernal Díaz del Castillo, *The Conquest of New Spain,* trans. J. M. Cohen (London: Penguin Books, 1963), 217.
5. Hernando Cortés, *Five Letters, 1519–1526,* trans. J. Bayard Morris (New York: Norton, 1991), 87.
6. Quoted in Irene Silverblatt, *Moon, Sun, and Witches: Gender Ideologies and Class in Inca and Colonial Peru* (Princeton, NJ: Princeton University Press, 1987), 10.
7. Quoted in Irene Silverblatt, *Moon, Sun, and Witches: Gender Ideologies and Class in Inca and Colonial Peru* (Princeton, N.J.: Princeton University Press, 1987), 10.

Religious Conversion

Religious conversion has two meanings that often get confused. The term can refer to the inner transformation an individual may feel on joining a new religious community or becoming revitalized in his or her religious belief. Conversions of this sort are often sudden and deeply emotional. In historical terms, they may be important when they transform the lives of prominent individuals.

In its other meaning, *religious conversion* refers to a change in the religious identity of an entire population, or a large portion of a population. This generally occurs slowly and is hard to trace in historical documents. As a result, historians have sometimes used superficial indicators to trace the spread of a religion. Doing so can result in misleading conclusions, such as considering the spread of the Islamic faith to be the result of forced conversion by Arab conquerors, or taking the routes traveled by Christian or Buddhist missionaries as evidence that the people they encountered adopted their spiritual message, or assuming that a king or chieftain's adherence to a new religion immediately resulted in a religious change among subjects or followers.

In addition to being difficult to document, religious conversion in the broad societal sense has followed different patterns according to changing circumstances of time and place. Historians have devised several models to explain the different conversion patterns. According to one model, religious labels in a society change quickly, through mass baptism, for example, but devotional practices remain largely the same. Evidence for this can be found in the continuation of old religious customs among people who identify themselves as belonging to a new religion. Another model sees religious change as primarily a function of economic benefit or escape from persecution. Taking this approach makes it difficult to explain the endurance of certain religious communities in the face of hardship and discrimination. Nevertheless, most historians pay attention to economic advantage in their assessments of mass conversion. A third model associates a society's religious conversion with its desire to adopt a more sophisticated way of life, by shifting, for example, from a religion that does not use written texts to one that does.

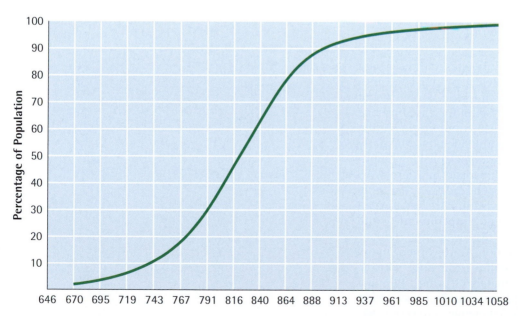

Figure 1   Conversion to Islam in Iran   *Source:* Richard W. Bulliet, *Conversion to Islam in the Medieval Period,* Cambridge, MA: Harvard University Press, 1979, 23. Copyright ©1979 by the President and Fellows of Harvard College.

One final conceptual approach to explaining the process of mass religious change draws on the quantitative models of innovation diffusion that were originally developed to analyze the spread of new technologies in the twentieth century. According to this approach, new ideas, whether in the material or religious realm, depend on the spread of information. A few early adopters—missionaries, pilgrims, or conquerors, perhaps—spread word of the new faith to the people they come in contact with, some of whom follow their example and convert. Those converts in turn spread the word to others, and a chain reaction picks up speed in what might be called a bandwagon effect. The period of bandwagon conversion tapers off when the number of people who have not yet been offered an opportunity to convert diminishes. The entire process can be graphed as a *logistic* or S-shaped curve. Figure 1, the graph of conversion to Islam in Iran based on changes from Persian (non-Islamic) to Arabic (Islamic) names in family genealogies, shows such a curve over a period of almost four centuries.

In societies that were largely illiterate, like those in which Buddhism, Christianity, and Islam slowly achieved spiritual dominance, information spread primarily by word of mouth. The proponents of the new religious views did not always speak the same language as the people they hoped to bring into the faith. Under these circumstances, significant conversion, that is, conversion that involved some understanding of the new religion, as opposed to forced baptism or imposed mouthing of a profession of faith, must surely have started with fairly small numbers.

Language was crucial. Chinese pilgrims undertook lengthy travels to visit early Buddhist sites in India. There they acquired Sanskrit texts, which they translated into Chinese. These translations became the core texts of Chinese Buddhism. In early Christendom, the presence of bilingual (Greek-Aramaic) Jewish communities in the eastern parts of the Roman Empire facilitated the early spread of the religion beyond its Aramaic-speaking homeland. By contrast, Arabic, the language of Islam, was spoken only in the Arabian peninsula and the desert borderlands that extended northwards from Arabia between Syria, Jordan, and Iraq. This initial impediment to the spread of knowledge about Islam dissolved only when intermarriage with non-Muslim, non-Arab women, many of them taken captive and distributed as booty during the conquests, produced bilingual offspring. Bilingual preachers of the Christian faith were similarly needed in the Celtic, Germanic, and Slavic language areas of western and eastern Europe.

This slow process of information diffusion, which varied from region to region, made changing demands on religious leaders and institutions. When a faith was professed primarily by a ruler, his army, and his dependents, religious leaders gave the highest priority to servicing the needs of the ruling minority and perhaps discrediting, denigrating, or exterminating the practices of the majority. Once a few centuries had passed and the new faith had become the religion of the great majority of the population, religious leaders turned to establishing popular institutions and reaching out to the common people. Historical interpretation can benefit from knowing where a society is in a long-term process of conversion.

These various models reinforce the importance of distinguishing between emotional individual conversion experiences and broad changes in a society's religious identity. New converts are commonly thought of as especially zealous in their faith, and that description is often apt in instances of individual conversion experiences. It is less appropriate, however, to broader episodes of conversion. In a conversion wave that starts slowly, builds momentum in the bandwagon phase, and then tapers off, the first individuals to convert are likely to be more spiritually motivated than those who join the movement toward its end. Religious growth depends as much on making the faith attractive to late converts as to ecstatic early converts.

PART FOUR

Interregional Patterns of Culture and Contact, 1200–1550

In Eurasia, overland trade along the Silk Road, which had begun before the Roman and Han empires, reached its peak during the era of the Mongol empires. Beginning in 1206 with the rise of Genghis Khan, the Mongols tied Europe, the Middle East, Russia, and East Asia together with threads of conquest and trade centered on Central and Inner Asia. For over a century and a half, some communities thrived on the continental connections that the Mongols fostered, while others groaned under the tax burdens and physical devastation of Mongol rule. But whether for good or ill, Mongol power was based on the skills, strategies, and technologies of the overland trade and life on the steppes.

The impact of the Mongols was also felt by societies that escaped conquest. In Eastern Europe, the Mediterranean coastal areas of the Middle East, Southeast Asia, and Japan, fear of Mongol attack stimulated societies to organize more intensively in their own defense, accelerating processes of urbanization, technological development, and political centralization that in many cases were already underway.

By 1500, Mongol dominance was past, and new powers had emerged. A new Chinese empire, the Ming, was expanding its influence in Southeast

Asia. The Ottomans had captured Constantinople and overthrown the Byzantine Empire. And the Christian monarchs who had defeated the Muslims in Spain and Portugal were laying the foundations of new overseas empires. With the fall of the Mongol Empire, Central and Inner Asia were no longer at the center of Eurasian trade.

As the overland trade of Eurasia faded, merchants, soldiers, and explorers took to the seas. The most spectacular of the early state-sponsored long-distance ocean voyages were undertaken by the Chinese admiral Zheng He. The 1300s and 1400s also saw African exploration of the Atlantic and Polynesian colonization of the central and eastern Pacific. By 1500 the navigator Christopher Columbus, sailing for Spain, had reached the Americas; within twenty-five years a Portuguese ship would sail all the way around the world. New sailing technologies and a sounder knowledge of the size of the globe and the contours of its shorelines made sub-Saharan Africa, the Indian Ocean, Asia, Europe, and finally the Americas more accessible to each other than ever before.

The great overland routes of Eurasia had generated massive wealth in East Asia and a growing hunger for commerce in Europe. These factors animated the development of the sea trade, too. Exposure to the achievements, wealth, and resources of societies in the Americas, sub-Saharan Africa, and Asia enticed the emerging European monarchies to pursue further exploration and control of the seas.

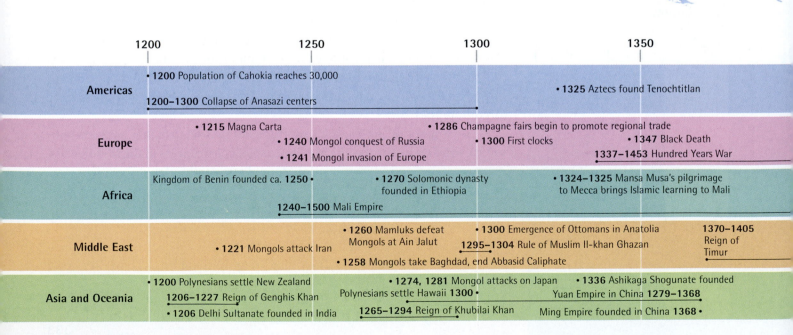

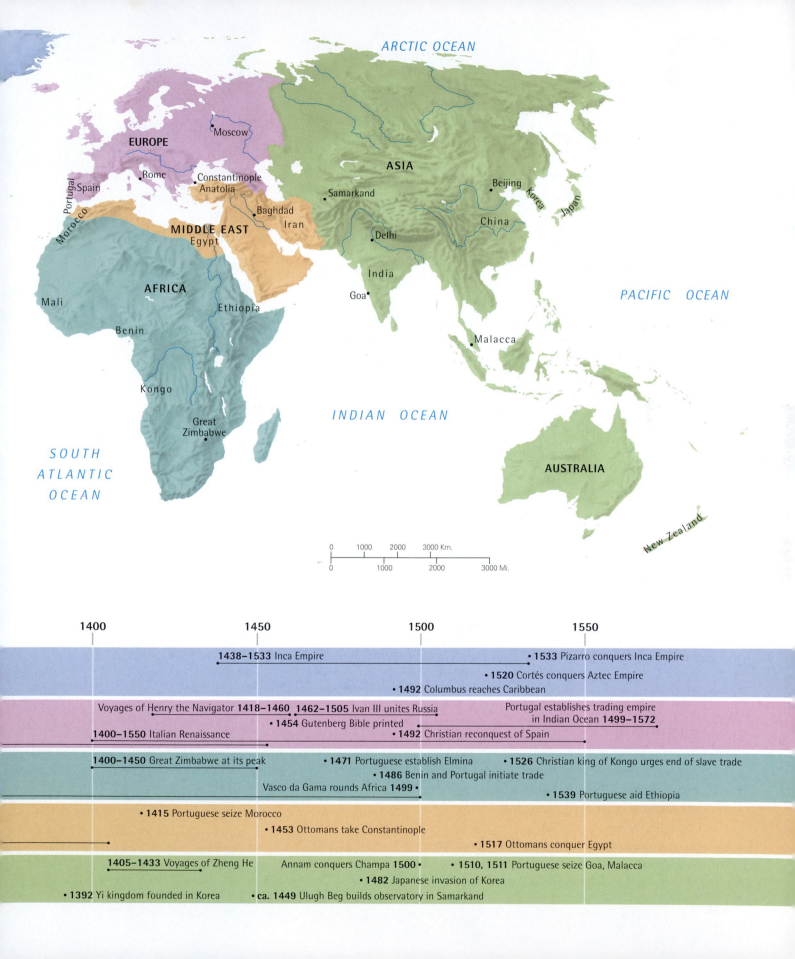

ARCTIC OCEAN

EUROPE
Moscow
Rome
Portugal
Spain
Morocco
Constantinople
Anatolia
MIDDLE EAST
Baghdad
Iran
Egypt

AFRICA
Mali
Benin
Ethiopia
Kongo
Great
Zimbabwe

SOUTH
ATLANTIC
OCEAN

ASIA
Samarkand
Beijing
Korea
Japan
China
Delhi
India
Goa

Malacca

INDIAN OCEAN

PACIFIC OCEAN

AUSTRALIA

New Zealand

| 0 | 1000 | 2000 | 3000 Km. |
| 0 | 1000 | 2000 | 3000 Mi. |

1400   **1450**   **1500**   **1550**

1438–1533 Inca Empire   • **1533** Pizarro conquers Inca Empire

• **1520** Cortés conquers Aztec Empire

• **1492** Columbus reaches Caribbean

Voyages of Henry the Navigator **1418–1460**   **1462–1505** Ivan III unites Russia   Portugal establishes trading empire
in Indian Ocean **1499–1572**

• **1454** Gutenberg Bible printed

1400–1550 Italian Renaissance   • **1492** Christian reconquest of Spain

1400–1450 Great Zimbabwe at its peak   • **1471** Portuguese establish Elmina   • **1526** Christian king of Kongo urges end of slave trade

• **1486** Benin and Portugal initiate trade

Vasco da Gama rounds Africa **1499** •   • **1539** Portuguese aid Ethiopia

• **1415** Portuguese seize Morocco

• **1453** Ottomans take Constantinople

• **1517** Ottomans conquer Egypt

1405–1433 Voyages of Zheng He   Annam conquers Champa **1500** •   • **1510, 1511** Portuguese seize Goa, Malacca

• **1482** Japanese invasion of Korea

• **1392** Yi kingdom founded in Korea   • **ca. 1449** Ulugh Beg builds observatory in Samarkand

13

Mongol Eurasia and Its Aftermath, 1200–1500

Defending Japan Japanese warriors board Mongol warships with swords to prevent the landing of the invasion force in 1281.

CHAPTER OUTLINE

When the Mongol leader Temüjin° was a boy, a rival group murdered his father. Temüjin's mother tried to shelter him (and protect him from dogs, which he feared), but she could not find a safe haven. At fifteen Temüjin sought refuge with the leader of the Keraits°, one of Mongolia's many warring confederations. The Keraits spoke Turkic and respected both Christianity and Buddhism. Gifted with strength, courage, and intelligence, Temüjin learned the importance of religious tolerance, the necessity of dealing harshly with enemies, and the variety of Central Asia's cultural and economic traditions.

In 1206 the **Mongols** and their allies acknowledged Temüjin as **Genghis Khan°,** or supreme leader. His advisers included speakers of many languages and adherents of all the major religions of the Middle East and East Asia. His deathbed speech, which cannot be literally true even though a contemporary recorded it, captures the strategy behind Mongol success: "If you want to retain your possessions and conquer your enemies, you must make your subjects submit willingly and unite your diverse energies to a single end."[1] By implementing this strategy, Genghis Khan became the most famous conqueror in history, initiating an expansion of Mongol dominion that by 1250 stretched from Poland to northern China.

Scholars today stress the immense impact Temüjin and his successors had on the later medieval world, and the positive developments that transpired under Mongol rule. European and Asian sources of the time, however, vilify the Mongols as agents of death, suffering, and conflagration, a still-common viewpoint based on reliable accounts of horrible massacres.

The tremendous extent of the Mongol Empire promoted the movement of people and ideas from one end of Eurasia to the other. Specialized skills developed in different parts of the world spread rapidly throughout the Mongol domains. Trade routes improved, markets expanded, and the demand for products grew. Trade on the Silk Road, which had declined with the fall of the Tang Empire (see Chapter 11), revived.

During their period of domination, lasting from 1218 to about 1350 in western Eurasia and to 1368 in China, the Mongols focused on specific economic and strategic interests and usually permitted local cultures to survive and continue to develop. In some regions, local reactions to Mongol domination and unification sowed seeds of regional and ethnic identity that grew extensively in the period of Mongol decline. Societies in regions as widely separated as Russia, Iran, China, Korea, and Japan benefited from the Mongol stimulation of economic and cultural exchange and also found in their opposition to the Mongols new bases for political consolidation and affirmation of cultural difference.

As you read this chapter, ask yourself the following questions:

- What accounts for the magnitude and speed of the Mongol conquests?

- What benefits resulted from the integration of Eurasia in the Mongol Empire?

- How did the effect of Mongol rule on Russia and the lands of Islam differ from its effect on East Asia?

- In what ways did the Ming Empire continue or discontinue Mongol practices?

THE RISE OF THE MONGOLS, 1200–1260

The environment, economic life, cultural institutions, and political traditions of the steppes (prairies) and deserts of Central and Inner Asia contributed to the expansion and contraction of empires. The Mongol Empire owes much of its success to these long-term conditions. Yet the interplay of environment and technology, on the one hand, and specific human actions, on the other, cannot easily be determined. The way of life known as **nomadism** gives rise to imperial expansion only occasionally, and historians disagree about what triggers these episodes. In the case of the Mongols, a precise assessment of the personal contributions of Genghis Khan and his followers remains uncertain.

Temüjin (TEM-uh-jin)   **Keraits** (keh-rates)
Genghis Khan (GENG-iz KAHN)

Nomadism in Central and Inner Asia

Descriptions of steppe nomads from as early as the Greek writer Herodotus in the sixth century B.C.E. portray them as superb riders, herdsmen, and hunters. Traditional accounts maintain that the Mongols put their infants on goats to accustom them to riding. Moving regularly and efficiently with flocks and herds required firm decision making, and the independence of individual Mongols and their families made this decision making public, with many voices being heard. A council with representatives from powerful families ratified the decisions of the leader, the *khan*. Yet people who disagreed with a decision could strike off on their own. Even during military campaigns, warriors moved with their families and possessions.

Menial work in camps fell to slaves—people who were either captured during warfare or who sought refuge in slavery to escape starvation. Weak groups secured land rights and protection from strong groups by providing them with slaves, livestock, weapons, silk, or cash. More powerful groups, such as Genghis Khan's extended family and descendants, lived almost entirely off tribute, so they spent less time and fewer resources on herding and more on warfare designed to secure greater tribute.

Leading families combined resources and solidified intergroup alliances through arranged marriages and other acts, a process that helped generate political federations. Marriages were arranged in childhood—in Temüjin's case, at the age of eight—and children thus became pawns of diplomacy. Women from prestigious families could wield power in negotiation and management, though they ran the risk of assassination or execution just like men (see Diversity and Dominance: Mongol Politics, Mongol Women).

Families often included believers in two or more religions, most commonly Buddhism, Christianity, or Islam. Virtually all Mongols observed the practices of traditional shamanism, rituals in which special individuals visited and influenced the supernatural world. Whatever their faith, the Mongols believed in world rulership by a khan who, with the aid of his shamans, could speak to and for an ultimate god, represented as Sky or Heaven. This universal ruler transcended particular cultures and dominated them all.

The Mongols were not unfamiliar with agriculture or unwilling to use products grown by farmers, but their ideal was self-sufficiency. Since their wanderings with their herds normally took them far from any farming region, self-sufficiency dictated foods they could provide for themselves—primarily meat and milk—and clothing made from felt, leather, and furs. Women oversaw the breeding and birthing of livestock and the preparation of furs.

Mongol dependency on settled regions related primarily to iron for bridles, stirrups, cart fittings, and weapons. They acquired iron implements in trade and reworked them to suit their purposes. As early as the 600s the Turks, a related pastoral people, had large iron-working stations south of the Altai Mountains in western Mongolia. Neighboring agricultural states tried to limit the export of iron but never succeeded. Indeed, Central Asians developed improved techniques of iron forging, which the agricultural regions then adopted. The Mongols revered iron and the secrets of ironworking. Temüjin means "blacksmith," and several of his prominent followers were the sons of blacksmiths.

Steppe nomads situated near settled areas traded wool, leather, and horses for wood, cotton and cottonseed, silk, vegetables, grain, and tea. An appreciation of the value of permanent settlements for growing grain and cotton, as well as for working iron, led some nomadic groups to establish villages at strategic points, often with the help of migrants from the agricultural regions. The frontier regions east of the Caspian Sea and in northern China thus became economically and culturally diverse. Despite their interdependence, nomads and farmers often came into conflict. On rare occasion such conflicts escalated into full-scale invasions in which the martial prowess of the nomads usually resulted in at least temporary victory.

The Mongol Conquests, 1215–1283

Shortly after his acclamation in 1206 Genghis set out to convince the kingdoms of Eurasia to pay him tribute. Two decades of Mongol aggression followed. By 1209 he had forced the Tanggut rulers of northwest China to submit, and in 1215 he captured the Jin capital of Yanjing, today known as Beijing. He began to attack the west in 1219 with a full-scale invasion of a Central Asian state centered on Khwarezm, an oasis area east of the Caspian Sea. By 1221 he had overwhelmed most of Iran. By this time his conquests had gained such momentum that Genghis did not personally participate in all campaigns, and subordinate generals sometimes led the Mongol armies, which increasingly contained non-Mongol nomads as well.

Genghis Khan died in 1227. His son and successor, the Great Khan Ögödei° (see Figure 13.1), continued to

Ögödei (ERG-uh-day)

C H R O N O L O G Y

	Mongolia and China	Central Asia and Middle East	Russia	Korea, Japan, and Southeast Asia
1200	**1206** Temüjin chosen Genghis Khan of the Mongols	**1221–1223** First Mongol attacks in Iran	**1221–1223** First Mongol attacks on Russia	
	1227 Death of Genghis Khan			
	1227–1241 Reign of Great Khan Ögödei			
	1234 Mongols conquer northern China		**1240** Mongols sack Kiev	
			1242 Alexander Nevskii defeats Teutonic Knights	
		1250 Mamluk regime controls Egypt and Syria		
		1258 Mongols sack Baghdad and kill the caliph		**1258** Mongols conquer Koryo rulers in Korea
	1271 Founding of Yuan Empire	**1260** Mamluks defeat Il-khans at Ain Jalut	**1260** War between Il-khans and Golden Horde	
	1279 Mongol conquest of Southern Song			**1274, 1281** Mongols attack Japan
				1283 Yuan invades Annam
1300		**1295** Il-khan Ghazan converts to Islam		**1293** Yuan attacks Java
		1349 End of Il-khan rule	**1346** Plague outbreak at Kaffa	**1333–1338** End of Kamakura Shogunate in Japan, beginning of Ashikaga
	1368 Ming Empire founded	**ca. 1350** Egypt infected by plague		
		1370–1405 Reign of Timur		**1392** Founding of Yi kingdom in Korea
1400				
	1403–1424 Reign of Yongle	**1402** Timur defeats Ottoman sultan		
	1405–1433 Voyages of Zheng He			
	1449 Mongol attack on Beijing	**1453** Ottomans capture Constantinople	**1462–1505** Ivan III establishes authority as tsar. Moscow emerges as major political center.	**1471–1500** Annam conquers Champa

DIVERSITY AND DOMINANCE

MONGOL POLITICS, MONGOL WOMEN

*W*omen in nomadic societies often enjoy more freedom *and wield greater influence than women in villages and towns. The wives or mothers of Mongol rulers traditionally managed state affairs during the interregnum between a ruler's death and the selection of a successor. Princes and heads of ministries treated such regents with great deference and obeyed their commands without question. Since a female regent could not herself succeed to the position of khan, her political machinations usually focused on gaining the succession for a son or other male relative.*

The History of the World-Conqueror *by the Iranian historian 'Ata-Malik Juvaini, elegantly written in Persian during the 1250s, combines a glorification of the Mongol rulers with an unflinching picture of the cruelties and devastation inflicted by their conquests. As a Muslim, he explains these events as God's punishment for Muslim sins. But this religious viewpoint does not detract from his frank depiction of the instruments of Mongol domination and the fate of those who tried to resist.*

When [Qa'an, i.e., Ögödei, Genghis Khan's son and successor] was on his hunting ground someone brought him two or three water-melons. None of his attendants had any [money] or garments available, but Möge Khatun [his wife], who was present, had two pearls in her ears like the two bright stars of the Lesser Bear when rendered auspicious by conjunction with the radiant moon. Qa'an ordered these pearls to be given to the man. But as they were very precious she said: "This man does not know their worth and value: it is like giving saffron to a donkey. If he is commanded to come to the *ordu* [residence] tomorrow, he will there receive [money] and clothing." "He is a poor man," said Qa'an, "and cannot bear to wait until tomorrow. And whither should these pearls go? They too will return to us in the end. . . ."

At Qa'an's command she gave the pearls to the poor man, and he went away rejoicing and sold them for a small sum, round about two thousand dinars [Note: this is actually a very large sum]. The buyer was very pleased and thought to himself: "I have acquired two fine jewels fit for a present to the Emperor. He is rarely brought such gifts as these." He ac-

cordingly took the pearls to the Emperor, and at that time Möge Khatun was with him. Qa'an took the pearls and said: "Did we not say they would come back to us?" . . . And he distinguished the bearer with all kinds of favours. . . .

When the decree of God Almighty had been executed and the Monarch of the World . . . . Qa'an had passed away, Güyük, his eldest son, had not returned from the campaign against the Qifchaq, and therefore in accordance with precedent the dispatch of orders and the assembling of the people took place at the door of the *ordu*, or palace of his wife, Möge Khatun, who, in accordance with the Mongol custom, had come to him from his father, Chinggiz-Khan. But since Töregene Khatun was the mother of his eldest sons and was moreover shrewder and more sagacious than Möge Khatun, she sent messages to the princes, i.e. the brothers and nephews of the Qa'an, and told them of what had happened and of the death of Qa'an, and said that until a Khan was appointed by agreement someone would have to be ruler and leader in order that the business of state might not be neglected nor the affairs of the commonweal thrown into confusion; in order, too, that the army and the court might be kept under control and the interests of the people protected.

Chaghatai [another of Genghis's sons] and the other princes sent representatives to say that Töregene Khatun was the mother of the princes who had a right to the Khanate; therefore, until a *quriltai* [family council] was held, it was she that should direct the affairs of the state, and the old ministers should remain in the service of the Court, so that the old and new *yasas* [imperial decrees] might not be changed from what was the law.

Now Töregene Khatun was a very shrewd and capable woman, and her position was greatly strengthened by this unity and concord. And when Möge Khatun shortly followed in the wake of Qa'an [i.e., died], by means of finesse and cunning she obtained control of all the affairs of state and won over the hearts of her relatives by all kind of favours and kindnesses and by the sending of gifts and presents. And for the most part strangers and kindred, family and army inclined towards her, and submitted themselves obediently and gladly to her commands and prohibitions, and came under her sway. . . .

And when Güyük came to his mother, he took no part in affairs of state, and Töregene Khatun still executed the decrees of the Empire although the Khanate was settled upon her son. But when two or three months had passed and the son was somewhat estranged from his mother on account of Fatima [see below], the decree of God the Almighty and Glorious was fulfilled and Töregene passed away. . . .

And at that time there was a woman called Fatima, who had acquired great influence in the service of Töregene Khatun and to whose counsel and capability were entrusted all affairs of state. . . .

At the time of the capture of the place [Mashhad, Iran] in which there lies the Holy Shrine of 'Ali ar-Riza [the eighth Shi'ite Imam], she was carried off into captivity. It so chanced she came to Qara-Qorum [Karakorum], where she was a procuress in the market; and in the arts of shrewdness and cunning the wily Delilah could have been her pupil. During the reign of Qa'an she had constant access to the *ordu* of Töregene Khatun; and when times changed and Chinqai [a high official] withdrew from the scene, she enjoyed even greater favour, and her influence became paramount; so that she became the sharer of intimate confidences and the depository of hidden secrets, and the ministers were debarred from executing business, and she was free to issue commands and prohibitions. And from every side the grandees sought her protection, especially the grandees of Khorasan [where Mashhad is located]. And there also came to her certain of the *sayyids* [i.e., descendants of Muhammad] of the Holy Shrine [the tomb of 'Ali ar-Riza], for she claimed to be of the race of the great *sayyids*.

When Güyük succeeded to the Khanate, a certain native of Samarqand, who was said to be an 'Alid [i.e., descendant of Muhammad], one Shira . . . hinted that Fatima had bewitched Köten [another of Töregene Khatun's sons], which was why he was so indisposed. When Köten returned, the malady from which he was suffering grew worse, and he sent a messenger to his brother Güyük to say that he had been attacked by that illness because of Fatima's magic and that if anything happened to him Güyük should seek retribution from her. Following on this message there came tidings of Köten's death. Chinqai, who was now a person of authority, reminded Güyük of the message, and he sent an envoy to his mother to fetch Fatima. His mother refused to let her go saying that she would bring her herself. He sent again several times, and each time she refused him in a different way. As a result his relations with his mother became very bad, and he sent the man from Samarqand with instructions to bring Fatima by force if his mother should still delay in sending her or find some reason for refusing. It being no longer possible to excuse herself, she agreed to send Fatima; and shortly afterwards she passed away. Fatima was brought face to face with Güyük, and was kept naked, and in bonds, and hungry and thirsty for many days and nights; she was plied with all manner of violence, severity, harshness and intimidation; and at last she confessed to the calumny of the slanderous talebearer and avowed her falseness . . . She was rolled up in a sheet of felt and thrown into the river.

And everyone who was connected with her perished also. And messengers were sent to fetch certain persons who had come from the Shrine and claimed to be related to her; and they suffered many annoyances.

This was the year in which Güyük Khan went to join his father, and it was then that 'Ali Khoja of Emil accused Shira of the same crime, namely of bewitching Khoja. He was cast into bonds and chains and remained imprisoned for nearly two years, during which time by reason of all manner of questioning and punishment he despaired of the pleasure of life. And when he recognized and knew of a certainty that this was [his] punishment he resigned himself to death and surrendering his body to the will of Fate and Destiny confessed to a crime which he had not committed. He too was cast into the river, and his wives and children were put to the sword. . . .

[I]n that same year, in a happy and auspicious hour, the Khanate had been settled upon Mengü Qa'an. . . . And when Khoja was brought to the Qa'an, a messenger was sent to 'Ali Khoja, who was one of his courtiers. Some other person brought the same accusation against him, and Mengü-Qa'an ordered him to be beaten from the left and the right until all his limbs were crushed; and so he died. And his wives and children were cast into the baseness of slavery and disgraced and humiliated.

And it is not hidden from the wise and intelligent man, who looks at these matters in the light of understanding and reflects and ponders on them, that the end of treachery and the conclusion of deceit, which spring from evil ways and wicked pretensions, is shameful and the termination thereof unlucky. . . . God preserve us from the like positions and from trespassing into the region of deliberate offenses!

QUESTIONS FOR ANALYSIS

1. How do the stories of Töregene Khatun and Fatima differ in their presentation of female roles?

2. What does the passage indicate concerning the respect of the Mongols for women?

3. What does Güyük's refusal to take over the affairs of state while his mother is still alive imply?

Source: Reprinted by permission of the publisher from 'Ala-ad-Din 'Ata-Malik Juvaini, *The History of the World-Conqueror*, vol. 1, trans. John Andrew Boyle (Cambridge, MA: Harvard University Press, 1958), 211–212, 239–248. Copyright © 1958 by Manchester University Press.

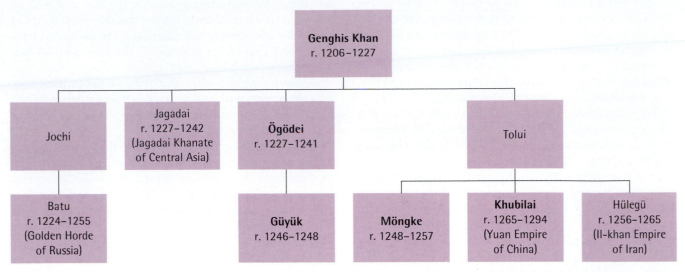

Figure 13.1   Mongol Rulers, 1206–1260   The names of the Great Khans are shown in bold type. Those who founded the regional khanates are listed with their dates of rule.

assault China. He destroyed the Tanggut and then the Jin and put their territories under Mongol governors. In 1236 Genghis's grandson Batu° (d. 1255) attacked Russian territories, took control of all the towns along the Volga° River, and within five years conquered Kievan Russia, Moscow, Poland, and Hungary. Europe would have suffered grave damage in 1241 had not the death of Ögödei compelled the Mongol forces to suspend their campaign. With Genghis's grandson Güyük° installed as the new Great Khan, the conquests resumed. By 1234 the Mongols controlled most of northern China and were threatening the Southern Song. In the Middle East they sacked Baghdad in 1258 and executed the last Abbasid caliph (see Chapter 9).

Although the Mongols' original objective may have been tribute, the scale and success of the conquests created a new historical situation. Ögödei unquestionably sought territorial rule. Between 1240 and 1260 his imperial capital at Karakorum° attracted merchants, ambassadors, missionaries, and adventurers from all over Eurasia. A European who visited in 1246 found the city isolated but well populated and cosmopolitan.

The Mongol Empire remained united until about 1265, as the Great Khan in Mongolia exercised authority over the khans of the Golden Horde in Russia, the khans of the Jagadai domains in Central Asia, and the Il-khans

in Iran (see Map 13.1). After Ögödei's death in 1241 family unity began to unravel. When Khubilai° declared himself Great Khan in 1265, the descendants of Jagadai and other branches of the family refused to accept him. The destruction of Karakorum in the ensuing fighting contributed to Khubilai's transferring his court to the old Jin capital that is now Beijing. In 1271 he declared himself founder of the **Yuan Empire.**

Jagadai's descendants, who continued to dominate Central Asia, had much closer relations with Turkic-speaking nomads than did their kinsmen farther east. This, plus a continuing hatred of Khubilai and the Yuan, contributed to the strengthening of Central Asia as an independent Mongol center and to the adoption of Islam in the western territories.

After the Yuan destroyed the Southern Song (see Chapter 11) in 1279, Mongol troops crossed south of the Red River and attacked Annam—now northern Vietnam. They occupied Hanoi three times and then withdrew after arranging for the payment of tribute. In 1283 Khubilai's forces invaded Champa in what is now southern Vietnam and made it a tribute nation as well. A plan to invade Java by sea failed, as did two invasions of Japan in 1274 and 1281.

In tactical terms, the Mongols did not usually outnumber their enemies, but like all steppe nomads for many centuries, they displayed extraordinary abilities

Batu (BAH-too)   **Volga** (VOHL-gah)   **Güyük** (gi-yik)
Karakorum (kah-rah-KOR-um)

Khubilai (KOO-bih-lie)

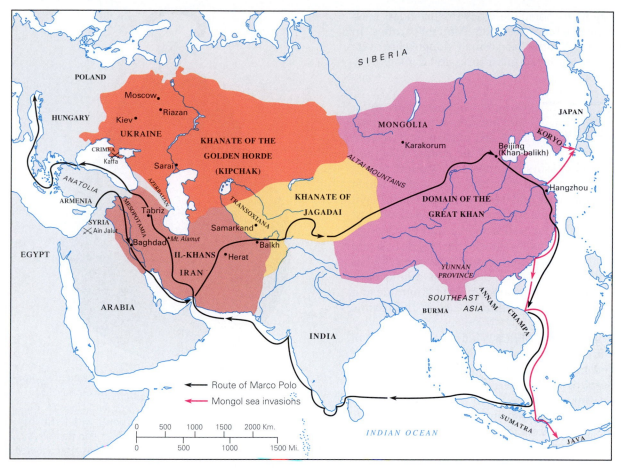

Map 13.1   The Mongol Domains in Eurasia in 1300   After the death of Genghis Khan in 1227, his empire was divided among his sons and grandsons. Son Ögödei succeeded Genghis as Great Khan. Grandson Khubilai expanded the domain of the Great Khan into southern China by 1279. Grandson Hülegü was the first Il-khan in the Middle East. Grandson Batu founded the Khanate of the Golden Horde in southern Russia. Son Jagadai ruled the Jagadai Khanate in Central Asia.

on horseback and utilized superior bows. The Central Asian bow, made strong by laminated layers of wood, leather, and bone, could shoot one-third farther (and was significantly more difficult to pull) than the bows used by their enemies in the settled lands.

Mounted Mongol archers rarely expended all of the five dozen or more arrows they carried in their quivers. As the battle opened, they shot arrows from a distance to decimate enemy marksmen. Then they galloped against the enemy's infantry to fight with sword, lance, javelin, and mace. The Mongol cavalry met its match only at the Battle of Ain Jalut°, where it confronted Mamluk forces whose war techniques shared some of the same traditions (see Chapter 9).

To penetrate fortifications, the Mongols fired flaming arrows and hurled enormous projectiles—sometimes flaming—from catapults. The first Mongol catapults, built on Chinese models, transported easily but had short range and poor accuracy. During western campaigns in Central Asia, the Mongols encountered a catapult design that was half again as powerful as the Chinese model. They used this improved weapon against the cities of Iran and Iraq.

Cities that resisted Mongol attack faced mass slaughter or starvation under siege. Timely surrender brought food, shelter, and protection. The bloodletting the Mongols inflicted on cities such as Balkh° (in present-day northern Afghanistan) spread terror and made it easier

Ain Jalut (ine jah-LOOT)

Balkh (bahlk)

for the Mongols to persuade cities to surrender. Each conquered area helped swell the "Mongol" armies. In campaigns in the Middle East a small Mongol elite oversaw armies of recently recruited Turks and Iranians.

Overland Trade and the Plague

Commercial integration under Mongol rule strongly affected both the eastern and western wings of the empire. Like their aristocratic predecessors in Inner Asia, Mongol nobles had the exclusive right to wear silk, almost all of which came from China. Trade under Mongol dominion brought new styles and huge quantities of silk westward, not just for clothing but also for wall hangings and furnishings. Abundant silk fed the luxury trade in the Middle East and Europe. Artistic motifs from Japan and Tibet reached as far as England and Morocco. Porcelain was another eastern luxury product that became important in trade and strongly influenced later cultural tastes in the Islamic world.

Traders from all over Eurasia enjoyed the benefits of Mongol control. Merchants encountered ambassadors, scholars, and missionaries over the long routes to the Mongol courts. Some of the resulting travel literature, like the account of the Venetian Marco Polo° (1254–1324), freely mixed the fantastic with the factual. Stories of fantastic wealth stimulated a European ambition to find easier routes to Asia.

Exchange also held great dangers. In southwestern China **bubonic plague** had festered in Yunnan province since the early Tang period. In the mid-thirteenth century Mongol troops established a garrison in Yunnan whose military and supply traffic provided the means for flea-infested rats to carry the plague into central China, northwestern China, and Central Asia. Marmots and other desert rodents along the routes became infected and passed the disease to dogs and people. The caravan traffic infected the oasis towns. The plague incapacitated the Mongol army during their assault on the city of Kaffa° in Crimea° in 1346. They withdrew, but the plague remained. From Kaffa rats infected by fleas reached Europe and Egypt by ship (see Chapter 15).

Typhus, influenza, and smallpox traveled with the plague. The combination of these and other diseases created what is often called the "great pandemic" of 1347–1352 and spread devastation far in excess of what the Mongols inflicted in war. Peace and trade, not conquest, gave rise to the great pandemic.

Marco Polo (mar-koe POE-loe) **Kaffa** (KAH-fah)
Crimea (cry-MEE-ah)

Passport The Mongol Empire facilitated the movement of products, merchants, and diplomats over long distances. Travelers frequently encountered new languages, laws, and customs. The *paisa* (from a Chinese word for "card" or "sign"), with its inscription in Mongolian, proclaimed that the traveler had the ruler's permission to travel through the region. Europeans later adopted the practice, thus making the *paisa* the ancestor of modern passports. (The Metropolitan Museum of Art, purchase bequest of Dorothy Graham Bennett, 1993 [1993.256]. Photograph 1997 The Metropolitan Museum of Art)

THE MONGOLS AND ISLAM, 1260–1500

From the perspective of Mongol imperial history, the issue of which branches of the family espoused Islam and which did not mostly concerns their political rivalries and their respective quests for allies. From the standpoint of the history of Islam, however, recovery from the political, religious, and physical devastation that culminated in the destruction of the Abbasid caliphate in Baghdad in 1258 attests to the vitality of the faith and the ability of Muslims to overcome adversity. Within fifty years of its darkest hour, Islam had reemerged as a potent ideological and political force.

Mongol Rivalry

By 1260 the **Il-khan**° state, established by Genghis's grandson Hülegü, controlled parts of Armenia and all of Azerbaijan, Mesopotamia, and Iran. The Mongols who had conquered southern Russia settled north of the Caspian Sea and established the capital of their Khanate of the **Golden Horde** (also called the Kipchak° Khanate) at Sarai° on the Volga River. There they established dominance over the indigenous Muslim Turkic population, both settled and pastoral.

Some members of the Mongol imperial family had professed Islam before the Mongol assault on the Middle East, and Turkic Muslims had served the family in various capacities. Indeed, Hülegü himself, though a Buddhist, had a trusted Shi'ite adviser and granted privileges to the Shi'ites. As a whole, however, the Mongols under Hülegü's command came only slowly to Islam.

The passage of time did little to reconcile Islamic doctrines with Mongol ways. Muslims abhorred the Mongols' worship of idols, a fundamental part of shamanism. Furthermore, Mongol law specified slaughtering animals without spilling blood, which involved opening the chest and stopping the heart. This horrified Muslims, who were forbidden to consume blood and slaughtered animals by slitting their throats and draining the blood.

Islam became a point of inter-Mongol tension when Batu's successor as leader of the Golden Horde declared himself a Muslim, swore to avenge the murder of the Abbasid caliph, and laid claim to the Caucasus—the region between the Black and Caspian Seas—which the Il-khans also claimed (see Map 13.2).

Some European leaders believed that if they helped the non-Muslim Il-khans repel the Golden Horde from the Caucasus, the Il-khans would help them relieve Muslim pressure on the crusader states in Syria, Lebanon, and Palestine (see Chapter 9). This resulted in a brief correspondence between the Il-khan court and Pope Nicholas IV (r. 1288–1292) and a diplomatic mission that sent two Christian Turks to western Europe as Il-khan ambassadors in the late 1200s. Many Christian crusaders enlisted in the Il-khan effort, but the pope later excommunicated some for doing so.

The Golden Horde responded by seeking an alliance with the Muslim Mamluks in Egypt (see Chapter 9) against both the crusaders and the Il-khans. These complicated efforts effectively extended the life of the crusader states; the Mamluks did not finish ejecting the crusaders until the fifteenth century.

Before the Europeans' diplomatic efforts could produce a formal alliance, however, a new Il-khan ruler, Ghazan° (1271–1304), declared himself a Muslim in 1295. Conflicting indications of Sunni and Shi'ite affiliation on such things as coins indicate that the Il-khans did not pay too much attention to theological matters. Nor is it clear whether the many Muslim Turkic nomads who served alongside the Mongols in the army were Shi'ite or Sunni.

Islam and the State

Like the Turks before them (see Chapter 9), the Il-khans gradually came to appreciate the traditional urban culture of the Muslim territories they ruled. Though nomads continued to serve in their armies, the Il-khans used tax farming, a fiscal method developed earlier in the Middle East, to extract maximum wealth from their domain. The government sold tax-collecting contracts to small partnerships, mostly consisting of merchants who might also work together to finance caravans, small industries, or military expeditions. The corporations that offered to collect the most revenue for the government won the contracts. They could use whatever methods they chose and could keep anything over the contracted amount.

Initially, the cost of collecting taxes fell, but over the long term, the exorbitant rates the tax farmers charged drove many landowners into debt and servitude. Agricultural productivity declined. The government had difficulty procuring supplies for the soldiers and resorted to taking land to grow its own grain. Like land held by religious trusts, this land paid no taxes. Thus the tax base shrank even as the demands of the army and the Mongol nobility continued to grow.

Ghazan faced many economic problems. Citing the humane values of Islam, he promised to reduce taxes, but the need for revenues kept the decrease from being permanent. He also witnessed the failure of a predecessor's experiment with the Chinese practice of using paper money. Having no previous exposure to paper money, the Il-khan's subjects responded negatively. The economy quickly sank into a depression that lasted beyond the end of the Il-khan state in 1349. High taxes caused widespread popular unrest and resentment. Mongol nobles competed fiercely among themselves for the decreasing revenues, and fighting among Mongol factions destabilized the government.

In the mid-fourteenth century Mongols from the Golden Horde moved through the Caucasus into the

---

Il-khan (IL-con)   **Kipchak** (KIP-chahk)   **Sarai** (sah-RYE)

Ghazan (haz-ZAHN)

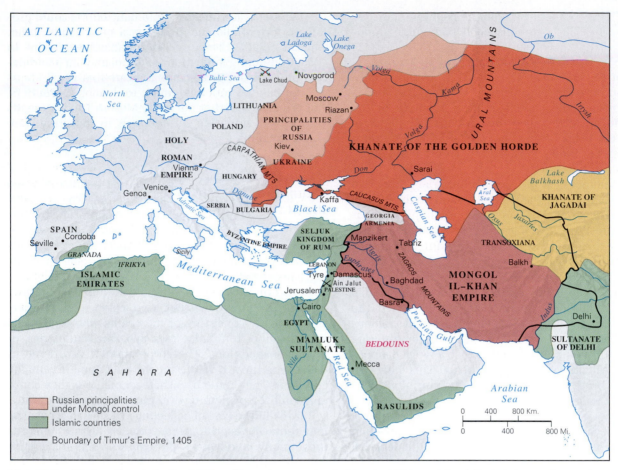

Map 13.2 Western Eurasia in the 1300s Ghazan's conversion to Islam in 1295 upset the delicate balance of power in Mongol domains. European leaders abandoned their hope of finding an Il-khan ally against the Muslim defenders in Palestine, while an alliance between the Mamluks and the Golden Horde kept the Il-khans from advancing west. This helped the Europeans retain their lands in Palestine and Syria.

western regions of the Il-khan Empire and then into the Il-khan's central territory, Azerbaijan, briefly occupying its major cities. At the same time a new power was emerging to the east, in the Central Asian Khanate of Jagadai (see Map 13.1). The leader **Timur°,** known to Europeans as Tamerlane, skillfully maneuvered himself into command of the Jagadai forces and launched campaigns into western Eurasia, apparently seeing himself as a new Genghis Khan. By ethnic background he was a Turk with only an in-law relationship to the family of the Mongol conqueror. This prevented him from assuming the title *khan,* but not from sacking the Muslim sultanate of Delhi in northern India in 1398 or defeating

the sultan of the rising Ottoman Empire in Anatolia in 1402. By that time he had subdued much of the Middle East, and he was reportedly preparing to march on China when he died in 1405. The Timurids (descendants of Timur) could not hold the empire together, but they laid the groundwork for the establishment in India of a Muslim Mongol-Turkic regime, the Mughals, in the sixteenth century.

Culture and Science in Islamic Eurasia

The Il-khans of Iran and Timurids of Central Asia presided over a brilliant cultural flowering in Iran, Afghanistan, and Central Asia based on the shar-

---

Timur (tem-EER)

Tomb of Timur in Samarqand   The turquoise tiles that cover the dome are typical of Timurid architectural decoration. Timur's family ornamented his capital with an enormous mosque, three large religious colleges facing one another on three sides of an open plaza, and a lane of brilliantly tiled Timurid family tombs in the midst of a cemetery. Timur brought craftsmen to Samarqand from the lands he conquered to build these magnificent structures.   (Sassoon/Robert Harding Picture Library)

The historian Juvaini° (d. 1283), the literary figure who noted Genghis Khan's deathbed speech, came from the city of Balkh, which the Mongols had devastated in 1221. His family switched their allegiance to the Mongols, and both Juvaini and his older brother assumed high government posts. The Il-khan Hülegü, seeking to immortalize and justify the Mongol conquest of the Middle East, enthusiastically supported Juvaini's writing. This resulted in the first comprehensive narrative of the rise of the Mongols under Genghis Khan.

Juvaini combined a florid style with historical objectivity—he often criticized the Mongols—and served as an inspiration to **Rashid al-Din°,** Ghazan's prime minister, when he attempted the first history of the world. Rashid al-Din's work included the earliest known general history of Europe, derived from conversations with European monks, and a detailed description of China based on information from an important Chinese Muslim official stationed in Iran. The miniature paintings that accompanied some copies of Rashid al-Din's work included depictions of European and Chinese people and events and reflected the artistic traditions of both cultures. The Chinese techniques of composition helped inaugurate the greatest period of Islamic miniature painting under the Timurids.

Rashid al-Din traveled widely and collaborated with administrators from other parts of the far-flung Mongol dominions. His idea that government should be in accord with the moral principles of the majority of the population buttressed Ghazan's adherence to Islam. Administratively, however, Ghazan did not restrict himself to Muslim precedents but employed financial and monetary techniques that roughly resembled those in use in Russia and China.

Under the Timurids, the tradition of the Il-khan historians continued. After conquering Damascus, Timur himself met there with the greatest historian of the age, Ibn Khaldun° (1332–1406), a Tunisian. In a scene reminiscent of Ghazan's answering Rashid al-Din's questions on the history of the Mongols, Timur and Ibn Khaldun exchanged historical, philosophical, and geographical viewpoints. Like Genghis, Timur saw himself as a world conqueror. At their capitals of Samarkand and Herat (in western Afghanistan), later Timurid rulers sponsored historical writing in both Persian and Turkish.

A Shi'ite scholar named **Nasir al-Din Tusi°** represents the beginning of Mongol interest in the scientific traditions of the Muslim lands. Nasir al-Din may have

ing of artistic trends, administrative practices, and political ideas between Iran and China, the dominant urban civilizations at opposite ends of the Silk Road. The dominant cultural tendencies of the Il-khan and Timurid periods are Muslim, however. Although Timur died before he could reunite Iran and China, his forcible concentration of Middle Eastern scholars, artists, and craftsmen in his capital, Samarkand, fostered advancement in some specific activities under his descendants.

Juvaini (joo-VINE-nee)   **Rashid al-Din** (ra-SHEED ad-DEEN)
Ibn Khaldun (ee-bin hal-DOON)
Nasir al-Din Tusi (nah-SEER ad-DEEN TOO-si)

Astronomy and Engineering   Observational astronomy went hand in hand not only with mathematics and calendrical science but also with engineering as the construction of platforms, instruments for celestial measurement, and armillary spheres became more sophisticated. This manual in Persian, completed in the 1500s but illustrating activities of the Il-khan period, illustrates the use of a plumb line with an enormous armillary sphere.   (Istanbul University Library)

he laid new foundations for algebra and trigonometry. Some followers working at an observatory built for Nasir al-Din at Maragheh°, near the Il-khan capital of Tabriz, used the new mathematical techniques to solve a fundamental problem in classical cosmology.

Islamic scholars had preserved and elaborated on the insights of the Greeks in astronomy and mathematics and adopted the cosmological model of Ptolemy°, which assumed a universe with the earth at its center surrounded by the sun, moon, and planets traveling in concentric circular orbits. However, the motions of these orbiting bodies did not coincide with predictions based on circular orbits. Astronomers and mathematicians had long sought a mathematical explanation for the movements that they observed.

Nasir al-Din proposed a model based on the idea of small circles rotating within a large circle. One of his students reconciled this model with the ancient Greek idea of epicycles (small circles rotating around a point on a larger circle) to explain the movement of the moon around the earth. The mathematical tables and geometric models devised by this student somehow became known to Nicholas Copernicus (1473–1543), a Polish monk and astronomer. Copernicus adopted the lunar model as his own, virtually without revision. He then proposed the model of lunar movement developed under the Il-khans as the proper model for planetary movement as well—but with the planets circling the sun.

Sponsorship of observational astronomy and the making of calendars had engaged the interest of earlier Central Asian rulers, particularly the Uighurs° and the Seljuks. Under the Il-khans, the astronomers of Maragheh excelled in predicting lunar and solar eclipses. Astrolabes, armillary spheres, three-dimensional quadrants, and other instruments acquired new precision.

The remarkably accurate eclipse predictions and tables prepared by Il-khan and Timurid astronomers reached the hostile Mamluk lands in Arabic translation. Byzantine monks took them to Constantinople and translated them into Greek, while Christian scholars working in Muslim Spain translated them into Latin. In India the sultan of Delhi ordered them translated into Sanskrit. The Great Khan Khubilai (see below) summoned a team of Iranians to Beijing to build an observatory for him. Timur's grandson Ulugh Beg° (1394–1449), who mixed science and rule, constructed a great observatory in Samarkand and actively participated in compiling observational tables that were later translated into Latin and used by European astronomers.

joined the entourage of Hülegü during a campaign in 1256 against the Assassins, a Shi'ite religious sect derived from the Fatimid dynasty in Egypt and at odds with his more mainstream Shi'ite views (see Chapter 9). Nasir al-Din wrote on history, poetry, ethics, and religion, but made his most outstanding contributions in mathematics and cosmology. Following Omar Khayyam° (1038?–1131), a poet and mathematician of the Seljuk° period,

---

Omar Khayyam (oh-mar kie-YAM)   Seljuk (SEL-jook)

Maragheh (mah-RAH-gah)   Ptolemy (TOHL-uh-mee)
Uigur (WEE-ger)   Ulugh Beg (oo-loog bek)

A further advance made under Ulugh Beg came from the mathematician Ghiyas al-Din Jamshid al-Kashi°, who noted that Chinese astronomers had long used one ten-thousandth of a day as a unit in calculating the occurrence of a new moon. This seems to have inspired him to employ decimal fractions, by which quantities less than one could be represented by a marker to show place. Al-Kashi's proposed value for *pi* (π) was far more precise than any previously calculated. This innovation arrived in Europe by way of Constantinople, where a Greek translation of al-Kashi's work appeared in the fifteenth century.

REGIONAL RESPONSES IN WESTERN EURASIA

Safe, reliable overland trade throughout Eurasia benefited Mongol ruling centers and commercial cities along the length of the Silk Road. But the countryside, ravaged by conquest, sporadically continuing violence, and heavy taxes, suffered terribly. As Mongol control weakened, regional forces in Russia, eastern Europe, and Anatolia reasserted themselves. All were influenced by Mongol predecessors, and all had to respond to the social and economic changes of the Mongol era. Sometimes this meant collaborating with the Mongols. At other times it meant using local ethnic or religious traditions to resist or roll back Mongol influence.

Russia and Rule from Afar

The Golden Horde established by Genghis's grandson Batu after his defeat of a combined Russian and Kipchak (a Turkic people) army in 1223 started as a unified state but gradually lost its unity as some districts crystallized into smaller khanates. The White Horde, for instance, came to rule much of southeastern Russia in the fifteenth century, and the Crimean khanate on the northern shore of the Black Sea succumbed to Russian invasion only in 1783.

Trade routes east and west across the steppe and north and south along the rivers of Russia and Ukraine conferred importance on certain trading entrepôts, as they had under Kievan Russia (see Chapter 10). The Mongols of the Golden Horde settled at (Old) Sarai, just north of where the Volga flows into the Caspian Sea (see Map 13.1). They ruled their Russian domains to the north and east from afar. To facilitate their control, they granted privileges to the Orthodox Church, which then helped reconcile the Russian people to their distant masters.

The politics of language played a role in subsequent history. Old Church Slavonic, an ecclesiastical language, revived; but Russian steadily acquired greater importance and eventually became the dominant written language. Russian scholars shunned Byzantine Greek, previously the main written tongue, even after the Golden Horde permitted renewed contacts with Constantinople. The Golden Horde enlisted Russian princes to act as their agents, primarily as tax collectors and census takers. Some had to visit the court of the Great Khans at Karakorum to secure the documents upon which their authority was based.

The flow of silver and gold into Mongol hands starved the local economy of precious metal. Like the Il-khans, the khans of the Golden Horde attempted to introduce paper money as a response to the currency shortage. This had little effect in a largely nonmonetary economy, but the experiment left such a vivid memory that the Russian word for money (*denga*°) comes from the Mongolian word for the stamp (*tamga*°) used to create paper currency. But commerce depended more on direct exchange of goods than on currency transactions.

Alexander Nevskii° (ca. 1220–1263), the prince of Novgorod, persuaded some fellow princes to submit to the Mongols. In return, the Mongols favored both Novgorod and the emerging town of Moscow, ruled by Alexander's son Daniel. These towns eclipsed devastated Kiev as political, cultural, and economic centers. This, in turn, drew people northward to open new agricultural land far from the Mongol steppe lands to the southwest. Decentralization continued in the 1300s, with Moscow only very gradually becoming Russia's dominant political center (see Map 13.2).

Russia was deeply affected by the Mongol presence. Bubonic plague became endemic among rodents in the Crimea. Ukraine°, a fertile and well-populated region in the late Kievan period (1000–1230), suffered severe population loss as Mongol armies passed through on campaigns against eastern Europe and raided villages to collect taxes.

Historians debate the Mongol impact on Russia. Some see the destructiveness of the Mongol conquests and the subsequent domination of the khans as isolating

---

Ghiyas al-Din Jamshid al-Kashi (gee-YASS ad-DIN jam-SHEED al-KAH-shee)

denga (DENG-ah)   *tamga* (TAHM-gah)   **Nevskii** (nih-EFF-skee)
Ukraine (you-CRANE)

Transformation of the Kremlin   Like other northern Europeans, the Russians preferred to build in wood, which was easy to handle and comfortable to live in. But they fortified important political centers with stone ramparts. In the 1300s, the city of Moscow emerged as a new capital, and its old wooden palace, the Kremlin, was gradually transformed into a stone structure.   (Novosti)

Russia and parts of eastern Europe from developments to the west. These historians refer to the "Mongol yoke" and hypothesize a sluggish economy and dormant culture under the Mongols.

Others point out that Kiev declined economically well before the Mongols struck and that the Kievan princes had already ceased to mint coins. Moreover, the Russian territories regularly paid their heavy taxes in silver. These payments indicate both economic surpluses and an ability to convert goods into cash. The burdensome taxes stemmed less from the Mongols than from their tax collectors, Russian princes who often exempted their own lands and shifted the load to the peasants.

As for Russia's cultural isolation, skeptics observe that before the Mongol invasion, the powerful and constructive role played by the Orthodox Church oriented Russia primarily toward Byzantium (see Chapter 10). This situation discouraged but did not eliminate contacts with western Europe, which probably would have become stronger after the fall of Constantinople to the Ottomans in 1453 regardless of Mongol influence.

The traditional structure of local government survived Mongol rule, as did the Russian princely families, who continued to battle among themselves for dominance. The Mongols merely added a new player to those struggles.

Ivan° III, the prince of Moscow (r. 1462–1505), established himself as an autocratic ruler in the late 1400s. Before Ivan, the title **tsar** (from "caesar"), of Byzantine origin, applied only to foreign rulers, whether the emperors of Byzantium or the Turkic khans of the steppe. Ivan's use of the title, which began early in his reign, probably represents an effort to establish a basis for legitimate rule with the decline of the Golden Horde and disappearance of the Byzantine Empire.

New States in Eastern Europe and Anatolia

The interplay between religion, political maneuvering, and new expressions of local identity affected Anatolia and parts of Europe confronted with the Mongol challenge as well. Raised in Sicily, the Holy Roman Emperor Frederick II (r. 1212–1250) appreciated Muslim culture and did not recoil from negotiating with Muslim rulers. When the pope threatened to excommunicate him unless he went on a crusade, Frederick nominally regained Jerusalem through a flimsy treaty with the Mamluk sultan in Egypt. This did not satisfy the pope, and the preoccupation of both pope and emperor with their quarrel left Hungary, Poland, and other parts of eastern Europe to deal with the Mongol onslaught on their own. Many princes capitulated and went to (Old) Sarai to offer their submission of Batu.

The Teutonic° Knights, however, resisted. Like the Knights Templar in the Middle East (see Chapter 9), the German-speaking Teutonic Knights had a crusading goal: to Christianize the Slavic and Kipchak populations of northern Europe, whose territories they colonized with thousands of German-speaking settlers. Having an interest in protecting Slav territory from German expansion, Alexander Nevskii cooperated in the Mongol campaigns against the Teutonic Knights and their Finnish allies. The latter suffered a catastrophic setback in 1242,

Ivan (ee-VAHN)   **Teutonic** (two-TOHN-ik)

when many broke through ice on Lake Chud (see Map 13.2) and drowned. This destroyed the power of the Knights, and the northern Crusades virtually ceased.

The "Mongol" armies encountered by the Europeans were barely Mongol other than in most command positions. Mongol recruitment and conscription created an international force of Mongols, Turks, Chinese, Iranians, a few Europeans, and at least one Englishman, who had gone to the Middle East as a crusader but joined the Mongols and served in Hungary.

Initial wild theories describing the Mongols as coming from Hell or from the caves where Alexander the Great confined the monsters of antiquity gave way to more sophisticated understanding as European embassies to the Golden Horde, the Il-khan, and the Great Khan in Mongolia reported on Mongol trade routes and the internal structure of Mongol rule. In some quarters terror gave way to awe and even idealization of Mongol wealth and power. Europeans learned about diplomatic passports, coal mining, movable type, high-temperature metallurgy, higher mathematics, gunpowder, and, in the fourteenth century, the casting and use of bronze cannon. Yet with the outbreak of bubonic plague in the late 1340s (see Chapter 15), the memory of Mongol terror helped ignite religious speculation that God might be punishing the Christians of eastern and central Europe with a series of tribulations.

In the fourteenth century several regions, most notably Lithuania° (see Map 13.2), escaped the Mongol grip. When Russia fell to the Mongols and eastern Europe was first invaded, Lithuania had experienced an unprecedented centralization and military strengthening. Like Alexander Nevskii, the Lithuanian leaders maintained their independence by cooperating with the Mongols. In the late 1300s Lithuania capitalized on its privileged position to dominate its neighbors—particularly Poland—and ended the Teutonic Knights' hope of regaining power.

In the Balkans independent and well-organized kingdoms separated themselves from the chaos of the Byzantine Empire and thrived amidst the political uncertainties of the Mongol period. The Serbian king Stephen Dushan (ca. 1308–1355) proved to be the most effective leader. Seizing power from his father in 1331, he took advantage of Byzantine weakness to raise the archbishop of Serbia to the rank of an independent patriarch. In 1346 the patriarch crowned him "tsar and autocrat of the Serbs, Greeks, Bulgarians, and Albanians," a title that fairly represents the wide extent of his rule. As in the case of Timur, however, his kingdom declined after his death

---

Lithuania (lith-oo-WAY-nee-ah)

in 1355 and disappeared entirely after a defeat by the Ottomans at the battle of Kosovo in 1389.

The Turkic nomads from whom the rulers of the **Ottoman Empire** descended had come to Anatolia in the same wave of Turkic migrations as the Seljuks (see Chapter 9). Though centered in Iran and preoccupied with quarrels with the Golden Horde, the Il-khans exerted great influence in eastern Anatolia. However, a number of small Turkic principalities emerged farther to the west. The Ottoman principality was situated in the northwest, close to the Sea of Marmara. This not only put them in a position to cross into Europe and take part in the internal dynastic struggles of the declining Byzantine state, but it also attracted Muslim religious warriors who wished to extend the frontiers of Islam in battle with the Christians. Though the Ottoman sultan suffered defeat at the hands of Timur in 1402, this was only a temporary setback. In 1453 Sultan Mehmet II captured Constantinople and brought the Byzantine Empire to an end.

The Ottoman sultans, like the rulers of Russia, Lithuania, and Serbia, seized the political opportunity that arose with the decay of Mongol power. The new and powerful states they created put strong emphasis on religious and linguistic identity, factors that the Mongols themselves did not stress. As we shall see, Mongol rule stimulated similar reactions in the lands of east and southeast Asia.

MONGOL DOMINATION IN CHINA, 1271–1368

After the Mongols conquered northern China in the 1230s, Great Khan Ögödei told a newly recruited Confucian adviser that he planned to turn the heavily populated North China Plain into a pasture for livestock. The adviser reacted calmly but argued that taxing the cities and villages would bring greater wealth. The Great Khan agreed, but he imposed the oppressive tax-farming system in use in the Il-khan Empire, rather than the fixed-rate method traditional to China.

The Chinese suffered under this system during the early years, but Mongol rule under the Yuan Empire, established by Genghis Khan's grandson Khubilai in 1271, also brought benefits: secure routes of transport and communication; exchange of experts and advisers between eastern and western Eurasia; and transmission of information, ideas, and skills.

The Yuan Empire, 1279–1368

Just as the Il-khans in Iran and the Golden Horde in Russia came to accept many aspects of Muslim and Christian culture, so the Mongols in China sought to construct a fruitful synthesis of the Mongol and Chinese religious and moral traditions. **Khubilai Khan** gave his oldest son a Chinese name and had Confucianists participate in the boy's education. In public announcements and the crafting of laws, he took Confucian conventions into consideration. Buddhist and Daoist leaders visited the Great Khan and came away believing that they had all but convinced him to accept their beliefs.

The teachings of Buddhist priests from Tibet called **lamas°** became increasingly popular with some Mongol rulers in the 1200s and 1300s. Their idea of a militant universal ruler bringing the whole world under control of the Buddha and thus pushing it nearer to salvation mirrored an ancient Central Asia idea of universal rulership.

Beijing, the Yuan capital, became the center of cultural and economic life. Where Karakorum had been remote from any major settled area, Beijing served as the eastern terminus of the caravan routes that began near Tabriz, the Il-khan capital, and (Old) Sarai, the Golden Horde capital. An imperial horseback courier system utilizing hundreds of stations maintained close communications along routes that were generally policed and safe for travelers. Ambassadors and merchants arriving in Beijing found a city that was much more Chinese in character than its predecessor in Mongolia.

Called Great Capital (Dadu) or City of the Khan (*khan-balikh°*, Marco Polo's "Cambaluc"), Khubilai's capital featured massive Chinese-style walls of rammed earth, a tiny portion of which can still be seen. Khubilai's engineers widened the streets and developed linked lakes and artificial islands at the city's northwest edge to form a closed imperial complex, the Forbidden City. For his summer retreat, Khubilai maintained the palace and parks at Shangdu°, now in Inner Mongolia. This was "Xanadu°" celebrated by the English poet Samuel Taylor Coleridge, its "stately pleasure dome" the hunting preserve where Khubilai and his courtiers practiced riding and shooting.

"China" as we think of it today did not exist before the Mongols. Before they reunified it, China had been divided into three separate states (see Chapter 11). The Tanggut and Jin empires controlled the north, the Southern Song most of the area south of the Yellow River. These states had different languages, writing systems, forms of government, and elite cultures. The Great Khans destroyed all three and encouraged the restoration or preservation of many features of Chinese government and society, thereby reuniting China in what proved to be a permanent fashion.

By law, Mongols had the highest social ranking. Below them came, in order, Central Asians and Middle Easterners, then northern Chinese, and finally southern Chinese. This apparent racial ranking also reflected a hierarchy of functions, the Mongols being the empire's warriors, the Central Asians and Middle Easterners its census takers and tax collectors. The northern Chinese outranked the southern Chinese because they had come under Mongol control almost two generations earlier.

Though Khubilai included some "Confucians" (under the Yuan, a formal and hereditary status) in government, their position compared poorly with their status as elite officeholders in pre-Mongol times. The Confucians criticized the favoring of merchants, many of whom were from the Middle East or Central Asia, and physicians. They regarded doctors as mere technicians, or even heretical practitioners of Daoist mysticism. The Yuan encouraged medicine and began the long process of integrating Chinese medical and herbal knowledge with western approaches derived from Greco-Roman and Muslim sources.

Like the Il-khan rulers in the Middle East, the Yuan rulers concentrated on counting the population and collecting taxes. They brought Persian, Arab, and Uighur administrators to China to staff the offices of taxation and finance, and Muslim scholars worked at calendar making and astronomy. For census taking and administration, the Mongols organized all of China into provinces. Central appointment of provincial governors, tax collectors, and garrison commanders marked a radical change by systematizing government control in all parts of the country.

The scarcity of contemporary records and the hostility of later Chinese writers make examination of the Yuan economy difficult. Many cities seem to have prospered: in north China by being on the caravan routes; in the interior by being on the Grand Canal; and along the coast by participation in maritime grain shipments from south China. The reintegration of East Asia (though not Japan) with the overland Eurasian trade, which had lapsed with the fall of the Tang (see Chapter 11), stimulated the urban economies.

The privileges and prestige that merchants enjoyed changed urban life and the economy of China. With only

---

lama (LAH-mah)   *khan-balikh* (kahn-BAL-ik)
Shangdu (shahng-DOO)   **Xanadu** (ZAH-nah-doo)

a limited number of government posts open to the old Chinese elite, great families that had previously spent fortunes on educating sons for government service sought other outlets. Many gentry families chose commerce, despite its lesser prestige. Corporations—investor groups that behaved as single commercial and legal units and shared the risk of doing business—handled most economic activities, starting with financing caravans and expanding into tax farming and lending money to the Mongol aristocracy. Central Asians and Middle Easterners headed most corporations in China in the early Yuan period; but as Chinese bought shares, most corporations acquired mixed membership, or even complete Chinese ownership.

The agricultural base, damaged by war, overtaxation, and the passage of armies, could not satisfy the financial needs of the Mongol aristocracy. Following earlier precedent, the imperial government issued paper money to make up the shortfall. But the massive scale of the Yuan experiment led people to doubt the value of the notes, which were unsecured. Copper coinage partially offset the failure of the paper currency. During the Song, exports of copper to Japan, where the metal was scarce, had caused a severe shortage in China, leading to a rise in value of copper in relation to silver. By cutting off trade with Japan, the Mongols intentionally or unintentionally stabilized the value of copper coins.

Gentry families that had previously prepared their sons for the state examinations moved from their traditional homes in the countryside to engage in urban commerce, and city life began to cater to the tastes of merchants instead of scholars. Specialized shops selling clothing, grape wine, furniture, and religiously butchered meats became common. Teahouses featured sing-song girls, drum singers, operas, and other entertainments previously considered coarse. Writers published works in the style of everyday speech. And the increasing influence of the northern, Mongolian-influenced Chinese language, often called Mandarin in the West, resulted in lasting linguistic change.

Cottage industries linked to the urban economies dotted the countryside, where 90 percent of the people lived. Some villages cultivated mulberry trees and cotton using dams, water wheels, and irrigation systems patterned in part on Middle Eastern models. Treatises on planting, harvesting, threshing, and butchering were published. One technological innovator, Huang Dao Po°, brought knowledge of cotton growing, spinning, and weaving from her native Hainan Island to the fertile Yangzi Delta. Some villagers came to revere such innovators as local gods.

Yet on the whole, the countryside did poorly during the Yuan period. After the initial conquests, the Mongol princes evicted many farmers and subjected the rest to brutal tax collection. As in Iran under the Il-khans, by the time the Yuan shifted to lighter taxes and encouragement of farming at the end of the 1200s, it was too late. Servitude or homelessness had overtaken many farmers. Neglect of dams and dikes caused disastrous flooding, particularly on the Yellow River.

According to Song records from before the Mongol conquest and the Ming census taken after their overthrow—each, of course, possibly subject to inaccuracy or exaggeration—China's population may have shrunk by 40 percent during eighty years of Mongol rule, with many localities in northern China losing up to five-sixths of their inhabitants. Scholars have suggested several causes, not all of them directly associated with Mongol rule: prolonged warfare, privations in the countryside causing people to resort to female infanticide, a southward movement of people fleeing the Mongols, and flooding on the Yellow River. The last helps explain why losses in the north exceeded those in the south and why the population along the Yangzi River markedly increased.

The bubonic plague and its attendant diseases, spread by the population movements, contributed as well. The Mongol incorporation of Yunnan°, a mountainous southwestern province where rodents commonly carried bubonic plague, into the centralized provincial system of government exposed the lowlands to plague (see Map 13.1). Cities seem to have managed outbreaks of disease better than rural areas as the epidemic moved from south to north in the 1300s.

Cultural and Scientific Exchange

Government officials in Yuan China maintained regular contact with their counterparts in Il-khan Iran and pursued similar economic and financial policies. While Chinese silks and porcelains affected elite tastes at the western end of the Silk Road, Il-khan engineering, astronomy, and mathematics reached China and Korea. Just as Chinese painters taught Iranian artists appealing new ways of drawing clouds, rocks, and trees, Muslims from the Middle East oversaw most of the weapons manufacture and engineering projects for

Huang Dao Po (hwahng DOW poh)

Yunnan (YOON-nahn)

Khubilai's armies. Similarly, the Il-khans imported scholars and texts that helped them understand Chinese technological advances, including stabilized sighting tubes for precisely noting the positions of astronomical objects, mechanically driven armillary spheres that showed how the sun, moon, and planets moved in relation to one another, and new techniques for measuring the movement of the moon. And Khubilai brought Iranians to Beijing to construct an observatory and an institute for astronomical studies similar to the Il-khans' facility at Maragheh. He made the state responsible for maintaining and staffing the observatory.

Muslim doctors and Persian medical texts—particularly in anatomy, pharmacology, and ophthalmology—circulated in China during the Yuan. Khubilai, who suffered from alcoholism and gout, accorded high status to doctors. New seeds and formulas from the Middle East stimulated medical practice. The traditional Chinese study of herbs, drugs, and potions came in for renewed interest and publication.

The Fall of the Yuan Empire

In the 1340s power contests broke out among the Mongol princes. Within twenty years farmer rebellions and feuds among the Mongols engulfed the land. Amidst the chaos, a charismatic Chinese leader, Zhu Yuanzhang°, mounted a campaign that destroyed the Yuan Empire and brought China under control of his new empire, the Ming, in 1368. Many Mongols—as well as the Muslims, Jews, and Christians who had come with them—remained in China, some as farmers or shepherds, some as high-ranking scholars and officials. Most of their descendants took Chinese names and became part of the diverse cultural world of China.

Many other Mongols, however, had never moved out of their home territories in Mongolia. Now they welcomed back refugees from the Yuan collapse. Though Turkic peoples were becoming predominant in the steppe region in the west of Central Asia, including territories still ruled by descendants of Genghis Khan, Mongols retained control of Inner Asia, the steppe regions bordering on Mongolia. Their reconcentration in this region fostered a renewed sense of Mongol unity. Some Mongol groups adopted Islam; others favored Tibetan Buddhism. But religious affiliation proved less important than Mongol identity.

The Ming thus fell short of dominating all the Mongols. The Mongols of Inner Asia paid tribute to the Ming only to the extent that doing so facilitated their trade.

The Mongols remained a continuing threat on the northern Ming frontier.

THE EARLY MING EMPIRE, 1368–1500

The history of the **Ming Empire** raises questions about the overall impact of the Mongol era in China. Just as historians of Russia and Iran divide over whether Mongol invasion and political domination retarded or stimulated the pace and direction of political and economic change, so historians of China have differing opinions about the Mongols. Since the Ming reestablished many practices that are seen as purely Chinese, they receive praise from people who ascribe central importance to Chinese traditions. On the other hand, historians who look upon the Mongol era as a pivotal historical moment when communication across the vast interior of Eurasia served to bring east and west together sometimes see the inward-looking Ming as less dynamic and productive than the Yuan.

Ming China on a Mongol Foundation

Zhu Yuanzhang, a former monk, soldier, and bandit, had watched his parents and other family members die of famine and disease, conditions he blamed on Mongol misrule. During the Yuan Empire's chaotic last decades, he vanquished rival rebels and assumed imperial power under the name Hongwu (r. 1368–1398). He ruled a highly centralized, militarily formidable empire.

Hongwu moved the capital to Nanjing° ("southern capital") on the Yangzi River, turning away from the Mongol's Beijing ("northern capital"; see Map 13.3). Though Zhu Yuanzhang the rebel had espoused a radical Buddhist belief in a coming age of salvation, once in power he used Confucianism to depict the emperor as the champion of civilization and virtue, justified in making war on uncivilized "barbarians."

Hongwu choked off the close relations with Central Asia and the Middle East fostered by the Mongols and imposed strict limits on imports and foreign visitors. Silver replaced paper money for tax payments and commerce. These practices, illustrative of an anti-Mongol ideology, proved as economically unhealthy as some of the Yuan economic policies and did not last. Instead, the Ming government gradually came to resemble the Yuan. Ming

---

Zhu Yuanzhang (JOO yuwen-JAHNG)

Nanjing (nahn-JING)

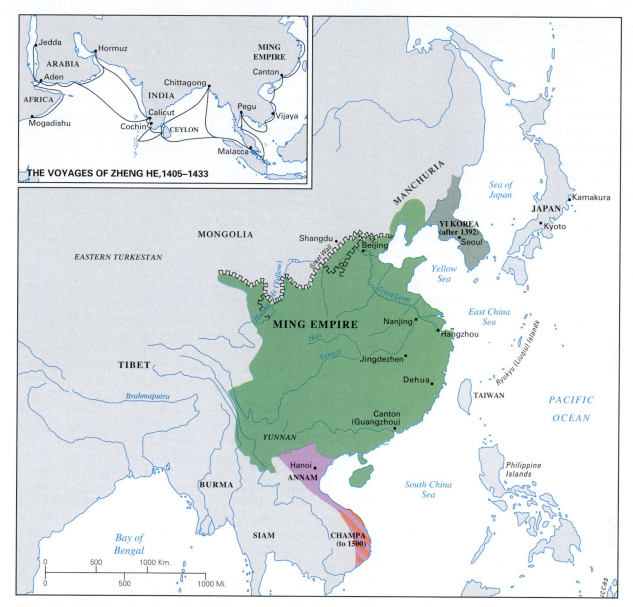

THE VOYAGES OF ZHENG HE, 1405–1433

Map 13.3   The Ming Empire and Its Allies, 1368–1500   The Ming Empire controlled China but had a hostile relationship with peoples in Mongolia and Inner Asia who had been under the rule of the Mongol Yuan emperors. Mongol attempts at conquest by seas were continued by the Ming mariner Zheng He. Between 1405 and 1433 he sailed to Southeast Asia and then beyond, to India, the Persian Gulf, and East Africa.

rulers retained the provincial structure and continued to observe the hereditary professional categories of the Yuan period. Muslims made calendars and astronomical calculations at a new observatory at Nanjing, a replica of Khubilai's at Beijing. The Mongol calendar continued in use.

Continuities with the Yuan became more evident after an imperial prince seized power through a coup d'état

to rule as the emperor **Yongle°** (r. 1403–1424). He returned the capital to Beijing, enlarging and improving Khubilai's imperial complex. The central area—the Forbidden City—acquired its present character, with moats, orange-red outer walls, golden roofs, and marble bridges.

Yongle (yoong-LAW)

Yongle intended this combination fortress, religious site, bureaucratic center, and imperial residential park to overshadow Nanjing, and it survives today as China's most imposing traditional architectural complex.

Yongle also restored commercial links with the Middle East. Because hostile Mongols still controlled much of the caravan route, Yongle explored maritime connections. In Southeast Asia, Annam became a Ming province as the early emperors continued the Mongol program of aggression. This focus on the southern frontier helped inspire the naval expeditions of the trusted imperial eunuch **Zheng He°** from 1405 to 1433.

A Muslim whose father and grandfather had made the pilgrimage to Mecca, Zheng He had a good knowledge of the Middle East; and his religion eased relations with the states of the Indian subcontinent, where he directed his first three voyages. Subsequent expeditions reached Hormuz on the Persian Gulf, sailed the southern coast of Arabia and the Horn of Africa (modern Somalia), and possibly reached as far south as the Strait of Madagascar (see Map 13.3).

On early voyages he visited long-established Chinese merchant communities in Southeast Asia in order to cement their allegiance to the Ming Empire and to collect taxes. When a community on the island of Sumatra resisted, he slaughtered the men to set an example. By pursuing commercial relations with the Middle East and possibly Africa, he also publicized Yongle's reversal of Hongwu's opposition to foreign trade.

The expeditions added some fifty new tributary states to the Ming imperial universe, but trade did not increase as dramatically. Sporadic embassies reached Beijing from rulers in India, the Middle East, Africa, and Southeast Asia. During one visit the ruler of Brunei° died and received a grand burial at the Chinese capital. Occasional expeditions continued until the 1430s, after the death of both Yongle and Zheng He, when they stopped.

Having demonstrated such abilities at long-distance navigation, why did the Chinese not develop seafaring for commercial and military gain? Contemporaries considered the voyages a personal project of Yongle, an upstart ruler who had always sought to prove his worthiness. Building the Forbidden City in Beijing and sponsoring gigantic encyclopedia projects might be taken to reflect a similar motivation. Yongle may also have been emulating Khubilai Khan, who had sent enormous fleets against Japan and Southeast Asia. This would fit with the rumor spread by Yongle's political enemies that he was actually a Mongol.

A less speculative approach to the question starts with the fact that the new commercial opportunities fell short of expectations, despite bringing foreign nations into the Ming orbit. In the meantime, Japanese coastal piracy intensified, and Mongol threats in the north and west grew. The human and financial demands of fortifying the north, redesigning and strengthening Beijing, and outfitting military expeditions against the Mongols ultimately took priority over the quest for maritime empire.

Technology and Population

Although innovation continued in all areas of the Ming economy, advances were less frequent and less significant than under the Song, particularly in agriculture. Agricultural production peaked around the mid-1400s and remained level for more than a century.

The Ming government limited mining, partly to reinforce the value of metal coins and partly to control and tax the industry. Farmers had difficulty obtaining iron and bronze for farm implements. The peace that had followed the Mongol conquest resulted in a decline in techniques for making high-quality bronze and steel, which were especially used for weapons. Central Asian and Middle Eastern technicians rather than Chinese cast the bronze instruments for Khubilai's observatory at Beijing. Japan quickly surpassed China in the production of extremely high-quality steel swords. Copper, iron, and steel became expensive in Ming China, leading to a lessened use of metal.

After the death of Emperor Yongle in 1424, shipbuilding also declined, and few advances occurred in printing, timekeeping, and agricultural technology. New weaving techniques did appear, but technological development in this field had peaked by 1500.

Reactivation of the examination system as a way of recruiting government officials (see Chapter 11) drew large numbers of educated, ambitious men into a renewed study of the Confucian classics. This reduced the vitality of commerce, where they had previously been employed, just as population increase was creating a labor surplus. Records indicating a growth from 60 million at the end of the Yuan period in 1368 to nearly 100 million by 1400 may not be entirely reliable, but rapid population growth encouraged the production of staples—wheat, millet, and barley in the north and rice in the south—at the expense of commercial crops such as cotton that had stimulated many technological innovations under the Song. Staple crops yielded lower profits, which further discouraged capital improvements. New

Zheng He (JEHNG HUH)   **Brunei** (broo-NIE)

Ming Porcelain Bowl   High-quality Chinese blue-and-white ware commanded an international market under the Ming Empire. This piece, bearing a Portuguese inscription showing that it was made in 1541 for the Portuguese governor of Malacca, is one of the earliest examples of works made specifically for a European.   (Collection, Junta de Baixo Alentago, Beja, Portugal)

foods, such as sweet potatoes, became available but were little adopted. Population growth in southern and central China caused deforestation and raised the price of wood.

The Mongols that the Ming confronted in the north fought on horseback with simple weapons. The Ming fought back with arrows, scattershot mortars, and explosive canisters. They even used a few cannon, which they knew about from contacts with the Middle East and later with Europeans (see Environment and Technology: From Gunpowder to Guns). Fearing that technological secrets would get into enemy hands, the government censored the chapters on gunpowder and guns in early Ming encyclopedias. Shipyards and ports shut down to avoid contact with Japanese pirates and to prevent Chinese from migrating to Southeast Asia.

A technology gap with Korea and Japan opened up nevertheless. When superior steel was needed, supplies came from Japan. Korea moved ahead of China in the design and production of firearms and ships, in printing techniques, and in the sciences of weather prediction and calendar making. The desire to tap the wealthy Ming market fueled some of these advances.

The Ming Achievement

In the late 1300s and the 1400s the wealth and consumerism of the early Ming stimulated high achievement in literature, the decorative arts, and painting. The Yuan period interest in plain writing had produced some of the world's earliest novels. This type of literature flourished under the Ming. *Water Margin*, which originated in the raucous drum-song performances loosely related to Chinese opera, features dashing Chinese bandits who struggle against Mongol rule, much as Robin Hood and his merry men resisted Norman rule in England. Many authors had a hand in the final print version.

Luo Guanzhong°, one of the authors of *Water Margin*, is also credited with *Romance of the Three Kingdoms*, based on a much older series of stories that in some ways resemble the Arthurian legends. It describes the attempts of an upright but doomed war leader and his followers to restore the Han Empire of ancient times and resist the power of the cynical but brilliant villain. *Romance of the Three Kingdoms* and *Water Margin* expressed much of the militant but joyous pro-China sentiment of the early Ming era and remain among the most appreciated Chinese fictional works.

Probably the best-known product of Ming technological advance was porcelain. The imperial ceramic works at Jingdezhen° experimented with new production techniques and new ways of organizing and rationalizing workers. "Ming ware," a blue-on-white style developed in the 1400s from Indian, Central Asian, and Middle Eastern motifs, became especially prized around the world. Other Ming goods in high demand included furniture, lacquered screens, and silk, all eagerly transported by Chinese and foreign merchants throughout Southeast Asia and the Pacific, India, the Middle East, and East Africa.

Luo Guanzhong (LAW GWAHB-JOONG)
Jingdezhen (JING-deh-JUHN)

ENVIRONMENT + TECHNOLOGY

From Gunpowder to Guns

Long before the invention of guns, gunpowder was used in China and Korea to excavate mines, build canals, and channel irrigation. Alchemists in China used related formulas to make noxious gas pellets to paralyze enemies and expel evil spirits. A more realistic benefit was eliminating disease-carrying insects, a critical aid to the colonization of malarial regions in China and Southeast Asia. The Mongol Empire staged fireworks displays on ceremonial occasions, delighting European visitors to Karakorum who saw them for the first time.

Anecdotal evidence in Chinese records gives credit for the introduction of gunpowder to a Sogdian Buddhist monk of the 500s. The monk described the wondrous alchemical transformation of elements produced by a combination of charcoal and saltpeter. In this connection he also mentioned sulfur. The distillation of naphtha, a light, flammable derivative of oil or coal, seems also to have been first developed in Central Asia, the earliest evidence coming from the Gandhara region (in modern Pakistan).

By the eleventh century, the Chinese had developed flamethrowers powered by burning naphtha, sulfur, or gunpowder in a long tube. These weapons intimidated and injured foot soldiers and horses and also set fire to thatched roofs in hostile villages and, occasionally, the rigging of enemy ships.

In their long struggle against the Mongols, the Song learned to enrich saltpeter to increase the amount of nitrate in gunpowder. This produced forceful explosions rather than jets of fire. Launched from catapults, gunpowder-filled canisters could rupture fortifications and inflict mass casualties. Explosives hurled from a distance could sink or burn ships.

The Song also experimented with firing projectiles from metal gun barrels. The earliest gun barrels were broad and squat and were transported on special wagons to their emplacements. The mouths of the barrels projected saltpeter mixed with scattershot minerals. The Chinese and then the Koreans adapted gunpowder to shooting masses of arrows—sometimes flaming—at enemy fortifications.

In 1280 weapons makers of the Yuan Empire produced the first device featuring a projectile that completely filled the mouth of the cannon and thus concentrated the explosive force. The Yuan used cast bronze for the barrel and iron for the cannonball. The new weapon shot farther and more accurately, and was much more destructive, than the earlier Song devices.

Knowledge of the cannon and cannonball moved westward across Eurasia. By the end of the thirteenth century cannon were being produced in the Middle East. By 1327 small, squat cannon called "bombards" were being used in Europe.

Launching Flaming Arrows   Song soldiers used gunpowder to launch flaming arrows.   (British Library)

CENTRALIZATION AND MILITARISM IN EAST ASIA, 1200–1500

Korea, Japan, and Annam, the other major states of East Asia, were all affected by confrontation with the Mongols, but with differing results. Japan and Annam escaped Mongol conquest but changed in response to the Mongol threat, becoming more effective and expansive regimes with enhanced commitments to independence.

As for Korea, just as the Ming stressed Chinese traditions and identity in the aftermath of Yuan rule, so Mongol domination contributed to revitalized interest in Korea's own language and history. The Mongols conquered Korea after a difficult war, and though Korea suffered socially and economically under Mongol rule, members of the elite associated closely with the Yuan Empire. After the fall of the Yuan, merchants continued the international connections established in the Mongol period, while Korean armies consolidated a new kingdom and fended off pirates.

Korea from the Mongols to the Yi, 1231–1500

In their effort to establish control over all of China, the Mongols searched for coastal areas from which to launch naval expeditions and choke off the sea trade of their adversaries. Korea offered such possibilities. When the Mongols attacked in 1231, the leader of a prominent Korean family assumed the role of military commander and protector of the king (not unlike the shoguns of Japan). His defensive war, which lasted over twenty years, left a ravaged countryside, exhausted armies, and burned treasures, including the renowned nine-story pagoda at Hwangnyong-sa° and the wooden printing blocks of the *Tripitaka*°, a ninth-century masterpiece of printing art. The commander's underlings killed him in 1258. Soon afterward the Koryo° king surrendered to the Mongols and became a subject monarch by linking his family to the Great Khan by marriage.

By the mid-1300s the Koryo kings were of mostly Mongol descent, and they favored Mongol dress, customs, and language. Many lived in Beijing. The kings, their families, and their entourages often traveled between China and Korea, thus exposing Korea to the philosophical and artistic styles of Yuan China: neo-Confucianism, Chan Buddhism (called *Sŏn* in Korea), and celadon (light green) ceramics.

Mongol control was a stimulus after centuries of comparative isolation. Cotton began to be grown in southern Korea; gunpowder came into use; and the art of calendar making, including eclipse prediction and vector calculation, stimulated astronomical observation and mathematics. Celestial clocks built for the royal observatory at Seoul reflected Central Asian and Islamic influences more than Chinese. Avenues of advancement opened for Korean scholars willing to learn Mongolian, landowners willing to open their lands to falconry and grazing, and merchants servicing the new royal exchanges with Beijing. These developments contributed to the rise of a new landed and educated class.

When the Yuan Empire fell in 1368, the Koryo ruling family remained loyal to the Mongols and had to be forced to recognize the new Ming Empire. In 1392 the **Yi**° established a new kingdom with a capital in Seoul and sought to reestablish a local identity. Like Russia and China after the Mongols, the Yi regime publicly rejected the period of Mongol domination. Yet the Yi government continued to employ Mongol-style land surveys, taxation in kind, and military garrison techniques.

Like the Ming emperors, the Yi kings revived the study of the Confucian classics, an activity that required knowledge of Chinese and showed the dedication of the state to learning. This revival may have led to a key technological breakthrough in printing technology.

Koreans had begun using Chinese woodblock printing in the 700s. This technology worked well in China, where a large number of buyers wanted copies of a comparatively small number of texts. But in Korea, the comparatively few literate men had interests in a wide range of texts. Movable wooden or ceramic type appeared in Korea in the early thirteenth century and may have been invented there. But the texts were frequently inaccurate and difficult to read. In the 1400s Yi printers, working directly with the king, developed a reliable device to anchor the pieces of type to the printing plate: they replaced the old beeswax adhesive with solid copper frames. The legibility of the printed page improved, and high-volume, accurate production became possible. Combined with the phonetic *han'gul*° writing system, this printing technology laid the foundation for a high literacy rate in Korea.

Yi publications told readers how to produce and use fertilizer, transplant rice seedlings, and engineer reservoirs. Building on Eurasian knowledge imported by the Mongols and introduced under the Koryo, Yi scholars

---

Hwanghnyong-sa (hwahng-NEEYAHNG-sah)
Tripitaka (tri-PIH-tah-kah)   **Koryo** (KAW-ree-oh)

Yi (YEE)   *han'gul* (HAHN-goor)

Movable Type   The improvement of cast bronze tiles, each showing a single character, eliminated the need to cast or carve whole pages. Individual tiles—the ones shown are Korean—could be moved from page frame to page frame and gave an even and pleasing appearance. All parts of East Asia eventually adopted this form of printing for cheap, popular books. In the mid-1400s Korea also experimented with a fully phonetic form of writing, which in combination with movable type allowed Koreans unprecedented levels of literacy and access to printed works.   (Courtesy, Yushin Yoo)

developed a meteorological science of their own. They invented or redesigned instruments to measure wind speed and rainfall and perfected a calendar based on minute comparisons of the systems of China and the Islamic world.

In agriculture, farmers expanded the cultivation of cash crops, the reverse of what was happening in Ming China. Cotton, the primary crop, enjoyed such high value that the state accepted it for tax payments. The Yi army used cotton uniforms, and cotton became the favored fabric of the Korean civil elite. With cotton gins and spinning wheels powered by water, Korea advanced more rapidly than China in mechanization and began to export considerable amounts of cotton to China and Japan.

Although both the Yuan and the Ming withheld the formula for gunpowder from the Korean government, Korean officials acquired the information by subterfuge. By the later 1300s they had mounted cannon on ships that patrolled against pirates and used gunpowder-driven arrow launchers against enemy personnel and the rigging of enemy ships. Combined with skills in armoring ships, these techniques made the small Yi navy a formidable defense force.

Political Transformation in Japan, 1274–1500

Having secured Korea, the Mongols looked toward Japan, a target they could easily reach from Korea and a possible base for controlling China's southern coast. Their first thirty-thousand-man invasion force in 1274 included Mongol cavalry and archers and sailors from Korea and northeastern Asia. Its weaponry included light catapults and incendiary and explosive projectiles of Chinese manufacture. The Mongol forces landed successfully and decimated the Japanese cavalry, but a great storm on Hakata° Bay on the north side of Kyushu° Island (see Map 13.4) prevented the establishment of a beachhead and forced the Mongols to sail back to Korea.

The invasion deeply impressed Japan's leaders and hastened social and political changes that were already under way. Under the Kamakura° Shogunate established in 1185—another powerful family actually exercised control—the shogun, or military leader, distributed land and privileges to his followers. In return they paid him tribute and supplied him with soldiers. This stable, but decentralized, system depended on the balancing of power among regional warlords. Lords in the north and east of Japan's main island were remote from those in the south and west. Beyond devotion to the emperor and the shogun, little united them until the alien and terrifying Mongol threat materialized.

After the return of his fleet, Khubilai sent envoys to Japan demanding submission. Japanese leaders executed them and prepared for war. The shogun took steps to centralize his military government. The effect was to increase the influence of warlords from the south and west of Honshu (Japan's main island) and from the island of Kyushu, because this was where invasion seemed most likely, and they were the local commanders acting under the shogun's orders.

Military planners studied Mongol tactics and retrained and outfitted Japanese warriors for defense against advanced weaponry. Farm laborers drafted from all over the country constructed defensive fortifications at Hakata and other points along the Honshu and Kyushu coasts. This effort demanded, for the first time, a national system to move resources toward western points rather than toward the imperial or shogunal centers to the east.

The Mongols attacked in 1281. They brought 140,000 warriors, including many non-Mongols, as well as thousands of horses, in hundreds of ships. However, the wall the Japanese had built to cut off Hakata Bay from the mainland deprived the Mongol forces of a reliable landing point. Japanese swordsmen rowed out and boarded the Mongol ships lingering offshore. Their superb steel swords shocked the invaders. After a prolonged standoff, a typhoon struck and sank perhaps half of the Mongol ships. The remainder sailed away, never again to harass Japan. The Japanese gave thanks to the "wind of the Gods"—*kamikaze*°—for driving away the Mongols.

Nevertheless, the Mongol threat continued to influence Japanese development. Prior to his death in 1294,

Hakata (HAH-kah-tah)   **Kyushu** (KYOO-shoo)
Kamakura (kah-mah-KOO-rah)   *kamikaze* (KUM-i-kuh-zee)

Map 13.4   Korea and Japan, 1200–1500   The proximity of Korea and northern China to Japan gave the Mongols the opportunity to launch enormous fleets against the Kamakura Shogunate, which controlled most of the three islands (Honshu, Shikoku, and Kyushu) of central Japan.

Khubilai had in mind a third invasion. His successors did not carry through with it, but the shoguns did not know that the Mongols had given up the idea of conquering Japan. They rebuilt coastal defenses well into the fourteenth century, helping to consolidate the social position of Japan's warrior elite and stimulating the development of a national infrastructure for trade and communication. But the Kamakura Shogunate, based on regionally collected and regionally dispersed revenues, suffered financial strain in trying to pay for centralized road and defense systems.

Between 1333 and 1338 the emperor Go-Daigo broke the centuries-old tradition of imperial seclusion and aloofness from government and tried to reclaim power from the shoguns. This ignited a civil war that destroyed the Kamakura system. In 1338, with the Mongol

Painting by Sesshu Sesshu Toyo (1420–1506) created a distinctive style of ink painting that contrasted with the Chinese styles that predominated earlier in Japan. Benefiting from growing Japanese commerce in the period of the Ashikaga Shogunate, he traveled to China as a youth and studied Chinese techniques. As he developed his style, a market for his art developed among merchant communities and other urban elites. (Collection of the Tokyo National Museum)

threat waning, the **Ashikaga Shogunate°**, took control at the imperial center of Kyoto.

Provincial warlords enjoyed renewed independence. Around their imposing castles, they sponsored the development of market towns, religious institutions, and schools. The application of technologies imported in earlier periods, including water wheels, improved plows, and Champa rice, increased agricultural productivity. Growing wealth and relative peace stimulated artistic creativity, mostly reflecting Zen Buddhist beliefs held by the warrior elite. In the simple elegance of architecture and gardens, in the contemplative landscapes of artists like Sesshu Toyo, and in the eerie, stylized performances of the No theater, the unified aesthetic code of Zen became established in the Ashikaga era.

Despite the technological advancement, artistic productivity, and rapid urbanization of this period,

Ashikaga (ah-shee-KAH-gah)

competition among warlords and their followers led to regional wars. By the later 1400s these conflicts resulted in the near destruction of the warlords. The great Onin War in 1477 left Kyoto devastated and the Ashikaga Shogunate a central government in name only. Ambitious but low-ranking warriors, some with links to trade with the continent, began to scramble for control of the provinces.

After the fall of the Yuan in 1368 Japan resumed trade with China and Korea. Japan exported raw materials as well as folding fans, invented in Japan during the period of isolation, and swords. Japan's primary imports from China were books and porcelain. The volatile political environment in Japan gave rise to partnerships between warlords and local merchants. All worked to strengthen their own towns and treasuries through overseas commerce or, sometimes, through piracy.

The Emergence of Vietnam, 1200–1500

Before the first Mongol attack in 1257, the states of Annam (northern Vietnam) and Champa (southern Vietnam) had clashed frequently. Annam (once called Dai Viet) looked toward China and had once been subject to the Tang. Chinese political ideas, social philosophies, dress, religion, and language heavily influenced its official culture. Champa related more closely to the trading networks of the Indian Ocean; its official culture was strongly influenced by Indian religion, language, architecture, and dress. Champa's relationship with China depended in part on how close its enemy Annam was to China at any particular time. During the Song period Annam was neither formally subject to China nor particularly threatening to Champa militarily, so Champa inaugurated a trade and tribute relationship with China that spread fast-ripening Champa rice throughout East Asia.

The Mongols exacted submission and tribute from both Annam and Champa until the fall of the Yuan Empire in 1368. Mongol political and military ambitions were mostly focused elsewhere, however, which minimized their impact on politics and culture. The two Vietnamese kingdoms soon resumed their warfare. When Annam moved its army to reinforce its southern border, Ming troops occupied the capital, Hanoi, and installed a puppet government. Almost thirty years elapsed before Annam regained independence and resumed a tributary status. By then the Ming were turning to meet Mongol challenges to their north. In a series of ruthless campaigns, Annam terminated Champa's independence, and by 1500 the ancestor of the modern state of Vietnam, still called Annam, had been born.

The new state still relied on Confucian bureaucratic government and an examination system, but some practices differed from those in China. The Vietnamese legal code, for example, preserved group landowning and decision making within the villages, as well as women's property rights. Both developments probably had roots in an early rural culture based on the growing of rice in wet paddies; by this time the Annamese considered them distinctive features of their own culture.

CONCLUSION

Despite their brutality and devastation, the Mongol conquests brought a degree of unity to the lands between China and Europe that had never before been known. Nomadic mobility and expertise in military technology contributed to communication across vast spaces and initially, at least, an often-callous disregard for the welfare of farmers, as manifested in oppressive tax policies. Trade, on the other hand, received active Mongol stimulation through the protection of routes and encouragement of industrial production. The Mongol regimes were characterized by an unprecedented openness, employing talented people irrespective of their linguistic, ethnic, or religious affiliations. As a consequence, the period of comparative Mongol unity, which lasted less than a century, saw a remarkable exchange of ideas, techniques, and products across the breadth of Eurasia. Chinese gunpowder spurred the development of Ottoman and European cannon; Muslim astronomers introduced new instruments and mathematical techniques to Chinese observatories.

However, rule over dozens of restive peoples could not endure. Where Mongol military enterprise reached its limit of expansion, it stimulated local aspirations for independence. Division and hostility among branches of Genghis Khan's family—between the Yuan in China and the Jagadai in Central Asia or between the Golden Horde in Russia and the Il-khans in Iran—provided opportunities for achieving these aspirations. The Russians gained freedom from Mongol domination in western Eurasia, and the general political disruption and uncertainty of the Mongol era assisted the emergence of the Lithuanian, Serbian, and Ottoman states. In the east, China, Korea, and Annam similarly found renewed political identity in the aftermath of Mongol rule, while Japan fought off two Mongol invasions and transformed its internal political and cultural identity in the process. In every case, the reality or threat of Mongol attack and domination encouraged centralization of government, improvement of military techniques, and renewed stress on local cultural identity. Thus, in retrospect, despite its traditional association with death and destruction, the Mongol period appears as a watershed establishing new connections between widespread parts of Eurasia and leading to the development of strong, assertive, and culturally creative regional states.

■ Key Terms

Mongols	tsar
Genghis Khan	Ottoman Empire
nomadism	Khubilai Khan
Yuan Empire	lama
bubonic plague	Beijing
Il-khan	Ming Empire
Golden Horde	Yongle
Timur	Zheng He
Rashid al-Din	Yi
Nasir al-Din Tusi	kamikaze
Alexander Nevskii	Ashikaga Shogunate

■ Suggested Reading

David Morgan's *The Mongols* (1986) affords an accessible introduction to the Mongol Empire. Morgan and Reuven Amitai-Preiss have also edited a valuable collection of essays, *The Mongol Empire and Its Legacy* (2000). Thomas T. Allsen has written more-specialized studies: *Mongol Imperialism: The Policies of the Grand Qan Möngke in China, Russia, and the Islamic Lands, 1251–1259* (1987); *Commodity and Exchange in the Mongol Empire: A Cultural History of Islamic Textiles* (2002); and *Culture and Conquest in Mongol Eurasia* (2001). Larry Moses and Stephen A. Halkovic, Jr., *Introduction to Mongolian History and Culture* (1985) links early and modern Mongol history and culture. Tim Severin, *In Search of Chinggis Khan* (1992), revisits the paths of Genghis's conquests.

William H. McNeill's *Plagues and Peoples* (1976) outlines the demographic effects of the Mongol conquests, and Joel Mokyr discusses their technological impact in *The Lever of Riches: Technological Creativity and Economic Progress* (1990). Connections between commercial development in Europe and Eurasian trade routes of the Mongol era within a broad theoretical framework inform Janet L. Abu-Lughod's *Before European Hegemony: The World System A.D. 1250–1350* (1989).

The only "primary" document relating to Genghis Khan, *Secret History of the Mongols*, has been reconstructed in Mongolian from Chinese script and has been variously produced in scholarly editions by Igor de Rachewiltz and Francis Woodman Cleaves, among others. Paul Kahn produced a readable prose English paraphrase of the work in 1984. Biographies of Genghis Khan include Leo de Hartog, *Genghis Khan, Conqueror of the World* (1989); Michel Hoang, *Genghis Khan*, trans. Ingrid Canfield (1991); and Paul Ratchnevsky, *Genghis Khan: His Life and*

Legacy, trans. and ed. Thomas Nivison Haining (1992), which is most detailed on Genghis's childhood and youth.

On Central Asia after the conquests see S. A. M. Adshead, *Central Asia in World History* (1993). The most recent scholarly study of Timur is Beatrice Manz, *The Rise and Rule of Tamerlane* (1989).

David Christian, *A History of Russia, Central Asia, and Mongolia* (1998), and Charles Halperin, *Russia and the Golden Horde: The Mongol Impact on Medieval Russian History* (1987), provide one-volume accounts of the Mongols in Russia. A more detailed study is John Lister Illingworth Fennell, *The Crisis of Medieval Russia, 1200–1304* (1983). See also Donald Ostrowski, *Muscovy and the Mongols: Cross-Cultural Influences on the Steppe Frontier* (1998). Religion forms the topic of Devin DeWeese, *Islamization and Native Religion in the Golden Horde* (1994). *The Cambridge History of Iran*: Volume 5, *The Saljuq and Mongol Periods*, ed. J. A. Boyle (1968) and Volume 6, *The Timurid and Safavid Periods*, eds. Peter Jackson and Laurence Lockhart (rprt 2001) contain detailed scholarly articles covering the period in Iran and Central Asia.

Translations from the great historians of the Il-khan period include Juvaini, 'Ala al-Din 'Ata Malek, *The History of the World-Conqueror,* trans. John Andrew Boyle (1958), and Rashid al-Din, *The Successors of Genghis Khan*, trans. John Andrew Boyle (1971). The greatest traveler of the time was Ibn Battuta; see C. Defremery and B. R. Sanguinetti, eds., *The Travels of Ibn Battuta, A.D. 1325–1354,* translated with revisions and notes from the Arabic text by H. A. R. Gibb (1994), and Ross E. Dunn, *The Adventures of Ibn Battuta, a Muslim Traveler of the 14th Century* (1986).

On Europe's Mongol encounter see James Chambers, *The Devil's Horsemen: The Mongol Invasion of Europe* (1979). Christopher Dawson, ed., *Mission to Asia* (1955; reprinted 1981), assembles some of the best-known European travel accounts. See also Marco Polo, *The Travels of Marco Polo* (many editions), and the controversial skeptical appraisal of his account in Frances Wood, *Did Marco Polo Really Go to China?* (1995). Morris Rossabi's *Visitor from Xanadu* (1992) deals with the European travels of Rabban Sauma, a Christian Turk.

For China under the Mongols see Morris Rossabi's *Khubilai Khan: His Life and Times* (1988). On the Mongol impact on economy and technology in Yuan and Ming China see Mark Elvin, *The Pattern of the Chinese Past* (1973); Joseph Needham, *Science in Traditional China* (1981). Also see the important interpretation of Ming economic achievement in Andre Gunder Frank, *ReORIENT: Global Economy in the Asian Age* (1998).

The Cambridge History of China, Vol. 8, The Ming Dynasty 1368–1644, part 2, ed. Denis Twitchett and Frederick W. Mote (1998), provides scholarly essays about a little studied period. See also Albert Chan, *The Glory and Fall of the Ming Dynasty* (1982), and Edward L. Farmer, *Early Ming Government: The Evolution of Dual Capitals* (1976).

On early Ming literature see Lo Kuan-chung, *Three Kingdoms: A Historical Novel Attributed to Luo Guanzhong,* translated and annotated by Moss Roberts (1991); Pearl Buck's translation of

Water Margin, entitled *All Men Are Brothers,* 2 vols. (1933), and a later translation by J. H. Jackson, *Water Margin, Written by Shih Nai-an* (1937); and Shelley Hsüeh-lun Chang, *History and Legend: Ideas and Images in the Ming Historical Novels* (1990).

Joseph R. Levenson, ed., *European Expansion and the Counter-Example of Asia, 1300–1600* (1967), recounts the Zheng He expeditions. Philip Snow's *The Star Raft* (1988) contains more recent scholarship, while Louise Levathes, *When China Ruled the Seas* (1993) makes for lively reading.

For a general history of Korea in this period see Andrew C. Nahm, *Introduction to Korean History and Culture* (1993); Ki-Baik Lee, *A New History of Korea* (1984); and William E. Henthorn, *Korea: The Mongol Invasions* (1963). On a more specialized topic see Joseph Needham et al., *The Hall of Heavenly Records: Korean Astronomical Instruments and Clocks, 1380–1780* (1986).

For a collection of up-to-date scholarly essays on Japan, see Kozo Yamamura, ed., *The Cambridge History of Japan, Vol. 3: Medieval Japan* (1990). See also John W. Hall and Toyoda Takeshi, eds., *Japan in the Muromachi Age* (1977); H. Paul Varley, trans., *The Onin War: History of Its Origins and Background with a Selective Translation of the Chronicle of Onin* (1967); Yamada Nakaba, *Ghenko, the Mongol Invasion of Japan, with an Introduction by Lord Armstrong* (1916); and the novel *Fûtô* by Inoue Yasushi, translated by James T. Araki as *Wind and Waves* (1989).

■ Notes

1. Quotation adapted from Desmond Martin, *Chingis Khan and His Conquest of North China* (Baltimore: The John Hopkins Press, 1950), 303.

14

Tropical Africa and Asia, 1200–1500

East African Pastoralists   Herding large and small livestock has long been a way of life in drier parts of the tropics.

CHAPTER OUTLINE

Tropical Lands and Peoples

New Islamic Empires

Indian Ocean Trade

Social and Cultural Change

DIVERSITY AND DOMINANCE: **Personal Styles of Rule in India and Mali**

ENVIRONMENT AND TECHNOLOGY: **The Indian Ocean Dhow**

Sultan Abu Bakr° customarily offered his personal hospitality to every distinguished visitor to his city of Mogadishu, an Indian Ocean port in northeast Africa. In 1331 he provided food and lodging for Muhammad ibn Abdullah ibn Battuta° (1304–1369), a young Muslim scholar from Morocco who had set out to explore the Islamic world. Before beginning his tour of the trading cities of the Red Sea and East Africa, Ibn Battuta had completed a pilgrimage to Mecca and had traveled throughout the Middle East. Subsequent travels took him through Central Asia and India, China and Southeast Asia, Muslim Spain, and sub-Saharan West Africa. Logging some 75,000 miles (120,000 kilometers) in twenty-nine years, Ibn Battuta became the most widely traveled man of his times. For this reason the journals he wrote about his travels provide valuable information about these lands.

Other Muslim princes and merchants welcomed Ibn Battuta as graciously as did the ruler of Mogadishu. Hospitality was a noble virtue among Muslims, and they ignored visitors' physical and cultural differences. Although the Moroccan traveler noted that Sultan Abu Bakr had skin darker than his own and spoke a different native language (Somali), that was of little consequence. They were brothers in faith when they prayed together at Friday services in the Mogadishu mosque, where the sultan greeted his foreign guest in Arabic, the common language of the Islamic world: "You are heartily welcome, and you have honored our land and given us pleasure." When Sultan Abu Bakr and his jurists heard cases after the mosque service, they decided them on the basis of the law code familiar in all the lands of Islam.

Islam was not the only thing that united the diverse peoples of Africa and southern Asia. They also shared a tropical environment itself and a network of land and sea trade routes. The variations in tropical environments led societies to develop different specialties, which stimulated trade among them. Tropical winds governed the trading patterns of the Indian Ocean. Older than Islam, these routes were important

Abu Bakr (a-BOO BAK-uhr) **Ibn Battuta** (IB-uhn ba-TOO-tuh)

for spreading beliefs and technologies as well as goods. Ibn Battuta made his way down the coast of East Africa in merchants' ships and joined their camel caravans across the Sahara to West Africa. His path to India followed overland trade routes, and a merchant ship carried him on to China.

As you read this chapter, ask yourself the following questions:

- How did environmental differences shape cultural differences in tropical Africa and Asia?

- How did cultural and ecological differences promote trade in specialized goods from one place to another?

- How did trade and other contacts promote state growth and the spread of Islam?

TROPICAL LANDS AND PEOPLES

To obtain food, the people who inhabited the tropical regions of Africa and Asia used methods that had proved successful during generations of experimentation, whether at the desert's edge, in grasslands, or in tropical rain forests. Much of their success lay in learning how to blend human activities with the natural order, but their ability to modify the environment to suit their needs was also evident in irrigation works and mining.

The Tropical Environment

Because of the angle of earth's axis, the sun's rays warm the **tropics** year-round. The equator marks the center of the tropical zone, and the Tropic of Cancer and Tropic of Capricorn mark its outer limits. As Map 14.1 shows, Africa lies almost entirely within the tropics, as do southern Arabia, most of India, and all of the Southeast Asian mainland and islands.

Lacking the hot and cold seasons of temperate lands, the Afro-Asian tropics have their own cycle of rainy and dry seasons caused by changes in wind patterns across the surrounding oceans. Winds from a permanent high-pressure air mass over the South Atlantic deliver heavy rainfall to the western coast of Africa during much of the year. In December and January large

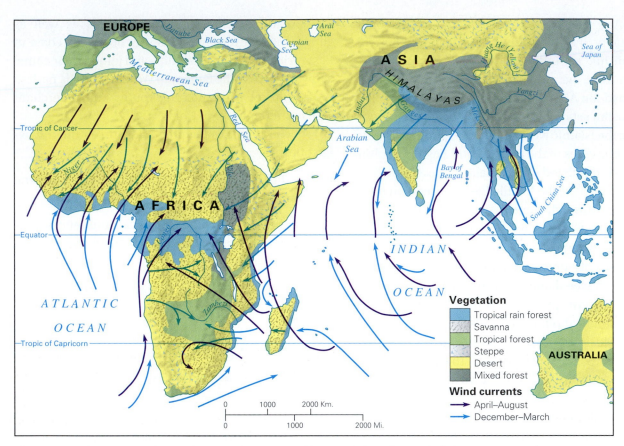

Map 14.1 Africa and the Indian Ocean Basin: Physical Characteristics Seasonal wind patterns control rainfall in the tropics and produce the different tropical vegetation zones to which human societies have adapted over thousands of years. The wind patterns also dominated sea travel in the Indian Ocean.

high-pressure zones over northern Africa and Arabia produce a southward movement of dry air that limits the inland penetration of the moist ocean winds.

In the lands around the Indian Ocean the rainy and dry seasons reflect the influence of alternating winds known as **monsoons.** A gigantic high-pressure zone over the Himalaya° Mountains that is at its peak from December to March produces a strong southward air movement (the northeast monsoon) in the western Indian Ocean. This is southern Asia's dry season. Between April and August a low-pressure zone over India creates a northward movement of air from across the ocean (the southwest monsoon) that brings southern Asia its heaviest rains. This is the wet season.

Areas with the heaviest rainfall—coastal West Africa and west-central Africa, Southeast Asia, and much of India—have dense rain forests. Lighter rains produce other

Himalaya (him-uh-LAY-uh)

tropical forests. The English word *jungle* comes from an Indian word for the tangled undergrowth in the tropical forests that once covered most of southern India.

Other parts of the tropics rarely see rain at all. The Sahara, the world's largest desert, stretches across northern Africa. This arid zone continues eastward across Arabia and into northwest India. Another desert zone occupies southwestern Africa. Most of the people of tropical India and Africa live between the deserts and the rain forests in lands that are favored with moderate amounts of moisture during the rainy seasons. These lands range from fairly wet woodlands to the much drier grasslands characteristic of much of East Africa.

Altitude produces other climatic changes. Thin atmospheres at high altitudes hold less heat than atmospheres at lower elevations. Snow covers some of the volcanic mountains of eastern Africa all or part of the year. The snowcapped Himalayas rise so high that they block cold air from moving south, thus giving northern

C H R O N O L O G Y

	Tropical Africa	Tropical Asia
1200		**1206** Delhi Sultanate founded in India
	1230s Mali Empire founded	
1300	**1270** Solomonic dynasty in Ethiopia founded	**1298** Delhi Sultanate annexes Gujarat
	1324–1325 Mansa Musa's pilgrimage to Mecca	
		1398 Timur sacks Delhi, Delhi Sultanate declines
1400	**1400s** Great Zimbabwe at its peak	
	1433 Tuareg retake Timbuktu, Mali declines	
1500		**1500** Port of Malacca at its peak

India a more tropical climate than its latitude would suggest. The many plateaus of inland Africa and the Deccan° Plateau of central India also make these regions somewhat cooler than the coastal plains.

The mighty rivers that rise in these mountains and plateaus redistribute water far from where it falls. Heavy rains in the highlands of Central Africa and Ethiopia supply the Nile's annual floods that make Egypt bloom in the desert. On its long route to the Atlantic, the Niger River of West Africa arcs northward to the Sahara's edge, providing waters to the trading cities along its banks. In like fashion, the Indus River provides nourishing waters from the Himalayas to arid northwest India. The Ganges° and its tributaries provide valuable moisture to northeastern India during the dry season. Mainland Southeast Asia's great rivers, such as the Mekong, are similarly valuable.

Human Ecosystems

Thinkers in temperate lands once imagined that surviving in the year-round warmth of the tropics was simply a matter of picking wild fruit off trees. In fact, mastering the tropics' many different environments was a long and difficult struggle. A careful observer touring the tropics in 1200 would have noticed that the many differences in societies derived from their particular ecosystems—that is, how people made use of the plants, animals, and other resources of their physical environments.

Domesticated plants and animals had been commonplace long before 1200, but people in some environments found it preferable to rely primarily on wild food that they obtained by hunting, fishing, and gathering. The small size of the ancient Pygmy° people in the dense forests of Central Africa permitted them to pursue their prey through dense undergrowth. Hunting also continued as a way of life in the upper altitudes of the Himalayas and in some desert environments. According to a Portuguese expedition in 1497, the people along the arid coast of southwestern Africa were well fed from a diet of "the flesh of seals, whales, and gazelles, and the roots of wild plants." Fishing was common along all the major lakes and rivers as well as in the oceans. The boating skills of ocean fishermen in East Africa, India, and Southeast Asia often led them to engage in ocean trade.

Tending herds of domesticated animals was common in areas too arid for agriculture. Unencumbered by bulky personal possessions and elaborate dwellings, they used their knowledge of local water and rain patterns to find adequate grazing for their animals in all but the severest droughts. Pastoralists consumed milk from their herds and traded hides and meat to neighboring farmers for grain and vegetables. The arid and semiarid lands of northeastern Africa and Arabia were home to the world's largest concentration of pastoralists. Like Ibn Battuta's host at Mogadishu, some Somali were urban dwellers, but most grazed their herds of goats and camels in the desert hinterland of the Horn of Africa. The western Sahara sustained

---

Deccan (de-KAN) **Ganges** (GAN-jeez)

Pygmy (PIG-mee)

herds of sheep and camels belonging to the Tuareg°, whose intimate knowledge of the desert also made them invaluable as guides to caravans, such as the one **Ibn Battuta** joined on the two-month journey across the desert. Along the Sahara's southern edge the cattle-herding Fulani° people gradually extended their range during this period. By 1500 they had spread throughout the western and central Sudan. Pastoralists in southern Africa sold meat to early Portuguese visitors.

By 1200 most Africans had been making their livelihood through agricultural for many centuries. Favorable soils and rainfall made farming even more dominant in South and Southeast Asia. High yields from intensive cultivation supported dense populations in Asia. In 1200 over 100 million people may have lived in South and Southeast Asia, more than four-fifths of them on the fertile Indian mainland. Though a little less than the population of China, this was triple the number of people living in all of Africa at that time and nearly double the number of people in Europe.

India's lush vegetation led one Middle Eastern writer to call it "the most agreeable abode on earth . . . its delightful plains resemble the garden of Paradise."[1] Rice cultivation dominated in the fertile Ganges plain of northeast India, in mainland Southeast Asia, and in southern China. Farmers in drier areas grew grains—such as wheat, sorghum, millet, and ensete—and legumes such as peas and beans, whose ripening cycle matched the pattern of the rainy and dry seasons. Tubers and tree crops characterized farming in rain-forest clearings.

Many useful domesticated plants and animals spread around the tropics. By 1200 Bantu-speaking farmers (see Chapter 8) had introduced grains and tubers from West Africa throughout the southern half of the continent. Bananas, brought to southern Africa centuries earlier by mariners from Southeast Asia, had become the staple food for people farming the rich soils around the Great Lakes of East Africa. Yams and cocoyams of Asian origin had spread across equatorial Africa. Asian cattle breeds grazed contentedly in pastures throughout Africa, and coffee of Ethiopian origin would shortly become a common drink in the Middle East.

Water Systems and Irrigation

In most parts of sub-Saharan Africa and many parts of Southeast Asia until quite recent times, the basic form of cultivation was extensive rather than intensive. Instead of enriching fields with manure and vegetable compost so they could be cultivated year after year, farmers abandoned fields every few years when the natural fertility of the soil was exhausted, and they cleared new fields. Ashes from the brush, grasses, and tree limbs that were cut down and burned gave the new fields a significant boost in fertility. Even though a great deal of work was needed to clear the fields initially, modern research suggests that such shifting cultivation was an efficient use of labor in areas where soils were not naturally rich in nutrients.

In other parts of the tropics, environmental necessity and population pressure led to the adoption of more intensive forms of agriculture. A rare area of intensive cultivation in sub-Saharan Africa was the inland delta of the Niger River, where large crops of rice were grown using the river's naturally fertilizing annual floods. The rice was probably sold to the trading cities along the Niger bend.

The uneven distribution of rainfall during the year was one of the great challenges faced by many Asian farmers. Unlike pastoralists who could move their herds to the water, they had to find ways of moving the water to their crops. Farmers in Vietnam, Java, Malaya, and Burma constructed special water-control systems to irrigate their terraced rice paddies. Villagers in southeast India built a series of stone and earthen dams across rivers to store water for gradual release through elaborate irrigation canals. Over many generations these canals were extended to irrigate more and more land. Although the dams and channels covered large areas, they were relatively simple structures that local people could keep working by routine maintenance. Other water-storage and irrigation systems were constructed in other parts of India in this period.

As had been true since the days of the first river-valley civilizations (see Chapter 2), the largest irrigation systems in the tropics were government public works projects. The **Delhi° Sultanate** (1206–1526) introduced extensive new water-control systems in northern India. Ibn Battuta commented appreciatively on one reservoir that supplied the city of Delhi with water. He reported that enterprising farmers planted sugar cane, cucumbers, and melons along the reservoir's rim as the water level fell during the dry season. A sultan in the fourteenth century built a network of irrigation canals in the Ganges plain that were not surpassed in size until the nineteenth century. These irrigation systems made it possible to grow crops throughout the year.

Since the tenth century the Indian Ocean island of Ceylon (modern Sri Lanka°) had been home to the greatest concentration of irrigation reservoirs and canals

---

Tuareg (TWAH-reg)   **Fulani** (foo-LAH-nee)

Delhi (DEL-ee)   **Sri Lanka** (sree LAHNG-kuh)

in the world. These facilities enabled the powerful Sinhalese° kingdom in arid northern Ceylon to support a large population. There was another impressive water-works in Southeast Asia, where a system of reservoirs and canals served Cambodia's capital city Angkor°.

These complex systems were vulnerable to disruption. Between 1250 and 1400 the irrigation complex in Ceylon fell into ruin when invaders from South India disrupted the Sinhalese government. The population of Ceylon then suffered from the effects of malaria, a tropical disease spread by mosquitoes breeding in the irrigation canals. The great Cambodian system fell into ruin in the fifteenth century when the government that maintained it collapsed. Neither system was ever rebuilt.

The vulnerability of complex irrigation systems built by powerful governments suggests an instructive contrast. Although village-based irrigation systems could be damaged by invasion and natural calamity, they usually bounced back because they were the product of local initiative, not centralized direction, and they depended on simpler technologies.

Mineral Resources

Throughout the tropics people mined and refined metal-rich ores, which skilled metalworkers turned into tools, weapons, and decorative objects. The more valuable metals, copper and gold, became important in long-distance trade.

Iron was the most abundant and useful of the metals worked in the tropics. Farmers depended on iron hoes, axes, and knives to clear and cultivate their fields and to open up parts of the rain forests of coastal West Africa and Southeast Asia for farming. Iron-tipped spears and arrows improved hunting success. Needles facilitated making clothes and leather goods; nails held timbers together. Indian metalsmiths were renowned for making strong and beautiful swords. In Africa the ability of iron smelters and blacksmiths to transform metal fostered a belief in their magical powers.

Copper and its alloys were of special importance in Africa. In the Copperbelt of southeastern Africa, the refined metal was cast into large X-shaped ingots (metal castings). Local coppersmiths worked these copper ingots into wire and decorative objects. Ibn Battuta described a town in the western Sudan that produced two sizes of copper bars that were used as a currency in place of coins. Skilled artisans in West Africa cast copper and brass (an alloy of copper and zinc) statues and heads that are considered among the masterpieces of world

King and Queen of Ife This copper-alloy work shows the royal couple of the Yoruba kingdom of Ife, the oldest and most sacred of the Yoruba kingdoms of southwestern Nigeria. The casting dates to the period between 1100 and 1500, except for the reconstruction of the male's face, the original of which shattered in 1957 when the road builder who found it accidentally struck it with his pick. (Andre Held, Switzerland)

art. These works were made by the "lost-wax" method, in which molten metal melts a thin layer of wax sandwiched between clay forms, replacing the "lost" wax with hard metal.

Africans exported large quantities of gold across the Sahara, the Red Sea, and the Indian Ocean. Some gold came from stream beds along the upper Niger River and farther south in modern Ghana°. In the hills south of the

---

Sinhalese (sin-huh-LEEZ)   **Angkor** (ANG-kor)

Ghana (GAH-nuh)

Zambezi° River (in modern Zimbabwe°) archaeologists have discovered thousands of mine shafts, dating from 1200, that were sunk up to 100 feet (30 meters) into the ground to get at gold ores. Although panning for gold remained important in the streams descending from the mountains of northern India, the gold and silver mines in India seem to have been exhausted by this period. For that reason, Indians imported considerable quantities of gold from Southeast Asia and Africa for jewelry and temple decoration.

Although they are rarely given credit for it, ordinary farmers, fishermen, herders, metalworkers, and others made possible the rise of powerful states and profitable commercial systems. Caravans could not have crossed the Sahara without the skilled guidance of desert pastoralists. The seafaring skills of the coastal fishermen underlay the trade of the Indian Ocean. Cities and empires rested on the food, labors, and taxes of these unsung heroes.

NEW ISLAMIC EMPIRES

The empires of Mali in West Africa and Delhi in South Asia were the largest and richest tropical states of the period between 1200 and 1500. Both utilized Islamic administrative and military systems introduced from the Islamic heartland, but in other ways these two Muslim sultanates were very different. **Mali** was founded by an indigenous African dynasty that had earlier adopted Islam through the peaceful influence of Muslim merchants and scholars. In contrast, the Delhi Sultanate was founded and ruled by invading Turkish and Afghan Muslims. Mali's wealth depended heavily on its participation in the trans-Saharan trade, but long-distance trade played only a minor role in Delhi.

Mali in the Western Sudan

The consolidation of the Middle East and North Africa under Muslim rule during the seventh and eighth centuries (see Chapter 9) greatly stimulated exchanges along the routes that crossed the Sahara. In the centuries that followed, the faith of Muhammad gradually spread to the lands south of the desert, which the Arabs called the *bilad al-sudan*°, "land of the blacks."

The role of force in spreading Islam south of the Sahara was limited. Muslim Berbers invading out of the desert in 1076 caused the collapse of Ghana, the empire that preceded Mali in the western Sudan (see Chapter 8), but their conquest did little to spread Islam. To the east, the Muslim attacks that destroyed the Christian Nubian kingdoms on the upper Nile in the late thirteenth century opened that area to Muslim influences, but Christian Ethiopia successfully withstood Muslim advances. Instead, the usual pattern for the spread of Islam south of the Sahara was through gradual and peaceful conversion. The expansion of commercial contacts in the western Sudan and on the East African coast greatly promoted the process of conversion. African converts found the teachings of Islam meaningful, and rulers and merchants found that the administrative, legal, and economic aspects of Islamic traditions suited their interests. The first sub-Saharan African ruler to adopt the new faith was in Takrur° in the far western Sudan, about 1030.

Shortly after 1200 Takrur expanded in importance under King Sumanguru°. Then in about 1240 Sundiata°, the upstart leader of the Malinke° people, handed Sumanguru a major defeat. Even though both leaders were Muslims, the Malinke epic sagas recall their battles as the clash of two powerful magicians, suggesting how much older beliefs shaped popular thought. The sagas say that Sumanguru was able to appear and disappear at will, assume dozens of shapes, and catch arrows in midflight. Sundiata defeated Sumanguru's much larger forces through superior military maneuvers and by successfully wounding his adversary with a special arrow that robbed him of his magical powers. This victory was followed by others that created Sundiata's Mali empire (see Map 14.2).

Like Ghana before it, Mali depended on a well-developed agricultural base and control of the lucrative regional and trans-Saharan trade routes. But Mali differed from Ghana in two ways. First, it was much larger. Mali controlled not only the core trading area of the upper Niger but the gold fields of the Niger headwaters to the southwest as well. Second, from the beginning its rulers were Muslims who fostered the spread of Islam among the political and trading elite of the empire. Control of the important gold and copper trades and contacts with North African Muslim traders gave Mali and its rulers unprecedented prosperity. The pilgrimage to Mecca of the ruler **Mansa Kankan Musa**° (r. 1312–1337), in fulfillment of his personal duty as a Muslim, also gave him an opportunity to display Mali's exceptional wealth. As befitted a powerful ruler, he

---

Zambezi (zam-BEE-zee) Zimbabwe (zim-BAHB-way)
bilad al-sudan (bih-LAD uhs–soo-DAN)

Takrur (TAHK-roor) Sumanguru (soo-muhn-GOO-roo)
Sundiata (soon-JAH-tuh) Malinke (muh-LING-kay)
Mansa Kankan Musa (MAHN-suh KAHN-kahn MOO-suh)

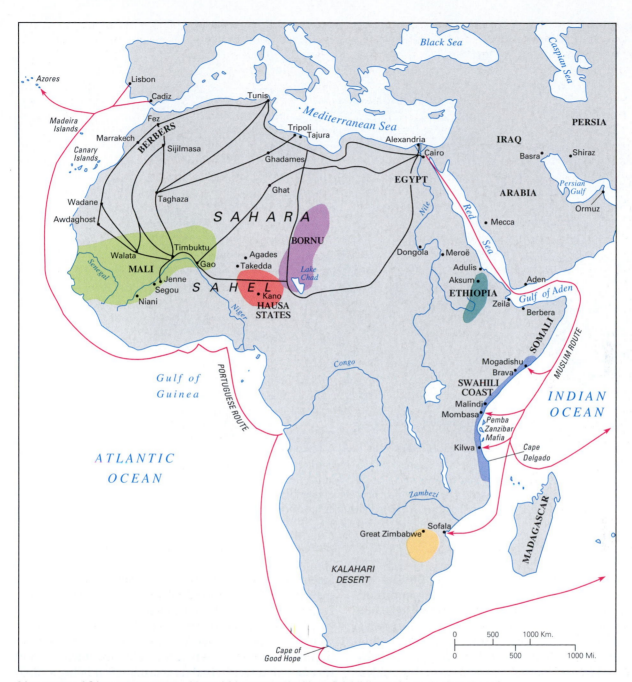

Map 14.2   Africa, 1200–1500   Many African states had beneficial links to the trade that crossed the Sahara and the Indian Ocean. Before 1500, sub-Saharan Africa's external ties were primarily with the Islamic world.

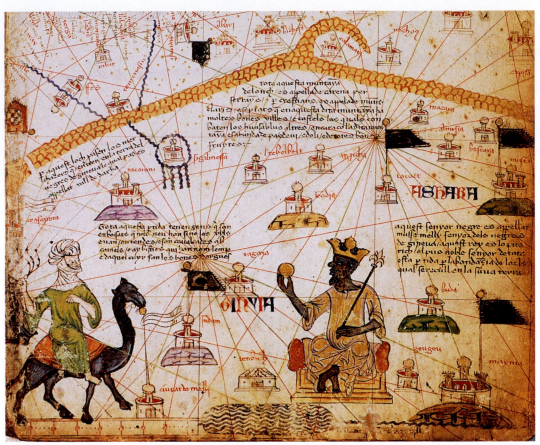

Map of the Western Sudan (1375)   A Jewish geographer on the Mediterranean island of Majorca drew this lavish map in 1375, incorporating all that was known in Europe about the rest of the world. This portion of the Catalan Atlas shows a North African trader approaching the king of Mali, who holds a gold nugget in one hand and a golden scepter in the other. A caption identifies the black ruler as Mansa Musa, "the richest and noblest king in all the land."   (Bibliothèque Nationale de France)

departed in 1324 with a large entourage. Besides his senior wife and 500 of her ladies in waiting and their slaves, according to one account, there were also 60,000 porters and a vast caravan of camels carrying supplies and provisions. For purchases and gifts he took eighty packages of gold each weighing 122 ounces (3.8 kilograms). In addition, 500 slaves each carried a golden staff. Mansa Musa was so lavish with his gifts when the entourage passed through Cairo that the value of gold there remained depressed for years.

After his return from the pilgrimage in 1325, Mansa Musa was eager to promote the religious and cultural influence of Islam in his empire. He built new mosques and opened Quranic schools in the cities along the Niger bend. When Ibn Battuta visited Mali from 1352 to 1354, during the reign of Mansa Musa's successor Mansa

Suleiman° (r. 1341–1360), he praised the Malians for their faithful recitation of Islamic prayers and for their zeal in teaching children the Quran.

Ibn Battuta also had high praise for Mali's government. He reported that "complete and general safety" prevailed in the vast territories ruled by Suleiman and that foreign travelers had no reason to fear being robbed by thieves or having their goods confiscated if they died. (For Ibn Battuta's account of the sultan's court and his subjects' respect see Diversity and Dominance: Personal Styles of Rule in India and Mali.)

Two centuries after Sundiata founded the empire, Mali began to disintegrate. When Mansa Suleiman's successors proved to be less able rulers, rebellions broke out

Mansa Suleiman (MAHN-suh SOO-lay-mahn)

among the diverse peoples who had been subjected to Malinke rule. Avid for Mali's wealth, other groups attacked from without. The desert Tuareg retook their city of Timbuktu° in 1433. By 1500 the rulers of Mali had dominion over little more than the Malinke heartland.

The cities of the upper Niger survived Mali's collapse, but some of the western Sudan's former trade and intellectual life moved east to other African states in the central Sudan. Shortly after 1450 the rulers of several of the Hausa city-states adopted Islam as their official religion. The Hausa states were also able to increase their importance as manufacturing and trading centers, becoming famous for their cotton textiles and leatherworking. Also expanding in the late fifteenth century was the central Sudanic state of Kanem-Bornu°. It was descended from the ancient kingdom of Kanem, whose rulers had accepted Islam in about 1085. At its peak about 1250, Kanem had absorbed the state of Bornu south and west of Lake Chad and gained control of important trade routes crossing the Sahara. As Kanem-Bornu's armies conquered new territories in the late fifteenth century, they also spread the rule of Islam.

The Delhi Sultanate in India

The arrival of Islam in India was more violent than in West Africa. Having long before lost the defensive unity of the Gupta Empire (see Chapter 7), the divided states of northwest India were subject to raids by Afghan warlords beginning in the early eleventh century. Motivated by a wish to spread their Islamic faith and by a desire for plunder, the raiders looted Hindu and Buddhist temples of their gold and jewels, kidnapped women for their harems, and slew Indian defenders by the thousands.

In the last decades of the twelfth century a new Turkish dynasty mounted a furious assault that succeeded in capturing the important northern Indian cities of Lahore and Delhi. The Muslim warriors could fire powerful crossbows from the backs of their galloping horses thanks to the use of iron stirrups. One partisan Muslim chronicler recorded, "The city [Delhi] and its vicinity was freed from idols and idol-worship, and in the sanctuaries of the images of the [Hindu] Gods, mosques were raised by the worshippers of one God."[2] The invaders' strength was bolstered by a ready supply of Turkish adventurers from Central Asia eager to follow individual leaders and by the unifying force of their common religious faith. Although Indians fought back bravely, their small states,

Salt Making in the Central Sahara For many centuries, people have extracted salt from the saline soils of places like Tegguida N'Tisent. Spring water is poured into shallow pits to dissolve the salt. The desert sun soon evaporates the water, leaving pure salt behind. (Afrique Photo, Cliché Naud, Paris)

often at war with one another, were unable to present an effective united front.

Between 1206 and 1236, the Muslim invaders extended their rule over the Hindu princes and chiefs in much of northern India. Sultan Iltutmish° (r. 1211–1236) consolidated the conquest of northern India in a series of military expeditions that made his empire the largest state in India (see Map 14.3). He also secured official recognition of the Delhi Sultanate as a Muslim state by the caliph of Baghdad. Although the looting and destruction of temples, enslavement, and massacres continued, especially on the frontiers of the empire, the Muslim invaders gradually underwent a transformation from brutal conquerors to more benign rulers. Muslim commanders accorded protection to the conquered, freeing them from persecution in return for payment of a special tax. Yet Hindus never forgot the intolerance and destruction of their first contacts with the invaders.

Timbuktu (tim-buk-TOO)
Kanem-Bornu (KAH-nuhm–BOR-noo)

Iltutmish (il-TOOT-mish)

우세인 은신처 방

파운드폭탄 4발 투하… 두 아들과 함께 사망 기

실진지 구축… 이틀째 시가戰

령이 대중 앞에 나타나거나 애국심
을 고취하는 노래만을 내보내던 방
송마저 중단됐다.

라크 전후 대
의에서는 전체
영국 주도로

DIVERSITY AND DOMINANCE

PERSONAL STYLES OF RULE IN INDIA AND MALI

Ibn Battuta wrote vivid descriptions of the powerful men who dominated the Muslim states he visited. Although his accounts are explicitly about the rulers, they also raise important issues about their relations with their subjects. The following account of Sultan Muhammad ibn Tughluq of Delhi may be read as a treatise on the rights and duties of rulers and ways in which individual personalities shaped diverse governing styles.

Muhammad is a man who, above all others, is fond of making presents and shedding blood. There may always be seen at his gate some poor person becoming rich, or some living one condemned to death. His generous and brave actions, and his cruel and violent deeds, have obtained notoriety among the people. In spite of this, he is the most humble of men, and the one who exhibits the greatest equity. The ceremonies of religion are dear to his ears, and he is very severe in respect of prayer and the punishment which follows its neglect. . . .

When drought prevailed throughout India and Sind, . . . the Sultan gave orders that provisions for six months should be supplied to all the inhabitants of Delhi from the royal granaries. . . . The officers of justice made registers of the people of the different streets, and these being sent up, each person received sufficient provisions to last him for six months.

The Sultan, notwithstanding all I have said about his humility, his justice, his kindness to the poor, and his boundless generosity, was much given to bloodshed. It rarely happened that the corpse of some one who had been killed was not seen at the gate of his palace. I have often seen men killed and their bodies left there. One day I went to his palace and my horse shied. I looked before me, and I saw a white heap on the ground, and when I asked what it was, one of my companions said it was the trunk of a man cut into three pieces. The sovereign punished little faults like great ones, and spared neither the learned, the religious, nor the noble. Every day hundreds of individuals were brought chained into his hall of audience; their hands tied to their necks and their feet bound together. Some of them were killed, and others were tortured, or well beaten . . . .

The Sultan has a brother named Masud Khan, [who] was one of the handsomest fellows I have even seen. The king suspected him of intending to rebel, so he questioned him, and, under fear of the torture, Masud confessed the charge. Indeed, every one who denies charges of this nature, which the Sultan brings against him, is put to the torture, and most people prefer death to being tortured. The Sultan had his brother's head cut off in the palace, and the corpse, according to custom, was left neglected for three days in the same place. The mother of Masud had been stoned two years before in the same place on a charge of debauchery or adultery. . . .

One of the most serious charges against this Sultan is that he forced all the inhabitants of Delhi to leave their homes. [After] the people of Delhi wrote letters full of insults and invectives against [him,] the Sultan . . . decided to ruin Delhi, so he purchased all the houses and inns from the inhabitants, paid them the price, and then ordered them to remove to Daulatabad. . . .

The greater part of the inhabitants departed, but [h]is slaves found two men in the streets: one was paralyzed, the other blind. They were brought before the sovereign, who ordered the paralytic to be shot away from a *manjanik* [catapult], and the blind man to be dragged from Delhi to Daulatabad, a journey of forty days' distance. The poor wretch fell to pieces during the journey, and only one of his legs reached Daulatabad. All of the inhabitants of Delhi left; they abandoned their baggage and their merchandize, and the city remained a perfect desert.

A person in whom I felt confidence assured me that the Sultan mounted one evening upon the roof of his palace, and, casting his eyes over the city of Delhi, in which there was neither fire, smoke, nor light, he said, "Now my heart is satisfied, and my feelings are appeased." . . . When we entered this capital, we found it in the state which has been described. It was empty, abandoned, and had but a small population.

In his description of Mansa Suleiman of Mali in 1353, Ibn Battuta places less emphasis on personality, a difference that may only be due to the fact that he had little personal contact with him. He stresses the huge social distance between the ruler and the ruled, between the master and the slave, and goes on to tell more of the ways in which Islam had altered life in Mali's cities as well as complaining about customs that the introduction of Islam had not changed.

The sultan of Mali is *Mansa* Suleiman, *mansa* meaning sultan, and Suleiman being his proper name. He is miserly, not a man from which one might hope for a rich present. It happened that I spent these two months without seeing him on account of my illness. Later on he held a banquet . . . to which the commanders, doctors, *qadi* and preacher were invited, and I went along with them. . . .

On certain days the sultan holds audiences in the palace yard, where there is a platform under a tree . . . carpeted with silk, [over which] is raised the umbrella, . . . surmounted by a bird in gold, about the size of a falcon. The sultan comes out of a door in a corner of the palace, carrying a bow in his hand and a quiver on his back. On his head he has a golden skull-cap, bound with a gold band which has narrow ends shaped like knives, more than a span in length. His usual dress is a velvety red tunic, made of the European fabrics called *mutanfas*. The sultan is preceded by his musicians, who carry gold and silver [two-stringed guitars], and behind him come three hundred armed slaves. He walks in a leisurely fashion, affecting a very slow movement, and even stops and looks round the assembly, then ascends [the platform] in the sedate manner of a preacher ascending a mosque-pulpit. As he takes his seat, the drums, trumpets, and bugles are sounded. Three slaves go at a run to summon the sovereign's deputy and the military commanders, who enter and sit down. . . .

The blacks are of all people the most submissive to their king and the most abject in their behavior before him. They swear by his name, saying *Mansa Suleiman ki* [by Mansa Suleiman's law]. If he summons any of them while he is holding an audience in his pavilion, the person summoned takes off his clothes and puts on worn garments, removes his turban and dons a dirty skullcap and enters with his garments and trousers raised knee-high. He goes forward in an attitude of humility and dejection, and knocks the ground hard with his elbows, then stands with bowed head and bent back listening to what he says. If anyone addresses the king and receives a reply from him, he uncovers his back and throws dust over his head and back, for all the world like a bather splashing himself with water. I used to wonder how it was that they did not blind themselves.

Among the admirable qualities of these people, the following are to be noted:

1. The small number of acts of injustice that one finds there; for the blacks are of all people those who most abhor injustice. The sultan pardons no one who is guilty of it.
2. The complete and general safety one enjoys throughout the land. The traveller has no more reason than the man who stays at home to fear brigands, thieves, or ravishers.
3. The blacks do not confiscate the goods of white men [i.e., North Africans and the Middle Easterners] who die in their country, not even when these consist of big treasure, They deposit them, on the contrary, with a man of confidence among the whites until those who have a right to the goods present themselves and take possession.
4. They make all their prayers punctually; they assiduously attend their meetings of the faithful, and punish their children if these should fail in this. On Fridays, anyone who is late at the mosque will find nowhere to pray, the crowd is so great. . . .
5. The blacks wear fine white garments on Fridays. If by chance a man has no more than one shirt or a soiled tunic, at least he washes it before putting it on to go to public prayer.
6. They zealously learn the Koran by heart. Those children who are neglectful in this are put in chains until they have memorized the Koran by heart. . . .

But these people have some deplorable customs, as for example:

1. Women servants, slave women, and young girls go about quite naked, not even covering their sexual parts. I saw many like this during Ramadan. . . .
2. Women go naked in the sultan's presence, too, without even a veil; his daughters also go about naked. On the twenty-seventh night of Ramadan I saw about a hundred women slaves coming out of the sultan's palace with food and they were naked. Two daughters of the sultan were with them, and these had no veil either, although they had big breasts.
3. The blacks throw dust and cinders on their heads as a sign of good manners and respect.
4. They have buffoons who appear before the sultan when his poets are reciting their praise songs.
5. And then a good number of the blacks eat the flesh of dogs and donkeys.

QUESTIONS FOR ANALYSIS

1. How would the actions of these rulers have enhanced their authority? To what extent do their actions reflect Islamic influences?
2. Although Ibn Battuta tells what the rulers did, can you imagine how one of their subjects would have described his or her perception of the same events and customs?
3. Which parts of Ibn Battuta's descriptions seem to be objective and believable? Which parts are more reflective of his personal values?

Source: The first excerpt is from Henry M. Elliot, *The History of India as Told by Its Own Historians* (London: Trübner and Co., 1869–1871) 3:611–614. The second excerpt is adapted from H. A. R. Gibb, ed., *Selections from the Travels of Ibn Battuta in Asia and Africa, 1325-1354* (London: Cambridge University Press, 1929), pp. 326–328. Copyright © 1929. Reprinted with permission of the Cambridge University Press.

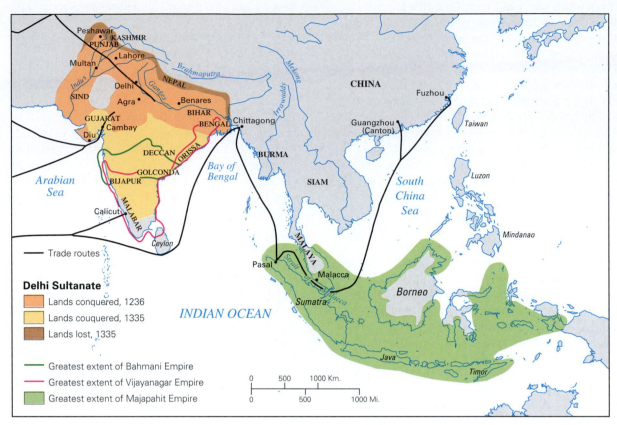

Map 14.3 South and Southeast Asia, 1200–1500 The rise of new empires and the expansion of maritime trade reshaped the lives of many tropical Asians.

To the astonishment of his ministers, Iltutmish passed over his weak and pleasure-seeking sons and designated his beloved and talented daughter Raziya° as his heir. When they questioned the unprecedented idea of a woman ruling a Muslim state, he said, "My sons are devoted to the pleasures of youth: no one of them is qualified to be king. . . . There is no one more competent to guide the State than my daughter.

In the event, her brother—whose great delight was riding his elephant through the bazaar, showering the crowds with coins—ruled ineptly for seven months before the ministers relented and put Raziya (r. 1236–1240) on the throne.

A chronicler who knew her explained why the reign of this able ruler lasted less than four years:

> Sultan Raziya was a great monarch. She was wise, just, and generous, a benefactor to her kingdom, a dispenser of justice, the protector of her subjects, and the leader of her armies. She was endowed with all

the qualities befitting a king, but that she was not born of the right sex, and so in the estimation of men all these virtues were worthless. May God have mercy upon her![3]

Doing her best to prove herself a proper king, Raziya dressed like a man and rode at the head of her troops atop an elephant. Nothing, however, could overcome the prejudice against a woman ruler. In the end the Turkish chiefs imprisoned her. Soon after she escaped, she died at the hands of a robber.

After a half-century of stagnation and rebellion, the ruthless but efficient policies of Sultan Ala-ud-din Khalji° (r. 1296–1316) increased his control over the empire's outlying provinces. Successful frontier raids and high taxes kept his treasury full; wage and price controls in Delhi kept down the cost of maintaining a large army; and a network of spies stifled intrigue. When a Mongol threat from the northeast eased, Ala-ud-din's forces extended the sultanate's southern flank, seizing the rich

Raziya (rah-ZEE-uh)

Ala-ud-din Khalji (uh-LAH–uh-DEEN KAL-jee)

Meenakshi Temple, Madurai, India   Some 15,000 pilgrims a day visit the large Hindu temple of Meenakshi (the fish-eyed goddess) in the ancient holy city of Madurai in India's southeastern province of Tamil Nadu. The temple complex dates from at least 1000 C.E., although the elaborately painted statues of these gopuram (gate towers) have been rebuilt and restored many times. The largest gopura rises 150 feet (46 meters) above the ground.   (Jean Louis NOU/akg-images)

trading state of **Gujarat**° in 1298. Then troops drove southward, briefly seizing the southern tip of the Indian peninsula.

At the time of Ibn Battuta's visit, Delhi's ruler was Sultan Muhammad ibn Tughluq° (r. 1325–1351), who received his visitor at his palace's celebrated Hall of a Thousand Pillars. The world traveler praised the sultan's piety and generosity, but also recounted his cruelties (see Diversity and Dominance: Personal Styles of Rule in India and Mali). In keeping with these complexities, the sultan resumed a policy of aggressive expansion that enlarged the sultanate to its greatest extent. He balanced that policy with religious toleration intended to win the loyalty of Hindus and other non-Muslims. He even attended Hindu religious festivals. However, his successor Firuz Shah° (r. 1351–1388) alienated powerful Hindus by taxing the Brahmins, preferring to cultivate good relations with the Muslim elite. Muslim chroniclers praised

him for constructing forty mosques, thirty colleges, and a hundred hospitals.

A small minority in a giant land, the Turkish rulers relied on terror more than on toleration to keep their subjects submissive, on harsh military reprisals to put down rebellion, and on pillage and high taxes to sustain the ruling elite in luxury and power. Though little different from most other large states of the time (including Mali) in being more a burden than a benefit to most of its subjects, the sultanate never lost the disadvantage of foreign origins and alien religious identity. Nevertheless, over time, the sultans incorporated some Hindus into their administration. Some members of the ruling elite also married women from prominent Hindu families, though the brides had to become Muslims.

Personal and religious rivalries within the Muslim elite, as well as the discontent of the Hindus, threatened the Delhi Sultanate with disintegration whenever it showed weakness and finally hastened its end. In the mid-fourteenth century Muslim nobles challenged the sultan's dominion and successfully established the

---

Gujarat (goo-juh-RAHT)   **Tughluq** (toog-LOOK)
Firuz Shah (fuh-ROOZ shah)

Bahmani° kingdom (1347–1482), which controlled the Deccan Plateau. To defend themselves against the southward push of Bahmani armies, the Hindu states of southern India united to form the Vijayanagar° Empire (1336–1565), which at its height controlled the rich trading ports on both coasts and held Ceylon as a tributary state.

The rulers of Vijayanagar and the Bahmani turned a blind eye to religious differences when doing so favored their interests. Bahmani rulers sought to balance devotion to Muslim domination with the practical importance of incorporating the leaders of the majority Hindu population into the government, marrying Hindu wives, and appointing Brahmins to high offices. Vijayanagar rulers hired Muslim cavalry specialists and archers to strengthen their military forces, and they formed an alliance with the Muslim-ruled state of Gujarat.

By 1351, when all of South India was independent of Delhi's rule, much of north India was also in rebellion. In the east, Bengal successfully broke away from the sultanate in 1338, becoming a center of the mystical Sufi tradition of Islam (see Chapter 9). In the west, Gujarat had regained its independence by 1390. The weakening of Delhi's central authority revived Mongol interests in the area. In 1398 the Turko-Mongol leader Timur (see Chapter 13) seized the opportunity to invade and captured the city of Delhi. When his armies withdrew the next year with vast quantities of pillage and tens of thousands of captives, the largest city in southern Asia lay empty and in ruins. The Delhi Sultanate never recovered.

For all its shortcomings, the Delhi Sultanate was important in the development of centralized political authority in India. It established a bureaucracy headed by the sultan, who was aided by a prime minister and provincial governors. There were efforts to improve food production, promote trade and economic growth, and establish a common currency. Despite the many conflicts that Muslim conquest and rule provoked, Islam gradually acquired a permanent place in South Asia.

INDIAN OCEAN TRADE

The maritime network that stretched across the Indian Ocean from the Islamic heartland of Iran and Arabia to Southeast Asia connected to Europe, Africa, and China. The Indian Ocean region was the world's richest maritime trading network and an area of rapid Muslim expansion.

Bahmani (bah MAHN-ee)　**Vijayanagar** (vee-juh-yah-NAH-gar)

Monsoon Mariners

The rising prosperity of Asian, European, and African states stimulated the expansion of trade in the Indian Ocean after 1200. Some of the growth was in luxuries for the wealthy—precious metals and jewels, rare spices, fine textiles, and other manufactures. The construction of larger ships also made shipments of bulk cargoes of ordinary cotton textiles, pepper, food grains (rice, wheat, barley), timber, horses, and other goods profitable. When the collapse of the Mongol Empire in the fourteenth century disrupted overland trade routes across Central Asia, the Indian Ocean routes assumed greater strategic importance in tying together the peoples of Eurasia and Africa.

Some goods were transported from one end of this trading network to the other, but few ships or crews made a complete circuit. Instead the Indian Ocean trade was divided into two legs: one from the Middle East across the Arabian Sea to India, and the other from India across the Bay of Bengal to Southeast Asia (see Map 14.4).

The characteristic cargo and passenger ship of the Arabian Sea was the **dhow**° (see Environment and Technology: The Indian Ocean Dhow). Ports on the Malabar coast of southwestern India constructed many of these vessels, which grew from an average capacity of 100 tons in 1200 to 400 tons in 1500. On a typical expedition, a dhow might sail west from India to Arabia and Africa on the northeast monsoon winds (December to March) and return on the southwest monsoons (April to August). Small dhows kept the coast in sight. Relying on the stars to guide them, skilled pilots steered large vessels by the quicker route straight across the water. A large dhow could sail from the Red Sea to mainland Southeast Asia in from two to four months, but few did so. Instead, cargoes and passengers normally sailed eastward to India in junks, which dominated travel in the Bay of Bengal and the South China Sea.

The largest, most technologically advanced, and most seaworthy vessel of this time, the junk had been developed in China. Junks were built from heavy spruce or fir planks held together with enormous nails. The space below the deck was divided into watertight compartments to minimize flooding in case of damage to the ship's hull. According to Ibn Battuta, the largest junks had twelve sails made of bamboo and carried a crew of a thousand men, of whom four hundred were soldiers. A large junk might have up to a hundred passenger cabins and could carry a cargo of over 1,000 tons. Chinese junks dominated China's foreign shipping to Southeast Asia

dhow (dow)

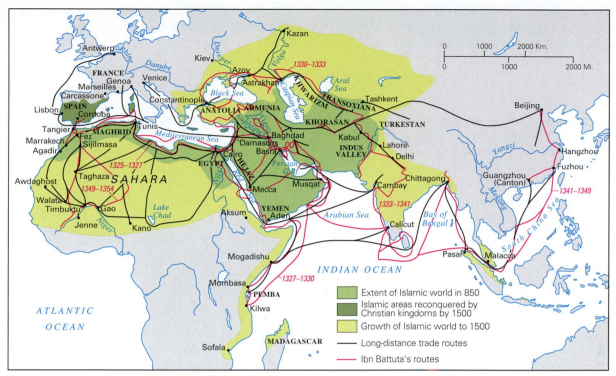

Map 14.4   Arteries of Trade and Travel in the Islamic World, to 1500 Ibn Battuta's journeys across Africa and Asia made use of land and sea routes along which Muslim traders and the Islamic faith had long traveled.

and India, but not all of the junks that plied these waters were Chinese. During the fifteenth century, vessels of this type came from shipyards in Bengal and Southeast Asia and were sailed by local crews.

The trade of the Indian Ocean was decentralized and cooperative. Commercial interests, rather than political authorities, tied several distinct regional networks together (see Map 14.4). Eastern Africa supplied gold from inland areas. Ports around the Arabian peninsula shipped horses and goods from the northern parts of the Middle East, the Mediterranean, and eastern Europe. At the center of the Indian Ocean trade, merchants in the cities of coastal India received goods from east and west, sold some locally, passed others along, and added vast quantities of Indian goods to the trade. The Strait of Malacca°, between the eastern end of the Indian Ocean and the South China Sea, was the meeting point of trade from Southeast Asia, China, and the Indian Ocean. In each region certain ports functioned as giant emporia, consolidating goods from smaller ports

and inland areas for transport across the seas. The operation of this complex trading system can best be understood by looking at some of the regions and their emporia in greater detail.

Africa: The Swahili and Zimbabwe

Trade expanded steadily along the East African coast from about 1250, giving rise to between thirty and forty separate city-states by 1500. As a result of this rising prosperity, new masonry buildings, sometimes three or four stories high, replaced many of the mud and thatch African fishing villages. Archaeology reveals the growing presence of imported glass beads, Chinese porcelain, and other exotic goods. As a result of trading contacts, many loan words from Arabic and Persian enriched the language of the coastal Africans, and the first to write in it used Arabic script. The visitors called these people "Swahili,"° from the Arabic name *sawahil*° *al-sudan*, meaning "shores of the blacks," and the name stuck.

Malacca (meh-LAK-eh)

Swahili (swah-HEE-lee)   *sawahil* (suh-WAH-hil)

The Indian Ocean Dhow

The sailing vessels that crossed the Indian Ocean shared the diversity of that trading area. The name by which we know them, *dhow*, comes from the Swahili language of the East African coast. The planks of teak from which their hulls were constructed were hewn from the tropical forests of South India and Southeast Asia. Their pilots, who navigated by stars at night, used the ancient technique that Arabs had used to find their way across the desert. Some pilots used a magnetic compass, which originated in China.

Dhows came in various sizes and designs, but all had two distinctive features in common. The first was hull construction. The hulls of dhows consisted of planks that were sewn together, not nailed. Cord made of fiber from the husk of coconuts or other materials was passed through rows of holes drilled in the planks. Because cord is weaker than nails, outsiders considered this shipbuilding technique strange. Marco Polo fancifully suggested that it indicated sailors' fear that large ocean magnets would pull any nails out of their ships. More probable explanations are that pliant sewn hulls were cheaper to build than rigid nailed hulls and were less likely to be damaged if the ships ran aground on coral reefs.

The second distinctive feature of dhows was their triangular (lateen) sails made of palm leaves or cotton. The sails were suspended from tall masts and could be turned to catch the wind.

The sewn hull and lateen sails were technologies developed centuries earlier, but there were two innovations between 1200 and 1500. First, a rudder positioned at the stern (rear end) of the ship replaced the large side oar that formerly had controlled steering. Second, shipbuilders increased the size of dhows to accommodate bulkier cargoes.

Dhow   This modern model shows the vessel's main features. (National Maritime Museum, London)

Royal Enclosure, Great Zimbabwe   Inside these oval stone walls the rulers of the trading state of Great Zimbabwe lived. Forced to enter the enclosure through a narrow corridor between two high walls, visitors were meant to be awestruck.   (Courtesy of the Department of Information, Rhodesia)

At the time of Ibn Battuta's visit, the southern city of Kilwa had displaced Mogadishu as the **Swahili Coast's** most important commercial center. The traveler declared Kilwa "one of the most beautiful and well-constructed towns in the world." He noted that its dark-skinned inhabitants were devout and pious Muslims, and he took special pains to praise their ruler as a man rich in the traditional Muslim virtues of humility and generosity.

Swahili oral traditions associate the coast's commercial expansion with the arrival of Arab and Iranian merchants, but do not say what had attracted them. In Kilwa's case the answer is gold. By the late fifteenth century the city was exporting a ton of gold a year. The gold was mined by inland Africans much farther south. Much of it came from or passed through a powerful state on the plateau south of the Zambezi River, whose capital city is known as **Great Zimbabwe.** At its peak in about 1400, the city, which occupied 193 acres (78 hectares), may have had 18,000 inhabitants.

Between about 1250 and 1450, local African craftsmen built stone structures for Great Zimbabwe's rulers, priests, and wealthy citizens. The largest structure, a walled enclosure the size and shape of a large football stadium, served as the king's court. Its walls of unmortared stone were up to 17 feet (5 meters) thick and 32 feet (10 meters) high. Inside the walls were many buildings, including a large conical stone tower. The stone ruins of Great Zimbabwe are one of the most famous historical sites in sub-Saharan Africa.

Mixed farming and cattle-herding was Great Zimbabwe's economic base, but, as in Mali, the state's wealth came from long-distance trade. Trade began regionally with copper ingots from the upper Zambezi Valley, salt, and local manufactures. The gold exports into the Indian Ocean in the fourteenth and fifteenth centuries brought Zimbabwe to the peak of its political and economic power. However, historians suspect that the city's residents depleted nearby forests for firewood while their cattle overgrazed surrounding grasslands. The resulting ecological crisis hastened the empire's decline in the fifteenth century.

Arabia: Aden and the Red Sea

The city of **Aden**° had a double advantage in the Indian Ocean trade. Most of the rest of Arabia was desert, but monsoon winds brought Aden enough rainfall to supply drinking water to a large population and to grow grain for export. In addition, Aden's location (see Map 14.2) made it a convenient stopover for trade with India, the Persian Gulf, East Africa, and Egypt. Aden's merchants sorted out the goods from one place and sent them on to another: cotton cloth and beads from India, spices from Southeast Asia, horses from Arabia and Ethiopia, pearls from the Red Sea, luxurious manufactures from Cairo, slaves, gold, and ivory from Ethiopia, and grain, opium, and dyes from Aden's own hinterland.

After visiting Mecca in 1331, Ibn Battuta sailed down the Red Sea to Aden, probably wedged among bales of trade goods. His comments on the great wealth of Aden's leading merchants include a story about the slave of one merchant who paid the fabulous sum of 400 dinars for a ram in order to keep the slave of another merchant from buying it. Instead of punishing the slave for this extravagance, the master freed him as a reward for outdoing his rival. Ninety years later a Chinese Muslim visitor, Ma Huan, found "the country . . . rich, and the people numerous," living in stone residences several stories high.

Common commercial interests generally promoted good relations among the different religions and cultures of this region. For example, in the mid-thirteenth century a wealthy Jew from Aden named Yosef settled in Christian Ethiopia, where he acted as an adviser. South Arabia had been trading with neighboring parts of Africa since before the time of King Solomon of Israel. The dynasty that ruled Ethiopia after 1270 claimed descent from Solomon and from the South Arabian princess Sheba. Solomonic Ethiopia's consolidation was associated with a great increase in trade through the Red Sea port of Zeila°, including slaves, amber, and animal pelts, which went to Aden and on to other destinations.

Friction sometimes arose, however. In the fourteenth century the Sunni Muslim king of Yemen sent materials for the building of a large mosque in Zeila, but the local Somalis (who were Shi'ite Muslims) threw the stones into the sea. The result was a year-long embargo of Zeila ships in Aden. In the late fifteenth century Ethiopia's territorial expansion and efforts to increase control over the trade provoked conflicts with Muslims who ruled the coastal states of the Red Sea.

India: Gujarat and the Malabar Coast

The state of Gujarat in western India prospered as its ports shared in the expanding trade of the Arabian Sea and the rise of the Delhi Sultanate. Blessed with a rich agricultural hinterland and a long coastline, Gujarat attracted new trade after the Mongol capture of Baghdad in 1258 disrupted the northern land routes. Gujarat's forcible incorporation into the Delhi Sultanate in 1298 had mixed results. The state suffered from the violence of the initial conquest and from subsequent military crackdowns, but it also prospered from increased trade with Delhi's wealthy ruling class. Independent again after 1390, Gujarat's Muslim rulers extended their control over neighboring Hindu states and regained their preeminent position in the Indian Ocean trade.

The state derived much of its wealth from its export of cotton textiles and indigo to the Middle East and Europe, largely in return for gold and silver. Gujaratis also dominated the trade from India to the Swahili Coast, selling cotton cloth, carnelian beads, and foodstuffs in exchange for ebony, slaves, ivory, and gold. During the fifteenth century traders expanded their trade from Gujarat eastward to the Strait of Malacca. These Gujarati merchants helped spread the Islamic faith among East Indian traders, some of whom even imported specially carved gravestones from Gujarat.

Unlike Kilwa and Aden, Gujarat was important for its manufactures as well as its commerce. According to the thirteenth-century Venetian traveler Marco Polo, Gujarat's leatherworkers dressed enough skins in a year to fill several ships to Arabia and other places and also made beautiful sleeping mats for export to the Middle East "in red and blue leather, exquisitely inlaid with figures of birds and beasts, and skilfully embroidered with gold and silver wire," as well as leather cushions embroidered in gold. Later observers considered the Gujarati city of Cambay the equal of cities in Flanders and northern Italy (see Chapter 15) in the size, skill, and diversity of its textile industries.

Gujarat's cotton, linen, and silk cloth, as well as its carpets and quilts, found a large market in Europe, Africa, the Middle East, and Southeast Asia. Cambay also was famous for its polished gemstones, gold jewelry, carved ivory, stone beads, and both natural and artificial pearls. At the height of its prosperity in the fifteenth century, this substantial city's well-laid-out streets and open places boasted fine stone houses with tiled roofs. Al-

---

Aden (AY-den) **Zeila** (ZEYE-luh)

though most of Gujarat's overseas trade was in the hands of its Muslim residents, members of its Hindu merchant caste profited so much from related commercial activities that their wealth and luxurious lives were the envy of other Indians.

More southerly cities on the Malabar Coast duplicated Gujarat's importance in trade and manufacturing. Calicut° and other coastal cities prospered from their commerce in locally made cotton textiles and locally grown grains and spices, and as clearing-houses for the long-distance trade of the Indian Ocean. The Zamorin° (ruler) of Calicut presided over a loose federation of its Hindu rulers along the Malabar Coast. As in eastern Africa and Arabia, rulers were generally tolerant of other religious and ethnic groups that were important to commercial profits. Most trading activity was in the hands of Muslims, many originally from Iran and Arabia, who intermarried with local Indian Muslims. Jewish merchants also operated from Malabar's trading cities.

Southeast Asia: The Rise of Malacca

At the eastern end of the Indian Ocean, the principal passage into the South China Sea was through the Strait of Malacca between the Malay Peninsula and the island of Sumatra (see Map 14.3). As trade increased in the fourteenth and fifteenth centuries, this commercial choke point became the object of considerable political rivalry. The mainland kingdom of Siam gained control of most of the upper Malay Peninsula, while the Java-based kingdom of Majapahit° extended its dominion over the lower Malay Peninsula and much of Sumatra. Majapahit, however, was not strong enough to suppress a nest of Chinese pirates who had gained control of the Sumatran city of Palembang° and preyed on ships sailing through the strait. In 1407 a fleet sent by the Chinese government smashed the pirates' power and took their chief back to China for trial.

Weakened by internal struggles, Majapahit was unable to take advantage of China's intervention. The chief beneficiary of the safer commerce was the newer port of **Malacca** (or Melaka), which dominated the narrowest part of the strait. Under the leadership of a prince from Palembang, Malacca had quickly grown from an obscure fishing village into an important port by means of a series of astute alliances. Nominally subject to the king of Siam, Malacca also secured an alliance with China that was sealed by the visit of the imperial fleet in 1407. The

Calicut (KAL-ih-cut)   **Zamorin** (ZAH-much-ruhn)
Majapahit (mah-jah-PAH-hit)   **Palembang** (pah-lem-BONG)

conversion of an early ruler from Hinduism to Islam helped promote trade with the Gujarati and other Muslim merchants who dominated so much of the Indian Ocean commerce. Merchants also appreciated Malacca's security and low taxes.

Malacca served as the meeting point for traders from India and China as well as an emporium for Southeast Asian trade: rubies and musk from Burma, tin from Malaya, gold from Sumatra, cloves and nutmeg from the Moluccas (or Spice Islands, as Europeans later dubbed them) to the east. Shortly after 1500, when Malacca was at its height, one resident counted eighty-four languages spoken among the merchants gathered there, who came from as far away as Turkey, Ethiopia, and the Swahili Coast. Four officials administered the large foreign merchant communities: one official for the very numerous Gujaratis, one for other Indians and Burmese, one for Southeast Asians, and one for the Chinese and Japanese. Malacca's wealth and its cosmopolitan residents set the standard for luxury in Malaya for centuries to come.

SOCIAL AND CULTURAL CHANGE

State growth, commercial expansion, and the spread of Islam between 1200 and 1500 led to many changes in the social and cultural life of tropical peoples. The political and commercial elites at the top of society grew more numerous, as did the slaves who served their needs. The spread of Islamic practices and beliefs affected social and cultural life—witness words of Arabic origin like *Sahara, Sudan, Swahili,* and *monsoon*—yet local traditions remained important.

Architecture, Learning, and Religion

Social and cultural changes typically affect cities more than rural areas. As Ibn Battuta observed, wealthy merchants and the ruling elite spent lavishly on new mansions, palaces, and places of worship.

Places of worship from this period exhibit fascinating blends of older traditions and new influences. African Muslims strikingly rendered Middle Eastern mosque designs in local building materials: sun-baked clay and wood in the western Sudan, coral stone on the Swahili Coast. Hindu temple architecture influenced the design of mosques, which sometimes incorporated pieces of older structures. The congregational mosque at Cambay, built in 1325, was assembled out of pillars,

Church of Saint George, Ethiopia King Lalibela, who ruled the Christian kingdom of Ethiopia between about 1180 and 1220, had a series of churches carved out of solid volcanic rock to adorn his kingdom's new capital (also named Lalibela). The church of Saint George, excavated to a depth of 40 feet (13 meters) and hollowed out inside, has the shape of a Greek cross.   (S. Sassoon/ Robert Harding Picture Library)

porches, and arches taken from sacked Hindu and Jain° temples. The culmination of a mature Hindu-Muslim architecture was the congregational mosque erected at the Gujarati capital of Ahmadabad° in 1423. It had an open courtyard typical of mosques everywhere, but the surrounding verandas incorporated many typical Gujarati details and architectural conventions.

Even more unusual than these Islamic architectural amalgams were the Christian churches of King Lalibela° of Ethiopia, constructed during the first third of the thirteenth century. As part of his new capital, Lalibela directed Ethiopian sculptors to carve eleven churches out of solid rock, each commemorating a sacred Christian site in Jerusalem. These unique structures carried on an old Ethiopian tradition of rock sculpture, though on a far grander scale.

Mosques, churches, and temples were centers of education as well as prayer. Muslims promoted literacy among their sons (and sometimes their daughters) so

that they could read the religion's classic texts. Ibn Battuta reported seeing several boys in Mali who had been placed in chains until they finished memorizing passages of the Quran. In sub-Saharan Africa the spread of Islam was associated with the spread of literacy, which had previously been confined largely to Christian Ethiopia. Initially, literacy was in Arabic, but in time Arabic characters were used to write local languages.

Islam affected literacy less in India, which had an ancient heritage of writing. Arabic served primarily for religious purposes, while Persian became the language of high culture and was used at court. Eventually, **Urdu**° arose, a Persian-influenced literary form of Hindi written in Arabic characters. Muslims also introduced papermaking in India.

Advanced Muslim scholars studied Islamic law, theology, and administration, as well as works of mathematics, medicine, and science, derived in part from ancient Greek writings. By the sixteenth century in the West African city **Timbuktu,** there were over 150 Quranic

---

Jain (jine)   **Ahmadabad** (AH-muhd-ah-bahd)
Lalibela (LAH-lee-BEL-uh)

Urdu (ER-doo)

schools, and advanced classes were held in the mosques and homes of the leading clerics. So great was the demand for books that they were the most profitable item to bring from North Africa to Timbuktu. At his death in 1536 one West African scholar, al-Hajj Ahmed of Timbuktu, possessed some seven hundred volumes, an unusually large library for that time. In Southeast Asia, Malacca became a center of Islamic learning from which scholars spread Islam throughout the region. Other important centers of learning developed in Muslim India, particularly in Delhi, the capital.

Even in conquered lands, such as India, Muslim rulers generally did not impose their religion. Example and persuasion by merchants and Sufis proved a more effective way of making converts. Many Muslims were active missionaries for their faith and worked hard to persuade others of its superiority. Islam's influence spread along regional trade routes from the Swahili Coast, in the Sudan, in coastal India, and in Southeast Asia. Commercial transactions could take place between people of different religions, but the common code of morality and law that Islam provided attracted many local merchants.

Marriage also spread Islam. Single Muslim men who journeyed along the trade routes often married local women and raised their children in the Islamic faith. Since Islam permitted a man to have up to four legal wives and many men took concubines as well, some wealthy men had dozens of children. In large elite Muslim households the many servants, both free and enslaved, were also required to be Muslims. Although such conversions were not fully voluntary, individuals could still find personal fulfillment in the Islamic faith.

In India Islamic invasions practically destroyed the last strongholds of long-declining Buddhism. In 1196 invaders overran the great Buddhist center of study at Nalanda° in Bihar° and burned its manuscripts, killing thousands of monks or driving them into exile in Nepal and Tibet. With Buddhism reduced to a minor faith in the land of its birth (see Chapter 8), Islam emerged as India's second most important religion. Hinduism was still India's dominant faith in 1500, but in most of maritime Southeast Asia Islam displaced Hinduism.

Islam also spread among the pastoral Fulani of West Africa and Somali of northeastern Africa, as well as among pastoralists in northwest India. In Bengal Muslim religious figures oversaw the conversion of jungle into farmland and thereby gained many converts among low-caste Hindus who admired the universalism of Islam.

Nalanda (nuh-LAN-duh)   **Bihar** (bee-HAHR)

The spread of Islam did not simply mean the replacement of one set of beliefs by another. Islam also adapted to the cultures of the regions it penetrated, developing African, Indian, and Indonesian varieties.

Social and Gender Distinctions

The conquests and commerce brought new wealth to some and new hardships to others. The poor may not have become poorer, but a significant growth in slavery accompanied the rising prosperity of the elite. According to Islamic sources, military campaigns in India reduced hundreds of thousands of Hindu "infidels" to slavery. Delhi overflowed with slaves. Sultan Ala-ud-din owned 50,000; Firuz Shah had 180,000, including 12,000 skilled artisans. Sultan Tughluq sent 100 male slaves and 100 female slaves as a gift to the emperor of China in return for a similar gift. His successor prohibited any more exports of slaves, perhaps because of reduced supplies in the smaller empire.

Mali and Bornu sent slaves across the Sahara to North Africa, including young maidens and eunuchs (castrated males). Ethiopian expansion generated a regular supply of captives for sale to Aden traders at Zeila. About 2.5 million enslaved Africans may have crossed the Sahara and the Red Sea between 1200 and 1500. Other slaves were shipped from the Swahili Coast to India, where Africans played conspicuous roles in the navies, armies, and administrations of some Indian states, especially in the fifteenth century. A few African slaves even found their way to China, where a Chinese source dating from about 1225 says that rich families preferred gatekeepers whose bodies were "black as lacquer."

With "free" labor abundant and cheap, most slaves were trained for special purposes. In some places, skilled trades and military service were dominated by hereditary castes of slaves, some of whom were rich and powerful. Indeed, the earliest rulers of the Delhi Sultanate rose from military slaves. A slave general in the western Sudan named Askia Muhammad seized control of the Songhai Empire (Mali's successor) in 1493. Less fortunate slaves, like the men and women who mined copper in Mali, did hard menial work.

Wealthy households in Asia and Africa employed many slaves as servants. Eunuchs guarded the harems of wealthy Muslims; female slaves were in great demand as household servants, entertainers, and concubines. Some rich men aspired to have a concubine from every part of the world. One of Firuz Shah's nobles was said to have two thousand harem slaves, including women from Turkey and China.

Indian Woman Spinning, ca. 1500   This drawing of a Muslim woman by an Indian artist shows the influence of Persian styles. The spinning of cotton fiber into thread—women's work—was made much easier by the spinning wheel, which the Muslim invaders introduced. Men then wove the threads into the cotton textiles for which India was celebrated.   (British Library, Oriental and Indian Office Library, Or 3299, f. 151)

Sultan Ala-ud-din's campaigns against Gujarat at the end of the thirteenth century yielded a booty of twenty thousand maidens in addition to innumerable younger children of both sexes. The supply of captives became so great that the lowest grade of horse sold for five times as much as an ordinary female slave destined for service, although beautiful young virgins destined for the harems of powerful nobles commanded far higher prices. Some decades later, when Ibn Battuta was given ten girls captured from among the "infidels," he commented: "Female captives [in Delhi] are very cheap because they are dirty and do not know civilized ways. Even the educated ones are cheap." It would seem fairer to say that such slaves were cheap because the large numbers offered for sale had made them so.

Hindu legal digests and commentaries suggest that the position of Hindu women may have improved somewhat overall. The ancient practice of sati°—in which an upper-caste widow threw herself on her husband's funeral pyre—remained a meritorious act strongly approved by social custom. But Ibn Battuta believed that sati was strictly optional, an interpretation reinforced by the Hindu commentaries that devote considerable attention to the rights of widows.

Indian parents still gave their daughters in marriage before the age of puberty, but consummation of the marriage was supposed to take place only when the young woman was ready. Wives were expected to observe far stricter rules of fidelity and chastity than were their husbands and could be abandoned for many serious breaches. But women often were punished by lighter penalties than men for offenses against law and custom.

A female's status was largely determined by the status of her male master—father, husband, or owner. Women usually were not permitted to play the kind of active roles in commerce, administration, or religion that would have given them scope for personal achievements. Even so, women possessed considerable skills within those areas of activity that social norms allotted to them.

Besides child rearing, one of the most widespread female skills was food preparation. So far, historians have paid little attention to the development of culinary skills, but preparing meals that were healthful and tasty required much training and practice, especially given the limited range of foods available in most places. One kitchen skill that has received greater attention is brewing, perhaps because men were the principal consumers. In many parts of Africa women commonly made beer from grains or bananas. These mildly alcoholic beverages, taken in moderation, were a nutritious source of vitamins and minerals. Socially they were an important part of male rituals of hospitality and relaxation.

Throughout tropical Africa and Asia women did much of the farm work. They also toted home heavy loads of food, firewood, and water for cooking, balanced on their heads. Other common female activities included making clay pots for cooking and storage and making clothing. In India the spinning wheel, introduced by the Muslim invaders, greatly reduced the cost of making yarn for weaving. Spinning was a woman's activity done in the home; the weavers were generally men. Marketing was a common activity among women, especially in West Africa, where they commonly sold agricultural products, pottery, and other craftwork in the markets.

Some free women found their status improved by becoming part of a Muslim household, while many others were forced to become servants and concubines. Adopting Islam did not require accepting all the social customs of the Arab world. Ibn Battuta was appalled that Muslim women in Mali did not completely cover their

sati (suh-TEE)

bodies and veil their faces when appearing in public. He considered their nakedness an offense to women's (and men's) modesty. In another part of Mali he berated a Muslim merchant from Morocco for permitting his wife to sit on a couch and chat with a male friend of hers. The husband replied, "The association of women with men is agreeable to us and part of good manners, to which no suspicion attaches." Ibn Battuta's shock at this "laxity" and his refusal to ever visit the merchant again reveal the patriarchal precepts that were dear to most elite Muslims. So does the fate of Sultan Raziya of Delhi.

CONCLUSION

Tropical Africa and Asia contained nearly 40 percent of the world's population and over a quarter of its habitable land. Between 1200 and 1500 commercial, political, and cultural expansion drew the region's diverse peoples closer together. The Indian Ocean became the world's most important and richest trading area. The Delhi Sultanate brought South Asia its greatest political unity since the decline of the Guptas. In the western Sudan, Mali extended the political and trading role pioneered by Ghana. This growth of trade and empires was closely connected with the enlargement of Islam's presence in the tropical world along with the introduction of greater diversity into Islamic practice.

But if change was an important theme of this period, so too was social and cultural stability. Most tropical Africans and Asians never ventured far outside the rural communities in which their families had lived for generations. Their lives followed the familiar pattern of the seasons, the cycle of religious rituals and festivals, and the stages from childhood to elder status. Custom and necessity defined occupations. Most people engaged in food production by farming, herding, and fishing; some specialized in crafts or religious leadership. Based on the accumulated wisdom about how best to deal with their environment, such village communities were remarkably hardy. They might be ravaged by natural disaster or pillaged by advancing armies, but over time most recovered. Empires and kingdoms rose and fell in these centuries, but the villages endured.

In comparison, social, political, and environmental changes taking place in the Latin West, described in the next chapter, were in many ways more profound and disruptive. They would have great implications for tropical peoples after 1500.

Key Terms

tropics	dhow
monsoon	Swahili Coast
Ibn Battuta	Great Zimbabwe
Delhi Sultanate	Aden
Mali	Malacca
Mansa Kankan Musa	Urdu
Gujarat	Timbuktu

Suggested Reading

The trading links among the lands around the Indian Ocean have attracted the attention of recent scholars. A fine place to begin is Patricia Risso, *Merchants and Faith: Muslim Commerce and Culture in the Indian Ocean* (1995). More ambitious but perhaps more inclined to overreach the evidence is Janet Abu-Lughod, *Before European Hegemony: The World System, A.D. 1250–1350* (1989), which may usefully be read with K. N. Chaudhuri, *Asia Before Europe: Economy and Civilization of the Indian Ocean from the Rise of Islam to 1750* (1991). Students will find clear summaries of Islam's influences in tropical Asia and Africa in Ira Lapidus, *A History of Islamic Societies*, 2d ed. (2002), part II, and of commercial relations in Philip D. Curtin, *Cross-Cultural Trade in World History* (1984).

Greater detail about tropical lands is found in regional studies. For Southeast Asia see Nicholas Tarling, ed., *The Cambridge History of Southeast Asia*, vol. 1 (1992); John F. Cady, *Southeast Asia: Its Historical Development* (1964); and G. Coedes, *The Indianized States of Southeast Asia*, ed. Walter F. Vella (1968). India is covered comprehensively by R. C. Majumdar, ed., *The History and Culture of the Indian People*, vol. 4, *The Delhi Sultanate*, 2d ed. (1967); with brevity by Stanley Wolpert, *A New History of India*, 6th ed. (1999); and from an intriguing perspective by David Ludden, *A Peasant History of South India* (1985). For advanced topics see Tapan Raychaudhuri and Irfan Habib, eds., *The Cambridge Economic History of India*, vol. 1, *c. 1200–c. 1750* (1982).

A great deal of new scholarship on Africa in this period is summarized in chapters 6 and 7 of Christopher Ehret's *The Civilizations of Africa: A History to 1800* (2002). See also the latter parts of Graham Connah's *African Civilizations: Precolonial Cities and States in Tropical Africa: An Archaeological Perspective* (1987), and, for greater depth, D. T. Niane, ed., *UNESCO General History of Africa*, vol. 4, *Africa from the Twelfth to the Sixteenth Century* (1984), and Roland Oliver, ed., *The Cambridge History of Africa*, vol. 3, *c. 1050 to c. 1600* (1977).

For accounts of slavery and the slave trade see Salim Kidwai, "Sultans, Eunuchs and Domestics: New Forms of Bondage in Medieval India," in *Chains of Servitude: Bondage and Slavery in India,* ed. Utsa Patnaik and Manjari Dingwaney (1985), and the first two chapters of Paul E. Lovejoy, *Transformations in Slavery: A History of Slavery in Africa*, 2d ed. (2000).

Three volumes of Ibn Battuta's writings have been translated by H. A. R. Gibb, *The Travels of Ibn Battuta, A.D. 1325–1354* (1958–1971). Ross E. Dunn, *The Adventures of Ibn Battuta: A Muslim of the 14th Century* (1986), provides a modern retelling of his travels with commentary. For annotated selections see Said Hamdun and Noël King, *Ibn Battuta in Black Africa* (1995).

The most accessible survey of Indian Ocean sea travel is George F. Hourani, *Arab Seafaring*, expanded ed. (1995). For a Muslim Chinese traveler's observations see Ma Huan, *Ying-yai Sheng-lan, "The Overall Survey of the Ocean's Shore" [1433]*, trans. and ed. J. V. G. Mills (1970). Another valuable contemporary account of trade and navigation in the Indian Ocean is G. R. Tibbetts, *Arab Navigation in the Indian Ocean Before the Coming of the Portuguese, Being a Translation of the Kitab al-Fawa'id . . . of Ahmad b. Majidal-Najdi* (1981).

■ Notes

1. Tarikh-i-Wassaf, in Henry M. Elliot, *The History of India as Told by Its Own Historians*, ed. John Dowson (London: Trübner and Co., 1869–1871), 2:28.
2. Hasan Nizami, Taju-l Ma-asir, in Elliot, *The History of India as Told by Its Own Historians*, 2:219.
3. Minhaju-s Siraj, Tabakat-i Nasiri, in Elliot, *The History of India as Told by Its Own Historians*, 2:332–333.

The Latin West, 1200–1500

Burying Victims of the Black Death   This scene from Tournai, Flanders, captures the magnitude of the plague.

CHAPTER OUTLINE

Rural Growth and Crisis

Urban Revival

Learning, Literature, and the Renaissance

Political and Military Transformations

DIVERSITY AND DOMINANCE: Persecution and Protection of Jews, 1272–1349

ENVIRONMENT AND TECHNOLOGY: The Clock

In the summer of 1454, a year after the Ottoman Turks had captured the Greek Christian city of Constantinople, Aeneas Sylvius Piccolomini° was trying to stir up support for a crusade to halt the Muslim advances that were engulfing southeastern Europe and that showed no sign of stopping. The man who in four years would become pope doubted that anyone could persuade the rulers of Christian Europe to take up arms together against the Muslims: "Christendom has no head whom all will obey;" he lamented, "neither the pope nor the emperor receives his due."

Aeneas Sylvius had good reason to believe that Latin Christians were more inclined to fight with each other than to join a common front against the Turks. French and English armies had been at war for more than a century. The German emperor presided over dozens of states that were virtually independent of his control. The numerous kingdoms and principalities of Mediterranean Europe had never achieved unity. With only slight exaggeration Aeneas Sylvius complained, "Every city has its own king, and there are as many princes as there are households."

He attributed this lack of unity to Europeans' being so preoccupied with personal welfare and material gain that they would never sacrifice themselves to stop the Turkish armies. During the century since a devastating plague had carried off a third of western Europe's population, people had become cynical about human nature and preoccupied with material things.

Yet despite all these divisions, disasters, and wars, historians now see the period from 1200 to 1500 (Europe's later Middle Ages) as a time of unusual progress. The avarice and greed Aeneas Sylvius lamented were the dark side of the material prosperity that was most evident in the splendid architecture, institutions of higher learning, and cultural achievements of the cities. Frequent wars caused havoc and destruction, but in the long run they promoted the development of more powerful weapons and more unified monarchies.

A European fifty years later would have known that the Turks did not overrun Europe, that a truce in the Anglo-French conflict would hold, and that explorers sent by Portugal and a newly united Spain would extend Europe's reach to other continents. In 1454 Aeneas Sylvius knew only what had been, and the conflicts and calamities of the past made him shudder.

Although their contemporary Muslim and Byzantine neighbors commonly called western Europeans "Franks," western Europeans ordinarily referred to themselves as "Latins." That term underscored their allegiance to the Latin rite of Christianity (and to its patriarch, the pope) as well as the use of the Latin language by their literate members. The **Latin West** deserves special attention because its achievements during this period had profound implications for the future of the world. The region was emerging from the economic and cultural shadow of its Islamic neighbors and, despite grave disruptions caused by plague and warfare, boldly setting out to extend its dominance. Some common elements promoted the Latin West's remarkable resurgence: competition, the pursuit of success, and the effective use of borrowed technology and learning.

As you read this chapter, ask yourself the following questions:

- How well did inhabitants of the Latin West deal with their natural environment?

- How did warfare help rulers in the Latin West acquire the skills, weapons, and determination that enabled them to challenge other parts of the world?

- How did superior technology in the Latin West promote excellence in business, learning, and architecture?

- How much did the region's achievements depend on its own people, and how much on things borrowed from Muslim and Byzantine neighbors?

Aeneas Sylvius Piccolomini (uh-NEE-uhs SIL-vee-uhs pee-kuh-lo-MEE-nee)

C H R O N O L O G Y		
Technology and Environment	**Culture**	**Politics and Society**

1200

Technology and Environment	Culture	Politics and Society
1200s Use of crossbows and longbows becomes widespread; windmills in increased use	**1210s** Religious orders founded: Teutonic Knights, Franciscans, Dominicans	**1200s** Champagne fairs flourish
		1204 Fourth Crusade launched
		1215 Magna Carta issued
	1225–1274 Thomas Aquinas, monk and philosopher	
	1265–1321 Dante Alighieri, poet	
	ca. 1267–1337 Giotto, painter	

1300

Technology and Environment	Culture	Politics and Society
1300 First mechanical clocks in the West	**1300–1500** Rise of universities	
	1304–1374 Francesco Petrarch, humanist writer	
1315–1317 Great Famine	**1313–1375** Giovanni Boccaccio, humanist writer	
	ca. 1340–1400 Geoffrey Chaucer, poet	**1337** Start of Hundred Years War
1347–1351 Black Death		
ca. 1350 Growing deforestation		**1381** Wat Tyler's Rebellion
	1389–1464 Cosimo de' Medici, banker	
	ca. 1390–1441 Jan van Eyck, painter	

1400

Technology and Environment	Culture	Politics and Society
1400s Large cannon in use in warfare; hand-held firearms become prominent		**1415** Portuguese take Ceuta
	1449–1492 Lorenzo de' Medici, art patron	**1431** Joan of Arc burned as witch
ca. 1450 First printing with movable type in the West	**1452–1519** Leonardo da Vinci, artist	
1454 Gutenberg Bible printed	**ca. 1466–1536** Erasmus of Rotterdam, humanist	**1453** End of Hundred Years War; Turks take Constantinople
	1472–1564 Michelangelo, artist	**1469** Marriage of Ferdinand of Aragon and Isabella of Castile
	1492 Explusion of Jews from Spain	**1492** Fall of Muslim state of Granada

RURAL GROWTH AND CRISIS

Between 1200 and 1500 the Latin West brought more land under cultivation, adopted new farming techniques, and made greater use of machinery and mechanical forms of energy. Yet for most rural Europeans—more than nine out of ten people were rural—this period was a time of calamity and struggle. Most rural men and women worked hard for meager returns and suffered mightily from the effects of famine, epidemics, warfare, and social exploitation. After the devastation caused from 1347 to 1351 by the plague known as the Black Death, social changes speeded up by peasant revolts released many persons from serfdom and brought some improvements to rural life.

Rural French Peasants Many scenes of peasant life in winter are visible in this small painting by the Flemish Limbourg brothers from the 1410s. Above the snow-covered beehives one man chops firewood, while another drives a donkey loaded with firewood to a little village. At the lower right a woman, blowing on her frozen fingers, heads past the huddled sheep and hungry birds to join other women warming themselves in the cottage (whose outer wall the artists have cut away).   (Musée Conde, Chantilly, France/Art Resource, NY)

Peasants and Population

Society was divided by class and gender. In 1200 most western Europeans were serfs, obliged to till the soil on large estates owned by the nobility and the church (see Chapter 10). Each noble household typically rested on the labors of from fifteen to thirty peasant families. The standard of life in the lord's stone castle or manor house stood in sharp contrast to that in the peasant's one-room thatched cottage containing little furniture and no luxuries. Despite numerous religious holidays, peasant cultivators labored long hours, but more than half of the fruits of their labor went to the landowner. Because of these meager returns, serfs were not motivated to introduce extensive improvements in farming practices.

Scenes of rural life show both men and women at work in the fields, although there is no reason to believe that equality of labor meant equality of decision making at home. In the peasant's hut, as elsewhere in medieval Europe, women were subordinate to men. The influential theologian Thomas Aquinas° (1225–1274) spoke for his age when he argued that, although both men and women were created in God's image, there was a sense in which "the image of God is found in man, and not in woman: for man is the beginning and end of woman; as God is the beginning and end of every creature."[1]

Rural poverty was not simply the product of inefficient farming methods and social inequality. It also re-

Aquinas (uh-KWY-nuhs)

sulted from the rapid growth of Europe's population. In 1200 China's population may have surpassed Europe's by two to one; by 1300 the population of each was about 80 million. China's population fell because of the Mongol conquest (see Chapter 13). Why Europe's more than doubled between 1100 and 1345 is uncertain. Some historians believe that the reviving economy may have stimulated the increase. Others argue that warmer-than-usual temperatures reduced the number of deaths from starvation and exposure, while the absence of severe epidemics lessened deaths from disease.

Whatever the causes, more people required more productive ways of farming and new agricultural settlements. One new technique gaining widespread acceptance in northern Europe increased the amount of farmland available for producing crops. Instead of following the custom of leaving half of their land fallow (uncultivated) every year to regain its fertility, some farmers tried a new **three-field system.** They grew crops on two-thirds of their land each year and planted the third field in oats. The oats stored nitrogen and rejuvenated the soil, and they could be used to feed plow horses. In much of Europe, however, farmers continued to let half of their land lie fallow and to use oxen (less efficient but cheaper than horses) to pull their plows.

Population growth also led to the foundation of new agricultural settlements. In the twelfth and thirteenth centuries large numbers of Germans migrated into the fertile lands east of the Elbe River and into the eastern Baltic states. Knights belonging to Latin Christian religious orders slaughtered or drove away native inhabitants who had not yet adopted Christianity. For example, during the thirteenth century, the Order of Teutonic Knights conquered, resettled, and administered a vast area along the eastern Baltic that later became Prussia (see Map 15.3). Other Latin Christians founded new settlements on lands conquered from the Muslims and Byzantines in southern Europe and on Celtic lands in the British Isles.

Draining swamps and clearing forests also brought new land under cultivation. But as population continued to rise, some people had to farm lands that had poor soils or were vulnerable to flooding, frost, or drought. As a result average crop yields declined after 1250, and more people were vulnerable to even slight changes in the food supply resulting from bad weather or the disruptions of war. According to one historian, "By 1300, almost every child born in western Europe faced the probability of extreme hunger at least once or twice during his expected 30 to 35 years of life."[2] One unusually cold spell led to the Great Famine of 1315–1317, which affected much of Europe.

The Black Death and Social Change

The **Black Death** cruelly resolved the problem of overpopulation by killing off a third of western Europeans. This terrible plague spread out of Asia and struck Mongol armies attacking the city of Kaffa° on the Black Sea in 1346 (see Chapter 13). A year later Genoese° traders in Kaffa carried the disease back to Italy and southern France. During the next two years the Black Death spread across Europe, sparing some places and carrying off two-thirds of the populace in others.

The plague's symptoms were ghastly to behold. Most victims developed boils the size of eggs in their groins and armpits, black blotches on their skin, foul body odors, and severe pain. In most cases, death came within a few days. To prevent the plague from spreading, town officials closed their gates to people from infected areas and burned victims' possessions. Such measures helped spare some communities but could not halt the advance of the disease across Europe (see Map 15.1). It is now believed that the Black Death was a combination of two diseases. One was anthrax, a disease that can spread to humans from cattle and sheep. The primary form of the Black Death was bubonic plague, a disease spread by contact with an infected person or from the bites of fleas that infest the fur of certain rats. But even if medieval Europeans had been aware of that route of infection, they could have done little to eliminate the rats, which thrived on urban refuse.

The plague left its mark on the survivors, bringing home how sudden and unexpected death could be. Some people became more religious, giving money to the church or flogging themselves with iron-tipped whips to atone for their sins. Others turned to reckless enjoyment, spending their money on fancy clothes, feasts, and drinking. Whatever their mood, most people soon resumed their daily routines.

Periodic returns of plague made recovery from population losses slow and uneven. By 1400 Europe's population regained the size it had had in 1200. Not until after 1500 did it rise above its preplague level.

In addition to its demographic and psychological effects, the Black Death triggered social changes in western Europe. Skilled and manual laborers who survived demanded higher pay for their services. At first authorities tried to freeze wages at the old levels. Seeing such repressive measures as a plot by the rich, peasants rose up against wealthy nobles and churchmen. During a widespread revolt in France in 1358 known as the Jacquerie,

---

Kaffa (KAH-fah)   **Genoese** (JEN-oh-eez)

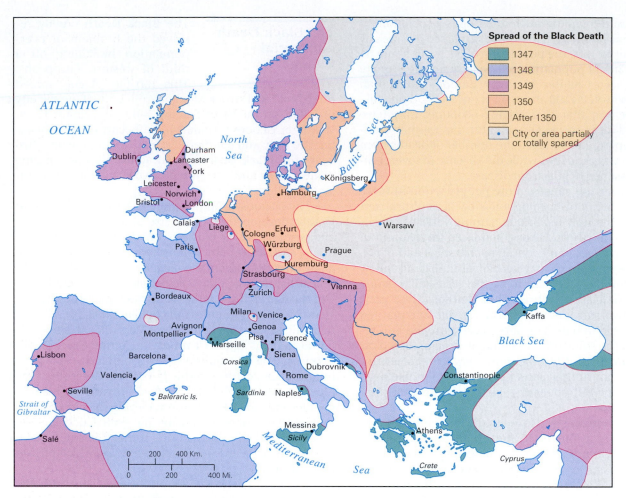

Map 15.1   The Black Death in Fourteenth–Century Europe   Spreading out of southwestern China along the routes opened by Mongol expansion, the plague reached the Black Sea port of Kaffa in 1346. This map documents its deadly progress year by year from there into the Mediterranean and north and east across the face of Europe.

peasants looted castles and killed dozens of persons. Urban unrest also took place. In a large revolt led by Wat Tyler in 1381, English peasants invaded London, calling for an end to all forms of serfdom and to most kinds of manorial dues. Angry demonstrators murdered the archbishop of Canterbury and many royal officials. Authorities put down these rebellions with even greater bloodshed and cruelty, but they could not stave off the higher wages and other social changes the rebels demanded.

Serfdom practically disappeared in western Europe as peasants bought their freedom or ran away. Free agricultural laborers used their higher wages to purchase land that they could farm for themselves. Some English landowners who could no longer afford to hire enough fieldworkers used their land to pasture sheep for their wool. Others grew less-labor-intensive crops or made greater use of draft animals and labor-saving tools. Because the plague had not killed wild and domesticated animals, more meat was available for each survivor and more leather for shoes. Thus the welfare of the rural masses generally improved after the Black Death, though the gap between rich and poor remained wide.

In urban areas employers had to raise wages to attract enough workers to replace those killed by the plague. Guilds (see below) found it necessary to reduce the period of apprenticeship. Competition within crafts also became more common. Although the overall econ-

Watermills on the Seine River in Paris Sacks of grain were brought to these mills under the bridge called the Grand Pont to be ground into flour. The water wheels were turned by the river flowing under them. Gears translated the vertical motion of the wheels into the horizontal motion of the millstones. (Bibliothèque Nationale de France)

omy shrank with the decline in population, per capita production actually rose.

Mines and Mills

Mining, metalworking, and the use of mechanical energy expanded so much in the centuries before 1500 that some historians have spoken of an "industrial revolution" in medieval Europe. That may be too strong a term, but the landscape fairly bristled with mechanical devices. Mills powered by water or wind were used to grind grain and flour, saw logs into lumber, crush olives, tan leather, make paper, and perform other useful tasks.

England's many rivers had some fifty-six hundred functioning watermills in 1086. After 1200 such mills spread rapidly across the western European mainland. By the early fourteenth century entrepreneurs had crammed sixty-eight watermills into a one-mile section of the Seine° River in Paris. The flow of the river below turned the simplest **water wheels.** Greater efficiency came from channeling water over the top of the wheel. Dams ensured these wheels a steady flow of water throughout the year. Some watermills in France and England even harnessed the power of ocean tides.

Windmills were common in comparatively dry lands like Spain and in northern Europe, where ice made water wheels useless in winter. Water wheels and windmills had long been common in the Islamic world, but people in the Latin West used these devices on a much larger scale than did people elsewhere.

Wealthy individuals or monasteries built many mills, but because of the expenses involved groups of investors undertook most of the construction. Since nature furnished the energy to run them for free, mills could be very profitable, a fact that often aroused the jealousy of their neighbors. In his *Canterbury Tales* the English poet Geoffrey Chaucer (ca. 1340–1400) captured millers' unsavory reputation (not necessarily deserved) by portraying a miller as "a master-hand at stealing grain" by pushing down on the balance scale with his thumb.[3]

Waterpower also made possible such a great expansion of iron making that some historians say Europe's real Iron Age came in the later Middle Ages, not in antiquity. Water powered the stamping mills that broke up the iron, the trip hammers that pounded it, and the bellows (first documented in the West in 1323) that raised temperatures to the point where the iron was liquid enough to pour into molds. Blast furnaces capable of producing high-quality iron are documented from 1380. The finished products included everything from armor and nails to horseshoes and agricultural tools.

Iron mining expanded in many parts of Europe to meet the demand. In addition, new silver, lead, and copper mines in Austria and Hungary supplied metal for coins, church bells, cannon, and statues. Techniques of deep mining that developed in Central Europe spread farther west in the latter part of the fifteenth century. To keep up with a building boom France quarried more

Seine (sen)

stone during the eleventh, twelfth, and thirteenth centuries than ancient Egypt had done during two millennia for all of its monuments.

The rapid growth of industry changed the landscape significantly. Towns grew outward and new ones were founded; dams and canals changed the flow of rivers; and the countryside was scarred by quarry pits and mines tunneled into hillsides. Pollution sometimes became a serious problem. Urban tanneries (factories that cured and processed leather) dumped acidic wastewater back into streams, where it mixed with human waste and the runoff from slaughterhouses. The first recorded antipollution law was passed by the English Parliament in 1388, although enforcing it was difficult.

One of the most dramatic environmental changes was deforestation. Trees were cut to provide timber for buildings and for ships. Tanneries stripped bark to make acid for tanning leather. Many forests were cleared to make room for farming. The glass and iron industries consumed great quantities of charcoal, made by controlled burning of oak or other hardwood. It is estimated that a single iron furnace could consume all the trees within five-eighths of a mile (1 kilometer) in just forty days. Consequently, the later Middle Ages saw the depletion of many once-dense forests in western Europe.

URBAN REVIVAL

In the tenth century not a single town in the Latin West could compare in wealth and comfort—still less in size—with the cities in the Byzantine Empire and the Islamic caliphates. Yet by the later Middle Ages wealthy commercial centers stood all along the Mediterranean, Baltic, and Atlantic, as well as on major rivers draining into these bodies of water (see Map 15.2). The greatest cities in the East were still larger, but those in the West were undergoing greater commercial, cultural, and administrative changes. Their prosperity was visible in impressive new churches, guild halls, and residences. This urban revival is a measure of the Latin West's recovery from the economic decline that had followed the collapse of the Roman Empire (see Chapter 10) as well as an illustration of how the West's rise was aided by its ties to other parts of the world.

Trading Cities

Most urban growth in the Latin West after 1200 was a result of the continuing growth of trade and manufacturing. Most of the trade was between cities and their hinterlands, but long-distance trade also stimulated urban revival. Cities in northern Italy in particular benefited from maritime trade with the bustling port cities of the eastern Mediterranean and, through them, with the great markets of the Indian Ocean and East Asia. In northern Europe commercial cities in the County of Flanders (roughly today's Belgium) and around the Baltic Sea profited from growing regional networks and from overland and sea routes to the Mediterranean.

Venice's diversion of the Fourth Crusade into an assault in 1204 against the city of Constantinople temporarily removed an impediment to Italian commercial expansion in the eastern Mediterranean. By crippling this Greek Christian stronghold, Venetians were able to seize the strategic island of Crete in the eastern Mediterranean and expand their trading colonies around the Black Sea.

Another boon to Italian trade was the westward expansion of the Mongol Empire, which opened trade routes from the Mediterranean to China (see Chapter 13). In 1271 the young Venetian merchant Marco Polo set out to reach the Mongol court by a long overland trek across Central Asia. There he spent many years serving the emperor Khubilai Khan as an ambassador and as the governor of a Chinese province. Some scholars question the truthfulness of Polo's later account of these adventures and of his treacherous return voyage through the Indian Ocean that finally brought him back to Venice in 1295, after an absence of twenty-four years. Few in Venice could believe Polo's tales of Asian wealth.

Even after the Mongol Empire's decline disrupted the trans-Asian caravan trade in the fourteenth century, Venetian merchants continued to purchase the silks and spices that reached Constantinople, Beirut, and Alexandria. Three times a year galleys (ships powered by some sixty oarsmen each) sailed in convoys of two or three from Venice, bringing back some 2,000 tons of goods. Other merchants began to explore new overland or sea routes.

Venice was not the only Latin city whose trade expanded in the thirteenth century. The sea trade of Genoa on the west coast of northern Italy probably equaled that of Venice. Genoese merchants established colonies on the shores of the eastern Mediterranean and around the Black Sea as well as in the western Mediterranean. In northern Europe an association of trading cities known as the **Hanseatic° League** traded extensively in the Baltic, including the coasts of Prussia, newly conquered by German knights. Their merchants ranged eastward to Novgorod in Russia and westward across the North Sea to London.

Hanseatic (han-see-AT-ik)

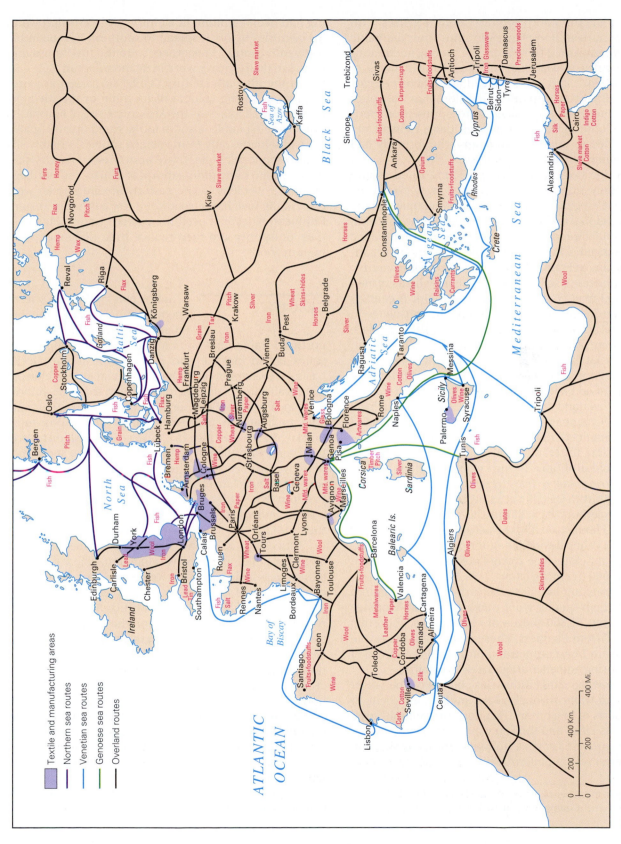

Map 15.2 Trade and Manufacturing in Later Medieval Europe The economic revival of European cities was associated with great expansion of commerce. Notice the concentration of wool and linen textile manufacturing in northern Italy, the Netherlands, and England; the importance of trade in various kinds of foodstuffs; and the slave-exporting markets in Cairo, Kiev, and Rostov.

By the late thirteenth century Genoese galleys from the Mediterranean and Hanseatic ships from the Baltic were converging on a third area, the trading and manufacturing cities in Flanders. In the Flemish towns of Bruges°, Ghent°, and Ypres° skilled artisans turned raw wool from English sheep into a fine cloth that was softer and smoother than the coarse "homespuns" from simple village looms. Dyed in vivid hues, these Flemish textiles appealed to wealthy Europeans who formerly had imported their fine textiles from Asia.

Along the overland route connecting Flanders and northern Italy, important trading fairs developed in the Champagne° region of Burgundy. The Champagne fairs began as regional markets, meeting once or twice a year, where manufactured goods, livestock, and farm produce were exchanged. When Champagne came under the control of the king of France at the end of the twelfth century, royal guarantees of safe conduct to all merchants turned the regional markets into international fairs. A century later fifteen Italian cities had permanent consulates in Champagne to represent the interests of their citizens. The fairs were also important for currency exchange and other financial transactions. During the fourteenth century the volume of trade grew so large that it became cheaper to send Flemish woolens to Italy by sea than to send them overland on pack animals. As a consequence, the fairs of Champagne lost some of their international trade but remained important regional markets.

In the late thirteenth century higher English taxes made it more profitable to turn wool into cloth in England than to export it to Flanders. Raw wool exports from England fell from 35,000 sacks at the beginning of the fourteenth century to 8,000 in the mid-fifteenth. With the aid of Flemish textile specialists and the spinning wheels and other devices they introduced, English exports of wool cloth rose from 4,000 pieces just before 1350 to 54,000 a century later.

Local banking families also turned Florence into a center for high-quality wool making. In 1338 Florence manufactured 80,000 pieces of cloth, while importing only 10,000 from Flanders. These changes in the textile industry show how competition promoted the spread of manufacturing and encouraged new specialties.

The growing textile industries channeled the power of wind and water through gears, pulleys, and belts to drive all sorts of machinery. Flanders, for example, used windmills to clean and thicken woven cloth by beating it in water, a process known as fulling. Another application of mill power was in papermaking. Although papermak-

ing had been common in China and the Muslim world for centuries before it spread to southern Europe in the thirteenth century, Westerners were the first to use machines to do the heavy work in its manufacturing.

In the fifteenth century Venice surpassed its European rivals in the volume of its trade in the Mediterranean as well as across the Alps into Central Europe. Its skilled craftspeople also manufactured luxury goods once obtainable only from eastern sources, notably silk and cotton textiles, glassware and mirrors, jewelry, and paper. At the same time, exports of Italian and northern European woolens to the eastern Mediterranean were also on the rise. In the space of a few centuries western European cities had used the eastern trade to increase their prosperity and then reduce their dependence on eastern goods.

Civic Life

Trading cities in Europe offered people more social freedom than did rural places. Most northern Italian and German cities were independent states, much like the port cities of the Indian Ocean basin (see Chapter 14). Other European cities held special royal charters that exempted them from the authority of local nobles. Because of their autonomy, they were able to adapt to changing market conditions more quickly than were cities in China and the Islamic world that were controlled by imperial authorities. Social mobility was also easier in the Latin West because anyone who lived in a chartered city for over a year might claim freedom. Thus cities became a refuge for all sorts of ambitious individuals, whose labor and talent added to their wealth.

Cities were also home to most of Europe's Jews. The largest population of Jews was in Spain, where earlier Islamic rulers had made them welcome. Many commercial cities elsewhere welcomed Jews for their manufacturing and business skills. Despite the official protection they received from Christian rulers and the church, Jews were subject to violent religious persecutions or expulsions (see Diversity and Dominance: Persecution and Protection of Jews, 1272–1349). Persecution peaked in times of crisis, such as during the Black Death. In the Spanish kingdom of Castile violent attacks on Jews were widespread in 1391 and brought the once vibrant Jewish community in Seville to an end. Terrified Jews left or converted to Christianity, but Christian fanaticism continued to rise over the next century, leading to new attacks on Jews and Jewish converts. In the Latin West only the papal city of Rome left its Jews undisturbed throughout the centuries before 1500.

Bruges (broozh)   **Ghent** (gent [hard *g* as in *get*])
Ypres (EE-pruh)   **Champagne** (sham-PAIN)

Flemish Weavers, Ypres   The spread of textile weaving gave employment to many people in the Netherlands. The city of Ypres in Flanders (now northern Belgium) was an important textile center in the thirteenth century. This drawing from a fourteenth-century manuscript shows a man and a woman weaving cloth on a horizontal loom, while a child makes thread on a spinning wheel.   (Stedelijke Openbare Bibliotheek, Ypres)

Opportunities for individual enterprise in European cities came with many restrictions. In most towns and cities powerful associations known as guilds dominated civic life. A **guild** was an association of craft specialists, such as silversmiths, or of merchants that regulated the business practices of its members and the prices they charged. Guilds also trained apprentices and promoted members' interests with the city government. By denying membership to outsiders and all Jews, guilds perpetuated the interests of the families that already were members. Guilds also perpetuated male dominance of most skilled jobs.

Nevertheless, in a few places women were able to join guilds either on their own or as the wives, widows, or daughters of male guild members. Large numbers of poor women also toiled in nonguild jobs in urban textile industries and in the food and beverage trades, generally receiving lower wages than men. Some women advanced socially through marriage. One of Chaucer's *Canterbury Tales* concerns a woman from Bath, a city in southern England, who became wealthy by marrying a succession of old men for their money (and then two other husbands for love), "aside from other company in youth." Chaucer says she was also a skilled weaver: "In making cloth she showed so great a bent, / She bettered those of Ypres and of Ghent."

By the fifteenth century a new class of wealthy merchant-bankers operated on a vast scale and specialized in money changing, loans, and investments. The merchant-bankers handled the financial transactions of a variety of merchants as well as of ecclesiastical and secular officials. They arranged for the transmission to the pope of funds known as Peter's pence, a collection taken up annually in every church in the Latin West. Their loans supported rulers' wars and lavish courts. Some merchant-bankers even developed their own news services, gathering information on any topic that could affect business.

Florence became a center of new banking services from checking accounts and shareholding companies

DIVERSITY AND DOMINANCE

PERSECUTION AND PROTECTION OF JEWS, 1272–1349

Because they did not belong to the dominant Latin Christian faith, Jews suffered from periodic discrimination and persecution. For the most part, religious and secular authorities tried to curb such anti-Semitism. Jews, after all, were useful citizens who worshipped the same God as their Christian neighbors. Still it was hard to know where to draw the line between justifiable and unjustifiable discrimination. The famous reviser of Catholic theology, St. Thomas Aquinas, made one such distinction in his Summa Theologica *with regard to attempts at forced conversion.*

Now, the practice of the Church never held that the children of Jews should be baptized against the will of their parents. . . . Therefore, it seems dangerous to bring forward this new view, that contrary to the previously established custom of the Church, the children of Jews should be baptized against the will of their parents.

There are two reasons for this position. One stems from danger to faith. For, if children without the use of reason were to receive baptism, then after reaching maturity they could easily be persuaded by their parents to relinquish what they had received in ignorance. This would tend to do harm to the faith.

The second reason is that it is opposed to natural justice . . . it [is] a matter of natural right that a son, before he has the use of reason, is under the care of his father. Hence, it would be against natural justice for the boy, before he has the use of reason, to be removed from the care of his parents, or for anything to be arranged for him against the will of his parents.

The "new view" Aquinas opposed was much in the air, for in 1272 Pope Gregory X issued a decree condemning forced baptism. The pope's decree reviews the history of papal protection given to the Jews, starting with a quotation from Pope Gregory I dating from 598, and decrees two new protections of Jews' legal rights.

Even as it is not allowed to the Jews in their assemblies presumptuously to undertake for themselves more than that which is permitted them by law, even so they ought not to suffer any disadvantage in those [privileges] which have been granted them.

Although they prefer to persist in their stubbornness rather than to recognize the words of their prophets and the mysteries of the Scriptures, and thus to arrive at a knowledge of Christian faith and salvation; nevertheless, inasmuch as they have made an appeal for our protection and help, we therefore admit their petition and offer them the shield of our protection through the clemency of Christian piety. In so doing we follow in the footsteps of our predecessors of happy memory, the popes of Rome—Calixtus, Eugene, Alexander, Clement, Celestine, Innocent, and Honorius.

We decree moreover that no Christian shall compel them or any one of their group to come to baptism unwillingly. But if any one of them shall take refuge of his own accord with Christians, because of conviction, then, after his intention will have been made manifest, he shall be made a Christian without any intrigue. For indeed that person who is known to come to Christian baptism not freely, but unwillingly, is not believed to possess the Christian faith.

Moreover, no Christian shall presume to seize, imprison, wound, torture, mutilate, kill, or inflict violence on them; furthermore no one shall presume, except by judicial action of the authorities of the country, to change the good customs in the land where they live for the purpose of taking their money or goods from them or from others.

In addition, no one shall disturb them in any way during the celebration of their festivals, whether by day or by night, with clubs or stones or anything else. Also no one shall exact any compulsory service of them unless it be that which they have been accustomed to render in previous times.

Inasmuch as the Jews are not able to bear witness against the Christians, we decree furthermore that the testimony of Christians against Jews shall not be valid unless there is among these Christians some Jew who is there for the purpose of offering testimony.

Since it occasionally happens that some Christians lose their Christian children, the Jews are accused by their enemies of secretly carrying off and killing these same Christian children, and of making sacrifices of the heart and blood of these very children. It happens, too, that the parents of these children, or some other Christian enemies of these Jews, secretly hide these very children in order that they may be able to injure these Jews, and in order that they may be able to extort from them a certain amount of money by redeeming them from their straits.

And most falsely do these Christians claim that the Jews have secretly and furtively carried away these children and killed them, and that the Jews offer sacrifice from the heart and the blood of these children, since their law in this matter precisely and expressly forbids Jews to sacrifice, eat, or drink the blood, or eat the flesh of animals having claws. This has been demonstrated many times at our court by Jews converted to the Christian faith: nevertheless very many Jews are often seized and detained unjustly because of this.

We decree, therefore, that Christians need not be obeyed against Jews in such a case or situation of this type, and we order that Jews seized under such a silly pretext be freed from imprisonment, and that they shall not be arrested henceforth on such a miserable pretext, unless—which we do not believe—they be caught in the commission of the crime. We decree that no Christian shall stir up anything against them, but that they should be maintained in that status and position in which they were from the time of our predecessors, from antiquity till now.

We decree, in order to stop the wickedness and avarice of bad men, that no one shall dare to devastate or to destroy a cemetery of the Jews or to dig up human bodies for the sake of getting money [by holding them for ransom]. Moreover, if anyone, after having known the content of this decree, should—which we hope will not happen—attempt audaciously to act contrary to it, then let him suffer punishment in his rank and position, or let him be punished by the penalty of excommunication, unless he makes amends for his boldness by proper recompense. Moreover, we wish that only those Jews who have not attempted to contrive anything toward the destruction of the Christian faith be fortified by the support of such protection. . . .

Despite such decrees violence against Jews might burst out when fears and emotions were running high. This selection is from the official chronicles of the upper-Rhineland towns.

In the year 1349 there occurred the greatest epidemic that ever happened. Death went from one end of the earth to the other, on that side and this side of the [Mediterranean] sea, and it was greater among the Saracens [Muslims] than among the Christians. In some lands everyone died so that no one was left. Ships were also found on the sea laden with wares; the crew had all died and no one guided the ship. The Bishop of Marseilles and priests and monks and more than half of all the people there died with them. In other kingdoms and cities so many people perished that it would be horrible to describe. The pope at Avignon stopped all sessions of court, locked himself in a room, allowed no one to approach him and had a fire burning before him all the time. And from what this epidemic came, all wise teachers and physicians could only say that it was the God's will. And the plague was now here, so it was in other places, and lasted more than a whole year. This epidemic also came to Strasbourg in the summer of the above mentioned year, and it is estimated about sixteen thousand people died.

In the matter of this plague the Jews throughout the world were reviled and accused in all lands of having caused it through the poison which they are said to have put into the water and the wells—that is what they were accused of—and for this reason the Jews were burnt all the way from the Mediterranean into Germany, but not in Avignon, for the pope protected them there.

Nevertheless they tortured a number of Jews in Berne and Zofingen who admitted they had put poison into many wells, and they found the poison in the wells. Thereupon they burnt the Jews in many towns and wrote of this affair to Strasbourg, Freibourg, and Basel in order that they too should burn their Jews. . . . The deputies of the city of Strasbourg were asked what they were going to do with their Jews. They answered and said that they knew no evil of them. Then . . . there was a great indignation and clamor against the deputies from Strasbourg. So finally the Bishop and the lords and the Imperial Cities agreed to do away with the Jews. The result was that they were burnt in many cities, and wherever they were expelled they were caught by the peasants and stabbed to death or drowned. . . .

On Saturday—that was St. Valentine's Day—they burnt the Jews on a wooden platform in their cemetery. There were about two thousand people of them. Those who wanted to baptize themselves were spared. Many small children were taken out of the fire and baptized against the will of their fathers and mothers. And everything that was owed to the Jews was cancelled, and the Jews had to surrender all pledges and notes that they had taken for debts. The council, however, took the cash that the Jews possessed and divided it among the working-men proportionately. The money was indeed the thing that killed the Jews. If they had been poor and if the feudal lords had not been in debt to them, they would not have been burnt.

QUESTIONS FOR ANALYSIS

1. Why do Aquinas and Pope Gregory oppose prejudicial actions against Jews?
2. Why did prejudice increase at the time of the Black Death?
3. What factors account for the differences between the views of Christian leaders and the Christian masses?

Source: First selection reprinted with permission of Pocket Books, an imprint of Simon & Schuster Adult Publishing Group, from *The Pocket Aquinas,* edited with translations by Vernon J. Bourke. Copyright © 1960 by Washington Square Press. Copyright renewed © 1988 by Simon & Schuster Adult Publishing Group. Second and third selections from Jacob R. Marcus, ed., *The Jew in the Medieval World: A Source Book, 315–1791* (Cincinnati: Union of American Hebrew Congregations, 1938), 152–154, 45–47. Reprinted with permission of the Hebrew Union College Press, Cincinnati.

to improved bookkeeping. In the fifteenth century the Medici° family of Florence operated banks in Italy, Flanders, and London. Medicis also controlled the government of Florence and were important patrons of the arts. By 1500 the greatest banking family in western Europe was the Fuggers° of Augsburg, who had ten times the Medici bank's lending capital. Starting out as cloth merchants under Jacob "the Rich" (1459–1525), the family branched into many other activities, including the trade in Hungarian copper, essential for casting cannon.

Christian bankers had to devise ways to profit indirectly from loans in order to get around the Latin Church's condemnation of usury (charging interest). Some borrowers agreed to repay a loan in another currency at a rate of exchange favorable to the lender. Others added a "gift" in thanks to the lender to the borrowed sum. For example, in 1501 papal officials agreed to repay a loan of 6,000 gold ducats in five months to the Fuggers along with a "gift" of 400 ducats, amounting to an effective interest rate of 16 percent a year. In fact, the return was much smaller since the church failed to repay the loan on time. Because they were not bound by church laws, Jews were important moneylenders.

Despite the money made by some, for most residents of western European cities poverty and squalor were the norm. Even for the wealthy, European cities generally lacked civic amenities, such as public baths and water supply systems, that had existed in the cities of Western antiquity and still survived in cities of the Islamic Middle East.

Gothic Cathedrals

Master builders were in great demand in the thriving cities of late medieval Europe. Cities vied to outdo one another in the magnificence of their guild halls, town halls, and other structures (see Environment and Technology: The Clock). But the architectural wonders of their times were the new **Gothic cathedrals,** which made their appearance in about 1140 in France.

The hallmark of the new cathedrals was the pointed Gothic arch, which replaced the older round Roman arch. External (flying) buttresses stabilized the high, thin stone columns below the arches. This method of construction enabled master builders to push the Gothic cathedrals to great heights and fill the outside walls with giant windows of brilliantly colored stained glass. During the next four centuries, interior heights went ever higher,

Medici (MED-ih-chee) Fuggers (FOOG-uhrz)

Strasbourg Cathedral Only one of the two spires originally planned for this Gothic cathedral was completed when work ceased in 1439. But the Strasbourg Cathedral was still the tallest masonry structure of medieval Europe. This engraving is from 1630. (Courtesy of the Trustees of the British Museum)

towers and spires pierced the heavens, and walls dazzled worshippers with religious scenes in stained glass.

The men who designed and built the cathedrals had little or no formal education and limited understanding of the mathematical principles of modern civil engineering. Master masons sometimes miscalculated, and parts of some overly ambitious cathedrals collapsed. For instance, the record-high choir vault of Beauvais Cathedral—154 feet (47 meters) in height—came tumbling down in 1284. But as builders gained experience, they devised new ways to push their steeples heavenward. The spire of the Strasbourg cathedral reached

ENVIRONMENT + TECHNOLOGY

The Clock

Clocks were a prominent feature of the Latin West in the late medieval period. The Song-era Chinese had built elaborate mechanical clocks centuries earlier (see Chapter 11), but the West was the first part of the world where clocks became a regular part of urban life. Whether mounted in a church steeple or placed on a bridge or tower, mechanical clocks proclaimed Western people's delight with mechanical objects, concern with precision, and display of civic wealth.

The word *clock* comes from a word for bell. The first mechanical clocks that appeared around 1300 in western Europe were simply bells with an automatic mechanical device to strike the correct number of hours. The most elaborate Chinese clock had been powered by falling water, but this was impractical in cold weather. The levers, pulleys, and gears of European clocks were powered by a weight hanging from a rope wound around a cylinder. An "escapement" lever regulated the slow, steady unwinding.

Enthusiasm for building expensive clocks came from various parts of the community. For some time, monks had been using devices to mark the times for prayer.

Employers welcomed chiming clocks to regulate the hours of their employees. Universities used them to mark the beginning and end of classes. Prosperous merchants readily donated money to build a splendid clock that would display their city's wealth. The city of Strasbourg, for example, built a clock in the 1350s that included statues of the Virgin, the Christ Child, and the three Magi; a mechanical rooster; the signs of the zodiac; a perpetual calendar; and an astrolabe—and it could play hymns, too!

By the 1370s and 1380s clocks were common enough for their measured hours to displace the older system that varied the length of the hour in proportion to the length of the day. Previously, for example, the London hour had varied from thirty-eight minutes in winter to eighty-two minutes in summer. By 1500 clocks had numbered faces with hour and minute hands. Small clocks for indoor use were also in vogue. Though not very accurate by today's standards, these clocks were still a great step forward. Some historians consider the clock the most important of the many technological advances of the later Middle Ages because it fostered so many changes during the following centuries.

Early Clock This weight-driven clock dates from 1454. (Bodleian Library Oxford, Ms. Laud Misc. 570, 25v.)

466 feet (142 meters) into the air—as high as a 40-story building. Such heights were unsurpassed until the twentieth century.

LEARNING, LITERATURE, AND THE RENAISSANCE

Throughout the Middle Ages people in the Latin West lived amid reminders of the achievements of the Roman Empire. They wrote and worshiped in a version of its language, traveled its roads, and obeyed some of its laws. Even the vestments and robes of medieval popes, kings, and emperors were modeled on the regalia of Roman officials. Yet early medieval Europeans lost touch with much of the learning of Greco-Roman antiquity. More vivid was the biblical world they heard about in the Hebrew and Christian scriptures.

A small revival of classical learning associated with the court of Charlemagne in the ninth century was followed by a larger renaissance (rebirth) in the twelfth century. The growing cities were home to intellectuals, artists, and universities after 1200. In the mid-fourteenth century the pace of intellectual and artistic life quickened in what is often called the **Renaissance,** which began in northern Italy and later spread to northern Europe. Some Italian authors saw the Italian Renaissance as a sharp break with an age of darkness. A more balanced view might reveal this era as the high noon of a day that had been dawning for several centuries.

Universities and Learning

Before 1100 Byzantine and Islamic scholarship generally surpassed scholarship in Latin Europe. When southern Italy was wrested from the Byzantines and Sicily and Toledo from the Muslims in the eleventh century, many manuscripts of Greek and Arabic works came into Western hands and were translated into Latin for readers eager for new ideas. These included philosophical works by Plato and Aristotle°; newly discovered Greek treatises on medicine, mathematics, and geography; and scientific and philosophical writings by medieval Muslims. Latin translations of the Iranian philosopher Ibn Sina° (980–1037), known in the West as Avicenna°, were particularly influential. Jewish scholars contributed significantly to the translation and explication of Arabic and other manuscripts.

Two new religious orders, the Dominicans and the Franciscans, contributed many talented professors to the growing number of new independent colleges after 1200. Some scholars believe that the colleges established in Paris and Oxford in the late twelfth and thirteenth centuries may have been modeled after similar places of study then spreading in the Islamic world—*madrasas,* which provided subsidized housing for poor students and paid the salaries of their teachers. The Latin West, however, was the first part of the world to establish modern **universities,** degree-granting corporations specializing in multidisciplinary research and advanced teaching.

Between 1300 and 1500 sixty new universities joined the twenty existing institutions of higher learning in the Latin West. Students banded together to found some of them; guilds of professors founded others. Teaching guilds, like the guilds overseeing manufacturing and commerce, set the standards for membership in their profession, trained apprentices and masters, and defended their professional interests.

Universities set the curriculum of study for each discipline and instituted comprehensive final examinations for degrees. Students who passed the exams at the end of their apprenticeship received a teaching diploma known as a "license." Students who completed longer training and successfully defended a scholarly treatise became "masters" or "doctors." The colleges of Paris were gradually absorbed into the city's university, but the colleges of Oxford and Cambridge remained independent, selfgoverning organizations.

Universally recognized degrees, well-trained professors, and exciting new texts promoted the rapid spread of universities in late medieval Europe. Because all university courses were taught in Latin, students and masters could move freely across political and linguistic lines, seeking out the university that offered the courses they wanted and that had the most interesting professors. Universities offered a variety of programs of study but generally were identified with a particular specialty. Bologna° was famous for the study of law; Montpellier and Salerno specialized in medicine; Paris and Oxford excelled in theology.

The prominence of theology partly reflected the fact that many students were destined for ecclesiastical careers, but theology was also seen as "queen of the sciences"—the central discipline that encompassed all knowledge. For this reason thirteenth-century theologians sought to synthesize the newly rediscovered philosophical works of Aristotle, as well as the commentaries of Avicenna, with the revealed truth of the Bible. Their

---

Aristotle (AR-ih-stah-tahl)   **Ibn Sina** (IB-uhn SEE-nah)
Avicenna (av-uh-SEN-uh)

Bologna (buh-LOHN-yuh)

daring efforts to synthesize reason and faith were known as **scholasticism°**.

The most notable scholastic work was the *Summa Theologica°*, issued between 1267 and 1273 by Thomas Aquinas, a brilliant Dominican priest who was a professor of theology at the University of Paris. Although Aquinas's exposition of Christian belief organized on Aristotelian principles was later accepted as a masterly demonstration of the reasonableness of Christianity, scholasticism upset many traditional thinkers. Some church authorities even tried to ban Aristotle from the curriculum. There also was much rivalry between the leading Dominican and Franciscan theological scholars over the next two centuries. However, the considerable freedom of medieval universities from both secular and religious authorities eventually enabled the new ideas of accredited scholars to prevail over the fears of church administrators.

Humanists and Printers

The intellectual achievements of the later Middle Ages were not confined to the universities. Talented writers of this era made important contributions to literature and literary scholarship. A new technology in the fifteenth century helped bring works of literature and scholarship to a larger audience.

Dante Alighieri° (1265–1321) completed a long, elegant poem, the *Divine Comedy*, shortly before his death. This supreme expression of medieval preoccupations tells the allegorical story of Dante's journey through the nine circles of hell and the seven terraces of purgatory (a place where the souls not deserving eternal punishment were purged of their sinfulness), followed by his entry into Paradise. His guide through hell and purgatory is the Roman poet Virgil. His guide through Paradise is Beatrice, a woman whom he had loved from afar since childhood and whose death inspired him to write the poem.

The *Divine Comedy* foreshadows some of the literary fashions of the later Italian Renaissance. Like Dante, later Italian writers made use of Greco-Roman classical themes and mythology and sometimes chose to write not in Latin but in the vernacular languages spoken in their regions, in order to reach broader audiences. (Dante used the vernacular spoken in Tuscany°.)

The English poet Geoffrey Chaucer was another vernacular writer of this era. Many of his works show the influence of Dante, but he is most famous for the *Canterbury Tales*, the lengthy poem written in the last dozen years of his life. These often humorous and earthy tales, told by fictional pilgrims on their way to the shrine of Thomas à Becket in Canterbury, are cited several times in this chapter because they present a marvelous cross-section of medieval people and attitudes.

Dante also influenced the literary movement of the **humanists** that began in his native Florence in the mid-fourteenth century. The term refers to their interest in the humanities, the classical disciplines of grammar, rhetoric, poetry, history, and ethics. With the brash exaggeration characteristic of new intellectual fashions, humanist writers such as the poet Francesco Petrarch° (1304–1374) and the poet and storyteller Giovanni Boccaccio° (1313–1375) claimed that their new-found admiration for the classical values revived Greco-Roman traditions that for centuries had lain buried under the rubble of the Middle Ages. This idea of a rebirth of learning long dead overlooks the fact that scholars at the monasteries and universities had been recovering and preserving all sorts of Greco-Roman learning for many centuries. Dante (whom the humanists revered) had anticipated humanist interests by a generation.

Yet it is hard to exaggerate the beneficial influences of the humanists as educators, advisers, and reformers. Their greatest influence was in reforming secondary education. Humanists introduced a curriculum centered on the languages and literature of Greco-Roman antiquity, which they felt provided intellectual discipline, moral lessons, and refined tastes. This curriculum dominated secondary education in Europe and the Americas well into the twentieth century. Despite the humanists' influence, theology, law, medicine, and branches of philosophy other than ethics remained prominent in university education during this period. After 1500 humanist influence grew in university education.

Believing the pinnacle of learning, beauty, and wisdom had been reached in antiquity, many humanists tried to duplicate the elegance of classical Latin or Greek. Others followed Dante in composing literary works in vernacular languages. Boccaccio is most famous for his vernacular writings, especially the *Decameron*, an earthy work that has much in common with Chaucer's boisterous tales. Under Petrarch's influence, however, Boccaccio turned to writing in classical Latin, including *De mulieribus claris (Famous Women)*, a chronicle of 106

---

scholasticism (skoh-LAS-tih-sizm)
Summa Theologica (SOOM-uh thee-uh-LOH-jih-kuh)
Dante Alighieri (DAHN-tay ah-lee-GYEH-ree)
Tuscany (TUS-kuh-nee)

Franceso Petrarch (fran-CHES-koh PAY-trahrk)
Giovanni Boccaccio (jo-VAH-nee boh-KAH-chee-oh)

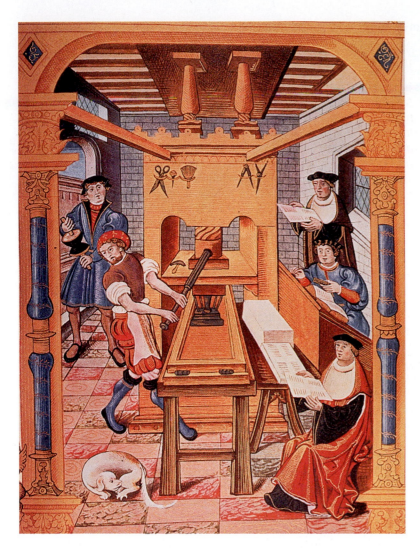

A French Printshop, 1537 A workman operates the "press," quite literally a screw device that presses the paper to the inked type. Other employees examine the printed sheets, each of which holds four pages. When folded, the sheets make a book. (Giraudon/Art Resource, NY)

famous women from Eve to his own day. It was the first collection of women's lives in Western literature.

Once they had mastered classical Latin and Greek, a number of humanist scholars of the fifteenth century worked to restore the original texts of Greco-Roman writers and of the Bible. By comparing many different manuscripts, they eliminated errors introduced by generations of copyists. To aid in this task, Pope Nicholas V (r. 1447–1455) created the Vatican Library, buying scrolls of Greco-Roman writings and paying to have accurate copies and translations made. Working independently, the respected Dutch scholar Erasmus° of Rotterdam (ca. 1466–1536) produced a critical edition of the New Testament in Greek.

Erasmus (uh-RAZ-muhs)

Erasmus was able to correct many errors and mistranslations in the Latin text that had been in general use throughout the Middle Ages. In later years this humanist priest and theologian also wrote—in classical Latin—influential moral guides including the *Enchiridion militis christiani* (*The Manual of the Christian Knight*, 1503) and *The Education of a Christian Prince* (1515).

The influence of the humanists was enhanced after 1450 because new printing technology increased the availability of their critical editions of ancient texts, literary works, and moral guides. The Chinese were the first to use carved wood blocks for printing (see Chapter 13), and block-printed playing cards from China were circulating in Europe before 1450. Then, around 1450, three technical improvements revolutionized printing: (1) mov-

The Medici Family   This detail of a mural painting of 1459 by Benozzo Gozzoli depicts the arrival of the Magi at the birthplace of the Christ Child, but the principal figures are important members of the wealthy Medici family of Florence and their entourage in costumes of their day. The bowman on the left suggests how common African servants and slaves became in southern Europe during the Renaissance.   (Art Resource, NY)

able pieces of type consisting of individual letters, (2) new ink suitable for printing on paper, and (3) the **printing press,** a mechanical device that pressed inked type onto sheets of paper.

The man who did most to perfect printing was Johann Gutenberg° (ca. 1394–1468) of Mainz. The Gutenberg Bible of 1454, the first book in the West printed from movable type, was a beautiful and finely crafted work that bore witness to the printer's years of diligent experimentation. As printing spread to Italy and France, humanists worked closely with printers. Erasmus worked for years as an editor and proofreader for the great scholar-printer Aldo Manuzio (1449–1515), whose press in Venice published critical editions of many classical Latin and Greek texts.

By 1500 at least 10 million printed copies had issued forth from presses in 238 towns in western Europe. Though mass-produced paperbacks were still in the future, the printers and humanists had launched a revolution that was already having an effect on students, scholars, and a growing number of literate people who could gain access to ancient texts as well as to unorthodox political and religious tracts.

Johann Gutenberg (yoh-HAHN GOO-ten-burg)

Renaissance Artists

The fourteenth and fifteenth centuries were as distinguished for their masterpieces of painting, sculpture, and architecture as they were for their scholarship. Although artists continued to depict biblical subjects, the spread of Greco-Roman learning led many artists, especially in Italy, to portray Greco-Roman deities and mythical tales. Another popular trend was depicting the scenes of daily life.

However, neither daily life nor classical images were entirely new subjects. Renaissance art, like Renaissance scholarship, owed a major debt to earlier generations. The Florentine painter Giotto° (ca. 1267–1337) had a formidable influence on the major Italian painters of the fifteenth century, who credited him with single-handedly reviving the "lost art of painting." In his religious scenes Giotto replaced the stiff, staring figures of the Byzantine style, which were intended to overawe viewers, with more natural and human portraits with whose emotions of grief and love viewers could identify. Rather than floating on backgrounds of gold leaf, his saints inhabit earthly landscapes.

Giotto (JAW-toh)

Another important contribution to the early Italian Renaissance was a new painting technology from north of the Alps. The Flemish painter Jan van Eyck° (ca. 1390–1441) mixed his pigments with linseed oil instead of the diluted egg yolk of earlier centuries. Oil paints were slower drying and more versatile, and they gave pictures a superior luster. Van Eyck's use of the technique for his own masterfully realistic paintings on religious and domestic themes was quickly copied by talented painters of the Italian Renaissance.

The great Italian Leonardo da Vinci° (1452–1519), for example, used oil paints for his famous *Mona Lisa*. Renaissance artists like Leonardo were masters of many media. His other works include the fresco (painting in wet plaster) *The Last Supper*, bronze sculptures, and imaginative designs for airplanes, submarines, and tanks. Leonardo's younger contemporary Michelangelo° (1472–1564) painted frescoes of biblical scenes on the ceiling of the Sistine Chapel in the Vatican, sculpted statues of David and Moses, and designed the dome for a new Saint Peter's Basilica.

The patronage of wealthy and educated merchants and prelates did much to foster an artistic blossoming in the cities of northern Italy and Flanders. The Florentine banker Cosimo de' Medici (1389–1464), for example, spent immense sums on paintings, sculpture, and public buildings. His grandson Lorenzo (1449–1492), known as "the Magnificent," was even more lavish. The church was also an important source of artistic commissions. Seeking to restore Rome as the capital of the Latin Church, the papacy° launched a building program culminating in the construction of the new Saint Peter's Basilica and a residence for the pope.

These scholarly and artistic achievements exemplify the innovation and striving for excellence of the Late Middle Ages. The new literary themes and artistic styles of this period had lasting influence on Western culture. But the innovations in the organization of universities, in printing, and in oil painting had wider implications, for they were later adopted by cultures all over the world.

POLITICAL AND MILITARY TRANSFORMATIONS

Stronger and more unified states and armies developed in western Europe in parallel with the economic and cultural revivals. In no case were transformations smooth and steady, and the political changes unfolded somewhat differently in each state (see Map 15.3). During and after the prolonged struggle of the Hundred Years War, French and English monarchs forged closer ties with the nobility, the church, and the merchants. The consolidation of Spain and Portugal was linked to crusades against Muslim states. In Italy and Germany, however, political power remained in the hands of small states and loose alliances.

Monarchs, Nobles, and Clergy

Thirteenth-century states still shared many features of early medieval states (see Chapter 10). Hereditary monarchs occupied the peak of the political pyramid, but their powers were limited by modest treasuries and the rights possessed by others. Below them came the powerful noblemen who controlled vast estates and whose advice and consent were often required on important matters of state. The church, jealous of its traditional rights and independence, was another powerful body within each kingdom. Towns, too, had acquired many rights and privileges. Indeed, the towns in Flanders, the Hanseatic League, and Italy were nearly independent from royal interference.

In theory, nobles were vassals of the reigning monarchs and were obliged to furnish them with armored knights in time of war. In practice, vassals sought to limit the monarch's power and protect their own rights and privileges. The nobles' privileged economic and social position rested on the large estates that had been granted to their ancestors in return for supporting and training knights in armor to serve in a royal army.

In the year 1200 knights were still the backbone of western European fighting forces, but two changes in weaponry were bringing their central military role, and thus the system of estates that supported them, into question. The first involved the humble arrow. Improved crossbows could shoot metal-tipped arrows with such force that they could pierce helmets and light body armor. Professional crossbowmen, hired for wages, became increasingly common and much feared. Indeed, a church council in 1139 outlawed the crossbow as being too deadly for use against Christians. The ban was largely ignored. The second innovation in military technology that weakened the feudal system was the firearm. This Chinese invention, using gunpowder to shoot stone or metal projectiles, further transformed the medieval army.

The church also resisted royal control. In 1302 the outraged Pope Boniface VIII (r. 1294–1303) went so far as to assert that divine law made the papacy superior to

---

Jan van Eyck (yahn vahn-IKE)
Leonardo da Vinci (lay-own-AHR-doh dah-VIN-chee)
Michelangelo (my-kuhl-AN-juh-low)   **papacy** (PAY-puh-see)

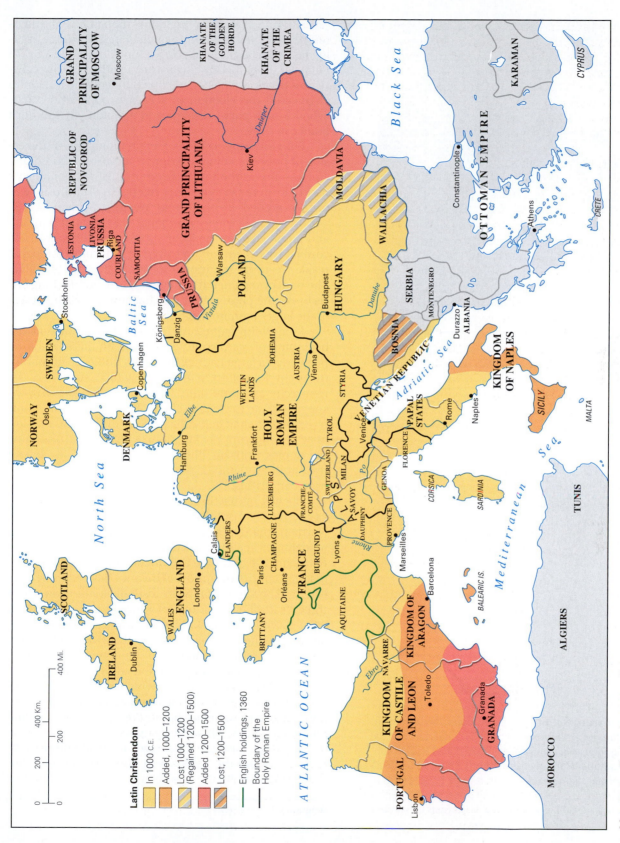

Latin Christendom

In 1000 C.E.	
Added, 1000–1200	
Lost 1000–1200 (Regained 1200–1500)	
Added 1200–1500	
Lost, 1200–1500	

— English holdings, 1360
— Boundary of the Holy Roman Empire

400 Mi.

400 Km.

GRAND PRINCIPALITY OF MOSCOW
• Moscow

KHANATE OF THE GOLDEN HORDE

KHANATE OF THE CRIMEA

KARAMAN

CYPRUS

REPUBLIC OF NOVGOROD

GRAND PRINCIPALITY OF LITHUANIA

Dnieper

• Kiev

Black Sea

• Constantinople

OTTOMAN EMPIRE

ESTONIA
LIVONIA
PRUSSIA
Riga
COURLAND
SAMOGITIA

MOLDAVIA

WALLACHIA

• Athens

CRETE

SWEDEN

Stockholm

Baltic Sea

Königsberg
Danzig
PRUSSIA

Warsaw •

Vistula

POLAND

Budapest •
HUNGARY

Danube

SERBIA
MONTENEGRO
Durazzo •
ALBANIA

Copenhagen •

NORWAY

Oslo •

DENMARK

Hamburg •

Elbe

BOHEMIA

AUSTRIA
Vienna •
STYRIA

BOSNIA

VENETIAN REPUBLIC

Adriatic Sea

KINGDOM OF NAPLES

SICILY

NORTH SEA

Frankfort •

Rhine

WETTIN LANDS

HOLY ROMAN EMPIRE

TYROL
SWITZERLAND
MILAN
Po
SAVOY
DAUPHINY

Venice •
PAPAL STATES

FLORENCE •

GENOA

Rome •

Naples •

MALTA

CORSICA

SARDINIA

Mediterranean Sea

TUNIS

SCOTLAND

WALES
ENGLAND
London •

IRELAND
Dublin •

Calais
FLANDERS

Paris •
CHAMPAGNE
LUXEMBURG
FRANCHE-COMTÉ
BURGUNDY
Lyons •
PROVENCE
Marseilles •

Orléans •
FRANCE

BRITTANY

AQUITAINE

Rhône

Barcelona •

BALEARIC IS.

ALGIERS

ATLANTIC OCEAN

NAVARRE
Ebro
KINGDOM OF ARAGON

Toledo •

KINGDOM OF CASTILE AND LEON

Granada •
GRANADA

PORTUGAL
Lisbon •

MOROCCO

Map 15.3   Europe in 1453   This year marked the end of the Hundred Years War between France and England and the fall of the Byzantine capital city of Constantinople to the Ottoman Turks. Muslim advances into southeastern Europe were offset by the Latin Christian reconquests of Islamic holdings in southern Italy and the Iberian Peninsula and by the conversion of Lithuania.

The Magna Carta One of four extant copies, this document shows the ravages of time, but the symbolic importance of the charter King John of England signed under duress in 1215 for English constitutional history has not been dimished. Originally a guarantee of the baron's feudal rights, it came to be seen as a limit on the monarch's authority over all subjects. (The National Archives, Public Record Office and Historical Manuscripts Commission)

"every human creature," including monarchs. This theoretical claim of superiority was challenged by force. Issuing his own claim of superiority, King Philip "the Fair" of France (r. 1285–1314) sent an army to arrest the pope. After this treatment hastened Pope Boniface's death, Philip engineered the election of a French pope who established a new papal residence at Avignon° in southern France in 1309.

With the support of the French monarchy, a succession of popes residing in Avignon improved church discipline—but at the price of compromising the papacy's neutrality in the eyes of other rulers. Papal authority was further eroded by the **Great Western Schism** (1378–1415), a period when rival papal claimants at Avignon and Rome vied for the loyalties of Latin Christians. The conflict was eventually resolved by returning the papal residence to its traditional location, the city of Rome. The papacy regained its independence, but the long crisis broke the pope's ability to challenge the rising power of the larger monarchies.

King Philip gained an important advantage at the beginning of his dispute with Pope Boniface when he persuaded a large council of French nobles to grant him the right to collect a new tax, which sustained the monarchy for some time. Earlier, by adroitly using the support of the towns, the saintly King Louis IX of France (r. 1226–1270) had been able to issue ordinances that applied throughout his kingdom without first obtaining the nobles' consent. But later kings' efforts to extend royal authority sparked prolonged resistance by the most powerful vassals.

English monarchs wielded more centralized power as a result of consolidation that had taken place after the Norman conquest of 1066. Anglo-Norman kings also extended their realm by assaults on their Celtic neighbors. Between 1200 and 1400 they incorporated Wales and reasserted control over most of Ireland. Nevertheless, English royal power was far from absolute. In the span of just three years the ambitions of King John (r. 1199–1216) were severely set back. First he was compelled to acknowledge the pope as his overlord (1213). Then he lost his bid to reassert claims to Aquitaine in southern France (1214). Finally he was forced to sign the Magna Carta ("Great Charter," 1215), which affirmed that monarchs were subject to established law, confirmed the independence of the church and the city of London, and guaranteed nobles' hereditary rights.

Separate from the challenges to royal authority by the church and the nobles were the alliances and conflicts generated by the hereditary nature of monarchial

Avignon (ah-vee-NYON)

rule. Monarchs and their vassals entered into strategic marriages with a view to increasing their lands and their wealth. Such marriages showed scant regard for the emotions of the wedded parties or for "national" interests. Besides unhappiness for the parties involved, these marriages often led to conflicts over far-flung inheritances. Although these dynastic struggles and shifting boundaries make European politics seem chaotic in comparison with the empires of Asia, some important changes were emerging from them. Aided by the changing technology of war, monarchs were strengthening their authority and creating more stable (but not entirely fixed) state boundaries within which the nations of western Europe would in time develop. Nobles lost autonomy and dominance on the battlefield but retained their social position and important political roles.

The Hundred Years War, 1337–1453

The long conflict between the king of France and his vassals known as the **Hundred Years War** (1337–1453) was a key example of the transformation in politics and warfare. This long conflict set the power of the French monarchy against the ambitions of his vassals, who included the kings of England (for lands that belonged to their Norman ancestors) and the heads of Flanders, Brittany, and Burgundy. In typical fashion, the conflict grew out of a marriage alliance.

Princess Isabella of France married King Edward II of England (r. 1307–1327) to ensure that this powerful vassal remained loyal to the French monarchy. However, when none of Isabella's three brothers, who served in turn as kings of France, produced a male heir, Isabella's son, King Edward III of England (r. 1327–1377), laid claim to the French throne in 1337. Edward decided to fight for his rights after French courts awarded the throne to a more distant (and more French) cousin. Other vassals joined in a series of battles for the French throne that stretched out over a century.

New military technology shaped the conflict. Early in the war, hired Italian crossbowmen reinforced the French cavalry, but arrows from another late medieval innovation, the English longbow, nearly annihilated the French force. Adopted from the Welsh, the 6-foot (1.8-meter) longbow could shoot farther and more rapidly than the crossbow. Although arrows from longbows could not pierce armor, in concentrated volleys they often found gaps in the knights' defenses or struck their less-well-protected horses. To defend against these weapons, armor became heavier and more encompassing, making it harder for a knight to move. A knight who

was pulled off his steed by a foot soldier armed with a pike (hooked pole) was usually unable to get up to defend himself.

Firearms became prominent in later stages of the Hundred Years War. Early cannon were better at spooking the horses than at hitting rapidly moving targets. As cannon grew larger, they proved quite effective in blasting holes through the heavy walls of medieval castles and towns. The first use of such artillery, against the French in the Battle of Agincourt (1415), gave the English an important victory.

A young French peasant woman, Joan of Arc, brought the English gains to a halt. Believing she was acting on God's instructions, she donned a knight's armor and rallied the French troops, which defeated the English in 1429 just as they seemed close to conquering France. Shortly after this victory, Joan had the misfortune of falling into English hands. English churchmen tried her for witchcraft and burned her at the stake in 1431.

In the final battles of the Hundred Years War, French forces used large cannon to demolish the walls of once-secure castles held by the English and their allies. The truce that ended the struggle in 1453 left the French monarchy in firm control.

New Monarchies in France and England

The war proved to be a watershed in the political history of France and England. The **new monarchies** that emerged differed from their medieval predecessors in having greater centralization of power, more fixed "national" boundaries, and stronger representative institutions. English monarchs after 1453 strove to consolidate control within the British Isles, though the Scots strongly defended their independence. French monarchs worked to tame the independence of their powerful noble vassals. Holdings headed by women were especially vulnerable. Mary of Burgundy (1457–1482) was forced to surrender much of her family's vast holdings to the king. Anne of Brittany's forced marriage to the king led to the eventual incorporation of her duchy° into France.

Changes in military technology helped undermine nobles' resistance. Smaller, more mobile cannon developed in the late fifteenth century blasted through their castle walls. More powerful hand-held firearms that could pierce even the heaviest armor hastened the demise of the armored knights. New armies depended less on knights from noble vassals and more on bowmen,

---

duchy (DUTCH-ee)

pikemen, musketeers, and artillery units paid by the royal treasury.

The new monarchies tried several strategies to pay for their standing armies. Monarchs encouraged noble vassals to make monetary payments in place of military service and levied additional taxes in time of war. For example, Charles VII of France (r. 1422–1461) won the right to impose a land tax on his vassals that enabled him to pay the costs of the last years of war with England. This new tax sustained the royal treasury for the next 350 years.

Taxes on merchants were another important revenue source. The taxes on the English wool trade, begun by King Edward III, paid most of the costs of the Hundred Years War. Some rulers taxed Jewish merchants and extorted large contributions from wealthy towns. Individual merchants sometimes curried royal favor with loans, even though such debts could be difficult or dangerous to collect. For example, the wealthy fifteenth-century French merchant Jacques Coeur° gained many social and financial benefits for himself and his family by lending money to important members of the French court, but he was ruined when his jealous debtors accused him of murder and had his fortune confiscated.

The church was a third source of revenue. The clergy often made voluntary contributions to a war effort. English and French monarchs gained further control of church funds in the fifteenth century by gaining the right to appoint important ecclesiastical officials in their realms. Although reformers complained that this subordinated the church's spiritual mission to political and economic concerns, the monarchs often used state power to enforce religious orthodoxy in their realms more vigorously than the popes had ever been able to do.

The shift in power to the monarchs and away from the nobility and the church did not deprive nobles of social privileges and special access to high administrative and military offices. Moreover, towns, nobles, and clergy found new ways to check royal power in the representative institutions that came into existence in England and France. By 1500 Parliament had become a permanent part of English government: the House of Lords contained all the great nobles and English church officials; the House of Commons represented the towns and the leading citizens of the counties. In France a similar but less effective representative body, the Estates General, represented the church, the nobles, and the towns.

Iberian Unification

The growth of Spain and Portugal into strong, centralized states was also shaped by struggles between kings and vassals, dynastic marriages and mergers, and warfare. But Spain and Portugal's **reconquest** of Iberia from Muslim rule was also a religious crusade. Religious zeal did not rule out personal gain. The Christian knights who gradually pushed the borders of their kingdoms southward expected material rewards. The spoils of victory included irrigated farmland, cities rich in Moorish architecture, and trading ports with access to the Mediterranean and the Atlantic. Serving God, growing rich, and living off the labor of others became a way of life for the Iberian nobility.

The reconquest advanced in waves over several centuries. Christian knights took Toledo in 1085. The Atlantic port of Lisbon fell in 1147 with the aid of English crusaders on their way to capture the Holy Land. It became the new capital of Portugal and the kingdom's leading city, displacing the older capital of Oporto, whose name (meaning "the port") is the root of the word *Portugal*. A Christian victory in 1212 broke the back of Muslim power in Iberia. During the next few decades Portuguese and Castilian forces captured the beautiful and prosperous cities of Cordova (1236) and Seville (1248) and in 1249 drove the Muslims from the southwestern corner of Iberia, known as Algarve° ("the west" in Arabic). Only the small kingdom of Granada hugging the Mediterranean coast remained in Muslim hands.

By incorporating Algarve in 1249, Portugal attained its modern territorial limits. After a long pause to colonize, Christianize, and consolidate this land, Portugal took the Christian crusade to North Africa. In 1415 Portuguese knights seized the port city of Ceuta° in Morocco, where they learned more about the trans-Saharan caravan trade in gold and slaves (see Chapter 14). During the next few decades, Portuguese mariners sailed down the Atlantic coast of Africa seeking access to this rich trade and alliances with rumored African Christians (see Chapter 16).

Although it took the other Iberian kingdoms much longer to complete the reconquest, the struggle served to bring them together and to keep their Christian religious zealotry at a high pitch. The marriage of Princess Isabella of Castile and Prince Ferdinand of Aragon in 1469 led to the permanent union of their kingdoms into Spain a decade later when they inherited their respective thrones. Their conquest of Granada in 1492 secured the final piece of Muslim territory in Iberia for the new kingdom.

Coeur (cur)

Algarve (ahl-GAHRV)   **Ceuta** (say-OO-tuh)

The year 1492 was also memorable because of Ferdinand and Isabella's sponsorship of the voyage led by Christopher Columbus in search of the riches of the Indian Ocean (see Chapter 16). A third event that year also reflected Spain's crusading mentality. Less than three months after Granada's fall, the monarchs ordered all Jews to be expelled from their kingdoms. Efforts to force the remaining Muslims to convert or leave led to a Muslim revolt at the end of 1499 that was not put down until 1501. Portugal also began expelling Jews in 1493, including many thousands who had fled from Spain.

CONCLUSION

From an ecological perspective, the later medieval history of the Latin West is a story of triumphs and disasters. Westerners excelled in harnessing the inanimate forces of nature with their windmills, water wheels, and sails. They mined and refined the mineral wealth of the earth, although localized pollution and deforestation were among the results. But their inability to improve food production and distribution as rapidly as their population grew created a demographic crisis that became a demographic calamity when the Black Death swept through Europe in the mid-fourteenth century.

From a regional perspective, the period witnessed the coming together of the basic features of the modern West. States were of moderate size but had exceptional military capacity honed by frequent wars with one another. The ruling class, convinced that economic strength and political strength were inseparable, promoted the welfare of the urban populations that specialized in trade, manufacturing, and finance—and taxed their profits. Autonomous universities fostered intellectual excellence, and printing diffused the latest advances in knowledge. Art and architecture reached peaks of design and execution that set the standard for subsequent centuries. Perhaps most fundamentally, later medieval Europeans were fascinated by tools and techniques. In commerce, warfare, and industry, new inventions and improved versions of old ones underpinned the region's continuing dynamism.

From a global perspective, these centuries marked the Latin West's change from a region dependent on cultural and commercial flows from the East to a region poised to export its culture and impose its power on other parts of the world. It is one of history's great ironies that many of the tools that the Latin West used to challenge Eastern supremacy had originally been borrowed from the East. Medieval Europe's mills, printing, firearms, and navigational devices owed much to Eastern designs, just as its agriculture, alphabet, and numerals had in earlier times. Western European success depended as much on strong motives for expansion as on adequate means. Long before the first voyages overseas, population pressure, religious zeal, economic motives, and intellectual curiosity had expanded the territory and resources of the Latin West. From the late eleventh century onward such expansion of frontiers was notable in the English conquest of Celtic lands, in the establishment of crusader and commercial outposts in the eastern Mediterranean and Black Seas, in the massive German settlement east of the Elbe River, and in the reconquest of southern Iberia from the Muslims. The early voyages into the Atlantic were an extension of similar motives in a new direction.

■ Key Terms

Latin West	universities
three-field system	scholasticism
Black Death	humanists (Renaissance)
water wheel	printing press
Hanseatic League	Great Western Schism
guild	Hundred Years War
Gothic cathedral	new monarchies
Renaissance (European)	reconquest

■ Suggested Reading

A fine guide to the Latin West (including its ties to eastern Europe, Africa, and the Middle East) is Robert Fossier, ed., *The Cambridge Illustrated History of the Middle Ages*, vol. 3, *1250–1520* (1986). George Holmes, *Europe: Hierarchy and Revolt, 1320–1450*, 2d ed. (2000), and Denys Hay, *Europe in the Fourteenth and Fifteenth Centuries*, 2d ed. (1989), are comprehensive overviews. For the West's economic revival and growth, see Robert S. Lopez, *The Commercial Revolution of the Middle Ages, 950–1350* (1976), and Harry A. Miskimin, *The Economy of Early Renaissance Europe, 1300–1460* (1975). For greater detail see *The New Cambridge Medieval History*, vol. 6, *1300–c.1415*, ed. M. Jones (1998), and vol. 7, *1415–1500*, ed. C. Allmand (1999).

For fascinating primary sources see James Bruce Ross and Mary Martin McLaughlin, eds., *The Portable Medieval Reader* (1977) and *The Portable Renaissance Reader* (1977). *The Notebooks of Leonardo da Vinci*, ed. Pamela Taylor (1960), show this versatile genius at work.

Technological change is surveyed by Arnold Pacey, *The Maze of Ingenuity: Ideas and Idealism in the Development of Technology* (1974); Jean Gimpel, *The Medieval Machine: The Industrial Revolution of the Middle Ages* (1977); and William H. McNeill, *The Pursuit of Power: Technology, Armed Force, and Society Since A.D. 1000* (1982). For a key aspect of the environment see Roland Bechmann, *Trees and Man: The Forest in the Middle Ages* (1990).

Charles Homer Haskins, *The Rise of the Universities* (1923; reprint, 1957), is a brief, lighthearted introduction; more detailed and scholarly is Olef Pedersen, *The First Universities: Studium Generale and the Origins of University Education in Europe* (1998). Johan Huizinga, *The Waning of the Middle Ages* (1924), is the classic account of the "mind" of the fifteenth century. A multitude of works deal with the Renaissance, but few in any broad historical context. Lisa Jardine, *Worldly Goods: A New History of the Renaissance* (1996), is well illustrated and balanced; see also John R. Hale, *The Civilization of Europe in the Renaissance* (1995).

For social history see Georges Duby, *Rural Economy and Country Life in the Medieval West* (1990), for the earlier centuries. George Huppert, *After the Black Death: A Social History of Early Modern Europe* (1986), takes the analysis past 1500. Brief lives of individuals are found in Eileen Power, *Medieval People*, new ed. (1997), and Frances Gies and Joseph Gies, *Women in the Middle Ages* (1978). More systematic are the essays in Mary Erler and Maryanne Kowaleski, eds., *Women and Power in the Middle Ages* (1988). Vita Sackville-West, *Saint Joan of Arc* (1926; reprint, 1991), is a readable introduction to this extraordinary person.

Key events in the Anglo-French dynastic conflict are examined by Christopher Alland, *The Hundred Years War: England and France at War, ca. 1300–ca. 1450* (1988). Joseph F. O'Callaghan, *A History of Medieval Spain* (1975), provides the best one-volume coverage; for more detail see Jocelyn N. Hillgarth, *The Spanish Kingdoms*, 2 vols. (1976, 1978). Barbara W. Tuchman, *A Distant Mirror: The Calamitous 14th Century* (1978), is a popular account of the crises of that era. Norman F. Cantor, *In the Wake of the Plague: The Black Death and the World It Made* (2001), supplies a thorough introduction.

The Latin West's expansion is well treated by Robert Bartlett, *The Making of Europe: Conquest, Colonization, and Cultural Change* (1993); J. R. S. Phillips, *The Medieval Expansion of Europe*, 2d ed. (1998); and P. E. Russell, *Portugal, Spain and the African Atlantic, 1343–1492* (1998).

Francis C. Oakley, *The Western Church in the Later Middle Ages* (1985), is a reliable summary of modern scholarship. Kenneth R. Stow, *Alienated Minority: The Jews of Medieval Latin Europe* (1992), provides a fine survey up through the fourteenth century. For pioneering essays on the Latin West's external ties see Khalil I. Semaan, ed., *Islam and the Medieval West: Aspects of Intercultural Relations* (1980).

◼ Notes

1. Quoted in Marina Warner, *Alone of All Her Sex: The Myth and Cult of the Virgin Mary* (New York: Random House, 1983), 179.
2. Harry Miskimin, *The Economy of the Early Renaissance, 1300–1460* (Englewood Cliffs, NJ: Prentice-Hall, 1969), 26–27.
3. Quotations here and later in the chapter are from Geoffrey Chaucer, *The Canterbury Tales*, trans. Nevill Coghill (New York: Penguin Books, 1952), 25, 29, 32.

The Maritime Revolution, to 1550

Columbus Prepares to Cross the Atlantic, 1492 This later representation shows Columbus with the ships, soldiers, priests, and seamen that were part of Spain's enterprise.

In 1511 young Ferdinand Magellan sailed from Europe around the southern tip of Africa and eastward across the Indian Ocean as a member of the first Portuguese expedition to explore the East Indies (maritime Southeast Asia). Eight years later, this time in the service of Spain, he headed an expedition that sought to demonstrate the feasibility of reaching the East Indies by sailing westward from Europe. By the middle of 1521 Magellan's expedition had achieved its goal by sailing across the Atlantic, rounding the southern tip of South America, and crossing the Pacific Ocean—but at a high price.

One of the five ships that had set out from Spain in 1519 was wrecked on a reef, and the captain of another deserted and sailed back to Spain. The passage across the vast Pacific took much longer than anticipated, resulting in the deaths of dozens of sailors due to starvation and disease. In the Philippines, Magellan himself was killed on April 27, 1521, while aiding a local king who had promised to become a Christian. Magellan's successor met the same fate a few days later.

To consolidate their dwindling resources, the expedition's survivors burned the least seaworthy of their remaining three ships and transferred the men and supplies from that ship to the smaller *Victoria*, which continued westward across the Indian Ocean, around Africa, and back to Europe. Magellan's flagship, the *Trinidad*, tried unsuccessfully to recross the Pacific to Central America. The *Victoria*'s return to Spain on September 8, 1522, was a crowning example of Europeans' new ability and determination to make themselves masters of the oceans. A century of daring and dangerous voyages backed by the Portuguese crown had opened new routes through the South Atlantic to Africa, Brazil, and the rich trade of the Indian Ocean. Rival voyages sponsored by Spain since 1492 had opened new contacts with the American continents. Now the unexpectedly broad Pacific Ocean had been crossed as well. A maritime revolution was under way that would change the course of history.

That new maritime skill marked the end of an era in which the flow of historical influences tended to move from east to west. Before 1500 most overland and maritime expansion had come from Asia, as had the most useful technologies and the most influential systems of belief. Asia also had been home to the most powerful states and the richest trading networks. The Iberians set out on their voyages of exploration to reach Eastern markets, and their success began a new era in which the West gradually became the world's center of power, wealth, and innovation.

The maritime revolution created many new contacts, alliances, and conflicts. Some ended tragically for individuals like Magellan. Some were disastrous for entire populations: Amerindians, for instance, suffered conquest, colonization, and a rapid decline in numbers. Sometimes the results were mixed: Asians and Africans found both risks and opportunities in their new relations with the visitors from Europe.

As you read this chapter, ask yourself the following questions:

- Why did Portugal and Spain undertake voyages of exploration?

- Why do the voyages of Magellan and other Iberians mark a turning point in world history?

- What were the consequences for the different peoples of the world of the new contacts resulting from these voyages?

GLOBAL MARITIME EXPANSION BEFORE 1450

Since ancient times travel across the salt waters of the world's seas and oceans had been one of the great challenges to people's technological ingenuity. Ships had to be sturdy enough to survive heavy winds and waves, and pilots had to learn how to cross featureless expanses of water to reach their destinations. In time ships, sails, and navigational techniques perfected in the more protected seas were tried on the vast, open oceans.

However complex the solutions and dangerous the voyages, the rewards of sea travel made them worthwhile. Ships could move goods and people more quickly and cheaply than any form of overland travel then possible. Because of its challenges and rewards, sea travel attracted adventurers. To cross the unknown waters, find

CHRONOLOGY

	Pacific Ocean	Atlantic Ocean	Indian Ocean
1400	**400–1300** Polynesian settlement of Pacific islands	**770–1200** Viking voyages **1300s** Settlement of Madeira, Azores, Canaries **Early 1300s** Mali voyages **1418–1460** Voyages of Henry the Navigator **1440s** Slaves from West Africa **1482** Portuguese at Gold Coast and Kongo **1486** Portuguese at Benin **1488** Bartolomeu Dias reaches Indian Ocean **1492** Columbus reaches Caribbean **1492–1500** Spanish conquer Hispaniola **1493** Columbus returns to Caribbean (second voyage) **1498** Columbus reaches mainland of South America (third voyage)	**1405–1433** Voyages of Zheng He **1497–1498** Vasco da Gama reaches India
1500		**1500** Cabral reaches Brazil **1513** Ponce de León explores Florida	**1505** Portuguese bombard Swahili Coast cities **1510** Portuguese take Goa **1511** Portuguese take Malacca **1515** Portuguese take Hormuz
	1519–1522 Magellan expedition	**1519–1520** Cortés conquers Aztec Empire **1531–1533** Pizarro conquers Inca Empire	**1535** Portuguese take Dui **1538** Portuguese defeat Ottoman fleet **1539** Portuguese aid Ethiopia

new lands, and open up new trade or settlements was an exciting prospect. For these reasons, some men on every continent had long turned their attention to the sea.

By 1450 much had been accomplished and much remained undone. Daring mariners had discovered and settled most of the islands of the Pacific, the Atlantic, and the Indian Oceans. The greatest success was the trading system that united the peoples around the Indian Ocean. But no individual had yet crossed the Pacific in either direction. Even the narrower Atlantic was a barrier that kept the peoples of the Americas, Europe, and Africa in ignorance of each other's existence. The inhabitants of Australia were likewise completely cut off from contact with the rest of humanity. All this was about to change.

The Pacific Ocean

The voyages of Polynesian peoples out of sight of land over vast distances across the Pacific Ocean are one of the most impressive feats in maritime history before 1450 (see Map 16.1). Though they left no written records, over several thousand years

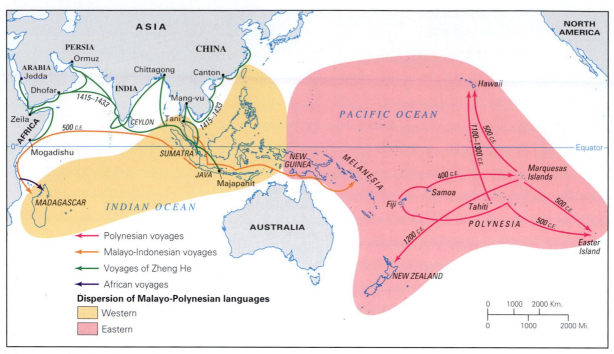

Map 16.1   Exploration and Settlement in the Indian and Pacific Oceans Before 1500   Over many centuries, mariners originating in Southeast Asia gradually colonized the islands of the Pacific and Indian Oceans. The Chinese voyages led by Zheng He in the fifteenth century were lavish official expeditions.

intrepid mariners from the Malay° Peninsula of Southeast Asia explored and settled the island chains of the East Indies and moved onto New Guinea and the smaller islands of Melanesia°. Beginning sometime before the Common Era (C.E.), a new wave of expansion from the area of Fiji brought the first humans to the islands of the central Pacific known as Polynesia. The easternmost of the Marquesas° Islands were reached about 400 C.E.; Easter Island, 2,200 miles (3,540 kilometers) off the coast of South America, was settled a century later. From the Marquesas, Polynesian sailors sailed to the Hawaiian Islands as early as 500 C.E. They settled New Zealand about 1200. Then, between 1100 and 1300, new voyages northward from Tahiti to Hawaii brought more Polynesian settlers across the more than 2,000 nautical miles (4,000 kilometers) to Hawaii.

Until recent decades some historians argued that Polynesians could have reached the eastern Pacific islands only by accident because they lacked navigational devices to plot their way. Others wondered how Polynesians could have overcome the difficulties, illustrated by

Magellan's flagship, *Trinidad*, of sailing eastward across the Pacific. In 1947 one energetic amateur historian of the sea, Thor Heyerdahl°, argued that Easter Island and Hawaii were actually settled from the Americas. He sought to prove his theory by sailing his balsa-wood raft, *Kon Tiki*, westward from Peru.

Although some Amerindian voyagers did use ocean currents to travel northward from Peru to Mexico between 300 and 900 C.E., there is now considerable evidence that the settlement of the islands of the eastern Pacific was the result of planned expansion by Polynesian mariners. The first piece of evidence is the fact that the languages of these islanders are all closely related to the languages of the western Pacific and ultimately to those of Malaya. The second is the finding that accidental voyages could not have brought sufficient numbers of men and women for founding a new colony along with all the plants and domesticated animals that were basic to other Polynesian islands.

In 1976 a Polynesian crew led by Ben Finney used traditional navigational methods to sail an ocean canoe from Hawaii south to Tahiti. The *Hokulea* was a 62-foot-

---

Malay (May-LAY)   **Melanesia** (mel-uh-NEE-zhuh)
Marquesas (mar-KAY-suhs)

Heyerdahl (HIGH-uhr-dahl)

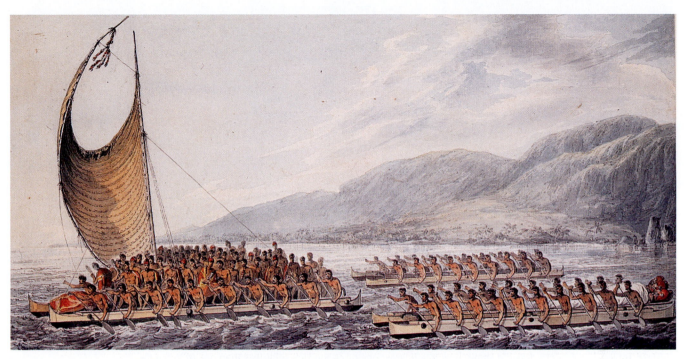

Polynesian Canoes   Pacific Ocean mariners sailing canoes such as these, shown in an eighteenth-century painting, made epic voyages of exploration and settlement. A large platform connects two canoes at the left, providing more room for the members of the expedition, and a sail supplements the paddlers.   ("Tereoboo, King of Owyhee, bringing presents to Captain Cook," D. L. Ref. p. xx 2f. 35. Courtesy, The Dixon Library, State Library of New South Wales)

long (19-meter-long) double canoe patterned after old oceangoing canoes, which sometimes were as long as 120 feet (37 meters). Not only did the *Hokulea* prove seaworthy, but, powered by an inverted triangular sail and steered by paddles (not by a rudder), it was able to sail across the winds at a sharp enough angle to make the difficult voyage, just as ancient mariners must have done. Perhaps even more remarkable, the *Hokulea*'s crew was able to navigate to their destination using only their observation of the currents, stars, and evidence of land.

The Indian Ocean

While Polynesian mariners were settling Pacific islands, other Malayo-Indonesians were sailing westward across the Indian Ocean and colonizing the large island of Madagascar off the southeastern coast of Africa. These voyages continued through the fifteenth century. To this day the inhabitants of Madagascar speak Malayo-Polynesian languages. However, part of the island's population is descended from Africans who had crossed the 300 miles (500 kilometers) from the mainland to Madagascar, most likely in the centuries leading up to 1500.

Other peoples had been using the Indian Ocean for trade since ancient times. The landmasses of Southeast Asia and eastern Africa that enclose the Indian Ocean on each side, and the Indian subcontinent that juts into its middle, provided coasts that seafarers might safely follow and coves for protection. Moreover, seasonal winds known as monsoons are so predictable and steady that navigation using sailing vessels called dhows° was less difficult and dangerous in ancient times than elsewhere.

The rise of medieval Islam gave Indian Ocean trade an important boost. The great Muslim cities of the Middle East provided a demand for valuable commodities. Even more important were the networks of Muslim traders that tied the region together. Muslim traders shared a common language, ethic, and law and actively spread their religion to distant trading cities. By 1400 there were Muslim trading communities all around the Indian Ocean.

The Indian Ocean traders operated largely independently of the empires and states they served, but in East Asia imperial China's rulers were growing more and more interested in these wealthy ports of trade. In 1368

dhow (dow)

Chinese Junk This modern drawing shows how much larger one of Zheng He's ships was than one of Vasco da Gama's vessels. Watertight interior bulkheads made junks the most seaworthy large ships of the fifteenth century. Sails made of pleated bamboo matting hung from the junk's masts, and a stern rudder provided steering. European ships of exploration, though smaller, were faster and more maneuverable. (Dugald Stermer)

the Ming dynasty overthrew Mongol rule and began expansionist policies to reestablish China's predominance and prestige abroad.

Having restored Chinese dominance in East Asia, the Ming next moved to establish direct contacts with the peoples around the Indian Ocean. In choosing to send out seven imperial fleets between 1405 and 1433, the Ming may have been motivated partly by curiosity. The fact that most of the ports the fleets visited were important in the Indian Ocean trade suggests that enhancing China's commerce was also a motive. Yet because the expeditions were far larger than needed for exploration or promoting trade, their main purpose probably was to inspire awe of Ming power and achievements.

The Ming expeditions into the Indian Ocean basin were launched on a scale that reflected imperial China's resources and importance. The first consisted of sixty-two specially built "treasure ships," large Chinese junks each about 300 feet long by 150 feet wide (90 by 45 meters). There were also at least a hundred smaller vessels, most of which were larger than the flagship in which Columbus later sailed across the Atlantic. Each treasure ship had nine masts, twelve sails, many decks, and a car-

rying capacity of 3,000 tons (six times the capacity of Columbus's entire fleet). One expedition carried over 27,000 individuals, including infantry and cavalry troops. The ships would have been armed with small cannon, but in most Chinese sea battles arrows from highly accurate crossbows dominated the fighting.

At the command of the expeditions was Admiral **Zheng He**° (1371–1435). A Chinese Muslim with ancestral connections to the Persian Gulf, Zheng was a fitting emissary to the increasingly Muslim-dominated Indian Ocean basin. The expeditions carried other Arabic-speaking Chinese as interpreters.

One of these interpreters kept a journal recording the customs, dress, and beliefs of the people visited, along with the trade, towns, and animals of their countries. He observed exotic animals such as the black panther of Malaya and the tapir of Sumatra; beliefs in legendary "corpse headed barbarians" whose heads left their bodies at night and caused infants to die; the division of coastal Indians into five classes, which correspond to the four Hindu varna and a separate Muslim class; and the fact

Zheng He (jung huh)

that traders in the rich Indian trading port of Calicut° could perform error-free calculations by counting on their fingers and toes rather than using the Chinese abacus. After his return, the interpreter went on tour in China, telling of these exotic places and "how far the majestic virtue of [China's] imperial dynasty extended."[1]

The Chinese "treasure ships" carried rich silks, precious metals, and other valuable goods intended as gifts for distant rulers. In return those rulers sent back gifts of equal or greater value to the Chinese emperor. Although the main purpose of these exchanges was diplomatic, they also stimulated trade between China and its southern neighbors. For that reason they were welcomed by Chinese merchants and manufacturers. Yet commercial profits could not have offset the huge cost of the fleets.

Interest in new contacts was not confined to the Chinese side. In 1415–1416 at least three trading cities on the Swahili° Coast of East Africa sent delegations to China. The delegates from one of them, Malindi, presented the emperor of China with a giraffe, creating quite a stir among the normally reserved imperial officials. Such African delegations may have encouraged more contacts, for the next three of Zheng's voyages were extended to the African coast. Unfortunately, no documents record how Africans and Chinese reacted to each other during these historic meetings between 1417 and 1433. It appears that China's lavish gifts stimulated the Swahili market for silk and porcelain. An increase in Chinese imports of pepper from southern Asian lands also resulted from these expeditions.

Had the Ming court wished to promote trade for the profit of its merchants, Chinese fleets might have continued to play a dominant role in Indian Ocean trade. But some high Chinese officials opposed increased contact with peoples whom they regarded as barbarians with no real contribution to make to China. Such opposition caused a suspension in the voyages from 1424 to 1431, and after the final expedition of 1432 to 1433, no new fleets were sent out. Later Ming emperors focused their attention on internal matters in their vast empire. China's withdrawal left a power vacuum in the Indian Ocean.

The Atlantic Ocean

The greatest mariners of the Atlantic in the early Middle Ages were the Vikings. These northern European raiders and pirates used their small, open ships to attack coastal European settlements for several centuries. They also dis-

covered and settled one island after another in the North Atlantic during these warmer than usual centuries. Like the Polynesians, the Vikings had neither maps nor navigational devices, but they managed to find their way wonderfully well using their knowledge of the heavens and the seas.

The Vikings first settled Iceland in 770. From there some moved to Greenland in 982, and by accident one group sighted North America in 986. Fifteen years later Leif Ericsson established a short-lived Viking settlement on the island of Newfoundland, which he called Vinland. When a colder climate returned after 1200, the northern settlements in Greenland went into decline, and Vinland became only a mysterious place mentioned in Norse sagas.

Some southern Europeans also used the maritime skills they had acquired in the Mediterranean and coastal Atlantic to explore the Atlantic. In 1291 two Vivaldo brothers from Genoa set out to sail through the South Atlantic and around Africa to India. They were never heard of again. Other Genoese and Portuguese expeditions into the Atlantic in the fourteenth century discovered (and settled) the islands of Madeira°, the Azores°, and the Canaries.

There is also written evidence of African voyages of exploration in the Atlantic in this period. The celebrated Syrian geographer al-Umari (1301–1349) relates that when Mansa Kankan Musa°, the ruler of the West African empire of Mali, passed through Egypt on his lavish pilgrimage to Mecca in 1324, he told of voyages to cross the Atlantic undertaken by his predecessor, Mansa Muhammad. Muhammad had sent out four hundred vessels with men and supplies, telling them, "Do not return until you have reached the other side of the ocean or if you have exhausted your food or water." After a long time one canoe returned, reporting that the others had been swept away by a "violent current in the middle of the sea." Muhammad himself then set out at the head of a second, even larger, expedition, from which no one returned.

In addition to sailing up the Pacific coast, early Amerindian voyagers from South America also colonized the West Indies. By the year 1000 Amerindians known as the **Arawak°** had moved up from the small islands of the Lesser Antilles (Barbados, Martinique, and Guadeloupe) into the Greater Antilles (Cuba, Hispaniola, Jamaica, and Puerto Rico) as well as into the Bahamas

---

Calicut (KAL-ih-kut)   **Swahili** (swah-HEE-lee)

Madeira (muh-DEER-uh)   **Azores** (A-zorz)
Mansa Kankan Musa (MAHN-suh KAHN-kahn MOO-suh)
Arawak (AR-uh-wahk)

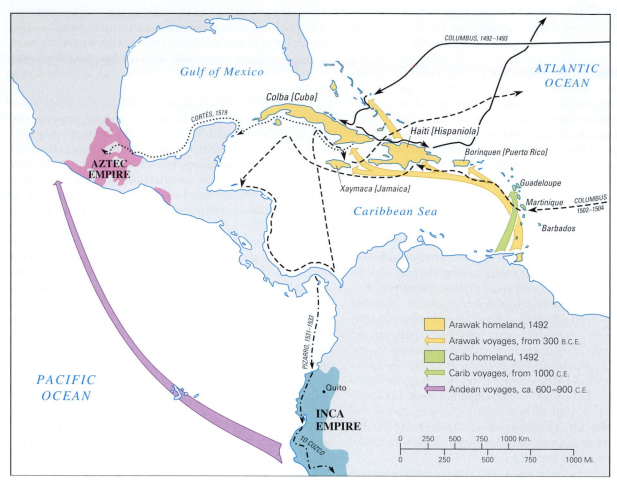

Map 16.2 Middle America to 1533 Early Amerindian voyages from South America brought new settlers to the West Indies and western Mexico. The arrival of Europeans in 1492 soon led to the conquest and depopulation of Amerindians.

(see Map 16.2). The Carib followed the same route in later centuries and by the late fifteenth century had overrun most Arawak settlements in the Lesser Antilles and were raiding parts of the Greater Antilles. From the West Indies Arawak and Carib also undertook voyages to the North American mainland.

EUROPEAN EXPANSION, 1400–1550

The preceding survey shows that maritime expansion occurred in many parts of the world before 1450. The epic sea voyages sponsored by the Iberian kingdoms

of Portugal and Spain are of special interest because they began a maritime revolution that profoundly altered the course of world history. The Portuguese and Spanish expeditions ended the isolation of the Americas and increased global interaction. The influence in world affairs of the Iberians and other Europeans who followed them overseas rose steadily in the centuries after 1500.

Iberian overseas expansion was the product of two related phenomena. First, Iberian rulers had strong economic, religious, and political motives to expand their contacts and increase their dominance. Second, improvements in their maritime and military technologies gave them the means to master treacherous and unfamiliar ocean environments, seize control of existing maritime trade routes, and conquer new lands.

Motives for Exploration

Why did Iberian kingdoms decide to sponsor voyages of exploration in the fifteenth century? Part of the answer lies in the individual ambitions and adventurous personalities of these states' leaders. Another part of the answer can be found in long-term tendencies in Europe and the Mediterranean. In many ways these voyages continued four trends evident in the Latin West since about the year 1000: (1) the revival of urban life and trade, (2) a struggle with Islamic powers for dominance of the Mediterranean that mixed religious motives with the desire for trade with distant lands, (3) growing intellectual curiosity about the outside world, and (4) a peculiarly European alliance between merchants and rulers.

The city-states of northern Italy took the lead in all these developments. By 1450 they had well-established trade links to northern Europe, the Indian Ocean, and the Black Sea, and their merchant princes had also sponsored an intellectual and artistic Renaissance. But there were two reasons why Italian states did not take the lead in exploring the Atlantic, even after the expansion of the Ottoman Empire disrupted their trade to the East and led other Christian Europeans to launch new religious wars against the Ottomans in 1396 and 1444. The first was that the trading states of Venice and Genoa preferred to continue the system of alliances with the Muslims that had given their merchants privileged access to the lucrative trade from the East. The second was that the ships of the Mediterranean were ill suited to the more violent weather of the Atlantic. However, many individual Italians played leading roles in the Atlantic explorations.

In contrast, the special history and geography of the Iberian kingdoms led them in a different direction. Part of that special history was centuries of anti-Muslim warfare that dated back to the eighth century, when Muslim forces overran most of Iberia. By about 1250 the Iberian kingdoms of Portugal, Castile, and Aragon had conquered all the Muslim lands in Iberia except the southern kingdom of Granada. United by a dynastic marriage in 1469, Castile and Aragon conquered Granada in 1492. These territories were gradually amalgamated into Spain, sixteenth-century Europe's most powerful state.

Christian militancy continued to be an important motive for both Portugal and Spain in their overseas ventures. But the Iberian rulers and their adventurous subjects were also seeking material returns. With only a modest share of the Mediterranean trade, they were much more willing than the Italians to take risks to find new routes through the Atlantic to the rich trade of Africa and Asia. Moreover, both were participants in the shipbuilding changes and the gunpowder revolution that were under way in Atlantic Europe. Though not centers of Renaissance learning, both were especially open to new geographical knowledge. Finally, both states were blessed with exceptional leaders.

Portuguese Voyages

Portugal's decision to invest significant resources in new exploration rested on well-established Atlantic fishing and a history of anti-Muslim warfare. When the Muslim government of Morocco in northwestern Africa showed weakness in the fifteenth century, the Portuguese went on the attack, beginning with the city of Ceuta° in 1415. This assault combined aspects of a religious crusade, a plundering expedition, and a military tournament in which young Portuguese knights displayed their bravery. The capture of the rich North African city, whose splendid homes, they reported, made those of Portugal look like pigsties, also made the Portuguese better informed about the caravans that brought gold and slaves to Ceuta from the African states south of the Sahara. Despite the capture of several more ports along Morocco's Atlantic coast, the Portuguese were unable to push inland and gain access to the gold trade. So they sought more direct contact with the gold producers by sailing down the African coast.

The attack on Ceuta was led by young Prince Henry (1394–1460), third son of the king of Portugal. Because he devoted the rest of his life to promoting exploration of the South Atlantic, he is known as **Henry the Navigator**. His official biographer emphasized Henry's mixed motives for exploration—converting Africans to Christianity, making contact with existing Christian rulers in Africa, and launching joint crusades with them against the Ottomans. Prince Henry also wished to discover new places and hoped that such new contacts would be profitable. His initial explorations were concerned with Africa. Only later did reaching India become an explicit goal of Portuguese explorers.

Despite being called "the Navigator," Prince Henry himself never ventured much farther from home than North Africa. Instead, he founded a sort of research institute at Sagres° for studying navigation and collecting information about the lands beyond Muslim North Africa. His staff drew on the pioneering efforts of Italian merchants, especially the Genoese, who had learned some of the secrets of the trans-Saharan trade, and of fourteenth-century Jewish cartographers who used information from Arab and European sources to produce remarkably

---

Ceuta (say-OO-tuh)   **Sagres** (SAH-gresh)

accurate sea charts and maps of distant places. Henry also oversaw the collection of new geographical information from sailors and travelers and sent out ships to explore the Atlantic. His ships established permanent contact with the islands of Madeira in 1418 and the Azores in 1439.

Henry devoted resources to solving the technical problems faced by mariners sailing in unknown waters and open seas. His staff studied and improved navigational instruments that had come into Europe from China and the Islamic world. These instruments included the magnetic compass, first developed in China, and the astrolabe, an instrument of Arab or Greek invention that enabled mariners to determine their location at sea by measuring the position of the sun or the stars in the night sky. Even with such instruments, however, voyages still depended on the skill and experience of the navigators.

Another achievement of Portuguese mariners was the design of vessels appropriate for the voyages of exploration. The galleys in use in the Mediterranean were powered by large numbers of oarsmen and were impractical for long ocean voyages. The square sails of the three-masted European ships of the North Atlantic were propelled by friendly winds but could not sail at much of an angle against the wind. The voyages of exploration made use of a new vessel, the **caravel**°. Caravels were small, only one-fifth the size of the largest European ships of their day and of the large Chinese junks. Their size permitted them to enter shallow coastal waters and explore upriver, but they were strong enough to weather ocean storms. When equipped with lateen sails, caravels had great maneuverability and could sail deeply into the wind; when sporting square Atlantic sails, they had great speed. The addition of small cannon made them good fighting ships as well. The caravels' economy, speed, agility, and power justified a contemporary's claim that they were "the best ships that sailed the seas."[2]

To conquer the seas, pioneering captains had to overcome crew's fears that the South Atlantic waters were boiling hot and contained ocean currents that would prevent any ship entering them from ever returning home. It took Prince Henry fourteen years—from 1420 to 1434—to coax an expedition to venture beyond southern Morocco (see Map 16.3). The crew's fears proved unfounded, but the next stretch of coast, 800 miles (1,300 kilometers) of desert, offered little of interest to the explorers. Finally, in 1444 the mariners reached the Senegal River and the well-watered and well-populated lands below the Sahara beginning at what they named "Cape Verde" (Green Cape) because of its vegetation.

In the years that followed, Henry's explorers made an important addition to the maritime revolution by learning how to return speedily to Portugal. Instead of battling the prevailing northeast trade winds and currents back up the coast, they discovered that by sailing northwest into the Atlantic to the latitude of the Azores, ships could pick up prevailing westerly winds that would blow them back to Portugal. The knowledge that ocean winds tend to form large circular patterns helped explorers discover many other ocean routes.

To pay for the research, the ships, and the expeditions during the many decades before the voyages became profitable, Prince Henry drew partly on the income of the Order of Christ, a military religious order of which he was governor. The Order of Christ had inherited the properties and crusading traditions of the Order of Knights Templar, which had disbanded in 1314. The Order of Christ received the exclusive right to promote Christianity in all the lands that were discovered, and the Portuguese emblazoned their ships' sails with the crusaders' red cross.

The first financial return from the voyages came from selling into slavery Africans captured by the Portuguese in raids on the northwest coast of Africa and the Canary Islands during the 1440s. The total number of Africans captured or purchased on voyages exceeded eighty thousand by the end of the century and rose steadily thereafter. However, the gold trade quickly became more important than the slave trade as the Portuguese made contact with the trading networks that flourished in West Africa and reached across the Sahara. By 1457 enough African gold was coming back to Portugal for the kingdom to issue a new gold coin called the *cruzado* (crusade), another reminder of how deeply the Portuguese entwined religious and secular motives.

By the time of Prince Henry's death in 1460, his explorers had established a secure base of operations in the uninhabited Cape Verde Islands and had explored 600 miles (950 kilometers) of coast beyond Cape Verde, as far as what they named Sierra Leone° (Lion Mountain). From there they knew the coast of Africa curved sharply toward the east. It had taken the Portuguese four decades to cover the 1,500 miles (2,400 kilometers) from Lisbon to Sierra Leone; it took only three decades to explore the remaining 4,000 miles (6,400 kilometers) to the southern tip of the African continent.

The Portuguese crown continued to sponsor voyages of exploration, but speedier progress resulted from the growing participation of private commercial interests. In 1469 a prominent Lisbon merchant named

---

caravel (KAR-uh-vel)

Sierra Leone (see- ER-uh lee-OWN)

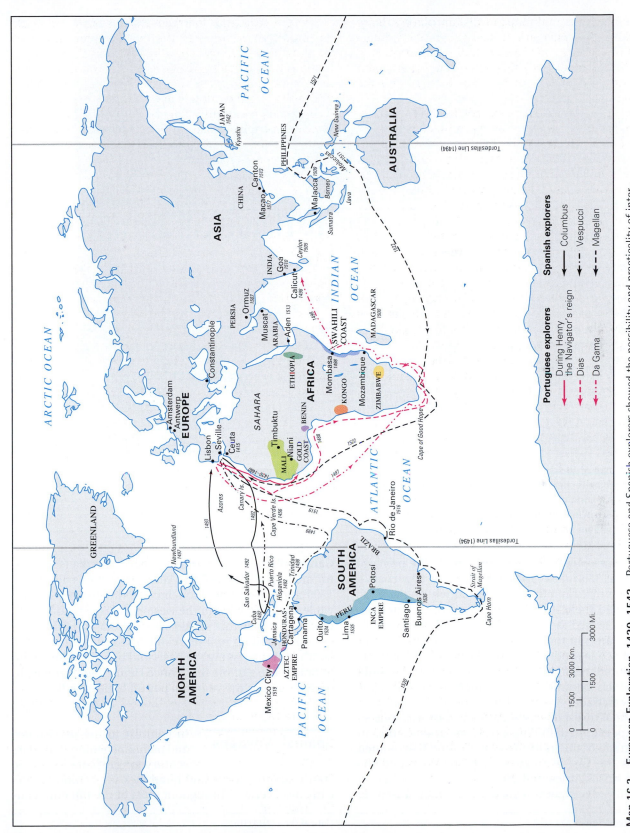

Map 16.3 European Exploration, 1420–1542 Portuguese and Spanish explorers showed the possibility and practicality of intercontinental maritime trade. Before 1540 European trade with Africa and Asia was much more important than that with the Americas, but after the Spanish conquest of the Aztec and Inca Empires transatlantic trade began to increase. Notice the Tordesillas line, which in theory separated the Spanish and Portuguese spheres of activity.

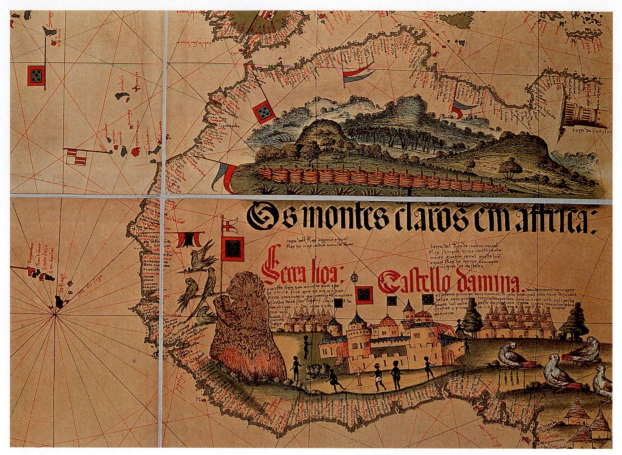

Portuguese Map of Western Africa, 1502   This map shows in great detail a section of African coastline that Portuguese explorers charted and named in the fifteenth century. The cartographer illustrated the African interior, which was almost completely unknown to Europeans, with drawings of birds and views of coastal sights: Sierra Leone (Serra lioa), named for a mountain shaped like a lion, and the Portuguese Castle of the Mine (Castello damina) on the Gold Coast.   (akg-images)

Fernão Gomes purchased from the Crown the privilege of exploring 350 miles (550 kilometers) of new coast a year for five years in return for a monopoly on the trade he developed there. During the period of his contract, Gomes discovered the uninhabited island of São Tomé° on the equator; in the next century it became a major source of sugar produced with African slave labor. He also explored what later Europeans called the **Gold Coast**, which became the headquarters of Portugal's West African trade.

The final thrust down the African coast was spurred by the expectation of finding a passage around Africa to the rich trade of the Indian Ocean. In 1488 **Bartolomeu Dias** was the first Portuguese explorer to round the southern tip of Africa and enter the Indian Ocean. In 1497–1498 a Portuguese expedition led by **Vasco da Gama** sailed around Africa and reached India (see Environment and Technology: Vasco da Gama's Fleet). In 1500 ships in an expedition under Pedro Alvares Cabral°, while swinging wide to the west in the South Atlantic to catch the winds that would sweep them around southern Africa and on to India, came on the eastern coast of South America, laying the basis for Portugal's later claim to Brazil. The gamble that Prince Henry had begun eight decades earlier was about to pay off handsomely.

Spanish Voyages

In contrast to the persistence and planning behind Portugal's century-long exploration of the South Atlantic, haste and blind luck lay behind Spain's early discoveries. Throughout most of the fifteenth cen-

São Tomé (sow toh-MAY)

Cabral (kah-BRAHL)

ENVIRONMENT + TECHNOLOGY

Vasco da Gama's Fleet

The four small ships that sailed for India from Lisbon in June 1497 may seem a puny fleet compared to the sixty-two Chinese vessels that Zheng He had led into the Indian Ocean ninety-five years earlier. But given the fact that China had a hundred times as many people as Portugal, Vasco da Gama's fleet represented at least as great a commitment of resources. In any event, the Portuguese expedition had a far greater impact on the course of history. Having achieved its aim of inspiring awe at China's greatness, the Chinese throne sent out no more expeditions after 1432. Although da Gama's ships seemed more odd than awesome to Indian Ocean observers, that modest fleet began a revolution in global relations.

Portugal spared no expense in ensuring that the fleet would make it to India and back. Craftsmen built extra strength into the hulls to withstand the powerful storms that Dias had encountered in 1488 at the tip of Africa. Small enough to be able to navigate any shallow harbors and rivers they might encounter, the ships were crammed with specially strengthened casks and barrels of water, wine, oil, flour, meat, and vegetables far in excess of what was required even on a voyage that would take the better part of a year. Arms and ammunition were also in abundance.

Three of da Gama's ships were rigged with square sails on two masts for speed and a lateen sail on the third mast. The fourth vessel was a caravel with lateen sails. Each ship carried three sets of sails and plenty of extra rigging so as to be able to repair any damages due to storms. The crusaders' red crosses on the sails signaled one of the expedition's motives.

The captains and crew—Portugal's most talented and experienced—received extra pay and other rewards for their service. Yet there was no expectation that the unprecedented sums spent on this expedition would bring any immediate return. According to a contemporary chronicle, the only immediate return the Portuguese monarch received was

Vasco da Gama's Flagship This vessel carried the Portuguese captain on his second expedition to India in 1505. (The Pierpont Morgan Library/Art Resource, NY)

"the knowledge that some part of Ethiopia and the beginning of Lower India had been discovered." However, the scale and care of the preparations suggest that the Portuguese expected the expedition to open up profitable trade to the Indian Ocean. And so it did.

tury, the Spanish kingdoms had been preoccupied with internal affairs: completion of the reconquest of southern Iberia; amalgamation of the various dynasties; and the conversion or expulsion of religious minorities. Only in the last decade of the century were Spanish monarchs ready to turn again to overseas exploration, by which time the Portuguese had already found a new route to the Indian Ocean.

The leader of their overseas mission was **Christopher Columbus** (1451–1506), a Genoese mariner. His four voyages between 1492 and 1502 established the existence of a vast new world across the Atlantic, whose existence few in "old world" Eurasia and Africa had ever suspected. But Columbus refused to accept that he had found unknown continents and peoples, insisting that he had succeeded in his goal of finding a shorter route to the Indian Ocean than the one the Portuguese had found.

As a younger man Columbus had gained considerable experience of the South Atlantic while participating in Portuguese explorations along the African coast, but he had become convinced there was a shorter way to reach the riches of the East than the route around Africa. By his reckoning (based on a serious misreading of a ninth-century Arab authority), the Canaries were a mere 2,400 nautical miles (4,450 kilometers) from Japan. The actual distance was five times as far.

It was not easy for Columbus to find a sponsor willing to underwrite the costs of testing his theory that one could reach Asia by sailing west. Portuguese authorities twice rejected his plan, first in 1485 following a careful study and again in 1488 after Dias had established the feasibility of a route around Africa. Columbus received a more sympathetic hearing in 1486 from Castile's able ruler, Queen Isabella, but no commitment of support. After a four-year study a Castilian commission appointed by Isabella concluded that a westward sea route to the Indies rested on many questionable geographical assumptions, but Columbus's persistence finally won over the queen and her husband, King Ferdinand of Aragon. In 1492 they agreed to fund a modest expedition. Their elation at expelling the Muslims from Granada may have put them in a favorable mood.

Columbus recorded in his log that he and his mostly Spanish crew of ninety men "departed Friday the third day of August of the year 1492," toward "the regions of India." Their mission, the royal contract stated, was "to discover and acquire certain islands and mainland in the Ocean Sea." He carried letters of introduction from the Spanish sovereigns to Eastern rulers, including one to the "Grand Khan" (meaning the Chinese emperor). Also on board was a Jewish convert to Christianity whose knowledge of Arabic was expected to facilitate communication with the peoples of eastern Asia. The expedition traveled in three small ships, the *Santa María*, the *Santa Clara* (nicknamed the *Niña*), and a third vessel now known only by its nickname, the *Pinta*. The *Niña* and the *Pinta* were caravels.

The expedition began well. Other attempts to explore the Atlantic west of the Azores had been impeded by unfavorable headwinds. But on earlier voyages along the African coast, Columbus had learned that he could find west-blowing winds in the latitudes of the Canaries, which is why he chose that southern route. After reaching the Canaries, he had the *Niña's* lateen sails replaced with square sails, for he knew that from then on speed would be more important than maneuverability.

In October 1492 the expedition reached the islands of the Caribbean. Columbus insisted on calling the inhabitants "Indians" because he believed that the islands were part of the East Indies. A second voyage to the Caribbean in 1493 did nothing to change his mind. Even when, two months after Vasco da Gama reached India in 1498, Columbus first sighted the mainland of South America on a third voyage, he stubbornly insisted it was part of Asia. But by then other Europeans were convinced that he had discovered islands and continents previously unknown to the Old World. Amerigo Vespucci's explorations, first on behalf of Spain and then for Portugal, led mapmakers to name the new continents "America" after him, rather than "Columbia" after Columbus.

To prevent disputes arising from their efforts to exploit their new discoveries and to spread Christianity among the people there, Spain and Portugal agreed to split the world between them. The Treaty of Tordesillas°, negotiated by the pope in 1494, drew an imaginary line down the middle of the North Atlantic Ocean. Lands east of the line in Africa and southern Asia could be claimed by Portugal; lands to the west in the Americas were reserved for Spain. Cabral's discovery of Brazil, however, gave Portugal a valid claim to the part of South America that bulged east of the line.

But if the Tordesillas line were extended around the earth, where would Spain's and Portugal's spheres of influence divide in the East? Given Europeans' ignorance of the earth's true size in 1494, it was not clear whether the Moluccas°, whose valuable spices had been a goal of the Iberian voyages, were on Portugal's or Spain's side of the line. The missing information concerned the size of the Pacific Ocean. By chance, in 1513 a Spanish adventurer named Vasco Núñez de Balboa° crossed the

Tordesillas (tor-duh-SEE-yuhs)   **Moluccas** (muh-LOO-kuhz)
Balboa (bal-BOH-uh)

isthmus (a narrow neck of land) of Panama from the east and sighted the Pacific Ocean on the other side. And the 1519 expedition of **Ferdinand Magellan** (ca. 1480–1521) was designed to complete Columbus's interrupted westward voyage by sailing around the Americas and across the Pacific, whose vast size no European then guessed. The Moluccas turned out to lie well within Portugal's sphere, as Spain formally acknowledged in 1529.

Magellan's voyage laid the basis for Spanish colonization of the Philippine Islands after 1564. Nor did Magellan's death prevent him from being considered the first person to encircle the globe, for a decade earlier he had sailed from Europe to the East Indies as part of an expedition sponsored by his native Portugal. His two voyages took him across the Tordesillas line, through the separate spheres claimed by Portugal and Spain—at least until other Europeans began demanding a share. Of course, in 1500 European claims were largely theoretical. Portugal and Spain had only modest settlements overseas.

Although Columbus failed to find a new route to the East, the consequences of his voyages for European expansion were momentous. Those who followed in his wake laid the basis for Spain's large colonial empires in the Americas and for the empires of other European nations. In turn, these empires promoted, among the four Atlantic continents, the growth of a major new trading network whose importance rivaled and eventually surpassed that of the Indian Ocean network. The more immediately important consequence was Portugal's entry into the Indian Ocean, which quickly led to a major European presence and profit. Both the eastward and the westward voyages of exploration marked a tremendous expansion of Europe's role in world history.

ENCOUNTERS WITH EUROPE, 1450–1550

European actions alone did not determine the consequences of the new contacts that Iberian mariners had opened. The ways in which Africans, Asians, and Amerindians perceived their new visitors and interacted with them also influenced their future relations. Some welcomed the Europeans as potential allies; others viewed them as rivals or enemies. In general, Africans and Asians had little difficulty in recognizing the benefits and dangers that European contacts might bring. However, the long isolation of the Amerindians from the rest of the world added to the strangeness of their encounter with the Spanish and made them more vulnerable to the unfamiliar diseases that these explorers inadvertently introduced.

Western Africa

Many Africans along the West African coast were eager for trade with the Portuguese. It would give them new markets for their exports and access to imports cheaper than those that reached them through the middlemen of the overland routes to the Mediterranean. This reaction was evident along the Gold Coast of West Africa, first visited by the Portuguese in 1471. Miners in the hinterland had long sold their gold to African traders, who took it to the trading cities along the southern edge of the Sahara, where it was sold to traders who had crossed the desert from North Africa. Recognizing that they might get more favorable terms from the new sea visitors, coastal Africans were ready to negotiate with the royal representative of Portugal who arrived in 1482 seeking permission to erect a trading fort.

The Portuguese noble in charge and his officers (likely including the young Christopher Columbus, who had entered Portuguese service in 1476) were eager to make a proper impression. They dressed in their best clothes, erected and decorated a reception platform, celebrated a Catholic Mass, and signaled the start of negotiations with trumpets, tambourines, and drums. The African king, Caramansa, staged his entrance with equal ceremony, arriving with a large retinue of attendants and musicians. Through an African interpreter, the two leaders exchanged flowery speeches pledging goodwill and mutual benefit. Caramansa then gave his permission for a small trading fort to be built, assured, he said, by the appearance of these royal delegates that they were honorable persons, unlike the "few, foul, and vile" Portuguese visitors of the previous decade.

Neither side made a show of force, but the Africans' upper hand was evident in Caramansa's warning that if the Portuguese failed to be peaceful and honest traders, he and his people would simply move away, depriving their post of food and trade. Trade at the post of Saint George of the Mine (later called Elmina) enriched both sides. From there the Portuguese crown was soon purchasing gold equal to one-tenth of the world's production at the time. In return, Africans received large quantities of goods that Portuguese ships brought from Asia, Europe, and other parts of Africa.

After a century of aggressive expansion, the kingdom of Benin in the Niger Delta was near the peak of its power when it first encountered the Portuguese. Its oba (king) presided over an elaborate bureaucracy from a spacious palace in his large capital city, also known as Benin. In response to a Portuguese visit in 1486, the oba sent an ambassador to Portugal to learn more about the homeland of these strangers. Then he established a royal monopoly on trade with the Portuguese, selling pepper and ivory tusks (to be taken back to Portugal) as well as stone beads, textiles, and prisoners of war (to be resold at Elmina). In return, the Portuguese merchants provided Benin with copper and brass, fine textiles, glass beads, and a horse for the king's royal procession. In the early sixteenth century, as the demand for slaves for the Portuguese sugar plantations on the nearby island of São Tomé grew, the oba first raised the price of slaves and then imposed restrictions that limited their sale.

Early contacts generally involved a mixture of commercial, military, and religious interests. Some African rulers were quick to appreciate that the European firearms could be a useful addition to their spears and arrows in conflicts with their enemies. Because African religions did not presume to have a monopoly on religious knowledge, coastal rulers were also willing to test the value of Christian practices, which the Portuguese eagerly promoted. The rulers of Benin and Kongo, the two largest coastal kingdoms, invited Portuguese missionaries and soldiers to accompany them into battle to test the Christians' religion along with their muskets.

Portuguese efforts to persuade the king and nobles of Benin to accept the Catholic faith ultimately failed. Early kings showed some interest, but after 1538 the rulers declined to receive any more missionaries. They also closed the market in male slaves for the rest of the sixteenth century. Exactly why Benin chose to limit its contacts with the Portuguese is uncertain, but the rulers clearly had the power to control the amount of interaction.

Farther south, on the lower Congo River, relations between the kingdom of Kongo and the Portuguese began similarly but had a very different outcome. Like the oba of Benin, the manikongo° (king of Kongo) sent delegates to Portugal, established a royal monopoly on trade with the Portuguese, and expressed interest in missionary teachings. Deeply impressed with the new religion, the royal family made Catholicism the kingdom's official faith. But Kongo, lacking ivory and pepper, had less to trade than Benin. To acquire the goods brought by Portugal and to pay the costs of the missionaries, it had to sell more and more slaves.

Soon the manikongo began to lose his royal monopoly over the slave trade. In 1526 the Christian manikongo, Afonso I (r. 1506–ca. 1540), wrote to his royal

---

manikongo (mah-NEE-KONG-goh)

Afro–Portuguese Ivory A skilled ivory carver from the kingdom of Benin probably made this saltcellar. Intended for a European market, it depicts a Portuguese ship on the cover and Portuguese nobles around the base. However European the subject, the craftsmanship is typical of Benin. (Courtesy of the Trustees of the British Museum)

"brother," the king of Portugal, begging for his help in stopping the trade because unauthorized Kongolese were kidnapping and selling people, even members of good families (see Diversity and Dominance: Kongo's Christian King). Alfonso's appeals for help received no reply from Portugal, whose interests had moved to the Indian Ocean. Some subjects took advantage of the manikongo's weakness to rebel against his authority. After 1540 the major part of the slave trade from this part of Africa moved farther south.

Eastern Africa

Different still were the reactions of the Muslim rulers of the trading coastal states of eastern Africa. As Vasco da Gama's fleet sailed up the coast in 1498, most rulers gave the Portuguese a cool reception, suspicious of the intentions of these visitors who painted crusaders' crosses on their sails. But the ruler of one of the ports, Malindi, saw in the Portuguese an ally who could help him expand the city's trading position and provided da Gama with a pilot to guide him to India. The suspicions of most rulers were justified seven years later when a Portuguese war fleet bombarded and looted most of the coastal cities of eastern Africa in the name of Christ and commerce, though they spared Malindi.

Another eastern African state that saw potential benefit in an alliance with the Portuguese was Christian Ethiopia. In the fourteenth and early fifteenth centuries, Ethiopia faced increasing conflicts with Muslim states along the Red Sea. Emboldened by the rise of the Ottoman Turks, who had conquered Egypt in 1517 and launched a major fleet in the Indian Ocean to counter the Portuguese, the talented warlord of the Muslim state of Adal launched a furious assault on Ethiopia. Adal's decisive victory in 1529 reduced the Christian kingdom to a precarious state. At that point Ethiopia's contacts with the Portuguese became crucial.

For decades, delegations from Portugal and Ethiopia had been exploring a possible alliance between their states based on their mutual adherence to Christianity. A key figure was Queen Helena of Ethiopia, who acted as regent for her young sons after her husband's death in 1478. In 1509 Helena sent a letter to "our very dear and well-beloved brother," the king of Portugal, along with a gift of two tiny crucifixes said to be made of wood from the cross on which Christ had died in Jerusalem. In her letter she proposed an alliance of her land army and Portugal's fleet against the Turks. No such alliance was completed by the time Helena died in 1522. But as Ethiopia's situation grew increasingly desperate, renewed appeals for help were made.

Finally, a small Portuguese force commanded by Vasco da Gama's son Christopher reached Ethiopia in 1539, at a time when what was left of the empire was being held together by another woman ruler. With Portuguese help, the queen rallied the Ethiopians to renew their struggle. Christopher da Gama was captured and tortured to death, but the Muslim forces lost heart when their leader was mortally wounded in a later battle. Portuguese aid helped the Ethiopian kingdom save itself from extinction, but a permanent alliance faltered because Ethiopian rulers refused to transfer their Christian affiliation from the patriarch of Alexandria to the Latin patriarch of Rome (the pope) as the Portuguese wanted.

As these examples illustrate, African encounters with the Portuguese before 1550 varied considerably, as much because of the strategies and leadership of particular African states as because of Portuguese policies. Africans and Portuguese might become royal brothers, bitter opponents, or partners in a mutually profitable trade, but Europeans remained a minor presence in most of Africa in 1550. By then the Portuguese had become far more interested in the Indian Ocean trade.

Indian Ocean States

Vasco da Gama's arrival on the Malabar Coast of India in May 1498 did not make a great impression on the citizens of Calicut. After more than ten months at sea, many members of the crew were in ill health. Da Gama's four small ships were far less imposing than the Chinese fleets of gigantic junks that had called at Calicut sixty-five years earlier and no larger than many of the dhows that filled the harbor of this rich and important trading city. The samorin (ruler) of Calicut and his Muslim officials showed mild interest in the Portuguese as new trading partners, but the gifts da Gama had brought for the samorin evoked derisive laughter. Twelve pieces of fairly ordinary striped cloth, four scarlet hoods, six hats, and six wash basins seemed inferior goods to those accustomed to the luxuries of the Indian Ocean trade. When da Gama tried to defend his gifts as those of an explorer, not a rich merchant, the samorin cut him short, asking whether he had come to discover men or stones: "If he had come to discover men, as he said, why had he brought nothing?"

Coastal rulers soon discovered that the Portuguese had no intention of remaining poor competitors in the rich trade of the Indian Ocean. Upon da Gama's return to Portugal in 1499, the jubilant King Manuel styled himself "Lord of the Conquest, Navigation, and Commerce of Ethiopia, Arabia, Persia, and India," setting forth the ambitious scope of his plans. Previously the Indian Ocean had been an open sea, used by merchants (and pirates) of all the surrounding coasts. Now the Portuguese crown intended to make it Portugal's sea, the private property of the Portuguese alone, which others might use only on Portuguese terms.

The ability of little Portugal to assert control over the Indian Ocean stemmed from the superiority of its ships and weapons over the smaller and lightly armed merchant dhows. In 1505 the Portuguese fleet of eighty-one ships and some seven thousand men bombarded Swahili Coast cities. Next on the list were Indian ports. Goa, on the

Portuguese in India   In the sixteenth century Portuguese men moved to the Indian Ocean basin to work as administrators and traders. This Indo-Portuguese drawing from about 1540 shows a Portuguese man speaking to an Indian woman, perhaps making a proposal of marriage.   (Ms. 1889, c. 97, Biblioteca Casanateunse Rome. Photo: Humberto Nicoletti Serra)

west coast of India, fell to a well-armed fleet in 1510, becoming the base from which the Portuguese menaced the trading cities of Gujarat° to the north and Calicut and other Malabar Coast cities to the south. The port of Hormuz, controlling the entry to the Persian Gulf, was taken in 1515. Aden, at the entrance to the Red Sea, used its intricate natural defenses to preserve its independence. The addition of the Gujarati port of Diu in 1535 consolidated Portuguese dominance of the western Indian Ocean.

Meanwhile, Portuguese explorers had been reconnoitering the Bay of Bengal and the waters farther east. The independent city of Malacca° on the strait between the Malay Peninsula and Sumatra became the focus of their attention. During the fifteenth century Malacca had become the main entrepôt° (a place where goods are stored or deposited and from which they are distributed) for the trade from China, Japan, India, the Southeast Asian mainland, and the Moluccas. Among the city's more than 100,000 residents an early Portuguese counted

eighty-four different languages, including those of merchants from as far west as Cairo, Ethiopia, and the Swahili Coast of East Africa. Many non-Muslim residents supported letting the Portuguese join this cosmopolitan trading community, perhaps to offset the growing solidarity of Muslim traders. In 1511, however, the Portuguese seized this strategic trading center with a force of a thousand fighting men, including three hundred recruited in southern India.

Force was not always necessary. On the China coast, local officials and merchants interested in profitable new trade with the Portuguese persuaded the imperial government to allow the Portuguese to establish a trading post at Macao° in 1557. Operating from Macao, Portuguese ships nearly monopolized the trade between China and Japan.

In the Indian Ocean, the Portuguese used their control of the major port cities to enforce an even larger trading monopoly. They required all spices, as well as all goods on the major ocean routes such as between Goa

---

Gujarat (goo-juh-RAHT)   **Malacca** (muh-LAH-kuh)
entrepôt (ON-truh-poh)

Macao (muh-COW)

and Macao, to be carried in Portuguese ships. In addition, the Portuguese also tried to control and tax other Indian Ocean trade by requiring all merchant ships entering and leaving one of their ports to carry a Portuguese passport and to pay customs duties. Portuguese patrols seized vessels that attempted to avoid these monopolies, confiscated their cargoes, and either killed the captain and crew or sentenced them to forced labor.

Reactions to this power grab varied. Like the emperors of China, the Mughal° emperors of India largely ignored Portugal's maritime intrusions, seeing their interests as maintaining control over their vast land possessions. The Ottomans responded more aggressively. From 1501 to 1509 they supported Egypt's fleet of fifteen thousand men against the Christian intruders. Then, having absorbed Egypt into their empire, the Ottomans sent another large expedition against the Portuguese in 1538. Both expeditions failed because the Ottoman galleys were no match for the faster, better-armed Portuguese vessels in the open ocean. However, the Ottomans retained the advantage in the Red Sea and Persian Gulf, where they had many ports of supply.

The smaller trading states of the region were even less capable of challenging Portuguese domination head on, since their mutual rivalry impeded the formation of any common front. Some chose to cooperate with the Portuguese to maintain their prosperity and security. Others engaged in evasion and resistance. Two examples illustrate the range of responses among Indian Ocean peoples.

The merchants of Calicut put up some of the most sustained local resistance. In retaliation, the Portuguese embargoed all trade with Aden, Calicut's principal trading partner, and centered their trade on the port of Cochin, which had once been a dependency of Calicut. Some Calicut merchants became adept at evading the patrol, but the price of resistance was the shrinking of Calicut's importance as Cochin gradually became the major pepper-exporting port on the Malabar Coast.

The traders and rulers of the state of Gujarat farther north had less success in keeping the Portuguese at bay. At first they resisted Portuguese attempts at monopoly and in 1509 joined Egypt's failed effort to sweep the Portuguese from the Arabian Sea. But in 1535, finding his state at a military disadvantage due to Mughal attacks, the ruler of Gujarat made the fateful decision to allow the Portuguese to build a fort at Diu in return for their support. Once established, the Portuguese gradually extended their control, so that by midcentury they were licensing and taxing all Gujarati ships. Even after the Mughals (who were Muslims) took control of Gujarat in

Mughal (MOO-gahl)

1572, the Mughal emperor Akbar permitted the Portuguese to continue their maritime monopoly in return for allowing one ship a year to carry pilgrims to Mecca without paying the Portuguese any fee.

The Portuguese never gained complete control of the Indian Ocean trade, but their domination of key ports and the main trade routes during the sixteenth century brought them considerable profit, which they sent back to Europe in the form of spices and other luxury goods. The effects were dramatic. The Portuguese sold the large quantities of pepper that they exported for less than the price charged by Venice and Genoa for pepper obtained through Egyptian middlemen, thus breaking the Italian cities' monopoly.

In Asia the consequences were equally startling. Asian and East African traders were at the mercy of Portuguese warships, but their individual responses affected their fates. Some were devastated. Others prospered by meeting Portuguese demands or evading their patrols. Because the Portuguese were ocean-based, they had little impact on the Asian and African mainlands, in sharp contrast to what was occurring in the Americas.

The Americas

In the Americas the Spanish established a vast territorial empire, in contrast to the trading empires the Portuguese created in Africa and Asia. This outcome had little to do with differences between the two Iberian kingdoms, except for the fact that the Spanish kingdoms had somewhat greater resources to draw on. The Spanish and Portuguese monarchies had similar motives for expansion and used identical ships and weapons. Rather, the isolation of the Amerindian peoples made their responses to outside contacts different from the responses of peoples in Africa and the Indian Ocean cities. In dealing with the small communities in the Caribbean, the first European settlers resorted to conquest and plunder rather than trade. This practice was later extended to the more powerful Amerindian kingdoms on the American mainland. The spread of deadly new diseases among the Amerindians after 1518 weakened their ability to resist.

The first Amerindians to encounter Columbus were the Arawak of Hispaniola (modern Haiti and the Dominican Republic) in the Greater Antilles and the Bahamas to the north (see Map 16.2). They cultivated maize (corn), cassava (a tuber), sweet potatoes, and hot peppers, as well as cotton and tobacco, and they met their other material needs from the sea and wild plants. Although they were skilled at mining and working gold, the Arawak did not trade gold over long distances as

Africans did, and they had no iron. The Arawak at first extended a cautious welcome to the Spanish but were unprepared to sell them large quantities of gold. Instead, they told Columbus exaggerated stories about gold in other places to persuade him to move on.

When Columbus made his second trip to Hispaniola in 1493, he brought several hundred settlers from southern Iberia who hoped to make their fortune and missionaries who were eager to persuade the Indians to accept Christianity. The settlers stole gold ornaments, confiscated food, and raped women, provoking the Hispaniola Arawak to war in 1495. In this and later conflicts, horses and body armor gave the Spaniards a great advantage. Tens of thousands of Arawak were slaughtered. Those who survived were forced to pay a heavy tax in gold, spun cotton, and food. Any who failed to meet the quotas were condemned to forced labor. Meanwhile, the cattle, pigs, and goats introduced by the settlers devoured the Arawak's food crops, causing deaths from famine and disease. A governor appointed by the Spanish crown in 1502 forced the Arawak remaining on Hispaniola to be laborers under the control of Spanish settlers.

The actions of the Spanish in the Antilles were reflections of Spanish actions and motives during the wars against the Muslims in Spain in the previous centuries: seeking to serve God by defeating nonbelievers and placing them under Christian control—and becoming rich in the process. Individual **conquistadors°** (conquerors) extended that pattern around the Caribbean. Some attacked the Bahamas to get gold and labor as both became scarce on Hispaniola. Many Arawak from the Bahamas were taken to Hispaniola as slaves. Juan Ponce de León (1460–1521), who had participated in the conquest of Muslim Spain and the seizure of Hispaniola, conquered the island of Borinquen (Puerto Rico) in 1508 and explored southeastern Florida in 1513.

An ambitious and ruthless nobleman, **Hernán Cortés°** (1485–1547), led the most audacious expedition to the mainland. Cortés left Cuba in 1519 with six hundred fighting men and most of the island's stock of weapons to assault the Mexican mainland in search of slaves and to establish trade. When the expedition learned of the rich Aztec Empire in central Mexico, Cortés brought to the American mainland, on a massive scale, the exploitation and conquest begun in the reconquest of Muslim Iberia and continued in the Greater Antilles.

The Aztecs themselves had conquered their vast empire only during the previous century, and many of the Amerindians they had subjugated were far from loyal subjects. Many resented the tribute they had to pay the

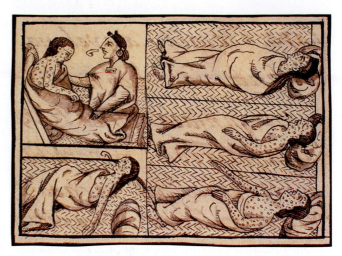

Death from Smallpox This Aztec drawing shows a healer attending smallpox victims. The little puffs coming from their mouths represent speech. (Biblioteca Medicea Laurenziana. Photo: MicroFoto, Florence)

Aztecs, the forced labor, and the large-scale human sacrifices to the Aztec gods. Many subject people saw the Spaniards as powerful human allies against the Aztecs and gave them their support. Like the Caribbean people, the Amerindians of Mexico had no precedent by which to judge these strange visitors.

Aztec accounts suggest that some believed Cortés to be the legendary ruler Quetzalcoatl°, whose return to earth had been prophesied, and treated him with great deference. Another consequence of millennia of isolation was far more significant: the lack of acquired immunity to the diseases of the Old World. Smallpox was the most deadly of the early epidemics that accompanied the Spanish conquistadors. It appeared for the first time on the island of Hispaniola late in 1518. An infected member of the Cortés expedition then transmitted smallpox to Mexico in 1519, where it spread with deadly efficiency.

From his glorious capital city Tenochtitlan°, the Aztec emperor **Moctezuma°** II (r. 1502–1520) sent messengers to greet Cortés and determine whether he was god or man, friend or foe. Cortés advanced steadily toward Tenochtitlan, overcoming Aztec opposition with cavalry charges and steel swords and gaining the support of thousands of Amerindian allies from among the unhappy subjects of the Aztecs. When the Spaniards

---

conquistador (kon-KEY-stuh-dor) **Cortés** (kor-TEZ)

Quetzalcoatl (ket-zahl-COH-ah-tal)
Tenochtitlan (teh-noch-TIT-lan)
Moctezuma (mock-teh-ZOO-ma)

Coronation of Emperor Moctezuma This painting by an unnamed Aztec artist depicts the Aztec ruler's coronation. Moctezuma, his nose pierced by a bone, receives the crown from a prince in the palace at Tenochtitlan. (Oronoz)

were near, the emperor went out in a great procession, dressed in all his finery, to welcome Cortés with gifts and flower garlands.

Despite Cortés's initial promise that he came in friendship, Moctezuma quickly found himself a prisoner in his own palace. The Spanish looted his treasury and melted down its golden objects. Soon a battle was raging in and about the capital between the Spaniards (helped by their new Amerindian allies) and the Aztecs and their supporters. Briefly the Aztecs gained the upper hand. They destroyed half of the Spanish force and four thousand of the Spaniards' Amerindian allies, and they sacrificed to their gods fifty-three Spanish prisoners and four horses, displaying their severed heads in rows on pikes. In the battle Moctezuma was killed.

The Spanish survivors retreated from the city and rebuilt their strength. Their successful capture of Tenochtitlan in 1521 was greatly facilitated by the spread of smallpox, which weakened and killed more of the city's defenders than died in the fighting. One source remembered that the disease "spread over the people as a great destruction." The bodies of the afflicted were covered with oozing sores, and large numbers soon died. It is likely that many Amerindians as well as Europeans blamed the devastating spread of this disease on supernatural forces.

After the capital fell, the conquistadors took over other parts of Mexico. Then some Spaniards began eyeing the vast Inca Empire, stretching nearly 3,000 miles (5,000 kilometers) south from the equator and containing half of the population in South America. The Inca had conquered the inhabitants of the Andes Mountains and the Pacific coast of South America during the previous century, and their rule was not fully accepted by all of the peoples they had defeated.

With the vast Pacific Ocean on one side of their realm and the sparsely inhabited Amazon forests on the other, it is not surprising that Inca rulers believed they controlled most of the world worth controlling. Theirs was a great empire with highly productive agriculture, exquisite stone cities (such as the capital, Cuzco), and rich gold and silver mines. The power of the Inca emperor was sustained by beliefs that he was descended from the Sun God and by an efficient system of roads and messengers that kept him informed about major events in the empire. Yet all was not well.

At the end of the 1520s, before even a whisper of news about the Spanish reached the Inca rulers, small-

DIVERSITY AND DOMINANCE

KONGO'S CHRISTIAN KING

The new overseas voyages brought conquest to some and opportunities for fruitful borrowings and exchanges to others. The decision of the ruler of the kingdom of Kongo to adopt Christianity in 1491 added cultural diversity to Kongolese society and in some ways strengthened the hand of the king. From then on Kongolese rulers sought to introduce Christian beliefs and rituals while at the same time Africanizing Christianity to make it more intelligible to their subjects. In addition, the kings of Kongo sought a variety of more secular aid from Portugal, including schools and medicine. Trade with the Portuguese introduced new social and political tensions, especially in the case of the export trade in slaves for the Portuguese sugar plantations on the island of São Tomé to the north.

Two letters sent to King João (zhwao) III of Portugal in 1526 illustrate how King Afonso of Kongo saw his kingdom's new relationship with Portugal and the problems that resulted from it. (Afonso adopted that name when he was baptized as a young prince.) After the death of his father in 1506, Afonso successfully claimed the throne and ruled until 1542. His son Henrique became the first Catholic bishop of the Kongo in 1521.

These letters were written in Portuguese and penned by the king's secretary João Teixera (tay-SHER-uh), a Kongo Christian, who, like Afonso, had been educated by Portuguese missionaries.

6 July 1526

To the very powerful and excellent prince Dom João, our brother:

On the 20th of June just past, we received word that a trading ship from your highness had just come to our port of Sonyo. We were greatly pleased by that arrival for it had been many days since a ship had come to our kingdom, for by it we would get news of your highness, which many times we had desired to know, . . . and likewise as there was a great and dire need for wine and flour for the holy sacrament; and of this we had had no great hope for we have the same need frequently. And

that, sir, arises from the great negligence of your highness's officials toward us and toward shipping us those things. . . .

Sir, your highness should know how our kingdom is being lost in so many ways that we will need to provide the needed cure, since this is caused by the excessive license given by your agents and officials to the men and merchants who come to this kingdom to set up shops with goods and many things which have been prohibited by us, and which they spread throughout our kingdoms and domains in such abundance that many of our vassals, whose submission we could once rely on, now act independently so as to get the things in greater abundance than we ourselves; whom we had formerly held content and submissive and under our vassalage and jurisdiction, so it is doing a great harm not only to the service of God, but also to the security and peace of our kingdoms and state.

And we cannot reckon how great the damage is, since every day the mentioned merchants are taking our people, sons of the land and the sons of our noblemen and vassals and our relatives, because the thieves and men of bad conscience grab them so as to have the things and wares of this kingdom that they crave; they grab them and bring them to be sold. In such a manner, sir, has been the corruption and deprivation that our land is becoming completely depopulated, and your highness should not deem this good nor in your service. And to avoid this we need from these kingdoms [of yours] no more than priests and a few people to teach in schools, and no other goods except wine and flour for the holy sacrament, which is why we beg of your highness to help and assist us in this matter. Order your agents to send here neither merchants nor wares, because it is our will that in these kingdoms there should not be any dealing in slaves nor outlet for them, for the reasons stated above. Again we beg your highness's agreement, since otherwise we cannot cure such manifest harm. May Our Lord in His mercy have your highness always under His protection and may you always do the things of His holy service. I kiss your hands many times.

From our city of Kongo. . . .

The King, Dom Afonso

18 October 1526

Very high and very powerful prince King of Portugal, our brother,

Sir, your highness has been so good as to promise us that anything we need we should ask for in our letters, and that everything will be provided. And so that there may be peace and health of our kingdoms, by God's will, in our lifetime. And as there are among us old folks and people who have lived for many days, many and different diseases happen so often that we are pushed to the ultimate extremes. And the same happens to our children, relatives, and people, because this country lacks physicians and surgeons who might know the proper cures for such diseases, as well as pharmacies and drugs to make them better. And for this reason many of those who had been already confirmed and instructed in the things of the holy faith of Our Lord Jesus Christ perish and die. And the rest of the people for the most part cure themselves with herbs and sticks and other ancient methods, so that they live putting all their faith in the these herbs and ceremonies, and die believing that they are saved; and this serves God poorly.

And to avoid such a great error, I think, and inconvenience, since it is from God and from your highness that all the good and the drugs and medicines have come to us for our salvation, we ask your merciful highness to send us two physicians and two pharmacists and one surgeon, so that they may come with their pharmacies and necessary things to be in our kingdoms, for we have extreme need of each and everyone of them. We will be very good and merciful to them, since sent by your highness, their work and coming should be for good. We ask your highness as a great favor to do this for us, because besides being good in itself it is in the service of God as we have said above.

Moreover, sir, in our kingdoms there is another great inconvenience which is of little service to God, and this is that many of our people, out of great desire for the wares and things of your kingdoms, which are brought here by your people, and in order to satisfy their disordered appetite, seize many of our people, freed and exempt men. And many times noblemen and the sons of noblemen, and our relatives are stolen, and they take them to be sold to the white men who are in our kingdoms and take them hidden or by night, so that they are not recognized. And as soon as they are taken by the white men, they are immediately ironed and branded with fire. And when they are carried off to be embarked, if they are caught by our guards, the whites allege that they have bought them and cannot say from whom, so that it is our duty to do justice and to restore to the free their freedom. And so they went away offended.

And to avoid such a great evil we passed a law so that every white man living in our kingdoms and wanting to purchase slaves by whatever means should first inform three of our noblemen and officials of our court on whom we rely in this matter, namely Dom Pedro Manipunzo and Dom Manuel Manissaba, our head bailiff, and Gonçalo Pires, our chief supplier, who should investigate if the said slaves are captives or free men, and, if cleared with them, there will be no further doubt nor embargo and they can be taken and embarked. And if they reach the opposite conclusion, they will lose the aforementioned slaves. Whatever favor and license we give them [the white men] for the sake of your highness in this case is because we know that it is in your service too that these slaves are taken from our kingdom; otherwise we should not consent to this for the reasons stated above that we make known completely to your highness so that no one could say the contrary, as they said in many other cases to your highness, so that the care and remembrance that we and this kingdom have should not be withdrawn. . . .

We kiss your hands of your highness many times.

From our city of Kongo, the 18th day of October,

The King, Dom Afonso

QUESTIONS FOR ANALYSIS

1. What sorts of things does King Afonso desire from the Portuguese?
2. What is he willing and unwilling to do in return?
3. What problem with his own people has the slave trade created and what has King Afonso done about it?
4. Does King Afonso see himself as an equal to King João or his subordinate? Do you agree with that analysis?

Source: From António Brásio, ed., *Monumenta Missionaria Africana: Africa Ocidental (1471–1531)* (Lisbon: Agência Geral do Ultramar, 1952), I:468, 470–471, 488–491. Translated by David Northrup.

pox claimed countless Amerindian lives, perhaps including the Inca emperor in 1530. Even more devastating was the threat awaiting the empire from **Francisco Pizarro°** (ca. 1478–1541) and his motley band of 180 men, 37 horses, and two cannon.

With limited education and some military experience, Pizarro had come to the Americas in 1502 at the age of twenty-five to seek his fortune. He had participated in the conquest of Hispaniola and in Balboa's expedition across the Isthmus of Panama. By 1520 Pizarro was a wealthy landowner and official in Panama, yet he gambled his fortune on more adventures, exploring the Pacific coast to a point south of the equator, where he learned of the riches of the Inca. With a license from the king of Spain, he set out from Panama in 1531 to conquer them.

In November 1532 Pizarro arranged to meet the new Inca emperor, **Atahualpa°** (r. 1531–1533), near the Andean city of Cajamarca°. With supreme boldness and brutality, Pizarro's small band of armed men seized Atahualpa off a rich litter borne by eighty nobles as it passed through an enclosed courtyard. Though surrounded by an Inca army of at least forty thousand, the Spaniards were able to use their cannon to create confusion while their swords sliced thousands of the emperor's lightly armed retainers and servants to pieces. The strategy to replicate the earlier Spanish conquest of Mexico was working.

Noting the glee with which the Spaniards seized gold, silver, and emeralds, the captive Atahualpa offered them what he thought would satisfy even the greediest among them in exchange for his freedom: a roomful of gold and silver. But when the ransom of 13,400 pounds (6,000 kilograms) of gold and 26,000 pounds (12,000 kilograms) of silver was paid, the Spaniards gave Atahualpa a choice: he could be burned at the stake as a heathen or baptized as a Christian and then strangled. He chose the latter. His death and the Spanish occupation broke the unity of the Inca Empire.

In 1533 the Spaniards took Cuzco and from there set out to conquer and loot the rest of the empire. The defeat of a final rebellion in 1536 spelled the end of Inca rule. Five years later Pizarro himself met a violent death at the hands of Spanish rivals, but the conquest of the mainland continued. Incited by the fabulous wealth of the Aztecs and Inca, conquistadors extended Spanish conquest and exploration in South and North America, dreaming of new treasuries to loot.

Pizarro (pih-ZAHR-oh)   **Atahualpa** (ah-tuh-WAHL-puh)
Cajamarca (kah-hah-MAHR-kah)

Patterns of Dominance

Within fifty years of Columbus's first landing in 1492, the Spanish had located and occupied all of the major population centers of the Americas, and the penetration of the more thinly populated areas was well under way. In no other part of the world was European dominance so complete. Why did the peoples of the Americas suffer a fate so different from that of peoples in Africa and Asia? Why were the Spanish able to erect a vast land empire in the Americas so quickly? Three factors seem crucial.

First, long isolation from the rest of humanity made the inhabitants of the Americas vulnerable to new diseases. The unfamiliar illnesses first devastated the native inhabitants of the Caribbean islands and then spread to the mainland. Contemporaries estimated that between 25 and 50 percent of those infected with smallpox died. Repeated epidemics inhibited Amerindians' ability to regain control. Because evidence is very limited, estimates of the size of the population before Columbus's arrival vary widely, but there is no disputing the fact that the Amerindian population fell sharply during the sixteenth century. The Americas became a "widowed land," open to resettlement from across the Atlantic.

A second major factor was Spain's military superiority. Steel swords, protective armor, and horses gave the Spaniards an advantage over their Amerindian opponents in many battles. Though few in number, muskets and cannon also gave the Spaniards a significant psychological edge. However, it should not be forgotten that the Spanish conquests depended heavily on large numbers of Amerindian allies armed with the same weapons as the people they defeated. Perhaps the Spaniards' most decisive military advantage came from the no-holds-barred fighting techniques they had developed during a long history of warfare at home.

The patterns of domination previously established in reconquest of Iberia were a third factor in Spain's ability to govern its New World empire. The forced labor, forced conversion, and system for administering conquered lands all had their origins in the Iberian reconquest.

The same three factors help explain the quite different outcomes elsewhere. Because of centuries of contacts before 1500, Europeans, Africans, and Asians shared the same Old World diseases. Only small numbers of very isolated peoples in Africa and Asia suffered the demographic calamity that undercut Amerindians' ability to retain control of their lands. The Iberians enjoyed a military advantage at sea, as the conquest of the Indian Ocean trade routes showed, but on land they had no decisive advantage against more numerous indigenous people who were not weakened by disease. Everywhere, Iberian religious zeal to conquer non-Christians went hand in hand with a desire for riches. In Iberia and America conquest brought wealth. But in Africa and Asia, where existing trading networks were already well established, Iberian desire for wealth from trade restrained or negated the impulse to conquer.

CONCLUSION

Historians agree that the century between 1450 and 1550 was a major turning point in world history. It was the beginning of an age to which they have given various names: the "Vasco da Gama epoch," the "Columbian era," the "age of Magellan," or simply the "modern period." During those years European explorers opened new long-distance trade routes across the world's three major oceans, for the first time establishing regular contact among all the continents. By 1550 those who followed them had broadened trading contacts with sub-Saharan Africa, gained mastery of the rich trade routes of the Indian Ocean, and conquered a vast land empire in the Americas.

As dramatic and momentous as these events were, they were not completely unprecedented. The riches of the Indian Ocean trade that brought a gleam to the eye of many Europeans had been developed over many centuries by the trading peoples who inhabited the surrounding lands. European conquests of the Americas were no more rapid or brutal than the earlier Mongol conquests of Eurasia. Even the crossing of the Pacific had been done before, though in stages.

What gave this maritime revolution unprecedented importance had more to do with what happened after 1550 than with what happened earlier. Europeans' overseas empires would endure longer than the Mongols' and would continue to expand for three-and-a-half centuries after 1550. Unlike the Chinese, the Europeans did not turn their backs on the world after an initial burst of exploration. Not content with dominance in the Indian Ocean trade, Europeans opened an Atlantic maritime network that grew to rival the Indian Ocean network in the wealth of its trade. They also pioneered regular trade across the Pacific. The maritime expansion begun in the period from 1450 to 1550 marked the beginning of a new age of growing global interaction.

■ Key Terms

Zheng He

Arawak

Henry the Navigator

caravel

Gold Coast

Bartolomeu Dias

Vasco da Gama

Christopher Columbus

Ferdinand Magellan

conquistadors

Hernán Cortés

Moctezuma

Francisco Pizarro

Atahualpa

■ Suggested Reading

There is no single survey of the different expansions covered by this chapter, but the selections edited by Joseph R. Levenson, *European Expansion and the Counter Example of Asia, 1300–1600* (1967), remain a good introduction to Chinese expansion and Western impressions of China. Janet Abu-Lughod, *Before European Hegemony: The World System, A.D. 1250–1350* (1989), provides a stimulating speculative reassessment of the importance of the Mongols and the Indian Ocean trade in the creation of the modern world system; she summarizes her thesis in the American Historical Association booklet *The World System in the Thirteenth Century: Dead-End or Precursor?* (1993).

The Chinese account of Zheng He's voyages is Ma Huan, *Ying-yai Sheng-lan: "The Overall Survey of the Ocean's Shores"* [1433], ed. and trans. J. V. G. Mills (1970). A reliable guide to Polynesian expansion is Jesse D. Jennings, ed., *The Prehistory of Polynesia* (1979), especially the excellent chapter "Voyaging" by Ben R. Finney, which encapsulates his *Voyage of Rediscovery: A Cultural Odyssey Through Polynesia* (1994). The medieval background to European intercontinental voyages is summarized by Felipe Fernandez-Armesto, *Before Columbus: Exploration and Colonization from the Mediterranean to the Atlantic, 1229–1492* (1987). Tim Severin, *The Brendan Voyage* (2000) vividly recounts a modern retracing of even earlier Irish voyages.

A simple introduction to the technologies of European expansion is Carlo M. Cipolla, *Guns, Sails, and Empires: Technological Innovation and the Early Phases of European Expansion, 1400–1700* (1965; reprint, 1985). More advanced is Roger C. Smith, *Vanguard of Empire: Ships of Exploration in the Age of Columbus* (1993).

The European exploration is well documented and the subject of intense historical investigation. Clear general accounts based on the contemporary records are Boies Penrose, *Travel and Discovery in the Age of the Renaissance, 1420–1620* (1952); J. H. Parry, *The Age of Reconnaissance: Discovery, Exploration, and Settlement, 1450–1650* (1963); and G. V. Scammell, *The World Encompassed: The First European Maritime Empires, c. 800–1650* (1981).

An excellent general introduction to Portuguese exploration is C. R. Boxer, *The Portuguese Seaborne Empire, 1415–1825* (1969). More detail can be found in Bailey W. Diffie and George D. Winius, *Foundations of the Portuguese Empire, 1415–1580*

(1977); A. J. R. Russell-Wood, *The Portuguese Empire: A World on the Move* (1998); and Luc Cuyvers, *Into the Rising Sun: The Journey of Vasco da Gama and the Discovery of the Modern World* (1998). John William Blake, ed., *Europeans in West Africa, 1450–1560* (1942), is an excellent two-volume collection of contemporary Portuguese, Castilian, and English sources. Elaine Sanceau, *The Life of Prester John: A Chronicle of Portuguese Exploration* (1941), is a very readable account of Portuguese relations with Ethiopia. The *Summa Oriental of Tomé Pires: An Account of the East, from the Red Sea to Japan, Written in Malacca and India in 1512–1515*, trans. Armando Cortesão (1944), provides a detailed firsthand account of the Indian Ocean during the Portuguese's first two decades there.

The other Iberian kingdoms' expansion is well summarized by J. H. Parry, *The Spanish Seaborne Empire* (1967). Samuel Eliot Morison's *Admiral of the Ocean Sea: A Life of Christopher Columbus* (1942) is a fine scholarly celebration of the epic mariner, and is also available in an abridged version as *Christopher Columbus, Mariner* (1955). More focused on the shortcomings of Columbus and his Spanish peers is Tzvetan Todorov, *The Conquest of America*, trans. Richard Howard (1985). Marvin Lunenfeld, ed., *1492: Discovery, Invasion, Encounter* (1991), critically examines contemporary sources and interpretations. William D. Phillips and Carla Rhan Phillips, *The Worlds of Christopher Columbus* (1992), examines the mariner and his times in terms of modern concerns. Peggy K. Liss, *Isabel the Queen: Life and Times* (1992), is a sympathetic examination of Queen Isabella of Castile. Detailed individual biographies of all of the individuals in Pizarro's band are the subject of James Lockhart's *Men of Cajamarca: A Social and Biographical Study of the First Conquerors of Peru* (1972). A firsthand account of Magellan's expedition is Antonio Pigafetta, *Magellan's Voyage: A Narrative Account of the First Circumnavigation*, available in a two-volume edition (1969) that includes a facsimile reprint of the manuscript.

Matthew Restall, *Seven Myths of the Spanish Conquests* (2003) uses indigenous sources to challenge traditional interpretations of New World conquests. The trans-Atlantic encounters of Europe and the Americas are described by J. H. Elliott, *The Old World and the New, 1492–1650* (1970). Alfred W. Crosby, *The Columbian Voyages, the Columbian Exchange, and Their Historians* (1987), available as an American Historical Association booklet, provides a brief overview of the first encounters in the Americas and their long-term consequences. The early chapters of Mark A. Burkholder and Lyman L. Johnson, *Colonial Latin America*, 2d ed. (1994), give a clear and balanced account of the Spanish conquest.

The perceptions of the peoples European explorers encountered are not as well documented. David Northrup, *Africa's Discovery of Europe, 1450–1850* (2002) and John Thornton, *Africa and Africans in the Making of the Atlantic World, 1400–1800*, 2d ed. (1998), examine Africans' encounters with Europe and their involvement in the Atlantic economy. *The Broken Spears: The Aztec Account of the Conquest of Mexico*, ed. Miguel Leon-Portilla (1962), presents Amerindian chronicles in a readable package, as does Nathan Wachtel, *The Vision of the Vanquished: The Spanish Conquest of Peru Through Indian Eyes* (1977). Anthony Reid, *Southeast Asia in the Age of Commerce, 1450–1680*, 2 vols. (1988, 1993), deals with events in that region.

■ Notes

1. Ma Huan, *Ying-yai Sheng-lan: "The Overall Survey of the Ocean's Shores,"* ed. Feng Ch'eng-Chün, trans. J. V. G. Mills (Cambridge, England: Cambridge University Press, 1970), 180.
2. Alvise da Cadamosto in *The Voyages of Cadamosto and Other Documents*, ed. and trans. G. R. Crone (London: Hakluyt Society, 1937), 2.

Climate and Population, to 1500

During the millennia before 1500 human populations expanded in three momentous surges. The first occurred after 50,000 B.C.E. when humans emigrated from their African homeland to all of the inhabitable continents. After that, the global population remained steady for several millennia. During the second expansion, between about 5000 and 500 B.C.E., population rose from about 5 million to 100 million as agricultural societies spread around the world (see Figure 1). Again population growth then slowed for several centuries before a third surge took world population to over 350 million by 1200 C.E. (see Figure 2).

For a long time historians tended to attribute these population surges to cultural and technological advances. Indeed, a great many changes in culture and technology are associated with adaptation to different climates and food supplies in the first surge and with the domestication of plants and animals in the second. However, historians have not found a cultural or technological change to explain the third surge, nor can they explain why creativity would have stagnated for long periods between the surges. Something else must have been at work.

Recently historians have begun to pay more attention to the impact of long-term variations in global climate. By examining ice cores drilled out of glaciers, scientists have been able to compile records of thousands of years of climate change. The comparative width of tree rings from ancient forests has provided additional data on periods of favorable and unfavorable growth. Such evidence shows that cycles of population growth and stagnation followed changes in global climate.

Historians now believe that global temperatures were above normal for extended periods from the late 1100s to the late 1200s C.E. In the temperate lands where most of the world's people lived, above-normal temperatures meant a longer growing season, more bountiful harvests, and thus a more adequate and reliable food supply. The ways in which societies responded to the medieval warm period are as important as the climate change, but it is unlikely that human agency alone would have produced the medieval surge. One notable response was that of the Vikings, who increased the size and range of their settlements in the North Atlantic, although their raids also caused death and destruction.

Some of the complexities involved in the interaction of human agency, climate, and other natural factors are also evident in the demographic changes that followed the medieval warm period. During the 1200s the Mongol invasions caused death and disruption of agriculture across Eurasia. China's population, which had been over 100 million in 1200, declined by a third or more by 1300. The Mongol invasions did not cause harm west of Russia, but climate changes in the 1300s resulted in population losses in Europe. Unusually heavy rains caused crop failures and a prolonged famine in northern Europe from 1315 to 1319.

The freer movement of merchants within the Mongol empire also facilitated the spread of disease across Eurasia, culminating in the great pandemic known as the Black Death in Europe. The demographic recovery underway in China was reversed. The even larger population losses in Europe may have been affected by the decrease in global temperatures to their lowest point in many millennia between 1350 and 1375. Improving economic conditions enabled population to recover more rapidly in Europe after 1400 than in China, where the conditions of rural life remained harsh.

Because many other historical circumstances interact with changing weather patterns, historians have a long way to go in deciphering the role of climate in history. Nevertheless, it is a factor that can no longer be ignored.

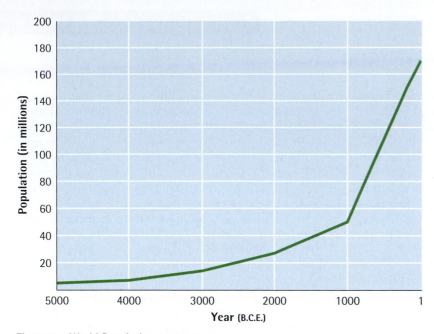

Figure 1 World Population, 5000–1 B.C.E.

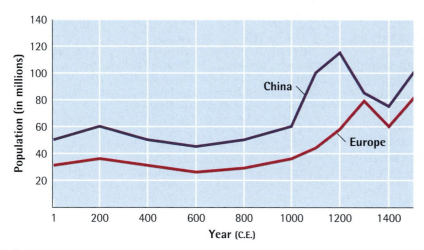

Figure 2 Population in China and Europe, 1–1500 C.E.

Glossary

The glossary for *The Earth and Its Peoples*, 3/e is for the complete text, Chapters 1 through 34.

Abbasid Caliphate   Descendants of the Prophet Muhammad's uncle, al-Abbas, the Abbasids overthrew the **Umayyad Caliphate** and ruled an Islamic empire from their capital in Baghdad (founded 762) from 750 to 1258.   (*p. 238*)

abolitionists   Men and women who agitated for a complete end to slavery. Abolitionist pressure ended the British transatlantic slave trade in 1808 and slavery in British colonies in 1834. In the United States the activities of abolitionists were one factor leading to the Civil War (1861–1865).   (*p. 650*)

acculturation   The adoption of the language, customs, values, and behaviors of host nations by immigrants.   (*p. 654*)

Acheh Sultanate   Muslim kingdom in northern Sumatra. Main center of Islamic expansion in Southeast Asia in the early seventeenth century, it declined after the Dutch seized **Malacca** from Portugal in 1641.   (*p. 545*)

Aden   Port city in the modern south Arabian country of Yemen. It has been a major trading center in the Indian Ocean since ancient times.   (*p. 384*)

African National Congress   An organization dedicated to obtaining equal voting and civil rights for black inhabitants of South Africa. Founded in 1912 as the South African Native National Congress, it changed its name in 1923. Though it was banned and its leaders were jailed for many years, it eventually helped bring majority rule to South Africa. (*p. 837*)

Afrikaners   South Africans descended from Dutch and French settlers of the seventeenth century. Their Great Trek founded new settler colonies in the nineteenth century. Though a minority among South Africans, they held political power after 1910, imposing a system of racial segregation called apartheid after 1949.   (*p. 758*)

Agricultural Revolution(s) (ancient)   The change from food gathering to food production that occurred between ca. 8000 and 2000 B.C.E. Also known as the Neolithic Revolution.   (*pp. 18, 610*)

agricultural revolution (eighteenth century)   The transformation of farming that resulted in the eighteenth century from the spread of new crops, improvements in cultivation techniques and livestock breeding, and the consolidation of small holdings into large farms from which tenants and sharecroppers were forcibly expelled.   (*p. 610*)

Aguinaldo, Emilio (1869–1964)   Leader of the Filipino independence movement against Spain (1895–1898). He proclaimed the independence of the Philippines in 1899, but his movement was crushed and he was captured by the United States Army in 1901.   (*p. 766*)

Akbar I (1542–1605)   Most illustrious sultan of the Mughal Empire in India (r. 1556–1605). He expanded the empire and pursued a policy of conciliation with Hindus.   (*p. 541*)

Akhenaten   Egyptian pharaoh (r. 1353–1335 B.C.E.). He built a new capital at Amarna, fostered a new style of naturalistic art, and created a religious revolution by imposing worship of the sun-disk. The Amarna letters, largely from his reign, preserve official correspondence with subjects and neighbors.   (*p. 86*)

Alexander (356–323 B.C.E.)   King of Macedonia in northern Greece. Between 334 and 323 B.C.E. he conquered the Persian Empire, reached the Indus Valley, founded many Greek-style cities, and spread Greek culture across the Middle East. Later known as Alexander the Great.   (*p. 143*)

Alexandria   City on the Mediterranean coast of Egypt founded by Alexander. It became the capital of the Hellenistic kingdom of the **Ptolemies.** It contained the famous Library and the Museum—a center for leading scientific and literary figures. Its merchants engaged in trade with areas bordering the Mediterranean and the Indian Ocean.   (*p. 145*)

Allende, Salvador (1908–1973)   Socialist politician elected president of Chile in 1970 and overthrown by the military in 1973. He died during the military attack.   (*p. 890*)

All-India Muslim League   Political organization founded in India in 1906 to defend the interests of India's Muslim minority. Led by Muhammad Ali Jinnah, it attempted to negotiate with the **Indian National Congress.** In 1940, the League began demanding a separate state for Muslims, to be called Pakistan. (See also **Jinnah, Muhammad Ali.**)   (*p. 841*)

amulet   Small charm meant to protect the bearer from evil. Found frequently in archaeological excavations in Mesopotamia and Egypt, amulets reflect the religious practices of the common people.   (*p. 36*)

Amur River   This river valley was a contested frontier between northern China and eastern Russia until the settlement arranged in Treaty of Nerchinsk (1689).   (*p. 562*)

anarchists   Revolutionaries who wanted to abolish all private property and governments, usually by violence, and replace them with free associations of groups.   (*p. 733*)

Anasazi   Important culture of what is now the Southwest United States (1000–1300 C.E.). Centered on Chaco Canyon in New Mexico and Mesa Verde in Colorado, the Anasazi culture built multistory residences and worshiped in subterranean buildings called kivas.   (*p. 317*)

aqueduct   A conduit, either elevated or underground, using gravity to carry water from a source to a location—usually a city—that needed it. The Romans built many aqueducts in a period of substantial urbanization.   (*p. 163*)

Arawak   Amerindian peoples who inhabited the Greater Antilles of the Caribbean at the time of Columbus.   (*p. 423*)

Arkwright, Richard (1732–1792)   English inventor and entrepreneur who became the wealthiest and most successful textile manufacturer of the early **Industrial Revolution.** He invented the water frame, a machine that, with minimal human supervision, could spin many strong cotton threads at once. (*p. 615*)

Armenia One of the earliest Christian kingdoms, situated in eastern Anatolia and the western Caucasus and occupied by speakers of the Armenian language. (*p. 226*)

Asante African kingdom on the **Gold Coast** that expanded rapidly after 1680. Asante participated in the Atlantic economy, trading gold, slaves, and ivory. It resisted British imperial ambitions for a quarter century before being absorbed into Britain's Gold Coast colony in 1902. (*p. 759*)

Ashikaga Shogunate (1336–1573) The second of Japan's military governments headed by a shogun (a military ruler). Sometimes called the Muromachi Shogunate. (*p. 362*)

Ashoka Third ruler of the **Mauryan Empire** in India (r. 270–232 B.C.E.). He converted to Buddhism and broadcast his precepts on inscribed stones and pillars, the earliest surviving Indian writing. (*p. 189*)

Asian Tigers Collective name for South Korea, Taiwan, Hong Kong, and Singapore—nations that became economic powers in the 1970s and 1980s. (*p. 896*)

Atahualpa (1502?–1533) Last ruling Inca emperor of Peru. He was executed by the Spanish. (*p. 440*)

Atlantic Circuit The network of trade routes connecting Europe, Africa, and the Americas that underlay the Atlantic system. (*p. 511*)

Atlantic system The network of trading links after 1500 that moved goods, wealth, people, and cultures around the Atlantic Ocean basin. (*p. 500*)

Augustus (63 B.C.E.–14 C.E.) Honorific name of Octavian, founder of the **Roman Principate,** the military dictatorship that replaced the failing rule of the **Roman Senate.** After defeating all rivals, between 31 B.C.E. and 14 C.E. he laid the groundwork for several centuries of stability and prosperity in the Roman Empire. (*p. 157*)

Auschwitz Nazi extermination camp in Poland, the largest center of mass murder during the **Holocaust.** Close to a million Jews, Gypsies, Communists, and others were killed there. (*p. 827*)

australopithecines The several extinct species of humanlike primates that existed during the Pleistocene era (genus *Australopithecus*). (*p. 6*)

ayllu Andean lineage group or kin-based community. (*p. 321*)

Aztecs Also known as Mexica, the Aztecs created a powerful empire in central Mexico (1325–1521 C.E.). They forced defeated peoples to provide goods and labor as a tax. (*p. 314*)

Babylon The largest and most important city in Mesopotamia. It achieved particular eminence as the capital of the Amorite king **Hammurabi** in the eighteenth century B.C.E. and the Neo-Babylonian king Nebuchadnezzar in the sixth century B.C.E. (*p. 29*)

balance of power The policy in international relations by which, beginning in the eighteenth century, the major European states acted together to prevent any one of them from becoming too powerful. (*p. 468*)

Balfour Declaration Statement issued by Britain's Foreign Secretary Arthur Balfour in 1917 favoring the establishment of a Jewish national homeland in Palestine. (*p. 784*)

Bannermen Hereditary military servants of the **Qing Empire,** in large part descendants of peoples of various origins who had fought for the founders of the empire. (*p. 708*)

Bantu Collective name of a large group of sub-Saharan African languages and of the peoples speaking these languages. (*p. 224*)

Batavia Fort established ca. 1619 as headquarters of Dutch East India Company operations in Indonesia; today the city of Jakarta. (*p. 548*)

Battle of Midway U.S. naval victory over the Japanese fleet in June 1942, in which the Japanese lost four of their best aircraft carriers. It marked a turning point in World War II. (*p. 821*)

Battle of Omdurman British victory over the Mahdi in the Sudan in 1898. General Kitchener led a mixed force of British and Egyptian troops armed with rapid-firing rifles and machine guns. (*p. 753*)

Beijing China's northern capital, first used as an imperial capital in 906 and now the capital of the People's Republic of China. (*p. 352*)

Bengal Region of northeastern India. It was the first part of India to be conquered by the British in the eighteenth century and remained the political and economic center of British India throughout the nineteenth century. The 1905 split of the province into predominantly Hindu West Bengal and predominantly Muslim East Bengal (now Bangladesh) sparked anti-British riots. (*p. 840*)

Berlin Conference (1884–1885) Conference that German chancellor Otto von Bismarck called to set rules for the partition of Africa. It led to the creation of the Congo Free State under King **Leopold II** of Belgium. (See also **Bismarck, Otto von.**) (*p. 755*)

Bhagavad-Gita The most important work of Indian sacred literature, a dialogue between the great warrior Arjuna and the god Krishna on duty and the fate of the spirit. (*p. 190*)

bin Laden, Usama Saudi-born Muslim extremist who funded the al Qaeda organization that was responsible for several terrorist attacks, including those on the World Trade Center and the Pentagon in 2001. (*p. 923*)

bipedalism The ability to walk upright on two legs, characteristic of hominids. (*p. 7*)

Bismarck, Otto von (1815–1898) Chancellor (prime minister) of Prussia from 1862 until 1871, when he became chancellor of Germany. A conservative nationalist, he led Prussia to victory against Austria (1866) and France (1870) and was responsible for the creation of the German Empire in 1871. (*p. 737*)

Black Death An outbreak of **bubonic plague** that spread across Asia, North Africa, and Europe in the mid-fourteenth century, carrying off vast numbers of persons. (*p. 395*)

Bolívar, Simón (1783–1830) The most important military leader in the struggle for independence in South America. Born in Venezuela, he led military forces there and in Colombia, Ecuador, Peru, and Bolivia. (*p. 634*)

Bolsheviks Radical Marxist political party founded by Vladimir Lenin in 1903. Under Lenin's leadership, the Bolsheviks seized power in November 1917 during the Russian Revolution. (See also **Lenin, Vladimir.**) (*p. 784*)

Bonaparte, Napoleon. See **Napoleon I.**

Bornu   A powerful West African kingdom at the southern edge of the Sahara in the Central Sudan, which was important in trans-Saharan trade and in the spread of Islam. Also known as Kanem-Bornu, it endured from the ninth century to the end of the nineteenth.   (*p. 520*)

Borobodur   A massive stone monument on the Indonesian island of Java, erected by the Sailendra kings around 800 C.E. The winding ascent through ten levels, decorated with rich relief carving, is a Buddhist allegory for the progressive stages of enlightenment.   (*p. 199*)

bourgeoisie   In early modern Europe, the class of well-off town dwellers whose wealth came from manufacturing, finance, commerce, and allied professions.   (*p. 457*)

Brant, Joseph (1742–1807)   Mohawk leader who supported the British during the American Revolution.   (*p. 589*)

Brazza, Savorgnan de (1852–1905) Franco-Italian explorer sent by the French government to claim part of equatorial Africa for France. Founded Brazzaville, capital of the French Congo, in 1880.   (*p. 755*)

British raj   The rule over much of South Asia between 1765 and 1947 by the East India Company and then by a British government.   (*p. 674*)

bronze   An alloy of copper with a small amount of tin (or sometimes arsenic), it is harder and more durable than copper alone. The term *Bronze Age* is applied to the era—the dates of which vary in different parts of the world—when bronze was the primary metal for tools and weapons. The demand for bronze helped create long-distance networks of trade.   (*p. 40*)

bubonic plague   A bacterial disease of fleas that can be transmitted by flea bites to rodents and humans; humans in late stages of the illness can spread the bacteria by coughing. Because of its very high mortality rate and the difficulty of preventing its spread, major outbreaks have created crises in many parts of the world. (See also **Black Death**.)   (*pp. 285, 344*)

Buddha (563–483 B.C.E.)   An Indian prince named Siddhartha Gautama, who renounced his wealth and social position. After becoming "enlightened" (the meaning of *Buddha*) he enunciated the principles of Buddhism. This doctrine evolved and spread throughout India and to Southeast, East, and Central Asia. (See also **Mahayana Buddhism, Theravada Buddhism**.)   (*p. 184*)

business cycles   Recurrent swings from economic hard times to recovery and growth, then back to hard times and a repetition of the sequence.   (*p. 626*)

Byzantine Empire   Historians' name for the eastern portion of the Roman Empire from the fourth century onward, taken from "Byzantion," an early name for Constantinople, the Byzantine capital city. The empire fell to the Ottomans in 1453. (See also **Ottoman Empire**.)   (*p. 254*)

caliphate   Office established in succession to the Prophet Muhammad, to rule the Islamic empire; also the name of that empire. (See also **Abbasid Caliphate; Sokoto Caliphate; Umayyad Caliphate**.)   (*p. 236*)

capitalism   The economic system of large financial institutions—banks, stock exchanges, investment companies—that first developed in early modern Europe. *Commercial capitalism*, the trading system of the early modern economy, is often distinguished from *industrial capitalism*, the system based on machine production.   (*p. 510*)

caravel   A small, highly maneuverable three-masted ship used by the Portuguese and Spanish in the exploration of the Atlantic.   (*p. 426*)

Cárdenas, Lázaro (1895–1970)   President of Mexico (1934–1940). He brought major changes to Mexican life by distributing millions of acres of land to the peasants, bringing representatives of workers and farmers into the inner circles of politics, and nationalizing the oil industry.   (*p. 847*)

Carthage   City located in present-day Tunisia, founded by **Phoenicians** ca. 800 B.C.E. It became a major commercial center and naval power in the western Mediterranean until defeated by Rome in the third century B.C.E.   (*p. 107*)

Caste War   A rebellion of the Maya people against the government of Mexico in 1847. It nearly returned the Yucatán to Maya rule. Some Maya rebels retreated to unoccupied territories where they held out until 1901.   (*p. 649*)

Catholic Reformation   Religious reform movement within the Latin Christian Church, begun in response to the **Protestant Reformation**. It clarified Catholic theology and reformed clerical training and discipline.   (*p. 453*)

Celts   Peoples sharing a common language and culture that originated in Central Europe in the first half of the first millennium B.C.E.. After 500 B.C.E. they spread as far as Anatolia in the east, Spain and the British Isles in the west, and later were overtaken by Roman conquest and Germanic invasions. Their descendants survive on the western fringe of Europe (Brittany, Wales, Scotland, Ireland).   (*p. 71*)

Champa rice   Quick-maturing rice that can allow two harvests in one growing season. Originally introduced into Champa from India, it was later sent to China as a tribute gift by the Champa state. (See also **tributary system**.)   (*p. 302*)

Chang'an   City in the Wei Valley in eastern China. It became the capital of the Qin and early Han Empires. Its main features were imitated in the cities and towns that sprang up throughout the Han Empire.   (*p. 171*)

Charlemagne (742–814)   King of the Franks (r. 768–814); emperor (r. 800–814). Through a series of military conquests he established the Carolingian Empire, which encompassed all of Gaul and parts of Germany and Italy. Though illiterate himself, he sponsored a brief intellectual revival.   (*p. 254*)

chartered companies   Groups of private investors who paid an annual fee to France and England in exchange for a monopoly over trade to the West Indies colonies.   (*p. 502*)

Chavín   The first major urban civilization in South America (900–250 B.C.E.). Its capital, Chavín de Huántar, was located high in the Andes Mountains of Peru. Chavín became politically and economically dominant in a densely populated region that included two distinct ecological zones, the Peruvian coastal plain and the Andean foothills.   (*p. 77*)

Chiang Kai-shek   (1886–1975) Chinese military and political leader. Succeeded Sun Yat-sen as head of the **Guomindang** in 1923; headed the Chinese government from 1928 to 1948; fought against the Chinese Communists and Japanese invaders. After 1949 he headed the Chinese Nationalist government in Taiwan.   (*pp. 792, 815*)

chiefdom   Form of political organization with rule by a hereditary leader who held power over a collection of villages and towns. Less powerful than kingdoms and empires, chiefdoms were based on gift giving and commercial links.   (*p. 318*)

Chimu   Powerful Peruvian civilization based on conquest. Located in the region earlier dominated by **Moche.** Conquered by **Inca** in 1465.   (*p. 323*)

chinampas   Raised fields constructed along lake shores in Mesoamerica to increase agricultural yields.   (*p. 309*)

city-state   A small independent state consisting of an urban center and the surrounding agricultural territory. A characteristic political form in early Mesopotamia, Archaic and Classical Greece, Phoenicia, and early Italy. (See also **polis.**)   (*p. 32*)

civilization   An ambiguous term often used to denote more complex societies but sometimes used by anthropologists to describe any group of people sharing a set of cultural traits.   (*p. 28*)

Cixi, Empress Dowager (1835–1908)   Empress of China and mother of Emperor Guangxi. She put her son under house arrest, supported antiforeign movements, and resisted reforms of the Chinese government and armed forces.   (*p. 743*)

clipper ship   Large, fast, streamlined sailing vessel, often American built, of the mid-to-late nineteenth century rigged with vast canvas sails hung from tall masts.   (*p. 684*)

Cold War (1945–1991)   The ideological struggle between communism (Soviet Union) and capitalism (United States) for world influence. The Soviet Union and the United States came to the brink of actual war during the **Cuban missile crisis** but never attacked one another. The Cold War came to an end when the Soviet Union dissolved in 1991. (See also **North Atlantic Treaty Organization; Warsaw Pact.**)   (*p. 831*)

colonialism   Policy by which a nation administers a foreign territory and develops its resources for the benefit of the colonial power.   (*p. 754*)

Columbian Exchange   The exchange of plants, animals, diseases, and technologies between the Americas and the rest of the world following Columbus's voyages.   (*p. 474*)

Columbus, Christopher (1451–1506)   Genoese mariner who in the service of Spain led expeditions across the Atlantic, reestablishing contact between the peoples of the Americas and the Old World and opening the way to Spanish conquest and colonization.   (*p. 430*)

Confederation of 1867   Negotiated union of the formerly separate colonial governments of Ontario, Quebec, New Brunswick, and Nova Scotia. This new Dominion of Canada with a central government in Ottawa is seen as the beginning of the Canadian nation.   (*p. 639*)

Confucius   Western name for the Chinese philosopher Kongzi (551–479 B.C.E.). His doctrine of duty and public service had a great influence on subsequent Chinese thought and served as a code of conduct for government officials.   (*p. 64*)

Congress of Vienna (1814–1815)   Meeting of representatives of European monarchs called to reestablish the old order after the defeat of **Napoleon I.**   (*p. 603*)

conquistadors   Early-sixteenth-century Spanish adventurers who conquered Mexico, Central America, and Peru. (See **Cortés, Hernán; Pizarro, Francisco.**)   (*p.436*)

Constantine (285–337 C.E.)   Roman emperor (r. 312–337). After reuniting the Roman Empire, he moved the capital to Constantinople and made Christianity a favored religion.   (*p. 166*)

Constitutional Convention   Meeting in 1787 of the elected representatives of the thirteen original states to write the Constitution of the United States.   (*p. 591*)

contract of indenture   A voluntary agreement binding a person to work for a specified period of years in return for free passage to an overseas destination. Before 1800 most **indentured servants** were Europeans; after 1800 most indentured laborers were Asians.   (*p. 687*)

Cortés, Hernán (1485–1547)   Spanish explorer and conquistador who led the conquest of Aztec Mexico in 1519–1521 for Spain.   (*p. 436*)

Cossacks   Peoples of the Russian Empire who lived outside the farming villages, often as herders, mercenaries, or outlaws. Cossacks led the conquest of Siberia in the sixteenth and seventeenth centuries.   (*p. 569*)

Council of the Indies   The institution responsible for supervising Spain's colonies in the Americas from 1524 to the early eighteenth century, when it lost all but judicial responsibilities.   (*p. 477*)

***coureurs des bois* (runners of the woods)**   French fur traders, many of mixed Amerindian heritage, who lived among and often married with Amerindian peoples of North America.   (*p. 493*)

creoles   In colonial Spanish America, term used to describe someone of European descent born in the New World. Elsewhere in the Americas, the term is used to describe all non-native peoples.   (*p. 483*)

Crimean War (1853–1856)   Conflict between the Russian and Ottoman Empires fought primarily in the Crimean Peninsula. To prevent Russian expansion, Britain and France sent troops to support the Ottomans.   (*p. 700*)

Crusades (1096–1291)   Armed pilgrimages to the Holy Land by Christians determined to recover Jerusalem from Muslim rule. The Crusades brought an end to western Europe's centuries of intellectual and cultural isolation.   (*p. 275*)

Crystal Palace   Building erected in Hyde Park, London, for the Great Exhibition of 1851. Made of iron and glass, like a gigantic greenhouse, it was a symbol of the industrial age.   (*p. 618*)

Cuban missile crisis (1962)   Brink-of-war confrontation between the United States and the Soviet Union over the latter's placement of nuclear-armed missiles in Cuba.   (*p. 869*)

cultural imperialism   Domination of one culture over another by a deliberate policy or by economic or technological superiority.   (*p. 937*)

Cultural Revolution (China) (1966–1969)   Campaign in China ordered by **Mao Zedong** to purge the Communist Party of his opponents and instill revolutionary values in the younger generation.   (*p. 881*)

culture   Socially transmitted patterns of action and expression. *Material culture* refers to physical objects, such as dwellings, clothing, tools, and crafts. Culture also includes arts, beliefs, knowledge, and technology.   (*p. 11*)

cuneiform   A system of writing in which wedge-shaped symbols represented words or syllables. It originated in Mesopotamia and was used initially for Sumerian and Akkadian but later was adapted to represent other languages of western Asia. Because so many symbols had to be learned, literacy was confined to a relatively small group of administrators and **scribes.** (*p. 37*)

Cyrus (600–530 B.C.E.) Founder of the Achaemenid Persian Empire. Between 550 and 530 B.C.E. he conquered Media, Lydia, and Babylon. Revered in the traditions of both Iran and the subject peoples, he employed Persians and Medes in his administration and respected the institutions and beliefs of subject peoples. (*p. 122*)

czar See **tsar.**

daimyo Literally, great name(s). Japanese warlords and great landowners, whose armed **samurai** gave them control of the Japanese islands from the eighth to the later nineteenth century. Under the **Tokugawa Shogunate** they were subordinated to the imperial government. (*p. 551*)

Daoism Chinese school of thought, originating in the Warring States Period with Laozi (604–531 B.C.E.). Daoism offered an alternative to the Confucian emphasis on hierarchy and duty. Daoists believe that the world is always changing and is devoid of absolute morality or meaning. They accept the world as they find it, avoid futile struggles, and deviate as little as possible from the *Dao,* or "path" of nature. (See also **Confucius.**) (*p. 64*)

Darius I (ca. 558–486 B.C.E.) Third ruler of the Persian Empire (r. 521–486 B.C.E.). He crushed the widespread initial resistance to his rule and gave all major government posts to Persians rather than to Medes. He established a system of provinces and tribute, began construction of Persepolis, and expanded Persian control in the east (Pakistan) and west (northern Greece). (*p. 123*)

Decembrist revolt Abortive attempt by army officers to take control of the Russian government upon the death of Tsar Alexander I in 1825. (*p. 706*)

Declaration of the Rights of Man (1789) Statement of fundamental political rights adopted by the French **National Assembly** at the beginning of the French Revolution. (*p. 595*)

deforestation The removal of trees faster than forests can replace themselves. (*p. 460*)

Delhi Sultanate (1206–1526) Centralized Indian empire of varying extent, created by Muslim invaders. (*p. 370*)

democracy A system of government in which all "citizens" (however defined) have equal political and legal rights, privileges, and protections, as in the Greek city-state of Athens in the fifth and fourth centuries B.C.E. (*p. 135*)

demographic transition A change in the rates of population growth. Before the transition, both birthrates and death rates are high, resulting in a slowly growing population; then the death rate drops but the birthrate remains high, causing a population explosion; finally the birthrate drops and the population growth slows down. This transition took place in Europe in the late nineteenth and early twentieth centuries, in North America and East Asia in the mid-twentieth, and, most recently, in Latin America and South Asia. (*p. 902*)

Deng Xiaoping (1904–1997) Communist Party leader who forced Chinese economic reforms after the death of **Mao Zedong.** (*p. 897*)

development In the nineteenth and twentieth centuries, the

economic process that led to industrialization, urbanization, the rise of a large and prosperous middle class, and heavy investment in education. (*p. 656*)

devshirme "Selection" in Turkish. The system by which boys from Christian communities were taken by the Ottoman state to serve as **Janissaries.** (*p. 530*)

dhow Ship of small to moderate size used in the western Indian Ocean, traditionally with a triangular sail and a sewn timber hull. (*p. 380*)

Diagne, Blaise (1872–1934) Senegalese political leader. He was the first African elected to the French National Assembly. During World War I, in exchange for promises to give French citizenship to Senegalese, he helped recruit Africans to serve in the French army. After the war, he led a movement to abolish forced labor in Africa. (*p. 837*)

Dias, Bartolomeu (1450?–1500) Portuguese explorer who in 1488 led the first expedition to sail around the southern tip of Africa from the Atlantic and sight the Indian Ocean. (*p. 428*)

Diaspora A Greek word meaning "dispersal," used to describe the communities of a given ethnic group living outside their homeland. Jews, for example, spread from Israel to western Asia and Mediterranean lands in antiquity and today can be found throughout the world. (*p. 101*)

Dirty War War waged by the Argentine military (1976–1982) against leftist groups. Characterized by the use of illegal imprisonment, torture, and executions by the military. (*p. 890*)

divination Techniques for ascertaining the future or the will of the gods by interpreting natural phenomena such as, in early China, the cracks on oracle bones or, in ancient Greece, the flight of birds through sectors of the sky. (*p. 60*)

division of labor A manufacturing technique that breaks down a craft into many simple and repetitive tasks that can be performed by unskilled workers. Pioneered in the pottery works of Josiah Wedgwood and in other eighteenth-century factories, it greatly increased the productivity of labor and lowered the cost of manufactured goods. (See also **Wedgwood, Josiah.**) (*p. 614*)

driver A privileged male slave whose job was to ensure that a slave gang did its work on a plantation. (*p. 506*)

Druids The class of religious experts who conducted rituals and preserved sacred lore among some ancient Celtic peoples. They provided education, mediated disputes between kinship groups, and were suppressed by the Romans as a potential focus of opposition to Roman rule. (See also **Celts.**) (*p. 73*)

durbar An elaborate display of political power and wealth in British India in the nineteenth century, ostensibly in imitation of the pageantry of the **Mughal Empire.** (*p. 676*)

Dutch West India Company (1621–1794) Trading company chartered by the Dutch government to conduct its merchants' trade in the Americas and Africa. (*p. 502*)

Edison, Thomas (1847–1931) American inventor best known for inventing the electric light bulb, acoustic recording on wax cylinders, and motion pictures. (*p. 726*)

Einstein, Albert (1879–1955) German physicist who developed the theory of relativity, which states that time, space, and mass are relative to each other and not fixed. (*p. 800*)

El Alamein Town in Egypt, site of the victory by Britain's Field Marshal Bernard Montgomery over German forces led by General Erwin Rommel (the "Desert Fox") in 1942–1943. (*p. 821*)

electricity A form of energy used in telegraphy from the 1840s on and for lighting, industrial motors, and railroads beginning in the 1880s. (*p. 726*)

electric telegraph A device for rapid, long-distance transmission of information over an electric wire. It was introduced in England and North America in the 1830s and 1840s and replaced telegraph systems that utilized visual signals such as semaphores. (See also **submarine telegraph cables.**) (*p. 620*)

encomienda A grant of authority over a population of Amerindians in the Spanish colonies. It provided the grant holder with a supply of cheap labor and periodic payments of goods by the Amerindians. It obliged the grant holder to Christianize the Amerindians. (*p. 482*)

English Civil War (1642-1649) A conflict over royal versus. Parliamentary rights, caused by King Charles I's arrest of his parliamentary critics and ending with his execution. Its outcome checked the growth of royal absolutism and, with the Glorious Revolution of 1688 and the English Bill of Rights of 1689, ensured that England would be a constitutional monarchy. (*p. 466*)

Enlightenment A philosophical movement in eighteenth-century Europe that fostered the belief that one could reform society by discovering rational laws that governed social behavior and were just as scientific as the laws of physics. (*pp. 456, 582*)

equites In ancient Italy, prosperous landowners second in wealth and status to the senatorial aristocracy. The Roman emperors allied with this group to counterbalance the influence of the old aristocracy and used the *equites* to staff the imperial civil service. (*p. 157*)

Estates General France's traditional national assembly with representatives of the three estates, or classes, in French society: the clergy, nobility, and commoners. The calling of the Estates General in 1789 led to the French Revolution. (*p. 593*)

Ethiopia East African highland nation lying east of the Nile River. (See also **Menelik II; Selassie, Haile.**) (*p. 226*)

ethnic cleansing Effort to eradicate a people and its culture by means of mass killing and the destruction of historical buildings and cultural materials. Ethnic cleansing was used by both sides in the conflicts that accompanied the disintegration of Yugoslavia in the 1990s. (*p. 922*)

European Community (EC) An organization promoting economic unity in Europe formed in 1967 by consolidation of earlier, more limited, agreements. Replaced by the European Union (EU) in 1993. (*p. 865*)

evolution The biological theory that, over time, changes occurring in plants and animals, mainly as a result of **natural selection** and genetic mutation, result in new species. (*p. 5*)

extraterritoriality The right of foreign residents in a country to live under the laws of their native country and disregard the laws of the host country. In the nineteenth and early twentieth centuries, European and American nationals living in certain areas of Chinese and Ottoman cities were granted this right. (*p. 701*)

Faisal I (1885–1933) Arab prince, leader of the Arab Revolt in World War I. The British made him king of Iraq in 1921, and he reigned under British protection until 1933. (*p.784*)

Fascist Party Italian political party created by Benito Mussolini during World War I. It emphasized aggressive nationalism and was Mussolini's instrument for the creation of a dictatorship in Italy from 1922 to 1943. (See also **Mussolini, Benito.**) (*p. 813*)

fief In medieval Europe, land granted in return for a sworn oath to provide specified military service. (*p. 263*)

First Temple A monumental sanctuary built in Jerusalem by King Solomon in the tenth century B.C.E. to be the religious center for the Israelite god Yahweh. The Temple priesthood conducted sacrifices, received a tithe or percentage of agricultural revenues, and became economically and politically powerful. The First Temple was destroyed by the Babylonians in 587 B.C.E., rebuilt on a modest scale in the late sixth century B.C.E., and replaced by King Herod's Second Temple in the late first century B.C.E. (destroyed by the Romans in 70 C.E.) (*p. 100*)

Five-Year Plans Plans that Joseph Stalin introduced to industrialize the Soviet Union rapidly, beginning in 1928. They set goals for the output of steel, electricity, machinery, and most other products and were enforced by the police powers of the state. They succeeded in making the Soviet Union a major industrial power before World War II. (See also **Stalin, Joseph.**) (*p. 806*)

foragers People who support themselves by hunting wild animals and gathering wild edible plants and insects. (*p. 12*)

Franklin, Benjamin (1706–1790) American intellectual, inventor, and politician He helped negotiate French support for the American Revolution. (*p. 585*)

free-trade imperialism Economic dominance of a weaker country by a more powerful one, while maintaining the legal independence of the weaker state. In the late nineteenth century, free-trade imperialism characterized the relations between the Latin American republics, on the one hand, and Great Britain and the United States, on the other. (*p. 768*)

Fujiwara Aristocratic family that dominated the Japanese imperial court between the ninth and twelfth centuries. (*p. 301*)

Funan An early complex society in Southeast Asia between the first and sixth centuries C.E. It was centered in the rich rice-growing region of southern Vietnam, and it controlled the passage of trade across the Malaysian isthmus. (*p. 198*)

Gama, Vasco da (1460?–1524) Portuguese explorer. In 1497–1498 he led the first naval expedition from Europe to sail to India, opening an important commercial sea route. (*p. 428*)

Gandhi, Mohandas K. (Mahatma) (1869–1948) Leader of the Indian independence movement and advocate of nonviolent resistance. After being educated as a lawyer in England, he returned to India and became leader of the **Indian National Congress** in 1920. He appealed to the poor, led nonviolent demonstrations against British colonial rule, and was jailed many times. Soon after independence he was assassinated for attempting to stop Hindu-Muslim rioting. (*p. 841*)

Garibaldi, Giuseppe (1807–1882) Italian nationalist and revolutionary who conquered Sicily and Naples and added them to a unified Italy in 1860. (*p. 736*)

Genghis Khan (ca. 1167–1227) The title of Temüjin when he ruled the Mongols (1206–1227). It means the "oceanic" or "universal" leader. Genghis Khan was the founder of the Mongol Empire. (*p. 337*)

gens de couleur Free men and women of color in Haiti. They sought greater political rights and later supported the Haitian Revolution. (See also **L'Ouverture, François Dominique Toussaint.**) (*p. 601*)

gentry In China, the class of prosperous families, next in wealth below the rural aristocrats, from which the emperors drew their administrative personnel. Respected for their education and expertise, these officials became a privileged group and made the government more efficient and responsive than in the past. The term *gentry* also denotes the class of landholding families in England below the aristocracy. (*pp. 171, 172, 459*)

Ghana First known kingdom in sub-Saharan West Africa between the sixth and thirteenth centuries C.E. Also the modern West African country once known as the Gold Coast. (*p. 221*)

global culture Cultural practices and institutions that have been adopted internationally, whether elite (the English language, modern science, and higher education) or popular (music, television, the Internet, food, and fashion). (*p. 939*)

globalization The economic, political, and cultural integration and interaction of all parts of the world brought about by increasing trade, travel, and technology. (*p. 920*)

Gold Coast (Africa) Region of the Atlantic coast of West Africa occupied by modern Ghana; named for its gold exports to Europe from the 1470s onward. (*p. 428*)

Golden Horde Mongol khanate founded by Genghis Khan's grandson Batu. It was based in southern Russia and quickly adopted both the Turkic language and Islam. Also known as the Kipchak Horde. (*p. 345*)

Gorbachev, Mikhail (b. 1931) Head of the Soviet Union from 1985 to 1991. His liberalization effort improved relations with the West, but he lost power after his reforms led to the collapse of communist governments in eastern Europe. (*p. 898*)

Gothic cathedrals Large churches originating in twelfth-century France; built in an architectural style featuring pointed arches, tall vaults and spires, flying buttresses, and large stained-glass windows. (*p. 404*)

Grand Canal The 1,100-mile (1,700-kilometer) waterway linking the Yellow and the Yangzi Rivers. It was begun in the **Han** period and completed during the Sui Empire. (*p. 282*)

Great Ice Age Geological era that occurred between ca. 2 million and 11,000 years ago. As a result of climate shifts, large numbers of new species evolved during this period, also called the Pleistocene epoch. (See also **Holocene.**) (*p. 8*)

"great traditions" Historians' term for a literate, well-institutionalized complex of religious and social beliefs and practices adhered to by diverse societies over a broad geographical area. (See also **"small traditions."**) (*p. 222*)

Great Western Schism A division in the Latin (Western) Christian Church between 1378 and 1417, when rival claimants to the papacy existed in Rome and Avignon. (*p. 412*)

Great Zimbabwe City, now in ruins (in the modern African country of Zimbabwe), whose many stone structures were built between about 1250 and 1450, when it was a trading center and the capital of a large state. (*p. 383*)

guild In medieval Europe, an association of men (rarely women), such as merchants, artisans, or professors, who worked in a particular trade and banded together to promote their economic and political interests. Guilds were also important in other societies, such as the Ottoman and Safavid empires. (*p. 401*)

Gujarat Region of western India famous for trade and manufacturing; the inhabitants are called Gujarati. (*p. 379*)

gunpowder A mixture of saltpeter, sulfur, and charcoal, in various proportions. The formula, brought to China in the 400s or 500s, was first used to make fumigators to keep away insect pests and evil spirits. In later centuries it was used to make explosives and grenades and to propel cannonballs, shot, and bullets. (*p. 296*)

Guomindang Nationalist political party founded on democratic principles by **Sun Yat-sen** in 1912. After 1925, the party was headed by **Chiang Kai-shek,** who turned it into an increasingly authoritarian movement. (*p. 791*)

Gupta Empire (320–550 C.E.) A powerful Indian state based, like its Mauryan predecessor, on a capital at Pataliputra in the Ganges Valley. It controlled most of the Indian subcontinent through a combination of military force and its prestige as a center of sophisticated culture. (See also **theater-state.**) (*p. 190*)

Habsburg A powerful European family that provided many Holy Roman Emperors, founded the Austrian (later Austro-Hungarian) Empire, and ruled sixteenth- and seventeenth-century Spain. (*p. 462*)

hadith A tradition relating the words or deeds of the Prophet Muhammad; next to the **Quran,** the most important basis for Islamic law. (*p. 243*)

Hammurabi Amorite ruler of **Babylon** (r. 1792–1750 B.C.E.). He conquered many city-states in southern and northern Mesopotamia and is best known for a code of laws, inscribed on a black stone pillar, illustrating the principles to be used in legal cases. (*p. 34*)

Han A term used to designate (1) the ethnic Chinese people who originated in the Yellow River Valley and spread throughout regions of China suitable for agriculture and (2) the dynasty of emperors who ruled from 206 B.C.E. to 220 C.E. (*p. 166*)

Hanseatic League An economic and defensive alliance of the free towns in northern Germany, founded about 1241 and most powerful in the fourteenth century. (*p. 398*)

Harappa Site of one of the great cities of the Indus Valley civilization of the third millennium B.C.E. It was located on the northwest frontier of the zone of cultivation (in modern

Pakistan), and may have been a center for the acquisition of raw materials, such as metals and precious stones, from Afghanistan and Iran. (*p. 49*)

Hatshepsut Queen of Egypt (r. 1473–1458 B.C.E.). She dispatched a naval expedition down the Red Sea to Punt (possibly northeast Sudan or Eretria), the faraway source of myrrh. There is evidence of opposition to a woman as ruler, and after her death her name and image were frequently defaced. (*p. 86*)

Hausa An agricultural and trading people of central Sudan in West Africa. Aside from their brief incorporation into the Songhai Empire, the Hausa city-states remained autonomous until the **Sokoto Caliphate** conquered them in the early nineteenth century. (*p. 520*)

Hebrew Bible A collection of sacred books containing diverse materials concerning the origins, experiences, beliefs, and practices of the Israelites. Most of the extant text was compiled by members of the priestly class in the fifth century B.C.E. and reflects the concerns and views of this group. (*p. 97*)

Hellenistic Age Historians' term for the era, usually dated 323–30 B.C.E., in which Greek culture spread across western Asia and northeastern Africa after the conquests of **Alexander** the Great. The period ended with the fall of the last major Hellenistic kingdom to Rome, but Greek cultural influence persisted until the spread of Islam in the seventh century C.E. (*p. 144*)

Helsinki Accords (1975) Political and human rights agreement signed in Helsinki, Finland, by the Soviet Union and western European countries. (*p. 870*)

Henry the Navigator (1394–1460) Portuguese prince who promoted the study of navigation and directed voyages of exploration down the western coast of Africa. (*p. 425*)

Herodotus (ca. 485–425 B.C.E.) Heir to the technique of *historia*—"investigation"—developed by Greeks in the late Archaic period. He came from a Greek community in Anatolia and traveled extensively, collecting information in western Asia and the Mediterranean lands. He traced the antecedents of and chronicled the **Persian Wars** between the Greek city-states and the Persian Empire, thus originating the Western tradition of historical writing. (*p. 136*)

Herzl, Theodore (1860–1904) Austrian journalist and founder of the Zionist movement urging the creation of a Jewish national homeland in Palestine. (*p. 784*)

Hidalgo y Costilla, Miguel (1753–1811) Mexican priest who led the first stage of the Mexican independence war in 1810. He was captured and executed in 1811. (*p. 637*)

Hidden Imam Last in a series of twelve descendants of Muhammad's son-in-law Ali, whom **Shi'ites** consider divinely appointed leaders of the Muslim community. In occlusion since ca. 873, he is expected to return as a messiah at the end of time. (*p. 538*)

hieroglyphics A system of writing in which pictorial symbols represented sounds, syllables, or concepts. It was used for official and monumental inscriptions in ancient Egypt. Because of the long period of study required to master this system, literacy in hieroglyphics was confined to a relatively small group of **scribes** and administrators. Cursive symbol-forms were developed for rapid composition on other media, such as **papyrus.** (*p. 44*)

Hinduism A general term for a wide variety of beliefs and ritual practices that have developed in the Indian subcontinent since antiquity. Hinduism has roots in ancient Vedic, Buddhist, and south Indian religious concepts and practices. It spread along the trade routes to Southeast Asia. (*p. 185*)

Hiroshima City in Japan, the first to be destroyed by an atomic bomb, on August 6, 1945. The bombing hastened the end of World War II. (*p. 823*)

history The study of past events and changes in the development, transmission, and transformation of cultural practices. (*p. 11*)

Hitler, Adolf (1889–1945) Born in Austria, Hitler became a radical German nationalist during World War I. He led the National Socialist German Workers' Party—the **Nazis**—in the 1920s and became dictator of Germany in 1933. He led Europe into World War II. (*p. 813*)

Hittites A people from central Anatolia who established an empire in Anatolia and Syria in the Late Bronze Age. With wealth from the trade in metals and military power based on chariot forces, the Hittites vied with New Kingdom Egypt for control of Syria-Palestine before falling to unidentified attackers ca. 1200 B.C.E. (See also **Ramesses II.**) (*p. 84*)

Holocaust Nazis' program during World War II to kill people they considered undesirable. Some 6 million Jews perished during the Holocaust, along with millions of Poles, Gypsies, Communists, Socialists, and others. (*p. 827*)

Holocene The geological era since the end of the **Great Ice Age** about 11,000 years ago. (*p. 21*)

Holy Roman Empire Loose federation of mostly German states and principalities, headed by an emperor elected by the princes. It lasted from 962 to 1806. (*pp. 267, 462*)

hominid The biological family that includes humans and humanlike primates. (*p. 7*)

Homo erectus An extinct human species. It evolved in Africa about 2 million years ago. (*p. 10*)

Homo habilis The first human species (now extinct). It evolved in Africa about 2.5 million years ago. (*p. 8*)

Homo sapiens The current human species. It evolved in Africa about 200,000 years ago. It includes archaic forms such as Neanderthals (now extinct) and all modern humans. (*p. 10*)

hoplite A heavily armored Greek infantryman of the Archaic and Classical periods who fought in the close-packed phalanx formation. Hoplite armies—militias composed of middle- and upper-class citizens supplying their own equipment—were for centuries superior to all other military forces. (*p. 133*)

horse collar Harnessing method that increased the efficiency of horses by shifting the point of traction from the animal's neck to the shoulders; its adoption favors the spread of horse-drawn plows and vehicles. (*p. 274*)

House of Burgesses Elected assembly in colonial Virginia, created in 1618. (*p. 489*)

humanists (Renaissance) European scholars, writers, and teachers associated with the study of the humanities (grammar, rhetoric, poetry, history, languages, and moral philosophy), influential in the fifteenth century and later. (*p. 407*)

Hundred Years War (1337–1453) Series of campaigns over

control of the throne of France, involving English and French royal families and French noble families. (*p. 413*)

Husain, Saddam (b. 1937) President of Iraq from 1979 until overthrown by an American-led invasion in 2003. Waged war on Iran from 1980 to 1988. His invasion of Kuwait in 1990 was repulsed in the Persian Gulf War in 1991. (*p. 893*)

Ibn Battuta (1304–1369) Moroccan Muslim scholar, the most widely traveled individual of his time. He wrote a detailed account of his visits to Islamic lands from China to Spain and the western Sudan. (*p. 370*)

Il-khan A "secondary" or "peripheral" khan based in Persia. The Il-khans' khanate was founded by Hülegü, a grandson of **Genghis Khan,** and was based at Tabriz in modern Azerbaijan. It controlled much of Iran and Iraq. (*p. 345*)

import-substitution industrialization An economic system aimed at building a country's industry by restricting foreign trade. It was especially popular in Latin American countries such as Mexico, Argentina, and Brazil in the mid-twentieth century. It proved successful for a time but could not keep up with technological advances in Europe and North America. (*p. 851*)

Inca Largest and most powerful Andean empire. Controlled the Pacific coast of South America from Ecuador to Chile from its capital of Cuzco. (*p. 327*)

indentured servant A migrant to British colonies in the Americas who paid for passage by agreeing to work for a set term ranging from four to seven years. (*p. 489*)

Indian Civil Service The elite professional class of officials who administered the government of British India. Originally composed exclusively of well-educated British men, it gradually added qualified Indians. (*p. 676*)

Indian National Congress A movement and political party founded in 1885 to demand greater Indian participation in government. Its membership was middle class, and its demands were modest until World War I. Led after 1920 by Mohandas K. Gandhi, it appealed increasingly to the poor, and it organized mass protests demanding self-government and independence. (See also **Gandhi, Mohandas K.**) (*pp. 681, 840*)

Indian Ocean Maritime System In premodern times, a network of seaports, trade routes, and maritime culture linking countries on the rim of the Indian Ocean from Africa to Indonesia. (*p. 213*)

indulgence The forgiveness of the punishment due for past sins, granted by the Catholic Church authorities as a reward for a pious act. Martin Luther's protest against the sale of indulgences is often seen as touching off the **Protestant Reformation.** (*p. 450*)

Industrial Revolution The transformation of the economy, the environment, and living conditions, occurring first in England in the eighteenth century, that resulted from the use of steam engines, the mechanization of manufacturing in factories, and innovations in transportation and communication. (*p. 609*)

investiture controversy Dispute between the popes and the Holy Roman Emperors over who held ultimate authority over bishops in imperial lands. (*p. 267*)

Irigoyen, Hipólito (1850–1933) Argentine politician, president of Argentina from 1916 to 1922 and 1928 to 1930.

The first president elected by universal male suffrage, he began his presidency as a reformer, but later became conservative. (*p. 850*)

Iron Age Historians' term for the period during which iron was the primary metal for tools and weapons. The advent of iron technology began at different times in different parts of the world. (*p. 82*)

iron curtain Winston Churchill's term for the Cold War division between the Soviet-dominated East and the U.S.-dominated West. (*p. 861*)

Iroquois Confederacy An alliance of five northeastern Amerindian peoples (six after 1722) that made decisions on military and diplomatic issues through a council of representatives. Allied first with the Dutch and later with the English, the Confederacy dominated the area from western New England to the Great Lakes. (*p. 492*)

Islam Religion expounded by the Prophet Muhammad (570–632 C.E.) on the basis of his reception of divine revelations, which were collected after his death into the **Quran.** In the tradition of Judaism and Christianity, and sharing much of their lore, Islam calls on all people to recognize one creator god—Allah—who rewards or punishes believers after death according to how they led their lives. (See also **hadith.**) (*p. 235*)

Israel In antiquity, the land between the eastern shore of the Mediterranean and the Jordan River, occupied by the Israelites from the early second millennium B.C.E. The modern state of Israel was founded in 1948. (*p. 97*)

Jackson, Andrew (1767–1845) First president of the United States to be born in humble circumstances. He was popular among frontier residents, urban workers, and small farmers. He had a successful political career as judge, general, congressman, senator, and president. After being denied the presidency in 1824 in a controversial election, he won in 1828 and was reelected in 1832. (*p. 643*)

Jacobins Radical republicans during the French Revolution. They were led by Maximilien Robespierre from 1793 to 1794. (See also **Robespierre, Maximilien.**) (*p. 596*)

Janissaries Infantry, originally of slave origin, armed with firearms and constituting the elite of the Ottoman army from the fifteenth century until the corps was abolished in 1826. (See also ***devshirme.***) (*pp. 530, 693*)

jati. See ***varna.***

Jesus (ca. 5 B.C.E.–34 C.E.) A Jew from Galilee in northern Israel who sought to reform Jewish beliefs and practices. He was executed as a revolutionary by the Romans. Hailed as the Messiah and son of God by his followers, he became the central figure in Christianity, a belief system that developed in the centuries after his death. (*p. 162*)

Jinnah, Muhammad Ali (1876–1948) Indian Muslim politician who founded the state of Pakistan. A lawyer by training, he joined the **All-India Muslim League** in 1913. As leader of the League from the 1920s on, he negotiated with the British and the **Indian National Congress** for Muslim participation in Indian politics. From 1940 on, he led the movement for the independence of India's Muslims in a separate state of Pakistan, founded in 1947. (*p. 844*)

joint-stock company A business, often backed by a government charter, that sold shares to individuals to raise money for its trading enterprises and to spread the risks (and profits) among many investors.   (*p. 459*)

Juárez, Benito (1806–1872)   President of Mexico (1858–1872). Born in poverty in Mexico, he was educated as a lawyer and rose to become chief justice of the Mexican supreme court and then president. He led Mexico's resistance to a French invasion in 1863 and the installation of Maximilian as emperor.   (*p. 646*)

junk   A very large flatbottom sailing ship produced in the **Tang, Ming,** and **Song Empires,** specially designed for long-distance commercial travel.   (*p. 295*)

Kamakura shogunate   The first of Japan's decentralized military governments. (1185–1333).   (*p. 302*)

kamikaze   The "divine wind," which the Japanese credited with blowing Mongol invaders away from their shores in 1281.   (*p. 361*)

Kangxi (1654–1722)   Qing emperor (r. 1662–1722). He oversaw the greatest expansion of the **Qing Empire.**   (*p. 559*)

karma   In Indian tradition, the residue of deeds performed in past and present lives that adheres to a "spirit" and determines what form it will assume in its next life cycle. The doctrines of karma and reincarnation were used by the elite in ancient India to encourage people to accept their social position and do their duty.   (*p. 183*)

keiretsu   Alliances of corporations and banks that dominate the Japanese economy.   (*p. 896*)

khipu   System of knotted colored cords used by preliterate Andean peoples to transmit information.   (*p. 321*)

Khomeini, Ayatollah Ruhollah (1900?–1989)   Shi'ite philosopher and cleric who led the overthrow of the shah of Iran in 1979 and created an Islamic republic.   (*p. 892*)

Khubilai Khan (1215–1294)   Last of the Mongol Great Khans (r. 1260–1294) and founder of the **Yuan Empire.**   (*p. 352*)

Kievan Russia   State established at Kiev in Ukraine ca. 879 by Scandinavian adventurers asserting authority over a mostly Slavic farming population.   (*p. 254*)

Korean War (1950–1953)   Conflict that began with North Korea's invasion of South Korea and came to involve the United Nations (primarily the United States) allying with South Korea and the People's Republic of China allying with North Korea.   (*p. 866*)

Koryo   Korean kingdom founded in 918 and destroyed by a Mongol invasion in 1259.   (*p. 301*)

Kush   An Egyptian name for Nubia, the region alongside the Nile River south of Egypt, where an indigenous kingdom with its own distinctive institutions and cultural traditions arose beginning in the early second millennium B.C.E. It was deeply influenced by Egyptian culture and at times under the control of Egypt, which coveted its rich deposits of gold and luxury products from sub-Saharan Africa carried up the Nile corridor.   (*p. 68*)

labor union   An organization of workers in a particular industry or trade, created to defend the interests of members through strikes or negotiations with employers.   (*p. 732*)

laissez faire   The idea that government should refrain from interfering in economic affairs. The classic exposition of laissez-faire principles is Adam Smith's *Wealth of Nations* (1776).   (*p. 627*)

lama   In Tibetan Buddhism, a teacher.   (*p. 352*)

Las Casas, Bartolomé de (1474–1566)   First bishop of Chiapas, in southern Mexico. He devoted most of his life to protecting Amerindian peoples from exploitation. His major achievement was the New Laws of 1542, which limited the ability of Spanish settlers to compel Amerindians to labor for them. (See also **encomienda.**)   (*p. 480*)

Latin West   Historians' name for the territories of Europe that adhered to the Latin rite of Christianity and used the Latin language for intellectual exchange in the period ca. 1000–1500.   (*p. 392*)

League of Nations   International organization founded in 1919 to promote world peace and cooperation but greatly weakened by the refusal of the United States to join. It proved ineffectual in stopping aggression by Italy, Japan, and Germany in the 1930s, and it was superseded by the **United Nations** in 1945.   (*p. 786*)

Legalism   In China, a political philosophy that emphasized the unruliness of human nature and justified state coercion and control. The **Qin** ruling class invoked it to validate the authoritarian nature of their regime and its profligate expenditure of subjects' lives and labor. It was superseded in the **Han** era by a more benevolent Confucian doctrine of governmental moderation.   (*p. 64*)

"legitimate" trade   Exports from Africa in the nineteenth century that did not include the newly outlawed slave trade.   (*p. 671*)

Lenin, Vladimir (1870–1924)   Leader of the Bolshevik (later Communist) Party. He lived in exile in Switzerland until 1917, then returned to Russia to lead the Bolsheviks to victory during the Russian Revolution and the civil war that followed.   (*p. 784*)

Leopold II (1835–1909)   King of Belgium (r. 1865–1909). He was active in encouraging the exploration of Central Africa and became the ruler of the Congo Free State (to 1908).   (*p. 755*)

liberalism   A political ideology that emphasizes the civil rights of citizens, representative government, and the protection of private property. This ideology, derived from the **Enlightenment,** was especially popular among the property-owning middle classes of Europe and North America.   (*p. 736*)

Library of Ashurbanipal   A large collection of writings drawn from the ancient literary, religious, and scientific traditions of Mesopotamia. It was assembled by the sixth century B.C.E. Assyrian ruler Ashurbanipal. The many tablets unearthed by archaeologists constitute one of the most important sources of present-day knowledge of the long literary tradition of Mesopotamia.   (*p. 97*)

Linear B   A set of syllabic symbols, derived from the writing system of **Minoan** Crete, used in the Mycenaean palaces of the Late Bronze Age to write an early form of Greek. It was used primarily for palace records, and the surviving Linear B tablets provide substantial information about the economic organization of Mycenaean society and tantalizing clues about political, social, and religious institutions.   (*p. 91*)

Li Shimin (599–649)   One of the founders of the **Tang Empire** and its second emperor (r. 626–649). He led the expansion of the empire into Central Asia.   (*p. 282*)

Little Ice Age   A century-long period of cool climate that began in the 1590s. Its ill effects on agriculture in northern Europe were notable.   *(p. 460)*

llama   A hoofed animal indigenous to the Andes Mountains in South America. It was the only domesticated beast of burden in the Americas before the arrival of Europeans. It provided meat and wool. The use of llamas to transport goods made possible specialized production and trade among people living in different ecological zones and fostered the integration of these zones by **Chavín** and later Andean states.   *(p. 77)*

loess   A fine, light silt deposited by wind and water. It constitutes the fertile soil of the Yellow River Valley in northern China. Because loess soil is not compacted, it can be worked with a simple digging stick, but it leaves the region vulnerable to devastating earthquakes.   *(p. 58)*

Long March (1934–1935)   The 6,000-mile (9,600-kilometer) flight of Chinese Communists from southeastern to northwestern China. The Communists, led by **Mao Zedong,** were pursued by the Chinese army under orders from **Chiang Kai-shek.** The four thousand survivors of the march formed the nucleus of a revived Communist movement that defeated the **Guomindang** after World War II.   *(p. 816)*

L'Ouverture, François Dominique Toussaint (1743–1803)   Leader of the Haitian Revolution. He freed the slaves and gained effective independence for Haiti despite military interventions by the British and French.   *(p. 601)*

ma'at   Egyptian term for the concept of divinely created and maintained order in the universe. Reflecting the ancient Egyptians' belief in an essentially beneficent world, the divine ruler was the earthly guarantor of this order. (See also **pyramid.**)   *(p. 43)*

Macartney mission (1792–1793)   The unsuccessful attempt by the British Empire to establish diplomatic relations with the **Qing Empire.**   *(p. 564)*

Magellan, Ferdinand (1480?–1521)   Portuguese navigator who led the Spanish expedition of 1519–1522 that was the first to sail around the world.   *(p. 431)*

Mahabharata   A vast epic chronicling the events leading up to a cataclysmic battle between related kinship groups in early India. It includes the Bhagavad-Gita, the most important work of Indian sacred literature.   *(p. 190)*

Mahayana Buddhism   "Great Vehicle" branch of Buddhism followed in China, Japan, and Central Asia. The focus is on reverence for **Buddha** and for bodhisattvas, enlightened persons who have postponed nirvana to help others attain enlightenment.   *(p. 185)*

Malacca   Port city in the modern Southeast Asian country of Malaysia, founded about 1400 as a trading center on the Strait of Malacca. Also spelled Melaka.   *(p. 385)*

Malay peoples   A designation for peoples originating in south China and Southeast Asia who settled the Malay Peninsula, Indonesia, and the Philippines, then spread eastward across the islands of the Pacific Ocean and west to Madagascar.   *(p. 196)*

Mali   Empire created by indigenous Muslims in western Sudan of West Africa from the thirteenth to fifteenth century. It was famous for its role in the trans-Saharan gold trade. (See also **Mansa Kankan Musa** and **Timbuktu.**)   *(p. 372)*

Malthus, Thomas (1766–1834)   Eighteenth-century English intellectual who warned that population growth threatened future generations because, in his view, population growth would always outstrip increases in agricultural production.   *(p. 902)*

Mamluks   Under the Islamic system of military slavery, Turkic military slaves who formed an important part of the armed forces of the **Abbasid Caliphate** of the ninth and tenth centuries. Mamluks eventually founded their own state, ruling Egypt and Syria (1250–1517).   *(p. 239)*

Manchu   Federation of Northeast Asian peoples who founded the **Qing Empire.**   *(p. 551)*

Mandate of Heaven   Chinese religious and political ideology developed by the **Zhou,** according to which it was the prerogative of Heaven, the chief deity, to grant power to the ruler of China and to take away that power if the ruler failed to conduct himself justly and in the best interests of his subjects.   *(p. 61)*

mandate system   Allocation of former German colonies and Ottoman possessions to the victorious powers after World War I, to be administered under League of Nations supervision.   *(p. 792)*

manor   In medieval Europe, a large, self-sufficient landholding consisting of the lord's residence (manor house), outbuildings, peasant village, and surrounding land.   *(p. 262)*

mansabs   In India, grants of land given in return for service by rulers of the **Mughal Empire.**   *(p. 542)*

Mansa Kankan Musa   Ruler of Mali (r. 1312–1337). His pilgrimage through Egypt to **Mecca** in 1324–1325 established the empire's reputation for wealth in the Mediterranean world.   *(p. 372)*

manumission   A grant of legal freedom to an individual slave.   *(p. 509)*

Mao Zedong (1893–1976)   Leader of the Chinese Communist Party (1927–1976). He led the Communists on the **Long March** (1934–1935) and rebuilt the Communist Party and Red Army during the Japanese occupation of China (1937–1945). After World War II, he led the Communists to victory over the **Guomindang.** He ordered the **Cultural Revolution** in 1966.   *(p. 815)*

maroon   A slave who ran away from his or her master. Often a member of a community of runaway slaves in the West Indies and South America.   *(p. 509)*

Marshall Plan   U. S. program to support the reconstruction of western Europe after World War II. By 1961 more than $20 billion in economic aid had been dispersed. *(p. 863)*

Marx, Karl (1818–1883)   German journalist and philosopher, founder of the Marxist branch of **socialism.** He is known for two books: *The Communist Manifesto* (1848) and *Das Kapital* (Vols. I–III, 1867–1894).   *(p. 732)*

mass deportation   The forcible removal and relocation of large numbers of people or entire populations. The mass deportations practiced by the Assyrian and Persian Empires were meant as a terrifying warning of the consequences of rebellion. They also brought skilled and unskilled labor to the imperial center.   *(p. 95)*

mass production   The manufacture of many identical products by the division of labor into many small repetitive tasks. This method was introduced into the manufacture of pottery by Josiah Wedgwood and into the spinning of cotton thread by Richard Arkwright. (See also **Arkwright, Richard; Industrial Revolution; Wedgwood, Josiah.**) (*p. 614*)

Mauryan Empire   The first state to unify most of the Indian subcontinent. It was founded by Chandragupta Maurya in 324 B.C.E. and survived until 184 B.C.E. From its capital at Pataliputra in the Ganges Valley it grew wealthy from taxes on agriculture, iron mining, and control of trade routes. (See also **Ashoka.**)   (*p. 188*)

Maya   Mesoamerican civilization concentrated in Mexico's Yucatán Peninsula and in Guatemala and Honduras but never unified into a single empire. Major contributions were in mathematics, astronomy, and development of the calendar.   (*p. 310*)

Mecca   City in western Arabia; birthplace of the Prophet **Muhammad,** and ritual center of the Islamic religion. (*p. 234*)

mechanization   The application of machinery to manufacturing and other activities. Among the first processes to be mechanized were the spinning of cotton thread and the weaving of cloth in late-eighteenth- and early-nineteenth-century England.   (*p. 615*)

medieval   Literally "middle age," a term that historians of Europe use for the period ca. 500 to ca. 1500, signifying its intermediate point between Greco-Roman antiquity and the Renaissance.   (*p. 254*)

Medina   City in western Arabia to which the Prophet Muhammad and his followers emigrated in 622 to escape persecution in Mecca.   (*p. 235*)

megaliths   Structures and complexes of very large stones constructed for ceremonial and religious purposes in **Neolithic** times.   (*p. 23*)

Meiji Restoration   The political program that followed the destruction of the **Tokugawa Shogunate** in 1868, in which a collection of young leaders set Japan on the path of centralization, industrialization, and imperialism. (See also **Yamagata Aritomo.**)   (*p. 744*)

Memphis   The capital of Old Kingdom Egypt, near the head of the Nile Delta. Early rulers were interred in the nearby **pyramids.**   (*p. 43*)

Menelik II (1844–1911)   Emperor of Ethiopia (r. 1889–1911). He enlarged Ethiopia to its present dimensions and defeated an Italian invasion at Adowa (1896).   (*p. 759*)

mercantilism   European government policies of the sixteenth, seventeenth, and eighteenth centuries designed to promote overseas trade between a country and its colonies and accumulate precious metals by requiring colonies to trade only with their motherland country. The British system was defined by the Navigation Acts, the French system by laws known as the *Exclusif.*   (*p. 627*)

Meroë   Capital of a flourishing kingdom in southern Nubia from the fourth century B.C.E. to the fourth century C.E. In this period Nubian culture shows more independence from Egypt and the influence of sub-Saharan Africa.   (*p. 69*)

mestizo   The term used by Spanish authorities to describe someone of mixed Amerindian and European descent. (*p. 487*)

Middle Passage   The part of the **Atlantic Circuit** involving the transportation of enslaved Africans across the Atlantic to the Americas.   (*p. 511*)

millenarianism   Beliefs, based on prophetic revelations, in apocalyptic global transformations associated with the completion of cycles of a thousand years.   (*p. 930*)

Ming Empire (1368–1644)   Empire based in China that Zhu Yuanzhang established after the overthrow of the **Yuan Empire.** The Ming emperor **Yongle** sponsored the building of the Forbidden City and the voyages of **Zheng He.** The later years of the Ming saw a slowdown in technological development and economic decline.   (*pp. 354, 557*)

Minoan   Prosperous civilization on the Aegean island of Crete in the second millennium B.C.E. The Minoans engaged in far-flung commerce around the Mediterranean and exerted powerful cultural influences on the early Greeks.   (*p. 88*)

mit'a   Andean labor system based on shared obligations to help kinsmen and work on behalf of the ruler and religious organizations.   (*p. 321*)

Moche   Civilization of north coast of Peru (200–700 C.E.). An important Andean civilization that built extensive irrigation networks as well as impressive urban centers dominated by brick temples.   (*p. 322*)

Moctezuma II (1466?–1520)   Last Aztec emperor, overthrown by the Spanish conquistador Hernán Cortés.   (*p. 436*)

modernization   The process of reforming political, military, economic, social, and cultural traditions in imitation of the early success of Western societies, often with regard for accommodating local traditions in non-Western societies.   (*p. 668*)

Mohenjo-Daro   Largest of the cities of the Indus Valley civilization. It was centrally located in the extensive flood-plain of the Indus River in contemporary Pakistan. Little is known about the political institutions of Indus Valley communities, but the large-scale of construction at Mohenjo-Daro, the orderly grid of streets, and the standardization of building materials are evidence of central planning.   (*p. 49*)

moksha   The Hindu concept of the spirit's "liberation" from the endless cycle of rebirths. There are various avenues—such as physical discipline, meditation, and acts of devotion to the gods—by which the spirit can distance itself from desire for the things of this world and be merged with the divine force that animates the universe.   (*p. 184*)

monasticism   Living in a religious community apart from secular society and adhering to a rule stipulating chastity, obedience, and poverty. It was a prominent element of medieval Christianity and Buddhism. Monasteries were the primary centers of learning and literacy in medieval Europe.   (*p. 268*)

Mongols   A people of this name is mentioned as early as the records of the **Tang Empire,** living as nomads in northern Eurasia. After 1206 they established an enormous empire under **Genghis Khan,** linking western and eastern Eurasia.   (*p. 337*)

monotheism   Belief in the existence of a single divine entity. Some scholars cite the devotion of the Egyptian pharaoh **Akhenaten** to Aten (sun-disk) and his suppression of traditional gods as the earliest instance. The Israelite worship of Yahweh developed into an exclusive belief in one god, and this concept passed into Christianity and Islam.   (*p. 101*)

monsoon   Seasonal winds in the Indian Ocean caused by the differences in temperature between the rapidly heating and cooling landmasses of Africa and Asia and the slowly changing ocean waters. These strong and predictable winds have long been ridden across the open sea by sailors, and the large amounts of rainfall that they deposit on parts of India, Southeast Asia, and China allow for the cultivation of several crops a year. (*pp. 180, 368*)

Morelos, José María (1765–1814) Mexican priest and former student of Miguel Hidalgo y Costilla, he led the forces fighting for Mexican independence until he was captured and executed in 1814. (See also **Hidalgo y Costilla, Miguel.**) (*p. 638*)

most-favored-nation status A clause in a commercial treaty that awards to any later signatories all the privileges previously granted to the original signatories. (*p. 709*)

movable type Type in which each individual character is cast on a separate piece of metal. It replaced woodblock printing, allowing for the arrangement of individual letters and other characters on a page, rather than requiring the carving of entire pages at a time. It may have been invented in Korea in the thirteenth century. (See also **printing press.**) (*p. 297*)

Mughal Empire Muslim state (1526–1857) exercising dominion over most of India in the sixteenth and seventeenth centuries. (*p. 541*)

Muhammad (570–632 C.E.) Arab prophet; founder of religion of Islam. (*p. 234*)

Muhammad Ali (1769–1849) Leader of Egyptian modernization in the early nineteenth century. He ruled Egypt as an Ottoman governor, but had imperial ambitions. His descendants ruled Egypt until overthrown in 1952. (*p. 668*)

mulatto The term used in Spanish and Portuguese colonies to describe someone of mixed African and European descent. (*p. 488*)

mummy A body preserved by chemical processes or special natural circumstances, often in the belief that the deceased will need it again in the afterlife. In ancient Egypt the bodies of people who could afford mummification underwent a complex process of removing organs, filling body cavities, dehydrating the corpse with natron, and then wrapping the body with linen bandages and enclosing it in a wooden sarcophagus. (*p. 48*)

Muscovy Russian principality that emerged gradually during the era of Mongol domination. The Muscovite dynasty ruled without interruption from 1276 to 1598. (*p. 566*)

Muslim An adherent of the Islamic religion; a person who "submits" (in Arabic, *Islam* means "submission") to the will of God. (*p. 566*)

Mussolini, Benito (1883–1945) Fascist dictator of Italy (1922–1943). He led Italy to conquer Ethiopia (1935), joined Germany in the Axis pact (1936), and allied Italy with Germany in World War II. He was overthrown in 1943 when the Allies invaded Italy. (*p. 821*)

Mycenae Site of a fortified palace complex in southern Greece that controlled a Late Bronze Age kingdom. In Homer's epic poems Mycenae was the base of King Agamemnon, who commanded the Greeks besieging Troy. Contemporary archaeologists call the complex Greek society of the second millennium B.C.E. "Mycenaean." (*p. 90*)

Napoleon I (1769–1832) Overthrew French Directory in 1799 and became emperor of the French in 1804. Failed to defeat Great Britain and abdicated in 1814. Returned to power briefly in 1815 but was defeated and died in exile. (*p. 597*)

Nasir al-Din Tusi (1201–1274) Persian mathematician and cosmologist whose academy near Tabriz provided the model for the movement of the planets that helped to inspire the Copernican model of the solar system. (*p. 347*)

National Assembly French Revolutionary assembly (1789–1791). Called first as the Estates General, the three estates came together and demanded radical change. It passed the **Declaration of the Rights of Man** in 1789. (*p. 594*)

nationalism A political ideology that stresses people's membership in a nation—a community defined by a common culture and history as well as by territory. In the late eighteenth and early nineteenth centuries, nationalism was a force for unity in western Europe. In the late nineteenth century it hastened the disintegration of the Austro-Hungarian and Ottoman Empires. In the twentieth century it provided the ideological foundation for scores of independent countries emerging from **colonialism.** (*p. 733*)

nawab A Muslim prince allied to British India; technically, a semi-autonomous deputy of the Mughal emperor. (*p. 671*)

Nazis German political party joined by Adolf Hitler, emphasizing nationalism, racism, and war. When Hitler became chancellor of Germany in 1933, the Nazis became the only legal party and an instrument of Hitler's absolute rule. The party's formal name was National Socialist German Workers' Party. (See also **Hitler, Adolf.**) (*p. 813*)

Nehru, Jawaharlal (1889–1964) Indian statesman. He succeeded Mohandas K. Gandhi as leader of the **Indian National Congress.** He negotiated the end of British colonial rule in India and became India's first prime minister (1947–1964). (*p. 842*)

Neo-Assyrian Empire An empire extending from western Iran to Syria-Palestine, conquered by the Assyrians of northern Mesopotamia between the tenth and seventh centuries B.C.E. They used force and terror and exploited the wealth and labor of their subjects. They also preserved and continued the cultural and scientific developments of Mesopotamian civilization. (*p. 93*)

Neo-Babylonian kingdom Under the Chaldaeans (nomadic kinship groups that settled in southern Mesopotamia in the early first millennium B.C.E.), **Babylon** again became a major political and cultural center in the seventh and sixth centuries B.C.E. After participating in the destruction of Assyrian power, the monarchs Nabopolassar and Nebuchadnezzar took over the southern portion of the Assyrian domains. By destroying the **First Temple** in Jerusalem and deporting part of the population, they initiated the **Diaspora** of the Jews. (*p. 110*)

neo-Confucianism Term used to describe new approaches to understanding classic Confucian texts that became the basic ruling philosophy of China from the **Song** period to the twentieth century. (*p. 296*)

neo-liberalism The term used in Latin America and other developing regions to describe free-market policies that include reducing tariff protection for local industries; the sale of public-sector industries, like national airlines and public utilities, to private investors or foreign corporations;

and the reduction of social welfare policies and public-sector employment. (*p. 894*)

Neolithic   The period of the Stone Age associated with the ancient **Agricultural Revolution(s). It** follows the **Paleolithic** period. (*p. 12*)

Nevskii, Alexander (1220–1263)   Prince of Novgorod (r. 1236–1263). He submitted to the invading Mongols in 1240 and received recognition as the leader of the Russian princes under the **Golden Horde.** (*p. 349*)

New Economic Policy   Policy proclaimed by Vladimir Lenin in 1924 to encourage the revival of the Soviet economy by allowing small private enterprises. Joseph Stalin ended the N.E.P. in 1928 and replaced it with a series of **Five-Year Plans.** (See also **Lenin, Vladimir.**) (*p. 788*)

New France   French colony in North America, with a capital in Quebec, founded 1608. New France fell to the British in 1763. (*p. 493*)

New Imperialism   Historians' term for the late-nineteenth- and early-twentieth-century wave of conquests by European powers, the United States, and Japan, which were followed by the development and exploitation of the newly conquered territories for the benefit of the colonial powers. (*p. 749*)

newly industrialized economies (NIEs)   Rapidly growing, new industrial nations of the late twentieth century, including the **Asian Tigers.** (*p. 897*)

new monarchies   Historians' term for the monarchies in France, England, and Spain from 1450 to 1600. The centralization of royal power was increasing within more or less fixed territorial limits. (*p. 413*)

nomadism   A way of life, forced by a scarcity of resources, in which groups of people continually migrate to find pastures and water. (*p. 337*)

nonaligned nations   Developing countries that announced their neutrality in the **Cold War.** (*p. 861*)

nongovernmental organizations (NGOs)   Nonprofit international organizations devoted to investigating human rights abuses and providing humanitarian relief. Two NGOs won the Nobel Peace Prize in the 1990s: International Campaign to Ban Landmines (1997) and Doctors Without Borders (1999). (*p. 934*)

North Atlantic Treaty Organization (NATO)   Organization formed in 1949 as a military alliance of western European and North American states against the Soviet Union and its east European allies. (See also **Warsaw Pact.**) (*p. 862*)

Olmec   The first Mesoamerican civilization. Between ca. 1200 and 400 B.C.E., the Olmec people of central Mexico created a vibrant civilization that included intensive agriculture, wide-ranging trade, ceremonial centers, and monumental construction. The Olmec had great cultural influence on later Mesoamerican societies, passing on artistic styles, religious imagery, sophisticated astronomical observation for the construction of calendars, and a ritual ball game. (*p. 75*)

Oman   Arab state based in Musqat, the main port in the southwest region of the Arabian peninsula. Oman succeeded Portugal as a power in the western Indian Ocean in the eighteenth century. (*p. 547*)

Opium War (1839–1842)   War between Britain and the **Qing Empire** that was, in the British view, occasioned by the Qing government's refusal to permit the importation of opium into its territories. The victorious British imposed the one-sided **Treaty of Nanking** on China. (*p. 708*)

Organization of Petroleum Exporting Countries (OPEC)   Organization formed in 1960 by oil-producing states to promote their collective interest in generating revenue from oil. (*p. 884*)

Ottoman Empire   Islamic state founded by Osman in north-western Anatolia ca. 1300. After the fall of the **Byzantine Empire,** the Ottoman Empire was based at Istanbul (formerly Constantinople) from 1453 to 1922. It encompassed lands in the Middle East, North Africa, the Caucasus, and eastern Europe. (*pp. 351, 526*)

Páez, José Antonio (1790–1873)   Venezuelan soldier who led Simón Bolívar's cavalry force. He became a successful general in the war and built a powerful political base. He was unwilling to accept the constitutional authority of Bolívar's government in distant Bogotá and declared Venezuela's independence from Gran Colombia in 1829. (*p. 643*)

Paleolithic   The period of the Stone Age associated with the **evolution** of humans. It predates the **Neolithic** period. (*p. 12*)

Pan-Slavism   Movement among Russian intellectuals in the second half of the nineteenth century to identify culturally and politically with the Slavic peoples of eastern Europe. (*p. 705*)

Panama Canal   Ship canal cut across the isthmus of Panama by United States Army engineers; it opened in 1915. It greatly shortened the sea voyage between the east and west coasts of North America. The United States turned the canal over to Panama on January 1, 2000. (*p. 771*)

papacy   The central administration of the Roman Catholic Church, of which the pope is the head. (*pp. 267, 450*)

papyrus   A reed that grows along the banks of the Nile River in Egypt. From it was produced a coarse, paperlike writing medium used by the Egyptians and many other peoples in the ancient Mediterranean and Middle East. (*p. 44*)

Parthians   Iranian ruling dynasty between ca. 250 B.C.E. and 226 C.E. (*p. 211*)

patron/client relationship   In ancient Rome, a fundamental social relationship in which the patron—a wealthy and powerful individual—provided legal and economic protection and assistance to clients, men of lesser status and means, and in return the clients supported the political careers and economic interests of their patron. (*p. 155*)

Paul (ca. 5–65 C.E.)   A Jew from the Greek city of Tarsus in Anatolia, he initially persecuted the followers of Jesus but, after receiving a revelation on the road to Syrian Damascus, became a Christian. Taking advantage of his Hellenized background and Roman citizenship, he traveled throughout Syria-Palestine, Anatolia, and Greece, preaching the new religion and establishing churches. Finding his greatest success among pagans ("gentiles"), he began the process by which Christianity separated from Judaism. (*p. 162*)

pax romana   Literally, "Roman peace," it connoted the stability and prosperity that Roman rule brought to the lands of the Roman Empire in the first two centuries C.E. The movement of people and trade goods along Roman roads and safe seas allowed for the spread of cultural practices, technologies, and religious ideas. (*p. 161*)

Pearl Harbor Naval base in Hawaii attacked by Japanese aircraft on December 7, 1941. The sinking of much of the U.S. Pacific Fleet brought the United States into World War II. (*p. 821*)

Peloponnesian War A protracted (431–404 B.C.E.) and costly conflict between the Athenian and Spartan alliance systems that convulsed most of the Greek world. The war was largely a consequence of Athenian imperialism. Possession of a naval empire allowed Athens to fight a war of attrition. Ultimately, Sparta prevailed because of Athenian errors and Persian financial support. (*p. 142*)

perestroika Policy of "openness" that was the centerpiece of Mikhail Gorbachev's efforts to liberalize communism in the Soviet Union. (See also **Gorbachev, Mikhail**.) (*p. 898*)

Pericles (ca. 495–429 B.C.E.) Aristocratic leader who guided the Athenian state through the transformation to full participatory democracy for all male citizens, supervised construction of the Acropolis, and pursued a policy of imperial expansion that led to the **Peloponnesian War.** He formulated a strategy of attrition but died from the plague early in the war. (*p. 138*)

Perón, Eva Duarte (1919–1952) Wife of **Juan Perón** and champion of the poor in Argentina. She was a gifted speaker and popular political leader who campaigned to improve the life of the urban poor by founding schools and hospitals and providing other social benefits. (*p. 852*)

Perón, Juan (1895–1974) President of Argentina (1946–1955, 1973–1974). As a military officer, he championed the rights of labor. Aided by his wife **Eva Duarte Perón,** he was elected president in 1946. He built up Argentinean industry, became very popular among the urban poor, but harmed the economy. (*p. 852*)

Persepolis A complex of palaces, reception halls, and treasury buildings erected by the Persian kings **Darius I** and Xerxes in the Persian homeland. It is believed that the New Year's festival was celebrated here, as well as the coronations, weddings, and funerals of the Persian kings, who were buried in cliff-tombs nearby. (*p. 124*)

Persian Wars Conflicts between Greek city-states and the Persian Empire, ranging from the Ionian Revolt (499–494 B.C.E.) through Darius's punitive expedition that failed at Marathon (490 B.C.E.) and the defeat of Xerxes' massive invasion of Greece by the Spartan-led Hellenic League (480–479 B.C.E.). This first major setback for Persian arms launched the Greeks into their period of greatest cultural productivity. **Herodotus** chronicled these events in the first "history" in the Western tradition. (*p. 138*)

personalist leaders Political leaders who rely on charisma and their ability to mobilize and direct the masses of citizens outside the authority of constitutions and laws. Nineteenth-century examples include José Antonio Páez of Venezuela and Andrew Jackson of the United States. Twentieth-century examples include Getulio Vargas of Brazil and Juan Perón of Argentina. (See also **Jackson, Andrew; Páez, José Antonio; Perón, Juan; Vargas, Getulio**.) (*p. 643*)

Peter the Great (1672–1725) Russian tsar (r. 1689–1725). He enthusiastically introduced Western languages and technologies to the Russian elite, moving the capital from Moscow to the new city of St. Petersburg. (*p. 569*)

pharaoh The central figure in the ancient Egyptian state. Believed to be an earthly manifestation of the gods, he used his absolute power to maintain the safety and prosperity of Egypt. (*p. 43*)

Phoenicians Semitic-speaking Canaanites living on the coast of modern Lebanon and Syria in the first millennium B.C.E. From major cities such as Tyre and Sidon, Phoenician merchants and sailors explored the Mediterranean, engaged in widespread commerce, and founded **Carthage** and other colonies in the western Mediterranean. (*p. 104*)

pilgrimage Journey to a sacred shrine by Christians seeking to show their piety, fulfill vows, or gain absolution for sins. Other religions also have pilgrimage traditions, such as the Muslim pilgrimage to **Mecca** and the pilgrimages made by early Chinese Buddhists to India in search of sacred Buddhist writings. (*p. 276*)

Pilgrims Group of English Protestant dissenters who established Plymouth Colony in Massachusetts in 1620 to seek religious freedom after having lived briefly in the Netherlands. (*p. 490*)

Pizarro, Francisco (1475?–1541) Spanish explorer who led the conquest of the **Inca** Empire of Peru in 1531–1533. (*p. 440*)

Planck, Max (1858–1947) German physicist who developed quantum theory and was awarded the Nobel Prize for physics in 1918. (*p. 800*)

plantocracy In the West Indian colonies, the rich men who owned most of the slaves and most of the land, especially in the eighteenth century. (*p. 505*)

polis The Greek term for a **city-state,** an urban center and the agricultural territory under its control. It was the characteristic form of political organization in southern and central Greece in the Archaic and Classical periods. Of the hundreds of city-states in the Mediterranean and Black Sea regions settled by Greeks, some were oligarchic, others democratic, depending on the powers delegated to the Council and the Assembly. (*p. 132*)

pop culture Entertainment spread by mass communications and enjoying wide appeal. (*p. 938*)

positivism A philosophy developed by the French count of Saint-Simon. Positivists believed that social and economic problems could be solved by the application of the scientific method, leading to continuous progress. Their ideas became popular in France and Latin America in the nineteenth century. (*p. 628*)

Potosí Located in Bolivia, one of the richest silver mining centers and most populous cities in colonial Spanish America. (*p. 480*)

printing press A mechanical device for transferring text or graphics from a woodblock or type to paper using ink. Presses using movable type first appeared in Europe in about 1450. See also **movable type.** (*p. 409*)

Protestant Reformation Religious reform movement within the Latin Christian Church beginning in 1519. It resulted in the "protesters" forming several new Christian denominations, including the Lutheran and Reformed Churches and the Church of England.   (*p. 450*)

proxy wars   During the **Cold War,** local or regional wars in which the superpowers armed, trained, and financed the combatants.   (*p. 888*)

Ptolemies   The Macedonian dynasty, descended from one of Alexander the Great's officers, that ruled Egypt for three centuries (323–30 B.C.E.). From their magnificent capital at Alexandria on the Mediterranean coast, the Ptolemies largely took over the system created by Egyptian pharaohs to extract the wealth of the land, rewarding Greeks and Hellenized non-Greeks serving in the military and administration.   (*p. 145*)

Puritans   English Protestant dissenters who believed that God predestined souls to heaven or hell before birth. They founded Massachusetts Bay Colony in 1629.   (*p. 490*)

pyramid   A large, triangular stone monument, used in Egypt and Nubia as a burial place for the king. The largest pyramids, erected during the Old Kingdom near Memphis with stone tools and compulsory labor, reflect the Egyptian belief that the proper and spectacular burial of the divine ruler would guarantee the continued prosperity of the land. (See also **ma'at**.)   (*p. 43*)

Qin   A people and state in the Wei Valley of eastern China that conquered rival states and created the first Chinese empire (221–206 B.C.E.). The Qin ruler, **Shi Huangdi,** standardized many features of Chinese society and ruthlessly marshaled subjects for military and construction projects, engendering hostility that led to the fall of his dynasty shortly after his death. The Qin framework was largely taken over by the succeeding **Han** Empire.   (*p. 166*)

Qing Empire   Empire established in China by Manchus who overthrew the **Ming Empire** in 1644. At various times the Qing also controlled Manchuria, Mongolia, Turkestan, and Tibet. The last Qing emperor was overthrown in 1911. (*p. 558*)

Quran   Book composed of divine revelations made to the Prophet Muhammad between ca. 610 and his death in 632; the sacred text of the religion of **Islam.**   (*p. 236*)

railroads   Networks of iron (later steel) rails on which steam (later electric or diesel) locomotives pulled long trains at high speeds. The first railroads were built in England in the 1830s. Their success caused a railroad-building boom throughout the world that lasted well into the twentieth century.   (*p. 723*)

Rajputs   Members of a mainly Hindu warrior caste from northwest India. The Mughal emperors drew most of their Hindu officials from this caste, and **Akbar I** married a Rajput princess.   (*p. 542*)

Ramesses II   A long-lived ruler of New Kingdom Egypt (r. 1290–1224 B.C.E.). He reached an accommodation with the **Hittites** of Anatolia after a standoff in battle at Kadesh in Syria. He built on a grand scale throughout Egypt.   (*p. 87*)

Rashid al-Din (d.1318)   Adviser to the **Il-khan** ruler Ghazan, who converted to Islam on Rashid's advice.   (*p. 347*)

recaptives   Africans rescued by Britain's Royal Navy from the illegal slave trade of the nineteenth century and restored to free status.   (*p. 671*)

reconquest of Iberia   Beginning in the eleventh century, military campaigns by various Iberian Christian states to recapture territory taken by Muslims. In 1492 the last Muslim ruler was defeated, and Spain and Portugal emerged as united kingdoms.   (*p. 414*)

Renaissance (European)   A period of intense artistic and intellectual activity, said to be a "rebirth" of Greco-Roman culture. Usually divided into an Italian Renaissance, from roughly the mid-fourteenth to mid-fifteenth century, and a Northern (trans-Alpine) Renaissance, from roughly the early fifteenth to early seventeenth century.   (*pp. 406, 449*)

Revolutions of 1848   Democratic and nationalist revolutions that swept across Europe. The monarchy in France was overthrown. In Germany, Austria, Italy, and Hungary the revolutions failed.   (*p. 604*)

Rhodes, Cecil (1853–1902)   British entrepreneur and politician involved in the expansion of the British Empire from South Africa into Central Africa. The colonies of Southern Rhodesia (now Zimbabwe) and Northern Rhodesia (now Zambia) were named after him.   (*p. 758*)

Robespierre, Maximilien (1758–1794)   Young provincial lawyer who led the most radical phases of the French Revolution. His execution ended the Reign of Terror. See **Jacobins.**   (*p. 596*)

Romanization   The process by which the Latin language and Roman culture became dominant in the western provinces of the Roman Empire. The Roman government did not actively seek to Romanize the subject peoples, but indigenous peoples in the provinces often chose to Romanize because of the political and economic advantages that it brought, as well as the allure of Roman success.   (*p. 161*)

Roman Principate   A term used to characterize Roman government in the first three centuries C.E., based on the ambiguous title *princeps* ("first citizen") adopted by Augustus to conceal his military dictatorship.   (*p. 157*)

Roman Republic   The period from 507 to 31 B.C.E., during which Rome was largely governed by the aristocratic **Roman Senate.**   (*p. 154*)

Roman Senate   A council whose members were the heads of wealthy, landowning families. Originally an advisory body to the early kings, in the era of the **Roman Republic** the Senate effectively governed the Roman state and the growing empire. Under Senate leadership, Rome conquered an empire of unprecedented extent in the lands surrounding the Mediterranean Sea. In the first century B.C.E. quarrels among powerful and ambitious senators and failure to address social and economic problems led to civil wars and the emergence of the rule of the emperors.   (*p. 154*)

Royal African Company   A trading company chartered by the English government in 1672 to conduct its merchants' trade on the Atlantic coast of Africa.   (*p. 400*)

sacrifice   A gift given to a deity, often with the aim of creating a relationship, gaining favor, and obligating the god to provide some benefit to the sacrificer, sometimes in order to sustain the deity and thereby guarantee the continuing vitality of the natural world. The object devoted to the deity could be as simple as a cup of wine poured on the ground, a live animal slain on the altar, or, in the most extreme case, the ritual killing of a human being.   (*p. 135*)

Safavid Empire   Iranian kingdom (1502–1722) established by Ismail Safavi, who declared Iran a Shi'ite state.   (*p. 536*)

Sahel   Belt south of the Sahara; literally "coastland" in Arabic.   (*p. 220*)

samurai   Literally "those who serve," the hereditary military elite of the **Tokugawa Shogunate.**   (*p. 551*)

Sandinistas   Members of a leftist coalition that overthrew the Nicaraguan dictatorship of Anastasia Somoza in 1979 and attempted to install a socialist economy. The United States financed armed opposition by the Contras. The Sandinistas lost national elections in 1990.   (*p. 890*)

Sanger, Margaret (1883–1966)   American nurse and author; pioneer in the movement for family planning; organized conferences and established birth control clinics.   (*p. 799*)

Sasanid Empire   Iranian empire, established ca. 226, with a capital in Ctesiphon, Mesopotamia. The Sasanid emperors established **Zoroastrianism** as the state religion. Islamic Arab armies overthrew the empire ca. 640.   (*p. 230*)

satrap   The governor of a province in the Achaemenid Persian Empire, often a relative of the king. He was responsible for protection of the province and for forwarding tribute to the central administration. Satraps in outlying provinces enjoyed considerable autonomy.   (*p. 123*)

savanna   Tropical or subtropical grassland, either treeless or with occasional clumps of trees. Most extensive in **sub-Saharan Africa** but also present in South America.   (*p. 222*)

schism   A formal split within a religious community. See **Great Western Schism.**   (*p. 256*)

scholasticism   A philosophical and theological system, associated with Thomas Aquinas, devised to reconcile Aristotelian philosophy and Roman Catholic theology in the thirteenth century.   (*p. 407*)

Scientific Revolution   The intellectual movement in Europe, initially associated with planetary motion and other aspects of physics, that by the seventeenth century had laid the groundwork for modern science.   (*p. 454*)

"scramble" for Africa   Sudden wave of conquests in Africa by European powers in the 1880s and 1890s. Britain obtained most of eastern Africa, France most of northwestern Africa. Other countries (Germany, Belgium, Portugal, Italy, and Spain) acquired lesser amounts.   (*p. 755*)

scribe   In the governments of many ancient societies, a professional position reserved for men who had undergone the lengthy training required to be able to read and write using **cuneiforms, hieroglyphics,** or other early, cumbersome writing systems.   (*p. 35*)

seasoning   An often difficult period of adjustment to new climates, disease environments, and work routines, such as that experienced by slaves newly arrived in the Americas.   (*p. 508*)

Selassie, Haile (1892–1975)   Emperor of Ethiopia (r. 1930–1974) and symbol of African independence. He fought the Italian invasion of his country in 1935 and regained his throne during World War II, when British forces expelled the Italians. He ruled **Ethiopia** as a traditional autocracy until he was overthrown in 1974.   (*p. 838*)

Semitic   Family of related languages long spoken across parts of western Asia and northern Africa. In antiquity these languages included Hebrew, Aramaic, and Phoenician. The most widespread modern member of the Semitic family is Arabic.   (*p. 32*)

"separate spheres"   Nineteenth-century idea in Western societies that men and women, especially of the middle class, should have clearly differentiated roles in society: women as wives, mothers, and homemakers; men as breadwinners and participants in business and politics.   (*p. 730*)

sepoy   A soldier in South Asia, especially in the service of the British.   (*p. 673*)

Sepoy Rebellion   The revolt of Indian soldiers in 1857 against certain practices that violated religious customs; also known as the Sepoy Mutiny.   (*p. 676*)

Serbia   The Ottoman province in the Balkans that rose up against **Janissary** control in the early 1800s. After World War II the central province of Yugoslavia. Serb leaders struggled to maintain dominance as the Yugoslav federation dissolved in the 1990s.   (*p. 693*)

serf   In medieval Europe, an agricultural laborer legally bound to a lord's property and obligated to perform set services for the lord. In Russia some serfs worked as artisans and in factories; serfdom was not abolished there until 1861.   (*pp. 262, 569*)

shaft graves   A term used for the burial sites of elite members of Mycenaean Greek society in the mid-second millennium B.C.E. At the bottom of deep shafts lined with stone slabs, the bodies were laid out along with gold and bronze jewelry, implements, weapons, and masks.   (*p. 90*)

Shah Abbas I (r. 1587–1629)   The fifth and most renowned ruler of the **Safavid** dynasty in Iran. Abbas moved the royal capital to Isfahan in 1598.   (*p. 538*)

shamanism   The practice of identifying special individuals (shamans) who will interact with spirits for the benefit of the community. Characteristic of the Korean kingdoms of the early medieval period and of early societies of Central Asia.   (*p. 300*)

Shang   The dominant people in the earliest Chinese dynasty for which we have written records (ca. 1750–1027 B.C.E.). Ancestor worship, divination by means of oracle bones, and the use of bronze vessels for ritual purposes were major elements of Shang culture.   (*p. 60*)

Shi Huangdi   Founder of the short-lived **Qin** dynasty and creator of the Chinese Empire (r. 221–210 B.C.E.). He is remembered for his ruthless conquests of rival states, standardization of practices, and forcible organization of labor for military and engineering tasks. His tomb, with its army of life-size terracotta soldiers, has been partially excavated.   (*p. 166*)

Shi'ites   Muslims belonging to the branch of Islam believing that God vests leadership of the community in a descendant of Muhammad's son-in-law Ali. Shi'ism is the state religion of Iran. (See also **Sunnis.**)   (*pp. 230, 537*)

Siberia   The extreme northeastern sector of Asia, including the Kamchatka Peninsula and the present Russian coast of the Arctic Ocean, the Bering Strait, and the Sea of Okhotsk.   (*p. 567*)

Sikhism   Indian religion founded by the guru Nanak (1469–1539) in the Punjab region of northwest India. After the Mughal emperor ordered the beheading of the ninth guru in 1675, Sikh warriors mounted armed resistance to Mughal rule.   (*p. 543*)

Silk Road   Caravan routes connecting China and the Middle East across Central Asia and Iran.   (*p. 209*)

Slavophiles   Russian intellectuals in the early nineteenth century who favored resisting western European influences and taking pride in the traditional peasant values and institutions of the Slavic people.   (*p. 705*)

"small traditions"   Historians' term for a localized, usually nonliterate, set of customs and beliefs adhered to by a single society, often in conjunction with a **"great tradition."**   (*p. 222*)

socialism   A political ideology that originated in Europe in the 1830s. Socialists advocated government protection of workers from exploitation by property owners and government ownership of industries. This ideology led to the founding of socialist or labor parties throughout Europe in the second half of the nineteenth century. (See also **Marx, Karl.**)   (*p. 732*)

Socrates   Athenian philosopher (ca. 470–399 B.C.E.) who shifted the emphasis of philosophical investigation from questions of natural science to ethics and human behavior. He attracted young disciples from elite families but made enemies by revealing the ignorance and pretensions of others, culminating in his trial and execution by the Athenian state.   (*p. 140*)

Sokoto Caliphate   A large Muslim state founded in 1809 in what is now northern Nigeria.   (*p. 667*)

Solidarity   Polish trade union created in 1980 to protest working conditions and political repression. It began the nationalist opposition to communist rule that led in 1989 to the fall of communism in eastern Europe.   (*p. 899*)

Song Empire   Empire in central and southern China (960–1126) while the Liao people controlled the north. Empire in southern China (1127–1279; the "Southern Song") while the Jin people controlled the north. Distinguished for its advances in technology, medicine, astronomy, and mathematics.   (*p. 292*)

Songhai   A people, language, kingdom, and empire in western Sudan in West Africa. At its height in the sixteenth century, the Muslim Songhai Empire stretched from the Atlantic to the land of the **Hausa** and was a major player in the trans-Saharan trade.   (*p. 519*)

Srivijaya   A state based on the Indonesian island of Sumatra, between the seventh and eleventh centuries C.E. It amassed wealth and power by a combination of selective adaptation of Indian technologies and concepts, control of the lucrative trade routes between India and China, and skillful showmanship and diplomacy in holding together a disparate realm of inland and coastal territories. (See also **theater-state.**)   (*p. 198*)

Stalin, Joseph (1879–1953)   Bolshevik revolutionary, head of the Soviet Communist Party after 1924, and dictator of the Soviet Union from 1928 to 1953. He led the Soviet Union with an iron fist, using **Five-Year Plans** to increase industrial production and terror to crush all opposition.   (*p. 805*)

Stalingrad   City in Russia, site of a Red Army victory over the German army in 1942–1943. The Battle of Stalingrad was the turning point in the war between Germany and the Soviet Union. Today Volgograd.   (*p. 819*)

Stanley, Henry Morton (1841–1904)   British-American explorer of Africa, famous for his expeditions in search of Dr. David Livingstone. Stanley helped King **Leopold II** establish the Congo Free State.   (*p. 755*)

steam engine   A machine that turns the energy released by burning fuel into motion. Thomas Newcomen built the first crude but workable steam engine in 1712. **James Watt** vastly improved his device in the 1760s and 1770s. Steam power was later applied to moving machinery in factories and to powering ships and locomotives.   (*p. 618*)

steel   A form of iron that is both durable and flexible. It was first mass-produced in the 1860s and quickly became the most widely used metal in construction, machinery, and railroad equipment.   (*p. 724*)

steppes   Treeless plains, especially the high, flat expanses of northern Eurasia, which usually have little rain and are covered with coarse grass. They are good lands for nomads and their herds. Living on the steppes promoted the breeding of horses and the development of military skills that were essential to the rise of the Mongol Empire.   (*p. 222*)

stirrup   Device for securing a horseman's feet, enabling him to wield weapons more effectively. First evidence of the use of stirrups was among the Kushan people of northern Afghanistan in approximately the first century C.E.   (*p. 213*)

stock exchange   A place where shares in a company or business enterprise are bought and sold.   (*p. 459*)

Stone Age   The historical period characterized by the production of tools from stone and other nonmetallic substances. It was followed in some places by the Bronze Age and more generally by the Iron Age.   (*p. 11*)

submarine telegraph cables   Insulated copper cables laid along the bottom of a sea or ocean for telegraphic communication. The first short cable was laid across the English Channel in 1851; the first successful transatlantic cable was laid in 1866. (See also **electric telegraph.**)   (*p. 724*)

sub-Saharan Africa   Portion of the African continent lying south of the Sahara.   (*p. 222*)

Suez Canal   Ship canal dug across the isthmus of Suez in Egypt, designed by Ferdinand de Lesseps. It opened to shipping in 1869 and shortened the sea voyage between Europe and Asia. Its strategic importance led to the British conquest of Egypt in 1882.   (*p. 749*)

Suleiman the Magnificent (1494–1566)   The most illustrious sultan of the **Ottoman Empire** (r. 1520–1566); also known as Suleiman Kanuni, "The Lawgiver." He significantly expanded the empire in the Balkans and eastern Mediterranean.   (*p. 528*)

Sumerians   The people who dominated southern Mesopotamia through the end of the third millennium B.C.E. They were responsible for the creation of many fundamental elements of Mesopotamian culture—such as irrigation technology, **cuneiform,** and religious conceptions—taken over by their **Semitic** successors.   (*p. 31*)

Sunnis   Muslims belonging to branch of Islam believing that the community should select its own leadership. The majority religion in most Islamic countries. (See also **Shi'ites.**)   (*p. 230*)

Sun Yat-sen (1867–1925)   Chinese nationalist revolutionary, founder and leader of the **Guomindang** until his death. He attempted to create a liberal democratic political movement in China but was thwarted by military leaders.   (*p. 791*)

Swahili   Bantu language with Arabic loanwords spoken in coastal regions of East Africa.   (*p. 547*)

Swahili Coast   East African shores of the Indian Ocean between the Horn of Africa and the Zambezi River; from the Arabic *sawahil,* meaning "shores."   (*p. 383*)

Taiping Rebellion (1853–1864)   The most destructive civil war before the twentieth century. A Christian-inspired rural rebellion threatened to topple the **Qing Empire.**   (*p. 710*)

Tamil kingdoms   The kingdoms of southern India, inhabited primarily by speakers of Dravidian languages, which developed in partial isolation, and somewhat differently, from the Aryan north. They produced epics, poetry, and performance arts. Elements of Tamil religious beliefs were merged into the Hindu synthesis.   (*p. 190*)

Tang Empire   Empire unifying China and part of Central Asia, founded 618 and ended 907. The Tang emperors presided over a magnificent court at their capital, Chang'an.   (*p. 282*)

Tanzimat   "Restructuring" reforms by the nineteenth-century Ottoman rulers, intended to move civil law away from the control of religious elites and make the military and the bureaucracy more efficient.   (*p. 696*)

Tecumseh (1768–1813)   Shawnee leader who attempted to organize an Amerindian confederacy to prevent the loss of additional territory to American settlers. He became an ally of the British in War of 1812 and died in battle.   (*p. 648*)

Tenochtitlan   Capital of the Aztec Empire, located on an island in Lake Texcoco. Its population was about 150,000 on the eve of Spanish conquest. Mexico City was constructed on its ruins.   (*p. 314*)

Teotihuacan   A powerful **city-state** in central Mexico (100 B.C.E.–750 C.E.). Its population was about 150,000 at its peak in 600.   (*p. 30*)

terrorism   Political belief that extreme and seemingly random violence will destabilize a government and permit the terrorists to gain political advantage. Though an old technique, terrorism gained prominence in the late twentieth century with the growth of worldwide mass media that, through their news coverage, amplified public fears of terrorist acts.   (*p. 923*)

theater-state   Historians' term for a state that acquires prestige and power by developing attractive cultural forms and staging elaborate public ceremonies (as well as redistributing valuable resources) to attract and bind subjects to the center. Examples include the **Gupta Empire** in India and **Srivijaya** in Southeast Asia.   (*p. 191*)

Thebes   Capital city of Egypt and home of the ruling dynasties during the Middle and New Kingdoms. Amon, patron deity of Thebes, became one of the chief gods of Egypt. Monarchs were buried across the river in the Valley of the Kings.   (*p. 43*)

Theravada Buddhism   "Way of the Elders" branch of Buddhism followed in Sri Lanka and much of Southeast Asia. Therevada remains close to the original principles set forth by the **Buddha;** it downplays the importance of gods and emphasizes austerity and the individual's search for enlightenment.   (*p. 185*)

third-century crisis   Historians' term for the political, military, and economic turmoil that beset the Roman Empire during much of the third century C.E.: frequent changes of ruler, civil wars, barbarian invasions, decline of urban centers, and near-destruction of long-distance commerce and the monetary economy. After 284 C.E. Diocletian restored order by making fundamental changes.   (*p. 163*)

Third World   Term applied to a group of developing countries who professed nonalignment during the **Cold War.**   (*p. 879*)

three-field system   A rotational system for agriculture in which one field grows grain, one grows legumes, and one lies fallow. It gradually replaced two-field system in medieval Europe.   (*p. 395*)

Tiananmen Square   Site in Beijing where Chinese students and workers gathered to demand greater political openness in 1989. The demonstration was crushed by Chinese military with great loss of life.   (*p. 897*)

Tibet   Country centered on the high, mountain-bounded plateau north of India. Tibetan political power occasionally extended farther to the north and west between the seventh and thirteen centuries.   (*p. 289*)

Timbuktu   City on the Niger River in the modern country of Mali. It was founded by the Tuareg as a seasonal camp sometime after 1000. As part of the **Mali** empire, Timbuktu became a major terminus of the trans-Saharan trade and a center of Islamic learning.   (*p. 386*)

Timur (1336–1405)   Member of a prominent family of the Mongols' Jagadai Khanate, Timur through conquest gained control over much of Central Asia and Iran. He consolidated the status of Sunni Islam as orthodox, and his descendants, the Timurids, maintained his empire for nearly a century and founded the **Mughal Empire** in India.   (*p. 346*)

Tiwanaku   Name of capital city and empire centered on the region near Lake Titicaca in modern Bolivia (375–1000 C.E.).   (*p. 323*)

Tokugawa Shogunate (1600–1868)   The last of the three shogunates of Japan.   (*p. 552*)

Toltecs   Powerful postclassic empire in central Mexico (900–1168 C.E.). It influenced much of Mesoamerica. Aztecs claimed ties to this earlier civilization.   (*p. 313*)

trans-Saharan caravan routes   Trading network linking North Africa with **sub-Saharan Africa** across the Sahara.   (*p. 219*)

Treaty of Nanking (1842)   The treaty that concluded the **Opium War.** It awarded Britain a large indemnity from the **Qing Empire,** denied the Qing government tariff control over some of its own borders, opened additional ports of residence to Britons, and ceded the island of Hong Kong to Britain.   (*p. 708*)

Treaty of Versailles (1919)   The treaty imposed on Germany by France, Great Britain, the United States, and other Allied Powers after World War I. It demanded that Germany dismantle its military and give up some lands to Poland. It was resented by many Germans.   (*p. 787*)

treaty ports   Cities opened to foreign residents as a result of the forced treaties between the **Qing Empire** and foreign signatories. In the treaty ports, foreigners enjoyed **extraterritoriality.**   (*p. 708*)

tributary system   A system in which, from the time of the **Han** Empire, countries in East and Southeast Asia not under the direct control of empires based in China nevertheless enrolled as tributary states, acknowledging the superiority of the emperors in China in exchange for trading rights or strategic alliances.   (*p. 285*)

tribute system   A system in which defeated peoples were forced to pay a tax in the form of goods and labor. This forced transfer of food, cloth, and other goods subsidized the development of large cities. An important component of the Aztec and Inca economies.   (*p. 315*)

trireme   Greek and Phoenician warship of the fifth and fourth centuries B.C.E. It was sleek and light, powered by 170 oars arranged in three vertical tiers. Manned by skilled sailors, it was capable of short bursts of speed and complex maneuvers.   (*p. 139*)

tropical rain forest   High-precipitation forest zones of the Americas, Africa, and Asia lying between the Tropic of Cancer and the Tropic of Capricorn.   (*p. 222*)

tropics   Equatorial region between the Tropic of Cancer and the Tropic of Capricorn. It is characterized by generally warm or hot temperatures year-round, though much variation exists due to altitude and other factors. Temperate zones north and south of the tropics generally have a winter season.   (*p. 367*)

Truman Doctrine   Foreign policy initiated by U.S. president Harry Truman in 1947. It offered military aid to help Turkey and Greece resist Soviet military pressure and subversion.   (*p. 866*)

tsar (czar)   From Latin *caesar,* this Russian title for a monarch was first used in reference to a Russian ruler by Ivan III (r. 1462–1505).   (*pp. 350, 567*)

Tulip Period (1718–1730)   Last years of the reign of Ottoman sultan Ahmed III, during which European styles and attitudes became briefly popular in Istanbul.   (*p. 536*)

Tupac Amaru II   Member of Inca aristocracy who led a rebellion against Spanish authorities in Peru in 1780–1781. He was captured and executed with his wife and other members of his family.   (*p. 496*)

tyrant   The term the Greeks used to describe someone who seized and held power in violation of the normal procedures and traditions of the community. Tyrants appeared in many Greek **city-states** in the seventh and sixth centuries B.C.E., often taking advantage of the disaffection of the emerging middle class and, by weakening the old elite, unwittingly contributing to the evolution of **democracy.** (*p. 134*)

Uighurs   A group of Turkic-speakers who controlled their own centralized empire from 744 to 840 in Mongolia and Central Asia.   (*p. 289*)

ulama   Muslim religious scholars. From the ninth century onward, the primary interpreters of Islamic law and the social core of Muslim urban societies.   (*p. 241*)

Umayyad Caliphate   First hereditary dynasty of Muslim caliphs (661 to 750). From their capital at Damascus, the Umayyads ruled an empire that extended from Spain to India. Overthrown by the **Abbasid Caliphate.**   (*p. 236*)

umma   The community of all Muslims. A major innovation against the background of seventh-century Arabia, where traditionally kinship rather than faith had determined membership in a community.   (*p. 235*)

underdevelopment   The condition experienced by economies that depend on colonial forms of production such as the export of raw materials and plantation crops with low wages and low investment in education.   (*p. 656*)

United Nations   International organization founded in 1945 to promote world peace and cooperation. It replaced the **League of Nations.**   (*p. 862*)

Universal Declaration of Human Rights   A 1946 United Nations covenant binding signatory nations to the observance of specified rights.   (*p. 933*)

universities   Degree-granting institutions of higher learning. Those that appeared in Latin West from about 1200 onward became the model of all modern universities.   (*p. 406*)

Ural Mountains   This north-south range separates Siberia from the rest of Russia. It is commonly considered the boundary between the continents of Europe and Asia. (*p. 567*)

Urdu   A Persian-influenced literary form of Hindi written in Arabic characters and used as a literary language since the 1300s.   (*p. 386*)

utopian socialism   A philosophy introduced by the Frenchman Charles Fourier in the early nineteenth century. Utopian socialists hoped to create humane alternatives to industrial capitalism by building self-sustaining communities whose inhabitants would work cooperatively. (See also **socialism.**)   (*p. 628*)

Vargas, Getulio (1883–1954)   Dictator of Brazil from 1930 to 1945 and from 1951 to 1954. Defeated in the presidential election of 1930, he overthrew the government and created Estado Novo ("New State"), a dictatorship that emphasized industrialization and helped the urban poor but did little to alleviate the problems of the peasants.   (*p. 851*)

varna/jati   Two categories of social identity of great importance in Indian history. *Varna* are the four major social divisions: the *Brahmin* priest class, the *Kshatriya* warrior/administrator class, the *Vaishya* merchant/farmer class, and the *Shudra* laborer class. Within the system of *varna* are many *jati*, regional groups of people who have a common occupational sphere, and who marry, eat, and generally interact with other members of their group.   (*pp. 182, 183*)

vassal   In medieval Europe, a sworn supporter of a king or lord committed to rendering specified military service to that king or lord.   (*p. 263*)

Vedas   Early Indian sacred "knowledge"—the literal meaning of the term—long preserved and communicated orally by Brahmin priests and eventually written down. These religious texts, including the thousand poetic hymns to various deities contained in the Rig Veda, are our main source of information about the Vedic period (ca. 1500–500 B.C.E.). (*p. 180*)

Versailles   The huge palace built for French King Louis XIV south of Paris in the town of the same name. The palace symbolized the preeminence of French power and architecture in Europe and the triumph of royal authority over the French nobility.   (*p. 466*)

Victorian Age   The reign of Queen Victoria of Great Britain (r. 1837–1901). The term is also used to describe late-nineteenth-century society, with its rigid moral standards and sharply differentiated roles for men and women and for middle-class and working-class people. (See also **"separate spheres."**) (*p. 730*)

Vietnam War (1954–1975) Conflict pitting North Vietnam and South Vietnamese communist guerrillas against the South Vietnamese government, aided after 1961 by the United States. (*p. 869*)

Villa, Francisco "Pancho" (1878–1923) A popular leader during the Mexican Revolution. An outlaw in his youth, when the revolution started, he formed a cavalry army in the north of Mexico and fought for the rights of the landless in collaboration with **Emiliano Zapata.** He was assassinated in 1923. (*p. 846*)

Wari Andean civilization culturally linked to **Tiwanaku,** perhaps beginning as a colony of Tiwanaku. (*p. 323*)

Warsaw Pact The 1955 treaty binding the Soviet Union and countries of eastern Europe in an alliance against the **North Atlantic Treaty Organization.** (*p. 866*)

Washington, George (1732–1799) Military commander of the American Revolution. He was the first elected president of the United States (1789–1799). (*p. 589*)

water wheel A mechanism that harnesses the energy in flowing water to grind grain or to power machinery. It was used in many parts of the world but was especially common in Europe from 1200 to 1900. (*p. 397*)

Watt, James (1736–1819) Scot who invented the condenser and other improvements that made the **steam engine** a practical source of power for industry and transportation. The watt, an electrical measurement, is named after him. (*p. 619*)

weapons of mass destruction Nuclear, chemical, and biological devices that are capable of injuring and killing large numbers of people. (*p. 923*)

Wedgwood, Josiah (1730–1795) English industrialist whose pottery works were the first to produce fine-quality pottery by industrial methods. (*p. 614*)

Western Front A line of trenches and fortifications in World War I that stretched without a break from Switzerland to the North Sea. Scene of most of the fighting between Germany, on the one hand, and France and Britain, on the other. (*p. 780*)

Wilson, Woodrow (1856–1924) President of the United States (1913–1921) and the leading figure at the Paris Peace Conference of 1919. He was unable to persuade the U.S. Congress to ratify the **Treaty of Versailles** or join the **League of Nations.** (*p. 785*)

witch-hunt The pursuit of people suspected of witchcraft, especially in northern Europe in the late sixteenth and seventeenth centuries. (*p. 453*)

Women's Rights Convention An 1848 gathering of women angered by their exclusion from an international antislavery meeting. They met at Seneca Falls, New York to discuss women's rights. (*p. 655*)

World Bank A specialized agency of the United Nations that makes loans to countries for economic development, trade promotion, and debt consolidation. Its formal name is the International Bank for Reconstruction and Development. (*p. 862*)

World Trade Organization (WTO) An international body established in 1995 to foster and bring order to international trade. (*p. 927*)

Wright, Wilbur (1867-1912), and Orville (1871-1948) American bicycle mechanics; the first to build and fly an airplane, at Kitty Hawk, North Carolina, December 7, 1903. (*p. 800*)

Xiongnu A confederation of nomadic peoples living beyond the northwest frontier of ancient China. Chinese rulers tried a variety of defenses and stratagems to ward off these "barbarians," as they called them, and finally succeeded in dispersing the Xiongnu in the first century C.E. (*p. 173*)

Yamagata Aritomo (1838–1922) One of the leaders of the **Meiji Restoration.** (*p. 746*)

Yi (1392–1910) The Yi dynasty ruled Korea from the fall of the **Koryo** kingdom to the colonization of Korea by Japan. (*p. 359*)

yin/yang In Chinese belief, complementary factors that help to maintain the equilibrium of the world. Yin is associated with feminine, dark, and passive qualities; yang with masculine, light, and active qualities. (*p. 65*)

Yongle Reign period of Zhu Di (1360–1424), the third emperor of the **Ming Empire** (r. 1403–1424). He sponsored the building of the **Forbidden City,** a huge encyclopedia project, the expeditions of **Zheng He,** and the reopening of China's borders to trade and travel. (*p. 355*)

Young Ottomans Movement of young intellectuals to institute liberal reforms and build a feeling of national identity in the Ottoman Empire in the second half of the nineteenth century. (*p. 703*)

Yuan Empire (1271–1368) Empire created in China and Siberia by **Khubilai Khan.** (*p. 342*)

Yuan Shikai (1859–1916) Chinese general and first president of the Chinese Republic (1912–1916). He stood in the way of the democratic movement led by **Sun Yat-sen.** (*p. 791*)

Zapata, Emiliano (1879–1919) Revolutionary and leader of peasants in the Mexican Revolution. He mobilized landless peasants in south-central Mexico in an attempt to seize and divide the lands of the wealthy landowners. Though successful for a time, he was ultimately defeated and assassinated. (*p. 846*)

Zen The Japanese word for a branch of **Mahayana Buddhism** based on highly disciplined meditation. It is known in Sanskrit as *dhyana*, in Chinese as *chan*, and in Korean as *son*. (*p. 296*)

Zheng He (1371–1433) An imperial eunuch and Muslim, entrusted by the Ming emperor **Yongle** with a series of state voyages that took his gigantic ships through the Indian Ocean, from Southeast Asia to Africa. (*pp. 356, 422*)

Zhou The people and dynasty that took over the dominant position in north China from the **Shang** and created the concept of the **Mandate of Heaven** to justify their rule. The Zhou era, particularly the vigorous early period (1027–771 B.C.E.), was remembered in Chinese tradition as a time of prosperity and benevolent rule. In the later Zhou period (771–221 B.C.E.), centralized control broke down, and warfare among many small states became frequent. (*p. 63*)

ziggurat A massive pyramidal stepped tower made of

mudbricks. It is associated with religious complexes in ancient Mesopotamian cities, but its function is unknown.   (*p. 36*)

Zoroastrianism   A religion originating in ancient Iran with the prophet Zoroaster. It centered on a single benevolent deity—Ahuramazda—who engaged in a twelve-thousand-year struggle with demonic forces before prevailing and restoring a pristine world. Emphasizing truth-telling, purity, and reverence for nature, the religion demanded that humans choose sides in the struggle between good and evil. Those whose good conduct indicated their support for Ahuramazda would be rewarded in the afterlife. Others would be punished. The religion of the Achaemenid and Sasanid Persians, Zoroastrianism may have spread within their realms and influenced Judaism, Christianity, and other faiths.   (*p. 128*)

Zulu   A people of modern South Africa whom King Shaka united in 1818.   (*p. 665*)

Index